Fourth Edition

The New Structural Social Work

Ideology, Theory, and Practice

Bob Mullaly
Marilyn Dupré

OXFORD
UNIVERSITY PRESS

OXFORD
UNIVERSITY PRESS

Oxford University Press is a department of the University of Oxford.
It furthers the University's objective of excellence in research, scholarship,
and education by publishing worldwide. Oxford is a registered trade mark of
Oxford University Press in the UK and in certain other countries.

Published in Canada by
Oxford University Press
8 Sampson Mews, Suite 204,
Don Mills, Ontario M3C 0H5 Canada

www.oupcanada.com

First Edition published in 1993 (McClelland & Stewart Ltd)
Second Edition published in 1997
Third Edition published in 2007

Library and Archives Canada Cataloguing in Publication

Mullaly, Robert P., author
The new structural social work : ideology, theory, and
practice / by Bob Mullaly & Marilyn Dupré. — Fourth edition.

Includes bibliographical references and index.
Issued in print and electronic formats.
ISBN 978-0-19-902294-6 (softcover).—ISBN 978-0-19-902295-3
(PDF)

1. Social service—Philosophy—Textbooks. 2. Social service—
Textbooks. 3. Social case work—Textbooks. 4. Textbooks. I. Dupré,
Marilyn, author II. Title.

HV40.M855 2018   361.001   C2018-901987-5
                   C2018-901988-3

Cover image: © iStock/ Qweek
Cover and interior design: Laurie McGregor

Oxford University Press is committed to our environment.
Wherever possible, our books are printed on paper which comes from
responsible sources.

Printed and bound in the United States of America

1 2 3 4 — 21 20 19 18

Contents

PART I   In Search of a Paradigm

1   The Social Work Vision: A Progressive View   2

2   Capitalism, Crises, and Paradigms   29

6 The Marxist Paradigm   145

7 Feminist, Anti-racist, and Postmodern Critiques   167

PART III Structural Social Work: Practice Elements

(11) Working within (and against) the System: Radical Humanism 296

(12) Working outside (and against) the System: Radical Structuralism and Working within Ourselves 340

Boxes

Acknowledgements

To write a book such as this, which calls for a social order and a social work approach different from those now dominant, requires a tremendous amount of angry energy. It is not enough to understand how our present set of social arrangements benefits a privileged minority (mainly white, bourgeois, entrepreneurial males) at the expense of the majority (mainly people living in poverty, racialized individuals, immigrants, people with disabilities, Indigenous persons, and the working class). One must be angry enough to want to do something about it. As argued in this book, anger can be a gift. To paraphrase Marx, it is not enough to understand the world as it is; the task is to change it. If channelled constructively, anger can be a powerful force for such change. It is what will enable those of us who are committed to a just society to translate our social justice ideals and goals into practice and to carry out the struggle for liberation.

So we wish to thank all those individuals and groups and organizations that have fuelled and sustained our sense of indignation and rage over attitudes and acts that unfairly and unnecessarily have denied so many people their essential human dignity and have blocked the realization of their human potential. Included among them are: conservative politicians of all stripes for pandering to the corporate agenda in exchange for monetary and political support, leaving millions of people to fend for themselves; business organizations such as the Canadian Manufacturers and Exporters, the Canadian Chamber of Commerce, and the Business Council on National Issues, which in their greed for higher and higher profits have created a social Darwinian business culture in society that has swelled the ranks of the underclass; right-wing think tanks that do not think at all (such as the Fraser Institute, the C.D. Howe Institute, and the Conference Board of Canada) but continue to recycle a 200-year-old socially pernicious economic doctrine of laissez-faire that has never worked; the mainstream media that trivialize alternative social arrangements and economic policies and brainwash people into accepting a social system that victimizes and oppresses them; and all those social work academics who smugly and arrogantly dismiss progressive forms of social work and continue to teach recycled, conventional theories of social work that implicitly accept an inhumane social order and attempt to fit people into it; they should know better.

Of course, anger by itself is not enough to sustain one's writing. Support, encouragement, and help are also required. So we wish to thank the hundreds of people in Canada, the United States, Australia, Britain, and elsewhere—other progressive social work writers, instructors, students, and activists—who took the time to give constructive feedback on the first three editions of this book. In particular, I (Bob) want to thank my co-author, Dr Marilyn Dupré, who worked with me through the entire project of writing this book. I first met Marilyn years ago when she was one of my BSW students at St Thomas University in Fredericton, NB. Subsequently, when I was appointed as dean of the Faculty of Social Work at the University of Manitoba, Marilyn was a student in their PhD program, and I agreed to be a member of her thesis committee. She was an outstanding student—one of the best among those with whom I've had the pleasure of working. She possesses a keen mind, superior writing abilities, exemplary research skills, and sound knowledge of oppression and privilege and of structural and other progressive social work approaches—so much so that I invited her to become co-author for this current edition of *The New Structural Social Work*. It was a pleasure to work with Marilyn, and I will miss our stimulating and energizing conversations on social theory, politics, and critical social work.

Throughout my academic career, I have often been asked by students (and others) how, living in a society replete with conservative attitudes, values, institutions, and practices that ridicule, dismiss, and punish persons who advocate for a more just set of social arrangements and a progressive social work approach, I am able to maintain my commitment to the pursuit of a more just and egalitarian society and to the development of an alternative practice of social work. I owe gratitude to those just mentioned for their support and encouragement, but I owe my greatest appreciation to my parents, Audrey and Clement Mullaly. Although neither had the opportunity to attend university, each possessed a keen mind, an insightful social analysis, and a well-developed social conscience. I grew up in one of the poorest areas in one of the poorest cities in Canada (Saint John, NB) where I experienced, directly and indirectly, discrimination, oppression, and punitive treatment from most of our social institutions and organizations on a daily basis. Most privileged individuals and groups blamed people in this area for their inferior living circumstances, but it was my parents who helped me to interpret these issues through a critical lens that did not blame victims of social injustice for living conditions that were imposed on them by social forces of over which they had no control. It was my mother and father who helped me to develop a critical understanding of social inequality, to better understand issues of oppression and privilege, and to become aware of structural forces that have such a powerful impact on our lives. Most of all, they helped me to develop an understanding and appreciation of the concept of social resistance and the importance of looking for ways to carry it out in constructive ways. This book is one form of such resistance. It is to their memory that I dedicate my portion of this book.

I (Marilyn Dupré) would like to thank Dr Robert (Bob) Mullaly for approaching me to contribute to this latest edition of *The New Structural Social Work: Ideology, Theory, and Practice*. I was privileged to be able to attend St Thomas University, Fredericton, back in the late 1980s when Bob was teaching his BSW theory course using the notes that would form the chapters of the first edition of the book *Structural Social Work: Ideology, Theory, and Practice*, published in 1993. Over the years our academic paths have crossed on several occasions. In 2003, I was accepted into the PhD program in the Faculty of Social Work, University of Manitoba, and discovered to my absolute delight that Bob had been hired as the new dean that same summer. Being Maritimers, we both "returned home from away" and kept in touch over the years. I had the privilege of becoming the director of the School of Social Work at St Thomas University in July 2014, and in contributing to the fifth edition of the book that inspired me as a student and as a practising social worker and now as an academic, I feel as though I have come full circle in my career. Just this year (2017) St Thomas University School of Social Work celebrated its 35th anniversary as an accredited school of social work. The mission of the school has changed little since Bob Mullaly and Noel Kinsella (former St Thomas faculty member and Speaker of the Senate of Canada) worked together with the university administration to establish a school of social work founded on a progressive social work vision. I would like to thank Bob Mullaly for continuing to promote and advance that vision, which I believe is more relevant than ever to our profession, given the changing socio-political and economic circumstances of our time. Therefore, I would like to thank Bob and all the students and social work practitioners who have kept the spirit and philosophy of structural social work thriving and developing in classroom discussions and presentations.

We wish to thank the reviewers, both named and anonymous, of the four editions of this book, including Brenda A. LeFrancois, Memorial University of Newfoundland; Karen McCauley, Laurentian University; Bharati Sethi, Western University; Kelly-Ann Spezowka, University of Windsor; and Anne Wagner, Nipissing University. We hope our revisions do their suggestions justice. We are very grateful to Leah-Ann Lymer of Oxford University Press, who worked with us throughout this entire project. She was quick to respond to all of our questions and concerns and provided us with helpful advice. And we want to extend our appreciation to our copy editor, Dorothy Turnbull, for her attention to detail and care in putting the finishing touches on our manuscript.

In solidarity,

bob mullaly
Fredericton

Marilyn Dupré
Fredericton

Preface

This book represents the third stage of the development of thinking and writing with respect to "structural social work." The first edition, *Structural Social Work: Ideology, Theory, and Practice*, published in 1993, followed a period of relative quiet from the progressive or radical social work camp. The second edition, published in 1997, was one of many progressive social work books that appeared around this time. This new edition, which is called *The New Structural Social Work*, raises the question: what is new about structural social work? To answer this, a brief overview of the development of progressive social work in Anglo-democracies is presented here.

Although progressive forms of social work date back to the Settlement House Movement of the late nineteenth and early twentieth centuries, the modern formulation of progressive social work began with the 1975 publication of Roy Bailey and Mike Brake's *Radical Social Work* in Britain, Jeffry Galper's *The Politics of Social Services* in the United States, and Harold Throssell's *Social Work: Radical Essays* in Australia. Despite being written independently from one another and in three different English-speaking countries, they contained a number of common themes that had emerged in the radical sixties. Each criticized capitalism as a social and economic system that was antithetical to human need; each criticized mainstream social work for being an unwitting agent for capitalism; and each called for emancipatory/radical forms of social work practice that would contribute to the transformation of capitalism to some form of socialism.

A flood of progressive social work writings appeared in the late 1970s and early 1980s that focused mainly on class struggle. From these writings the progressive social work agenda was clear. The critical analysis of capitalism would be further developed to show not only its oppressive effects but also its contradictions, which would provide the levers and latitude for the practice of radical social work. The critique of mainstream social work practices would also be further developed to show how they actually covered up many of the oppressive features of capitalism by helping people to cope with it, adjust to it, or fit back into it. These critical analyses of capitalism and mainstream social work would, in turn, be used to develop radical/progressive theories and practices of social work at both the personal and the political level. This would include raising the consciousness of social services users of how capitalism exploited them and encouraging them to organize and mobilize against it; joining with the trade union movement, which was seen as the major vehicle for overthrowing capitalism; building up the welfare state that had need rather than profit as its criterion for production and distribution; and electing social democratic political parties, which were viewed as more committed to social justice than were bourgeois parties. Also, radical social work in the 1970s was responding to the criticism by feminist social workers that it was gender-neutral and in the early 1980s to the criticism by mainly black social workers that it was colour-neutral. In varying degrees, most social work educational programs incorporated some of these progressive ideas and analyses into parts of their curriculum, but for the most part, they occupied marginal or token positions alongside mainstream social work ideas and practices.

By the mid-1980s, it was clear that the progressive project of radical social work was being undermined by the worldwide economic crisis and right-wing social policies brought about by the oil crisis in 1973 along with the inflation-fuelling Vietnam War. Led by "big business" and bourgeois governments, economic restructuring was initiated to address a worldwide recession and inflation (i.e., stagflation). Capitalism was transformed from its rigid and centralized postwar form to a flexible (for the capitalists at least) and global form (Harvey, 1989), thus making much of the earlier critical analyses of capitalism outdated and irrelevant. We witnessed, as Leonard (1997) pointed out, the ascendancy of neo-conservatism on a global scale and the virtual collapse of leftist politics, a reduced welfare state, increasing disparities between rich and poor, national trade unions in disarray, and massive economic uncertainty. Given the irrelevance of much of its analysis of capitalism, the diminished political power of the trade union movement, continuous cutbacks in the welfare state, and the election of neo-conservative governments, not only did the development of radical social work halt, but the whole radical social work movement seemed to have gone underground.

Though never dead, radical social work underwent a period of inactivity and virtual invisibility (roughly during the 1980s) before an important book was published in Britain in 1989. *Radical Social Work Today* contained a number of articles by various radical writers and practitioners that reassessed the need for radical social work in its new socio-economic–political context and identified what the various contributing authors believed to be the essential elements of a radical social work strategy in the 1990s. In our view, this book breathed new life into progressive social work. The title of its opening chapter, "Whatever Happened to Radical Social Work?" addressed the questions that so many progressive social workers had. What *did* happen to radical social work? To what extent is it still relevant? Which aspects should be modified and/or rejected, given the events of the previous decade and the new realities facing social work? The editors of the book (Mary Langan and Phil Lee), who were also the authors of the first chapter, identified a number factors that, in their view, would have to be considered and addressed before radical social work could move on.

One of these factors, of course, was the changed practice context in which social work operated, such as dramatic increases in the workloads of social workers, criticism and condemnation of social workers from conservative politicians and the mainstream media, the drive to push social workers into a more coercive and interventionist role in policing "deviant" families, and a growing criticism from members of oppressed groups such as women, racialized individuals, persons with disabilities, and older people that their interests had not been adequately articulated by the radical social work movement. A major criticism of the 1970s radical social work was that it was strong on critique but short on practice. Although this criticism seemed to underestimate how necessary the critique was and the constructive role it played, by 1989 it was obvious that radical social work had to translate its critical analysis into practice if it were to move on. Several other books appeared around this time that furthered the critical analysis of social work and the social welfare state but did not really address the practice of radical social work: Fiona Williams's 1989 book from Britain, *Social Policy: A Critical Introduction: Issues of Race, Gender, and Class*; Ben Carniol's second edition of *Case Critical* (1990) from Canada; and George Martin's *Social Policy in the Welfare State* (1990) from the US.

It was shortly after the publication of *Radical Social Work Today* that the first edition of *Structural Social Work* (1993) appeared. It attempted to address many of the criticisms made of radical social work in Langan and Lee's book, but in particular it focused on the inconsistent treatment that radical social work had received in the literature until that time and the criticism that it had not moved much beyond a critique of conventional social work. This first edition attempted to clarify the clutter of the existing radical social literature by providing a framework that integrated its ideological context, its theoretical base, and its political practice. As well, it attempted to advance the existing theoretical and practice bases of radical social work beyond that which existed in the literature at that time by linking social work practice with individuals, families, and groups to contribute simultaneously to fundamental changes of structures in society. As its theoretical base, critical social theory was chosen, and as its framework, a particular school of radical social work was chosen that had been pioneered in Canada by Maurice Moreau, which he termed "structural social work." Critical social theory was selected because it, unlike mainstream social theory, goes beyond attempting to simply explain and understand social phenomena to a political purpose of changing social conditions and challenging oppression.

The label "structural social work" was chosen for several reasons. First, the term "structural" is descriptive of the nature of social problems in that they are an inherent part of our neo-conservative/liberal, capitalist society and do not reside in the individual. Second, the term is prescriptive because it indicates that the focus for change is mainly on the structures of society, not on the personal characteristics of the individual. Third, structural social work has more potential for integrating various theoretical concepts and political practices because it does not establish hierarchies of oppression but is concerned with all oppressed groups. Fourth, it is a dialectical approach to social work practice and, therefore, does not get trapped within false dichotomies or binary opposites. Finally, most of the development of structural social work had occurred in Canada, and it was increasingly becoming a major social work perspective.

Coincidentally, another book on radical social work was published in Australia the same year as the first edition of *Structural Social Work*. Jan Fook's *Radical Casework* focused primarily on the practice (at the micro level) of radical social work and de-emphasized theory whereas *Structural Social Work* was stronger on theory than it was on practice. Many radical social work instructors in Australia and Canada used the two books together because they complemented each other. As well, these two books are widely credited as representing an important milestone in the development of radical forms of social work theory and practice, as evidenced by the plethora of books on progressive social work that were published a few years after 1993. However, *Radical Casework* is still one of the best books written on the practice of radical social work.

The first edition of *Structural Social Work* proved immensely popular because, in our view, it filled a large gap in the literature. There were many, many social work practitioners and academics committed to fundamental social change and to social work practices that did not blame people experiencing social problems for their situations who were looking for a workable progressive form of social work. However, this first edition contained a number of limitations and over time required further development. For example, it did not contain a full analysis of the transformation of capitalism from its previous postwar form, when it existed almost on a nation-by-nation basis, to its global form. Thus, the book represented a reaction to the negative consequences of globalization without a full understanding of what was happening or how to challenge it. Although the first edition acknowledged other forms of oppression and furthered the analysis of social problems beyond those associated with class, it still did not sufficiently emphasize other forms and sources of oppression, such as patriarchy, racism, and ageism, which not only existed in society but were also present in the postwar welfare state and in social work practice. As well, the first edition of *Structural Social Work* was conceptualized within a modernist framework, since postmodernism was just beginning to appear in the social work literature. Thus, it did not contain any of the insights of postmodernism and, in fact, was based on the emancipatory narrative of Western modernity with certain claims to unqualified universalisms and essentialisms and with a linear view of history and progress.

In late 1997, the second edition of *Structural Social Work* was published. Among other changes, an attempt was made to address the limitations of the first edition and in doing so to further the development of structural social work theory and practice. An overview of the transformation process from postwar capitalism to its global form was included (thanks to David Harvey, 1989), which outlined the latter's negative consequences on vulnerable populations, the welfare state, and social work. Given this analysis, at least social work now knew what it was up against and who the beneficiaries and victims of globalization were. Without such understanding, it is difficult to challenge or influence any such movement. The second edition also included a chapter on oppression, which was presented as the primary focus of structural social work. In other words, it is not capitalism or class relations that constitute the major source of social problems and exclusion. Rather, it is the exploitation and oppression based on dominant–subordinate relations that result in social problems. Classism is one form and source of oppression but not the only one. Also included was the postmodern critique of modernist thinking, which had influenced earlier forms of radical (and mainstream) social work. It was argued that it was not a matter of modernist versus postmodernist thought but that both were necessary because each informed and provided a corrective to the other. Several other books on progressive social work were published around the same time as the second edition of *Structural Social Work* so that by the late 1990s there was a substantial body of literature on various schools of progressive social work, including structural social work.

In spite of attending to the limitations of the earlier edition, the 1997 version of *Structural Social Work* still contained gaps and weaknesses. Although the analysis of the transformation of capitalism was retained, the book did not include any real plan or strategy of what to do about it beyond caring for its victims. Although it was argued that postmodernism had to be a part of any progressive school of social work, the dominant paradigms that have played such an important part of our approach to structural social work were still steeped in modernist concepts and contained elements of universalism, essentialism, and linear progress with respect to the pursuit of social justice and equality. Some critics contended that the chapters on practice were not sufficiently nuanced to address the complexities of real-world practice and that the book did not address the micro-politics of practice sufficiently. Another criticism was that little attention had been given to issues of identity and subjectivity and to the structural social worker as a person or to the social location of the worker and how this might affect their practice.

In the third edition, which appeared in 2007, an attempt was made to address these criticisms. And because the third edition was sufficiently different from the previous two editions and because the context of social work was also sufficiently different from what it was when the previous edition was published 10 years earlier, the title was changed to *The New Structural Social Work*.

In the interim, many observers and commentators, such as Canada's John Ralston Saul, had argued that globalization had run its course and was now on the decline. It had not delivered the goods it promised, and very few people expected that it could. Many countries had opted out of the globalization process and were reasserting their national autonomy over economic and social affairs. Some of the leaders of the globalization movement had not only lost credibility because of their exorbitant salaries and benefits, but many of them were before the courts answering to charges of corruption, fraud, and other white-collar crimes. In addition to the decline of globalization as an economic theology or religion, there were other hopeful signs that had not been present 10 years before. For example, Canada, instead of being in a deficit situation as it had been a decade before, was recording surpluses in the billions of dollars in each of the previous eight years, so government deficits could no longer be used as the excuse for cutting social services. As well, the anti-globalization movement, once considered by corporate and government elites as a rag-tag group of extreme anarchists and radicals, showed that people can organize, challenge large movements, and make changes in the face of formidable odds. What was made by an elite few can be unmade and remade.

In addition to a different economic and political context in 2007, there was also a new intellectual context. When the 1997 version of *Structural Social Work* was published, there was a seemingly unalterable tension between modernist and postmodern ideas as they applied to ideas and ideals such as social justice, emancipation, and solidarity that were crucial to the modernist notion of a progressive social work. In 2007, there were several versions of postmodernism, ranging from a nihilistic and individualistic form on one end of the continuum to a critical postmodernism on the other end whereby writers and theorists were attempting to bridge the positive and liberating aspects of the critical social theory tradition with those of postmodernism. This developing epistemology called for: work on the interstices of materialist philosophies and postmodernism; a retention of the ideals of social justice, emancipation, and equality in ways that respect difference, diversity, and inclusion; and an avoidance of totalizing belief systems and essentialisms, on the one hand, and politically disabling fragmentation and witless relativism on the other hand. Most progressive social work writers had moved beyond a modernist versus postmodernist dichotomy. This perspective is the one that guided the new structural social work. This is not to say that antagonisms did not exist between the two, but many believed that a healthy tension existed rather than a binary opposition or dualism.

However, there were also limitations and new social changes that occurred after the 2007 edition was published, requiring an updating. For example, there was a global financial crisis in 2007–8, which negatively affected the welfare state of every Western country, and elections in Canada, the UK, and the US resulted in new federal governments with different approaches to social welfare. These and other updates are included in the current (2018) edition. As well, the new edition includes a major addition—"privilege" as a major cause of oppression, social problems, social inequality, and social injustice. Oppression and privilege are opposite sides of the same coin. We have oppression because we have privilege, and if we want to eliminate oppression, we must do something about privilege. This is a relatively new perspective in social work, which has dramatic implications for social work theory, practice, and pedagogy.

Part 1 of the present work shows how and why current social work theory and practice are parts of the larger crisis of global capitalism and oppression and what it must do to contribute to the resolution of social problems. Chapter 1 differentiates two major social work perspectives— the conventional view and the progressive view. The former accepts our social system, and the latter seeks to transform it. Structural social work is based on the progressive view and believes that an alternative vision of society must exist in advance of practice as a necessary prerequisite to social transformation. An outline of such a vision based on a progressive view of social work values and principles is developed and articulated, and a progressive critique of the Canadian Association of Social Workers (CASW) 2005 *Code of Ethics* is provided.

The transformation to global capitalism and the devastating effects that it and neo-conservative policies have imposed on the labour market, the autonomy of communities, the social welfare state, the social work profession, and historically marginalized groups are examined in Chapter 2. To date, social work has been ineffective in dealing with the deleterious consequences of the "fiscal crisis of the state" and, therefore, is itself in a state of crisis. This situation has resulted in considerable soul-searching within social work with respect to many of its comfortable assumptions about the nature of society, the nature of social problems, and the nature of social work practice. And although many social workers have fallen back on victim-blaming explanations for social problems, there has been considerable criticism of our present set of social arrangements and our conventional social work practices, and there is a significant call for alternative models and practices. The concept of paradigm is presented in Chapter 2 as a means of exploring alternative models of society more in keeping with human well-being, alternative explanations for social problems more in keeping with people's lived realities, and alternative theories of social work practice more in keeping with social emancipation than social control. There are hopeful signs today on the national and international scenes that were not present a decade ago, and they are presented in Chapter 2. Potentially, they could alleviate some of the devastation incurred since the mid-1970s by global capitalism and ease some of the pressure that social workers have experienced over the past four decades because of the fiscal crisis of the state.

Chapters 3 to 6 examine the ideologies of four dominant societal paradigms (neo-conservatism, liberalism, social democracy, and Marxism) along with how each paradigm views human nature, the nature of society, the role of the state, and the concepts of social justice and social change. Also presented is an explanation that each paradigm offers for the existence of social problems, the ideal social welfare system consistent with each paradigm's ideology and interpretation of social problems, and the nature and form of social work practice dictated by each paradigm.

Chapter 7 presents three critiques of the four paradigms: the feminist critique (i.e., the paradigms are gender-neutral), the anti-racist critique (i.e., the paradigms are colour-neutral), and the postmodern critique (i.e., the paradigms are steeped in modernist thought where there is no respect for diversity and difference and oppressed groups are subjugated under working-class oppression). An argument is made that the progressive paradigms (social democracy and Marxism) must be reconstructed to accommodate these critiques.

Part 2 presents the theoretical basis of structural social work, with oppression as its focus. Chapter 8 compares and contrasts the four paradigms with each other and with the elements of the progressive social work vision outlined in Chapter 1. It is concluded that progressive social work is much more congruent with the socialist paradigms (social democracy and Marxism) than it is with the capitalist paradigms (neo-conservatism and liberalism). However, it must be a *revitalized socialism* and not the "old" socialism of the twentieth century, which reflected a project of emancipation rooted in domination. This revitalized socialism must engage with post-modernism along with feminist, anti-racist, and other struggles against domination and demand the acknowledgement and celebration of diversity in cultures, sexualities, races, ages, abilities, and other human characteristics that were excluded, suppressed, or discriminated against within an unreconstructed modernist version of socialism. The remainder of Chapter 8 discusses the fundamental components of structural social work theory—its socialist ideology, its radical social work heritage, its critical social theory base (including modernism and postmodernism), its conflict or change perspective, its dialectical analysis, its inclusion of all forms of oppression, and a conceptual framework that incorporates these components into social transformative and emancipatory forms of social work practice.

Chapter 9 argues that oppression is an issue of social justice and is the fundamental source of social problems. Rejected are the neo-conservative individual deficiency explanation and the liberal social disorganization explanation of social problems. Presented also are the nature of oppression; its causes, sources and forms; its production and reproduction; the three levels at which it occurs (personal, cultural, and institutional); its dynamics; its effects on oppressed groups, including its internalization; coping mechanisms used by oppressed persons; and the social functions it carries out in the interests of the dominant groups in society. Anti-oppressive social work is a prominent part of this chapter.

Chapter 10 is a new chapter that focuses on "privilege" and argues that it is the underlying source of oppression. Anti-privilege scholarship has a much shorter history than anti-oppressive social work, although both are important components of today's structural social work. This formulation and incorporation of both anti-oppression and anti-privilege as integral parts of structural social work is what makes this book innovative and timely. It acts as a call to all social workers to join in the pursuit of a society characterized by social equality and social justice.

Part 3 outlines several practice elements of structural social work that are derived from its theoretical base. Chapter 11 focuses on structural social work practice within (and against) the system, and Chapter 12 deals with structural social work practice outside (and against) the system as well as some personal characteristics of structural social workers. Chapter 11 discusses several structural social work practice elements to be used with service users that differentiate structural practice from conventional practice. The chapter also looks at how structural social workers can survive in a workplace that they are attempting to politicize and democratize. Issues and strategies of protecting oneself from reprisal while trying to radicalize the workplace are discussed. Chapter 12 considers several arenas for struggle outside the workplace where structural social workers can contribute to social transformation and presents a number of personal attributes that are essential for carrying out structural social work practice. It is argued in the final section of the chapter that structural social work is much more than a technique or a practice modality. It is a way of life.

When the first edition of *Structural Social Work* appeared in 1993, there were only a few social work programs in Canada (and elsewhere) that might have had a single course on radical or progressive social work. Today, there are entire social work programs that advertise themselves as structural or anti-oppressive or some other variation of progressive social work. Times have changed, and so has structural social work. We hope that this edition of *The New Structural Social Work* reflects and contributes to these changes.

It should be noted that throughout this book, we use the plural "they/their" instead of the singular "he/she" or "his/her." Basically, we have decided to so because the use of "he/she" or "his/her" tends to privilege male over female and also constructs a two-gender world view as normal and natural. "They/their" challenges sexism and gender as binary, is inclusive of all people, and is congruent with the content of this book. The use of "they" and "their" is a change from the previous edition of this book. We appreciate the fact that Oxford University Press is willing to be progressive by allowing us to present a counter-hegemony with respect to gender and sexism.

PART I
In Search of a Paradigm

1 The Social Work Vision: A Progressive View

We do not anticipate the world with our dogmas but instead attempt to discover the new world through the critique of the old.

— Karl Marx (1844)

Introduction

The purpose of this chapter is twofold: (1) to present an argument that social work needs an alternative vision of society, one that is more in accordance with the social, emotional, cultural, physical, and spiritual well-being of all people (not just a privileged minority); and (2) to outline such a vision based on the espoused values of the social work profession. By itself, this twofold purpose is impossible to carry out because social work is not a unitary profession. There is no consensus within social work with respect to the ideal nature of society, or the nature and functions of the welfare state, or the nature and political consequences of social work practice. As the title of this chapter suggests, the analysis and discourse presented here are derived from the progressive wing of the social work profession as opposed to the conventional wing.

Conventional and Progressive Perspectives within Social Work

Modern-day social work has two traditions that date back to the latter part of the nineteenth century: the Charity Organization Society movement that began in 1877 in the United States and the Settlement House movement that began in 1884 in England (Chandler, 1995). Although both were products of industrialization and urbanization, each adopted a different view of and approach to the problem of poverty and those experiencing poverty.

The Charity Organization Society movement believed that a rational system of coordinated, private, and scientific philanthropy supplemented by an army of "friendly visitors" would do much to diminish destitution, hardship, and begging. Coordination was viewed as important because otherwise, people living in poverty might take advantage of a fragmented charity system and obtain duplicative goods and services. All decisions regarding this system were made by the "right" people in the community (i.e., mainly white, middle-class businessmen) because people living in poverty could not be trusted to make responsible decisions affecting their lives; their poverty, after all, was seen as evidence of this inability. (The United Way in Canada is the modern version of a Charity Organization Society.) The role of the friendly visitors (who were mainly volunteer women of high socio-economic status) was to visit people who were experiencing poverty in their homes and teach them life skills, thrift, and moral behaviour. Obviously, the explanation for poverty was one of character defect and moral deficiency, and the solution was to reform the individual. Out of this heritage came one of social work's primary methods (arguably, the primary method) of intervention, a type of casework with individuals and families that focused on coping, adjustment, and restoration of those living in poverty rather than a change of social conditions.

The Settlement House movement's approach to the problem of poverty and to those experiencing it rested on a different assumption from that of the Charity Organization Society movement. Rather than seeing people as makers of their own misfortune, it believed that they were victims of an unjust social order that discriminated against large numbers of people so that a few might benefit. In other words, the capitalist system caused poverty, not the people experiencing

Box 1.1 *Bleeding Hearts and Do-Gooders*

Social workers are sometimes portrayed in negative stereotypes and called such names as "bleeding hearts," "busybodies," and "do-gooders." In the early nineties, I (Bob) was teaching at St Thomas University in Fredericton, New Brunswick. Over the course of a few months there was a particular individual in the community who wrote a series of derogatory letters about social workers to the local newspaper, which were printed on the "Letters to the Editor" page. Referring to social workers as "do-gooders" was his major mantra. One day I'd had enough and wrote my own letter to the editor in response to his letters. The following is a modified version of my letter.

Dear Editor:
I wish to respond to the derogatory, uninformed, and prejudicial letters written by Mr Anti–Social Worker that have appeared in your paper over the past few months. In those letters he constantly refers to social workers and other community-minded people as "do-gooders." It seems to me that the label "do-gooder" suggests there are three kinds of people in the world: those who do good, those who do bad, and those who do nothing. Since Mr Anti–Social Worker is obviously not in the do-good group, I wonder if he could tell us which of the other two groups he belongs to.

A reply from Mr Anti–Social Worker did not follow, and no more social worker–bashing letters from this person appeared.

poverty. People involved in the Settlement House movement established houses in slum neighbourhoods and worked directly with families in attempts to do something about poor sanitary conditions, slum housing, crime, poverty, sweatshop work conditions, and so on. Their focus was on reforming society rather than on reforming the person. Out of this heritage came another of social work's primary methods of intervention, a self-help model of community organization that focused on participation of people living in poverty, community development, and social action.

When social work emerged in the 1940s in Canada as a profession requiring a university-based education, it was faced with the task of trying to reconcile these two different approaches to social problems and to integrate them into the curricula of schools of social work. For a variety of reasons (i.e., the theories of Sigmund Freud and the medical model were the dominant scientific bases of knowledge at that time, and the schools of social work were established mainly by social agencies that were part of the Charity Organization Society system), the casework "reform-the-person" approach became dominant. One only has to look at the disproportionate share of faculty and resources allocated to direct practice courses in most schools of social work today, or to the existing social work literature, or to the current practices employed in most social agencies to see the dominance of casework with its individual reform-the-person approach.[1]

From the above two traditions, modern social work has always had two major competing views of society, social welfare, and social work practice[2]—the conventional view and the progressive or critical view. The conventional view, which has always been held by the majority, is influenced by and reflective of popular beliefs and attitudes about the nature of the individual, of society, and of the relationship between the two. According to this perspective, our present social order, although not perfect, is the best there is, and it ought to be preserved. Society is viewed as comprising social institutions that serve the individual as long as they make full use of available opportunities for personal success. This view acknowledges that social problems do exist but defines them in terms of personal difficulties or immediate environmental issues that require social work intervention either to help people cope with or adjust to existing institutions or to modify existing policies in a limited fashion. Carniol (2010), a progressive Canadian social work scholar, points out that the conventional approach is adopted by those who believe that our institutions are responsive to and capable of meeting people's needs. Obviously, the political function of conventional social work practice is such that by conforming to established institutions, it reinforces, supports, and defends the status quo. This is not to say that there is no disagreement within the conventional view. Most of the political debate about social welfare has been conducted within a liberal–conservative framework, with the former seeing more services as a good thing and the latter seeing fewer services as a good thing (Galper, 1975). Neither liberalism nor conservatism questions the legitimacy of the present capitalist social order, however.

In contrast to the conventional view, the progressive or critical view does not believe that our present social institutions are capable of adequately meeting human need. Social workers with this view are quick to point out that in spite of a social welfare state and social work interventions that have existed for most of the last century and the early part of this century, social problems are not decreasing but, on the contrary, appear to be worsening. Thirty-five years ago there were no soup kitchens or food banks in Canada, nor were there emergency shelters to feed and house any other than derelict populations. Today these residual means of meeting basic needs have become institutionalized. Progressive social workers also point to the growing gap between rich and poor, to the worsening plight of traditionally disadvantaged groups, to the resurrection of conservatism, and to the social control functions of welfare programs and social work practice as proof that the present set of social arrangements does not work for large numbers of people. Although there has always been a progressive or radical contingent within social work, it has been a minority voice. However, in recent years and in the face of the fiscal crisis of the state, its numbers have been growing as have their challenges to the conventional view.

Carniol (2010, p. 13) believes that the scope, quantity, and areas of injustice, both in Canada and globally, have deep roots and are not easily dislodged.

> Some people reap handsome benefit from injustice, and usually work hard to protect, enlarge, and entrench their well-established privilege. They will also try to ridicule, marginalize, intimidate, and silence individuals, networks, and organizations that expose this unfair privilege.

However, Carniol is optimistic that these injustices are being challenged in significant ways, with many people and groups concluding that equity, inclusion, and democratic accountability are not only possible and desirable but also critically urgent. Social transformation in support of social justice is the ultimate goal of progressive/critical social work, and the pursuit of this goal is a major theme of this book. However, there are disagreements within the progressive camp on how best to achieve this goal. For example, although the elimination of oppression and inequality may be a common goal, feminists, Marxists, social democrats, racialized groups, and so on have often disagreed on the fundamental source of oppression and on the strategies to overcome oppression and inequality. This is further discussed in Chapters 9 and 10.

Social Work Is a Political Profession

Historical overviews of social work perspectives and approaches that have been used in Canada have been discussed elsewhere (Hick, 2010; Jennissen & Lundy, 2011) and, therefore, will not be reproduced here. Instead, some of the major theories or approaches of social work are grouped in Table 1.1 according to the main focus or unit of analysis and change of each. There are two schools of conventional social work. One focuses on the individual or individuals as both the source of and the solutions to problems and has as its goal to help the individual cope with, fit into, and/or adjust to society. The other focuses on the "goodness of fit" between the individual and their environment. This approach seeks change either in the individual or in the individual's limited environment (i.e., within the family, the community, the school, the workplace, etc.). No thought is given to the possibility that maybe the system itself (i.e., society) is unjust and unfixable and that the solution might be to transform it fundamentally to one based on a different set of values and social dynamics.

It is important to note here that although the conventional approaches outlined in Table 1.1 have historically reinforced the status quo, they can be used in progressive ways, as will be discussed in Chapter 8. In fact, widespread agreement exists that social work has responsibility

Table 1.1 Selected Conventional and Progressive Social Work Perspectives/Approaches

Conventional (consensus-based)		Progressive (conflict/change)
personal change	*person-in-environment (personal change and/or limited social change)*	*fundamental social change/transformation**
• psychodynamic	• general systems	• feminist theory
• behavioural	• ecosystems (ecological)	• Marxist
• client-centred	• life model	• radical
• psychosocial	• problem-solving	• structural
• clinical	• strengths perspective	• anti-racist
• family therapies		• anti-oppressive
• casework		• critical
		• post-colonial
		• Indigenous
		• narrative
		• just therapy

Note: Any of the above can be used within a critical or progressive framework, although traditionally this has rarely occurred.

* Progressive social work today recognizes that fundamental social change cannot occur without fundamental personal change also occurring. Earlier versions of progressive social work tended to emphasize structural changes and psychological preparation to participate in social change activities but gave little or no consideration to the impact of oppressive structures on oppressed groups and how to respond to them in a way that was meaningful.

for both individual and structural (social change) interventions (Trainor, 1996). Today countless social work bodies and publications assert the need for social work to be involved in broader political action and social change (Schneider & Lester, 2001). The principles governing the International Federation of Social Workers (IFSW) and the social work codes of ethics in Australia, the US, and to a lesser extent Canada all include strong statements in favour of social justice. Many social workers have become involved in political and social action within formal structures of political parties. Therefore, social work must be viewed as a highly political practice in which social problems and their solutions are shaped by access to power and resources.

> To politicize something or someone is to introduce the idea that everything has political elements; that is, to introduce the idea that nothing is neutral and everything involves an overt or covert struggle over power, resources, and affirming identities. . . . When an issue is politicized rather than just thought of as an unfortunate social problem or individual shortcoming, individuals and groups can more easily analyze and act upon it. At the very core of social work's existence are conflicts between competing social-political groups and forces over defining needs and how to interpret and meet needs (Baines, 2011, p. 6).

Box 1.2 *Limitations of Systems and Ecological Perspectives*

- They are not theories because they are descriptive only and have no explanatory or predictive capacities.
- They are so vague and general that they offer little specific guidance for practice.
- They do not deal with or explain power relationships (i.e., power differentials).
- They do not accommodate or deal with conflict. All social units (or subsystems) are viewed as interacting in harmony with each other and with the larger system (i.e., society). The whole purpose of a systems approach is to eliminate any conflict that disrupts the system.
- They operate to maintain the status quo, since the goal is to restore the system to normal functioning.
- Social problems are believed to be a result of a breakdown between individuals and the subsystems (e.g., family, school, peer group, welfare office) with which they interact.
- The focus on the here-and-now situation and possibilities for intervention contributes to a neglect of history.
- There is no recognition or analysis of oppressive social structures that produce inequality.

Unfortunately, systems theory and ecological perspectives (under the "person-in-environment" subheading in Table 1.1), which have now been around for more than 40 years, are still presented as core social work theory in many schools of social work in North America. Box 1.2 outlines a number of serious limitations and flaws with this perspective that have been cited in the progressive literature for more than two decades (see, e.g., Pease, 2003; Finn & Jacobson, 2003). These and other limitations are discussed more fully in Chapter 8.

Need for a Progressive Social Work Vision

Over the past 30 years, we have witnessed an increasing body of social science writings criticizing our present social order because of its failure to provide satisfying levels of living for large numbers of citizens. These criticisms are important for social work because they identify and illuminate the sources of and reasons for many of our social problems and show us what we are struggling against. However, although critical analysis may show us what we are fighting against, by itself it does not show us what we are fighting for. It may be possible to resist dominant forces by engaging in the powerfully negative act of saying "no." But without a clear vision or alternative, that accomplishment of saying "no," while immensely important in terms of building confidence and capacities for struggle, only postpones the battle. To shift from the defensive to the offensive requires a vision of a different kind of future. However, visions are not blueprints for future societies but provide the guiding principles of social justice "that may be implemented in different ways by different societies, at different times and places, and at different stages of knowledge and technological development" (Gil, 2013, p. 34).

We are passing through a period of history when societal visions or Utopian models of society have not been widely discussed. At present, many of our comfortable and cherished assumptions about the nature of our society and its ability to respond genuinely to human needs are in doubt. The global justice movement has experienced significant success, but it continues to be divided over its political and organizational direction; there are major difficulties in maintaining coalitions, agreeing to solutions to problems, and devising strategies that will have a real impact (Staggenborg, 2012). We need visions of alternative societies. Without such alternatives or visions, there is a danger that we will become victims of distorted notions of justice, well-being, and solidarity, thus denying many people their rightful place in society. Fortunately, given the apparent collapse of (or at least reconstituted) globalism, there is a return to discussions of visions or ideas of a different type of world—one based on social justice—as evidenced by such works as Ferguson, Lavalette, and Whitmore's book *Globalisation, Global Justice and Social Work* (2005), and Dominelli's *Social Work in a Globalizing World* (2010).

Because social work often deals with the casualties and victims of society, it too must become involved in questioning our present social arrangement. Given social work's belief in the inherent dignity and worth of the person, it must ask itself what type of society best promotes this ideal. Given social work's belief that people have a right to develop fully and freely their inherent human potential and to live productive and satisfying lives free from domination and exploitation by others, those in social work must ask what social arrangements best accommodate these values. In other words, what type of society best promotes the values, ideals, principles, and beliefs espoused by the social work profession? What is the vision that social work should pursue?

Unfortunately, it would be impossible to reach consensus among social workers on such a vision of society. A major obstacle to developing and articulating a universally accepted social work vision is the existence of the two incompatible views of current society, social welfare, and social work. Not even a common value base or a professional code of ethics is enough to unify the profession with respect to the coexisting conventional and progressive views. However, all social workers have a role to play in advocating for a world that is rooted in equality and can become allies in struggles for liberation and the elimination of structural inequalities that impede human growth and development (Dominelli, 2010, p. 171).

A Code of Ethics for Progressive Social Workers

If the espoused values of social work were to be used to formulate a social work vision, the nature and form of that vision would differ depending on whether a conventional or progressive view was used. The 2005 Canadian Association of Social Workers (CASW) *Code of Ethics* reflects a "liberal-humanist" approach to social work that seeks to comfort victims of social problems rather than a critical approach that seeks fundamental social change (i.e., transformation). Many of the changes to the Canadian *Code* were made in support of a competency-based framework for overseeing practice that has been developed by the Canadian Council of Social Work Regulators (CCSWR), a group formed by a national association of provincial regulatory bodies. The council has developed entry-level competencies for the social work profession in Canada, arguing that professional regulation is necessary to protect citizens from persons who are "unqualified, incompetent or unfit to practice" (CCSWR, 2012). The council states that a further benefit of a competency-based framework is that education and training will be guided by regulation. In reality, Canadian social work educational institutions are being coerced into developing academic programs with more emphasis on learning about a variety of intervention techniques and assessments related to determining eligibility for services than on understanding the importance of connecting social work theory with practice. The definition and context of social work practice being advocated within the Competency Profile is based on an ecological perspective, which has been criticized for its serious limitations and flaws (Box 1.2).

> Social workers provide social services to a broad range of clients specifically focusing on their social development and the improvement or restoration of their social functioning, in particular by psychosocial evaluations and social intervention, by means of an approach focused in the interactions with the environment (CCSWR, 2012).

The current Canadian Association of Social Workers' *Code of Ethics* (2005) has retreated to an era when there was no vision or articulation of what social work wanted, when no statement of social philosophy existed, and when the primary task of social work was to help people cope with, adjust to, and/or fit back into the very society that caused them problems in the first place. In other words, the *Code* emphasizes residual ideas and regressive practices. Mullaly (2006) outlines a number of its major limitations:

1.   *No philosophical statement or vision.* Without a vision, what type of society should social work have as its goal? What is it that gives social work a sense of direction? The *Code* is silent on this issue. It does state in its preamble (p. 3) that "[t]he social work profession is dedicated to the welfare and self-realization of all people," but it does not offer an opinion on what type or kind of society would best promote this principle. Is it our current North American society with its value base of individualism and cutthroat competition? Or is it a society based on a different set of values that are more consistent with social work values? Without such social ideals, what is it that inspires social work? What is its social raison d'être? Why doesn't the *Code* have a vision statement along the following lines?

> The vision of the profession of Social Work is to help create and contribute to a world where there are no great inequalities of wealth or income, where economic and political power is more evenly distributed, where human need is the central value of distribution of society's resources, where diversity of culture is celebrated, where people have greater control over their own lives, and where all persons are afforded maximum opportunity to enrich their physical, spiritual, psychological, and intellectual well-being.
>
> (taken from the *Vision Statement* of the Faculty of Social Work,
> University of Manitoba, http://law.robsonhall.com/chrr/experts/social-work/)

2. *The client is no longer the primary professional obligation.* The *Code* states, "Social workers maintain the best interests of clients as *a priority* with due regard to the respective interests of others" (p. 3; emphasis added). In other words, the client is no longer the primary obligation of the social worker but just one "other" priority. Given that the best interests of the client often conflict with the interests of the agency (or of more powerful others), whose interests are likely to win out in such conflicts—the client's or one's employer?

3. *The fallacy of equal opportunity or universal impartiality.* A regressive stance in the *Code* is found in "Value 4: Integrity in Practice," in which it is stated that "Social Workers strive for *impartiality* in their professional practice" (p. 6; emphasis added). Impartiality is a liberal-humanist notion that was adopted as a professional norm by mainstream social work dating back to at least 1958 when Wilensky and Lebeaux called for it to become part of the social work "professional self." The notion of professional impartiality specifies the desirability of providing social work services to people without regard to gender, class, race, sexuality, age, and so on. In other words, all people should be treated equally. However, as Galper pointed out in 1975, and as feminists and anti-racist writers argued in the 1980s and 1990s, although perhaps well-intentioned this mandate carries with it a limited notion of fairness. By treating people equally, we are assuming that the standard of equality is "equality of opportunity," thus ignoring important social differences. Equality of opportunity assumes that people start from the same place and compete equally for resources, including social welfare benefits and social work services. Persons and/or groups may be equal before the law, but not all people or groups start out at the same position, which means that not all people or groups are able to exercise their rights or access resources or use their opportunities to the same extent as more privileged groups. If some groups are in a better position to use opportunities because of their social position and the resources available to them, then notions of impartiality and equal opportunity discriminate against other groups (e.g., Indigenous groups, people living in poverty, racialized individuals, refugees, and disabled persons) who have been historically marginalized in our society. The whole fallacy of the impartiality position is that social groups differ with respect to their ability or capacity to use opportunities and to access services. To treat all social groups as if they were all the same is to maintain the inequalities that exist among them.

4. *Acknowledgement of diversity.* Ethical Guideline 1.2 in the *Code*, titled "Demonstrate Cultural Awareness and Sensitivity," contains a subclause 1.2.2: "Social Workers *acknowledge* the diversity within and among individuals, communities and cultures" (p. 4; emphasis added). Given our so-called pluralistic or multicultural Canadian society and the fact that the present white majority is predicted to become a minority within 20 years, why does the *Code* not make a stronger and more positive statement about culture, such as "Social Workers celebrate and promote the diversity of culture"? Use of the word "acknowledge" could be interpreted to mean "recognize" only or "tolerate" rather than appreciate. Recognition or acknowledgement of diversity is part of the multicultural model of social work that now has more than 10 years of critique from the feminist, anti-racist, post-colonial, postmodern, Indigenous, and other progressive social work perspectives, and this model has been rejected in favour of an anti-oppressive or "politics of difference" approach to diversity (see Mullaly, 2010).

5. *Limited self-determination.* The *Code* states under Ethical Guideline 1.3, "Promote Client Self-Determination and Informed Consent," that with respect to agency records, "Social Workers . . . provide them [clients] with honest and accurate information regarding . . . the client's right to view professional records and to seek avenues of complaint" (p. 5), but this does not go far enough. If we are talking about promoting or maximizing "client self-determination," the *Code* should stipulate that service users have the right to write their own recordings or tell their stories and have them placed in the file along with any other document they may wish to have placed there. By not clearly stating so, we continue to privilege professional knowledge over personal experience—something for which the profession has been criticized by various service user groups and contemporary social theorists.

Given this critique of the 2005 CASW *Code of Ethics*, what kind of code of ethics would suit social workers who are interested in fundamental social change (i.e., social transformation)? Jeffry Galper developed such a code back in 1975. More recently, two Australian progressive social workers, Heather Fraser and Linda Briskman (2004), developed a code that would be more relevant to progressive social work practice in the new millennium (Box 1.3). They point out that this code is not a definitive or final declaration but a way to open discussion with progressive social workers around the world. The code is presented here so that a comparison might be made with the CASW 2005 *Code of Ethics*.

Box 1.3 *Code of Ethics for Progressive Social Workers*

1. We regard our primary obligation to be the welfare of all humankind, across the globe, not just those in our immediate vicinity.
2. We understand the contradictions inherent in delivering social work services in a capitalist society. We know that the state can be both oppressive and supportive.
3. We never claim to be "apolitical" or "neutral" and we define social justice in political, material and global terms, not just psychological terms.
4. We respect the need for resources and decision-making processes to be fairly shared, and we realize that this will be hard to achieve given the current political order.
5. We recognize the importance of language and try to show sensitivity through the words that we use. However, we realize that we might "get it wrong."
6. We value processes as much as "products" or "outcomes" and we are—at the very least—skeptical of using violence to deal with conflict.
7. We define power in possessive and relational ways. This means that while we are wary of calling anyone "powerless," we are also aware of the way dominant groups can exercise power over people who are oppressed on the basis of race, gender, class, ability, age, sexual orientation and geographical location.

Continued

8. Because we strive to live in a society where people are able to exercise their human rights, we try to democratize our professional relationships as well as our personal ones.

9. We do not see financial profit as the primary motive in life. Thus, we do not uphold the tenets of global capitalism nor do we value paid work over that which is unpaid.

10. While we appreciate the importance of group bonds, we are wary of the way national- ism can be used to deride and exclude others. In so doing, we seek to work with people from diverse backgrounds in equitable and culturally sensitive ways.

11. We value education for the ways it can be used to develop critical consciousness.

12. We respect the need for oppressed groups to sometimes "go it alone." Yet, we do not presume this will always be their preference. Instead, we are open to providing support/resources to oppressed groups in a manner that they suggest will be useful.

13. While developing knowledge that will be useful to social transformation, we speak up whenever we can about acts of unfairness that we see, using all sorts of media to broadcast our observations and ideas.

14. We recognize the potentially conservative nature of all methods of social work and strive to radicalize all forms of social work that we undertake. As we do this, we avoid individual acts of heroism or martyrdom, preferring instead to work in collaboration with others.

15. We do not see ourselves sitting outside society, or as liberators of the "needy" or the "downtrodden." Rather, we try to use the benefits derived from our professional status to work against the exploitation of individuals and groups.

16. We try to do all this in everyday, reflexive ways, without posturing as self-appointed experts.

17. Given the obstacles that confront us, we realize that fatalism, cynicism and despair may set in. To prevent this we try to keep a sense of humour, have fun with others and incorporate self-care activities into our lives.

Source: Fraser & Briskman (2004).

Another example of a progressive code of ethics is that of the Radical Social Work Group (Morgaine & Capous-Desyllas, 2015). This organization, founded in 2008, is a New York City–based collective and community of social service workers and activists who organized for social justice and human rights. Its mission is to promote social change by challenging the systems of injustice that they and their service users face and to transform society by using radical social work principles and practices. This group lists the following values and points of unity that guide the practices of members of the Radical Social Work Group:

- We believe in anti-racist, anti-oppressive social work practice that challenges the insti- tutions which social work contributes to.

- Base our work on the common values of human rights and social justice.
- Creating a space free of coercion; respecting one another's self-determination: politics, identity and choices.
- Moving beyond our fears and being independent of the institutions that use social work and social workers as a means of control.
- Creating a worldview that avoids designation of identity, stereotypes, or prejudgments.
- Be allies & honor culture, ethnicity, race, class, gender, sexual orientation, etc.
- We are committed to a true democracy; we are committed to transparency & consensus.
- Stay accountable to the people we work for, with each other, ourselves, and the planet.
- Work to move away from being "anti___" towards the creation of something.
- We understand that there's conflict and resistance in social work schools & programs to transform the field and combat conservatism.
- We will not reduce human beings to "cases" to be "managed," manipulated or coerced, or ourselves to mere "workers."

— From https://radicalsocialwork.org

We present these two progressive codes here to show: (1) how mainstream codes of ethics are inadequate for practices of progressive social work; and (2) that there are other social work writers and groups that are developing progressive codes of ethics.

The Fundamental Values of Social Work

Values consist of beliefs, preferences, or assumptions about what is good or desirable for people. They are not assertions or descriptions of the way the world is but rather of how the world ought to be. Values do not stand alone but exist in systems of thought and are organized in such a way that they have a relative importance to other values. Fundamental or primary values represent ideals or goals that a profession attempts to achieve—that is, the end product. Secondary or instrumental values specify the means to achieve these goals or desired ends.

There are many social workers who believe that codes of ethics focus on an individual professional's behaviour and that they serve to pathologize practitioners when many of the problems they encounter in promoting best practice may be structural (Dominelli, 2010). Workers are made to feel individually accountable for judgments made. The prominence of personal responsibility results in the creation of practitioners who work at developing strong decision-making skills. However, ethical dilemmas that involve structural inadequacies may be viewed as personal dilemmas rather than as part of broader societal factors. As a result, social work practitioners may view ethics as being primarily a personal rather than a communal responsibility, supported by codes that place the blame for inadequacies squarely on the shoulders of individual practitioners (Weinberg, 2010, p. 36). However, ethics is also concerned with oppression as a process within groups that has the power to limit the lives, experiences, and opportunities of groups in an unjust way.

Matters of conduct, ethical judgment and decision making of individual professionals cannot be abstracted from the political and policy contexts in which they take place. Individual professionals are both influenced by and help create the ethical discourses of the organizations where they work and the policy frameworks within which they practice. There is a tendency in some of the ethics literature to focus on the individual practitioner making difficult ethical decisions in cases that are sometimes constructed in ways that are decontextualized, both from the character and motives of the individual people involved and from the organization, policy, political and social context (Banks, 2008, p. 1245).

The International Federation of Social Workers' (IFSW) definition of social work (2012) supports principles of human rights and social justice as being fundamental to social work. Although both the IFSW and the CASW codes of ethics identify the pursuit of social justice as a value, they present a limited and limiting view of social justice. That is, social justice is defined only in terms of distributing or redistributing society's resources (i.e., distributive or redistributive justice), which excludes doing anything about the social institutions, policies, processes, and practices responsible for the inequitable distribution in the first place. A (re)distributive view of social justice simply compensates victims of social injustice and does nothing to change a society characterized by inequality along lines of race, class, gender, age, sexuality, and so on.

Social Justice

In her classic book *Justice and the Politics of Difference* (1990), American philosopher and feminist Iris Marion Young contends that contemporary philosophical theories of justice do not conceive justice broadly enough. Instead, they restrict themselves to an interpretation of social justice as the morally proper distribution of benefits and burdens among all society's members. The benefits to be distributed would include both material resources, such as wealth and income, and non-material social goods, such as rights, opportunities, and power. Issues of distributive justice are analogous to persons dividing a stock of goods and comparing the amount or size of the portions. Injustice, according to this distributive notion of social justice, would be defined as a situation in which one group has a monopoly over a particular good. Equating the scope of social justice only with distribution is misleading in two ways: (1) the social processes and practices that caused the maldistribution in the first place are ignored; and (2) the limits of the logic of extending the notion of distribution to such non-material goods and resources as rights and opportunities are not recognized.

Young notes that the distributional view of justice assumes a social atomist or individualist perspective of people in that they are externally related to the goods they possess and only related to one another in terms of a comparison of the amounts of goods they possess. The institutional contexts within which distribution occurs are ignored. These institutional contexts include all social structures and practices, the rules and norms that guide them, and the language and symbols that mediate social interactions within them. This context affects distribution—what is distributed, how it is distributed, who distributes it, who receives it, and what the outcome is. An example presented by Young (1990, p. 23) is economic inequality. Discussions of distribution often omit the decision-making structures that determine economic relations in society.

> Economic domination in our society occurs not simply because persons have more wealth and income than others, as important as this is. Economic domination derives at least as much from the corporate and legal structures and procedures that give some persons the power to make decisions about investment, production, marketing, employment, interest rates, and wages that affect millions of other people. Not all who make these decisions are wealthy or even privileged, but the decision-making structure operates to reproduce distributive inequality and the unjust constraints on people's lives.

Welfare capitalism and conventional social work have adopted the distributional concept of social justice in that their focus has been on the distribution and redistribution of income and other resources (often defined in terms of some kind of social minimum). Discussion has tended to centre on inequalities of wealth and income and the extent to which the state can or should alleviate the suffering of the poor and disadvantaged. Indeed, the immediate provision of basic goods and services for people suffering severe deprivation must be a first priority for any group or program seeking social justice. Any conception of justice must take into account the vast differences in the amount of material goods that exist in our society, where thousands starve and live on the streets while others can have anything they want (Young, 1990).

Limits of Extending Distribution to the Non-material

Advocates of the distributive theory of justice claim that any issue of justice, including such non-material things as rights and opportunities, may be treated as "goods" or some aggregate of things to be possessed and/or distributed and redistributed. Young argues that such treatment produces a misleading conception of the issues of justice involved because it reifies aspects of social life that are better understood as functions of rules, relations, and processes than as things. Distributing or redistributing rights and opportunities is not the same as distributing or redistributing income because rights and opportunities are not possessions. Some groups may have rights and opportunities that other groups do not have, but extending them to the groups that do not have them does not entail that the formerly privileged group must surrender some of its rights and/or opportunities as it does in the case of a redistribution of income. Rights are not things but relationships; rights are institutionally defined rules specifying what people can do in relation to others. "Rights refer to doing more than having, to social relationships that enable or constrain action" (Young, 1990, p. 25). In other words, people may have certain rights but be unable to exercise them because of particular constraints based on class, gender, race, and so on. For example, a person living in poverty may have a right to a fair trial but be unable financially to hire proper legal counsel.

Similarly, opportunity refers to doing rather than to having. It is a condition of enablement rather than of possession and usually involves a system of social rules and social relations, as well as an individual's skills and abilities. Having opportunities may lead to securing material goods such as food, shelter, and a job, but it is no guarantee that these goods and services will be secured. Just as people may have certain rights but are unable to exercise them, so too might people have certain opportunities but be constrained from using them because of particular social relations and practices. For example, in Canada we may say that Indigenous persons have the opportunity to obtain an education, but education occurs in a complex context of social relations. Indigenous people tend to have inferior schools, fewer material resources, and less access to tutors and computers, as well as the experience of culture shock in off-reserve schools. This is not to say that distribution is irrelevant to educational opportunities, but that opportunity has a wider scope than distribution (Young, 1990).

Certainly, then, the distributive theory of social justice contains a major limitation. By focusing on something that must be identifiable and assignable, it reifies social relations and processes and institutional rules. It gives primacy to substance over relations, rules, and processes by conceiving of people as social atoms, thus failing to appreciate that individual identity and capacities are themselves the products of social relations and processes (Taylor, 1985, cited in Young, 1990). Such an atomistic social ontology ignores or obscures the importance of institutional contexts, rules, social relations, and processes for understanding issues of social justice. An adequate conception of social justice must understand and evaluate these social phenomena as well as the substance of distribution (Young, 1990).

Heller (1987) suggests a conception of justice that includes social phenomena. She views justice as primarily the virtue of citizenship wherein persons collectively consider problems and issues facing them within their institutions and actions, under conditions free from oppression and domination, with reciprocity and mutual tolerance of differences. Young argues that this conception of justice shifts the focus from distribution issues to procedural issues of participation in deliberation and decision-making.

- A norm would be just only if people who follow it have an effective voice in its consideration and acceptance.
- A social condition would be just only if it enabled all people to meet their needs and exercise their freedoms.
- A social process would be just only if it were an inclusive process with respect to different social groupings.
- A social practice would be just only if it is in accordance with how people carrying it out would like to be treated themselves.

Social injustice from this perspective entails not only an unfair distribution of goods and resources but includes any norm, social condition, social process, or social practice that interferes with or constrains one from fully participating in society—that is, from becoming a full citizen. This concept of social justice is empowering because it goes beyond a concern with distribution to include the institutional conditions necessary for the development and exercise of individual capacities and collective communication and cooperation (Young, 1990). A society may be evaluated as just to the degree that it contains and supports the institutional conditions necessary for the promotion of the universal value that everyone is of equal intrinsic worth.

Egalitarianism

Although more than one meaning can be ascribed to the term "egalitarianism,"[3] the one that forms part of a progressive social work ideology is that of "social equality." David Gil (1976; 1998) has written eloquently and extensively on the notion of social equality from a social work perspective. He argues that if we wish to establish a society based on social equality, we need to explicate the meaning of this overused, yet elusive, concept. The central value premise of social equality is that every person is of equal intrinsic worth and should therefore be entitled to equal civil, political, social, and economic rights, responsibilities, and treatment.

Implicit is the belief "that every individual should have the right and the resources to develop freely and fully, to actualize his [or her] inherent human potential, and to lead as fulfilling a life [as possible] free of domination, control and exploitation by others" (Gil, 1976, p. 4). Social equality is a correlate of humanism because the dignity of the person cannot be achieved if some people have control over others, have preferred access to life chances, or have more power concerning public affairs: "Genuine democracy, liberty and individuality for all are simply not feasible without social equality" (Gil, 1976, p. 4). A society based on social inequality is based on the value premise that people differ in intrinsic worth and therefore are entitled to different rights and to as much power, control, and material goods as they can gain in competition with others. Humanistic ideals cannot be reached in such a society.

Social equality does not mean monotonous uniformity; rather, it aims at the realization of individual differences in innate potentialities, not at the division of available resources into identical parts for every member of society. The key element in arriving at a humanistic and egalitarian society is the development of a true collectivist spirit. This means taking seriously the fact that people form a social entity called a society when they live together. This does not mean uniform blandness or submission to the group, but it recognizes that decisions made in those areas affecting the whole must be subjected to collective thought and to collective action in the light of collective needs and resources.[4] Collectivism implies participatory decision-making, not hierarchical decisions made at the top and passed down. People should have a say in the decisions that affect any area of their lives—social, economic, political, work, the distribution of society's resources, and so on. This type of decision-making cannot occur in a society based on social inequality.

Humanism

The CASW *Code of Ethics* (2005, p. 4) states that "social work is founded on a long-standing commitment to respect the inherent dignity and worth of persons." Humanism (used interchangeably in the social work literature with the term "humanitarianism"[5]) is defined as "a system of views based on the respect for the dignity and rights of man [*sic*], his value as a personality, concern for his welfare, his all-round development, and the creation of favourable conditions for social life" (Saiflin & Dixon, 1984). This view of the person recognizes that the individual should be the focus of all societal decisions. A society based on humanism would not only recognize the universal nature of human need but would actively attempt to provide to everyone conditions conducive to physical survival, mental health, self-respect, dignity, love, a sense of identity, the opportunity to use one's intellect, and happiness (Hardy, 1981a). Such a commitment must be based on social equality, cooperation, and collective orientation (Gil, 1976), and consideration of all economic decisions ought to be based on their implications for human welfare (Galper, 1975).

Goroff (1981) has articulated his view of a society based on humanism as one in which: (1) each individual is seen as a person with inherent dignity and worth and not as an object with utility; (2) relationships among human beings are non-exploitative, cooperative, and egalitarian; (3) resources created by human beings through their labour are distributed so as to provide each person with the goods and services to meet his or her needs without denying others theirs; and (4) each individual has equal opportunities to develop his or her fullest human potential. There is consensus in the social welfare and social work literatures that our present North American society does not contain these humanistic characteristics.[6]

Because it has been suggested by some writers on the subject of the philosophy of social work that the values of social work are firmly rooted in humanism (e.g., Payne, 1997; Ife, 1997), we should be aware of the limitations of humanism. A common criticism of humanism is that it is ahistorical and does not consider the social context of people's lives—that is, it overlooks the implications of inequalities (Clark & Asquith, 1985; Rojek, Peacock, & Collins, 1988) and does not contain a structural analysis of oppression (Ife, 1997). Certainly, notions of "acceptance" in social work have been influenced by humanism in that social work practice has often excluded concern for the material hardships of service users (Biehal & Sainsbury, 1991). Psychoanalytic, client-centred, and family therapies, for the most part, have focused on introspection, self-realization, and interpersonal dynamics rather than on the social context of people's lives. An example of overlooking material impoverishment and social context is the fact that poverty was rediscovered in the 1960s by people other than social workers.[7]

Another criticism of humanism comes from post-colonial writers (see Gandhi, 1998, for a discussion of this point), who point out that humanism is a Western concept that assumes a Western superiority over all other cultures and societies. As well, postmodernists criticize humanism (particularly radical humanism) for overlooking discourse, subjectivity, and subject position (Pease, 2003). However, the position adopted here is that there are different versions of humanism and that such forms as a critical humanism (Ife, 1997) or a radical humanism (Howe, 1987; Mullaly & Keating, 1991), which emphasize dominant ideology and consciousness, are essential for developing progressive forms of social work. Bob Pease (2003) argues that radical forms of humanism can contribute to progressive forms of social work practice if they are supplemented by critical theory traditions of materialist perspectives emphasizing material conditions and lived experiences, Marxist and feminist Freudian views emphasizing the unconscious and repression, and postmodern perspectives emphasizing discourse, subjectivity, and subject position. Also, radical humanism must be accompanied by another perspective on social interpretation and social change—that is, radical structuralism. An elaboration of these ideas is presented in Chapter 8.

In sum, humanism and social equality must form the twin pillars of an ideal social work society. These fundamental values, and not inequality, rugged individualism, and cutthroat competition, support the dignity and intrinsic worth of people. To realize these fundamental values, society must be arranged according to the principles of collectivism, participatory decision-making, and cooperation and not according to the practices of exploitation, distribution of resources according to economic profit rather than social need, and hierarchical, elitist decision-making. A social work vision of society is based on the premise that the present set of social arrangements is not a natural phenomenon but is, instead, the result of person-made decisions. "People can be self-determining about social forms and can shape and reshape them to meet their current needs" (Galper, 1975, p. 151). In other words, given the political will, a society can develop a social order that promotes human welfare. In addition to meeting people's individual needs, it is part of the progressive social work mission to promote this political will. Gil (1990, pp. 20–21) reminds us that social work practice cannot be politically neutral: "it either confronts and challenges established societal institutions or it conforms to them openly or tacitly. [Social work] practitioners should avoid the illusion of neutrality and should consciously choose and acknowledge their political philosophy."

The Secondary (Instrumental) Values of Social Work

Social work's secondary or instrumental values stem from its fundamental values and contribute to the goal of social justice premised on humanism and egalitarianism. "They dictate the ways the [social] worker should interact with others in carrying out his [or her] professional activities so as to actualize the primary values, that is to achieve the desired ends or goals" (Pincus & Minahan, 1973, p. 39). Secondary values highlighted within the principles of the International Federation of Social Workers' *Statement of Principles* (2005) are respect, self-determination, and acceptance of difference. The operationalization of these three values is assumed to contribute to the situation in which the worth and dignity of people are realized. We affirm people's worth and dignity by showing respect for them, by allowing them maximum feasible self-determination, and by accepting their individualities.

Statham (1978, p. 34) argues that these instrumental values are meaningless in societies based on economic individualism rather than on social equality:

> Social workers affirm their belief in the worth of each person by virtue of their humanity and see them as having needs in common, but the society in which they operate distributes rewards unequally, not because of faulty mechanisms which can be remedied by social work or reform, but because the allocation of rewards is intended to operate in this way.

Do we not negate the respect we extend to clients in our interpersonal relationships with them if we accept a social order based on economic individualism with its inevitable consequences of poverty, homelessness, deprivation, and unemployment? By accepting a person's individuality, are we also accepting their social and economic conditions? And how can we practice self-determination with people who do not possess the economic and social resources necessary for choices to be realized? Self-determination often has meaning only for those possessing the economic resources and social status necessary to implement choice. In a society based on inequality, self-determination is not possible for persons who are powerless "to resolve, by their individual efforts, the problems created, for instance, by inadequate income, housing, or by unemployment" (Statham, 1978, p. 27).

It would seem, then, that social work's instrumental values are illusory if, as Biehal and Sainsbury (1991, p. 249) suggest, "They are not seen in the context of people's lives—notably the context of differences in power." It is not enough to show respect and acceptance for people and offer them choices restricted by their social position in society. Cries for acceptance of rights for people are empty slogans if the reality of power (to exercise rights) is ignored. Social work must also be concerned with realizing a society that promotes social work values rather than one that negates or compromises them. It would seem that only a society founded on humanitarian and egalitarian ideals can accommodate these secondary values. Surely, an imperative for social work is to work toward the establishment of a social vision based on its own value position.

A Progressive Perspective of Social Work Ideology

An ideology is a consistent set of social, economic, and political beliefs. It serves as the foundation and determines the nature and world view of particular social paradigms. Social work has historically been practised in an arena of conflicting beliefs. There has always been some degree of conflict between the social, economic, and political beliefs of the larger society and those espoused by the social work profession in general and by the progressive sector of the profession in particular. Social workers currently operate at the meeting place of the conflict between the dominant values of liberal capitalism and the dominant social work values of humanism and egalitarianism.[8]

Many social workers also experience conflict within their own social, economic, and political beliefs. For example, social workers may subscribe to social beliefs about the dignity and worth of people but also subscribe to our present capitalist economic system based on competition and exploitation, without realizing the inherent conflict between their humanitarian social beliefs and their capitalist economic beliefs. As well, many social workers may believe that self-determination is a laudable goal but will not question our present system of representative democracy in which self-determination and meaningful participation are not options for large numbers of people.

Although social workers espouse many humanitarian and egalitarian beliefs, insufficient attention has been paid to integrating these beliefs in any consistent fashion. Thus, an articulation of social work ideology must entail a delineation of specific social beliefs, economic beliefs, and political beliefs that are consistent with one another. Otherwise, the present hodge-podge of beliefs will continue to present conflict, inconsistency, and uncertainty to social workers in their everyday practice and will do nothing in terms of informing social workers of the nature and form that society would assume if it were to be congruent with social work ideology.

Social Beliefs

David Gil (1976, p. 242) has described in humanistic and egalitarian terms the nature of the relationship between people and the society in which they live:

> All humans, everywhere, despite their manifest differences and their uniqueness as individuals, should be considered of equal intrinsic worth. Hence, they should be deemed entitled to equal social, economic, civil, and political rights, liberties and obligations. Societal institutions . . . should assure and facilitate the exercise of these equal rights, and the free, autonomous, and authentic development of all humans.

This view of people is one in which persons are considered social beings. John Friedmann (1973) contrasts this view of social beings with economic individualism, which perceives people as independent, gratification-maximizing individuals with no social responsibility for others. What distinguishes people as social beings from people as economic individualists is that the former view is based on the notion of community and the latter on the notion of the "rugged individual." Whereas the economic individualist equates public well-being with the mere aggregation of individual interests, the social view of persons recognizes public well-being as a more complex construct made up of not only the aggregate of its members but also the relationships among them.

Friedmann argues that the view of people as social beings is essentially moral whereas the view of people as economic individualists is essentially amoral. As a social being, a person is a thinking and feeling animal who stands in relation to others as a person. A person's recognition of the other person as one like them establishes the manner in which their relationship will be fulfilled. People will treat others as they themselves would want to be treated. A society built on the image of economic individualism would be simply "a bundle of functional roles . . . superordinated, subordinated, or equal and either useful to you or not," a relationship based on a "suspicion of mutual exploitation" (Friedmann, 1973, pp. 6, 5). In the economic individualist view, the notion of the public well-being is arrived at by summing the individual utilities in the marketplace. The worth of a person is judged mainly by what they earn and/or own. Community, which is the cornerstone of civilized life, is not possible with such an amoral foundation. "Without community, there can be no justice, and without justice, life becomes brutish and destructive of both the self and others" (Friedmann, 1973, p. 4).

Economic Beliefs

In *The Politics of Social Services* (1975), Jeffry Galper outlines a set of economic beliefs consistent with social work values. He contrasts these beliefs with the practices of competitive and capitalist economy, which is based on the criterion of profitability. Galper contends that if we are to be successful in creating a world conducive to human well-being, then we must find a way to dominate, rather than be dominated by, economics. Neither the invisible hand of the marketplace nor the present partnership of government and big business ensures that social priorities will dominate economic decision-making.

Galper (1975, pp. 142–143) argues that in our present economic system, the goods produced, the decisions made, and the number and nature of jobs available for people are determined on the basis of profitability. The consequences of this system are:

> an overabundance of goods that do not add up to a fundamental sense of well-being for most people, an absence of goods that we need but that are not profitable to produce, jobs that are destructive to people who hold them, a national psychology organized around competition and consumption, ecological destruction, and exploitation of large parts of the rest of the world to enable us to maintain our standards of material achievement. Human well-being is not, as it should be, the rationale for our actions.

Galper contrasts our present economic system with one in which all decisions of production are based on the criterion of human need. In other words, decisions about what should be produced and in what quantities, as well as when, where, and how, should be made according to their impact on our overall well-being. Galper uses two examples: (1) the decision to produce cars would not be made exclusively on the basis of their saleability but on the basis of such social criteria as the relative emphasis to be given to private versus public transportation, pollution, use of raw materials, safety, and the nature of the work experience for people; and (2) a new factory would be located not just according to the availability of raw materials, labour, and transportation, or for political gain, but according to the development needs of the various regions of the country. An economic system consistent with social work ideals would assure each person full economic rights, and the distribution of wealth, goods, and resources would be much more equitable than it is at present.

In sum, to be consistent with social work ideals, the economic system must be rationalized from a social perspective. It must be viewed as the means to achieve those social goals to which social work aspires, not as an end in itself. Goods must be produced for their utility rather than their profitability, and consideration should be given to all the costs (social, economic, ecological, and so on) of production. Finally, the distribution of wealth, rather than following social Darwinian notions, must be done according to social determinations—those factors that contribute to the well-being of all citizens, not just of those who own the means of production. These principles are, of course, contradictory to and inconsistent with the laissez-faire principles of our present liberal-capitalist economic system.

Political Beliefs

Social work subscribes to the democratic ideals of self-determination, participation, and an equal distribution of political power. In fact, much of social work practice is directed toward individuals and groups, helping them to gain or regain autonomy and control over their lives. However, there are basically two methods by which democracy can be practised: representative democracy and participatory democracy.

We all are used to the representative form of government. Pateman (1970, cited in Hardy, 1981b, p. 17) describes and analyzes this system of democracy:

> The characteristically democratic element . . . is the competition of leaders for the votes of the people at periodic, free elections. Elections are crucial to the democratic method for it is primarily through elections that the majority can exercise control over their leaders through loss of office. . . . The decisions of leaders can also be influenced by active groups bringing pressure to bear during inter-election periods. "Political equality" in the theory [of representative democracy] refers to universal suffrage and to the existence of equality of opportunity of access to channels of influence over leaders. . . . The level of participation by the majority should not rise much above the minimum level necessary to keep the democratic method working; that is, it should remain at about the level that exists in Anglo-American democracies.

Although this model of democracy is relatively efficient in terms of the time it takes to make decisions, its weaknesses have been well documented in the literature (Galper, 1975; Hardy, 1981b; Naiman, 1997; Wharf & Cossom, 1987). (1) Political elites at times make decisions that are not responsive to the wishes of the electorate. (2) Interest pressure groups may gain some sectional advantage at the expense of more general welfare. (3) Unorganized sections of society may be ignored or exploited by powerful, organized sections. (4) The right to vote every few years is inconsistent with the notion of democracy. (5) Such a system promotes and relies on a considerable degree of passivity in the majority of people. (6) In the absence of participatory principles, those who make decisions will be those who have benefited most from the system and, therefore, have the least commitment to changing it. "Though democratic in the way it is chosen, representative government has been shown to be elitist in the way that it operates" (Lees, 1972, p. 39).

By way of contrast, participatory democracy would produce a very different world (Hardy, 1981b). It would permit and encourage greater popular participation in non-governmental bodies like industry, trade unions, political parties, corporations, schools, universities, and the like (Lees, 1972; Naiman, 1997). In addition, it would delegate a larger share of public power to local communities small enough to permit effective and meaningful general participation in decision-making:

> Participation in politics would provide individuals with opportunities to take part in making significant decisions about their everyday lives. It would build and consolidate a sense of genuine community that would serve as a solid foundation for government. The first and most important step is to recognize that personal self-development is the moral goal of democracy and that direct popular participation is the chief means of achieving it. When this is generally accepted, then society can get on with the largely technical job of thinking up new and better means for increasing popular participation (Lees, 1972, p. 41).

Surely, given social work's values and ideals with respect to egalitarianism, self-determination, and so on, participatory democracy rather than representative democracy is the preferred form of democracy.

Summary of Social Work Ideology

The amalgam of the above social, economic, and political beliefs comprises social work's ideology. Social beliefs are based on the person as a social being. Economic beliefs are based on the notion that human well-being is the major criterion for economic decision-making. And political beliefs are based on people having the right and the responsibility to participate in those decisions that affect their lives. Taken together, these beliefs constitute social work's ideology for progressive social workers (see Table 1.2). This ideology comprises an interdependent, consistent, and mutually reinforcing set of ideas and ideals that should underpin the type of society that best promotes social work's fundamental values of humanism and egalitarianism.

Social Work and Social Problems

All social work activity is concerned with social problems—that is, with alleviating, eliminating, or preventing social problems and the deleterious effects they have on people. However, although poverty, mental health issues, and deprivation may constitute objective phenomena, the analyses, interpretations, and explanations of these phenomena are subjective. In other words, a social problem may be seen as a set of objective circumstances, but it includes a subjective interpretation. Such interpretations are defined largely in terms of ideology and group interests.

Table 1.2 Overview of Progressive Social Work Ideals and Beliefs

Social Beliefs	Humanitarianism (humanism)
	Community
	Equality
Economic Beliefs	Government intervention
	Social priorities dominate economic decisions
	Equitable distribution of society's resources
Political Beliefs	Participatory democracy (self-determination) in both governmental and non-governmental areas
View of Social Welfare	An instrument of equality, solidarity, and community
	Ideal = social welfare
Principles of Social Work Practice	Treat people with respect
	Enhance dignity and integrity
	Facilitate self-determination and self-realization
	Accept differences
	Advocate and promote social justice

For example, the existence of poverty will be explained differently by a conservative than by a Marxist, the former attributing poverty to a defective individual and the latter attributing it to a defective social arrangement (i.e., capitalism). The implication for social work is that the individual living in poverty would be treated in a punitive or remedial manner by a conservative social worker but would be treated as a victim of an oppressive social order by a progressive or critical social worker.

Although the values of social work are generally considered progressive and humanistic, its definitions or explanations of social problems have not always been progressive or humanistic. Because social work has been reluctant to elevate the discussion of its values to a societal level, there has been no agreed-upon goal or product with respect to the type and form of society social work is seeking. In the absence of a publicly articulated social vision, social work falls victim to the prevailing paradigm. That is, without a clear vision of itself and of the society within which it exists, social work has tended to accept as a given the current social order or paradigm. This means that social work "theory and practice become accommodated only to that which is possible within existing organizational constraints" (Moreau & Leonard, 1989, p. 235). With no alternative social order defined or articulated, social work becomes part of the existing social order, helping people to adjust to it or cope with it or attempting to make small changes within the system rather than attempting to make fundamental changes that transform the system.

Social work, by being part of the present paradigm and in the absence of an alternative, tends to take on the prevailing definitions or explanations of social problems. In Canada and the United States, social problems have been defined mainly within conservative-liberal perspectives. Most internally derived social work theory-building has been in the methods or means of social work practice rather than in the goals or desired ends of social work practice. As long as social work avoids the task of articulating its desired ends or vision, it will continue to treat objective social problems with the subjective prescriptions of the prevailing paradigm. To date in North America, most social work explanations of social problems and most social work interventions have been based either on "individual pathology" (conservative ideology) or "general systems/ecological explanations" (liberal ideology) of social problems. Such approaches, of course, do not guarantee that social problems experienced by large numbers of people will be dealt with adequately or effectively. Radical or critical explanations of social problems have only recently become part of the social work theory landscape, but they still occupy a minority position. This is because, to date, socialist/Marxist, feminist, anti-racist, anti-oppressive, and queer ideas and analyses have not been major parts of the prevailing paradigms in North America.

In sum, although social work espouses a set of values considered progressive, its approach to resolve social problems has not been progressive. In the absence of an articulated social vision or goal consistent with its value base, social work has accepted by default the mainstream definitions and explanations of social problems, which have come from the prevailing North American ideologies of conservatism and liberalism. The critical question arising from this situation is whether or not social work ideology is consistent with either conservatism or liberalism. Or is it more consistent with an ideology that does not prevail in North America? A related question is whether or not social work's progressive and humanistic ideology is consistent with or in conflict with its current theory base and practice.

The Ideal Social Welfare System: A Progressive View

Every industrial democracy in the Western world has developed a social welfare system to deal with the vagaries of the market economy. Although all states have policies of intervention, the forms of these interventions often differ, as do their purposes. Furniss and Tilton (1977) have aggregated the different forms of intervention into three models of social welfare states: the positive state, the social security state, and the social welfare state. These models are described below in terms of the type of intervention employed, the groups in society benefiting from the intervention, and the vision of society that inspires each model. The first two models correspond to Wilensky and Lebeaux's (1965) typology of the residual model (the positive state) and the institutional model (the social security state). The third model corresponds to Mishra's (1981) description of the structural model of welfare.

The Positive State or Residual Model of Welfare

The main goal of the positive state is to protect the interests of business from the difficulties of unprotected markets and from potential redistributive demands. The policy emphasis is on government–business collaboration for economic growth. Business yields much of its market decisions to government in return for financial assistance at home and political support abroad. The positive state aims at minimal full employment to keep consumption up, labour costs down, and labour unions weak. The current process of globalization is being driven, in large part, by values and principles of the positive state.

The preferred social welfare instrument is social insurance, which is consistent with economic efficiency and encourages "proper" work habits. As well, it functions as social control by tying people's eligibility for social insurance benefits to their participation in the labour market. The beneficiaries of the positive state tend to be those who, under conditions of laissez-faire individualism, prosper most readily. The vision of the positive state is not at all similar to that of social work. Rather, it is one of rugged individualism within the context of balanced economic growth and protection of business interests (Mishra, 1981). It is the model of welfare favoured by neo-conservatives. The United States best typifies this model.

The Social Security State or Institutional Model of Welfare

The key concept of the social security state is that everyone who is a casualty of the industrial order has a right to a guaranteed minimum of social security. This collective responsibility for individual maintenance recognizes that a society based on competitive capitalism cannot provide universal security and that the state has a duty to fill this void. Theoretically, it is possible to eliminate poverty by establishing the national minimum income at an adequate level. The vision of a social security state is based on government–business cooperation whereby the guaranteed national minimum is financed by pursuing an economic policy of maximal full employment and public employment as a last resort. These economic and social policies are intended to be of direct benefit to every citizen and to overcome the limitations of social insurance provisions.

The social security state does not contain egalitarian social and economic ideals. The governing principle is "equality of opportunity" whereby all are equal in status before the law but unequal in material resources, life chances, and political power. It represents what Furniss and Tilton (1977) call "a modern and noble version of the Liberal ideal." Great Britain (before Thatcherism) and Canada and Australia (before Howard), to a lesser extent, typify the social security state, although there has been a drift toward the positive state in all three jurisdictions.

The Social Welfare State or Structural Model of Welfare

Unlike the goal of minimalist–full employment of the positive state or of maximalist–full employment of the social security state, the social welfare state has as its goal full employment. This requires government–union cooperation in the labour market. Equally important to the social welfare state are two other policies: environmental planning (in its most comprehensive form) and solidaristic wages. Environmental planning encompasses regulation of property to preserve amenities, prohibition of activities resulting in pollution, urban planning, and development of new communities. In short, this policy represents an effort to inject collective and social values into a society founded on the good life of the individual. The solidaristic wage policy counteracts the tendency toward concentration of assets and income, narrows differentials among groups of wage-earners, and extracts for labour a larger piece of the national income.

The social welfare state aims to promote equality and solidarity. It seeks more than a national minimum for citizens in attempting to achieve a general equality of living conditions. It substitutes public services, such as the public provision of health care, child care, and legal services, for social insurance programs. These services are available to all, not just to the underprivileged. The social welfare state envisions extending the locus of political and economic power and increasing citizen participation in all areas of living. It is similar to what Mishra (1981) calls the structural model of welfare. Although no country at present typifies the social welfare state, Sweden best approximates it among Western industrial democracies.

Social work must reject the positive state as a welfare system because it violates its fundamental values of humanism and egalitarianism and its corresponding set of social, economic, and political beliefs. The social security state contains some humanistic elements but lacks egalitarian ideals. The social welfare state, on the other hand, is most congruent with social work values, beliefs, and principles. Thus, progressive social workers must work toward and attempt to achieve this form of society if they are to remain true to their own ideals. However, the social welfare state or the structural model of welfare cannot be achieved in our present society because it rests on a set of values contradictory to those of neo-conservative or liberal capitalism.

Conclusion

In this chapter, the two major approaches to social work, the mainstream and progressive views, were presented. Using the progressive perspective as a point of departure, the argument here is that social work needs a progressive vision of society and social work practice if it is to be true to its primary values of humanitarianism and egalitarianism. The 2005 CASW *Code of Ethics* contains little potential to develop such a view. The question for social work is which of the major societal paradigms is most congruent with a concept of social justice premised on creating societal conditions in which people are free from oppression and domination. In other words, is there a paradigm that approximates or is consistent with social work's primary values of humanitarianism and egalitarianism, as well as its secondary or instrumental values? These instrumental values include respect for the individual as a social being, the domination of economic decisions by societal decisions, participatory democracy, and a social welfare system that contributes to equality, solidarity, and community. The next four chapters will examine various social paradigms in an attempt to answer this question.

Critical Questions

1. What does a "progressive view" mean, and why is it important to social work?
2. Why does social work need a code of ethics?
3. Why does social work need a professional association? Why doesn't social work organize itself into a union instead of a professional association?
4. How do you respond to the charge that social workers advocate for more spending on social programs only to guarantee themselves jobs?
5. Why has social work not been able to exert a significant influence on social policy decisions?
6. How and in what direction do the media influence people's opinions about social work and social programs?

2 Capitalism, Crises, and Paradigms

Subjects enter a social world they didn't make, but they are able to act upon it provided they can understand how it is made, and in so doing, develop a revolutionary praxis to free themselves.

—Peter Leonard (1997), paraphrasing Karl Marx

Introduction

This chapter presents an overview of the economic, social, and political crises that occurred over the last quarter of the twentieth century and the first decade and a half of the twenty-first century as capitalism transformed from its postwar (1945–73) welfare state form to a globalized version, which, as will be argued, peaked around 1995. Starting with the oil crisis and the Yom Kippur (October) War between Israel and its Arab neighbours in 1973, along with the inflation-fuelled Vietnam War, the chapter traces the latest mutation of capitalism, from when the nation-state was largely able to contain the worst excesses of capitalism by Keynesian interventions to the shift to a global economy. This process of economic globalization has reduced the autonomy of nation-states, limited the power of the trade union movement, resulted in a retrenched welfare state, and brought a crisis in confidence in social work among people both within and outside the profession. Some of the negative consequences of this new form of capitalism are presented. These consequences include vulnerability in the labour market, a re-emphasis of the subordinate positions of historically disadvantaged groups such as women and racialized individuals, draconian cuts in social services at a time of increased need, and an ineffective response by social work because it had no widely accepted theoretical analysis of the crises to respond to them. An overview of the "globalization thesis" suggests that globalization is normal, natural, inevitable, and irreversible and, therefore, should not be resisted.

Following a discussion of the various social, economic, and political crises that resulted from and/or were part of the globalizing of capitalism, we consider a number of hopeful signs that emerged during the decade of 1995–2006. Discussed are the successes of the anti-globalization movement, the "collapse of the globalism thesis," and the fact that the federal government, in Canada at least, went from a deficit to a surplus position in 1997 and had experienced eight successive budget surpluses in the billions of dollars. Government deficits could no longer be used as the reason or excuse for cutting back on social programs. However, these hopeful signs and an improved financial situation were erased by the 2008 worldwide financial crisis—the greatest worldwide recession since the Great Depression of the 1930s—and by the Harper Conservative government's responses to this crisis in particular. A number of draconian economic, social, environmental, and political policies were enacted during its term of government (2006–15). An overview of these regressive policies and their social, economic, and political impact on Canada, along with an outlook on what might be expected from the Trudeau government (elected in October 2015), will be presented here. Also discussed in this chapter are some optimistic signs that have emerged recently in Canada and elsewhere and that should give hope to people who are concerned with social justice. They include the defeat of the Harper Conservative government, a renewed environmental movement, the anti-globalization movement, the collapse of the "globalism thesis," and the recent "Idle No More" movement, which is one of the largest Indigenous mass movements in Canadian history.

The crises of the last quarter of the twentieth century and first part of the twenty-first century have brought about considerable soul-searching in social work with respect to many of its comfortable assumptions about the nature of people, society, the state, and the relationships among them. And although some social workers have fallen back on victim-blaming explanations for social problems, with others having drifted toward new models of regressive and oppressive forms of social work such as the "competency movement" (to be discussed in a subsequent chapter) and still others having clung tenaciously to old models of practice, such as ecological perspectives and systems theory, there has been a significant call for new or alternative social work theory and practice models that are relevant to today's economic, social, political, cultural, and intellectual reality.

The two concepts adopted here as a point of departure in response to this call for alternative theories and models of practice are those of "ideology" and "paradigm." These are not new concepts, and, in fact, their use has been criticized by many groups and writers as being part of the modernist tradition, which has inherent oppressive qualities (discussed in subsequent chapters). However, an attempt is made here to use postmodern and other forms of modernist critique to inform all analyses based on the concepts of ideology and paradigm. Behaviour, social organization, social movements, and so on are often influenced by ideology. Thus, ideological positions with respect to politics, political parties, and social attitudes, including those toward the state and social welfare, are examined in this chapter. Finally, the concept of "paradigm" is explained in terms of how it helps to organize social thought in general and social work analysis, theory, and practice in particular.

The Changing Face of Capitalism

Keynesian (Welfare) Capitalism

Something significant has changed since the early 1970s in the way capitalism has been working, or not working. Although seldom steady and never free from tensions and conflicts, postwar capitalism managed to maintain an economic boom from 1945 until 1973. This long boom, to a certain extent, benefited unionized labour, raised material living standards for much of the population living in advanced capitalist countries, and provided a relatively stable environment for corporate profit-making. The particular set of labour control practices, consumption patterns, and configurations of political and economic power that characterized postwar capitalism depended on a series of compromises on the part of its key players: the corporate sector, the trade union movement, and the nation-state. In his celebrated book, *The Condition of Postmodernity* (1989), David Harvey outlines the nature of these compromises and the roles played by their major actors.

For its part, large corporate power was to assure steady increased investments that would enhance productivity, guarantee economic growth, and raise living standards for the general populace. This involved a commitment to ongoing technological development, mass fixed capital investments in plants and equipment, increased managerial experience in production and marketing, and mobilization of economies of scale through standardization of products. Scientific management—in the form of Taylorism[1] and Fordism[2]—of all areas of corporate activity became the cornerstone of bureaucratic rationality, and the massing of workers in large-scale factories became the modus operandi of productive processes. This, in turn, required hierarchical work relations and a deskilled workforce.

The trade union movements in North America, like those in most other advanced capitalist regions, have never been marked by total solidarity or homogeneity. There have always been radical working-class movements, but they have been in the minority and, like the larger trade union movement, have been brought under strict legal discipline by way of state industrial relations and labour legislation. Although unions may have won considerable power in the area of collective bargaining, they have done so in return for adopting a collaborative stance with the corporate and state sectors. That is, the trade union movement would collaborate with capitalist ownership and bourgeois governments and not pursue radical social or economic reform. In exchange for real wage gains and job security from employers and for social insurance and minimum wage benefits from the state, trade union leaders undertook to control their membership and collaborate with business in plans to increase productivity using scientific management principles and techniques.

The state, for its part, assumed a variety of obligations to both the corporate sector and workers. It was to create relatively stable consumer demand conditions by curbing business cycles of "boom and bust" through an appropriate mix of fiscal and monetary policies—that is, by applying Keynesian[3] economic principles. The state was to invest in areas such as transportation and public utilities, which are vital to mass production and mass consumption. Likewise, it was to ensure a certain level of social protection by providing programs of social insurance, health care, education, and housing.

In sum, "the long postwar boom . . . was built upon a certain set of labour control practices, technological mixes, consumption habits, and configurations of political-economic power" (Harvey, 1989, p. 124). This model of capitalism can reasonably be called "Keynesian capitalism" but is also known as "welfare capitalism" because it reflected a belief that a welfare state could exist within capitalism (although there are competing explanations as to the real function of the welfare state, i.e., social care vs social control). These competing views will be explored in some detail in later chapters of this book. The major assumption of this model was that of infinite economic growth manifested by the production and consumption of more and more products, which in turn would be followed by more and more jobs, increased profits, higher wages, and more government revenue for an ever-expanding welfare state. Furthermore, as noted by Mishra (1999),

Keynesian macroeconomic management presupposed a relatively closed national economy that could be regulated by the national government. Thus, although nation-states may have had close and cooperative relations with other nations in the postwar era, the nation-state itself was considered the basic unit of economic and political life (McBride, 2001).

Global Capitalism

Cracks were already appearing in the postwar Keynesian capitalist economy by the early 1970s. The Vietnam War fuelled inflation both in the United States and abroad. The sharp recession of 1973 that resulted from the OPEC oil crisis saw a quadrupling in the price of oil brought about by the 1973 Yom Kippur War between Israel and its Arab neighbours. These events set in motion a whole set of processes that shattered the "grand corporate–labour–state accord" that underpinned Keynesian capitalism. Suddenly, the economy was no longer growing (Lightman, 2003). The corporate sector was the first to act and began a process whereby capitalism shifted away from its Keynesian form, with national governments managing their respective economies, to a global form in which national governments have less control over their own national economies. In the face of unstable economic growth, inflation, and a worldwide recession, the corporate sector began to rationalize and restructure its operations. Technological change, automation, downsizing, mergers, acceleration of capital turnover, and moves to countries with cheaper and more manageable labour became the strategies for corporate survival (Harvey, 1989). These changes have re-emphasized the vulnerability of historically disadvantaged groups, particularly women, children, immigrants, racialized groups, and people living in poverty. The changes in the organization of the labour market and industry have also weakened the trade union movement, which has lost core, full-time members in the face of the transition to a more flexible labour force (i.e., an increased reliance on part-time, casual, and subcontracted workers). The labour movement has also experienced some political repression through legislative curbs on union power and by the geographical relocation of many businesses to underdeveloped countries. And, of course, with a weakened and reduced trade union movement, class consciousness is reduced as well.

Governments also felt the effects of the transformation in capitalism. The "stagflation" (a combination of high inflation and high unemployment) that occurred in the mid-1970s could not be explained by Keynesian economic theory and did not seem amenable to the usual practices of government intervention. Also, partly because of economic decline, governments began to receive less tax revenue than in the past but were confronted with growing numbers of people hurt by the recession and subsequent corporate restructuring who were in need of government-sponsored social programs. Critics of Keynesianism argued that governments that continue to provide services at a cost higher than a country's economic growth invite a serious fiscal crisis of overload. Faced with mounting deficits, governments could either raise taxes and extend the tax base (as some European countries did) or reduce government expenditures. Right-wing governments were elected in 1979 in Britain, in 1980 in the United States, and in 1984 in Canada. All three governments voiced similar priorities to deal with their respective economic crises. Thatcher's Conservatives stressed the values of "self-reliance," Reagan's Republicans aimed "to get big government off the backs of people," and Mulroney's Progressive Conservatives declared that "Canada was open for business." These governments chose to reduce expenditures rather than raise taxes, and all three targeted the welfare state as a major area of cost containment and/ or cost reduction. Subsequent governments of nominally different political stripes in each of these countries have continued with cost-containment policies. Australia, under the Hawke and Keating Labour governments, although implementing such policies a little later and a little more slowly, went down the same road, but with the Howard Liberal government elected in 1996 that country pursued the same course at a much more accelerated rate. As a result of these policy choices, the welfare state in all four countries underwent (and continues to undergo) a "crisis of legitimation."[4] That is, it is seen as an unaffordable luxury by many people and organizations of the New Right (i.e., a range of right-wing groups and organizations that advocate free-market principles, anti-welfare policies, and the supremacy of individual rights over those of the common good). Survival in the global economy now seems to take precedence over meeting human and social needs.

The Globalization Thesis

There is by now a vast literature on globalization, and no attempt will be made to summarize it. Instead, a critical view of the dominant explanation for the present course of globalization and its accompanying discourse of inevitability will be provided, along with some of the social and economic effects resulting from globalization. It should be noted here, however, that the concept of globalization and the explanation for the process that it has taken are contestable. For example, globalization is viewed by some (e.g., big business) as a positive phenomenon; others view it as a negative phenomenon (e.g., many persons who hold social programs dear); still others view it as neither inherently positive nor negative (e.g., Lightman, 2003; Mishra, 1999). An example of the latter view is provided by Lightman (2003), who argues that globalization processes can be positive or negative. He contends that the European Union (EU) is an example of positive economic integration because the participating nations built into their treaty social protections for workers. An example of negative economic integration, according to Lightman, is the North American Free Trade Agreement (NAFTA), which is based on free-market principles and does not include any direct social or political concerns. The position taken here concurs with that of Lightman (2003) and Mishra (1999), which is that globalization is neither inherently good nor evil. Rather, the problem is the dominant ideology underpinning the specific forms and processes of globalization. To date, globalization has been led by the United States and is based largely on that nation's dominant ideology of free markets, individualism, a minimal welfare state, and meeting corporate interests.

From the above, it is obvious that there is no single universal definition of globalization. Globalization may be viewed as primarily an economic process involving cross-border transactions in goods and services, international capital flows, and the rapid spread of technology. This view has been adopted by the International Monetary Fund (IMF) (Ferguson, Lavalette, & Mooney, 2002). Most social welfare and social work writers, however, view globalization as a much more complex phenomenon involving not only economic factors but also cultural, political, and ideological processes (see, for example, Ferguson et al., 2002; George & Wilding, 2002;

Mishra, 1999). It is nonetheless important to understand the dominant view of globalization because this view is used by corporations, governments, and others to rationalize reductions in social services spending. A critique of this dominant view will be presented in a subsequent section of this chapter. The following outlines nine components of what Ferguson et al. (2002) call the "globalization thesis."

The Triumph of Capitalism over Socialist Alternatives

The first major component of the dominant explanation of globalization, as identified by Mishra (1999), is the collapse of communism and the retreat of the socialist alternative. The collapse of the Soviet Union in the last decade of the twentieth century signified for many the emergence of a new world order in which capitalism had triumphed—we had reached what Fukuyama (1992) described as the end of history because there was no further basis for any ideological struggles against capitalism. "Globalization and the triumph of the market would benefit us all" (Ferguson et al., 2002, p. 136).

The Ideological Foundation of Globalization

A second major component of the current form and process of globalization is its ideological foundation—neo-conservatism or neo-liberalism. (Although these terms are often used inter-changeably, which causes some confusion to students of social work and social policy, there are differences between the two, which are outlined in Note 5. We choose to use the term "neo-conservatism" for reasons given in this endnote. The main difference between the two is that neo-conservatism refers to a complete set of social, economic, and political beliefs [these beliefs are presented in Chapter 8], whereas neo-liberalism is mainly an economic doctrine. However, we recognize that many writers use the term "neo-liberalism" to mean essentially the same set of ideas.) "Contemporary globalization expresses, promotes and legitimates a particular ideology—neoliberalism [or neo-conservatism]—which has had . . . a profound effect on social policy" (George & Wilding, 2002, p. 56).[5] The values of economic growth and private gain are extolled at the expense of broader economic and social development (George & Wilding, 2002). There is broad consensus in the literature that neo-conservative ideology has been driving the present course of globalization since the 1970s. Mishra (1999), for example, points out that what neo-conservatism presents as ideology, globalization makes into a virtue and a necessity. John Gray (1998) argues that the global economy did not emerge spontaneously but that human agency played a critical role in engineering its development. Emphasizing the roles of Thatcher and Reagan, he argues that globalization was part of a deliberate (neo-conservative) ideological project to destroy the Keynesian state interventions that had dominated economic and social affairs at the national level during the postwar years.

Economic Determinism

An important component of globalization is that its logic and ideology are framed within a particular *discourse*[6] that justifies this new global capitalism—a discourse of economic determinism.

The central message of this discourse is that global capitalism is a natural, normal, evolutionary, and inevitable process. Therefore, it should not be interfered with or resisted (especially by unions or governments) but instead should be embraced. Any form of Keynesian intervention is now dead because no one has control over the determining effects of global market forces, since they are the products of impersonal economic relations, new technologies, and new means of communication (Leonard, 1997)—or so we are told by neo-classical economists, the mainstream press, the corporate sector, and its government allies. The global economy is spoken about in terms of *economic laws* (e.g., the law of supply and demand, the laws of competition) and mystical market forces that presumably come from a higher source than humankind—perhaps nature or even Divine Providence. The dominant discourse of the new economy also speaks of the joys of entrepreneurial innovation and the economic necessity of worker adjustment. At the same time, it is made to appear imperative that any resistance to global economic changes must be overcome by whatever means are at hand (Head, 1996).

Regulated by the Natural Laws of the Marketplace

The discourse of globalization uses Hobbesian and Darwinian language[7] to urge us to accept that competitive life, although nasty and brutish, is necessary for survival in the global economy (Leonard, 1997). We are told that we must accept the negative consequences of the development of globalization on employment, wages, community, and class relations because the consequences would even be worse if we did not compete successfully in the global market. Growing poverty is deemed unsolvable because it is the product of an "underclass" subculture (Fisher & Karger, 1997). Economic development is part of the discourse applied to exploitation of the developing world by global corporate capitalism, yet this latter world continues to provide cheap resources just as it did in the days of colonial rule. A significant part of the globalization discourse is to present the market and social investment as a contradiction. That is, how can a lean national economy that must compete in the global marketplace support a welfare state? The predictable answer, of course, is that it cannot. Leonard (1997, p. 113) comments on this position:

> The old ideas which ruled the modern welfare state—universality, full employment, increasing equality—are proclaimed to be a hindrance to survival. They are castigated as ideas which have outlived their usefulness: they are no longer appropriate to the conditions of a global capitalist economy.

The discourse of inevitability or economic determinism perfectly suits neo-conservatism. It justifies free markets, unfettered competition, individualism, anti-unionism, and a reduced welfare state. (Neo-conservative ideology is covered in some detail in Chapter 3.) Another part of the globalization discourse is that its proponents proclaim that free and prosperous markets will both increase the living standards of all participant nations and turn dictatorships into democracies. With respect to the latter claim, however, David McNally (2002) points out that none of the international economic accords, from the North American Free Trade Agreement (NAFTA) to the World Trade Organization (WTO), contains one clause that would establish a single addition to the civil or human rights of people. With respect to increased standards of living, the evidence suggests that free markets have led less to international prosperity than to increased international social inequality.

Globalization Helps to Spread Democracy

The globalization thesis tends to equate free markets with democracy. The belief is that increased prosperity coming from free markets will lift impoverished and oppressed people out of poverty and provide them with the means to convert dictatorships into democracies. Steger (2003) argues that globalization affirms the compatibility of these two concepts (i.e., free markets and democracy) and treats this compatibility as "common sense," which precludes any challenge to it in public discourse, as evidenced by the following examples:

> The level of economic development resulting from globalization is conducive to the creation of complex civil societies with a powerful middle class. It is this class and societal structure that facilitates democracy.
> — Francis Fukuyama, John Hopkins University, cited in Steger (2003, p. 110)

> The emergence of new businesses and shopping centers in former communist countries should be seen as the backbone of democracy.
> — Hillary Rodham Clinton, US Senator from New York [and presidential candidate of the Democratic Party in the 2016 election], cited in Steger (2003, p. 110)

Globalization Benefits Everyone

A contention of the globalization thesis is that global markets, freed from narrow national interests and restrictive regulations, will bring forth waves of trade, which in turn will "unleash a broad economic-social tide that would raise all ships, whether of our Western poor or for the developing world in general" (Saul, 2004, p. 34). Steger (2003, p. 104) quotes Alan Greenspan, the long-time head of the US Federal Reserve who finally stepped down in 2006, as representative of many "globalists" who connect their arguments supporting globalization to the alleged economic benefits resulting from market liberalization: "There can be little doubt that the extraordinary changes in global finance on balance have been beneficial in facilitating significant improvements in economic structures and living standards throughout the world."

Political and Economic Sovereignty Surrendered to Global Markets

An important component of the globalization thesis is that the power of the nation-state was on its way out, to be replaced by that of global markets. Economics, not politics, would determine the course of human events. In other words, transnational corporations, not nation-states, would rightfully determine economic policies and markets, and they would do a better job of managing them with major rewards trickling down to the masses. The laws of the free market would necessarily supersede the laws of any particular nation-state.

Welfare State No Longer Affordable or Desirable

Another component of the globalization thesis is that the welfare state on a national level is no longer sustainable. For almost the past 100 years, the state was considered to be the major provider of welfare and the key player in directing the economy. However, since the 1970s this view has come under constant attack from multinational capital and New Right governments, the argument being that interference in the economy by governments is the major cause of economic problems. The relationship between globalization and the welfare state is discussed in the next section of this chapter.

Deregulation of the Economy and Regulation of Trade Unions

Ferguson et al. (2002, p. 136) summarize the final component (i.e., deregulation of the economy, accompanied by regulation of trade unions) of the globalization thesis:

> The globalization thesis is . . . part and parcel of neo-liberal [or neo-conservative] ideology. To expand and deepen capitalism, the free flow of capital, the "opening up" of national economies and markets, the deregulation of economies and labour markets and the marginalization of illegitimate monopolies (such as trade unions) are seen as vital—they are the guiding principles of economic activity. These principles in turn require only minimal state "interference" and where there has been state intervention this should be dismantled or "rolled back"—markets represent the most efficient state distributive mechanism and any interference in markets brings disequilibrium into the system which, in turn, will increase the probability of breakdown and short-term economic crisis.

Given what we know of the globalization thesis, it may be asked: what have been the effects of globalization to date?

A report by Oxfam International (2016) entitled *An Economy for the 1%* presents some updated figures on wealth and inequality that show inequality getting worse on an international and national level. Using data from Credit Suisse and the *Forbes* list of the world's wealthiest individuals, it highlights shifts in wealth concentration that have occurred over the past several decades. Among its findings are that:

- The richest 62 people hold the same amount of wealth as the 3.5 billion people who make up the bottom 50 per cent. By comparison, 80 people had as much wealth as the bottom half in 2015; in 2014 the figure was 85 people, and in 2010 it was 388, showing that these excessive discrepancies in wealth inequality continue to increase on a yearly basis.
- The wealth of the richest 62 people has risen by 45 per cent since 2010, while the wealth of the bottom half (i.e., the poorest 3.5 billion people) fell by 38 per cent.

- The richest 1 per cent of the world's population controls more wealth than the rest of the world's population combined. The average wealth of each of the 72 million adults who make up the richest 1 per cent was $1.7 million compared to $5,000 for the 6.48 billion people in the bottom 90 per cent.
- The world economy is heavily skewed in favour of the rich in that far from trickling down, wealth and income are moving upwards at an alarming rate. Once there, an elaborate system of "tax havens" and an industry of wealth managers ensure that it stays there. One recent estimate (Zucman, 2014, cited in Oxfam 2016) is that $7.6 trillion of individual wealth—more than the combined GDP of Germany and the UK—is currently held offshore (i.e., outside a country's national boundaries). These offshore tax havens take money that could be used for social welfare programs.
- Rising economic inequality compounds other forms of inequality. The International Monetary Fund (IMF) found recently that countries with higher income inequality also have larger gaps between men and women with respect to education, health, labour market participation, and representation in government institutions.

Oxfam concludes its report by stating that because our current economic system benefits only the richest 1 per cent, it is broken, and because it is failing the majority of people, it is failing the planet. It goes on to state that this crisis of inequality is not inevitable, since it is the result of deliberate policy choices made by our leaders acting in the best interests of the richest 1 per cent of people. What was made by policy choices can be unmade by policy choices. It is time to act and make policy choices that further the interests of the majority.

The Crisis of the Welfare State in an Age of Globalization

The economic, social, and political effects of global capitalism have had a profound effect on the welfare states of all Western democracies. The welfare states in Canada, the United Kingdom, Australia, and the United States, for example, have been in a state of crisis and restructuring for well over three decades. The growth that Western welfare states had experienced since World War II has been curtailed in some jurisdictions, halted in others, and even reversed in still others. Most writers on the subject pinpoint the mid-1970s as the starting point of the crisis of the welfare state, a result of the larger crisis of the slumping international economy brought on by sharp increases in oil prices, followed by stagflation and economic decline (Gough, 1979; Harvey, 1989; Lightman, 2003; Mishra, 1984, 1999; Riches, 1986). This combination undermined general confidence in the Keynesian-led economy and the welfare state.

The rash of social legislation enacted after World War II via the Beveridge Report in Britain, the New Deal in the United States, the Whitlam reforms in Australia, and the Green Book proposals for Canadian postwar reconstruction marked for many the beginning of a new era, variously referred to as "post-industrial society," the "mixed economy," "welfare capitalism," "Fordist or Keynesian capitalism," or, more commonly, the "welfare state." The Great Depression had

Box 2.1 *The Welfare State in Crisis*

Ferguson, Lavalette, and Mooney (2002) outline the elements of the welfare state in crisis in the UK. However, these same elements (and crisis) may be found in the welfare states of all Anglo-democracies today.

- Pension benefits for elderly persons are under threat.
- Health services face a continuous crisis of underfunding.
- Educational provision is becoming increasingly fragmented because of privatization.
- Higher education continues to be associated with higher fees, leaving students with massive debts and reducing access.
- Workfare is becoming a primary means to social assistance.
- Homelessness continues to increase and is now a massive problem.
- Social workers are required to practise in more punitive ways and to handle ever-growing caseloads and consequently are becoming more stressed.
- Privatization of social services, along with its deleterious consequences, continues to increase.

shown that, left on its own, a laissez-faire state with its free market could not function properly. The economic and social costs associated with cyclical recessions, the inefficiency and waste associated with unfettered monopoly development, and the political and social instability associated with civil unrest led to a profound transformation in the economy, in society, and in the role of the modern state. Indeed, World War II was viewed by many in Canada as a fight for a better society than that which existed under the free-market economy prior to the war (Guest, 1997). From this historical context, the welfare state represented a new deal or social consensus among government, capital, and labour whereby government would use public funds to provide a wide array of services and programs to protect citizens from many social hazards associated with a complex modern society. A history of Canada's welfare state is detailed elsewhere (Guest, 1997; McGilly, 1998; Teeple, 2000; Chappel, 2013).

As Mishra (1984) indicates in *The Welfare State in Crisis*, the postwar welfare state rested on two pillars: the Keynesian economic component and the Beveridge social component. Keynesian economic theory argued for "state intervention" to ensure a high level of economic activity and full employment. Beveridge (1942) in his Beveridge Report, which became the foundation for the modern welfare state in almost all English-speaking democracies, argued for "state intervention" to protect people on a universal, comprehensive, and adequate basis against those contingencies that were part of a modern industrial society and further argued that social welfare benefits were to be provided as a right to all and not as a form of charity to a few. Social welfare developed in most Western industrialized nations on the assumption that a harmonious relationship could exist between capitalism and the social welfare sector (thus the terms "mixed economy" and "welfare capitalism"). However, following the oil crisis of 1973, slower rates of economic growth, government deficits, excessive unemployment, inflation, and high interest rates brought this assumption into question and discredited Keynesianism.

The crisis of the welfare state can only be understood by seeing it within the larger international crisis in capitalism. Gough (1979, p. 32) notes that from the end of 1973 until 1975 the world capitalist economy experienced a slump greater than any since the Great Depression:

> The combined GNP of the OECD countries fell by 5 per cent, industrial output plummeted, and world trade declined by 14 per cent. Unemployment climbed to a staggering 15 million in all OECD countries combined. At the same time inflation accelerated and the advanced capitalist world experienced a growing collective trade deficit.

As Callaghan (2000) and other writers point out, the action of most (but not all) advanced capitalist governments has been to retreat from their postwar policies of state intervention and to return to the pre-war free-market philosophy. Riches (1986, p. 105) writes:

> In response to this [international economic] crisis . . . rugged individualism, in the guise of neo-conservatism, fanned into life by Thatcher, in the United Kingdom, Reagan in the United States and the Fraser Institute and Premier Bennett in British Columbia, came to dominate economic and social policy thinking in Canada. . . . Neo-conservatism has been largely responsible for the collapse of the public safety net in Canada by rejecting Keynesianism and calling into question the legitimacy of the welfare state.

Demise of the American Welfare State

In a special issue of the *Journal of Sociology and Social Welfare* devoted to an examination of the effects of Ronald Reagan's policies and programs on the American welfare state, Midgely (1992) outlined some of the efforts made by the Reagan administration to disengage the state from welfare. These included substantial budget cuts to welfare programs, a reduction in benefit levels, and stricter eligibility criteria. As a result, more than 1 million people lost their eligibility for food stamps; unemployment insurance, child nutrition programs, and food stamp expenditures were reduced; and homelessness, infant mortality, and hunger increased.

The attack on the American welfare state did not stop with the end of the Reagan administration. The first President George Bush's "kinder, gentler nation" was anything but kinder and gentler toward disadvantaged groups, and President Bill Clinton's promised social reform translated into further erosion of America's social safety net. For example, in August of 1996, after claiming that he was going "to end welfare as we know it," Clinton signed a piece of regressive welfare legislation (the PRWORA—the Personal Responsibility and Work Opportunity Act) that imposed a number of cuts and limitations to welfare programs. The Republicans welcomed this piece of regressive legislation, complaining only that it did not go far enough. George W. Bush, elected as president of the United States (the Florida electoral fiasco notwithstanding) in 2000, continued the assault on the American social welfare state by privatizing health care, resisting any movement toward a public health care system even though 40 million Americans were without health care coverage, and continuing the Reagan–Bush–Clinton policy of using police and prisons as the preferred way of dealing with the inevitable rise in poverty and homelessness that resulted from the massive cuts in social programs (McNally, 2002).

President Barak Obama curtailed some of the welfare retrenchment that occurred before his election to the office of president in November 2008, but inequality of wealth, income, and living standards continued to increase during his term of office. The recession of 2008, a hostile Congress, and expensive military involvement in a number of Middle Eastern countries dashed the hope held by many Americans that the government would renew its efforts to address the social welfare needs of underserved populations (Ambrosino, Heffernan, Shuttlesworth, & Ambrosino, 2015). Even Obama's signature piece of social legislation, the Affordable Care Act, signed into law in 2010, is not a universal health care plan because it only covers 90 per cent of the population (approximately 30 million people are not covered) and relies on private insurance. The United States continues to be the "welfare laggard" of Western democratic countries. It taxes less and spends less on social welfare programs than most other Western democracies. Thus, the welfare system does less to reduce poverty and inequality than that in any other affluent Western democracy. It is the only country without a family allowance program, a parental leave program, paid sick benefits, or a universal health care system—rights that are assured to most workers across the developed world (Morgan, 2013). President Donald Trump had only been in power for approximately a year at the time of this writing (November 2017) and has not yet directed much attention to the welfare state. Early indications are that Trump's priorities will be tightening up immigration, building up the military, cuts to environmental protection, a massive overhaul of the income tax system, and the reduction or elimination of the Affordable Care Act, which will see 24 million people dropped from any kind of health insurance.

Demise of the British Welfare State

The Thatcher government came to power in Britain in 1979, a year and a half before Reagan assumed the US presidency. It was one of the earliest critics of the Keynesian–Beveridge welfare state and sought to retrench big government by reversing the advance of the welfare state and by giving market forces freer play in the allocation of resources and rewards. Like Reagan's, Thatcher's anti-welfare rhetoric was greater than the actual welfare retrenchment effected by her government. However, as with Reagan, the negative impact on the welfare state was considerable. Commenting on the early days of the crisis of the welfare state in Great Britain, Gough (1979, p. x) stated:

> Certainly the signs of crisis are everywhere to be seen . . . in the welfare field, social expenditure is being cut back whilst here and abroad a rising tide of criticism engulfs the major institutions of the welfare state. The goals of liberal education are questioned, social workers are vilified in the right-wing press, and a welfare backlash develops.

Ferguson et al. (2002, p. 161) describe the grim outcome of the assault on the welfare state carried out by the Conservative governments under Margaret Thatcher and her successor John Major over 18 years (1979–97):

> when we cast our minds back to the period of Conservative rule in the 1980s and 1990s, among the most enduring memories will be of lengthening queues for NHS [National Health Service] treatment, school and hospital closures, long lines of the unemployed and other claimants at social security and other benefits offices and continual reports of others in need being refused benefits or being forced to live on the most meager state incomes. Lying behind these stark images is a story of increasing attacks on working class living standards and the degradation and casualisation of work—at a time when the rich saw their incomes rise dramatically.

In 1997, the Labour Party (calling itself New Labour) under the leadership of Tony Blair was elected to government on a wave of resentment against the 18 years of Conservative rule and social welfare cuts. However, Labour, the party of social reform and the party most clearly associated with the welfare state, continued with the previous Conservative government's economic policies of downsizing the public sector, extending privatization of public services, increasing the number of leading businessmen in key government posts, and committing itself to freeing up the market (Ferguson et al., 2002). New Labour also deemed many of the postwar welfare reforms (brought about by previous Labour and Conservative governments) as failures. Although Blair and his intellectual champion, Anthony Giddens, claimed that the Third Way represented a renewal of social democracy, several respected writers maintain that the Third Way had simply adopted neo-conservative policies and principles (Hay, 1999; Hattersley, 2001; Marquand, 1999; Vincent, 1998, cited in Bastow & Martin, 2003). The evidence for this view rests on the Blair government having adopted the policies of the Thatcher neo-conservative government on crime, education, and public service funding and on its refusal to renationalize the public services she had privatized. With respect to social policy, while New Labour reduced the role of the state in some areas of social and economic life, it extended the power of the state in other areas that can only be described as draconian. For example, the Blair government increased law-and-order spending on such things as curfews, blaming society's social problems on the "breakdown of the family unit," and implementing a policy of parenting classes for parents of "delinquent" or "anti-social" children.

David Cameron, leader of the Conservative Party, became prime minister of Great Britain in May of 2010, heading a coalition government comprising the Conservatives and the Liberal Democratic Party. Cameron described himself as a "modern compassionate conservative" (Freedland, 2005) and admitted to being a "big Thatcher fan." In May 2015 his Conservative Party won the election and became a majority government. Cameron's approach to social welfare followed the Thatcher tradition, but he was able to articulate his regressive welfare reform acts and packages of 2011, 2012, and 2015 in slightly less offensive terms than those of Thatcher. Still, the orientation was the same—cost containment, pathologizing and stigmatizing persons in receipt of social benefits, imposing stringent eligibility criteria for a number of assistance programs, cutting child tax credits, lowering the benefit cap of social assistance, and reducing access to social security benefits for EU migrants, among other austerity measures. His stated goal was to create a "Big Society" in contrast to "Big Government" or "Big Labour" in which the private and voluntary sectors would carry more responsibility for meeting the social needs of the British population. Following a very close vote to leave the European Union in June of 2016 by the UK population in the Brexit (abbreviation for "British Exit") campaign, Cameron resigned as prime minister, since it was he who promoted the vote, promising that the result would see the UK remaining in the EU. A month later, Theresa May was appointed leader of the Conservative Party and prime minister of the UK (in July 2016) and to date has not made any significant changes to the British welfare state because she is preoccupied with terrorist activities in Britain and its withdrawal from the European Union initiated by the Brexit vote.

Demise of the Canadian Welfare State

The Mulroney Years (1984–93)

Although Riches (1986) presented an impressive amount of evidence that led him to conclude that Canada's safety net (though never fully developed) had collapsed, several respected Canadian social policy writers at that time suggested that Canada had not followed in the footsteps of Britain and the United States in attempting to dismantle the Canadian welfare state (Jenson, 1989; Lightman & Irving, 1991; Mishra, 1990). This suggestion loses all validity, however, when one examines the aspects of the 1990 budget of the Mulroney Progressive Conservative government (or the Chrétien Liberal government budget of 1995 and the Harper budget of 2012) that dealt with the Canadian welfare system. In 1990 alone, the federal government of Mulroney ended its contribution to the unemployment insurance fund, increased the waiting period for unemployment benefits, and decreased the duration of benefits for many areas of the country; it reduced contributions to voluntary women's and Native groups; it cut funding for social housing by 15 per cent; it froze transfer payments to the provinces for health and education; it capped funding for social services for three provinces; it froze legal aid funds for two years at 1989 rates; and it "clawed back" family allowance and old age security payments from persons with annual incomes of more than $50,000 (*Perception*, 1991). In its 9 December 2013 edition, the *Toronto Star* published an article by Les Whittington entitled "Conservatives Dismantling Social Programs Built over Generations" that pulled together a detailed account of the range of cuts made by the Harper government that continued the retrenchments made by Mulroney and Chrétien with respect to Canada's welfare state. (See below for summaries of cuts made by the Chrétien and Harper governments.)

The Chrétien Years (1993–2003)

The federal election of 1993 saw the Liberals returned to office, with reduction of the federal deficit as its primary goal (Lightman, 2003). The 1995 budget of Finance Minister Paul Martin cut $7.5 billion from provincial transfer payments for social assistance, health care, and post-secondary education. The Liberals continued a systematic attack on Canada's unemployment insurance system, renaming it Employment Insurance and calling for a 10 per cent cut in expenditures, the fourth cut in the 1990s alone (Wiggins, 1996). The effects on the unemployed have been dramatic. In 1989 when the cuts to the program began, 83 per cent of unemployed workers qualified for benefits. This number had dropped to 49.7 per cent by 1995 (Canadian Centre for Policy Alternatives, 1995). The federal government also announced the end of the Established Programs Financing Act under which it funded post-secondary education and health care. And, most draconian of all, it announced the end of the Canada Assistance Plan—the cornerstone of social assistance and social services in Canada for 30 years. In the place of these programs, the Canada Health and Social Transfer, which lumps together into one block fund the federal transfer payments to the provinces for health, post-secondary education, and social assistance and social services, was enacted on 1 April 1996. By 1998 the federal government had eliminated its deficit but at the direct expense of the provinces, which in turn downloaded their responsibilities to municipalities and the public at large. In 1999 the vastly downsized federal government introduced another social reform that many critics claim puts an end to its role as the dominant social welfare player in the federal state. Rather than another cut to social spending, the Social Union Framework Agreement (SUFA) was put in place. It focuses on process; that is, before the federal government can introduce a new social program, at least six provinces have to approve it. Lightman (2003) argues that this program requirement ensured that Ottawa's hands were tied with respect to enacting any new federal social program, thereby ending its role as the major social policy player.

In 2005 a report was issued by the Canadian Feminist Alliance for International Action (FAFIA), which tracked the effects of federal government budgets over a 10-year (1995–2004) period. The report measured the federal government's performance against the explicit commitments it had made to gender equality in 1995 when it adopted the Beijing Platform for Action that set out a detailed plan for addressing women's poverty, economic security, and health. The report looked at the budgets of the deficit era (1995–7) and those of the surplus era (1998–2004) and found that massive spending cuts unduly hurt women in the deficit era and that women's interests had been largely ignored since Ottawa began posting surpluses. Almost $12 billion a year was cut from Employment Insurance, the Child Tax Benefit, social housing, and the Canada Health and Social Transfer during the deficit era, and when the government began registering surpluses it allocated $152 billion to tax cuts, another $61 billion to pay down the debt, and $42 billion on new program spending on initiatives such as defence and innovation. The FAFIA report concluded that promises made to women were not kept.

The effects of governments reducing social expenditures in Canada during the Mulroney and Chrétien years are obvious to all who either depend on or work within social services. The very nature of the welfare state itself has changed. "Deregulation and privatization increased: costs were cut, but so were service levels in education, health, and welfare" (Lightman, 2003, p. 23). By reducing their involvement and by transferring much of their responsibility to the private sector, governments have relinquished their responsibility for assuring that many people's social rights are protected. Voluntarism, privatization, and self-help replaced many statutory programs, including the provision of basic, life-sustaining benefits and services. In other words, the welfare state has moved closer to a charity model such as existed in many countries before World War II.

The Harper Years (2006–15)

In Canada, successive Progressive Conservative and Liberal governments in the 1980s and 1990s carried out neo-conservative policies and programs—unemployment, social assistance, and child and family caseloads increased while freezes on public-sector hirings exacerbated the situation. The fact that Liberal governments were no more progressive than Conservative governments throughout the 1980s and 1990s gives credence to the NDP's claim that while Liberal parties may sound like social democrats when they are out of office, they act like conservatives when they are in office. Government retrenchment during this period led to the formation of Depression-type soup kitchens, food banks, and clothing depots, while the number of homeless people continued to increase. Churches and voluntary organizations had to pick up the slack. This is the current situation facing those of us who thought that the "fight for our daily bread" was over when the welfare state was put in place. The absurdity of soup kitchens and food banks should make us question an economic and political system that takes an enormous endowment of natural resources and immense human potential and converts them not into happiness, security, and abundance but into misery, want, and scarcity. The great irony of the welfare state crisis is that we seem to be returning to the very conditions that gave rise to the welfare state in the first place.

Just when it seemed that it could not get any worse in Canada in terms of austerity measures and social welfare cutbacks, Stephen Harper became prime minister in 2006. He was the first prime minister to represent the new Conservative Party of Canada, having dropped the word "progressive" from use after 60 years. Harper was the quintessential conservative (see Chapter 3 for coverage of conservatism/neo-conservatism), who followed in the traditions of Margaret Thatcher and Ronald Reagan. All three set out to fundamentally change the political culture of their respective countries by undoing the progressive developments that had occurred in the Western world after the Second World War when social democracy and the welfare state rose to prominence, driven by the values of social justice and collective well-being (Gutstein, 2014; Jeffrey, 2015). Each leader recognized that they could not change society without changing the intellectual climate within which politics operates. Gutstein (2014) claims that they did this by entering into a symbiotic relationship with conservative think tanks through which free-market ideas were shared with like-minded political, economic, and social allies (i.e., sympathetic politicians, academics, journalists, and researchers). Gutstein's research uncovers the relationship between these right-wing think tanks and the neo-conservative governments of the UK, the US, and Canada. A small group of free marketers formed the Mount Pelerin Society (MPS) in Britain in 1947 to undo the progressive developments that had occurred after the war, which, in turn, led to the establishment of the first neo-conservative think tank, the London-based Institute of Economic Affairs (IEA) in the mid-1950s. The IEA's pro-market and anti-welfare ideas greatly influenced both Margaret Thatcher and Ronald Reagan and were adopted by the Heritage Foundation, an American think tank established to influence elite and public opinion in the US along neo-conservative lines. The Canadian version of a conservative think tank is the Fraser Institute, which along with its allied think tanks spends upwards of $26 million a year to promote neo-conservative ideas in Canada alone (Gutstein, 2014).

During his three terms as prime minister, two as head of a minority government and the third as leader of a majority government, Harper carried out much of his goal of transforming Canada, including the welfare state, from a liberal/social democratic form to a neo-conservative society. In his 2014 book, *Harperism: How Harper and His Think Tank Colleagues Have Transformed Canada*, Gutstein reveals a number of ways by which Harper fundamentally modified the relationship between state and society. Some of them are presented below.

- *Convince Canadians that economic freedom is more important than political freedom,* which rationalizes, among other things, minimal government interference in the marketplace and, conversely, rationalizes such excesses of capitalism as gross inequality of wealth and income, rape of the environment, global warming and pollution, attacks on labour unions and the public service, exploitation of workers, privatization of public goods such as health care, dismantling of social programs such as pensions and public housing, the creation of monopolies, an erosion of human and civil rights, and a concentration of political power.
- *Send in the (neo-conservative) think tanks to win the battle of ideas.* Harper confided that he was a disciple of the Fraser Institute. This institute and other Canadian right-wing think tanks have regularly pumped out articles and studies that promote Harper's agenda to transform Canada into a market-oriented country. It is funded by corporations that benefit from the kinds of changes the institute calls for and has validated Harper's social, economic, and political agenda.
- *Reject unions and prosper.* Like most neo-conservative governments, the Harper government viewed unions as an impediment to free markets and economic growth (critics claimed that there was no evidence that unions caused economic damage and that Harper's attacks on unions were done for ideological reasons). Despite significant public support for unions, "[N]o federal government has gone after unions as comprehensively as Harper's, upsetting long-standing labour practices, intervening in in contract negotiations, slashing the federal workforce, reducing union membership, and threatening right-to-work legislation" (Gutstein, 2014, p. 105).
- *Counter the environmental threat to the market.* Because neo-conservatives believe so strongly in free markets, they are reluctant to become involved in environmental development. The following are a few examples of Stephen Harper resisting environmental protections and positive developments. Canada was active in the negotiations that led to the Kyoto Accord in 1997, which was ratified in Parliament under a Liberal government in 2002. Countries that signed the accord committed to reducing their greenhouse emissions by particular agreed-upon amounts (Canada's target was 6 per cent) beginning in 2005. Calling the accord "a socialistic scheme to suck money out of wealth-producing nations" and referring to it as "the job-killing, economy-destroying Kyoto Accord" (De Souza, 2007), the Harper government withdrew from the accord in December 2011, making it the only country that had signed the accord to repudiate it. This move and other anti-environmental actions acceptable to the Canadian public were made possible by a 25-year campaign funded by fossil-fuel companies and wealthy conservatives to

manufacture uncertainty and cause confusion among the public about the reality of global warming. Part of this campaign was to muzzle scientists who worked within the government, forbidding them to publish the results of their research on the environment, and to reduce the number of scientists, along with cutting many environmental research programs. Another part of this propaganda program was to label environmentalists as "radical activists" who worked outside the mainstream and were not to be trusted or believed. Given the lack of attention to greenhouse gas emissions by the federal government, Canada ranks seventh out of 186 countries in terms of per capita greenhouse gas emissions and has a rate of warming about twice the global rate (a 2°C increase globally and a 3–4°C increase for Canada).

- *Attacks on First Nations' health, welfare, and safety.* Stephen Harper showed disregard for Indigenous peoples' well-being through a number of cuts and inaction in various areas designed to deal with the gross inequalities between Indigenous and non-Indigenous populations. Examples include the elimination of the Kelowna Accord—an agreement between first ministers and Indigenous leaders that identified priority concerns of First Nations, Inuit, and Métis peoples, which was reached in April 2004 after 18 months of consultation (Mitchell & Curtis, 2013). It included health, education, housing, and economic development, with a $5.1-billion financial commitment from the federal government. Before it could be passed into legislation, however, the newly elected government of Stephen Harper refused to implement it. Another example occurred in 2012 when the Harper government cut funding for the National Aboriginal Health Organization—an organization founded in 2000 that brought together Indigenous groups with a common purpose of "improving the health of the unhealthiest, most disenfranchised people in the country" (Picard, 2012). One final example (there are many, many more) of Harper attacks on the health and well-being of Indigenous people was his refusal to establish an inquiry into the disappearance and murder of more than 1000 Indigenous women, with Harper claiming that most of the cases had been solved and that the idea of an inquiry was misguided, since the issue of missing (Indigenous) persons was a law-and-order issue and not a "sociological" issue.

- *Deny income inequality.* Economic freedom is a core value of neo-conservatism and takes precedence over political freedom. However, economic freedom leads to and requires economic inequality, which leads to incentives to work harder, invest more, and get more education. Without these incentives the economy would not operate at efficient levels. There has always been a moral argument against excessive income inequality (e.g., Pope Francis and President Barak Obama have spoken against it in recent years), but lately an economic argument has been made that questions the belief that a trade-off exists between inequality and economic progress. This argument was presented in a 2011 study (Berg & Ostry, 2011) by the International Monetary Fund (IMF) that found that over the long term, the trade-off between efficiency and equality may not exist and, in fact, equality appears to be an important factor in promoting and sustaining growth. The authors of the study go even further and argue that the 2008 global financial crisis may have resulted from the increase in economic inequality. They contend that as inequality rises, people at the bottom of the income scale tend to borrow more to keep afloat, which in turn increases the risk of a major economic crisis. As well, excessive inequality causes social unrest that can lead to political instability, which decreases foreign investment. Severe inequality can also reduce economic growth if these gaps mean that a country is not fully utilizing the skills and capabilities of its citizens. Even though income inequality has increased in Canada over the past 20 years, unlike Obama, Harper was silent on the issue and had adopted a do-nothing approach. In fact, he had worsened the problem by giving large tax cuts to rich Canadians and cutting back on public services, which hurt middle- and low-income Canadians. In recent years and in spite of the Conservatives' lack of interest in the subject, inequality has risen up the political agenda, as indicated by mentions in major Canadian daily newspapers, and although both the Liberals and the NDP have talked about the suffering middle class, neither has talked about the working class or has made inequality a major issue. It will be interesting to see how the current Liberal government deals with income inequality, which has risen to a point where Canada now ranks 12th out of 17 of the world's richest countries.

From a Needs-Based Welfare State to a Privilege-Based Welfare State

Although cuts to existing social programs are obvious, Mullaly argued as far back as 1994 and again in 2007 that something more is happening. Using Richard Titmuss's (1963) classic work on the "social division of welfare," Mullaly extends the notion of social welfare beyond a simple collection of programs and services for disadvantaged and low-income groups. Titmuss described three class-based welfare systems that developed over time but independent from one another: (1) fiscal welfare that benefits mainly the capitalist class (i.e., the corporate sector); (2) occupational welfare that benefits mainly persons with good, full-time jobs; and (3) general welfare that is aimed primarily at unemployed and underemployed workers.

Fiscal Welfare

Fiscal welfare is the most lucrative welfare system and operates mainly through the Income Tax Act. Portions of corporate income are allowed to escape taxation by way of exemptions, deductions, deferrals, allowances, write-offs, and reduced taxation rates. Because there is no visible government spending involved, and because governments do not publish the amounts of money involved (i.e., not collected as tax revenues), it has been called Canada's "hidden welfare system" (National Council of Welfare, 1975; 1979). It is estimated that for every $100 the federal government spends, it forgoes (does not collect) $30 to $50 in potential corporate tax revenue—which amounted to $30–$50 billion in 1985 alone (McKenna, 1985). Whereas the corporate sector generally views welfare programs for the poor as government handouts, it sees tax breaks as an unquestionable right and a mark of good business practice (National Council of Welfare, 1975). Although it claims that tax breaks represent investments in the economy, the evidence indicates that they are used to increase dividends of corporate owners, not investment (McKenna, 1985). While it is impossible to know its exact size because of its hidden nature, the fiscal welfare system continues to grow (National Council of Welfare, 1979). For example, it went from $6 billion in 1979 to $8 billion in 1980 (*Canadian Business*, 1985). By 1990 it was estimated to be around $16 billion. Esping-Andersen (1989) contends that countries governed by neo-conservative political parties emphasize fiscal welfare, given the electoral importance (and political contributions) of those who receive it.

Occupational Welfare

Occupational welfare consists of occupational fringe benefits, such as health benefits and pensions, distributed through the workplace. Other forms are such "perks" as housing allowances, interest-free loans, and company cars and expense accounts, which are usually given only to executives and other top-echelon workers. These benefits are based on one's position in the work organization and not on need. Businesses finance these fringe benefits by passing their costs on to the consumers of their goods or services and/or by deducting their costs as business expenses from their taxes. Thus, the costs of the occupational welfare system are paid by consumers and by the general public, who must make up this lost money when they pay their own taxes. Occupational welfare fragments the working class, since one sector has good pay and work-related fringe benefits and, therefore, does not feel the need to have an adequate general welfare system. The other sector does not have access to these fringe benefits and must rely on an ever-diminishing welfare system. Occupational welfare also creates in many workers, especially the professional and managerial groups, a sense of loyalty to the corporate sector and its call for reduced social expenditures. The whole tendency of occupational welfare is "to divide loyalties, to nourish privilege, and to narrow the social conscience" (Titmuss, 1963, p. 52).

General Welfare

Titmuss's third welfare system is the one people generally think of when they hear the term "social welfare" but is referred to as "general welfare" by Titmuss. Consistent with Titmuss, "general welfare" is the term used here as well. It consists of modest universal transfers, means-tested programs, and minimal social insurance plans oriented mainly to low-income and other vulnerable populations. Its major aim is to relieve poverty by providing a safety net for those who cannot meet their basic needs in the market and who do not have access to private or occupational welfare benefits. It is the welfare system most oriented to people's basic needs. However, unlike the other two welfare systems, general welfare imposes a stigma on those who must rely on it. Whereas fiscal welfare, which serves principally the rich, has been thriving during the transformation from rigid Fordist capitalism to its new flexible form, and occupational welfare, which serves mostly the managerial and middle classes, has continued to grow, general welfare in Canada and other modern capitalist countries has been savaged (Mullaly, 1994).

Any true understanding of the current restructuring of the welfare state must take into account all of its components—that which caters to the rich, that which serves the well-paid middle and working classes with good permanent jobs, and that which is targeted at the growing number of the working class with low-paid, marginal jobs or no jobs at all. An awareness that there is more to this restructuring than simple cuts to general welfare and that, in fact, there has been a redistribution of money and resources away from the general welfare system to the other two systems opens up other possibilities for dealing with the fiscal crisis than the current "slashing and burning" of social programs. Mishra (1990) makes this point by noting that although rising budget deficits, increasing inflation, economic stagnation, and high unemployment may constitute "objective" phenomena, the analyses, explanations, and interpretations of these phenomena are "subjective." In other words, a crisis may be seen as an objective set of facts, but it includes a subjective interpretation. Such interpretations are usually based on particular ideologies and/or group interests.

A major theme of this book is that the welfare state is a social construction based on subjective and ideological grounds and not on objective and scientific grounds. Evidence of this is that not all countries affected by the international economic crisis have responded in the same way. Mishra (1990) notes two different ideological responses to it—one from the right and one from the left. Right-wing governments have called for a return to a pure form of capitalism—the rigour and discipline of the marketplace—including unemployment as natural and inevitable, privatization, a lean if not mean social welfare system, and reliance on non-governmental sectors for meeting social needs. Progressive governments have responded by attempting to maintain and consolidate the welfare component (high employment, progressive taxation, equity, adequate minimum wages, and a high level of social expenditures) of welfare capitalism. Each response "represents a different cluster of values and a different pattern of the distribution of power and privilege in society" (Mishra, 1990, p. 12). Britain, the United States, Australia, and Canada fall within the first response. Sweden, Norway, and Austria are examples of countries that chose the second response.

The notion that interpretations of crises and problems are subjective phenomena defined in terms of ideology and group interests is crucial for students of social welfare and social work. Every Western industrial country has a social welfare state, but no two countries have identical welfare systems. There is tremendous variation in levels of expenditures, in goals, and in the form and administration of the welfare state of various countries. The welfare states of all countries exist to deal with social and economic problems. However, although the problems may constitute objective criteria, the interpretations of and solutions to these problems are defined in ideological and subjective terms. In other words, welfare states represent socially constructed responses to social and economic problems.

Social Work in Crisis

The responses by right-wing governments to the crisis in capitalism have also created a crisis in social work. The ongoing restructuring of the welfare state since the 1980s means that the context for social work practice continues to change. The changes in the economic, political, and social environment are seen by many to be fundamentally in opposition to the values of the profession. Social workers often find themselves in unfriendly and hostile practice environments for people who sincerely believe that the role of social work is to make the world a better place for larger numbers of people and to further the cause of social justice by helping disadvantaged groups to empower themselves (Ife, 1997). The crisis in social work is manifest at all levels and in all areas of social work activity.

In 1997, Jim Ife discussed the hostile context that existed in the 1990s within which social workers were attempting to practise or, in many cases, simply survive. He outlines four inter-related components of this context: (1) economic rationalism; (2) managerialism; (3) modernist rationality; and (4) competencies. These components remain major issues for social work and for all those concerned with social justice because they are still discussed today by such writers as Canadians Ben Carniol (2010), Donna Baines (2011), and Marilyn Dupré (2013), Australian Karen Healy (2002), and J. Harris (2003) and Iain Ferguson (2008), both from Britain.

Economic Rationalism

"Economic rationalism" is the Australian term for neo-conservatism, an ideology that gives primacy to the marketplace as the determinant of individual choice, freedom, and well-being. Government spending, especially on welfare, undermines the market, drains the economy, and reduces individual initiative. Social work services are not highly valued in such a policy environment because they are perceived to represent unnecessary costs and intrusions on people's fundamental rights and freedoms. For social workers who may have thought that their work was actually improving individual well-being and an overall quality of life for society, it is a cruel irony to be labelled as "villains" or "wimps" (Franklin, 1989, cited in Ife, 1997) rather than as heroes in the struggle for a just and fair society.

Managerialism

"Managerialism" is the belief that all that is needed to make organizations (including social services organizations) more effective and efficient is a generic set of business and entrepreneurial skills. Hence, social services managers do not need to know anything about social work practice or the nature of social services. This philosophy has resulted in:

- people with no background in social work assuming managerial responsibilities for social services organizations;
- managers with social work backgrounds identifying themselves more as professional managers than as professional social workers and de-emphasizing such social work values as human well-being, equity, and human rights in favour of managerial values of efficiency, effectiveness, and cost containment;
- many social work positions now defined as "case managers," with top-down control and authority replacing notions of self-determination, empowerment, and democracy;
- a loss of autonomy with respect to creative, innovative, and empowering social work practice, especially within large governmental bureaucracies;
- a belief that social problems can be solved by technical means (e.g., organizational change) rather than these problems being seen as moral, political, and structural problems that are not amenable to managerial solutions.

Modernist Rationality

"Modernist rationality" is the third component of the social work practice environment of the 1990s (and spilling over into the twenty-first century) identified by Ife. It is similar to economic rationalism, but rather than believing in the primacy of economics as the determinant of policy-making, it focuses on rationality itself, whether economic or otherwise. It assumes that organizational and policy decision-making ought to be based on the logical analysis of objective data only and not on value considerations. This technical approach to policy development and service delivery does not always fit the norms of social work practice, which historically has been a normative activity. The modernist rational approach is based on the belief that there is one best answer to any problem or question if the logical steps in deductive reasoning are applied. This one best answer is then imposed on the entire population. Of course, this approach minimizes or ignores the importance of cultural, regional, class, and other diversities that are important considerations for good social work practice.

Competencies

The fourth component of the context for social work practice in the 1990s and which remains as a major issue today is that of "competencies." The competency movement is based on the notion that occupations should be defined according to the competencies or "best practices" required to perform them. This movement breaks social work behaviours and tasks down to the smallest feature in order to obtain economical and cost-effective social work practices (Baines, 2011; Dupré, 2013). Many social work jobs are now advertised and filled in accordance with required competencies rather than in terms of educational qualifications, practice experience, or the professional affiliations of persons applying for them. This is leading to a deprofessionalization of the social work profession. Jobs previously restricted to those possessing a social work degree are now being filled by those who can demonstrate the specified competencies.

In a competency-based job market, there would be no need for extended professional education for social work students, since they would not have to learn about the social and political context of their work, critical or social analysis, social and cultural diversity, innovative alternatives, and the like. Ife notes that "social workers under this system readily become seen as cogs in the machine, to be controlled and regulated." Rossiter and Heron (2011, p. 306) argue that "[T]he foundations of social work—thinking, reflecting and making complex judgments—cannot be represented in the form of competencies." Aronson and Hemingway (2011, p. 283) comment on the experience of other countries that have longer histories with social work competencies: "[I]n the U.K., Australia, and New Zealand, . . . competency-based frameworks have been found to reduce practice to prescribed behaviours requiring minimal professional judgment (e.g., Dominelli, 2007; Lymbery et al., 2000; van Heugten, 2011, cited in Aronson & Hemingway 2011). Observers note that they have enhanced neither the welfare of communities nor the morale and efficacy of practitioners. Jan Fook (2011) questions why competencies are conceptualized only in behavioural terms, and we (Marilyn and Bob) wonder why contextual factors, power relations, structural variables, community work, social action, advocacy, social justice, and ethical decision-making are ignored.

This critique of competencies does not mean that we are against "competence" or for "incompetence." What it does mean is that we believe that society, the people living within it, and the relationship between the two are too complex to be reduced to a simple recipe book of competencies or to a how-to-do-it procedure manual. In effect, under a competency-based framework social work becomes a trade based on a set of clearly defined basic skills rather than a profession based on critical thinking and analysis, innovative and independent problem-solving, and ethical and creative decision-making. We wonder why there is not more resistance from the social work profession to the competency movement here in Canada and elsewhere. We think that when the time comes when non-social work–educated persons with competency training start taking jobs away from professional social workers, more resistance will develop. We hope that by then it will not be too late.

Changes in the Delivery of Social Work Services

The current crisis in social work, which was initially described by Fabricant and Burghardt (1992) as manifest at all levels and in all areas of social work activity, remains so today (Baines, 2011; Ferguson, 2008; Ferguson & Woodward, 2009; Carniol, 2010). At the delivery level, there have been cuts in social expenditure and decreased funding of programs (Herbert, 2003), increased categorization and targeting of programs, privatization of many public services, special investigations of welfare recipients (Mullaly, 1984), imposition of user fees, and cutbacks in public-sector social work employment. Along with these changes, social needs have increased because of demographic changes, changing social roles, increased unemployment and underemployment, and inequalities in earnings (Borland, Gregory, & Sheehan, 2001; Hunsley, 1987). The net effect is that it is now impossible to address the economic and social needs of increasing numbers of people in a meaningful way—particularly people living in poverty, disadvantaged people, and those most exploited, which include women, immigrants, racialized individuals, and the unemployed.

Not only does this situation make it more difficult for people in need, it has also made the job of social workers more frustrating as more time is spent on refusing clients' requests, as absurd systems of priorities are worked out, as better coordination is emphasized, as service delivery is increasingly defined from a managerial perspective emphasizing efficiency, cost containment, and worker control. The negative effects of these changes have been well documented by Rees and Rodley in Australia (1995), Dominelli (1996) in Britain, Baines (2011), Tudiver (1993), and the Canadian Association of Social Workers (CASW) (2004a; 2004b; 2005) in Canada, with many social workers reporting increasing levels of stress, burnout, and low morale.

Crisis on the Organizational Level

On an organizational level (as discussed in the previous chapter), the Canadian Association of Social Work and many provincial social work associations have abandoned their social justice mandate and their political leadership role and now spend most of their time dealing with organizational issues along with pursuing and promoting professional interests. With a depoliticized leadership, an absence of any political mission, and an abdication of a vision of a just society, it is no wonder that the crisis in social work as outlined here continues unabated. Planning annual meetings, electing boards of directors, and developing endless standards of practice may all be necessary work, but they leave the profession without direction in terms of working toward the kind of society that would be characterized by a progressive view of social justice rather than social injustice. As noted by Lundy (2004) and Bonneycastle (2006), although the current CASW *Code of Ethics* mentions social justice and human rights, there is no indication of how these concepts should be put into place. Loose or vacuous statements by the CASW and other professional social work bodies about social justice are no substitute for a statement of philosophy or articulation of a vision of the kind of society that social work wants for the people it serves. Without such a vision, others will decide for us the type of society they want, and history shows us that liberal and neo-conservative views are not conducive to meeting the needs of large numbers of people or for dealing effectively with social problems because they are oriented toward maintaining the current set of social arrangements—arrangements that favour dominant groups.

As employees, social workers are being affected by the society's priorities, which lie in industrial enrichment and public order rather than in the well-being of the general population (Carniol, 2010; Baines, 2011; Garrett, 1999; Simpkin, 1979). To meet these priorities, social workers are asked not only to sacrifice their own living standards through wage control but to police the casualties of unemployment, inflation, economic neglect, and policies that place private profit above human need. Changes in the context of social work practice have meant larger (unmanageable) caseloads, declassification of professional social work jobs, increased use of part-time, casual, and contract social work positions, greater use of volunteers delivering services, and more decisions being made at the political level, which are passed down to social workers to implement. Some writers have termed this process the "proletarianization of social work" (Fabricant & Burghardt, 1992), the "deprofessionalization of social work" (Dominelli, 1996), and the "deskilling of social work" (Fisher & Karger, 1997). As discussed above, the deprofessionalization of social work results in many traditional social work tasks and functions being carried out by professionally untrained persons (Aronson & Sammon, 2000; Dominelli, 1996).

Crisis on the Professional Level

On a professional level, social workers have experienced an increasing loss of autonomy in the workplace (Baines, 2011; Lundy, 2011). Although never totally autonomous, social work has experienced a tendency toward increased bureaucracy in recent years. Neo-conservative policies made at the political level are passed down to social workers to implement, and often these policies violate our deeper impulses as human beings and contradict our professional beliefs and values. A study by Aronson and Sammon (2000) on social workers in the province of Ontario found that those within the child welfare and health areas often feel that they have to enforce decisions about entitlement that may contradict their own professional and political beliefs. Social workers are more and more today expected to use standardized organizational technology that is perceived to be cost-effective (Fisher & Karger, 1997; Harris, 1998). For example, the DSM (Diagnostic and Statistical Manual of Mental Disorders) in the US is mainly used to diagnose, catalogue, and treat service users on the basis of the symptoms described and defined in the manual. Leaning toward psychological variables, the DSM minimizes macro-contextual factors (e.g., poverty) and dismisses symptoms that defy categorization. Fisher and Karger (1997, p. 154) refer to this as an example of "the dominance of [organizational] production over human need."

Another example is the increasing use of "risk assessments"—a standardized instrument used by social workers to assess particular groups of people (e.g., parents in child welfare situations or persons in contact with the criminal justice system) according to "risk factors" contained in the risk assessment. These risk factors, however, are directed toward pathological or dysfunctional characteristics of individuals, and larger structural factors are minimized or ignored. The key concern associated with risk assessments is for the social worker to make a "defensible decision" (by following prescribed rules and procedures), not necessarily the correct decision (Callahan & Swift, 2006; Parton, 1999). Fabricant and Burghardt (1992) argue that social workers today are being transformed from thinking, reflective problem-solvers to specialized, automatic, and mechanized technicians who are subordinated to inferior work roles. Often, their prescribed activities are based on conservative notions of individual pathology or blaming-the-victim assumptions. Some employing agencies today do not understand social work roles or the complexity of social work practice (Herbert, 2003). Stephenson, Rondeau, Michaud, and Fiddler (2000) found in their study of Canadian social work organizations and social workers that job performance has become quantified through the use of outcome measurement tools, with an increased focus on accountability and an expectation for social workers to rationalize their decisions consistent with these measurement tools.

Working Conditions

A CASW review of the literature from 1994 to 2004 identified the following current working conditions for social workers and for social work practice, both in Canada and internationally: high caseloads, inadequate financial resources, increased complexity of the needs of service users, increased use of contract positions, supervision that is more administrative than professional, lack of opportunity for advancement. These conditions had several negative effects:

- job dissatisfaction, burnout, vicarious traumatization (i.e., a reaction to repeated exposure to the traumatic experience of service users);
- difficulty maintaining a work–life balance, physical and mental exhaustion, sleep disturbance, anxiety, dehumanizing service users;
- role conflict (i.e., a lack of a distinct identity for social workers);
- lack of opportunity to develop quality working relationships with service users;
- competing time demands that lead to increasingly crisis-oriented social work practice;
- feelings of increased isolation, of not being supported, and of vulnerability.

Although the precise nature of the crisis of the welfare state and its attendant crisis in social work are recognized by many social workers, what is less obvious is any theory or strategy to deal with these crises. Some writers see social work in its current state as under threat (Parton, 1994). Ife (1997, p. 9) describes the current situation in discussing social work's commitment to social justice and the worth of the individual:

it is important to emphasize that social work has consistently been defined as a normative activity. It does not simply do what political leaders and managers tell it to do, but rather it works towards a better society, defined in its own terms. It is thus more than a technical activity, and is out of place in an environment of increasing bureaucratic and managerial control, where "accountability" is defined as accountability to management rather than accountability to the community or the consumer. The current environment of practice does not readily allow for the kind of dissent, creativity and seeking of alternatives which are a natural consequence of social work's primary commitment to [its] value position.

Given the contradictions between social work values and its current work environment, what should social work do? How should it handle these contradictions and competing demands? Even though the neo-conservative ideology of welfare (or diswelfare) offends social work's traditional commitment to compassion, to social justice, and to preserving the dignity and autonomy of individuals (Mishra, 1989), social work has been, for the most part, ineffective in challenging the crisis confronting it. In the absence of a theory, strategy, or critical analysis, social work has tended to adjust to the retrenchment of the welfare state rather than look for (and fight for) alternative measures. Haynes and Mickelson (1992) present some examples of this adjustment in the United States, which are just as applicable in Canada. With the re-emergence of hunger and homelessness as issues, social workers have participated in establishing food banks, soup kitchens, and temporary emergency shelters rather than mounting large-scale campaigns to expand social assistance benefits and public housing. The effect of this action has been to institutionalize hunger, begging, and homelessness.

Inability to Deal with Present Crises

Several writers have presented reasons why social work has been unable to deal adequately with the present crises. Karger (1987) believes that the profession, before the crisis, thought that capitalism could be reformed and therefore was left unprepared to present any progressive alternatives to welfare capitalism. Similarly, others have cited its (supportive) relationship to the dominant ideology as the reason for social work's state of inertia in trying out new perspectives and roles. A number of writers analyzed the ideology–social work nexus when the crises began in the 1970s (Dykema, 1977; Findlay, 1978; George & Wilding, 1976; Leonard, 1975; Pritchard & Taylor, 1978). Subsequently, Burghardt (1982) wrote that part of the problem was found within the methodologies and practice frameworks taught to social workers. Too many of them contain abstract propositions for action, such as "link the social with the personal" or "see the individual in his or her environment," and do not go beyond these declarations themselves. Jones (1975, pp. 5–6) wrote that the crises were forcing social work to question some of its comfortable assumptions about the relationship between the individual and the state and the role of the state in securing the welfare of the individual and that "a process of soul-searching has begun in social work." Others were more specific about the content of this "soul-searching" and claimed, as Corrigan and Leonard (1978, p. 90) did, that "The inability of many social workers to act effectively derives in part from the fact that their analysis of the state and its welfare functions remains at a relatively undeveloped level."

In a previous edition of this book, I (Bob) stated my agreement with such writers as Carniol (1984), De Maria (1982), Lowenberg (1984), and Pritchard and Taylor (1978), who argued that in order to deal with this crisis not only must social workers learn about the nature and role of the state and social work's relation to it but there must also be a reformulation of social work theory. According to these writers, this reformulation must include: (1) an explication of social work's ideology as a necessary step in building knowledge; (2) knowledge about the nature and role of the state and social work's relation to the state; and (3) transformational knowledge of how social work practice can contribute to changing society from an entity that creates and perpetuates poverty, inequality, and humiliation to one that is more consistent with social work's fundamental values of humanism and egalitarianism. Although I still agree with this position, I now believe that, by itself, it is incomplete. In addition to being undermined by the massive and disruptive economic and social changes that have accompanied global capitalism, social work (particularly its progressive forms) has been challenged on another front as well. "Postmodernism," with its ironic distrust of large theories and sweeping ideologies and its eclectically relativist view of the human condition, has challenged many of the ideals, concepts, and discourses that underpinned the notions of the welfare state as a progressive project (Leonard, 1997) and of social work as a progressive practice (Fook, 2002; Healy, 2000; Howe, 1994; McLaren & Leonard, 1993; Leonard, 1994; Pease & Fook, 1999).

Hopeful Signs

Before looking at the concepts of "ideology" and "paradigm" that help to frame our approach to progressive social work practice in general and to structural social work in particular, we want to present a few hopeful signs that we believe cut through some of the "doom and gloom" messages that have been part of the globalization discourse and thesis over the past four and a half decades. Specifically, we want to look at: (1) the anti-globalization movement; (2) the Idle No More movement; (3) the "collapse of globalism" thesis of John Ralston Saul; and (4) the current economic situation of the government of Canada.

Anti-Globalization and Other Movements

As the twentieth century drew to a close, anti-globalization arguments began to receive more attention and credence in the public discourse on globalization—especially when it was becoming clear that globalization was producing extreme corporate profits that "were leading to widening global disparities in wealth and well-being" (Steger, 2003, p. 113). Throughout the 1980s and much of the 1990s, the resistance efforts by anti-globalization proponents were no match for the dominant globalization paradigm. The globalization discourse labelled them as groups of radicals who were out of touch with reality. However, since 1999 globalization has come under sustained attack by its opponents.

Cracks were already showing in the globalization thesis by 1999 (see Saul, 2005, for an overview of the decline of the globalization thesis) when the opponents of globalization began their concerted and well-orchestrated series of international demonstrations to protest meetings of those organizations and groups (e.g., the World Trade Organization [WTO], the International Monetary Fund [IMF], the World Bank, and the G-8 leaders)[8] that were leading the globalization movement. The first notable confrontation occurred on 18 June 1999 when various labour, environmental, and human rights groups organized international protests to coincide with the G-8 economic summit in Cologne, Germany. The financial districts of major cities in Europe and North America were subjected to large street demonstrations along with more than 10,000 "cyber-attacks" perpetrated by sophisticated computer hackers against the computer systems of large corporations.

This protest was followed six months later by demonstrations against a WTO meeting by 40,000 to 50,000 people in the streets of Seattle. This eclectic alliance of anti-globalists comprised more than 700 organizations and groups that included student organizations, labour unions, environmental groups, human rights proponents, consumer activists, feminist organizations, anti-racist groups, animal rights organizations, church groups, advocates of Third World debt relief, and social justice groups. They protested the WTO's neo-conservative position on agriculture, multilateral investments, and intellectual property rights, as well as the massive wealth accumulation for the leaders of globalization that came at the expense of reduced health, education, social services, and decent jobs for many in both the developed and the developing worlds. The demonstrators made it difficult for delegates to access the conference centre where the WTO meetings were being held. In spite of it being a well-organized, non-violent demonstration, the police overreacted against the demonstrators with flailing batons, rubber bullets, and pepper spray.

Negotiations inside the conference centre did not proceed smoothly and began later than scheduled because of the demonstrations. Steger (2003, p. 126) articulates the significance of the Battle of Seattle with respect to social protest and the use of technology in the new millennium:

> Ironically, the Battle of Seattle proved that many of the new technologies hailed by the globalists as the true hallmark of globalization could also be employed in the service of antiglobalist forces and their political agenda. For example, the Internet has enabled the organizers of events like the one in Seattle to arrange for new forms of protest such as a series of demonstrations held simultaneously in various cities around the globe. Individuals and groups can utilize the Internet to readily and rapidly recruit new members, establish dates, share experiences, arrange logistics, identify and publicize targets—activities that only 15 years ago would have demanded much more time and money. Other new technologies, like mobile phones, allow demonstrators not only to maintain close contact throughout the event, but also to react quickly and effectively to shifting police tactics. This enhanced ability to arrange and coordinate protests without the need of a central command, a clearly defined leadership, a large bureaucracy, and significant financial resources has added an entirely new dimension to the nature of street demonstrations.

Several large-scale demonstrations against globalization took place all over the world in rapid succession after the Seattle protest, which we interpret as a hopeful sign with respect to social justice and democracy. These and other demonstrations stunned the architects of and true believers in globalization—they could be publicly humiliated by non-professionals (Steger, 2003).

The demonstrations also changed the discourse of the proponents of globalization from one of enthusiastic optimism and inevitability to one of negativity and defensiveness (Saul, 2005). Leaders of the IMF were suddenly astonished to find themselves and their ideology being blamed for the myriad social problems that accompanied the globalization process. In contrast, the protestors were no longer seen as disconnected from reality. In fact, Jim Wolfensohn, president of the World Bank, publicly expressed his concern for those left behind by globalization and noted that the Seattle protestors were not just a "group of radicals" but spoke for some "very legitimate views" (*Financial Times*, 2000, cited in Saul, 2005, p. 168). In sum, the anti-globalization movement successfully challenged many aspects of both the ideology and the laissez-faire process of globalization.

The Environmental Movement

The environmental movement has been around since the early 1800s when people began to become concerned with the smoke pollution caused by the emergence of factories during the Industrial Revolution. However, this movement was slow to develop because it has always been resisted by the capitalist class, which feared that its profits would be curtailed by any form of environmental legislation. They were able to convince governments and the general population (and themselves) that priority should be given to economic development at the unfortunate but necessary expense of the environment. From about 1950 onwards, the movement grew as more and more people became concerned about such environmental issues as air and water pollution, noise pollution, radiation, pesticides, waste disposal, dwindling energy supplies, and so on. However, it has only been since around 2000 that widespread concern with issues of global warming and climate control accelerated the growth of the environmental movement internationally, culminating in the signing of the Paris Agreement on Earth Day (22 April 2016) by 177 member countries of the UN Framework Convention on Climate Change (UNFCCC). The purpose of this agreement is to control average global temperatures and greenhouse gas emissions and to increase the ability to adapt to the adverse effects of climate change. The environmental movement in general and the signing of an international agreement to reduce greenhouse gas emissions and control the rate of global warming in particular does much to loosen the chains that capitalism has historically had on the economies of the world and to shift emphasis away from unfettered economic development (i.e., more and more profits) to enhanced human well-being. This movement continues to be an ever-growing hopeful sign with respect to removing capitalism as an impediment to the development of the welfare state.

Recently, there have been a number of grassroots movements initiated by particular groups that have been historically oppressed, with standards of living well below those of mainstream society. Two such movements in North America are the Idle No More movement that originated among Canada's Indigenous peoples in December 2012 and the Black Lives Matter movement that originated in the African-American community of the United States in 2012. For purposes of brevity and because it originated in Canada, we only present the Idle No More movement here.

Idle No More Movement

This movement was created by Canada's Indigenous peoples—First Nations, Métis, and Inuit peoples along with their non-Indigenous allies and supporters. It began as a series of teach-ins in Saskatchewan in November 2012 by four female activists to protest impending legislation that would erode Indigenous sovereignty and environmental protections. The specific piece of legislation that outraged the Indigenous peoples was the federal Conservative government's omnibus Bill C-45. Among its many provisions was one whereby the number of federally protected waterways was reduced. Indigenous peoples were not consulted on this matter as is required by historical treaties between Indigenous peoples and the Crown, and they saw it as a threat to the environment and to their sovereignty. What began as a series of teach-ins quickly became one of the largest Indigenous mass movements in Canadian history. A National Day of Action was called for on 10 December 2012, which inspired thousands to action and to commit themselves to ongoing peaceful resistance to neo-colonialism.

The Idle No More movement continues to be active today, and among its calls for change are the following:

- Repeal provisions of Bill C-45 (including changes to the Indian Act and Navigable Waters Act, which infringe on environmental protections, Aboriginal and Treaty rights) and abandon all pending legislation that does the same.
- Deepen democracy in Canada through practices such as proportional representation and consultation on all legislation concerning collective rights, and environmental protections, and include legislation which restricts corporate interests.
- In accordance with the United Nations Declaration on the Rights of Indigenous Peoples' Principal [*sic*] of free, prior, and informed consent, respect the rights of Indigenous peoples to say no to development on their territory.
- Honour the spirit and intent of the historic Treaties. Officially repudiate the racist Doctrine of Discovery and the Doctrine of Terra Nullius, and abandon their use to justify the seizure of Indigenous lands and wealth.

— Excerpt from www.IdleNoMore.ca

The Idle No More website states that the movement

seeks to provide ongoing information on the historical and contemporary context of colonialism, and provide an analysis of the interconnections of race, gender, sexuality, class, and other identity constructions in ongoing oppression. . . . Idle No More has provided hope and love at a time when global corporate profits rule. We invite everyone to join in this movement.

The relevance of this social movement to social work should be obvious to all, especially those social workers who are part of the structural social work and/or anti-oppressive social work movements.

The "Collapse of Globalism Thesis"

In his book, *The Collapse of Globalism and the Reinvention of the World* (2005), the Canadian historian and philosopher John Ralston Saul makes a compelling case that although many of its effects (both positive and negative) are still with us, globalization as it was originally conceived and predicted by its supporters is now dead. Another Canadian writer, Adam Harmes, makes many of the same arguments in his 2004 book, *The Return of the State*. This does not mean, as Saul (2005, p. 204) points out, that the global economy is coming to an end. "What it does mean is that the Globalization model of the 1970s and 80s has faded away. It is now, at best, a regional project—that region being the West. But even there, the moves to reregulation and the return of nationalism are carrying the twenty or so old democracies in quite unexpected directions." Saul argues that after a long period of twitching, it finally died in January 2003 when the US Secretary of State, Colin Powell, announced to the economic forum at Davos, Switzerland, that the US would invade Iraq even if other countries would not join with it. In other words, the United States, the leader of the globalization movement, declared that it would go it alone if need be and other countries were free to act in their own self-determined interests. Contrary to the globalization thesis, this declaration signalled that nation-states rule; economics do not. And so the economic system that once had the status of a religion (Saul calls it "crucifixion economic theory") died at the age of 30 years, after a nasty, brutish, and short life. Saul bases his arguments on numerous events and occurrences that contradict and negate the globalization orthodoxy or globalization thesis. Some of these are outlined here.

(1) One of the tenets of globalization was that nation-states would lose power to global economic inevitability and the international institutions (WTO, World Bank, IMF) that were set up to regulate international trade and other global forces. However, by the turn of the century, it was obvious that nationalism and the nation-state were stronger in both democratic and non-democratic countries than they had been when globalization began. For example, Scotland voted in 1996 to create its own Parliament after being integrated for 290 years into one of the world's most centralized states.

(2) The experience of Latin America contradicts the neo-conservative economic theory and prescriptions that underpin the international lending institutions and debt mechanisms. In the year 2000, the social and economic problems in Latin America multiplied. For more than 12 years, most Latin American governments tried to follow the instructions laid down by the IMF, Western governments, and private banks. The "crucifixion economics" eventually produced some solid growth, but the divide between rich and poor grew even larger. Eventually, the recovery in each case was followed, a few years later, by even greater economic collapse. "So after all of the liberalizations, privatizations, and inflation-stabilization programs, growth in Latin America in the late nineties was a little over half what it had been before the reforms" (Saul, 2004, p. 40). Latin American countries such as Argentina, Chile, and Brazil are now designing their own economic solutions. Latin America no longer believes in globalization.

(3) Two gigantic developing countries—India (a socialist and bureaucratic country) and China (a communist country)—are benefiting from global trade as their exports are exploding, high-tech jobs are flowing their way, poverty is shrinking, and the middle class is growing. However, Saul argues that the world's two most populous countries have done well by not following the economic principles of globalization. They had controls on capital and various limitations on movements and investments. Whatever market reforms they have employed have come in the context of nation-state interests. The Chinese government controls more than half the country's

industrial assets, invests heavily in infrastructure, and shapes economic and social development. The Indian government does the same but to a lesser extent. Both countries view economic development as the means to deal with social problems rather than accepting the globalization approach of achieving economic development as an end in itself.

(4) In 1999, the electorate in New Zealand, which had formally embraced the full ideology of globalization in 1984, voted to change direction by electing a strong interventionist government devoted to a mix of national social policies, enforceable economic regulations, and a stable private sector. After 15 years of following the economic doctrine of globalization, New Zealanders concluded that it was a failure. Its national industries had been sold off to foreigners, which created a drain of money abroad. The economy was in decline, and its standard of living had been stagnant throughout the 15-year experiment. Young people were emigrating so fast that the national population was in decline. The divide between rich and poor took on dramatic proportions, and New Zealand had accumulated one of the highest levels of national debt in the developed world. By abandoning the globalization project, a small country had actually reversed the global inevitability claim.

(5) In 1998, in the face of an economic meltdown in Asia, the leaders of Malaysia refused to continue down the masochistic road of globalization. The prime minister, Mahathir Mohamad, went about breaking most of the rules of globalization. He pulled the Malaysian currency off the world market, made it unconvertible, and pegged it low enough to favour exports. He stabilized the country's economy by blocking the export of foreign capital, and he raised tariffs. He adjusted regulations and strengthened and weakened controls as needed in a manner consistent with Keynesianism. All sorts of globalization proponents wrote off Malaysia as an economic basket case, declared Mohamad to be mentally unstable, and waited for the inevitable collapse of its economy. It never came. Mohamad thumbed his nose at the West's need for simple economic truths as the economic crisis in his country eased. Investments grew, and production and exports increased. The Malaysian case showed that economic determinism was only wishful thinking and that nation-states were capable of making their own choices and succeeding through unconventional actions.

(6) One of the correlates of globalization has been the rise of a culture of corporate greed, especially among the executives of the largest corporations. Deregulation and the establishment of self-serving corporate regulations have been used to normalize the most basic forms of corruption. There has been an explosion in the use of share options by executives, along with executive salaries and benefits that have swelled way beyond any services rendered. Surveys of public opinion in many Western democracies report that private-sector leaders and elected officials compete for the two bottom spots with respect to trust, respect, and contributions to the public good. This is a relatively new phenomenon and is tied to a marginalization of ethics that has been part of the globalization process. At one time we would not question the integrity of our corporate masters. However, today there has been a backlash that began in the mid-1990s. In recent years there has been constant public criticism of the failures of corporate leadership and resentment of such things as the fact that two-thirds of American corporations paid no federal income tax in spite of record profits. Not surprisingly, this atmosphere of greed spilled over into fraud, as in the Enron case or with the accusations against Conrad Black and his management of

the Hollinger newspaper empire. The fall of many corporate leaders from public trust and respect has cast doubt on the globalization project itself.

From Deficit to Surplus to Purposeful Deficit

As discussed earlier, a major reason for retrenchment of the welfare state has been rising government deficits that originated in the mid-1970s. In the case of Canada, the Liberal government of Jean Chrétien inherited a deficit of $28 billion in 1993, which grew to $42 billion by 1996. Although successive Canadian governments talked about deficit reduction, it was not until Finance Minister Paul Martin's infamous deficit-slashing budget of 1995 with its major cuts to social programs that the fiscal house of Canada was finally brought under control (Lightman, 2003). At the time the previous edition of this book was written (2005–6), the surplus was projected at $8.2 billion, rising to $11.3 billion by 2010–11, with the total amount of surpluses over this period projected to be $54.5 billion (Government of Canada, 2005). I (Bob) wrote at that time that given the new (2006) Conservative minority government's Throne Speech and stated priorities, it was unlikely that these projected surpluses would change very much. What it would give away in the form of tax relief (e.g., 1 per cent drop in the GST) it would make up in program cuts (e.g., its less expensive daycare plan).

Because the surplus position during the first couple of years of the Conservative government was so substantial, it represented a totally different context with respect to the Canadian welfare state from what existed from the mid-1970s to the mid-1990s. For decades, cuts to social programs had been rationalized as a necessary evil to deal with government deficits, but the federal government was now faced with the situation of what to do with its large surpluses. During the 2005–6 Canadian federal election campaign, all political parties, in varying degrees, promised new social programs or extensions to existing social programs. None of the parties proposed cutbacks because there was no economic reason for doing so any longer. Some parties, notably the governing Liberals and the victorious Conservatives, promised tax relief for various groups of the electorate, but these proposals were more attempts to gain favour with voters than efforts to contribute to the development of an overall tax system based on equity rather than political considerations. Other nation-states, such as the United Kingdom and the United States, were also in better economic situations than they had been before 1995 (costs of the Iraq War and the War on Terrorism notwithstanding). The main point I (Bob) tried to make in the earlier edition is that over the long term, a surplus situation is more hopeful than a deficit situation with respect to devising and/or developing health, education, income maintenance, housing, and other systems that are responsive to human need. Nevertheless, deficits may be helpful in the short run as indicated below.

During the first two years of the Harper mandate, the economy looked promising in terms of growth and budget surpluses. However, no one predicted that the largest worldwide recession since the Great Depression of the 1930s would occur in 2008, just two years after the Conservatives took office. How the Harper government undid much of the progressive nature of Canadian political culture, including its social welfare state, was presented previously in this chapter when the demise of the welfare state was discussed. Justin Trudeau was elected Liberal Prime Minister of Canada on 19 October 2015 on a platform of "Real (and progressive) Change." To achieve this goal, Trudeau completely reversed the Conservative fixation on attaining a surplus at the expense of many social programs by deciding to run deficits for three years to finance infrastructure programs, promising to balance the books by 2019. This deficit financing would include $60 billion on roads, bridges, transit, and other projects. The Liberals also promised: to cut personal income tax (the Conservatives promised to cut business taxes); to invest in a youth employment strategy; to reduce employment insurance premiums; to replace the regressive income tax splitting and the Universal Child Care Benefit with a Canada Child Benefit that would benefit all families; to establish a new Seniors Price Index to guarantee that seniors' benefits would keep up with their rising costs; and to expand immediately the number of government-sponsored Syrian refugees to 25,000. They also made a number of promises in the health care, environment, and Indigenous peoples areas. These and other promises, if carried out, would greatly enhance Canada's social welfare state and put it back on a progressive road.

At the time of this writing (November 2017), the Trudeau Liberals have been in power for a little over two years. It is too early to see if they will make good on all their electoral promises, but the following are some of their social welfare/social policy promises that have been kept (www .liberal.ca/27-liberal-promises-kept):

- Introduced a new Canada Child Benefit that gives more money to 9 out of 10 Canadian families and lifts almost 300,000 children out of poverty.
- Lowered taxes to benefit almost 9 million middle-class Canadians every year.
- Increased taxes for the wealthiest 1 per cent of Canadians, which gives middle-class Canadians a tax break and makes taxes a little fairer.
- Achieved an agreement with the provinces to strengthen the Canada Pension Plan.
- Returned the eligibility age for Old Age Security and the Guaranteed Income Supplement to 65 years.
- Increased Guaranteed Income Supplement payments to approximately 900,000 single senior citizens.
- The 2016 budget provided new funding for emergency shelters and transition homes.
- Launched a National Inquiry into Missing and Murdered Indigenous Women and Girls.
- Increased funding for "Nutrition North" that will provide better support for food security to Canadian families living in isolated northern communities.
- Legalized medical assistance in dying to eligible patients who are suffering intolerably and offers them the choice to die with dignity.
- Committed $2.6 billion for primary and secondary education on First Nations reserves.
- Signed an international agreement (the Paris Climate Change Agreement) to combat climate change.

There have been a number of polls, analyses, and opinions expressed with respect to how well the new government is keeping its promises. To date, the opinions are mixed—Conservative and many progressive groups (e.g., NDP) and individuals say the Liberals are not keeping their promises, whereas, of course, the Liberals maintain they are. What most observers do agree on is that the tone of the new government is much better than the previous Conservative government in that it is not as adversarial, antagonistic, secretive, dismissive, arrogant, and mean-spirited. Many voters were influenced as much by the Harper government's tone as they were by its policies (The Star.com, 17 June 2014).

The Concepts of Ideology and Paradigm

Ideology

A significant literature focuses on ideology as a point of departure when discussing the state, social welfare, and social work. An ideology is defined here as "a consistent set of social, economic, and political beliefs." Armitage (2003), Djao (1983), Drover and Woodsworth (1978), George and Wilding (1985; 1994), Williams (1989), Mendes (2003), and Mishra (1984) have presented comparative analyses of ideological perspectives on the welfare state. Finn and Jacobson (2003), Pritchard and Taylor (1978), Galper (1975; 1980), De Maria (1982), Carniol (2010), and Kerans (1978) have presented comparative analyses of ideological perspectives in social work. Ife (1997) refers to social work as an "ideological activity." Lundy (2004) echoes Bricker-Jenkins's (1997) claim that every social work practice model has an ideological core. However, the large number of ideologies underpinning social work also presents a problem for the profession. Lowenberg (1984) and Carniol (1979) point out that, to date, social work has not been successful in reducing the social problems with which it deals. Part of the reason, according to Lowenberg, is the eclectic theory base of social work; Carniol cites the "jumble of confusion" taught to social work students when it comes to ideological analysis. Finn and Jacobson (2003) argue that the predominant theories and perspectives that guide the practice of social work are inadequate for meeting the current issues we face. These issues include increasing economic globalization and inequality, social exclusion and dislocation, continued trends toward privatization and profitability in the social service sector, and the precarious position of basic human rights. They point out that social work scholars and practitioners are engaged in debates over epistemology, theory, priorities, and the general relevance of the profession. They call for a new social work paradigm to confront these challenges, tensions, and contradictions based on a "fundamental rethinking of the nature and direction of social work practice as we come to grips with the rapidly changing environment in which we live and work" (Finn & Jacobson, 2003, p. 58).

The task of reformulating social work theory, then, is to bring some sense of order to the field of social work knowledge and to develop alternative theories and approaches that can respond to the challenges of the twenty-first century. This is not to say that social work's currently confused theory base can or ought to be unified but that an attempt must be made to develop what De Maria (1982) terms "meaningful patterns" from its present non-unified theory base. A number of theories and ideologies focus on the state. There are several models of social welfare and various explanations of social problems. A plethora of mid-range theories of social work intervention may be applied differently according to whether one subscribes (advertently or inadvertently) to a consensus or conflict view of society. A host of micro theories focus on human agency, and various macro theories emphasize structural variables. How is the social worker to make sense out of this jungle of ideas, theories, perspectives, practices, and ideologies? We need to challenge our certainties, acknowledge our uncertainties, and open up new ways of looking at and thinking about social problems and how the structuring of individuals and institutions are time-specific and contextually embedded.

Paradigms

The point of departure taken here relies on the concept of "paradigm." Thomas Kuhn's *The Structure of Scientific Revolutions* (1962; 1970) attacked the idea that scientific knowledge develops in a linear accumulation of facts and insights about natural phenomena. Struck by the amount of disagreement among scientists over the nature of their work and methods, Kuhn (1970, p. viii) wrote that "Attempting to discover the source of that difference led me to recognize the role in scientific research of what I call 'paradigms.' These I take to be universally recognized scientific achievements that for a time provide model problems and solutions to a community of practitioners."

By his own admission, Kuhn provided only a loose definition of paradigm. Masterman (1970) found 21 different usages of the term in Kuhn's book. Consequently, the use of the term "paradigm" has become almost faddish.[9] We speak of research paradigms, educational paradigms, paradigms of social welfare, sociological paradigms, and so on. In spite of the semantic conflict over the ambiguity of the term, the meaning ascribed to it by some writers would appear fruitful for the development of social work knowledge: a paradigm represents a "taken-for-granted reality" (Ford, 1975) or world view that consists of the entire constellation of beliefs, values, and techniques shared by a scientific community (Tornebohm, 1977). This does not refer to the beliefs of an entire discipline, as Kuhn points out, but to those that are dominant within the discipline (or profession). In other words, a paradigm represents a specific type of cognitive framework from which a discipline or profession views the world and its place in it. This framework allows for an analysis of the relationship between the scientific thought of a discipline and the social context in which it arises. Paradigms are the "taken-for-granted contexts, within which one locates facts and methods and ascribes meanings to them" (Bandopadhyay, 1971, p. 8).

A paradigm is not a fixed or rigid social category but rather an abstraction—an "ideal type" comprised of a reasonably consistent set of social, political, and economic ideas, beliefs, and values (in other words, an ideology) that provides an explanation of the world. Different paradigms include different ideologies, which, in turn, provide different interpretations of the world. "Ideologies provide a link between the world of ideas and the concrete realm of political action—for example, political parties, interest groups, mass movements, and constitutional systems" (Sigurdson, 2002, p. 115). That is not to say that people neatly fall into a single paradigm or subscribe to a single ideology. But people do tend to favour or adhere to many (but not all) of the ideas, beliefs, and values of a particular ideology. A primary function of an ideology is to explain the key problems facing a society and to interpret important events. For example, who or what is responsible for poverty? Are people living in poverty the architects of their own misfortune? Or is poverty caused by social events that are largely beyond the control of individuals? Conservative ideology would promote the former explanation, whereas social democratic ideology would promote the latter.

The Ideological Continuum

It is conventional to use the terms *right*, *left*, and *centre* to refer to the political orientation of a person or group according to where they fall on a continuum of ideological or political positions (see Figure 2.1).[10] The concept of a continuum helps us to understand that values and ideals overlap between adjacent positions on the continuum (e.g., between conservative and liberal) and that being on the left or the right ideologically is a matter of degree. While more than one set of measures can be used to locate persons or groups along the continuum, a popular measure is attitude toward social change, including both the degree and direction of change. The more conservative individuals and groups are located on the right. They desire the least radical change to the status quo. In contrast, the radicals on the left seek far-reaching and often revolutionary change, while the moderates are in the centre. There is a range of radical beliefs, depending on the extent of the change desired and the means to achieve it. Thus, anarchists and communists are further to the left than socialists, and social democrats are closer to the centre than others in the radical group. Radicals (anarchists, communists, Marxists, social democrats) often refer to themselves as progressives, since the changes they seek are forward-looking, inclusive, and intended to improve the well-being of all people in society, particularly poor and oppressed groups. This book is situated within the radical camp.

The centre of the political spectrum is occupied by politically moderate individuals and groups who fall within the generic name of liberalism. As with the left and right wings, liberals hold a variety of political views. On the left are reform-minded liberals, who, like social democrats, favour progressive social change and believe that government should be used to improve the well-being of all people in society through various kinds of social intervention and regulation. They favour an extensive welfare state, a mixed economy (private ownership along with some public corporations), and Keynesian fiscal policy (the use of public funds and regulations to prime the economy or slow it down). Reform liberals are also known as "welfare liberals." More to the right within the liberal range are "classical" or "market" liberals, who are concerned primarily with the right to private property and the protection of individual liberty against intrusive government interference. There is not much difference between classical liberals and contemporary neo-conservatives, since both wish to "conserve" a free-market capitalist economic system. This overlap between a classical liberal and a neo-conservative is confusing but is made even more confusing by use of the term "neo-liberalism" for the re-emergence of classical liberal ideas and doctrines. These terms are discussed and differentiated more fully in Chapters 3 and 4.

The traditional conservative position believes in social inequality and aristocracy. Conservatives place order and authority above liberty in their hierarchy of values. They are

FIGURE 2.1 The Left–Right Continuum

relatively content with the way things are and are skeptical of any attempts to change social institutions or to improve life through "social engineering" (i.e., social intervention). They lament such progressive social movements as feminism, the trade union movement, same-sex marriages, multiculturalism, and so on. Conservatism is discussed more fully in Chapter 3. The political reactionary, on the other hand, is not content with the way things are but wants to return to a day when things were better—real or imagined. Like the progressives, reactionaries seek widespread social change but in the opposite direction. They would reduce equality and inclusiveness along with democracy. They usually favour government by an elite few, preferably by military leaders. This is the ideology of the far right and is usually characterized by racism, xenophobia, and ultra-nationalism (Sigurdson, 2002). The Nazis in Germany and the Fascists in Italy are examples of reactionary political parties. Skinheads, white supremacists, and paramilitary organizations are contemporary examples of reactionary groups.

Attitude toward the State Continuum

An alternative continuum for distinguishing ideologies is the location of an individual's or group's attitude towards the state—that is, to what degree should government be involved in the affairs of individuals and society? Figure 2.2 depicts this continuum. Those on the left (Marxists and some social democrats) are more comfortable with the use of state power to promote social well-being than are those on the right. For example, they would support a well-developed welfare state and would call for total public ownership and full state control of the economy. Those on the right (classical liberals and neo-conservatives but not anarchists), on the other hand, would oppose almost all government intervention and regulation, believing that a free market is the best instrument for regulating the economy and for distributing goods, services, and opportunities. Those toward the moderate centre (social democrats, reform liberals, and traditional conservatives) would support a considerable amount of government intervention and regulation but for different reasons. Social democrats place their faith in a mixed economy as a strategy to move toward a socialist economy in an incremental manner. Traditional conservatives would allow a considerable amount of government control to ensure order and stability in society. Reform liberals would support a moderate amount of social reform in order to improve or refine present social arrangements rather than change them substantially. Fascists and anarchists are anomalies with respect to their attitude toward the state. Fascists would use a strong state to promote their views, but these views are the polar opposite to those of Marxists and social democrats—fascist ideology promotes xenophobia, racial purity, and social hierarchy. Similarly, anarchism is on the right wing along with classical liberalism and neo-conservatism in its desire for less government, but it shares many of the values of Marxism and social democracy, including the wish to free people from the constraints of capitalism in order to promote the public good. Libertarianism also fits on the same side of the continuum as anarchism because it stands for the maximization of individual freedom and the absence of a coercive state. However, its motivations are different because it promotes minimal state intervention for capitalistic reasons, defending the inalienable right to acquire and own property without interference from the state. In this way, it is similar to the right-wing ideologies of conservatism and classical liberalism. President

FIGURE 2.2 Attitude toward the State

Ronald Reagan associated libertarianism with conservatism, but he would never associate anarchism with conservatism.

Figure 2.3 locates a number of political ideologies along the left–right ideological continuum. With the exceptions of anarchism and fascism, these ideologies will be discussed in subsequent chapters with regard to defining social problems, developing social welfare solutions to alleviate or eliminate these problems, and determining social work practices to deal with social problems and people who experience them.

A number of ideologies, as shown in Figure 2.3, do not comfortably fit on the left–right continuum. *Feminism*, for example, is found both within (e.g., liberal feminism, socialist feminism) and outside (e.g., radical feminism) the traditional ideologies. Although all feminisms decry the subjugation of women, the various forms of feminism hold different views with respect to their analysis of the causes of and remedies for gender inequality. However, even those branches of the broad feminist movement aligned with traditional ideologies have as their major concern gender inequality, which was omitted by the traditional ideologies. The feminist critique of traditional ideologies is contained in Chapter 7. *Anti-racist* or *black liberation ideology* also does not fall within the traditional ideologies, since the latter were developed mainly in Europe at a time when the vast majority of the population was Caucasian (and where segments of the white population held almost total economic and political power). Thus, issues of race were not a part of the social reality of European social, philosophical, and political thought as they are today. The anti-racist critique regarding the traditional ideologies being colour-blind is also considered in Chapter 7. Persons who subscribe to *environmentalism* as an ideology claim that it is not on the left, right, or centre and is the only ideology that does not advocate the domination of nature by humanity for purposes of humanity. In other words, environmentalists challenge the "human-centred approach" of exploiting the environment, which all traditional ideologies hold, preferring instead an alternative, earth-centred philosophy.

The development of a distinct perspective based on a school of Indigenous research and theory, which originated in the 1980s, is currently replacing many of the perspectives, analyses, and reports of mainstream writers who wrote from the traditional ideological foundations (Armitage, 2003). While contributions from liberal, socialist, feminist, environmental, and anti-racist ideologies or perspectives are part of the Indigenous perspective, a distinct school of analysis of the Indigenous reality based on their own experiences can be seen in Indigenous writing and scholarship (see, for example, the works of Cree scholar and social work professor Michael Hart from the Faculty of Social Work, University of Manitoba, 2002; 2006; 2007). Today, the traditional Eurocentric political ideologies are subordinate to Indigenous perspectives.

FIGURE 2.3 The Ideological Continuum

Although none of these newer perspectives fits neatly on the left–right continuum, it is safe to say that, generally, they lean toward the left rather than the right side of the ideological divide.

Paradigms and Political Parties

Political parties tend to be organized, more or less, around a consistent set of ideological beliefs, values, and ideals. In fact, some parties in Anglo-democracies originally named themselves after the particular ideology to which they subscribed, such as the Liberals and Conservatives in Canada. This is usually somewhat confusing to students unfamiliar with political ideologies or parties. The name of a political party is usually capitalized (e.g., the Liberal Party or the Conservative Party), whereas an ideology (e.g., liberalism, conservatism) is not. Over time, the original name of a political party may change. For example, the Conservative Party of Canada became the Progressive Conservative Party in 1942 because it championed some progressive measures and sought Manitoba Premier John Bracken, a Progressive, as its leader. Many years later, in 2003, the party dropped the "Progressive" part of its name when it amalgamated with the much more right-wing Canadian Alliance Party. In addition to name changes over time, it is not uncommon for political parties to move away from their original respective sets of ideological beliefs. For example, the Liberal Party in Australia may have been based on liberal ideology at one time, but today it is a right-leaning neo-conservative party in spite of its name. During good economic times, when revenue is available for some social programs, most political parties will shift a little to the left on the political continuum and support popular social programs. As evidence of this, after eight years of successive large budget surpluses at the federal level, all Canadian federal political parties were promising to expand the welfare state in one way or another during the 2005–6 federal election campaign. When times are economically difficult, however, almost all political parties will shift slightly to the right by cutting back on social programs in an effort to bring public spending in line with shrinking revenues.

Paradigm Shifts

As with politics, so with the knowledge and scholarship within an academic discipline: although more than one paradigm can exist at the same time within a discipline or profession, usually one "dominant paradigm" provides the discipline with a framework for viewing the world. This dominant paradigm also provides the criteria for selecting and defining problems for inquiry, guides scientific practice by providing laws and theories and models for their application, and is transmitted throughout the discipline or profession by practitioners and in the textbooks used for schooling new members of the discipline. Members of a discipline/profession often are not aware of the dominant paradigm because it tends to be viewed as the taken-for-granted reality. Because it is viewed as the only reality, phenomena that do not fit into the paradigm are often not perceived or are rejected as being metaphysical, as lying outside the boundaries of one's discipline, or as being too problematic to be worth the effort of considering (Tornebohm, 1977). In this way, a paradigm can "insulate the community [discipline] from those socially important problems that are not reducible to puzzle form [of the paradigm], because they cannot be stated in terms of the conceptual and instrumental tools the paradigm supplies" (Kuhn, 1962, p. 37). Thus, the person who brings any anomaly to the attention of the discipline or profession is to blame, not the reality (i.e., not the dominant paradigm).

How, then, do dominant paradigms change or become discarded? Kuhn contends that only when anomalies can no longer be explained away or when they become so numerically overwhelming does the discipline begin to explore the area of anomaly that has violated its "paradigm-induced expectations" governing normal practice (Kuhn, 1962, pp. 52–53). This exploration ends when the paradigm has been adjusted to accommodate the anomaly or when the dominant paradigm has been discarded in favour of another. And, Kuhn asserts, this adjustment or exchange of paradigms is generally preceded and followed by periods of resistance.

According to Kuhn (1962, p. 6), development of a new paradigm occurs "when the profession can no longer evade anomalies that subvert the existing tradition of scientific practice. Then begin the extraordinary investigations that lead the profession at least to a new set of commitments, a new basis for practice." Alternative interpretations are posed, which leads to a competition between the present dominant paradigm and the new revolutionary paradigm. "Each revolution necessitates the rejection (not without resistance) of prior frameworks and rules in favour of new ones. The new paradigm is not simply grafted on to the old one: acceptance requires rejection of the old. When the transition is complete the profession will have changed its view of the field, its methods and its goals" (De Maria, 1982, p. 33). Shifts of paradigms bring members of a discipline/profession to see the world around them in a new light. To present an alternative paradigm is the ultimate revolutionary act.

Although we speak above of a "paradigm shift" occurring within a profession, it can also occur within an individual apart from a profession. For example, during the course of our respective careers as a social work academics and teachers, we have observed many, many times students who, because they were born into and raised within a particular dominant paradigm (usually a combination of conservativism and liberalism), held mainstream views about society, individuals living within that society, and the relationship between the two. However, when exposed to a different paradigm with a different view of society, a different explanation of social problems, and a different approach to social work, they would shift from the dominant paradigm to a more progressive paradigm such as those discussed below. This "shift" does not occur easily, however, as evidenced by the many students who upon being exposed to a more enlightened and progressive paradigm are still not able to think and act outside the dominant paradigm. During classroom discussions of more progressive paradigms and forms of social work, each of us has personally witnessed the power of the dominant paradigm with respect to its hold over many students who could not imagine any other way of viewing social situations, as evidenced by their verbalized and defensive and angry resistance to the fact that their view of the world was being challenged and/or threatened. Fortunately, there are many students who are able to make this shift and who engage in a social work practice that goes beyond individual explanations for social problems and beyond regressive treatment programs that blame victims of social problems for the situations in which they find themselves through no fault of their own.

Obviously, paradigms, in the social sciences at least, are not laws and do not represent right or wrong but are choices people make based on their own particular set of social, cultural, and

FIGURE 2.4 Political Parties along the Ideological Continuum

Notes:
1.   Individuals and groups tend to organize themselves politically based on particular shared ideologies.
2.   Not all persons who belong to a particular political party will agree with all its values, ideals, policies, etc., however.
3.   Political parties are not located at a particular point on the ideological continuum (as is shown above) but occupy a space on both sides of the point. There is a range of political positions within each party. For example, the Conservative Party of Canada comprises a group known as "red Tories" who are socially progressive and a group of former Alliance members who are socially regressive.
4.   Given that political parties occupy a space along the continuum, those adjacent spaces may even overlap with each other. For example, some progressive-minded Conservatives are more progressive than some Liberals on the right wing of their party. Thus, it is not that uncommon to have some politicians switch political parties even after they have been elected. Examples include Belinda Stronach, a "red Tory" who switched from the Conservative Party to the Liberal Party in 2005, and David Emerson, a cabinet minister in the Paul Martin Liberal government who switched to the victorious Conservatives almost immediately after the 2006 election to become a cabinet minister and was given the same portfolio (industry) that he had held in the Liberal cabinet.
5.   The Green Party of Canada does not fit comfortably on the ideological continuum because its major issue is the environment, which attracts both progressive-minded and conservative-minded individuals. However, the Green Party is mostly associated with progressive-minded people.
6.   The fact that the Liberal Party of Canada occupies the centre location on the political continuum makes it easier for it than for other parties to shift either left or right of centre, thus capitalizing on the mood of the electorate at any given time. Many political scientists attribute the electoral success that the Liberals enjoyed for most of the twentieth century to their central position on the continuum.

political beliefs or preferences. Unfortunately, this choice is too often imposed on us by virtue of being born into and growing up in a particular dominant paradigm. We become captives to it because alternative paradigms are not part of school curriculum, nor are they usually discussed, and when they are it is usually in a dismissive or ridiculed way.

The crisis of capitalism and the ensuing crises in social welfare and social work may be viewed in terms of paradigms. Prior to World War II, the dominant paradigm in North America was conservatism, with its emphasis on an unfettered market economy, and charity, the Poor Laws, and voluntarism were the major means of addressing social need. The Great Depression of the 1930s brought this paradigm into disrepute, and after the war liberalism or welfare capitalism (see Chapter 4), complete with a modern welfare state, gradually became the dominant paradigm. In turn, the recession and oil crisis of the early 1970s brought about a questioning of welfare capitalism and in the ensuing years a shift back to conservatism (i.e., neo-conservatism; see Chapter 3). However, this shift is by no means complete because we continue (thus far) to have significant government intervention into the economy and a welfare state (albeit reduced). There is consensus within social work that neo-conservatism is contradictory to social work values and beliefs. Is there a more compatible paradigm for social work? If so, what can we do to halt the present paradigmatic shift? What contributions can we make to transform our current society to one that is more sensitive to, and more capable of, meeting human need? These are a few of the questions addressed in this book.

Utility of the Paradigm Concept for Social Work

In view of the international economic crisis and the ensuing crises of the welfare state and social work, how does the concept of paradigm help social work deal with the problems it faces, including its own tangled web of ideological, political, and theoretical confusion? And how does it address the intellectual challenges that postmodernism presents to progressive forms of social work based on principles of social justice? It is our belief that the application of the paradigm concept can perform three major functions for social work in helping it to confront, understand, and deal with these crises.

First, as noted by Carniol (1984; 2010), ideological critiques and analyses at the level of social work methods abound in the literature. These critiques and analyses might be better appreciated, however, if they were presented within a framework that not only compares ideologies but also allows the student to compare and contrast the different views of the nature of social problems, of social welfare approaches, and of social work practices emanating from different ideologies. The concept of paradigm should help the student make the connection between ideology and social work practice—that is, how an ideology largely determines the nature and form of social work practice. In other words, it should help the student understand that there is no one universal approach to social work practice, nor is there only one explanation for social problems or one ideal type of social welfare system. Postmodernism teaches us that there are always multiple claims to truth. Using the concept of a paradigm helps us to compare and contrast different approaches to dealing with social problems and different claims as to what form both the welfare state and social work practice ought to take.

Second, one of the purposes of the above-mentioned comparison is to become aware of alternative ways of integrating economic and human welfare with that which is currently being offered by neo-conservatives (Mishra, 1989). A major theme of this book is that our present social order is not the natural and inevitable product of some evolutionary process; rather, there are alternatives. Sweden, for example, is representative of a paradigm different from that which exists in North America, and it has demonstrated that an efficient market economy does not have to be constructed at the expense of social welfare. It is to be hoped that an awareness of alternative world views—paradigms—will open everything to challenge and change, including our present social order, our present structure of social services, and the nature of our present social work practice. These things should not be predetermined by either present statistics or current power relationships. "The shape of events is determined by people, all of us, and by our willingness to understand and seek to change the world for the better" (Burghardt, 1982, p. 20). Indeed, several writers have argued that an alternative vision is a prerequisite for meaningful social change (Berger & Luckmann, 1966; Ferguson & Lavalette, 2005; Mishra, 1989; Moreau & Leonard, 1989; Mullaly, 2001; Wineman, 1984). Such a vision, if consistent with social work ideals, values, and beliefs, could provide a goal and a direction for social work. An articulation of such a vision was presented in Chapter 1.

The third function that the concept of paradigm may carry out for social work is to enhance our understanding of the dynamics of change, especially fundamental change. De Maria (1982, p. 34) informs us that "The concept of paradigm, particularly the causal link between social context and knowledge, has a history in philosophy, sociology and political science." For example, De Maria attempts to show how Kuhn's view of scientific development is similar to the Marxist view of social change. He states, "Whether it be a social revolution in the Marxian sense or a scientific revolution in the Kuhnian sense, the dynamics appear to be the same, with the existing paradigm or the Marxist notion of epoch carrying within itself the potentiality for a new order" (p. 35). Three examples of characteristics of paradigms that have implications for understanding the dynamics of social change follow. First, the fact that one paradigm (e.g., neo-conservatism) usually is dominant over others means that it is the taken-for-granted reality of most people in society—including social workers. Second, only when the dominant paradigm can no longer explain away certain anomalies (such as decreasing levels of well-being for many in an expanding global economy) can a shift of paradigms begin to occur. And third, an acceptance of a new paradigm does not occur without resistance. Understanding these dynamics of change should help social work to make a transition in its view of society, in its theory, and in its practice. These are a few of the tasks taken up here.

Two assumptions are made here. First, critical theory and ideological analysis in the modernist tradition can make important contributions in critiquing the dominant paradigm and in conceptualizing social work theory and practice so that they can adequately deal with the crises outlined in this chapter. Second, by themselves modernist critical theory and ideological analysis are inadequate for carrying out these tasks. In fact, as many social work writers (e.g., Fook, 2000, 2002; Healy, 2000; Pease & Fook, 1999; Leonard, 1997) have argued and as many social movements have shown (e.g., trade union movement, socialist movement), modernist critical theories and progressive ideological analyses based on a singular idea of truth can be just as oppressive as social structures and social relations based on inequality and domination. They must be informed, supplemented, and complemented by the contributions of postmodernism, post-structuralism, feminism, and anti-racism, which by themselves are also insufficient for formulating emancipatory forms of social work theory and practice. Rather than viewing modernism and postmodernism as a dichotomy, the position adopted in this book is that each serves as a corrective for the weaknesses and limitations of the other. In other words, rather than an "either-or" situation, they represent a dialectic,[11] a set of opposing forces that, taken together, help us to deconstruct and reconstruct social welfare and social work as emancipatory projects and activities within a progressive discourse. This position is similar to that of several other writers (Ife, 1997; P. Leonard, 1995, 1997; S. Leonard, 1990; Mullaly, 2001, 2002) and is discussed more fully in Chapter 9.

Conclusion

In this chapter an overview of the events surrounding the transformation of capitalism from its postwar form to a global form was presented, along with the deleterious effects that this new form of capitalism has imposed on so many social institutions (including the welfare state) and on so many social groups (including oppressed people and social work). The field of social work, generally, has been unprepared to confront social and economic change and has lacked the analytical or theoretical framework to understand global capitalism and to deal with its negative consequences. Thus, there is a need to develop new and alternative forms of social work that reflect more closely the current social, economic, and political circumstances. A number of hopeful signs have emerged since the mid-1990s, and the concepts of ideology and paradigm offer potential for developing alternative forms of social work theory and practice, provided that this project is informed by the insights of postmodernism, post-structuralism, and other such epistemologies.

Critical Questions

1. Is the main reason for globalization economic or ideological? Explain.
2. Why is it important that social workers be knowledgeable about globalization?
3. Instead of cutting back on social programs, what else could governments have done to deal with their economic problems? For example, why didn't they raise taxes on profitable corporations and wealthy individuals?

4. How do the concepts of ideology and paradigm help us to understand social policy and social welfare choices?

5. List the political parties that exist in Canada. What ideology is characteristic of each, and what is the view of social welfare held by each party?

6. Although the welfare state in all Anglo-democracies was under attack for more than two decades, it has in large measure survived. Why?

3 The Neo-conservative Paradigm

I did not mean that Conservatives are generally stupid; I meant, that stupid persons are generally Conservative.

— John Stuart Mill (1866)

Introduction

This chapter presents an overview of the traditional concept of "conservatism" as was originally conceived in the late eighteenth and early nineteenth centuries and compares it to its modern form or what has come to be known as "neo-conservatism." Also presented is a summary of what conservatives believe about the inherent nature of human beings, the nature of society, the role of the nation-state, the substance of social justice, and social change. Neo-conservative ideology is deconstructed into its constituent parts or sets of social, economic, and political beliefs, and an attempt is made to show how these beliefs underpin and shape the explanations neo-conservatives hold about social problems and the role and nature of the welfare state. A picture of what social work practice would look like within a neo-conservative context is outlined, as is a critique of neo-conservative beliefs. Finally, neo-conservative ideals are compared to those of progressive forms of social work.

Conservatism

Conservatism is a set of beliefs that "springs from a desire to conserve existing things, held to be either good in themselves, or better than the likely alternatives, or at least safe, familiar, and the objects of trust and affection" (Scruton, 1982, p. 90). This view implies a distrust of sudden or radical change. Conservatives prefer to maintain traditional institutions and processes, which should only be modified with extreme caution. The political consequences of these beliefs are suspicion of state interference, sympathy toward property rights, and acceptance of inequalities with respect to class, education, status, and wealth (Roberts, 1971).

The purest source of conservative principles is found in Edmund Burke's *Reflections on the Revolution in France*, published in 1790 (Rossiter, 1968). Burke (1729–97) wrote during a time of turmoil (the 1780s) in France—a parliamentary system was created, the Declaration of the Rights of Man was adopted, the last remnants of feudalism were abolished, the property of the Catholic Church was nationalized, and the rationalism of the Enlightenment replaced tradition as the surest guide to human conduct. These changes occurred with lightning rapidity and caused Burke to predict correctly that turmoil and despotism would follow such a radical break from the past (Dickerson & Flanagan, 1986). "The result was the emergence of a political faith that celebrated the beauties of stability and tradition" (Rossiter, 1968, p. 294).

Burke's conservatism, an amalgam of economic liberalism (free-market economy) and social conservatism (respect for the past and a hierarchical view of society), has been adopted by most Anglo-American conservatives (Dickerson & Flanagan, 1986). Benjamin Disraeli, a late nineteenth-century prime minister of Britain, John Adams, second president of the United States, and John A. Macdonald and Georges-Étienne Cartier, two of the chief "Fathers of Confederation" in Canada, are examples of political leaders who subscribed to the Burkean world of order, tradition, hierarchy, private property, laws, and customs. Conservatism in these terms is often found to be the ideological foundation of conservative political parties such as the Conservative Party of Britain, the Republican Party of the United States, the Liberal Party of Australia, and the Conservative Party of Canada.

Conservatism was the dominant ideology in nineteenth-century Britain and North America, where conservative parties were elected, and although it started to wane in the latter part of the nineteenth century, it remained dominant until the Great Depression of the 1930s. Then, many conservative notions fell into disrepute and were replaced by liberal ideals and beliefs, including a new economic theory developed by John Maynard Keynes and a new social policy direction contained in the Beveridge Report of 1942. Following World War II, the state was seen as a force for implementing a more just and equitable society, and a growing welfare state represented the means of implementation (Dickerson & Flanagan, 1986). The absence of serious recession, steady economic growth, and full employment (with some national fluctuations) made it seem that "the old order of capitalism with its crude dogma of laissez-faire, endemic business cycles of boom and bust and chronic unemployment had . . . been left behind in a major evolutionary advance" and that acceptance of "[t]he mix of values and institutions represented by the welfare state . . . symbolized the new social order" (Mishra, 1989, p. 172).

In light of such beliefs, the events of the 1970s, such as the oil crisis, a worldwide recession, stagflation, and the fiscal crisis of the state, came as a real shock and were not resolved by reformist liberal mechanisms and policies. Although never dead, conservative ideas and rhetoric have been revived as a way of explaining what went wrong with the mixed economy of the welfare state and as a guide to economic recovery and prosperity (Mishra, 1989). Political parties advocating conservative ideas and solutions have been elected in Britain (1979, 1983, 1987, 1991, 2015), the United States (1980, 1984, 1988, 2000, 2004, 2016), Australia (1996, 1998, 2001, 2004, 2013, 2016), and Canada (1984, 1988, 2006). Within the past three decades, even political parties traditionally advocating more progressive forms of welfare capitalism have pursued neo-conservative policies when elected: the federal Democratic Party elected in the US in 1992 and 1996; the federal Liberal Party elected in Canada in 1993, 1997, 2000, and 2004; the Australian Labour Party elected in 1983, 1984, 1987, 1990, 1993, 2007, and 2010; the British Labour Party elected in 1997, 2001, and 2005.

Neo-conservatism

The resurgence of conservative ideas, policies, and rhetoric, along with an attack on the welfare state, has been variously referred to as anti-collectivism (George & Wilding, 1976; 1985), rugged individualism (Djao, 1983), and the New Right (Mishra, 1984) but will be referred to here as neo-conservatism, which is more consistent with popular usage. Basing their economic and social views on the classical doctrines of laissez-faire and individualism, neo-conservatives have called for a return to the economic values of the private marketplace. Their solutions to the current crises are to attack government deficits by cutting profligate social spending, to rely on the private sector to restore economic growth, to eliminate or reduce the power of unions, to deregulate industry, and to limit the controls on multinational corporations (Riches, 1986).

Resnick (1984) describes three different but complementary elements running through neo-conservative thought. (1) People's excessive expectations are seen as a threat to representative government. Hence, government's role should be reduced, individual rights diminished, and more traditional values, such as authority and obedience, reinstated. (2) The state should follow laissez-faire policies and reject government interventions; demand management of the economy should be replaced by supply-side economics; deregulation, privatization, and severe limits on government spending should be imposed; and balanced budgets should be the central goal. (3) Traditional concepts of morality and religion should be asserted to control the permissiveness of modern society, and school prayers, the sacredness of pregnancy, law and order, and anti-communism should be the four foundations of the good society. Rossiter (1968) has identified some of the persistent philosophical themes of modern conservatism:

- the imperfect nature of people, where unreason and sin lie under the mask of civilized behaviour;
- the natural inequality of people in mind, body, and character;
- the necessity for social classes;
- the need for a ruling and serving elite;
- the existence of a universal moral order supported by organized religion;
- the primacy of private property;
- the limitations of human reason and the consequent need for traditions, institutions, symbols, and prejudices.

Traditional Conservatism and Neo-conservatism

What, then, is new about neo-conservatism? That is, what are the differences between the conservatism of the nineteenth century and the first half of the twentieth and the neo-conservatism of the 1980s, 1990s, and 2000s? Most writers suggest that there is little difference. Dickerson and Flanagan (1986, p. 105), for example, state, "We continue to use the traditional term conservatism because we see no fundamental change in ideology, even though popular support for conservative views has increased." Mishra (1984, p. 173) contends that the only difference is the context (i.e., welfare capitalism) and that the doctrine is the same: "Remove the context and the associated rhetoric and there is little that is new—that cannot, for example, be traced back to the classical doctrines of Adam Smith (individualism and free market) and Herbert Spencer (social Darwinism)." Most writers suggest that neo-conservatism represents a more sophisticated presentation of conservative doctrine rather than a different doctrine (Mishra, 1989).

Neo-conservatives have blamed much of the economic crisis on the welfare state. Mishra (1989, p. 171) says, "It is one thing when economic growth stops . . . and governments find that they have to economize on social [expenditure]. . . . It is quite another thing when economic recession . . . becomes[s] the occasion for a general attack on the basic principles and practices of the postwar welfare state." Neo-conservatives have argued that the welfare state has created both economic and social problems. The American neo-conservative writer Charles Murray (1984, cited in Rice & Prince, 2000) argued that the welfare system ignored three (conservative) premises: that people respond to sticks (disincentives) and carrots (incentives); that people are inherently amoral and would rather not work; and that people must be held accountable for their actions. Economically, neo-conservatives argue that the welfare state is too big and too expensive—and also inefficient because it allows (or encourages) workers to drop out of the labour market, thus depriving the economy of needed labour and increasing welfare costs at the same time. Socially, neo-conservatives contend that the welfare state has fractured traditional family life, eroded the work ethic, legitimated unearned leisure time without shame or penalty, and encouraged un-desirable behaviour (Stoesz & Karger, 1990). For example, the US attorney general in the admin-istration of George H.W. Bush blamed the 1992 Los Angeles race riots, which followed the "not guilty" verdict in the trial of the policemen who beat Rodney King, on the liberal social programs of the Kennedy and Johnson administrations. Social expenditures were cited as encouraging too many inner-city black females to have children out of wedlock, and these children, the products of sexual abandonment without proper families, it was claimed, were responsible for the looting and rioting. To the neo-conservative, then, social welfare programs represent the cause rather than the cure for many social problems.[1]

A difference between traditional conservatives and neo-conservatives is that the latter group is much more sophisticated in its criticisms and attacks on the welfare state. Traditional conservatives were content to snipe at social programs from the sidelines, using clichés about welfare cheats, bleeding-heart social workers, and self-interested bureaucrats (Stoesz & Karger, 1990). Right-wing think tanks that attempt to give neo-conservative ideas intellectual legitimacy have emerged in all Anglo-democracies. They include the London Institute of Economic Affairs and the Centre for Policy Studies in Britain; the Hoover Institute, the Cato Institute, and the Heritage Foundation in the United States; the Australian Institute for Public Policy, the Centre for Independent Studies (CIS), and the Institute of Public Affairs (IPA) in Australia (Mendes, 2003); and the moderately conservative C.D. Howe Institute and the more right-wing Fraser Institute in Canada, both of which are funded mainly by "big business" (Naiman,1997; Rice & Prince, 2000). All have made serious proposals to restructure the welfare state (consistent with market solutions for social problems) rather than to eliminate it. Examples of such proposals include: to transfer as much welfare responsibility as possible from the federal government to lower levels of government and to the private sector; to transfer money from welfare to work-fare programs; to encourage the involvement and participation of private citizens in the provi-sion of many welfare services (i.e., food banks, soup kitchens, emergency shelters, and so on). Mullaly (1994) has argued that the current restructuring of the welfare state is occurring along class lines, with money being taken out of general welfare programs for the working class and redirected into fiscal welfare—i.e., grants, tax breaks, and the like for corporations and wealthy individuals—and into occupational welfare—i.e., perks and fringe benefits for the managerial and professional sectors of the working class, which are subsidized through the tax system. The result of this restructuring is that social benefits are redistributed away from those most in need (people living in poverty) to those least in need (the wealthy). The class nature of this restructured welfare state is, of course, consistent with the neo-conservative belief in hierarchy and/or aristocracy (Sigurdson, 2002).

Neo-conservatism and Neo-liberalism

Given the confusion over use of the terms "neo-conservatism" and "neo-liberalism," what is the difference between them? It was pointed out in Chapter 2 that some writers maintain that there is no difference and show that the two terms are often used interchangeably. However, there is, in fact, a crucial difference. Although both perspectives subscribe to similar economic ideas and principles—that is, to fiscal conservatism in conservative terms and classical free-market doctrine in liberal terms—they differ with respect to social doctrine (see Table 3.1). Whereas neo-liberalism is mainly an economic ideology (shared with neo-conservatives but not as extreme or as absolute) that advocates an economic arena free from government control or restriction, neo-conservatism is just as much a social ideology (Green, 2000). The latter calls for a return to the value norms of the traditional two-parent family and to traditional male and female roles and decries the progressive changes that have come about from such social movements as feminism, gay and lesbian rights, and multiculturalism (Sigurdson, 2002). This social ideology also is hostile toward easier divorce laws and same-sex relationships—especially same-sex marriage (Lavalette & Pratt, 1997). These ideas have found their way into the Conservative Party of Canada via its previous Reform Party/Canadian Alliance base, as well as the Republican Party in the United States. The Conservative Harper government (2006–15) espoused the virtues of the traditional family with a stay-at-home parent but objected to measures recognizing unpaid household labour. The question of unpaid work in the long-form census had been the result of a long campaign by women's organizations to have women's contributions in the home made more visible. When the long-form census was cancelled in 2010, this question was deleted (Porter, 2012).

In early 2005, the Republican branches of government (federal and state) in the United States sought to interfere with the judicial system in a case in which a husband in Florida gave permission to turn off the life-support system attached to his wife (Terri Schiavo), who had been in a vegetative state for more than a decade. President George W. Bush and his brother, Jeb Bush, the governor of Florida, were part of this intervention, with the president claiming that he was upholding a sacred Republican belief in "a culture of life" (i.e., anti-abortion and anti-euthanasia). This claim is truly ironic when one considers that President Bush ordered the invasion of Iraq, that the United States is one of the very few Western democracies that employ capital punishment, and that the state of Texas, where he was governor, executes more people than any other state. This social ideology of neo-conservatism is also the bedrock of the so-called "Moral Majority"—the religious, fundamentalist right wing of the American population—one leader of which, the televangelist Pat Robertson, in 2005 called for the assassination of Venezuela's democratically elected leftist president, Hugo Chavez. Neo-liberals, for the most part, do not subscribe to this fundamentalist religious belief system or to this extreme ideology. They still prefer a reform brand of liberalism (albeit a watered-down version) that seeks to keep the free market but to purge it from some of its worst abuses (to be discussed in the next chapter).

Table 3.1 Neo-conservatism: Fiscal Conservatism plus Social Conservatism

Conservative Focus	Values
Fiscal conservatism	Espouses classical liberal economic doctrine but in more extreme/absolute form
	Views a free market as the means of distribution of income, resources, and life chances
	Sees government "intervention" as government "interference"
	Believes in restricted public spending and monetarist economic policy
	Champions global free trade
	Wants only minimal taxation and a minimal (residual) welfare state
	Expresses hostility toward labour unions
	Insists on private ownership of the means of production
	Believes that profit is the purpose of production
	Upholds private property and inheritance rights
Social conservatism	Believes that the traditional heterosexual, married couple with children is the cornerstone of society
	Claims that the ideal society is hierarchical, patriarchal, authoritarian, and inequitable
	Is skeptical about immigration, especially when it involves racialized groups
	Expresses hostility toward same-sex relationships, divorce laws, and multiculturalism
	Accommodates the religious right with its literal interpretations of the Bible, strong views on sin, and rejection of non-Christian religions
	Sees human life as sacred from conception to death; thus, abortion and euthanasia are wrong/sinful
	Abhors the changes that have occurred because of such social movements as the women's movement, the gay and lesbian rights movement, and the human rights movement
	Views poverty not as an economic problem but as culturally determined through values, behaviours, attitudes, and a lack of ambition transmitted across generations

Before we consider the specific ideological (social, economic, and political) beliefs of neo-conservatives, a brief overview of the views that neo-conservatives hold with respect to human nature, the nature of society and the state, social justice, and social change will be presented. The relationship between these neo-conservative views and the neo-conservative social, economic, and political ideals that constitute neo-conservative ideology is symbiotic. In other words, these views and ideals are mutually supportive of each other and interrelated, with each contributing to the overall neo-conservative world view or paradigm.

Views of the Nature of Humans, Society, the State, Social Justice, and Social Change

As mentioned in Chapter 1, what we believe about *human nature* largely determines how we think we should be governed (Sigurdson, 2002). It also determines our explanations for social problems, our social welfare solutions for dealing with those problems, and the nature and forms of our social work practices. What, then, do neo-conservatives believe about what it means to be human—in other words, what is our human essence? Thomas Hobbes (1588–1679) gave the classic conservative (and neo-conservative) view of human nature. He wrote that humans are isolated and selfish creatures, driven by the twin forces of appetites (pleasures or desires) and aversions (pains). Individuals are motivated by gain (profit) and power (control of others), and if they were left to their own devices, their lives would be "solitary, poor, nasty, brutish, and short" (Hobbes, 1981 [1651], pp. 185–186). Thus, Hobbes concludes that to avoid the violence and anxiety and constant war "of every man [person] against every man [person]" (p. 185) that comes from this natural condition, the only rational course of action is to give up or trade some individual freedom and live in a formally organized state to gain the security needed to satisfy individual needs. In other words, civil society is only an expedient or necessary evil and not a conservative value or ideal. Jeremy Bentham (1748–1832) further developed this notion of human nature by arguing that all human behaviour can be explained by the two primary motives of pleasure and pain (theory of psychological hedonism). He argued that it was only "rational" (natural) for the individual to pursue self-interest over the interests of all others and that one must use his or her "reason" in this pursuit. Bentham believed that community or society interests were a fiction, for by nature there only existed the sum of the individual interests of its members.

The *nature of society*, as suggested by Bentham, is only equal to the sum of individual interests. It has no rights or values or collective interests in and of itself. Bentham and David Ricardo (1772–1823), an early political economist who developed the classical school of economic theory further than anyone before him, argued that society is simply a convenient way of referring to the sum of the contracts that free individuals entered into with one another. Milton Friedman, the twentieth-century neo-conservative economist and adviser to Reagan in the US and Thatcher in Britain, held that there are no social goals other than the aggregate of individual goals. In this way, society is reduced to so many contracts and agreements between the individuals who, in total, comprise the society.

It does not stand above or apart from individuals. There is no idea that the whole is greater than the sum of its parts. There is no "sociological imagination" (Mills, 1959). Margaret Thatcher once remarked, when asked a question about society, that "there is no such thing as society; there are only individuals" who live within a particular state or nation. Although conservatives grudgingly accept the existence of classes, they have tended to de-emphasize the class concept by downplaying the importance of the concept of society; that is, society is comprised mostly of individuals, not classes. Ironically, conservatives subscribe to notions of hierarchy and aristocracy and the maintenance of such. Rather than social classes, however, conservatives have tended to see individuals who are either morally superior or inferior. Burke, who had an aristocratic belief in a natural hierarchy of persons, characterized the morally superior as "the wiser, the more expert, and the more opulent" and the morally inferior as "the weaker, the less knowing, and the less provided with the goods of fortune." Of course, with this distinction those who had wealth were regarded as morally superior and those without "opulence" were regarded as morally inferior. Thus, a conservative imperative was to maintain the position of each group. In other words, the status quo was to be "conserved" because it would not be good for the morally inferior to obtain positions of power.

If, as neo-conservatives claim, society only represents the sum of individual contracts, then what is *the role of the nation-state* (government)? Hobbes partially answered this when he stated that in exchange for some security, which was necessary for them to meet their individual needs, individuals must give up some freedoms to the state. Thus, to the neo-conservative the primary role of the state is to maintain law and order for the orderly management of trade and commerce. It is to act as impartial arbiter in trade and contract disputes. But anything beyond protecting people's lives and property by maintaining law and order becomes, in the eyes of neo-conservatives, a threat to liberty (Sigurdson, 2002). And, of course, part of the task of maintaining law and order was and is to assure the compliance of subordinate groups (individuals) with the goals, needs, and interests of the ruling class (i.e., the morally superior, the aristocracy, the bourgeoisie, and other elites).

Social justice, to neo-conservatives, is based on the belief in individual responsibility. That is, all individuals have a responsibility to look after themselves. Only when people do not carry out this responsibility do problems such as unemployment, lack of resources, and inadequate housing occur. Neo-conservatives would guarantee a formal equality of right to participate in the free market and then rely on the free market to provide an equilibrium of societal benefits (Sigurdson, 2002). That is, there should be no legal discrimination banning groups such as racialized individuals or women from applying to educational programs or running for office. Further, a fair system of competition will produce fair results, and, therefore, the state should not be used to provide specific advantages for historically disadvantaged groups (Sigurdson, 2002). Affirmative action programs are viewed as socially unjust by neo-conservatives because they are seen as programs of reverse discrimination. Social equality is not a value choice of neo-conservatives. They believe that material inequality can be a good thing. In 1786, for instance, Joseph Townsend, an influential clergyman in England, published anonymously a little book called *A Dissertation on the Poor Laws by a Well-Wisher to Mankind* in which he argued that "poverty was a necessary spur [incentive] to human activity" (cited in de Schweinitz, 1943, p. 115).

Neo-conservatives are relatively content with the way things are (i.e., with the status quo) and would defend institutions from reformers. The status quo—traditional social values and accepted ways of doing things—best serves the interests of the market, and any attempt to change the fundamental institutions is regarded as a threat to existing social relations (i.e., to the existence of a morally superior dominant group and a morally inferior subordinate group). Neo-conservatives are highly skeptical of attempts to improve life through social policy and social intervention, which they call "social engineering." They prefer the tried and true to the new and experimental. Conservatives place great emphasis on punishment and retribution, and as a consequence, scientific evidence on the rates of recidivism or rehabilitation is viewed as irrelevant (Jeffrey, 2015). In 2014 the *Annual Report* of the Office of the Correctional Investigator for Corrections Canada was scathing in its criticism of the Conservative government's failure to address the growth in the size, complexity, and diversity of the offender population in Canada. The report made the observation that while the correctional budget swelled to finance the construction of new prison units, there were no new investments in community corrections focused on the reintegration of offenders into the community.

Neo-conservatives realize that some change is inevitable but insist that *social change* should be gradual and evolutionary rather than rapid and revolutionary. Neo-conservatives point out that biological evolution has occurred over millions of years (since creation for many religious conservatives, especially in the US) and, therefore, contend that social change should follow the same course of normal, natural, divine, and evolutionary change.

Table 3.2 summarizes neo-conservative beliefs with respect to human nature, the nature of society, the state, social justice, and social change.

Table 3.2 A Summary of Neo-conservative Views

Concept	Views
Human nature	Isolated and selfish individuals
	Behaviours determined by pleasure and pain
	Motivated by gain (profit) and power (control over others)
	Not natural (but necessary) for humans to live in society
	Individuals are either morally superior or inferior
Society	No such thing as society, only individuals
	Equal to the sum of individual interests (no collective interests)
	Series of individual contracts that individuals enter into with one another
Nation-state	Necessary evil that maintains law and order
	Referee role in trade and contract disputes
	Assures conformity of subordinate groups to interests of dominant groups
Social justice	Individuals have responsibility to look after themselves
	There are no social problems, only personal problems that occur when individuals do not look after themselves
	Every individual should have the right (and responsibility) to participate in the free market
	Affirmative action is reverse discrimination, socially unjust
	Poverty is a good thing because it teaches discipline and provides incentive
Social change	Content with existing social institutions and social relations
	Skeptical of social engineering (i.e., social intervention)
	Any social change should be slow and evolutionary

The next three sections look at specific ideological beliefs of neo-conservatism along social, economic, and political lines. Some of these beliefs overlap with the views outlined above. These views and the subsequent ideological beliefs are mutually reinforcing. Taken together, they represent the neo-conservative position today. When compared to the progressive perspective of social work presented in Chapter 1, it is obvious that there is little, if any, agreement or common ground between neo-conservatism and progressive social work.

Social Beliefs

The central social values of neo-conservatism are freedom or liberty, individualism, and inequality (George & Wilding, 1976; 1985). Liberty is seen primarily as the absence of coercion. People must be as free as possible to exert themselves to the utmost limit of their abilities to the advantage of the individual person, which in turn will have a beneficial effect for society (in economic terms, a trickle-down effect). Any government promotion of social values that interfere with one's freedom is counterproductive. Yet if coercion is to be avoided, there must be sanctions against those who would use it. The state, therefore, uses the threat of coercion to avoid coercion by any individual. This institutionalization of coercion is perceived by neo-conservatives as benefiting everyone equally in spite of the stratified nature of society and the concentration of power within certain groups. Thus, one of the inherent contradictions of a neo-conservative society is that coercion by the state is the instrument of liberty.

Individualism is a necessary correlate of liberty. The dominant theme of individualism is that the individual must have as much liberty as possible to pursue his or her own interests and to bear the consequences of his or her actions. If everyone in society adheres to the principle of the pursuit of self-interest without harming others, then society will run smoothly. Only when people fail to carry out their obligations or when government interferes with one's liberty do problems occur for the individual and for society. Individualism perceives people as imperfect beings who, therefore, must be controlled by sanctions and rules enforced by the state. Individualism also attributes a large role in the socialization of people to voluntary organizations and to institutions such as the family, the school, and the church. When these voluntary institutions fail in their socialization function, the coercive role of the state is invoked.

Social equality and liberty are seen by neo-conservatives as contradictory. They fear that equality of incomes from work will destroy people's work incentives, including the social esteem that accompanies certain occupations. Politically, social equality implies that powerful groups would have to share their political power, which could only occur through government coercion. Thus, to achieve social equality necessitates interference with the equality of freedom (including the freedom to be poor rather than being coerced into affluence by the state). Equality of freedom is the only equality accepted by neo-conservatives and, in fact, is their supreme value. But this equality of freedom is bound to produce material and political inequality. Thus, neo-conservatives support equality of freedom and social inequality. Obviously, these values foster a social Darwinian "survival of the fittest" view that any form of state intervention into people's freedoms is contrary to the laws of nature, leading potentially to a restriction on the power and authority of the fittest members of society and an enhancement of the weak and unfit.

Economic Beliefs

The fundamental economic values of neo-conservatism are laissez-faire economics, competitive capitalism, and private property accumulation. Descriptively, the term "laissez-faire" (leave alone) refers to minimal government interference (as opposed to intervention) in the lives and activities of private citizens, especially with regard to their economic activities. The role of the state is to ensure the provision of the basic conditions for free competitive capitalism by maintaining law and order, enforcing contracts, protecting property rights, and defending the nation against attacks by other nations. It does not interfere in the economy by either holding back the successful or helping the unsuccessful.

Laissez-faire is a prerequisite for competitive capitalism. Reference is often made by neo-conservatives to the "natural laws" of the competitive marketplace (laws of supply, demand, and price determination). A society that ignores or interferes with these natural laws, it is assumed, will run into trouble as surely as a person who ignores the law of gravity. Neo-conservatives believe that competitive capitalism, based on voluntary exchange rather than on coercion, is the best model for an economic system (Friedman, 1962, cited in Djao, 1983). The free market protects everyone's interests: the consumer, the seller, the employee, and the employer. The consumer is protected because they can buy from other sellers. The seller is protected because there are other potential consumers. The employee is protected because there are other employers they can work for, and so on. This whole economic process is carried out unfettered by any authority. If government were to interfere by attempting to regulate and restrict competition, or to hamper the efficient and successful, or to help the inefficient and unsuccessful, the results would be to upset the delicate but perfectly balanced natural economic system. All society would suffer and be poorer for it. The best economic policy of government is to leave the economy alone.

One of the freedoms cherished by neo-conservatives is the right to acquire, accumulate, and own property (land, material and natural resources, means of production, and so on) and to use one's property as one sees fit. For example, the reduction of carbon emissions to reduce global warming is viewed as interference with property rights and the market, according to the conservative viewpoint. In Canada, the Standing Committee on Environment and Sustainable Development (2014) reported that the Conservative government did not introduce promised regulations in the oil and gas sectors—where emissions were growing the fastest. Private ownership is not only consistent with neo-conservative social beliefs of liberty, individualism, and inequality, it also is the driving force behind the economic system. Private ownership provides the means for making profits and thus is the incentive in a competitive free market for persons to work hard to maximize their material and spiritual well-being. If people were not allowed to keep the fruits of their labour and to dispose of them in any fashion they wish, there would be reduced incentive to work hard, and the economy, as a whole, would suffer. Individuals are responsible for providing for themselves out of resources they manage to control. This notion forces people to attempt to increase their share of available resources, since any increase in property is perceived as an increase in material security and social status. To the neo-conservatives, the appropriation of material resources is the fundamental principle around which a society's system of provision and the entire social order should be constructed.

Political Beliefs

The major political beliefs of neo-conservatism are: rule by a governing elite; subjugation of the political system to the economic system; law, order, and stability; and paternalism. Conservatives have always found the concept of democracy problematic, and it is important to remember that when modern democracy as we know it—that is, representative democracy—first appeared on the world stage, only property-owning males were allowed the vote. Politics is restricted in meaning to the "art of governing," which is too important to be left to anyone but the most able and best prepared, who, of course, are inevitably members of the elite ruling class. To extend political rights to the masses is to run the risk of decisions being made by the wrong people—that is, by non-members of the established elite, who, therefore, cannot be legitimate rulers. The Family Compact of Upper Canada (Ontario) in the nineteenth century and the hierarchy of the Roman Catholic Church of Lower Canada, which dominated Quebec life well into the twentieth century, are examples of conservative ruling elites in Canada.

The belief in ruling elites is no mere relic of political history but is used today by neo-conservatives as a political explanation for the economic and social crises confronting Western industrial societies. "A ruling class, unlike a democratically elected government, is expected to serve the interests of those who control the economy" (Marchak, 1981, p. 71). In a democracy, political parties must compete with one another for votes. In this electoral competition, excessive expectations are made on governments, pushing them further and further into responsibility for everything. The result, according to neo-conservative thought, is government overload: demands on government far exceed its capacity to meet them effectively. This situation is characterized by public expenditure out of control or by government itself expanded out of control and has been brought about by increasing democratization (Mishra, 1984). The neo-conservatives would like to see this process reversed or, at least, curtailed.

Neo-conservatives blame much of the recent fiscal crisis discussed in Chapter 2 on excessive government intervention and regulation. They would resolve this crisis by curtailing democratization of the political process and by depoliticizing the economy. If society is to benefit from economic activity, then, it is claimed, we must put up with the costs (e.g., unemployment, inadequate wages, questionable labour practices) of a free market. The role of government should be to protect, to support, to assure, and to enhance the workings of a free market. It should not be the role of government to regulate, interfere with, or explicitly allow unions, professional associations, or other interest groups to modify the spontaneous workings of the market. Thus, although neo-conservatives believe in a strong central state, its sphere of activities must be restricted to such things as national defence and protecting individual rights and freedoms.

Neo-conservatives place a premium on the maintenance of a social hierarchy, and much of past conservative effort has been to *conserve* rather than reform the legal, political, social, and economic status quo. Originally, such a perspective was justified on religious grounds, but today there is a strong psychological attraction for conserving rather than reforming (Pritchard & Taylor, 1978). In other words, much of neo-conservative rhetoric is based on the assumption that people have a basic psychological need for security and will opt for a social system they are familiar with, even though it may contain many flaws, rather than take a chance on one they have not experienced and are unfamiliar with. Thus, much of neo-conservative political rhetoric is focused on law and order and on preserving the "old" ways and values. Any change or reform is perceived as a threat to social stability and social continuity.

Another political belief of neo-conservatives is "paternalism for those whom society designates as not responsible" (George & Wilding, 1976, p. 32) or, in Poor Law terminology, "the deserving poor." This form of government activity is seen as a necessary evil (the alternative is to let people die) rather than as a means of reducing inequalities. Although the risk of abuse is great (in terms of expanding the categories of people considered as not capable of taking responsibility for themselves), there is no avoiding the need for some degree of paternalism. The amount of assistance must be the lowest acceptable to society. In return for this *noblesse oblige*, the neo-conservative ruling elite would expect conformity and loyalty from its citizenry.

View of Social Problems

In accordance with its views of human nature and society and its social, economic, and political beliefs, neo-conservatism holds that people should provide for themselves by exercising their individual freedoms and choices in the competitive marketplace. In other words, everyone should provide for their own needs through work, savings, and the acquisition of property. Only those persons who do not carry out these obligations (the unfit, the lazy, and the inferior) encounter problems. Even if people become ill and cannot look after themselves, the judgment is often that they should have made arrangements to cover such contingencies and it is up the family to look after them in the first instance. And because these problems are of their own making, they do not deserve help from government or from hard-working, responsible, and honest taxpayers. In fact, neo-conservatives believe that helping those who fail to provide for themselves reinforces idleness and dependence on government and encourages others to avoid efforts to support themselves. An exception to this rule is that if people are judged to be in difficulty through no fault of their own (i.e., disabled persons, dependent children, older persons), they may be eligible for some help through a residual welfare system (discussed in Chapter 1). History has shown, however, that this group of "deserving poor" has always been numerically under-represented.

The neo-conservative view of social problems seldom considers structural or environmental sources of social and economic problems but attributes such problems to individual weakness, deviance, or heredity. Social problems are viewed as personal problems, and the focus is on the troublesome person or family. The problem is supposed to be caused by defects of the mentally ill person or the drug addict or the poor person or the criminal. The family is also seen as the source of personal problems because, consistent with social Darwinian thought, unfit parents will produce unfit children. In other words, parents who are lazy, dishonest, and inferior will produce children with similar characteristics. Neo-conservative writer George Gilder (1981) contends that welfare programs and the decline of traditional family values and traditional family patterns (not sexism, racism, or unemployment) cause poverty and that any cause–effect relationship between racism or sexism and poverty is a myth perpetrated by social workers and feminists. In all cases, the analysis of social problems is the same. The individual is separated from society, and a biographical portrait of deficiencies is constructed as the source of the person's troubles.

The neo-conservative view of social problems is consistent with the "social pathology" perspective that was central to the thinking of early American sociologists. Their work was infused with moral indignation formulated in terms of a medical model wherein many social problems were the work of sick or pathological individuals—that is, people who are defective, delinquent, dependent, and deficient. The solution to social problems according to these early sociologists was to educate the pathological troublemakers in middle-class morality (Rubington & Weinberg, 2010). This perspective on social problems, which is often referred to as the "personal deficiency approach," has informed the diagnostic, functional, and psychosocial traditions in social work (Coates, 1991). The impact that the larger social environment has on personal problems is not considered.

Box 3.1 *The Double Standard of Neo-conservatives*

From approximately 1985 to 1995, I (Bob) was chair of the Social Work Department at St Thomas University in Fredericton, New Brunswick. During that time I was a frequent media commentator on various social policy issues. I often found myself on panels discussing the impacts of provincial or federal budgets or new legislation or particular social policies. Along with myself, the panels usually consisted of a businessman (never a businesswoman), an accountant or economist, a right-wing academic (usually a political scientist or management professor), and someone from the Chamber of Commerce or the Real Estate Board. Given this makeup of panel members, it is obvious that I was the "token" left-winger whose views would be out of step with the others, who were usually conservative in their positions. Inevitably, I found myself being written off and/or patronized by the other panel members, including the media person who chaired the panel. I like to think that I held my own in these panel discussions not only because I knew my stuff and was relatively articulate in expressing my views but also because the (neo-conservative) positions of the others were usually indefensible.

I remember one particular radio panel when we were discussing a recent provincial budget in which there were several cutbacks (again) to social programs. I took my usual position that these cuts were morally bankrupt, short-sighted in terms of social arithmetic because they would lead to higher social and economic costs over time, discriminatory because they picked on vulnerable groups, and so on. The business leader on the panel said to me in a patronizing way, "Well now, Bob, you have to understand that when you give someone something for nothing, you don't do them any favours. You just make them lazy, irresponsible parasites. Why would you want to reward them for doing nothing?" Because of his patronizing attitude, *I decided to go for his jugular!*

I said to Mr Big Business Leader, "Could I ask you a somewhat personal question that relates to what you just said?" Looking a little bewildered, he replied, "Yes, I guess so." I asked him, "When you die, I assume that you will not leave your children anything which you own. Is this right?" He stated in a rather annoyed manner. "Of course I will. Why would you even ask that?" To which I replied, "Well, you just made the argument that giving someone something for nothing will damage their character by making them lazy, dependent, and irresponsible. And, since I am sure you love your children, I assumed that you wouldn't want to do that to them or reward them for doing nothing. You know that it would be better if they worked for whatever they got rather than you giving it to them on a silver platter."

There was a long silence on the part of everyone on the panel, while Mr Big Business Leader, who now realized that he was hoisted on his own petard, was looking very uncomfortable and at a loss as to what to say. The moderator intervened and said, "We should perhaps move on." But having been patronized, I didn't want to move on, so I said, "No, I asked this guy a question, and I want to hear his answer. He just condemned everyone who has had to suffer the indignity of seeking some kind of help from society, and I want to know how he justifies this *double standard* where it is okay to help his children even when they are not in need but it is a big social sin to help others out who are in need." Another long silence. Finally, the moderator said that we *really* had to move on. I don't recall Mr Big Business Leader saying too much for the rest of the panel discussion.

View of Social Welfare

George and Wilding (1985; 1994) explain how neo-conservatives are fundamentally hostile to a developed social welfare state. Any provision of more than basic government services is believed to have unnecessary and undesirable social, economic, and political consequences. Socially, the more services the state provides, the more it weakens the traditional sources of welfare: the family and local voluntary organizations such as the churches. These sources will not only disappear over time but so, too, will the individual's ability and willingness to provide for their own needs. Economically, government assistance, above a basic subsistence level, diverts human and capital resources from the productive sector, undermines work incentives, is provided inefficiently, and encourages consumption of unneeded services. Politically, social welfare undermines individual freedom, weakens public respect for government and the political process, and may lead to dictatorial regimes. In essence, the neo-conservatives see the "welfare state" as a misnomer because government intervention actually leads to a state of "diswelfare."

The free-market system, according to the neo-conservatives, is the main source and origin of welfare. Even social services should be delivered through the market by private commercial practitioners/entrepreneurs. The model of social welfare most consistent with neo-conservative thought, and that has the free market as its central concept, is "residual" (Wilensky & Lebeaux, 1958). This is based on the neo-conservative belief that social welfare programs (both private and public) should only come into play when the normal channels for meeting needs—the family and the market economy—break down. When these preferred structures of supply are not functioning properly or when an individual cannot make use of them because of illness or old age, a third mechanism for fulfilling need—the social welfare system—is brought into play. This residual structure attends to emergency functions only, and it is expected to withdraw when the two normal or regular structures, the family and the economic system, are again working properly. All social welfare assistance should be minimal and must not threaten or undermine the operations of the marketplace, nor must it erode wage-earners' sense of responsibility for themselves and their families.

Because of its temporary, residual, and substitute nature, social welfare often carries a stigma of charity and abnormality. This concept of social welfare formed the basis of the Elizabethan Poor Laws, which divided the poor into two groups: the deserving (dependent children, the elderly, the disabled) and the non-deserving (employable adults). The former group might have been eligible for residual welfare; the second group was not. That this model of social welfare is consistent with such neo-conservative values as individual responsibility, the free market, and minimal government intervention is readily apparent. The residual model of welfare is similar to Furniss and Tilton's (1977) "positive state" model of social welfare described in Chapter 1, where it was argued that it should be rejected by the social work profession because it is based on value premises diametrically opposed to those of social work.

Mishra (1989, p. 174) contends that neo-conservatism challenges all persons who believe in an adequate and fair welfare state:

> neo-conservatism is openly and unashamedly partisan and one-sided. It has forced upon the world of social welfare the realization that what we are involved in is essentially a contest over values, beliefs and interests rather than some objective necessity dictated by the economy. In breaking the consensus of ideas and practices over the welfare state it has thrown an open challenge to those on the side of social welfare to make an adequate ideological response.

Social Work Practice within the Neo-conservative Paradigm

Given: (1) the neo-conservative views on the nature of human beings, society, the state, social justice, and social change; (2) such neo-conservative values as individual responsibility, inequality, survival of the fittest, and laissez-faire; (3) a neo-conservative view of social problems as originating from individual weakness and deviance; and (4) a neo-conservative conception of social welfare as temporary, abnormal, and residual, then the nature of social work practice within neo-conservatism would be one of control and coercion of people. Emphasis would be placed on getting people to accept their personal, family, and social obligations and not on social or environmental reform.

Because the nature of human beings is viewed as contentious, competitive, and self-absorbed, social work must use coercive measures to make sure that people look after themselves. All other sources of assistance must be explored before a person would be considered eligible for any kind of financial help. A means test is an integral part of the residual model of welfare. Separation of the deserving poor from the non-deserving poor would be a primary function of social workers in a neo-conservative society. Investigation and monitoring of people's living, work, and financial situations would occur regularly to control abuse of social welfare systems and programs. Because of the belief that social problems are mainly due to individual fault and deviance, then suspicion, moralism, and punitive attitudes would be qualities held by social workers. The primary task of social work under neo-conservatism would be to teach people how to do without the welfare state.

Individual behaviour within the neo-conservative paradigm is seen within a limited social context that hardly extends beyond an individual's family. In other words, neo-conservatives attribute problems to an individual's dysfunctional family, and it is not likely that the source of personal/social problems will be considered to extend beyond the boundary of the family. A dysfunctional family is not viewed as a victim of the social order but as a pathological social unit. Social work with pathological families would consist of coercing, cajoling, and convincing individual family members to adjust their behaviours and to carry out their individual responsibilities to themselves, to one another, and to society. Threats of removing children and other intimidation tactics would be major tools used in working with families.

Rather than focusing on helping, social work would emphasize control of people's behaviour by way of such methods as "case management" in order to remove any threat to the established social order. This is so because, according to the neo-conservatives, society can only function effectively and efficiently as long as everyone carries their own weight. Once the principle of individual responsibility starts to break down, then the whole society is in danger of collapsing. If individual pathology cannot be controlled by social work, then it must be neutralized by other state mechanisms such as asylums and prisons.

One possible exception to the controlling and coercive nature of social work within the neo-conservative paradigm would be its treatment of the so-called "deserving poor." Because a judgment has been made that the deserving poor are in need through no fault of their own, they would likely not be treated as punitively as their "non-deserving" counterparts. However, there is always the problem of determining who is deserving and who is not. As well, the history of the Poor Laws tells us that those judged deserving have always been numerically under-represented. Even in working with the deserving poor, social workers would be expected to exhort and cajole as much money and help as possible from the poor person's family for the maintenance of its unfortunate member.

Iatridis (1983, p. 101) sums up the effects of neo-conservatism on social work:

> neo-conservatism creates a special crisis for social workers because this ideology is the antithesis of social work theory, practice, philosophy, values, objectives, and commitments—of everything, in fact, for which the profession stands.

Critique of the Neo-conservative Paradigm

Neo-conservative thought forms much of the intellectual support for recent social policy in Canada, the United States, and Britain. An excellent overview of the criticisms of neo-conservative doctrine has been presented by Mishra (1984) and is summarized here.

(1) Although there may be a grain of truth in many neo-conservative arguments, there is a tendency to exaggerate this grain of truth and to generalize on the basis of insufficient evidence. For example, neo-conservatives often convey the impression that budget deficits have been occurring regularly since World War II because of Keynesian economic practices, when, in fact, it has only been since the recession of the 1970s that sizable deficits began to emerge.

(2) Neo-conservative thought and argument vary in terms of theoretical sophistication but, on the whole, tend to be one-sided and based on highly selective evidence. For example, neo-conservatives often blame Britain's economic ills on its welfare state, but no mention is made of other European countries such as Germany and Austria with well-developed welfare states that also enjoy excellent economic growth, low inflation, and low unemployment. They are simply ignored.

(3) Neo-conservatives offer a biased view of how government functions. They criticize governments for not being decisive enough and for not taking quick action. They fail to see that government is not the same kind of undertaking as a business seeking profit. Hence, what is presented as government failure—for example, "weakened" authority because of greater democracy and more participation—may in fact be government's strength.

(4) Neo-conservatives possess an inadequate conception of the role of democracy and politics in modern societies. It was mentioned earlier that neo-conservatives would like to see the capitalist market economy depoliticized as much as possible—that is, that elected governments should not be allowed to interfere in the market. This would be a reversal of the growth of the modern state and of citizenship that has been occurring over the past 100 years. It would negate the responsibility a democratically elected government has for the nation's well-being by not allowing it to exercise control and regulation over the economy.

(5) Based on the values of individualism, liberty, private property, and inequality, neo-conservatism has little appreciation of the concepts of social justice and social cohesion as vital elements of modern, industrial democracies.

Conclusion

This chapter presented an overview of conservative ideology and showed how it shaped neo-conservative beliefs about the reasons that we have social problems and what to do about them. It also provided an overview of neo-conservative beliefs about the nature of people and society, the role of the state, the meaning of social justice, and social change. The social, economic, and political beliefs of neo-conservatives were outlined, as were the neo-conservative views of the welfare state and the proper role of social work. Table 3.3 outlines the principal beliefs of neo-conservatism and contrasts them with the fundamental beliefs of progressive social work. After examining the major beliefs and ideals of each, one can conclude only that neo-conservatism and progressive social work are incompatible. The social, economic, and political beliefs of each contradict one another, as do their respective views of the welfare state. Although social work practice does contain coercive and controlling elements, they tend to be imposed by outside bodies such as the state and the authorizing agency. They are not self-directed functions of progressive social work. Neo-conservatism's eighteenth-century assumptions about economic, human, and social behaviour conflict with those of social welfare and are the antithesis of progressive social work.

Table 3.3 Overview of Neo-conservative and Social Work Ideals

	Neo-conservatism	Social Work
Social Beliefs	Freedom (from government coercion) Individualism Inequality	Humanitarianism (humanism) Community Equality
Economic Beliefs	Free market Competitive capitalism Private ownership	Government intervention Social priorities dominate economic decisions Equitable distribution of society's resources
Political Beliefs	Elite rule Depoliticization of economic system Law, order, and stability Paternalism	Participatory democracy in both governmental and non-governmental areas
View of Social Welfare	Fundamentally hostile Ideal = residual model	An instrument of equality, solidarity, and community Ideal = structural model
Nature of Social Work Practice	Use of coercive measures to make people look after themselves Control people's behaviour Poor Law treatment of separating deserving from non-deserving Emphasize investigation and monitoring to prevent cheating the system	Treat people with respect Enhance dignity and integrity Facilitate self-determination and self-realization Accept differences Advocate and promote social justice

Critical Questions

1. How closely do you think the following political parties adhere to conservative ideology?
   - federal Conservative Party in Canada
   - Republican Party in the US
   - federal Liberal Party in Australia
   - Conservative Party in the UK

2. The term "human nature" suggests that certain innate characteristics or traits are common to all people. For example, conservatives claim that humans are *by nature* greedy individuals and competitive. However, socialists claim that humans are *by nature* social beings and cooperative. Is there any such thing as a human nature, and, if so, what is it? Or are human traits and characteristics socially determined?

3. How would neo-conservatives explain street crime in low-income areas? How would they explain white-collar crime such as cheating on your income tax? How would they explain corporate crime such as manipulating markets or dipping into shareholders' money? Are any of these crimes more respectable in a neo-conservative's eyes than others? Why?

4. Why does neo-conservatism continue to be so successful in influencing social policy?

5. Which groups in society are most supportive of neo-conservative ideas?

6. How would you respond to the following neo-conservative claims?
   - If we abolished the minimum wage, we would increase youth employment.
   - Too many teenaged girls are having babies so they can get welfare.
   - Indigenous people will never get ahead as long as government gives them welfare, free housing, and free education and doesn't collect any taxes from them.

4

The Liberal and Neo-liberal Paradigms

There's no place for the state in the bedrooms of the nation.

— Pierre Elliott Trudeau (1967)

Liberals believe in the ability of government to be a force for good in society.

— Justin Trudeau (Liberal Party Platform, 2015)

Introduction

This chapter presents a brief historical overview of liberalism and attempts to clarify and differentiate among several forms of liberalism such as classical or market liberalism, contemporary or reform liberalism, welfare liberalism, and neo-liberalism. It also provides an overview of liberal views or beliefs about human nature, the nature of society, the role of the nation-state, the meaning of social justice, and social change. The social, economic, and political beliefs that constitute liberal ideology are examined, and we explore how these beliefs shape the explanations of liberals with respect to the causes of social problems and the nature and role of the welfare state. A picture of social work practice within the liberal paradigm is presented along with a discussion of how mainstream social work thought and practice developed within a liberal discourse. Even today, the bulk of social work education, literature, and practice is shaped by and reflects liberal ideology. In Canada, the election of a Liberal federal government in October 2015 has reaffirmed that the majority of Canadians still believe that the state has a positive role to play in civil society. A critique of liberalism is provided in this chapter, and a comparison and contrast of liberal ideals is made with those of progressive social work.

Liberalism(s)

Liberalism comes from the Latin word "liber," meaning free. It comprises a set of beliefs based on the assumption that there should be as much individual freedom as possible in any civilized society while allowing for essential constraints (Roberts, 1971). Although liberalism developed as a coherent system of ideals and practical goals mainly in the eighteenth and nineteenth centuries, it has a long and rich tradition (Smith, 1968). It has roots in Greek philosophy and literature, in Roman law, and in several religious traditions, including Christianity, and was fostered by the Renaissance and the Reformation. It is the result of the convergence of a number of broad social and political trends and forces. Today, the term "liberalism" is confusing, made only more confusing when the word is preceded by the prefix "neo," meaning "new." John Gray (1998, cited in O'Brien & Penna, 1998) claims that it is more realistic to think in terms of "liberalisms" in the plural. To some it means individualism in the extreme, whereby the only goal of social organization is to maximize individual autonomy and freedom; to others it means the promotion of collective strategies for social development while maintaining a commitment to individual freedom (O'Brien & Penna, 1998). In this chapter, we distinguish among the terms "liberalism," "neo-liberalism," "classical liberalism," and "reform liberalism," but the major emphasis will be on "reform liberalism," since this form guided the development of the twentieth-century welfare state, at least in North America, and reform liberalism is what separates the neo-conservative from the neo-liberal.

Major Differences between Classical Liberalism and Reform Liberalism

When discussing liberalism, it is important to distinguish the older classical liberalism from contemporary or reform liberalism. As mentioned in the previous chapter, classical liberal economic doctrine is today referred to as neo-liberalism. Classical liberalism, sometimes called "market" liberalism, is similar to conservatism as both developed in the eighteenth and nineteenth centuries, mainly in Britain and western Europe, and both used the same writers and thinkers as the source for many of their ideas and theories.[1] Reform liberalism, which developed in the twentieth century, acknowledged the role of the state in allowing the capitalist free market to function (Naiman, 1997). Whereas classical liberals saw the state in negative terms as a threat to individual freedom, reform liberals view the state in positive terms as promoting freedom for those who otherwise might not achieve it. Great inequalities in market power make one person's freedom another person's oppression. Also, reform liberals view the state as a means to remedy some of the abuses of the free market, such as child labour, slum housing, tainted food, and so on (Smith, 1968). Thus, economic freedom and the free market are not accorded the same primacy in reform liberalism as in classical liberalism (Dickerson & Flanagan, 1986).

Another major difference between classical and reform liberalism lies in the concept of equality that each holds. Equality to the classical liberal means only that everyone abides by the same rules (laws) and does not extend to a desire or responsibility to ameliorate inequality of wealth, status, or power. This is similar to the neo-conservative belief that there should be an equality of right (and responsibility) to participate (i.e., work) in the market. Equality to the reform liberal means equal opportunity—that is, everyone should have the same opportunity to compete in the marketplace for wealth, power, and prestige (Naiman, 1997). Such competition will lead to a status hierarchy in which one's location is determined by a system of meritocracy. Thus, liberals accept inequality. The reform liberal does not wish to eliminate inequality but seeks to reduce its excesses by using the power of the state to provide opportunities, such as public education and public health, that would not be available to some people without government intervention. In short, reform liberalism tries to modify the free market without abolishing it. Table 4.1 outlines some of the major "liberalisms."

Table 4.1 Liberalism(s)

Classical Liberalism (developed alongside the growth of early capitalism)	Shared origins with conservatism (history, place, intellectual foundations)
	Economic doctrine (i.e., free market) is similar to fiscal conservatism but not as extreme or absolute
	Government spending distorts market forces and causes budget deficits
	Unemployment is caused by government interference (giving workers an alternative to employment) and by the behaviour of unemployed people (voluntary withdrawal from job market)
	Business should be privately owned and be free from government interference in order to make a profit and create jobs
	Corporate taxes, minimum wages, and workplace legislation squeeze out jobs
	Unfettered laissez-faire capitalism is the ideal economic system
	Social doctrine espouses individualism, inequality, and guaranteed freedoms
	Poverty is desirable because it provides a labouring class
Reform Liberalism	Recognizes that the state can play a positive role in helping to reduce the worst excesses of a competitive market system by employing Keynesian economic policy, i.e., by planning and regulating capital, but keeping private ownership and profits
	Recognizes that capitalism produces winners and losers and believes that the state should be used to provide fair chances (i.e., equal opportunity) to compete by ensuring that no individual be discriminated against on the basis of gender, race, class, etc. Thus, human rights legislation is a liberal goal
	Believes that capitalism causes social problems for many and that the state should provide a minimum living standard (i.e., a welfare state) for those hurt by capitalism
	Believes in the social doctrine of liberty, individualism, and inequality but that they should be modified on humanitarian (concern for the individual) and pragmatic (concern for society as a whole) grounds
	The state can be used to mediate the struggle between capital and labour and bring about an accord between the two
Neo-liberalism	This is a modified amalgam of the doctrines of classical liberalism and reform liberalism
	Fiscal crisis led to a repudiation of Keynesian economic policy and a return to the belief that a free-market economy is necessary to provide the resources for social programs and government services
	The goals of reform liberalism are still laudable, but many are impractical and some can only be achieved (afforded) if we return to classical liberal economic principles and practices and reduce the scope and level of assistance of social programs

From their inception in Canada, Britain, and the United States, conservative thought and ideology helped to shape the welfare states and continue to exert a great deal of influence today. However, the dominant paradigm that accompanied the emergence of the postwar welfare state in Canada and the United States, and to a lesser extent in Britain,[2] is reform liberalism. Although challenged by neo-conservatism today, reform liberalism is still the dominant social ideology in Canada. In other words, Canadians live in a liberal society where both the existing social welfare state and social work practices have been influenced mainly by reform liberal ideology since World War II. Therefore, it is crucial for the social work profession to be informed of, and to understand, the social, economic, and political beliefs that in large part shape our welfare state and determine the nature of our practice.

Liberalism as Reluctant Collectivism

George and Wilding (1985) believe that the term "liberalism" stands for such a wide spectrum of political ideology that it has lost all meaning. Instead, they use the term "reluctant collectivism." Djao (1983) follows the lead of George and Wilding and refers to liberalism as "modified individualism." The term "liberalism" will be used in this book, however, because, as with "conservatism," it is more consistent with popular usage and is more widely used in Canadian social, economic, and political literature. Nevertheless, the terms "reluctant collectivism" and "modified individualism" are useful in distinguishing liberalism from conservatism and at the same time suggest what they have in common. Whereas conservatives subscribe to an absolute form of individualism, liberals, particularly reform liberals, subscribe to a modified version of individualism and/or to a reluctant form of collectivism.

As noted above, reform liberals share many of the same values with neo-conservatives: beliefs in freedom, in individualism, and in competitive private enterprise. However, they hold fewer absolute values in that they accept intervention into the economy on the basis of pragmatism and humanism. Their pragmatism is based on a conviction that although capitalism may be the best economic system, it is not self-regulating. It requires regulation and control to function efficiently and fairly. Their humanism is based on recognition that capitalism is hurtful to many people. Concern for the human implications of capitalism led John Maynard Keynes and William Henry Beveridge in Britain, John Kenneth Galbraith in the US, and Leonard Marsh and Harry Cassidy in Canada to lead British and North American societies to reject conservative thought and to adopt the reform liberal paradigm (George & Wilding, 1985).

The views of liberals with respect to the nature of human beings, society, the state, social justice, and social change are presented below. Again, these views are common to both reform liberalism and neo-liberalism, although they are less strictly applicable to neo-liberal thought.

Views of the Nature of Humans, Society, the State, Social Justice, and Social Change

Whereas neo-conservatives share a belief in the imperfection of *human nature*, seeing in the individual varying degrees of weakness, immorality, and irrationality (Sigurdson, 2002), liberals hold a more favourable view of human beings. They assume that people are naturally moral and rational (Bastow & Martin, 2003) and that, given certain social conditions (e.g., equal opportunity and freedom from societal interference), individuals can improve themselves. In this way, liberals implicitly connect the well-being of society to the well-being of the individual. L.T. Hobhouse (1864–1929), one of the great historians of British political thought and a founding father of British sociology, and the English philosopher Jeremy Bentham (1748–1832) argued that the liberal notion of "individuality" could not be realized without the state taking action "to secure the conditions of self-maintenance for the normal healthy citizen" (Hobhouse, 1994, p. 174). Individualism and social needs were thus conceived as mutually self-sustaining (Bastow & Martin, 2003). Human nature is dual in that it is both egoistic (self-interest) and altruistic (concern for others). In other words, decisions made by an individual go beyond a simple notion of economic greed to include a moral concern for others. Although inequality of life circumstances is a normal outcome of fair competition in the market, persons should not become so destitute that they are unable look after themselves.

The Nature of Society

Similar to neo-conservatism, liberalism holds an atomistic view of *the nature of society* whereby individuals interact with each other to satisfy their individual interests, but liberals differ from neo-conservatives with respect to their view that there is also a collective interest. Unlike conservatives, who developed a doctrine of social Darwinism based on Darwin's notion of "survival of the fittest," reform liberals were influenced by Charles Darwin's work that stressed cooperation and evolution and developed a theory of society in which collectivism represented a higher stage of human evolution. This theory allowed liberals to justify state welfare and social reform as part of the progressive logic of social development and to ground their normative theory in the "objective" terms of scientific theory. Twentieth-century liberalism also drew from the science of biology the notion of society as an "organism" or entity of mutually interdependent parts. This notion reinforced the view of liberal reformers (mentioned above) that the well-being of the individual cannot be considered apart from the health of the entire organism (Freeden, 1978, cited in Bastow & Martin, 2003). It is important to note that twentieth-century reform liberalism was challenged by socialist ideas and movements, which undoubtedly made it more receptive to notions of collectivism and social reform. Unlike classical liberals, reform liberals recognize the existence of classes, but they rationalize this by claiming that equality of opportunity means that people can climb the social ladder if they really try.

The Role of the State

Given the reform liberal's belief in social development, collective interests, and a mutual relationship between the well-being of the individual and that of society, then *the role of the state* goes beyond that of an umpire or arbiter of disputes among individuals with respect to contracts made between them. It includes a role of intervening into and regulating (to a degree) the social, economic, and political life. The major role of the state would be to operationalize the concept of "equal opportunity" and make the race of life fairer by implementing human rights legislation, placing legal restraints on corporate and professional conduct, providing public programs for all citizens such as public education and health care, and helping those disadvantaged by capitalism (Bastow & Martin, 2003; Naiman, 1997).

Social justice to the reform liberal is based on a distribution or redistribution of resources, which, of course, is consistent with a belief in equal opportunity. Liberals, by way of state intervention, would redistribute income and some goods and services through the tax system and/or social welfare system. No attention is given to the source or cause of the maldistribution in the first place, only to its consequences. Part of a just society is that individual rights are protected in legislation such as Canada's Charter of Rights and Freedoms and provincial human rights statutes, and a major human right is the right to participate/compete in society without being discriminated against on the basis of race, class, gender, and so on. Inequalities of circumstances are acceptable as long as they are based on merit or effort (i.e., competing successfully on a level playing field) and not on heredity or some other social characteristic. That is, unequal rewards go to those with unequal skills and effort.

Social Change

Whereas neo-conservatives would defend society and institutions from any attempts by reformers to bring about *social change*, preferring instead slow, evolutionary change, reform liberals would use the instrument of government to modify society in order to make it fairer for individuals to compete in the market. However, only modest alterations to society would be made. In the end, both conservatives and liberals accept current social arrangements and would not attempt to make fundamental social change. In other words, liberals would make changes *within* the system rather than changes *of* the system—it would remain the same system. After any liberal social change, we would still have a capitalist society in which structured inequality is acceptable (Naiman, 1997). Reform liberals would make changes in order to help society function better— that is, they would fine-tune society but not change its fundamental nature. Liberal social intervention would be designed to help the individual cope with, adjust to, or fit into the existing society. Galper argued in 1975 that liberal social reform is an illusion because the present society is not reformed by liberal social change; rather, it is consolidated and/or reinforced.

The next three sections look at the specific ideological beliefs of reform liberalism along social, economic, and political dimensions. These reform liberal values are tempered today by classical liberal economic principles. In other words, the drive for social reform and a well-developed welfare state is not as great today as during the three decades following World War II.

Table 4.2 A Summary of Liberal Views

Concept	Views
Human nature	Moral and rational
	Egoistic and altruistic
	Competitive and cooperative
	Motivated by self-development and progress
	Requires a healthy social environment to flourish
	A complex organism with interdependent parts
	Can be modified by government intervention
	Classes are recognized but can be transcended by effort
Nation-state	Promotes fair competition among members via state intervention
	Protects and enhances our natural rights
	Acts in best interests of all society
	Reduces the worst excesses of capitalism by (limited) regulation of the economy and by developing a welfare state
	Promotes consensus and harmony among interdependent parts of society
Social justice	(Re)distributive model of social justice
	Individual rights are protected by legislation
	A modern welfare state compensates victims of capitalism
	Equal opportunity provides everyone with the means to succeed
	Individual success and upward mobility occur on the basis of individual effort and merit
Social change	Social reform is valued as long as it improves society for individuals but does not fundamentally change its nature; i.e., social change must be ameliorative, not transformative
	Social reform is needed to attend to the socially defined needs of the population—public health care, pensions, unemployment assistance, student aid, etc.

With its emphasis on individualism (albeit in a modified form from that of conservatism), on inequality of circumstances, and on maintaining an economic system that victimizes some groups of people, there is an obvious disjuncture between liberalism and progressive social work, as outlined in Chapter 1.

Social Beliefs

The central social values of liberalism are essentially the same as those of neo-conservatism, but they differ in degree. Both groups believe in freedom and individualism, and both are non-egalitarian. As mentioned above, however, liberals modify or qualify these values somewhat by pragmatic and humanistic concerns. For example, while neo-conservatives and liberals regard freedom as an essential value, neo-conservatives view freedom simply as freedom from the arbitrary power of governments, whereas liberals include in their value the freedom from such social evils as unemployment, disease, and squalor. To protect this latter freedom would obviously necessitate some form of state intervention that would be unacceptable to neo-conservatives.

Individualism is a key value of liberals. All government action should have as its goal the maximization of an individual's pursuit of self-interest. The purpose of government intervention is to maximize individual welfare and to remove obstacles to self-sufficiency. Whereas neo-conservatives measure the total well-being of society by simply summing up the well-being of all individuals in that society, reform liberalism also has a collective interest. There is recognition that a healthy social environment is related to individual well-being. Classical liberals do not speak of classes because society is viewed as a collection of individuals rather than as a class or stratified society. This view helps to absolve people from responsibility for the well-being of others in society. Anything done for others is carried out either on pragmatic grounds (i.e., it is more efficient or it will dispel social unrest) or on humanitarian grounds, which often leaves people needing help reliant on the vagaries of charity and the paternalistic whims of others.

Those liberals who do recognize that classes exist and that some classes fare much better than others in a capitalist society would contend that social and economic mobility is possible because of equal opportunity. In other words, some people in society may be suffering, but if they work hard and take advantage of the opportunities available to them, they can get out of their present situation and move to a higher class ("socio-economic position" in liberal terms). Liberals accept inequality of circumstances because of their profound belief in equal opportunity, which means that we are all equal before the law. No one has any more freedoms or liberties than anyone else. Everyone has access to education, the job market, health care, social services, and so on. If a person fails in society, it is because they did not take advantage of available opportunities. Liberals do not consider the possibility that some people in society, because of their social position and resources, may be in a better position to exploit these so-called available opportunities than others. To use an analogy, if one person has a 50-metre head start in a 100-metre race, it is not likely that the other person will ever catch up. A small number of individuals, because of their great wealth, control the race and set it up in such a way as to prevent most people from winning. Furthermore, the children of the wealthiest people start the race so close to the finish line that they can be the slowest runners and still win (Naiman, 1997). The Achilles heel of the equal opportunity concept is that not everyone starts out at the same place in life. Therefore, some people have an unfair advantage and preferred access to these "equal" opportunities. Karger (1987, p. 8) states, "The fallacy of the entire argument is that true equality of opportunity is unattainable in an unequal society."

Although liberals are not egalitarians, they do think that inequalities should and could be reduced based on humanistic and/or pragmatic grounds. Humanistically, liberals are aware of the ugliness of poverty and would seek to eliminate it, which is a different concern from the search for equality. Pragmatically, a wider distribution of income will: (a) increase aggregate demand, thus lessening unemployment; and (b) reduce social tension. From this point of view, however, egalitarianism destroys incentives, weakens social cohesion, and threatens the freedom of the individual (George & Wilding, 1985).

Economic Beliefs

The fundamental economic value of liberalism is competitive capitalism based on free enterprise but with some government regulation. This type of economic system is often called a mixed economy as opposed to the neo-conservative's laissez-faire economy. Although both neo-conservatives and liberals subscribe to a capitalist economy, liberals do not share the neo-conservative belief that an unregulated free enterprise system works well.

Liberals have four major criticisms of capitalism (George & Wilding, 1985). (1) Capitalism is not self-regulating. Without state intervention, it cannot solve the economic problems it has created for itself, such as cyclical recession, structural unemployment and underemployment, inflation, large discrepancies in wealth and income, and regional disparity. (2) Capitalism is wasteful and inefficient and misallocates resources. With each recession the productive capacity of nations is wasted as factories and people lie idle. If left by itself, capitalism will result in private affluence and public squalor, which are morally unacceptable to humanistic liberals and politically dangerous because public squalor can lead to crime, violence, and social unrest. (3) Capitalism will not by itself eliminate poverty and injustice. By its very nature (material acquisition, competition, survival of the fittest), capitalism produces and perpetuates poverty and inequality. (4) Capitalism leads to the interests of the economically dominant groups being identified as the national interest. These groups have, for example, convinced government and the people that industrial development, which is of interest to the capitalists, is really in the national interest. Consequently, giant corporations have little difficulty getting government to spend money on roads, technological development, research, and so on, while the care of older people on fixed incomes, people who are ill, people with disabilities, and those living in poverty is neglected because no economically powerful group has spoken in their interests.

In spite of these significant criticisms of capitalism, liberals do not believe that it should be abolished. Rather, they believe it should be regulated because the faults of capitalism, in their view, are technical in nature rather than fundamental and can be made good by government action. However, liberals would still place limitations on this government action because they believe that: (1) once the technical problems of capitalism are solved, the system will regulate itself; (2) capitalism is naturally superior as a source of initiative and liberty; and (3) government action, while necessary for freedom, is always a potential threat to freedom (George & Wilding, 1985).

Because liberals do not seek to change the given economic system, most of their interventions into the economy will be symptom-focused and ameliorative rather than structural. Fiscal and monetary actions will be designed to compensate for such instabilities inherent in capitalism as recessions, unemployment, and inflation and will not be designed to overcome the systemic roots of these problems (Gil, 1976). In other words, government intervention into the economy is intended to fine-tune it rather than to change its basic nature.

Political Beliefs

The fundamental political beliefs of liberalism lie in representative democracy and pluralism (Marchak, 2011). Liberals argue that direct participation in the day-to-day business of government by the electorate is impossible. Rather, the essence of modern-day democracy rests in the popular control of elected representatives. Control is exercised through the competition of people running for office, selection by the people of representatives in periodic elections, limitations on the power elected representatives can exercise while in office, and removal of the incumbent representatives if they fail to perform to the people's satisfaction. In sum, the ultimate control within a representative democracy rests with the people who elect and hold accountable a representative government.

Representative democracy is based on the principles of free and regular elections, a broad suffrage, and the existence of a party capable of forming an alternative government (Lees, 1972). A fuller discussion and analysis of representative democracy was presented in Chapter 1 where it was contrasted with the concept of participatory democracy. In addition, it was argued that social work ideology is more consistent with participatory democracy as a model than with the liberal choice of representative democracy.

According to liberals, universal suffrage has led to a transformation of political systems in Western democracies from institutionalized ruling-class governments of the eighteenth and nineteenth centuries to open and democratic structures whereby ordinary citizens now have direct and immediate access to their elected representative. However, "modern society has become considerably more complex during the twentieth century and 'political power' has become more 'diffused' and more 'corporate'" (Pritchard & Taylor, 1978, p. 93). In other words, governments are more involved in a whole range of issues and areas, and a host of competing interests and pressure groups have emerged with the aim of influencing the decisions of elected representatives.

The above brings us to the second fundamental political belief of liberals—that in a representative (liberal) democracy, political power is divided among competing interest groups so that no one group dominates another, let alone dominates the government. This view of political power is called pluralism. The government acts as an independent arbitrator (umpire) of these competing interest groups, controlling their activities by a set of rules called the law through which it acts as the guardian of the public interest and of individual rights. Thus, it is claimed, no government can fail to respond to the wishes of its citizens because the individual is heard through his or her membership in particular interest groups and at election time.

Few serious commentators believe that liberal democracies are totally accessible. Some of the limitations of the pluralist view are: (1) as with any type of competition, there will be winners and losers so that the strongest and best-organized interest groups will have their interests prevail over their counterparts; (2) not everyone belongs to an organized interest group; (3) some powerful interest groups may gain sectional advantage at the expense of the general welfare; and (4) the elites within the various interest groups may make decisions that are not responsive to the needs or wishes of the memberships.

View of Social Problems

Unlike neo-conservatives, liberals do not place the blame for social problems squarely on the shoulders of the individual or their family. "They accept the failure of the market to meet basic needs, the inability of the contemporary family to meet needs it supposedly met in the past and that economic growth will not, on its own, abolish poverty" (George & Wilding, 1976, pp. 62–63). The imperfections of capitalism cause problems for some people, and this perception is different from the neo-conservative belief that it is individuals who cause problems for themselves. In other words, whereas neo-conservatives attribute social problems to the weakness, deviance, or heredity of the individual, liberals attribute such problems to social disorganization inherent in an urbanized and industrialized capitalist society and a globalized economy.

Although liberals focus more on society as the source of social problems, the personal deficiency view is not dropped completely. Society is viewed as a complex whole or organism consisting of individuals interacting within numerous interdependent social systems such as the family, the workplace, and the school. Liberals believe that these systems are based on consensus and have legitimate functions that contribute to the healthy functioning of society because they are expected to integrate individuals into the larger society (Carniol, 1984). They recognize, however, that the numerous interdependent social systems that comprise society are not perfect and may not adequately provide the resources needed for healthy functioning. The various systems may get out of tune with one another in a society that experiences urbanization, industrialization, technological change, migration, globalization, and so on. These movements or forces upset the equilibrium among systems and between people and social systems, thus precipitating social disorganization. In turn, this social disorganization produces stress and personal disorganization: mental health issues, alcoholism, family breakdown, crime, spousal and child abuse, even community disintegration (Rubington & Weinberg, 1995). Because social problems are caused by some systems out of tune with one another, the solution to the problem is to fine-tune these systems and restore equilibrium. This may involve personal change and/or system change, but in all cases "such changes are accommodative to the status quo" (Carniol, 1984, p. 188).

From the disciplinary vantage point of social work, the social disorganization view of social problems is an improvement over the personal deficiency view held by neo-conservatives because it recognizes the role that society plays in creating social problems. The systems perspective of liberalism is found in most major introductory social work texts and in the curriculum of most schools of social work. An outgrowth of this perspective is the ecological view of social problems, which assumes an "optimal goodness of fit" between the individual and society (Germain, 1979). Thus, if personal disorganization occurs, the social worker would try to change either the individual or a particular subsystem or both. This approach has contributed to a plethora of generalist and/or eclectic social work approaches. However, because liberals believe that our present liberal democratic social order, although flawed, is superior to all others, then any social change proposed by the liberal worker will be limited to fine-tuning the system rather than overhauling it. Any change will occur within the system and will not involve a fundamental change of the system. That is, after the change, liberal capitalism will still be intact.

In short, liberals believe that social problems occur mainly because of instrumental or technical flaws in the capitalist system that cause personal disorganization for some people. They also believe that the capitalist system is the most efficient form of economic organization and must be preserved. Therefore, the response to social problems is not to alter the system dramatically but to: (1) purge it of as many inefficiencies as possible by way of minor social reform (i.e., system-tinkering); and (2) purge it of injustices by tending to those persons who are hurt by the system.

This view of social problems is much more humane and benign than that held by neo-conservatives. Liberals believe that even when people conform to their roles in society and attempt to carry out their social responsibilities, they will sometimes experience problems because of events (technological change, cultural changes, etc.) beyond their control. Thus, weaker members of society may succumb to the stresses they experience and will require care, cure, and protection. This approach to social problems has been termed "humanist liberal" (Lee, 1986) and "liberal humanist" (Coates, 1991). In spite of this humanistic aspect, liberals share two views with neo-conservatives with respect to social problems. First, liberals see individuals rather than social classes or social groupings as casualties of capitalism. Individuals remain the central unit of analysis rather than sexism, racism, and so on. Second, neither liberals nor neo-conservatives give serious consideration to the possibility that the unequal distribution of resources in society may have a connection to social problems (George & Wilding, 1985).

View of Social Welfare

Liberals accept the social welfare state as an instrument for correcting and modifying the negative aspects of capitalism. They do not see the welfare state as a means for pursuing social equality or for promoting social or economic change (George & Wilding, 1985). Its role is to be reactive (i.e., to deal with existing social problems) rather than to be proactive (i.e., to use the welfare state to achieve greater equality or to extend democracy into areas outside of the political sphere).

A primary goal of a liberal social welfare state is to achieve for all citizens the "social minimum." This concept has been described by Leonard Marsh (1950, p. 35), architect of Canada's social security system, as "the realization that in a civilized society, there is a certain minimum of conditions without which health, decency, happiness and a 'chance in life' are impossible."[3] In other words, society should use the welfare state to guarantee a minimum income to purchase the basic necessities of life and to ensure that everyone has access to basic (minimum) levels or standards of health care, housing, and education. However, liberals do not believe that governments are responsible for providing more than a minimum. A social welfare system that has as its primary goal a social minimum was described in Chapter 1. It was argued that such a welfare system, termed the "social security state" or "institutional model," although containing some humanistic elements, must be rejected by progressive social workers because of its lack of egalitarian ideals. It does not seek to reduce inequalities above the social minimum, nor does it promote solidarity or attempt to extend social, economic, or political democracy.

The "institutional conception" of welfare is based on the assumption that industrialization and urbanization are natural processes of human progress (Wilensky & Lebeaux, 1965), and while they have brought higher standards of living to many people, they have also brought disruption to some people who have had to bear most of the social costs of industrial progress. These people, it is argued by liberals, should be protected and compensated by state welfare programs. Unlike the neo-conservative residual conception of welfare, people in need are not considered lax, immoral, or irresponsible but are considered genuinely in need. Therefore, there is a reduced use of the humiliating means test, little suggestion of abnormalcy, and decreased stigma attached to social welfare programs. The institutional conception does not do away with family responsibility, but it recognizes that in a modern, complex industrial society, families may need help in carrying out their obligations. Social welfare programs represent a first line of defence against the exigencies of a capitalist society, not a residual function. That is, the institution of welfare should take its place alongside all other social institutions in society rather than coming into play only after all other social institutions have failed. This view dispenses with moralizing about the shortcomings of people in need. In short, industrialization, urbanization, and the development of the welfare state are viewed as normal, logical, evolutionary, and inevitable processes in human progress. The purpose of the welfare state, according to this view, is not to change society but to make good for its defects.

Social Work Practice within the Liberal Paradigm

Because we in Canada live in a liberal democratic state, most of our social work practice is determined by the values, beliefs, and tenets of liberalism. Galper (1975) argues that the greatest determinant of the kind of practice that social workers will engage in is the social-economic-political culture in which social work operates. In other words, not only is the social welfare system a reflection of the larger society, so, too, is social work practice. Taken together they form a paradigm, and in the case of Canada it is a liberal paradigm.

The above is not to suggest that social work practice in Canada is based purely on liberalism. Social work ideology is another major determinant of the nature of social work practice. For example, social work subscribes to egalitarianism, and some of our social work practice in Canada lies outside the liberal paradigm, especially that which seeks to transform our capitalist system. (Certainly, however, this is not yet an integral part of many social workers' practice.) Two other determinants of the nature of social work practice are historical continuity and competing paradigms. Canada was a conservative society before World War II; thus, our social welfare system and our social work practice have retained some features of control and coercion. The paradigms competing with liberalism in Canada are neo-conservatism, which supports the retention of coercive social work practices, and social democracy, which supports transforming Canada from a capitalist to a social democratic state. In spite of these other influences, however, social work practice today in Canada is based primarily on liberal values.

Social workers carry out basically three activities within the liberal paradigm: (1) personal reform based mainly on general systems theory; (2) limited social reform based mainly on the ecological model of practice; and (3) advocacy based on a pluralist view of society. The nature of these activities is determined by the liberal's belief that social problems are caused by social disorganization, an undesirable but unavoidable outcome of capitalism. And because they can do nothing about the occurrence of social disorganization, social workers must focus their attention on its negative consequences.

One way of dealing with the effects of social disorganization is to take those people who have fallen out of the game and direct them back to the starting point. They must be counselled and helped to learn more effective methods and patterns of communication so that they can enter into and maintain healthy relationships in all areas of their life. Or they must be rehabilitated or resocialized so that their attitudes and behaviour are more congruent with the expectations that society places on them. Or they must undergo psychotherapy and have their ego defence mechanisms strengthened so that they can better cope with competing and conflicting demands imposed on them. General systems theory is widely used by social workers in this area because of its assumption that the system (society) is basically okay but that some people need help getting back into it or coping with it.

Another possible way of helping people who are negatively affected by social disorganization is to try to make some changes in the person's immediate environment. Given that the capitalist system has some flaws, it may be possible to make minor reforms without affecting the working of the overall system. This could mean the removal of a family member, for example, in the case of family tension and dysfunction. Or it might mean a change in a public school's policy or program to better accommodate children from a disadvantaged group. Or it could mean some labour legislation to make work conditions less stressful. These changes are reactive because they focus on the effects of social disorganization, not on its causes. Many would argue that the root cause is the capitalist system itself. The ecological approach is often used with this activity because the ecological model assumes that a "goodness of fit" or natural harmony exists between the person and society. What is not considered is that the system itself could be bad and that we are looking for a goodness of fit between a person and a bad system.

A third area within the liberal paradigm where social workers often find themselves working is that of advocacy. Much time and effort is expended by social workers in attempting to obtain programs, services, compensation, and/or recognition for various individuals and groups in society who are injured by the capitalist system. Promoting the well-being of the homeless by advocating for housing programs and lobbying government for job protection legislation for minorities are examples of advocacy work, which again focuses on the consequences and not the causes of social disorganization. It is based on the pluralist view that society consists of competing interest groups, with some winning and others losing. It is often the job of social workers to help the losers get back into the competition.

These three areas of social work are based on the belief that the liberal-capitalist system is superior although it causes problems for some people. The job of social work is to work with capitalism's casualties for mainly humanitarian reasons. By doing so, social workers working within the liberal paradigm do not connect these people with economic structure, class, race, or gender. To make these connections, we must look to paradigms other than neo-conservatism and liberalism.

Canada as a Liberal State

The political science literature reveals that there are three major political ideologies in Canada: conservatism, liberalism, and socialism (Horowitz, 1968, cited in Campbell & Christian, 1999; McCready, 1980). There has been influence from other ideological perspectives, such as populism, progressivism, social credit, and nationalism, but they have not been as influential, as distinct, or as long-lasting as the three major political ideologies. And although Canada has three major political ideologies, they have not been and are not now of equal strength. There is agreement in the literature that the dominant and pervasive political ideology in Canada since World War II has been liberalism (see Campbell & Christian, 1999; Horowitz, 1996; Marchak, 2011). As Bell and Tepperman (1979, p. 232) emphasize, "liberalism is not just numerically dominant [in Canada]. It dominates because it is the ideology of the dominant class: it has the full force of the state, church, media, and educational system behind it: it has been trained into all of us."

On 19 October 2015, the Canadian electorate voted for a platform of "Real Change" and elected the federal Liberal Party to power under the leadership of Justin Trudeau after 10 years of Conservative government. Much of the election platform of the Liberal Party focused on modernizing how government works by improving accessibility to and transparency of government data and information, strengthening parliamentary committees, implementing a more open process for appointments to the Senate and the Supreme Court, and ensuring higher standards and better treatment for Canadians accessing government services (Liberal Party Platform, 2015). Early into the first year of the Liberal mandate, the government had fulfilled its promises to "unmuzzle scientists," to reinstate the long-form census, to create a cabinet with an equal number of women and men, and to include more Indigenous peoples and minority groups in positions of leadership. The view of this Liberal federal government is congruent with reform liberal values and beliefs in that "Real Change" is about making modifications to the existing system—for example, how government works so that it will function better (more focus on harmony and diversity) and create a level playing field in the provision of public programs and services (improved accessibility and enhanced performance standards for public servants).

The fact that liberalism has been and is the dominant and pervasive political ideology in Canada is of considerable importance in understanding the development of the Canadian social welfare state. As liberalism replaced conservatism as the dominant ideology of Canada beginning in the 1940s, Canada's social welfare state gradually shifted away from a residual form toward an institutional form of welfare[4] (notwithstanding some of the regressive policies of federal and provincial governments in Canada during the past 35 years). Social policy or social welfare choices are limited or bound by the social, economic, and political beliefs of liberalism. Obviously, those who subscribe to an established dominant ideology will not purposely seek its transformation or undoing. In fact, the elite or dominant class will attempt to protect and strengthen their ideology because, in so doing, they protect and strengthen their own positions in society. Thus, social policy in Canada does not threaten individualism, capitalism, inequality, or any other pre-eminent value of liberalism. In sum, even though there has been a shift to the right on the part of all major political parties, Canada remains a liberal society, and its social welfare system not only reflects liberalism and its attendant values, it reinforces them as well.

Critique of the Liberal Paradigm

A few words must be said about the theoretical incapacity of the liberal paradigm to explain certain social, economic, and political phenomena in a liberal society. Marchak (2011) provides an impressive amount of data that reveal some of the realities of Canadian society that liberalism does not explain: there is poverty in the midst of affluence; there is evidence of interference in the political process by privately owned corporations; there is a persistent division of the population along economic lines that liberals refuse to recognize as a class division but that is inexplicable otherwise; and the decisions of large corporations more profoundly affect the lives of people than do the actions of politicians. These empirical facts of a liberal society are not accounted for by liberal ideology.

Liberalism accounts for differences among individuals in terms of quality of life as due to individual differences in talent or effort or due to imperfections in the system. According to liberals, the consequences of the former can be alleviated and of the latter can be corrected or reformed. However, the evidence does not substantiate these beliefs but suggests, rather, that there are consistent and persistent differences among identifiable groups in Canada with respect to wealth, power, and access to goods, services, and social institutions. The evidence also shows that these differences are attributable not to individual characteristics but to social characteristics such as ethnicity, gender, age, place of residence, and family of origin (Curtis, Grabb, Guppy, & Gilbert, 1988; Marchak, 2011). The foremost criticism of liberalism is that it has failed to reform the system to correct the causes of these differences.

A major criticism of welfare capitalism (i.e., the welfare state in a liberal-capitalist society) is that although it was set up to modify (i.e., humanize) the negative impact of capitalism on people, it actually reinforces capitalism and thus, indirectly, contributes to many of the problems it seeks to eliminate. The reason for this is hardly surprising. The social welfare state is like any other social institution. It was established within the social, economic, and political context of liberalism and is bound to reflect and support the context from which it comes and within which it operates. In addition to attending to the immediate needs of some people who are hurt by capitalism, it also carries out socialization, social control, and stabilization functions for the prevailing social order by reinforcing the norms, behaviours, institutions, and values of liberalism.[5]

> Paradoxically, then, implicit in the social services is the affirmation of oppression and exploitation of humans by humans, and the negation of equality of rights, responsibilities, and dignity and of genuine liberty and self-actualization for all. The social services [welfare state] are thus revealed not as part of the solution of issues of provision in our society, but as a factor in the maintenance of the human problems they pretend to treat and prevent (Gil, 1976, p. 60).

Table 4.3 compares and contrasts the ideals of social work with those of liberalism. The differences between the two sets of ideals are not as great as those between neo-conservatism and social work. However, the differences and contradictions between liberalism and social work ideals are too great to be reconciled. With respect to social beliefs, although liberalism believes in a certain amount of humanism, it also subscribes to individualism and inequality, which contradict social work's beliefs in community and equality. And although liberalism subscribes to a limited amount of government intervention, it does not believe that society's resources should be distributed equitably among all citizens. Liberalism's belief in representative democracy and pluralism contrasts with social work's belief in participatory democracy. As a consequence of the above differences in ideals and values, liberalism holds a different view of the nature and purpose of the welfare state than does social work. Whereas liberalism perceives the social welfare state as a means of providing people with the social minimum, progressive social work believes the purpose of the social welfare state is to go beyond providing a bare minimum by promoting equality of living conditions, solidarity among citizens, and a sense of community.

With respect to social work practice, it has been suggested here that: (1) a liberal society actually causes many of the problems that social work seeks to resolve; and (2) social work practice within liberal boundaries actually reinforces and perpetuates many of the inequities social work claims to be against. Thus, it seems that the social work profession should reject the liberal paradigm if it is to remain true to its own values, beliefs, and principles. This does not mean that social work should abandon the three basic social work activities practised within the liberal paradigm—personal reform, social reform, and advocacy. It does mean, however, that the limitations of these activities must be recognized and that another dimension of social work practice must accompany them. This other dimension, referred to in this book as structural (or transformational) practice, is the subject of later chapters.

Table 4.3 Overview of Liberalism and Social Work Ideal

	Liberalism	Social Work
Social Beliefs	Freedom Individualism Inequality (all the above modified by humanitarianism and pragmatism)	Humanitarianism (humanism) Community Equality
Economic Beliefs	Competitive capitalism with some government intervention (i.e., mixed economy)	Government intervention Social priorities dominate economic decisions Equitable distribution of society's resources
Political Beliefs	Representative democracy Pluralism	Participatory democracy in both governmental and non-governmental areas
View of Social Welfare	An instrument to modify negative capitalism Ideal = institutional model Provides a social minimum	An instrument to promote equality, solidarity, and community Ideal = structural model
Nature of Social Work Practice	Personal reform Limited social reform Advocacy	Treat people with respect Enhance dignity and integrity Facilitate self-determination and self-realization Accept differences Advocate and promote social justice

Liberal Hegemony in Social Work

One of the characteristics of a dominant paradigm is that it is able to reproduce itself by so-cializing members of society into accepting the structures and social relationships it espouses. Literature and the media, for example, shape the thoughts and understandings of members of society. This socialization or reproduction is not necessarily a conspiratorial activity on the part of the ruling elite. However, it is only logical to expect that the people who run the media and people who write books and articles will reflect their world views and understandings of subjects in their work. Social workers are no different. Most social work educators and writers in North America have been socialized not only into liberal societies but into a liberal view of social welfare and social work as well.

Box 4.1 *An Example of Liberal Hegemony in Social Work*

One day while working on this chapter, I (Bob) decided to share my critique of systems theory and the ecological approach with my colleagues by way of an email in order to stimu-late thinking and discussion about the nature of social work practice. One colleague replied by email, expressing her disagreement that systems/ecological approaches essentially humanized the system rather than changed it fundamentally. A slightly modified version of her argument follows.

> Bob—Systems/ecological theory has as one of its tasks to examine ways to effect change *in the system* [emphasis added] so it can better meet the needs of clients. For example, the social worker can do this through advocacy with another agency in regard to how its policies are being interpreted for a client; the clients can also be encouraged or coached to work *to make changes in one of their systems (family, school, friendship network, etc.)* [emphasis added]. In some approaches to family therapy, parents are coached to advocate on behalf of a child with the school system, the justice system, etc.

In my view, my colleague has given the classic description of liberal social work. Although the work she speaks about is important, by itself it does not fundamentally challenge or change the larger social system in any way. The changes that my colleague seeks are all changes *within the system* and not changes *of the system*—a critical distinction. No thought is given to the possibility that the source of problems lies not within the system but is the system itself because of its various forms and sources of oppression (the subject of Chapter 9). My colleague, in my view, equates any kind of change brought about by a social worker as structural change, when in fact *it is the nature of the change* that differentiates mainstream (liberal) social work from progressive/structural social work. The former attempts to make life a little better for people by tinkering with or fine-tuning or adjusting the system. The latter attempts to make a contribution to fundamental change of the system itself—that is, to make a dent in the situations or processes of social inequality that fall along lines of class, gender, age, race, and so on.

Canadian social work students tend to be exposed to one or more of the standard American introductory social work textbooks that make prominent use of liberal approaches to social work systems theory, ecological models, eclectic methods, and so on. Many Canadian textbooks on social work are similar in orientation (i.e., liberal humanism) to most American texts. Tuula Heinonen and Len Spearman's *Social Work Practice: Problem Solving and Beyond* (2009) is framed within the ecological perspective, as is Nicole Ives, Myriam Denov, and Tamara Sussman's *Introduction to Social Work in Canada* (2015). There is no questioning in any of these books of the fundamental nature of our present liberal-capitalist society or any suggestion that social work should consider a different paradigm. A more recent example of a more progressive social work textbook is Donna Baines's edited text, *Doing Anti-Oppressive Practice: Social Justice Social Work* (2011) in which she proposes a social justice–oriented social work practice framework that is progressive and that recognizes social work as a highly political practice with the goal of social transformation. According to Baines, social work knowledge and practice need to be "assessed in relation to critical approaches in order to ensure that we are building lasting change and not intentionally reproducing various kinds of oppression" (Baines, 2011, p. 7).

Conclusion

In conclusion, social workers, like all Canadian citizens, are socialized into a liberal paradigm (although the nature of this paradigm has shifted to the right under a Conservative government and the influence of neo-liberal economics). Recent neo-liberal trends in Canadian social welfare have reduced the level and scope of many social programs. One example is the elimination of the Canada Assistance Plan (CAP), which was a cornerstone of the Canadian welfare state. It was a cost-shared grant program between the federal government and the provinces that encouraged the development of social programs and spending on social services. 1995 saw the beginning of the erosion of the CAP when it was combined with Established Program Financing (EPF) to become a block transfer known as the Canada Health and Social Transfer (CHST) with a reduced funding arrangement. In 2004, the CHST was divided into the Canada Health Transfer (CHT) and the Canada Social Transfer (CST), with funding allocated to provinces in a ratio of 62 per cent for health services and 38 per cent for post-secondary education and social programs not directly related to health (Government of Canada, 2014). These block transfers to the provinces are limited by federal legislation to an increase of 3 per cent per year. The way that the funding is distributed to the provinces, by an equal per capita cash allocation, does not take into account regional differences in population growth, levels of poverty, the increase in an aging population, the proportion of Indigenous or immigrant population, or the incidence of various diseases. The gap in adequate funding for social and health programs has allowed governments to promote ideas and polices that expand opportunities for businesses and corporations in the provision of human services (Baines, 2011). For example, private health clinics have proliferated in several provinces, creating a two-tiered health system that primarily serves the needs of those who can pay for their health care and avoid growing waiting lists (but not growing needs) for medical treatment.

Rather than challenging inequality or the capitalist system, which is based on inequality, social work in Canada has historically favoured large-scale government programs to compensate for the chronic and acute ills of an industrial liberal society and to ameliorate the resultant suffering. However, social service organizations, particularly in the public sector, have adopted management models, institutional values, and business approaches in response to managerialism. Viewing social problems as business or technical matters rather than as political or moral problems, Canadian social workers have become planners, researchers, administrators, and front-line workers focused on the reduction of waste and inefficiency within social service bureaucracies. In the next two chapters, it will be argued that the social democratic and Marxist paradigms provide an alternative vision of social welfare in which the issue is not one of more or fewer social services but one of a different social order.

Critical Questions

1. What is the difference between "Liberal" and "liberal"?
2. In order to promote a certain concept of equality, Western democracies have developed a number of codes or categories of rights such as civil rights, political rights, human rights, social rights, the Canadian Charter of Rights and Freedoms, and so on. What makes these different sets of rights a liberal idea? From a social justice and/or progressive social work point of view, what is their major limitation?
3. Should men and women always and in all ways be treated equally?
4. List the major textbooks used in your social work courses. Can you identify the dominant ideological perspective of each book? How many books tend to be liberal; how many are progressive? If a book does not state or imply a political position, do you think it supports a status quo or a social change position?

5 The Social Democratic Paradigm

*Courage, my friends, 'tis not too late to make
a better world.*

—Inscription on tombstone of Tommy Douglas
(1904–86)

Introduction

Because social democracy and the next paradigm to be examined, Marxism, are associated with socialist ideology, a section on socialism precedes the discussion of social democracy. The major reason for including an overview of socialism is to dispel the following myths sometimes associated with socialism—that it represents a single unified social doctrine; that it is anti-democratic and totalitarian; and that the events in eastern Europe during the 1980s, which led to the dissolution of the Soviet Union at the end of 1991 with 14 countries declaring their independence, prove that socialism is unworkable and all but dead. As with the neo-conservative and liberal/neo-liberal paradigms in the previous two chapters, a summary is presented of what social democrats believe about human nature, the nature of society, the role of the state, the meaning of social justice, and social change. As well, social democratic ideology is examined along the lines of its social, economic, and political beliefs and how these beliefs affect their particular views on the causes and remedies of social problems, the nature and role of the welfare state, and the nature of social work practice that is in accordance with the social democratic paradigm. A comparison is made between social democratic ideals and those of progressive social work, and a critique of social democracy is presented. Finally, the current status of social democracy in the UK, the US, and Canada is presented, which includes an assessment of Tony Blair's claim that his "Third Way" politics represents an advanced form of social democracy.

Socialism

Socialism to North Americans is probably the least understood and most misunderstood of all schools of political thought. The terms associated with the range of political and theoretical positions within socialism, such as anarchism, communism, Marxism, social democracy, and syndicalism, cause confusion. As well, through our North American liberal/conservative socialization, socialism has been presented to us by the media, by our educational system, by our politicians, and by our other social institutions as totalitarian and atheistic. This is especially so in the United States, where a psychology of Cold War paranoia existed for so many years.

The United States is probably the only Western democracy without a socialist political party at the national level. Canada does have a national socialist party, the New Democratic Party, but it has never won a national election, although it has historically been the third largest national party and did become the official opposition party in 2011 but fell back to third place during the election of 2015. There have been socialist governments, however, in almost all of the provinces.[1]

In spite of the vagueness and the negative picture painted of it in North America, socialism has strong appeal to many people all over the world, with national socialist governments having been democratically elected on all continents except North America. Even in North America, socialist values such as community and social justice have been popular with many groups, including progressive social workers. As a political theory, socialism is a relative newcomer, but it emerged in the twentieth century as a set of ambitious philosophical and political doctrines with a vision of human nature that connects the two (Scruton, 1982). One noted writer (Nove, 1989, p. 170) has defined socialism as:

> an alternative to a society still based largely on private ownership and private profit. Generations of reformers and revolutionaries envisaged a world in which there would be no great inequalities of income and wealth, where common ownership would prevail, where economic (and political) power would be more evenly distributed, where ordinary people would have greater control over their lives and over the conditions of their work, in which deliberate planning for the common good of society would replace (at least in part) the elemental forces of the marketplace.

There are certain characteristics that all schools of socialist thought accept, although in varying degrees. Four of particular importance are: (1) a planned economy geared toward the fulfillment of the human need of all rather than a free market geared to profits for a few; (2) public ownership (or control by regulation) of productive property for the benefit of all rather than private ownership for the benefit of a restricted circle of private owners; (3) equality of condition, or at least a serious effort to reduce, as much as possible, major inequalities of wealth, income, social status, and political influence; and (4) a belief that selfishness is the result of living in our present flawed social institutions and that social change can produce less selfish people who are concerned with the welfare of others (Dickerson & Flanagan, 1986). These four characteristics or objectives result from and, at the same time, support each other. Flowing from these characteristics are certain socialist policy objectives, such as elimination of privilege in all its forms, opposition to inheritance, defence of the welfare state, and a strong affiliation with the labour movement (Scruton, 1982).

While these characteristics represent the major areas of consensus among all schools of socialism, there is a fundamental source of disagreement among socialists: how to obtain and maintain the political power necessary to realize their common objectives. Disagreement among socialists tends to occur mainly over the means to achieve certain ends and not on the ends or goals themselves. A few historical events of modern socialism are highlighted below to distinguish for the reader some of the differences among the major socialist camps.[2]

Marx and Engels

Although socialism has a long history dating back to an early association with Christianity, it was given its classic formulation by Karl Marx and Friedrich Engels in their *Communist Manifesto* (1848). They departed from their Utopian socialist predecessors by rejecting the belief that social change for the betterment of humanity could occur by appealing to reason. Marx and Engels believed that socialism could only come about by the political victory of the working class (i.e., the proletariat). Marx's attitude toward capitalism was one of total rejection rather than reform, and he devoted most of his intellectual efforts to proving how it was both inhuman and unworkable.

Marx believed that the contradictions of capitalism—its association with imperialism and wars, overproduction, cyclical and deepening recessions, worsening conditions of workers—and the alienation of the working class would eventually become so intolerable that the working class, led by socialist intellectuals such as Marx himself, would eventually take over the state and use it to abolish capitalism. A system of social and economic collectivism termed communism would then be instituted by the proletariat. This system would involve communal ownership of all property and a classless social structure, and work would be directed by and performed willingly in the interests of the community as a whole—"from each according to his/her ability, to each according to his/her needs" (Roberts, 1971, p. 38). At this advanced stage of development, the state would wither away as "people would learn to conduct their affairs without a centralized apparatus of coercion" (Dickerson & Flanagan, 1986, p. 116). According to Marx, all forms of domination and hierarchy would disappear.

Marx did not believe that the transformation from capitalism to socialism could be automatic; rather, it would require a deliberate political struggle on the part of the proletariat. Marx's view of the nature of this political struggle has been a source of major disagreement among Marxist scholars. One group makes the case that, based on the number of times Marx (and Engels) advocated forcible measures (i.e., violent revolution) as the means for workers to assume political power and based on the number of times that Marx denounced reform as the means to transcend capitalism, there can be little doubt that his real convictions lay in revolutionary socialism (Becker & Barnes, 1978). Other Marxist scholars point out the occasions when Marx and Engels suggest or admit that a peaceful overturn of the social order might be possible and conclude that Marx actually had a dual approach to the gaining of power: (1) *revolutionary socialism* (use of forcible measures) in countries where constitutionalism and rule of law did not exist; and (2) *evolutionary socialism* (election of an organized workers' political party) in constitutional countries with a parliamentary system (Dickerson & Flanagan, 1986). The revolutionary socialist writers explain Marx's comments on peaceful means as tactical concessions he made to the reformist wing of the socialist party so that it would not split from the major party.

Evolutionary Socialism and Social Democracy

Whether or not Marx's revolutionary theory excluded peaceful means, his emphasis on forcible revolution caused a group of English socialists to repudiate revolutionary socialism and to advocate evolutionary socialism instead. This group formed the Fabian Society in England (1884), which developed social democracy in Britain and eventually created the country's official social democratic political party—the Labour Party (1906). The Fabian Society represents one of the earliest divisions among socialists and was based on disagreement, not with the goals of social-ism but with the means of achieving them. Evolutionary socialism in the form of social democracy spread to Germany in the latter part of the nineteenth century and soon after became the dominant form of socialism in Europe. Only in Russia did the revolutionary socialists remain in the majority (Becker & Barnes, 1978).

Social democratic parties have been elected in most western European countries and have actually governed for most of the postwar era in the Scandinavian countries. In 1999, nine of the eleven European Union governments were dominated by social democratic parties, and they have not hesitated to use their new-found powers to assert changes in the political order that the neo-conservative regimes of the early 1990s had attempted to establish (Rundle, 1999). Socialism, in the form of social democracy, is a familiar part of contemporary politics, but it has been con-siderably diluted from its original Marxian version. The modern-day social democratic para-digm is presented in the next section of this chapter.

Revolutionary Socialism and Russian Communism

Although social democracy has become the major school of socialist thought in western Europe, revolutionary socialism held sway in Russia. The absence of a parliament and a constitution in Russia during the early years of the twentieth century made evolutionary socialism irrelevant in that country. There were no democratic institutions or legal working-class organizations that could be used as the base of operations to transform Russian society from within. In February 1917, Czar Nicholas II was dethroned and a constitutional democracy established, and in October of the same year Vladimir Lenin led the Bolshevik Revolution and seized control of the state. Lenin deviated from Marx's theory of revolutionary socialism because the conditions in Russia were so different from those of western Europe. Faced with an economically and industrially backward country with a small working class and with a large peasant class, Lenin believed the socialist party had to be controlled from the top and that revolutionary consciousness had to be transmitted by intellectuals to the working class (Dickerson & Flanagan, 1986). This, of course, was inconsistent with Marx's belief that the revolution was to grow from the spontaneous class consciousness of the proletariat or working class.

To solidify his control over the country and the socialist party, Lenin centralized political power, calling it "democratic centralism." Lenin rationalized this action as being consistent with Marx's revolutionary theory. Marx believed that there had to be a transition period between the end of capitalism and the beginning of advanced communism. Marx did not believe that people could throw off the yoke of capitalism one day and live as adjusted, productive commun-ists the next day. A period of adjustment and transition was needed for the technological and social foundations to be put in place that would be necessary for the achievement of an advanced communist state. The old state machinery had to be destroyed and a new state constructed to serve as the means to attain the final communist commonwealth where there would be neither oppressor nor oppressed (Becker & Barnes, 1978). Marx's strategy for this transition period was for a government comprising workers to be set up that would actually function as a "dictatorship of the proletariat." This government/dictatorship would ignore the rules of law until the revolutionary fervour and violence subsided and would gradually phase itself out as the transition to communism was made (i.e., the state would wither away).[3] Marx called this transition period socialism. During this transitional stage between capitalism and advanced communism, the means of production would be taken into public ownership, and the provisional government would oversee a new order of legality and a new system of rights that would allow the emergence of true common ownership and the eventual abolition of the state (Scruton, 1982).

Lenin exercised Marx's notion of dictatorship of the proletariat and outlawed all political opposition, even socialist opposition. His extensive use of dictatorship and his constant postponement of the withering away of the state appalled socialists of western Europe. As a result, the world socialist movement split irreparably. Those who approved of Lenin and his methods organized themselves in communist parties in every country and adopted Marxism modified by Leninism as the official party ideology. Those who opposed Lenin regrouped under the social democratic banner and became the most prominent school of socialism in the Western world. Russian communism, with an extended dictatorship of the proletariat, was implemented by Lenin, developed by Stalin, and imposed by force on the less advanced nations of eastern Europe using a distorted version of Marx's theory of revolutionary socialism as a rationale. Fourteen semi-autonomous regions and countries in eastern Europe and western Asia were eventually annexed by Russia under the title of the Union of Soviet Socialist Republics (USSR).

Eurocommunism

Communist parties still exist in most western European countries. The label applied to them today is "Eurocommunism," and they differ from Russian communism in the very important area of political freedom. Although Soviet leaders did bring many reforms to the economic system in line with Marxist egalitarian ideology, they did not do the same in the political arena. Public ownership replaced private ownership, and inequalities in wealth, income, and life chances were greatly reduced in the Soviet Union. However, the egalitarian and democratic elements of Marxism did not spread to the political life of the Soviet Union. Its political system may be described as totalitarian and monistic. No political parties except for the Communist Party were legally allowed, no other ideologies were permitted expression, and civil and political rights were denied. In effect, the Soviet Union had a socialist economy and a totalitarian political system so that any social security experienced by citizens was overshadowed by the existence of political insecurity (Mishra, 1981). This totalitarian nature of Soviet society violated Marxist socialism, and Eurocommunist parties took exception to it. Eurocommunism, unlike Soviet communism, subscribes to a pluralistic and parliamentary democracy in which more than one ideology and one political party are allowed.

Aftermath of the Fall of Russian Communism

The fall of the Russian-led Soviet empire is now history. However, as this brief description of socialism suggests, the fall of Russian communism does not represent the fall of socialism or of its ideas. Russian communism represented one school of socialist thought, albeit a prominent school. Many would argue that it represented a distorted view of socialism because all that was achieved politically was the transfer of control from an old ruling class of aristocrats to a new elite of bureaucrats. Socialism originated as a doctrine concerned about the oppression of the working class. It would be difficult to find a true socialist today who would argue that the Russian experience contributed to the political emancipation of the proletariat in the former Soviet Union. However, the Communist (or socialist) governments did reduce inequalities in Russia and guaranteed the general population a modicum of universal health care, pensions, jobs, and education. Socialist ideology did influence all spheres of life except for the political life of the Russian population.

In sum, socialism does not represent a single unified ideology, and it is not anti-democratic. Although the goals of socialism are essentially common to all schools, the major area of disagreement is the appropriate means to transcend capitalism. The fall of the Soviet bloc does not represent a failure of socialism (Mishra, 1999). Its economic failures are due more to its centralized "command-administrative" socialism, which failed to generate stable growth and development, stifled workers' initiative, lagged behind in technological innovation, and misdirected new investment (van Houton, 1992). Its political failures were due more to its totalitarian practices. With the Soviet type of socialism gone, most socialists today hope that socialism will be able to learn from the mistakes of the Soviet experience, to reaffirm its claim to democracy, and to re-establish itself as the logical "political expression for collectivist and egalitarian impulses" (Jacques, 1990, p. 16).

Although there are several schools of socialist thought, the two major schools appear to be social democracy and Marxism (Mishra, 1999). Many social welfare and social work writers divide socialists ideologically into these two groups: (1) social democrats, who believe that social transformation of capitalism can occur by using the working-class institutions within capitalism such as the welfare state, trade unions, and the election of social democratic political parties; and (2) Marxists, who believe that social transformation can occur only by using alternative organizations to state bureaucracies (George & Wilding, 1985; Mullaly & Keating, 1991; Pritchard & Taylor, 1978). This division of socialists is adopted in this book: social democracy is the focus of this chapter; Marxism is the focus of the next chapter.

Social Democracy

Just as socialism consists of a range of theoretical and political divisions, social democracy occupies a wide area on the political spectrum, bordering on liberalism at one end and Marxism at the other end. The divisions between social democracy and these other ideologies are not always clear (George & Wilding, 1994). For many people, social democracy is only a well-developed form of liberalism, and they question whether or not social democracy is even a form of socialism. For others, social democracy is only a few steps away from Marxism. This chapter and the next will clarify these issues by presenting the similarities and the differences between social democracy and liberalism and between social democracy and Marxism.

Most Canadian, Australian, and British social policy writers, when writing about social democracy, use British Fabian social democracy as their reference point. This may be reasonable in terms of gaining an understanding of British social democratic values, beliefs, and principles. The danger, however, is that the British experience with a social democratic government may become the expectation for social democratic governments in all countries. The Labour Party first became government in the UK in 1924, but it has never fulfilled the expectations that many socialists anticipated. The Marxists (and many social democrats) now believe that capitalism cannot be transformed into socialism with a social democratic government. However, if one looks beyond Britain to Sweden, which has had a social democratic government for almost all the years since 1932, one might draw a different conclusion. This issue will be taken up later in this chapter.

It should be noted here that although there is not a "neo–social democracy" as such, there is another variant of social democracy that emerged in the 1990s, which is commonly known as the "Third Way." Anthony Giddens is the intellectual architect of the Third Way, and Tony Blair, the Labour prime minister of England, was the social democratic political leader who developed and implemented Third Way policies more than any other national leader. Third Way thinking and policies have influenced social democratic parties in Canada and Australia as well as Bill Clinton's social policies when he was the president of the United States. Basically, Third Way supporters claim that it is a new left-of-centre political ideology that incorporates the best aspects of social democracy and neo-conservatism or neo-liberalism. Third Way detractors argue that it is closer to neo-conservatism than it is to a progressive social doctrine or even a more humane form of neo-liberalism. The Third Way is discussed more fully in the section "Current Status of Social Democracy in Anglo-democracies" in this chapter.

The following section provides an overview of social democratic views on the nature of human beings, society, the state, social justice, and social change. Since social democracy and Marxism are both socialist paradigms, there is an overlap between them with respect to their views, beliefs, and fundamental values. This will become more evident in the next chapter.

Views of the Nature of Humans, Society, the State, Social Justice, and Social Change

What is our basic *human nature*? Are we independent individuals or social beings? Contrary to the neo-conservative belief that humans are by nature independent individuals for whom group membership is voluntary or to the liberal belief that humans are by nature independent individuals who require a healthy community to develop their individuality, social democrats (and all socialists) believe that humans are by nature social beings. The former position was championed by those early writers who were instrumental in formulating both conservativism and classical liberalism as ideologies, such as Thomas Hobbes (1588–1679), John Locke (1632–1704), and Edmund Burke (1729–97). The latter position (called communitarianism) can be traced to Aristotle (384–322 BCE), Jean-Jacques Rousseau (1712–78), and Karl Marx (1818–83), among others. Aristotle argued that only a beast or a god (the subhuman or the superhuman) could live without being a member of a community, for it is only in commune with our fellow citizens that we attain our full human potential (Sigurdson, 2002). In short, "all humans need other humans to achieve their humanity" (Berry, 1986, p. 6). Socialists believe that human nature is good and inherently perfectible and that humans may realize their inherent potential if the right environment is created by using their capacities for responsible and rational action (Sigurdson, 2002). A question that arises here is that if humans are essentially good, then why is it so difficult for us to get along? Whereas neo-conservatives adhere to Hobbes's argument that it is because we are by nature selfish and avaricious, socialists would subscribe to Rousseau's argument that it is because humans have introduced private property into their lives, which has led to inequality, selfishness, and the concentration of power in the hands of a few. In other words, Rousseau's thesis is that humans are basically good but have been corrupted by the socio-economic–political environment, which today is characterized by capitalism, patriarchy, racism, ageism, and so on. Socialists believe that this goodness can be recaptured if social conditions are put right by humans using their inherent human capacity for cooperation and consensus (Sigurdson, 2002). However, as indicated above and as will be discussed below, socialists disagree on the means (evolution vs revolution) of putting social conditions right.

The Nature of Society

Socialists, including social democrats, subscribe to Marx's argument that the *nature of society* or community is not some optional extra; rather, it is definitive, and outside this arena the individual is an unreal abstraction. The collective good is considered primary because it determines, in large part, the well-being of individuals. Society is not owned or controlled by a powerful few because such a system would violate the collective human nature of people. Given this collective nature, all persons would participate in its governance. Like Aristotle, socialists believe that because humans are by nature social beings, then society is natural. Without society individuals would not be what they are because any individual talent or ability still requires the cooperation of others for it to be effectively exercised (Berry, 1986). As well, we can only develop a sense of self or identity by associating or interacting with others because our sense of self is largely determined by feedback from others and comparisons with others.

Role of the State

Unlike neo-conservatives and liberals, social democrats believe that the *role of the state* is to promote the collective good and play a positive role in the economy. Social democrats believe that the state should carry out public control (not necessarily public ownership) of the major means of production to meet social needs rather individual profit, regulate the market and bring about greater equality in the distribution of society's resources, increase democracy in both the political and economic spheres, and protect the environment through centralized planning. Underpinning this role of the state is an emphasis on cooperation and a corresponding de-emphasis on competition. Social democrats do not see this role of the state being carried out satisfactorily in a capitalist society but believe that by electing social democratic governments and building the welfare state, the preconditions for a socialist society can be put in place as part of the transformation from capitalism to socialism.

Michael Meacher (1977, p. 36, cited in Berry, 1986, p. 8) articulates the *nature of a just society* from a socialist or communitarian perspective as one in which the members of that society govern their interrelationships according to the ideals of "sharing, co-operation, altruism" and in which the values are "more equal sharing of the material benefits of society, greater sharing in the key decisions rather than subjection to artificial hierarchies of command, and greater sharing of opportunities to develop one's full potentials." Such a society, Meacher claims, "abhors class domination and individualist aggrandizement at the expense of others." Sigurdson (2002, p. 102) states that "while liberals are content with an equality of opportunity, socialist justice requires an actual equality of condition," although he points out that for social democrats this "is more of an ideal than a practical goal." Although class inequality is a major source of injustice, social democrats recognize and seek to eliminate other sources of injustice and oppression, such as patriarchy, racism, sexism, ageism, ableism, and xenophobia.

Although socialists agree that capitalism must be transformed to a socialist society, they disagree on the *nature of social change* to carry out this transformation. Whereas communists, some Marxists, and other radical socialist camps believe in the necessity for total, revolutionary change, sometimes through violent means, social democrats insist on working within the parliamentary system and achieving socialism through democratic and evolutionary change. Social democrats would promote a variety of redistributive measures such as graduated or progressive tax systems, full employment policies, and well-developed social welfare programs. Social democrats would progressively develop the welfare state and use it as a stepping stone toward a socialist society. Social democratic social change would gradually transform existing social institutions and practices from those that serve individual interests to those that serve collective needs and ends.

As with the chapters on neo-conservatism and liberalism, the next three sections here look at the specific ideological beliefs of social democracy along social, economic, and political lines. Unlike neo-conservatism and liberalism, both of which accept competitive capitalism and its associated inequality, social democracy, like Marxism, seeks to transform the current set of unequal social relations to a socialist society. This is not to say that social democrats or Marxists believe that socialism represents a Utopian society in which everyone is happy and makes the same wages and where there are no social problems or bad behaviours. In fact, as mentioned above, there will be considerable variability among socialist societies depending on the unique set of cultural and historical characteristics of each (Naiman, 1997). Just as each capitalist society is unique, so each socialist society will be unique. However, all social democratic societies will have, to some degree, the views outlined in the section above and the beliefs outlined below.

Social Beliefs

Social democrats stress three central values—equality, freedom, and fellowship—and two derivative values—democratic participation (the derivative of equality and freedom) and humanitarianism (the derivative of equality and fellowship) (George & Wilding, 1985).

Equality

Arguably, the primary social democratic value is equality, which rests on four interrelated grounds—social integration, economic efficiency, natural rights, and individual self-realization. With respect to social integration, social democrats believe that a reduction in inequalities reduces feelings of isolation or alienation and creates a greater sense of belonging or social cohesion (George & Wilding, 1985). With respect to economic efficiency, a society characterized by gross inequalities experiences little social mobility, which means that many talented people will not rise to a position where they can use their talents and abilities. With respect to natural rights, inequality means that some people have greater opportunity and/or greater power than others, not because of merit but because of the luck of the genetic lottery in that some are born into families of wealth and influence. Finally, inequality often denies the individual the opportunity to realize their full potential, which in effect diminishes people's basic humanity. In spite of a consensus that there must be greater equality in all areas of life, social democrats do not agree on a definition of equality or on how much equality is desirable (George & Wilding, 1985). Whereas liberals are content with an equality of opportunity, social democrats talk about equality of condition but more as an ideal than a practical goal. The social democratic objective is to narrow the gap as much as possible between the rich and people living in poverty (Sigurdson, 2002).

Table 5.1 Summary of Social Democratic Views

Concept	Views
Human nature	Humans are social beings
	Rational, free-willed, and responsible
	Cooperative and consensual
	Inherently good
	Humans tend to actualize potentials in a supportive environment
(Socialist) society	Communal in nature
	Characterized by equality, solidarity, and cooperation
	Competitive capitalism and inequality are antithetical to a healthy society
	The common or collective good is primary
	Widespread participation in decision-making
Nation-state	Role is to regulate the economy, level out society's social and economic inequalities, and protect the environment
	Used to promote participation of citizenry in economic and non-economic decision-making
	Resources of the state are used to pursue goals of equality, social justice, democracy
	Balances the interests of different groups in society, ensuring that no group becomes dominant
Social justice	Equality of condition as a social goal
	Absence of a ruling class or group
	Entitlement (to society's resources) tied to individual need and not to the nature or worth of work
	All forms and sources of oppression must be challenged
Social change	Society is a human rather than a transcendental construct
	Capitalism must be transformed into a socialist society using peaceful means
	Mode of social transformation should be evolutionary

Freedom

Among the key social values social democrats hold, freedom ranks with equality. David Gil (1976) argues convincingly that freedom for all is the central socialist value but can only be achieved if greater social equality is attained first. If some people have greater resources than others, they have greater freedom to control their conditions of life, which conversely means that some people have less control or freedom to make choices with respect to their life conditions. Social democrats believe that genuine freedom for all can come about only through government action rather than, as neo-conservatives believe, through government inaction. Only government, according to social democrats, can create the conditions of social equality vital for the attainment of freedom for all.

Fellowship or Collectivism

The third central social value of social democrats is fellowship or collectivism, which means "cooperation rather than competition, an emphasis on duties rather than rights, on the good of the community rather than on the rights of the individual, on altruism rather than selfishness" (George & Wilding, 1985, p. 74). A capitalist society does not subscribe to the value of solidarity. Rather, it encourages people to use their power and abilities for self-interest and to treat others not as people but as commodities to be bought, sold, or used to further one's own end. Social democrats reject such attitudes and behaviour.

Democratic Participation and Humanitarianism

Two other social values strongly held by social democrats—democratic participation and humanitarianism—were noted earlier. Democratic participation should extend to all areas of life, not just to the political and economic areas. For example, in the workplace employees should have a voice in the conditions of their work, and employers should not be able to exercise arbitrary power or control over workers. In the areas of health and social services, lay people should have a say in formulating policies about the delivery of these services, since they are the actual and potential beneficiaries. Social democrats also believe that people should be able to enjoy certain minimum standards of living and that social distress should be eliminated. Therefore, they would like to see a higher proportion of the nation's wealth spent on these goals, with proportionately more spent on deprived groups (George & Wilding, 1985).

Economic Beliefs

The central economic beliefs of social democrats are government intervention, public control of the means of production and distribution, and a more equitable distribution of income and opportunities. Just as social democrats do not agree on how much equality is desirable, they do not agree on how much government intervention should occur, or on the extent of public control of the means of production and distribution, or on how equitable the distribution of income should be. Opinions vary from the Marxist belief that total public ownership is necessary to achieve socialist goals to the liberal belief that regulated capitalism is all that is necessary to achieve socialist goals.

George and Wilding (1985) present five criticisms that social democrats have of a free-market economy. (1) There is no social purpose or collective goal because individuals pursue their own interests, which results in social misery for many. (2) The free market is fundamentally unjust because it has no clear principles for distributing rewards other than a moral right to extract what one can without breaking the law. (3) The free market is undemocratic because decisions important to many, if made at all, are made by an elite few in privacy. (4) The free market is inefficient because without government regulation it leads to environmental devastation, regional economic disparities, periodic economic recessions, an oversupply of fundamentally useless products, and an undersupply of socially necessary goods and services. (5) The distribution of goods and services in a free-market economy does not include goods and services needed by those experiencing illness, old age, or life circumstances such as widowhood.

To overcome these inherent deficiencies of a free-market economy, social democrats would attempt to replace the anarchy of capitalism and the motives of private gain with rational economic and social planning for the common good. In other words, economic mechanisms would be put in place to control the means of production and distribution. These mechanisms could include the Marxist notion of state ownership (i.e., nationalization of private ownership) as well as government regulation of private ownership and the development of workers' co-operatives, consumers' associations, and credit unions. The question of nationalization has caused a division in the social democratic camps, fundamentalists believing that nationalization is the only way to achieve socialist goals and reformists claiming that separation between ownership and control can achieve the same goals.

Both fundamentalist and reformist social democrats condemn gross inequalities of income, opportunities, and living conditions. Pay equity, progressive taxation policies, the elimination of inheritance of large fortunes, an emphasis on human rights, and affirmative action programs are mechanisms favoured by social democrats to reduce inequality. Again, the questions of how much redistribution of resources is equitable and how far the wealth of the rich should be reduced are not answered unanimously by the social democrats.

Political Beliefs

The fundamental political beliefs of social democrats are: (1) the state has a positive role to play in society; (2) capitalism can be transformed into socialism by a social democratic government; and (3) the state should encourage broad participatory decision-making in all areas of life.

Social democrats view the state as an agent for redistributing benefits and resources. It is seen as acting independent of, and often in opposition to, market mechanisms (Djao, 1983). Only the state, through legislation and government action, can protect the freedoms of the less powerful citizen from the ravages of the more powerful, and only the state can bring about certain changes and promote an ethic of collective preference over that of individual interest (Mendes, 2003).

Through the state, the political process governs the economic process rather than the reverse, that of economics determining politics. The rationality of planning, under a social democratic regime, guides society, not the magical forces of laissez-faire.

Social democrats believe that government planning can transform capitalism into socialism without endangering individual freedom, contrary to the belief of neo-conservatives (George & Wilding, 1985). Social democrats believe that it is just as possible to plan for freedom as it is to plan for tyranny. Many social democrats claim that a social democratic government could use the state machinery (the government, the civil service, and the judiciary) to implement radical changes in capitalist society[4] and that over time, with proper public education about the bene-fits of its radical program, the citizenry would accept these changes and true democracy would flourish more than it does under capitalism. Social democrats, on the whole, believe that these changes must come through peaceful means and that violence would only contaminate social-ism. Social democrats also believe that one of the major ways of transforming capitalism into socialism is to develop the social welfare state, which emphasizes distribution according to need and not according to one's social position.

Social democrats subscribe to the principle and practice of participatory decision-making in both the economic and political spheres (Naiman, 1997). It is believed that this form of decision-making would spread responsibility, reduce power concentration, and increase pro-ductivity (George & Wilding, 1985). Social democrats would promote more worker control in industry and work organizations, more service-user involvement in the delivery of public servi-ces such as health and social services, and more community development directed at boosting the power of people with respect to local, regional, and national governments. Of course, these involvements would essentially be of a decision-making nature and not merely of a cosmetic consultative nature.

View of Social Problems

Basically, two competing sets of theories in the sociological literature attempt to explain the nature of society and the nature and cause of social problems. "Ultimately, all social theories, whether they acknowledge it or not, either support the present social arrangements or advocate changing them" (Naiman, 1997, p. 18). These two competing sets of theories are the *order* and *conflict* (or change) perspectives of society (Reasons & Perdue, 1981; Sears & Cairns, 2015), which are rooted in nineteenth-century history and social thought. Essentially, order theories are of a social system characterized by equilibrium, stability, continuity, consensus, integration, and social control. Order theories perceive social problems as caused when members of a society do not learn to revere its institutions or respect its rules (Reasons & Perdue, 1981; Sears & Cairns, 2015). Functionalism or structural functionalism, with its roots in the sociology of August Comte, Herbert Spencer, Max Weber, Émile Durkheim, and Talcott Parsons, is probably the best known of the order theories (Naiman, 1997). As will be discussed in Chapter 8, neo-conservatism and (neo-)liberalism adhere to order interpretations of society and social problems, whereas social democracy and Marxism adhere to conflict interpretations.

Conflict or Change Theories

Conflict or change theories view the nature of society as a contested struggle among groups with opposed aims and perspectives (Horton, 1966; Sears & Cairns, 2015). In pursuing their own interests, they are often in conflict with one another. Reasons and Perdue (1981) set out some of the major tenets of conflict theory. In the contested struggle among groups, the state is an important agent because it is used as an instrument of oppression by the dominant class for its own benefit. Social inequality is a consequence of coercive institutions that favour the dominant groups, and this social inequality is a primary source of conflict. In sum, conflict theorists see society as conflict-ridden rather than as stable, orderly, and integrated, and they question a social order marked by differences of race, class, gender, age, and so on. All conflict or change theories are informed by the ideas of Karl Marx (Naiman, 1997).

Although there are several schools of conflict/change thought, the two main theories, according to George & Wilding (1985), are the social conflict and the class conflict schools. The social conflict school believes that the sources of conflict are diverse and numerous and include such elements as race, religion, profession, region, gender, and economic status. Social democrats subscribe to the social conflict school. The class conflict school sees the conflict between the two major economic classes—the owners of production and those who must work for them—as the most important conflict in society. And because class conflict originates from the production system of capitalism, the only way it can be resolved is to abolish the capitalist system itself. Class conflict theory is, of course, synonymous with Marxist theory.

Racism, poverty, pollution, and other social problems, from the social conflict view, are actually contests among various groups over the acquisition or control of desirable resources such as wealth, privilege, and political power. Because these issues are actually clashes of interest, they represent political conflicts. Conflict theorists would prefer to call these conflicts "political conflicts" or "social conflicts" because the term "social problems" implies some kind of social sickness that can be treated more successfully by the "dispassionate intervention of experts" than by political action (Rule, 1971).

In short, social problems, according to social democrats, are not the result of deviance, as the neo-conservatives believe, or of industrialization, as the liberals believe, but are normal consequences of the way society is organized. Thus, they cannot be dealt with by technical means or administrative reforms. They can only be resolved by a reorganization of the society that caused the problems (conflicts) in the first place.

View of Social Welfare

When talking about socialist views of the welfare state, a distinction must be made between a welfare state within a socialist society and a welfare state within a capitalist society. For all socialists (Marxists and social democrats), the ideal welfare system, which would be consistent with socialist values and an integral part of a socialist society, is what Mishra (1981) calls a "structural model" of welfare. Although both social democrats and Marxists subscribe to this ideal socialist model of welfare, they differ in their views on the nature and functions of our present capitalist welfare state. Mishra (1981, p. 133) outlines the socialist conception of a welfare state:

> Central to the socialist view of welfare is the notion that "to each according to his [sic] needs" should be the guiding principle of distribution. In other words collective consumption—that is, typically universal, comprehensive and free social services such as health and education—constitutes the basic model of distribution under socialism.

Social democrats believe that the above form of equal distribution of societal resources is possible only after the production and distribution of all resources has come under state control (either by nationalization or by regulation). Only then will the market, the family, and private property cease to be the basic means of distribution of income and opportunities. The main feature of the structural model of welfare is that it considers welfare (distribution according to need) a central social value. The users of social services are not merely citizens entitled to a basic minimum of civilized life (as liberals believe) but are members of a socialist community whose needs are to be met to the fullest extent possible (Mishra, 1981).

Citizen Participation

Consistent with the socialist principle of participation of people in all areas of life, the structural model of welfare includes citizen participation in social services decision-making rather than strict control by administrators and experts. This emphasis on lay power or deprofessionalization of the social services would necessitate a demystification of professional knowledge (e.g., medical knowledge) and a decrease in the power, status, and authority of professionals in the social welfare field. This does not mean that lay people would be delivering health, education, and other social services but that they would have a much greater say in how they are to be delivered and how they are to be administered.

Preventive Services

Another vital principle of the structural welfare state is prevention. Many socialists (particularly Marxists) do not believe that preventive services can be established in a capitalist system because: (1) social services are viewed by socialists as institutions that tend to problems created by a system that neglects human needs; and (2) when the social welfare state is controlled by professionals, primary consideration is given to professional interests rather than to service-user interests. For example, Mishra (1981) contends that the Soviet Union placed much greater emphasis on preventive medicine because lay people had more say than professionals concerning health policies.

Social Democratic View of Welfare Capitalism

Although it is instructive to become informed about the social democratic ideal or preferred model of welfare, progressive social workers need to know the social democratic view of welfare capitalism. How does the welfare state in capitalist societies relate to the structural welfare model and to social democratic beliefs, principles, and values? If a social democratic party were elected to national office in Canada, for example, what would have to be done to its present welfare state to achieve social democratic goals?

Social democrats consider the welfare state to have followed a course of historical pragmatism (Mishra, 1981). In other words, social problems have accompanied industrialization, urbanization, and technological change and have had to be attended to by the state. In the course of dealing with these problems, the state has had to reconcile various group conflicts by compromise or by siding with one group and ultimately instituting a social policy to deal with the problem. Over time, this method of piecemeal social engineering has produced an accumulation of social policies that constitutes the welfare state.[5]

Social democrats value the welfare state for what it can and does achieve within a capitalist state. However, they want the welfare state to do more. Social welfare should further justice and prevent problems rather than deal only with situations of injustice and the treatment of problems; social welfare should promote equality of opportunity; social welfare should reduce all inequalities, not just eliminate poverty; and social welfare should promote greater control of social services by lay people rather than by administrators and experts (George & Wilding, 1985).

Perhaps the major belief of social democrats with respect to the social welfare state in a capitalist society is that it can be used as a stepping stone toward a socialist society. Because social welfare programs and services represent a break with the free-market doctrine of distribution, social democrats think that the advantages of such a system would be seen by the general public as preferable to that of the free market, thus aiding in the transformation from a capitalist to a socialist society. Social democrats are aware that a welfare state, by itself, will not provide a just society. This can occur only if the means of production and distribution come under public control, either by ownership or by regulation. However, the failure of the Labour governments in Britain to live up to the expectations placed on them by social democrats has been interpreted by some to indicate that the welfare state only supports and strengthens capitalism, while others now see the road from capitalism to socialism as longer and more perilous than originally perceived.

It should be noted here that although the welfare state was widely assumed by social democrats to be an emancipatory project in that the state would provide a wide range of public services to even up the life chances of individuals and groups, it has been criticized by feminists, racialized groups, postmodernists, and others as being another institution of domination. Beneath the socialist rhetoric of liberation and equality and universalistic ideas underpinning the modern welfare state, postmodernists, along with feminists, racialized individuals, and other oppressed groups, have criticized the welfare state for not acknowledging and/or for suppressing and discriminating against "diversity in cultures, sexualities, abilities, ages and other human characteristics" (Leonard, 1997, p. xiii). Any attempt by social democrats to reconstruct the welfare state as an emancipatory project must take into consideration these criticisms. More will be said about postmodern deconstruction and reconstruction of the welfare state in Chapter 7.

Social Work Practice within the Social Democratic Paradigm

The nature of social work practice within our present capitalist society will be determined by the view of social democracy that one holds. If one views social democracy as a well-developed extension of liberalism (as many writers contend was the view of British Fabians), then that person's practice of social work will be quite different from that of one who believes that capitalism must be transformed into socialism in order to deal effectively with our modern social problems. The former would concentrate on a social work practice of individual and humanitarian care while the latter, in addition to performing tasks of individual and humanitarian care, would seek to create forces that would contribute to the transformation of capitalism to socialism.

Fabian social democracy, as will be argued below, violates too many principles of socialism even to be considered as socialism. Therefore, social work practice according to this view will not be discussed here, for it would not differ significantly from liberal social work practice. Rather, an overview of social work practice based on the social democratic belief that the welfare state can be used as a stepping stone toward socialism is presented here.

Social democratic social work practice has a dual function: (1) to tend to the immediate and legitimate needs of people or groups of people who lose out in the ongoing group conflicts that occur in capitalist society over the acquisition of material resources and power; and (2) to work toward the transformation of capitalist society to one that adheres to the social, economic, and political beliefs and values of social democracy. That is, social work must aim at the creation of a socialist state. Underpinning this view of social work practice is the belief that our present set of social arrangements can be transformed by working through the existing political and social institutions, which, according to the social democrats, "are relatively accessible, are democratic, and are therefore capable of radical reform" (Pritchard & Taylor, 1978, pp. 96–97). This is a basic tenet of social democracy that goes back to Marx (although he, himself, did not believe in it) and is reiterated by such modern-day political economy writers as Greg Olsen (2002) and Richard Sigurdson (2002) in Canada and Ferguson, Lavalette, and Mooney (2002) in Britain.

The above belief is different from that of Marxists, who believe that alternative organizations and institutions must be established outside the existing system to challenge the power of the capitalist state. In other words, social democrats believe that social work can contribute to radical changes in society by working within the existing system, but Marxists tend to believe that social work must operate outside the existing system or else it will become incorporated into the present social order and end up protecting it rather than changing it.

The dual function of social democratic social work—to provide practical, humanitarian care and to further the democratization and restructuring of society along socialist lines—means a politicized and radical social work profession. This does not mean, however, that the two functions are mutually exclusive, that you cannot carry out both at the same time. Indeed, as a reforming profession, social work must help simultaneously both the individual and society to evolve along more socially concerned lines. For example, a social democratic social worker may work with someone who is considered deviant or disruptive. The task would be to help this non-conformist to cope with their non-conforming but not necessarily to abandon it—an important qualification, as Pritchard and Taylor (1978) point out. The non-conforming behaviour may not be at fault but rather society's rules, norms, or expectations. More will be said about this in Chapter 8.

Much of social democratic social work practice at the micro level would be to normalize and depersonalize the problematic situations in which many people find themselves. In other words, the social worker would explore the social context of the situation with the service user and analyze it along social democratic lines to see if a relationship exists between the problem and capitalism. For example, if the problem is unemployment and more than 1 million Canadians are unemployed, this does not mean that we have more than 1 million unique personal problems. Rather, we have one social problem affecting more than 1 million workers and their families. In other words, "the personal is political." As well as the incidence of unemployment, the reasons why capitalism needs and produces unemployment would be discussed with the service user. Subsequently, a plan of action would be jointly determined and would include helping the person to deal with their individual situation of unemployment, at the same time exploring ways that can contribute to a transformation of the existing capitalist system. At the macro level, social democratic social workers, through their professional organization or association, would act:

> as a legitimate pressure-group operating within the present socio-political structure and campaigning for both specific policies and a general reorientation of strategy and/ or philosophy (i.e., for policies based upon a more egalitarian, redistributive system which would also be far more concerned than at present with the achievements of social justice, the extension of welfare services and the protection of the rights of the under-privileged in society generally) (Pritchard & Taylor, 1978, p. 4).

The macro or political task, then, is to mobilize as much support as possible for social democracy, in general, and for social progress among social services users, in particular. Social democrats believe it is important to educate "both 'advantaged persons' and 'disadvantaged persons' in an acceptance of the interdependency of different sections of society" (Pritchard & Taylor, 1978, p. 95). The social work profession, therefore, must join forces with other socialistic organizations and institutions, such as the labour movement and social democratic political parties, to gain an ever-increasing control of the various institutions of the state and move eventually to a position where the attainment of a fully socialist system becomes possible. Such a project, however, must be informed by the postmodern deconstruction/critique of social democracy in general and the modern welfare state in particular so that it does not continue to be an institution of social exclusion and domination (see Chapter 7). If the welfare state is to become a radical force for progressive social and political change (i.e., a stepping stone to socialism), it is absolutely imperative that social work become politicized and radicalized. This is so because social work is a key sector within the welfare state structure and has an important influence on welfare state ideology.

Box 5.1 *Socialism and Atheism*

Since teaching social work from an explicitly political position (i.e., socialist), I (Bob) have experienced a number of hostile reactions from a few students (and from a few parents) over the years, especially on those occasions when I would claim that, given the collectivist principles and lifestyle of Jesus Christ, he would be called a socialist today. I remember one occasion in the mid-1980s when I was teaching in the social work program at St Thomas University, which is a small Catholic, liberal arts university located in Fredericton, New Brunswick. The president of the university at that time was a Roman Catholic priest. There were a few first- and second-year students in my Introduction to Social Welfare class who were offended by my socialist approach to social welfare and social work. They were also under the belief that all socialists were atheists, since this was part of the myth and stereotype attached to socialism at the time by many uninformed North Americans. They decided among themselves that they would go to the president and complain that there was a socialist and atheist who was teaching in his Catholic university and that they did not think they should have to be subjected to heretical and sinful views in the classroom. At the time I was a practising Roman Catholic who attended Mass in the university chapel every Sunday morning. The president's response to the student complaint was that he did not care about Dr Mullaly's political views but, for their information, he did see him at Mass every Sunday but could not remember seeing any of them. (God bless this president!)

Critique of the Social Democratic Paradigm

Some of the major criticisms levelled at social democracy are: it does not move capitalist society closer to a socialist society but only changes the face of capitalism; its anti-nationalization stance is inconsistent with one of the basic tenets of socialism; it leads to a centralized and elitist control of planning and decision-making; and the welfare state has not produced the desired reduction in inequalities. An overview of these criticisms and a response to each of them follows.

A common criticism of British social democracy is that although the social democratic Labour Party was the dominant political force in Britain for most of the 1960s and 1970s, it did not use this power to create an alternative to capitalism but adapted the labour movement to an acceptance of the existing system. Legitimation and public acceptance of social democracy in Britain seem to have gained at the expense of socialism (Pritchard & Taylor, 1978). However, as mentioned previously, it does not logically follow that the course of social democracy in Britain must be the course of social democracy everywhere.[6] Writing from Sweden on that country's experience with a social democratic government for all the years between 1932 and the present (except for 1976–82 and a brief period in the 1990s), Himmelstrand, Ahrne,

Lundberg, and Lundberg (1981, pp. 26–27) state that there are good theoretical and empirical reasons for "rejecting the simplistic notion of social democracy simply as a tool of capitalist development." The authors present some recent Swedish social democratic reforms concerning the work environment and the relative power of labour and capital that would seem to change significantly the relations of production in a socialistic direction. Based on the Swedish experience, it would seem that social democracy may be used as a path to a socialist state, though this path is longer and more complex than originally conceived by social democrats.

A second criticism of social democracy, that its anti-nationalization stance is antithetical to socialism, is also rebutted by the Swedish example. Swedish social democratic policy has been to separate ownership of the means of production from its control. Rather than risking a huge backlash as a result of nationalizing industry, the Swedish social democratic government has gained control of industry through legislation and regulation. In other words, by regulating industry the Swedes can in practice achieve the same economic and social goals as if they owned industry. In fact, the Swedes would point to the British experience of nationalization as contributing to capitalist development in that the compensation paid to the capitalists for nationalizing their firms was profitably reinvested elsewhere. One of the effects, then, was to see public industry subsidize private capitalism (Hughes, 1973). All this is not to say that Swedish social democrats are not interested in the labour force gaining capital ownership. Some of the recent Swedish workplace reforms move in this direction but without use of the draconian action of nationalization.[7]

The criticism that social democracy leads to a centralized and elitist control of planning and decision-making is also based on the British experience with social democracy. The trade union section of the Labour Party emphasized the democratic role of the working class within the transition to socialism, but the Fabians, who gained political control, actually opposed the idea of working-class control and mass participatory democracy. The Fabians believed that the working class was an alien mass incapable of understanding the complexities of modern society. British social democracy thus consisted of substituting for the capitalist class an elite of disinterested experts to control the new socialist society subject to control by the people through the parliamentary system (Pritchard & Taylor, 1978). Again, this elitist form of social democracy can be contrasted with the massive participation that goes into the decision-making process in Sweden. At any one time, 200 to 300 parliamentary-sanctioned commissions of study[8] are looking at various public policy issues. All relevant individuals, organizations, and interest groups are consulted before a preliminary report is drafted. They are consulted again on the contents of the preliminary report, after which a final report is drafted and presented to parliament for debate and policy formulation. The point to be made is that one of the fundamental social-political values of social democracy is participation in decision-making. It seems illogical to dismiss social democracy as elitist and undemocratic on the basis of what happened in one country's experience.

Another criticism is that social democracy has not produced a significant reduction of inequalities. It was originally thought by social democrats that many socialist objectives, including greater equality, could be achieved through the welfare state. But as Ferguson and Woodward (2009) point out, the British welfare state has failed to achieve a significant redistribution of income and opportunity to the working class. In fact, most of the distribution has been upward to the wealthy classes, and income inequality has not decreased but increased. This has occurred in most Western democracies, including Canada and the US. Market forces have counteracted the effects of egalitarian policies (for example, fringe benefits or occupational welfare has reduced the levelling effects of a progressive income tax system). Inequalities of income and wealth stubbornly persist in Britain and other social democratic countries. The universality of social services has meant that both rich people and people living in poverty have benefited from them. And social welfare has not resulted in an inter-class transfer of resources. "Those who use the social services by and large pay for them" (Pritchard & Taylor, 1978, p. 65). The response of the social democrats to this criticism is to acknowledge that there are deficiencies in the present welfare state. But they would argue that the welfare state is the creation of the Labour Party; without it many people would be much worse off than they are today, and with more time and the proper political will, the welfare state can be further developed to the point where its socialistic aims can be achieved. Other social democratic writers, such as Furniss and Tilton (1977) and Esping-Andersen (1990) argue that social democracy can achieve socialistic goals and point to the social democratic Scandinavian countries and their respective social welfare states because they have achieved much greater equality of income and opportunity than most other Western democracies. More recent writers (e.g., Olsen, 2002), who do not declare their political ideology but who write in the area of political ideologies, also identify those countries with a social democratic ideology such as the Scandinavian countries as having achieved much greater equality of income and opportunity than other Western democracies.

A final criticism of the social democratic paradigm to be looked at here is part of the critique that postmodernism has of all paradigms or ideological thought structures or "grand narratives." Although more will be said about this critique in subsequent chapters, its basic criticism of left (socialist) politics and social democratic welfare states is presented here. An essential idea of nineteenth- and twentieth-century socialism was that it was a unifying concept that could mobilize mass populations for the historic task of transforming capitalism. The socialist/social democratic political party was considered the vehicle for this transformative process. However, socialist parties also reflected in their organization and culture the forms of domination and exclusion that existed in the larger society. In particular, white males provided the leadership of such parties (Leonard, 1995), with *others* being excluded on the basis of culture, race, gender, sexuality, and so on—resulting in a situation, as Peter Leonard (1997, p. 18) states, in which "their voices [were] silenced, their very existence as active subjects erased from 'history.'" The social democratic view of the welfare state was that of an ever-expanding universalism that would improve the life chances of the entire population but especially the working class. It became, as Giddens (1994) points out, a welfare state based on a model of traditional family and gender patterns with programs aimed primarily at supporting male participation in the paid labour force with a secondary set of programs oriented toward families without a male breadwinner. In other words, the welfare state was essentially an institution used by social democrats in their "class struggle." Any reconstruction or reconceptualization of the welfare state as a project of emancipation must be informed by this postmodern critique. It must avoid the modernist illusion of essentialism, the practice of social exclusion, the tendency to privilege Eurocentric views of the world, and it must involve all oppressed groups in a dialogue of liberation.

Table 5.2 shows that, unlike with neo-conservatism and liberalism, there is a high degree of compatibility between the social democratic and social work paradigms. They share many of the same social, economic, and political beliefs, and there are no contradictions between the two sets of ideologies. Both have the same attitude toward the nature and some of the functions of the social welfare state. It would appear that social democracy (and eventually socialism) is one possibility as the kind of society that best meets and actualizes social work's values, principles, and ideals. If this is so, then a heavy emphasis would be placed on the structural components (restructuring society along socialist lines) of social work practice. In other words, social work practice would become much more like that described in this chapter.

Table 5.2 Overview of Social Democratic and Social Work Paradigms

	Social Democracy	Social Work
Social Beliefs	Humanitarianism Collectivism Equality Freedom Democratic participation	Humanitarianism (humanism) Community Equality
Economic Beliefs	Government intervention Public control of the means of production and distribution Equitable distribution of income and opportunities	Government intervention Social priorities dominate economic decisions Equitable distribution of society's resources
Political Beliefs	Participatory decision-making in all areas of life Capitalism can be transformed by a social democracy The state has a positive role to play in society	Participatory democracy in both governmental and non-governmental areas
View of Social Welfare	Welfare capitalism can be used as a stepping stone to a socialist state Ideal = social welfare state or structural model	An instrument to promote equality, solidarity, and community Ideal = structural model
Nature of Social Work Practice	Provide practical humanitarian care to casualties of capitalism Further the democratization and restructuring of society along socialist lines	Treat people with respect Enhance dignity and integrity Facilitate self-determination and self-realization Accept differences Advocate and promote social justice

Current Status of Social Democracy in Three Anglo-democracies

Almost all countries in western Europe, along with Australia and New Zealand, have had social democratic governments at various times since the end of World War I. This section looks at the recent experiences of three Anglo-democratic countries (UK, US, and Canada) with respect to social democracy to get a sense of the role and influence that social democracy has played within the political cultures of these countries, which are all related in many ways, not the least of which is that they emanate from the legacy of British colonialism.

United Kingdom

The Labour Party is a centre-left political party, which grew out of the trade union movement and the socialist parties of the nineteenth century. It quickly replaced the Liberal Party as the main opposition party to the Conservative Party and formed minority governments in 1924 and 1929 and served in the wartime coalition from 1940 to 1945, after which it formed a majority government. The Labour Party has historically, as its name suggests, been the party of labour (i.e., working class) and the welfare state (i.e., advancing welfare programs for the working class). The Labour Party was last in government from 1997 to 2010 under Tony Blair and Gordon Brown.

It was Tony Blair who broke with the traditional Labour Party approach to welfare development, which was to introduce programs and services through the public sector to address poverty and inequality. Blair's approach to government policy-making was to adopt a model that is commonly called the "Third Way," which broke with the binary or oppositional approaches of relying either on the public sector or the private sector as the basis of decision-making. For example, should the welfare state be developed within the public sector via government-run programs or within the private sector via private organizations and charities? In breaking with this "either-or" binary, Blair adopted the Third Way, which was associated with the New Left (also called New Labour in the UK and Australia) as opposed to the Old Left (or Old Labour). Third Way proponents claim that they are not part of the traditional oppositional left–right confrontation between particular values and policy choices because they use both the "market" and the "state" in a governing partnership by emphasizing both "rights" and "responsibilities" in their concept of citizenship and by focusing on both the "individual" and the "community" as the basis of social order (Bastow & Martin, 2003).

A full explanation of the Third Way is beyond the scope of this book, but in the previous edition an extensive overview was presented. The reason why the chapter on the Third Way is omitted in this edition is that the Labour Party was voted out of office in 2010 and replaced by the Conservatives under David Cameron, who de-emphasized Third Way social policy and, in fact, implemented an austerity program that reduced spending on the welfare state. Many writers (Bastow & Martin, 2003; Jordan, 2000; Mendes, 2003; White, 2001) have rejected the Third Way as having any potential for a progressive politics since, as outlined by Ferguson and Woodward (2009), it adheres to a fundamental belief in capitalism and a mixed economy.

Given the fact that the Labour Party with its Third Way policies has been replaced by the Conservative Party, and given the extensive criticisms of the Third Way, it was concluded in the previous edition of *The New Structural Social Work* (2007) that Third Way policies are not progressive even though they are cloaked in such terms of progressive rhetoric as "citizenship" and "social inclusion." Any paradigm or approach that provides social services in partnership with business, and that does not seek greater substantive equality, cannot be considered progressive. Not only must structural social work reject the Third Way on ideological grounds, it must also do so because Third Way politics does not deal with such issues as race, gender, and long-term structural inequalities that are identified in Chapter 7 as omissions in the traditional paradigms. In sum, the Third Way is not progressive, nor is it sensitive to feminist, anti-racist, and postmodernist concerns. And it is not progressive enough nor does it contain enough fundamental social democratic values and policies to be considered social democracy.

After Tony Blair stepped down from the position of prime minister, Gordon Brown succeeded him as leader of the Labour Party and as prime minister for a few years. The Brown government turned away from an emphasis on Third Way decision-making and returned, in part, to traditional Labour policies by de-emphasizing the market solutions of the Third Way and by promoting state solutions to social issues and problems. And when the Conservatives under David Cameron came to power in 2010, traditional Conservative social policies were implemented, which all but eliminated any progressive element that Third Way social democracy might have held.

At the time of this writing (winter of 2018), the Labour Party is the official opposition party in the UK, but it had been in a state of crisis. The leader of the party, Jeremy Corbyn, was strongly criticized for not being more active for the "Remain" campaign during the Brexit referendum (see Chapter 2), resulting in many of his shadow cabinet members resigning and the majority of his Labour MPs calling for his resignation. The party became preoccupied with organizational problems rather than social policy issues. However, its fortunes turned around when Prime Minister Theresa May, in an effort to increase her party's slim 17-seat majority, called a snap election for 8 June 2017. This moved backfired, however, because of a number of events at that time, including several terrorist attacks, a number of unpopular election promises made by May, and a lacklustre campaign by May coupled with an energized performance and presence by Labour Leader Jeremy Corbyn. May's Conservative Party lost 12 seats along with its governing majority and was forced to seek a coalition with Northern Ireland's Democratic Unionist Party (DUP), promising it 1 billion pounds in extra funding. Labour, on the other hand, increased its standing by 29 seats, translated into approximately 40 per cent of the popular vote compared with the Conservatives' 42 per cent. For social democrats and all those who support a strong welfare state, the resurgence of social democracy in the UK is good news.

United States

As mentioned earlier in this chapter, the US is the only Western democracy without a social democratic party at the federal level. It is also the country that has been most resistant to socialist ideas or values, preferring instead the purest form of a capitalist society in the Western world.

Socialism has long been vilified as a political doctrine in the US because it was considered totalitarian or the antithesis of liberty and was equated with atheism and with Soviet-style communism. The relationship between the US and the Union of Soviet Socialist Republics was so deeply antagonistic between the end of World War II and the dissolution of the Soviet Union in 1991 that that period of time was referred to as the "Cold War" between the two superpowers of the world. The Soviet Union with its socialist-style government became associated by Americans with the "evil empire" that had as its political goal the takeover of the free world. Thus, it represented all that was unholy, bad, and anti-democratic and was a country to be watched closely. If a politician or political party did not want a particular piece of proposed legislation, especially social welfare, one of the surest ways of defeating it would be to brand it as socialist. The classic example is that the US is the only Western democracy that does not have a public health care system for the total population because it was (and is) viewed by many as a socialist program, with its detractors referring to universal health care as "socialized medicine," which to Americans is a synonym for "socialist medicine." During the Cold War (and even today), many Americans use the terms "socialist" and "communist" interchangeably, and one of the worst insults was to call someone a socialist or a "commie." Given these attitudes and beliefs about socialism, it is not difficult to see why the Americans have been the welfare laggards in the Western world, preferring to meet people's needs through the private and charitable sectors, which are more consistent with the private market than they are with the public or state sector.

As mentioned earlier in the chapter, President Bill Clinton enacted a few Third Way social programs such as the Family and Medical Leave Act (1993) and the Violence against Women Act (1994), and he attempted to enact universal health insurance for all Americans. However, it was opposed by conservatives and the health care industry and was defeated in Congress. Although he is often associated with Third Way social welfare programs under the term "the New Progressivism," much of his welfare reform can only be described as punitive and moralistic. For example, his Personal Responsibility and Work Opportunity Reconciliation Act (1996) imposed time-limited welfare payments, compulsory workfare programs, and the denial of benefits to unmarried teenage mothers along with assigning them to the care of government-appointed guardians or trustees. The sole purpose of this scheme seemed to be to push recipients off the welfare rolls (O'Connor, 1999, cited in Mendes, 2003). In contrast, Tony Blair's Third Way welfare reform was much more non-punitive and rehabilitative, since sole parents were not required to participate in welfare-to-work programs and there was a stronger emphasis on job creation, wage subsidies, and the provision of education and training programs for welfare recipients. So at best, Clinton's New Progressivism represented a minimum of Third Way socialism and a modicum of conservativism and liberalism.

Even Barack Obama, whom many consider a progressive, is really a liberal given his adherence to the free market and private enterprise. His signature social program, the Affordable Health Care Act (also known as Obamacare), signed on 23 March 2010, is considered by many an example of a progressive American social welfare program. However, although it was designed to provide quality and affordable health care to Americans, it left 15 per cent of Americans without coverage, and it operated through the private insurance sector. This lack of universality of health care along with its dependence on the private sector are two violations of social democratic philosophy and principles. The US continues to be the only Western democracy without a universal health care program and without a social democratic political party.

At the time of writing this book (winter 2018), Donald Trump has been president for a little over one year. To date he has not proposed any progressive social legislation and, in fact, is more preoccupied with attempting to repeal Obamacare and replace it with a scheme (the American Health Care Act) whereby an estimated 54 million people would lose their current health care by 2020, according to a March 2017 Congressional Budget Office (CBO) report. Under Trump, the US continues to be the only Western democracy without a universal health care program and without a social democratic political party. His major legislative triumph to date has been to overhaul the income tax system by passing into law the Tax Cuts and Jobs Act on 22 December 2017. The law reduces corporate tax rates permanently and individual tax rates temporarily; it will benefit high-income earners most of all, and low-income earners will actually pay more in taxes after 2025. It is forecast to increase the federal deficit by 1.5–2.0 trillion dollars. Trump has focused on such issues as immigration to the exclusion of social welfare programs, although he has supported a few punitive measures such as work-for-welfare and a ban on transgender people serving in the military.

One of the surprising developments arising from the 2016 US presidential election (and there were many) was the popularity of Bernie Sanders and his progressive platform. This 74-year-old candidate for leader of the Democratic Party is a self-described socialist or what he calls a "democratic socialist" (the equivalent of a social democrat as described in this book) who was an Independent in Congress before joining the Democratic Party. His opponent for (and eventual winner of) the race to become the Democratic Party's nominee for president was Hillary Clinton. During the Cold War and for many years after, Sanders would have been laughed out of the country if he had run as a socialist and/or if he had proposed the platform he did in April 2015 when he announced his candidacy for the Democratic presidential nomination. Calling his campaign "the political revolution," his platform sounded more like a Nordic model of social democracy (a model that he admires). It included tackling such issues as income inequality, climate change, affordable housing, LGBTTQ equality, a universal health care system, free college and university tuition, and a fair and humane immigration policy as well as a promise to fight for women's and Indigenous rights and for racial justice (from <htpps://berniesanders.com>).

Canada

Canada has a relatively long history with socialism in general and with social democracy in particular. The Socialist Party of Canada, founded in 1904, was the first Canadian-based socialist political party. The Social Democratic Party of Canada was formed in 1911 out of frustration with the more radical and revolutionary Socialist Party of Canada, preferring instead an evolutionary form of socialism. (Earlier in this chapter, the two main approaches to socialism—the revolutionary and evolutionary schools—were presented.) Over the years, a number of Canadian political parties have arisen claiming to be socialist, most of which have followed the peaceful, evolutionary tradition of socialism that has come to be known as social democracy.

The Co-operative Commonwealth Federation (CCF) was formed in 1932 as a response to the Great Depression and quickly became the most popular and influential left-wing party in

Canada. Led by Tommy Douglas in Saskatchewan, the CCF became the first socialist government in North America when it was elected in 1944. It pioneered medicare in that province, the forerunner of medicare in Canada. In 1961, it joined with the Canadian Labour Congress to form the New Democratic Party (NDP). The CCF and the NDP are largely credited with creating Canada's universal health care system, much of its pension system, the development of its human rights code, and many of its social welfare programs. The NDP has become one of the three major federal political parties (along with the Liberals and the Conservatives) and has been in power in every province except Newfoundland and Labrador, New Brunswick, and Prince Edward Island. Although it has never been in power at the federal level, it has been very influential in persuading various federal governments to enact a range of social welfare measures, especially during minority governments.

Until the 2011 election, the federal NDP had never ranked higher than third place, but, as stated above, it played a significant role in the enactment of social welfare legislation. It has been called the "party of social programs" and the "conscience of the federal Parliament." However, in the 2011 election under the leadership of Jack Layton, the NDP won the second-most seats in the House of Commons and attained Official Opposition status. The new leader of the NDP, Thomas Mulcair, performed admirably as the leader of the Opposition, and just prior to the 2015 election one of the major election questions was whether the NDP would win, thus giving Canada a social democratic government. The mood of the country suggested a wish for a progressive government after nearly 10 years of a Conservative government under Stephen Harper, which many viewed as regressive, punitive, and moralistic (see Chapter 2 for an overview of this government and its record of social policy). However, the new Liberal leader, Justin Trudeau (son of former Prime Minister Pierre Trudeau) read the mood of the electorate and ran on a progressive platform that came close to rivalling the NDP platform. Given the popularity of the new Liberal leader, its progressive platform, and a number of organizational and electoral gaffes on the part of the NDP's leadership, the Liberals won the election, coming from third place in the House of Commons.

The NDP dropped back to third place in the election, which resulted in Tom Mulcair losing a vote of confidence by more than 50 per cent at a contentious convention held in April 2016 in Edmonton. This prompted him to announce his resignation from the party, to take effect in June 2018, and paved the way for a leadership race to replace him. A former Ontario NDP politician, Jagmeet Singh, was elected leader of the party at a leadership convention on 1 October 2017. He is the first racialized person as well as the first of the Sikh faith to lead a major federal party in Canada.

The NDP is currently adjusting to a new leader as well as attempting to heal some hard feelings among various groups within the party that emerged with the party falling to third place. Even though it went from 103 to 44 seats after the 2015 election, it maintains considerable popularity and has increased its membership since the election of Singh as party leader. Most pundits acknowledge that a few exceptional happenstances occurred during the election that diminished support for the party, even though many progressive Canadians supported its election platform. Additionally, a sizable number of Canadians hold progressive views, and only time will tell whether or not the Trudeau government can meet the needs and wishes of a progressive population. The Liberals, by definition, subscribe to liberal ideals and beliefs that include an acceptance of the free market, a modicum of government intervention, inequality, individualism, a residual welfare state, and so on. Only the NDP, as a social democratic political party, can go beyond the limits that liberalism places on progressive thinking and policy.

Conclusion

This chapter presented an overview of social democracy as a prominent school of socialism. An attempt was made to dispel some of the negative myths held about socialism, especially in North America. It examined social democratic beliefs about human nature, the nature of society, the role of the state, the meaning of social justice, and social democratic attitudes toward social change. It also looked at social democratic ideology and how social democrats would view and treat social problems, and it described the nature and role of social work from the social democratic paradigm. As well, it compared social democratic ideals with those of progressive social work and concluded that there was much more convergence between the two than exists between progressive social work and either neo-conservative or liberal ideals. Finally, the current state of social democracy in three countries with similar cultures and that share a British colonial history was presented.

Critical Questions

1. Socialism is all about equality, but no socialist would call for total and complete equality in all aspects of life. How much equality do you think is desirable or acceptable?

2. Jesus Christ has been described as a radical and a socialist because he lived according to collectivist principles, wanted more sharing of society's resources, challenged (and was crucified by) the status quo. However, it is often the most conservative groups in society such as the religious right or the Moral Majority who most decry socialism and support conservative causes. How do you account for this apparent contradiction?

3. The NDP in Canada and the Labour parties in Britain and Australia call themselves social democratic parties. How close do you think the particular social democratic party in your country comes to the social democratic ideals, beliefs, values, and social policies described in this chapter? Has there been a shift (right or left) in their positions over time? If so, why?

4. Early socialists based their analysis on the premise of a "class struggle"—that there were irreconcilable differences between the two classes in society—i.e., the capitalist class (bourgeoisie) and the working class. What are the major limitations of this analysis today?

5. What do your family (nuclear and extended) and your friends think or believe about socialism? Is there any difference in the opinions of the two groups? If so, what are they, and why do you think they exist?

6   The Marxist Paradigm

. . . the philosophers have only interpreted the world, in various ways; the point is to change it.

—Karl Marx (1975 [1845])

Introduction

This chapter presents a brief introduction to Karl Marx, the times in which he lived, and how the man and his era contributed to the school of social and socialist thought called Marxism. It also provides an overview of Marxist beliefs with respect to human nature, the nature of society, the role of the state, the meaning of social justice, and the Marxist attitude toward social change. An examination is made of the Marxist view of welfare, both in capitalist and socialist societies, and of the explanation for social problems held by Marxists. A picture of social work practice in accordance with Marxism is painted, and an overview of the development of Marxist-based social work in Anglo-democracies and its contributions to social work theory and practice is presented. Finally, a contemporary critique of Marxism is outlined, and a comparison of Marxist ideals with those of progressive social work is made.

Marxism

As mentioned in the previous chapter, the two most important schools of socialist thought are social democracy and Marxism. Marxism includes Karl Marx's own writings as well as the writings of others whose ideas and analyses are close to those of Marx. Marx's basic philosophy was humanistic because he was deeply concerned about the well-being and life chances of the working class in Victorian England. With the rise of capitalism, he saw the increasing degradation of industrial workers, who had no control over their work process or product and who had to live in squalor, insecurity, and poverty (see Box 6.1). At the same time that workers' lives were reduced to a subsistence level, the industrial landowners (i.e., the capitalists) became enormously wealthy and their lives greatly enriched materially and politically (Djao, 1983). Marx's attitude toward this system was one of total rejection rather than of reform, and he devoted most of his working life to seeking to prove that capitalism was both unworkable and inhuman (Mishra, 1981).

Marx's view of welfare or well-being is that it is a social norm based on the values of solidarity and cooperation. "In concrete terms, welfare manifests itself in the social recognition of human need and in the organization of production and distribution in accordance with the criterion of need" (Mishra, 1981, p. 69). In a Marxist society, production would be governed by

> ## Box 6.1 *The Communist Manifesto*
>
> The year is 1848. In Ireland, thousands of people are starving to death. Thousands more are migrating to swell the slums and warrens of English cities. Manchester, Liverpool, and all of the other rapidly expanding urban centres of English capitalist production are paradoxical places. They have pleasant shopping centres, leafy suburbs, and grand architectural monuments to the rich and powerful. They also seethe with poverty and pollution, disease and dissent. In France, King Louis Philippe has abdicated the throne, and Paris is burning behind barricades erected by the people against government forces. In Germany there is rebellion, counter-rebellion, and slaughter. All over Europe dissatisfaction with political and economic oppression erupts here and there into insurrection and war. In the English Parliament sits a Whig (classical Liberal) government, glowing with ideological fervour over its free-market theories and policies, determined to keep control over economic life and expand the riches flowing into the coffers of the bourgeois class. Its Poor Law system of welfare relief maintains the shackles of stigma and penury around those unable to find, or unable to carry out, paid labour. In London, a young philosopher, Karl Marx, and his colleague and patron, Friedrich Engels, present to the Communist League, a small group of left-wing radicals, a manifesto for transforming the world: the Manifesto of the Communist Party. It is a document filled with ominous warnings for the complacent bourgeoisie, rich in the rhetoric of revolution. From its opening portent—"There is a spectre haunting Europe— the spectre of Communism"—to its closing call to arms, it is both a brilliant piece of political propaganda and the key that unlocks the whole of Marxist theory.
>
> Source: O'Brien & Penna (1998, p. 46).

social criteria, and the fruits of labour, produced through cooperation, would be distributed according to the needs of people. Thus, a welfare society in the Marxist sense is one in which the well-being of people is of primary consideration and the mode of production is set up to meet human need rather than to make profits. To Marx, capitalism represented the very antithesis of a welfare society (Mishra, 1981).

For Marx, the central feature of any society is its mode of production—the way its system of productivity is organized. The mode of production determines the structure of society and its processes. In other words, the way society earns its living accounts for its political system, its educational system, the nature of its art and music, its ideology, its riches, its poverty, and how people relate to each other. The capitalist mode of production consists of the following structural (inherent) elements through which wealth, poverty, and inequality are generated and reproduced: private ownership of the means of production; production for profit; private property and inheritance; and the distribution of income and resources through the market mechanism (Mishra, 1981).

Marx did not believe that a welfare society could exist under capitalism. The dominance of the market as a distributive mechanism of income and life chances denies human need and social solidarity altogether. Coercion and competition rather than cooperation and solidarity are the bases of capitalist social organization. Welfare, as a central value, cannot make much headway in such a society. If welfare were to be institutionalized as a central value (i.e., production governed by social criteria and distribution determined by human need), private ownership of the means of production would have to transfer to public ownership. There are different interpretations of how Marx saw this transformation occurring: by reform or by revolution. This has been the source of much debate by contemporary Marxists.

In sum, Marxism is relevant to social welfare and social work on two counts. First, it provides a comprehensive theory of society that explains directly the nature and development of the welfare state and, indirectly, the nature and functions of social work practice in capitalist society. Second, it offers a normative theory about the transcendence of capitalism and the establishment of a welfare society whose central feature is to meet human need (Mishra, 1981).

The following section provides an overview of Marxist views on the nature of human beings, society, the state, social justice, and social change. As mentioned in the previous chapter, because social democracy and Marxism are both socialist paradigms, there is an overlap between them with respect to their views, beliefs, and fundamental values. As will become evident, however, there are also differences.

Views of the Nature of Humans, Society, the State, Social Justice, and Social Change

Human Nature

For Marx, the essence of *human nature* is that people are creative producers. This is not an individual attribute of people but a communitarian trait—by activating this essence, people create a true community of human beings. "To produce as an authentic human being is to express this deep communality" (Berry, 1986, p. 4). Not only is production an expression of an individual's own activity, but this individual satisfies the needs of another human being through this productive activity. And, Marx argued, by satisfying the needs of another, the producer is acknowledged as a complement to (even a necessity of) their own self. This process is mutual, and by attaining such complementarity between and among people, they are realizing their "human communal nature." "Accordingly all humans need other humans to achieve their humanity. Their interrelationship is thus one of basic complementarity" (Berry, 1986, p. 6). This communal production is what makes humans distinct. Although animals and insects may produce under the compulsion of physical need, they lack the self-consciousness, autonomy, and free will of human beings. Humans, then, are active creators of self and their social environment. Marx recognized that human nature is not static, however, because it changes with different social contexts, becoming competitive under capitalism and cooperative under socialism. It is when humans lose control over the production process and the product of their labour (through a forced division of labour and exploitation perpetrated by capitalism) that the person becomes alienated from their true essence and from society. De-alienation requires the radical transformation of society and its fundamental institutions.

The Nature of Society

For Marx and Engels, production is not only the basis of individual human nature but of the *nature of society* or collective life as well. "Every society has to produce food, goods, shelter, and so on, in order to reproduce both its individual members and its social system" (O'Brien & Penna, 1998, p. 50). The way in which a society organizes its production processes is called the *mode of production*. A mode of production consists of a combination of the means of production and the relations of production. The means of production include labour, land, tools, machines, factories, and so on that are organized in particular ways. For example, in a capitalist society the mode of production is privately owned, with the class structure, in its most simple form, consisting of owners and those who must work for them. Thus, the relations of production are characterized by a confrontation between the two camps because they have competing interests (i.e., profits vs wages). The relations of production in a capitalist society are unequal and take the form of a class struggle between the owners of production (the bourgeoisie or ruling class) and the workers who produce (the proletariat). In a socialist society, the means of production would be publicly owned, and because there would be no owners and everyone would contribute according to their ability and receive according to their needs, the relations of production would be characterized by social equality whereby there would be no economic class structure. The nature of a socialist society from a Marxist perspective is the same as that described in the previous chapter in regard to social democratic views and beliefs.

The Nature or Role of the State

The Marxist perspective of *the nature or role of the state* in a socialist society is similar to that of social democrats. The Marxist view of the role of the state in a capitalist society, however, differs from that of social democrats in that Marxists are much more skeptical about the state having any transformative potential. The state and other social institutions are seen "to act in opposition to the real interests of all members of society by constituting an 'illusory community,' which then serves to disguise the real struggles that classes wage against each other" (O'Brien & Penna, 1998, pp. 55–56). Over the course of history, each particular method of production gave rise to a political situation that furthered the interests of the economically dominant group. During feudalism, the interests of the aristocracy or landowners were protected by the law, the monarchy, the army, the suppression of the serfs, and so on. During the period of capitalism, the interests of the capitalists are protected by the law, the churches, the family, the education system, the political system, the media, a false sense of social consciousness perpetrated on workers, and so on. Marx and Engels referred to the "executive (leadership) of the modern state" as nothing "but a committee for managing the affairs of the whole bourgeoisie" (i.e., capitalists or ruling class) (O'Brien & Penna, 1998, p. 56). In sum, the role of the state in a capitalist society is viewed by Marxists as a tool and servant of the ruling class used to control the working class in that all laws, political decisions, policies, and actions of government are in the interest of the capitalists—that is, the ruling class. It is as Marx and Engels wrote, "The ideas of the ruling class are in every epoch the ruling ideas" (Marx & Engels, 1976).

Social Justice

The concept of *social justice*, from a Marxist perspective, is similar to that from a social democratic point of view and is best captured in Marx's statement about how goods in society ought to be distributed: "From each according to his [one's] ability, to each according to his [one's] needs" (Marx, 1970 [1875]). Marx did not believe that it was fair when workers, who worked to produce the goods, received so little for their labour and the capitalists, who did not work to produce the goods, received a disproportionate share of the product's value. Marx believed that entitlement should not be tied to the nature of work or the worth of work but to individual need itself. In this way, individual contribution to social wealth was separate from social consumption. These assumptions are based on a model of human nature different from those held by conservatives and liberals. Marx believed that individuals had a claim on society's resources, not on the basis of unequal individual endowment but on the basis that everyone is equal by virtue of being a human being. Thus, the ultimate or ideal form of a just society to Marx was a classless society.

Social Change

Social change, according to the Marxist perspective, is constantly occurring and is brought about directly through class struggle. In their earlier writings, Marx and Engels claimed that capitalism was doomed because the internal and inherent contradictions of capitalism (emphasis on accumulation, exploitation of workers, imperative of growth leading to overproduction) would eventually lead to its self-destruction. The leading force for this destruction would be a self-conscious, organized, and majority-size working class who would seize the means of production and turn these means to the service of its own needs. In their more analytical works, however, Marx and Engels acknowledged that the logic of capitalism was much more complex and adaptive. Both struggle and counter-struggle existed, with the classes mobilizing forces and developing strategies to further their own interests. In other words, much of the working class bought into capitalism and attempted to get as much out of it as they could. This co-optation, of course, fragmented the working class, reduced its class consciousness, and made the idea of social transformation seem unrealistic. This topic has been the subject of a number of distinct philosophical schools of Marxism or neo-Marxism (e.g., the Frankfurt School of critical theory, the existentialism of Jean-Paul Sartre, structuralism, the cultural Marxism of Antonio Gramsci and the Birmingham Centre for Contemporary Cultural Studies, political economy perspectives, feminist and anti-racist perspectives, and so on). These schools and perspectives have moved Marxism well beyond a simple class analysis by encouraging a series of reconstructions and re-formulations of Marxist theory. Unfortunately, too many social workers and social work writers have not informed themselves of these developments and have dismissed Marxism as an interesting but outdated theory of society and social change. *Nothing could be further from the truth.*

Table 6.1 A Summary of Marxist Views

Concept	Views
Human nature	Humans are communal beings
	Creative producers (production is the basis of human nature)
	Active creators of self and their social environment
	Conscious, autonomous, and free-willed
	Human nature changes with different social contexts
Society	Production is the basis of the nature of society
	Mode/organization of production (i.e., the means and the relations of production) determines the nature of society
Role of the state	Same as social democratic view regarding a socialist state
	State in a capitalist society furthers the interests of the economically dominant group
	Social institutions used to control and co-opt the working class and other subordinate groups in capitalist society
Social justice	From each according to one's ability, to each according to one's needs
	Entitlement not tied to worth of work but to human need
	People are valued on the basis of being human, not on the basis of some notion of superiority/inferiority
	Ideal form of social justice is a classless society
Social change	Social change is constantly occurring and is brought about by class struggle
	Inherent contradictions of capitalism are the leading force for its destruction
	Capitalism has, so far, been able to mutate and adapt and thus co-opt many of its opponents
	There are several neo-Marxist schools of social change

Social Beliefs

Marxists adhere to the three central values of socialism: liberty, equality, and fraternity. Liberty, to the Marxists, can only exist if certain other conditions are present in society (George & Wilding, 1985). Without a substantial degree of economic security and equality, freedom is an illusory concept. Without these conditions, some people will have more resources than others and, therefore, will have more privileges, more influence, and more liberties. Whereas neo-conservatives and liberals believe that civil rights are synonymous with liberty or freedom, Marxists believe that these rights or liberties can only be exercised fairly if they are complemented by social freedom—freedom from want, freedom from unemployment, and so on—and by opportunities to work, to earn, to develop oneself, to enjoy life.

The Marxists do not believe that true liberty for all can occur in a capitalist society based on inequality. Thus, while neo-conservatives equate liberty with inequality and liberals equate liberty with equal opportunity, Marxists equate liberty with equality of economic circumstances or human emancipation that can only be achieved under socialism. George and Wilding present the Marxist concept of equality based on the writings of two Marxist writers, Harold Laski (1925) and John Strachey (1936). Equality does not mean sameness to Marxists; rather, it means the absence of special privilege and the availability of opportunities to all. Differences in wealth or status are consistent with Marxism as long as they can be reasonably explained, all can attain them, and they are necessary for the common good. Economic equality does not mean equal incomes, for it would not be fair to reward unequal efforts exactly the same and it would not be fair to reward unequal needs with the same amount of social benefit. Also, a strict interpretation of "distribution according to individual need" is recognized as problematic because individual need is difficult to define. Rather than "absolute equality," some Marxists view equality as "relative equality," with every need related to the social or civic minimum that, when not met, prevents one from attaining effective citizenship. These needs must be satisfied before dealing with needs above the social minimum and, after the satisfaction of basic needs, differences in reward must be built into the system to acknowledge varying contributions of individuals in different occupations.

The third central social value, solidarity or collectivism, reflects the communitarian nature of people and is antithetical to individualism. It views the individual as a social being in the sense that their thoughts and actions are influenced by those of others and vice versa. Collectivism recognizes people's need for each other and suggests that a good society is one without barriers to people living harmoniously and cooperatively with one another. According to this view of people, government intervention is legitimate, necessary, and beneficial.

Economic Beliefs

The major economic beliefs of Marxists are public ownership of the means of production (brought about by nationalization of private enterprises), distribution of resources according to need, industrial democracy, and a planned economy.

Public Ownership of the Means of Production

Unlike social democrats, Marxists do not believe that the means of production can be controlled by regulation in a capitalist society. Private ownership creates two main classes—the capitalist class and the working class—locked in a structurally antagonistic relationship because their basic interests (profits versus wages) conflict with each other. Class conflict, then, is an inherent part of capitalism and can only be abolished by the abolition of the private ownership of the means of production.

The means of attaining public ownership advocated by the Marxists is nationalization, which they justify on both political and economic grounds (George & Wilding, 1985). The private ownership of the means of production has resulted in a concentration of economic power in the hands of the capitalist class in Britain, the United States, Australia, and Canada, and this inevitably has meant a concentration of political power in the same hands. Also, it is considered immoral by Marxists that profits are produced through the labour of the workers but are reaped by shareholders who do not have to work. In this way, workers feel alienated from the work process and suffer psychologically, which in turn reduces economic production. To deal effectively with these political and economic problems, the Marxists would nationalize private enterprise.

Distribution of Resources According to Need

The second Marxist economic belief flows from the Marxist notion of social justice outlined above: "each person should contribute to society according to his or her abilities and be rewarded by society according to his or her needs." Although this principle is problematic in its implementation, most Marxists would adhere to it in some form. For example, some Marxists would establish minimal standards of living necessary to retain full citizenship in society and would ensure that everyone in society was living up to these standards before dealing with needs above the social or civic minimum (Laski, 1925, cited in George & Wilding, 1985). Other Marxists would follow Marx's theory of revolutionary socialism by distinguishing between distribution according to the quality of work done under socialism (i.e., the transformation stage of socialism) and distribution according to individual need under communism (i.e., the final stage of socialism when capitalism has been abolished) (Strachey, 1936, cited in George & Wilding, 1985). These Marxists point out, however, that distribution according to need requires both economic affluence on the part of the state and a different value system than that which underpins capitalism.

Industrial Democracy

Industrial democracy—that is, a democratic workplace—is a third Marxist economic belief. Marxists generally accept that nationalized industries in a socialist society must be democratically run with maximum participation on the part of workers. As George and Wilding point out, the benefits of industrial democracy are many and varied—it extends and gives real meaning to political democracy; it reduces industrial conflict and promotes industrial cooperation; it enhances individual work satisfaction; and it increases work productivity, which in turn increases the overall standard of living of society.

A Planned Economy

The final Marxist economic belief is that government planning with the widest form of participation must be a central feature of a socialist society (George & Wilding, 1985). Rather than laissez-faire or free enterprise, the Marxists aspire to a planned economy (as part of a planned society) whereby the market is subordinated to purposes upon which members of society have agreed. The Marxists believe that, contrary to the neo-conservative argument, planning enhances democracy and efficiency and is less susceptible to government corruption (George & Wilding, 1985). Obviously, the combination of nationalization and industrial democracy would make it easier for governments to formulate and integrate economic and social policies.

Political Beliefs

The central political beliefs of the Marxists are government planning, a participatory democracy, a parliamentary system of government, and the view that capitalism can be transformed only by class conflict. The Marxist belief in government planning was discussed above, and the Marxist attitude toward participatory democracy is similar to that of the social democrats.

The suppression of parliamentary democracy during the Soviet era in eastern European countries, which were referred to as socialist by much of the media and by many commentators in capitalist countries (understandably, since the leader of the Eastern Bloc was the Union of Soviet *Socialist* Republics), caused many people to believe that Marxism is anti-democratic (George & Wilding, 1985). However, a belief in parliamentary democracy by most contemporary Marxists is unmistakable, as evidenced by its acceptance in western Europe's communist parties. The idea of a one-party socialist state is inconsistent with the concept of democratic socialism.

The Marxists believe that any significant social change can come about only through class conflict. This belief is different from that of the social democrats, who believe that capitalism can be transformed by social conflict between racial, religious, and other interest groups (including classes), aided by a progressive social democratic government. Although early Marxists recognized other conflicts in society in addition to that which exists between exploited wage-earners and the owners of the means of production, they believed these other conflicts could be resolved within the legal conditions of capitalism. Early Marxists were united in their belief that class conflict would sooner or later lead to the downfall of capitalism. Neo-Marxists are not as absolute in this regard. For example, Marxist feminists view patriarchy and classism as twin evils and do not think that the elimination of one would necessarily mean the end of the other. Similarly, anti-racist theorists do not think that the abolition of class exploitation will end racism. They point to the example of Jewish people who, as a group, have achieved middle-class status, which means that they receive higher than average incomes (Blalock, 1967) that tend to tie them in more with capitalism. However, anti-Semitism remains a primary hate crime in Canada. Given modern developments of Marxist theory and analysis, the road to social transformation is not as clear as it was 100 years or even 50 years ago. This change may come peacefully or violently, although most contemporary Marxist writers advocate peaceful means. Unlike social democrats, who believe that the welfare state can be used as a vehicle for socialist change, most Marxists view the welfare state as a social institution supporting capitalism (see below). They would, instead, focus their efforts on labour as the primary vehicle for socialist change but would not rule out other social movements contributing to this goal.

View of Social Problems

Unlike neo-conservatives, Marxists do not see so-called social problems as the result of individual fault. Nor do they view social problems as the result of industrialization, as the liberals do, or as the result of social conflict among various groups, as the social democrats do. Rather, social problems are "the result of the capitalist form of production and its accompanying forms of social relationships" (George & Wilding, 1985, pp. 109–110). Marxists believe that the term "social problem" mystifies structural issues of inequality, oppression, and alienation by turning them into individualistic issues of deviance, inadequacy, or pathology.

For example, a Marxist analysis of poverty shows that it will never be resolved or eliminated in a capitalist society because capitalism needs poverty. Poverty carries out the following functions for capitalism:

- Poverty helps to keep wages down and profits up. When people are poor, they will accept low wages to purchase basic necessities, and when there are many people living in poverty, one of the ways they will compete for jobs is by working for lower wages than the other person.
- Capitalism needs a workforce that will perform its dangerous work and carry out its menial tasks. People living in poverty often have to perform these tasks just to survive. For example, a disproportionate number of African Americans, Hispanic Americans, and white people living in poverty are on the front lines in fighting America's wars (with affluent white men occupying positions as generals, Pentagon officials, and White House politicians). Similarly, those who work in coal mines are decidedly not the sons of the well-to-do. Meanwhile, right-wing American politicians (such as Donald Trump, who was elected as president of the US in November 2016) rail against illegal Mexican migrants and pursue the construction of a border barrier fence costing billions of dollars for "security." It is these same migrants who do the dirty or dangerous jobs that others refuse. And it is often poverty-stricken (and illegal) immigrants and racialized individuals who are employed to clean public washrooms and pick up cigarette butts and Styrofoam coffee cups around university campuses and other public areas.
- Poverty enhances feelings of superiority (i.e., self-righteousness) of the non-poor.
- People living in poverty are often used as scapegoats for societal ills. For example, government deficits of the 1970s and 1980s were often blamed on generous social welfare programs that were needed because people living in poverty were considered too lazy to work.
- Programs developed to deal with poverty employ large numbers of people, thus contributing to a lower unemployment level.
- Many private organizations make profits via government contracts in delivering services to people living in poverty. (There is a good deal of money in poverty, yet people who are most affected by poverty are not getting much of it.)
- People living in poverty are often pointed out as examples of what will happen to a person if they do not conform to the (capitalist) society's expectations, such as becoming a productive member of the workforce (see Box 6.2).

Marxists believe that by focusing on the victims of inequality, oppression, and alienation and calling them criminals, drug addicts, or people living in poverty, we are actually labelling them as troublemakers. Consequently, we neglect the social conditions of inequality, powerlessness, and institutional violence that form the basis of our troubled society. Instead, the Marxists would trace these problems back to the social relationships determined by capitalism, not to the individual. Personal problems are rooted in capitalist politics. For some problems, such as poverty, the explanation is direct and simple; for others, such as crime, it is less direct and more complex.

Box 6.2 *"Shape up or You Will End up in the Poor House!"*

I (Bob) grew up in Saint John, New Brunswick, during the 1950s. Near the house in which I lived was a body of water called Courtney Bay. Right across the bay from our house was an old "Municipal Home" operated by the county. It was, in fact, a poor house, since the Poor Laws in New Brunswick were not repealed until 1960. Living in the "Home" were older people who had been there for years. They had originally been committed or forced to enter the poor house because they had no other means of support. On sunny days they would sit outside in front of the Home where they would be on display for people going by. They looked decrepit, forlorn, and very old, especially to a young boy driving by on his bicycle. My father, as one of his forms of discipline, would take me outside our house, point across the bay to the poor house, and say "If you don't behave yourself better, you will end up in that poor house." Of course, this terrified me, and I would be on my best behaviour—for a day or two.

In sum, Marxists believe that social problems are caused by the capitalist system. Therefore, they cannot be abolished by social policy in a capitalist society but only by the abolition of capitalism.

Critical Social Theory

Marx is arguably the founder of a body of social theory called "critical social theory." His ideas and emancipatory intentions have been extended by many notable theorists. As its name suggests, critical theory is critical of existing social institutions and practices and locates the sources of social problems (i.e., domination) within them. Critical social theory seeks to change a society whose institutions, practices, and processes are exploitative and discriminatory to one that is emancipatory and free from domination. Marxism is perhaps the earliest form of critical social theory and was based on an analysis of capitalism and its exploitation of workers. More recent forms of critical theory are emancipatory forms of feminism, anti-racism, anti-oppression, liberation theology, post-colonialism, and structural social work (Mullaly & West, 2018). Some of these theories accord primacy to one particular form and source of oppression (e.g., anti-racist perspectives); others attempt to accommodate multiple forms of oppression in their analyses and theories (e.g., anti-oppression and structural social work). More will be said about critical social theory in Chapter 8.

View of Social Welfare

Ideal Welfare System

The ideal social welfare system in the Marxist view is the same as that espoused by social democrats or by any socialist group—the structural model of welfare. Its major attributes are that social services should be distributed according to need; they should be universal, comprehensive, adequate, and free; prevention is a primary social welfare principle; and there should be participation on the part of lay people in determining policy.

Traditional Welfare State Props up Capitalism

Marxists, however, as noted previously, do not agree with the social democrats that the welfare state under capitalism provides a stepping stone to a socialist society. Instead, Marxists believe that although the welfare state does provide minimal help to some people, its main function is to support and strengthen the liberal-capitalist system. The welfare state represents one of the contradictions of capitalism. On the one hand, it works toward greater degrees of human well-being by tending to the immediate needs of some people. On the other hand, it denies and frustrates the pursuit of a just society because it supports and reinforces conformity to the very institutions and values that generate the problems the welfare state was established to deal with in the first place.

Two obvious questions arise from the Marxist contention that the welfare state does not move capitalist society any closer to a socialist society but, instead, supports and strengthens capitalism. Why does the welfare state prop up capitalism? How does it do this? The simple explanation of why the welfare state supports capitalism is that this is its principal raison d'être in a capitalist society—to protect capitalism. The welfare state is established within a certain political and economic context. Because of that liberal-capitalist context, the welfare state is part of a symbiotic relationship with all other major (liberal-capitalist) institutions in society. All activities and reform efforts of the welfare state are governed by the logic and requirements of capitalism. Marxists perceive all capitalist social institutions as functioning to promote conformity to capitalism. This perception is part of the fundamental Marxist belief that the government in a capitalist state represents the interests of the capitalist class. How the welfare state promotes conformity is described below.

Functions That the Traditional Welfare State Carries out for Capitalism

According to Marxists, the welfare state in a capitalist society operates (1) to reduce working-class antagonism to the existing social order, (2) to increase efficiency of the economic system, and (3) to underwrite many of the costs that the owners of capital incur. Marxists believe that many of our social welfare measures are actually tactical concessions made to labour to avert social disruption or other threats to the social order. The classic example is the social insurance reforms introduced by Otto von Bismarck in Germany in the late nineteenth century. These reforms were initiated to crush revolutionary socialism—a growing political force in Germany—and to win over German workers. Some Marxists view social welfare reforms as ransom for social harmony that the working class has squeezed out of the government, while other Marxists believe they are given freely by government but with an ulterior motive—co-optation of the working class. In either case, the effect is to cool down any drastic social reform efforts that would challenge capitalism.

Marxist analysis argues that the capitalist welfare state acts as a corrective for the inherent inefficiency of capitalism. Left on its own, the capitalist system of production tends toward regular cycles of depressions and recessions, overproduction, under-consumption, falling profits, and stagflation. The state is forced to intervene to enable the capitalist system to overcome these recurrent tendencies toward economic crisis. The more advanced the economy, the more government intervention seems to be needed. Thus, the welfare state, in this analysis, is largely the result of the functional needs of capitalism.

The welfare state also enhances the profitability of capitalist businesses by underwriting many of the costs associated with the capitalist system of production. Through public spending in the areas of education and health, the private sector has available to it an educated and healthy workforce without any direct costs to it. As well, our social insurance and other public financial assistance programs put money directly into the hands of consumers of the goods and services produced by the private sector, which keeps consumption at a higher level than it would be without social welfare programs. The welfare state also reduces costs to the private sector associated with accidents on the job (workers' compensation) and unsafe working conditions. Of course, publicly financed health care picks up the tab for the medical costs associated with these casualties (Finn, 1979, cited in Buchbinder, 1981).

Many social programs certainly subsidize private enterprise indirectly. James O'Connor (1973, p. 6) offers a more complete explanation of how the welfare state props up capitalism. He argues that the capitalist state must try to carry out two basic but apparently contradictory functions—accumulation and legitimation:

> The state must try to maintain or create the conditions in which profitable capital accumulation is possible. However, the state also must try to maintain or create the conditions for social harmony. A capitalist state that openly uses its coercive forces to help one class accumulate capital at the expense of other classes loses its legitimacy and hence undermines the basis of loyalty and support. But a state that ignores the necessity of assisting the process of capital accumulation risks drying up the source of its own power, the economy's surplus production capacity and the taxes drawn from this surplus. . . . the state must involve itself in the accumulation process, *but it must either mystify its policies by calling them something that they are not, or it must try to conceal them* [emphasis added].

O'Connor separates the economic (capital accumulation) functions of the state from the social welfare functions. The former aim at serving the needs of capital by helping to increase profit, by offering tax incentives, by encouraging labour mobility, and the like. However, a government seen to attend only to the interests of the minority but powerful capitalist class will not be accepted by the working class. To legitimize itself to the working class, therefore, the government must also appear to represent their interests. It does this, in part, by developing a welfare state that the government claims strives toward fairness, equity, and justice. Marxists believe, however, that the welfare state does not live up to these claims because, in fact, much of the government's social welfare activities actually enhance capital accumulation.

Thus, the functions of capital accumulation and legitimation may appear to be contradictory, but Marxists would argue that experience has shown they are mutually reinforcing and favour the capitalists.

Marxist critics have no difficulty citing evidence to substantiate their claim that the welfare state is the same as any other liberal-capitalist social institution in that it functions in such a manner as to protect dominant class interests. Galper (1975) provides an insightful analysis of how social welfare programs support and nurture liberal capitalism. Most public financial assistance programs support the labour market by making people's eligibility for assistance dependent on their past experience and present relationship to the job market. Even programs such as daycare depend on the needs of the dominant class for labour because daycare spaces tend to increase during periods of low unemployment and are cut back during recessions. Eligibility for many social welfare programs also depends on conforming to society's prevailing values. For example, public assistance regulations are often used to control the behaviour of recipients in such areas as parenting, sexual conduct, and market purchases. The fact that social welfare programs are often underfunded and provide minimal assistance gives the message to those who depend on such programs that people who cannot make it in the private market cannot really count on a public support system for much help. Also, they had better behave in a socially acceptable manner or they could easily lose the minimal benefits they do receive.

Even government actions that have no obvious effect on increasing profits or ensuring a ready workforce for private enterprise are viewed skeptically by Marxists. For example, the factory legislation enacted during Karl Marx's time in England was often not enforced. A contemporary example of governments appearing to act in the best interests of all citizens but not interfering with the capital accumulation of private enterprise is found in the fact that some very good anti-pollution legislation exists but is often not enforced when it is violated by large industries.

Mishra (1981) sums up the main features of the Marxist view of welfare:

1. True welfare (i.e., a social norm based on solidarity, cooperation, and human need) involves the regulation of working and living conditions and the distribution of society's resources based on human need.
2. As a socio-economic–political system, capitalism is the antithesis of true welfare.
3. True welfare can begin to be partially established in a capitalist society through the collective efforts of workers. Given the nature of capitalism, however, the chances for meaningful and lasting reform are slight.
4. In a class-divided society, the government and society largely attend to the interests of the dominant class. However, the universality of the state requires it to act (or appear to act) on behalf of all classes. Thus, the capitalist state is two-faced with respect to welfare. Social programs may be accepted in form but not realized in substance.
5. True welfare can be established fully as a social norm only after the means of production have been nationalized and the free-market/private-property system abolished.

6. Social welfare in a capitalist society contributes to the efficiency and smooth working of the capitalist economy.

7. Social welfare in a capitalist society has an important social control function—to moderate class conflict and stabilize the social order.

8. Not surprisingly, the initiative for social welfare programs often comes from sectors of the dominant class.

9. Attempts to reform the capitalist system only lead to new economic and social contradictions. The welfare state has stabilizing as well as destabilizing effects on the capitalist social structure.

10. To avoid wrongful ideological conclusions, welfare activities in a capitalist society must be seen in conjunction with its other interventions and activities.

In light of these beliefs about welfare, orthodox Marxists reject the notion that the welfare state in a capitalist society holds any potential for socialism. They differ, therefore, from social democrats, who believe that the welfare state, the trade union movement, and social democratic parties all have potential for socialist transformation and should be used in this fashion. However, not all Marxists reject the welfare state out of hand as a vehicle for socialism. It depends on whether one has adopted a revolutionary or an evolutionary Marxist perspective.

Social Work Practice within the Marxist Paradigm

The crucial question for the Marxist social worker is whether or not radical social and political change can come about through the social welfare institution in a capitalist society. The answer depends on whether one is a "revolutionary" or an "evolutionary" Marxist.[1] Although both types of Marxists favour the attainment of a socialist state, they differ on the means of such attainment. The evolutionary Marxist believes that a socialist state can be created by working within existing social institutions and organizations that have potential for socialism, such as the trade union movement and the welfare state. The revolutionary Marxist does not believe that any socialist potential is inherent in any capitalist social institution (except the trade unions, which constitute a working-class movement) and, therefore, seeks to create and develop counter-institutions and organizations to challenge the power of the state.

It is difficult to see how a revolutionary Marxist could even practise social work in a capitalist society. Since social work occurs within the welfare state, which is rejected as a base of operations by revolutionary Marxists, what or where would be the basis of attempts to stimulate, create, and develop socialist institutions and organizations? Revolutionary Marxists maintain that social work has political potential for socialism only if it disposes of its social reform illusions and joins in the "revolutionary movement." However, they do not say how this could be done or who would employ revolutionary social workers. Unless one is self-supporting or employed by a radical union, there do not appear to be many opportunities for revolutionary Marxists to practise social work in a capitalist state. Social work practice within the social welfare institution is seen by orthodox (revolutionary) Marxists as perpetuating an unworkable and undesirable system of capitalism because it is used as "a mechanism for identifying and absorbing potential social revolt against the status quo" (Pritchard & Taylor, 1978, p. 5).

Evolutionary Marxists do not reject the capitalist state as a vehicle for socialist change:

> There is, indeed, a significant number of evolutionary Marxian socialists arguing . . . for the creation of a socialist system . . . through the relatively untainted and indigenous institutions of the working class; most notably the trade unions and the welfare state (Pritchard & Taylor, 1978, pp. 89–90).

In other words, evolutionary Marxists believe that the welfare state can be used as a stepping stone toward socialism. In this regard, they appear to have much in common with those social democratic social workers who attempt to create forces in their social work practices that would contribute to the transformation of capitalism.

The differences between social democratic social work practice and evolutionary Marxist social work practice would be more of degree and emphasis than of kind. Both would attend to the needs of people who have been hurt by capitalism, and both would attempt to restructure society along socialist lines. However, the evolutionary Marxist social workers would undoubtedly emphasize the latter task more than would their social democratic counterparts.

> The ultimate function of [Marxist] social work must be to raise community, and thus ultimately political, consciousness by exposing the assumed class nature of existing society . . . the greater the "awareness" the greater the potential for conflict between working-class activists and "authority" (Pritchard & Taylor, 1978, p. 85).

To reiterate the Marxist position on social work practice, both revolutionary and evolutionary Marxists would attempt to raise socialist political consciousness. However, the revolutionary Marxist social worker, as part of this process, would attempt to undermine the acceptance of, and support for, the very institution of which his or her profession is a part—as Pritchard and Taylor (1978, p. 109) point out, "a dangerous but not altogether ignoble role!" Evolutionary Marxist social workers, on the other hand, would join their radical social democratic counterparts and attempt to radicalize the power structure within the welfare state by means of increased participation, decentralization, and democratization and "to extend and fortify the working-class and socialist incursions into capitalism" (Pritchard & Taylor, 1978, p. 107). Eventually, it is believed, such actions would lead to a position where the attainment of a fully socialist state becomes possible. Most of the recent Marxist or neo-Marxist social welfare and social work literature falls within the "evolutionary" school but does not ignore the revolutionary Marxist skepticism when analyzing the welfare state and social work as instruments for emancipation of oppressed groups.

Table 6.2 Overview of Marxist and Social Work Ideals

	Marxism	Social Work
Social Beliefs	Liberty Collectivism Equality	Humanitarianism (humanism) Community Equality
Economic Beliefs	Public ownership of means of production Industrial democracy Distribution of resources according to need Planned economy	Government intervention Social priorities dominate economic decisions Equitable distribution of society's resources
Political Beliefs	Government planning Participatory democracy Parliamentary system of government Transformation of capitalism by class conflict	Participatory democracy in both governmental and non-governmental areas
View of Social Welfare	Welfare capitalism props up capitalism but also represents the fruits of working-class efforts Ideal = social welfare state or structural model	An instrument to promote equality, solidarity, and community Ideal = structural model
Nature of Social Work Practice	Revolutionary Marxists see no social change role for social workers in capitalist society Evolutionary Marxists' practice of social work is similar to that of social democrats but emphasizes "class conflict" more	Treat people with respect Enhance dignity and integrity Facilitate self-determination and self-realization Accept differences Advocate and promote social justice

Critique of the Marxist Paradigm

As a social theory, Marxism is "probably the best single theory available for a critical understanding of capitalist society. That is its major strength" (Mishra, 1984, p. 97). Part of this critical understanding is the way in which the Marxist view locates the welfare state within capitalism rather than seeing it in isolation. The view of the welfare state as a necessity for capitalism because it makes capitalism more efficient and productive while controlling the workforce and legitimizing capitalism is a major contribution of Marxism. However, as a theory of building a socialist state it "remains sadly inadequate" (Mishra, 1984, p. 97). It has not come to terms with the entire historical experience of existing socialism. In fact, as Mishra points out, the actually existing socialism (i.e., Soviet socialism) was for many years an embarrassment to Western

Marxists. There is no working model of advanced socialism that Marxists can point to. There are, however, many social democratic countries that have been influenced by Marxist ideas. In fact, most western European states are social democratic, but, as mentioned above, Marxists do not consider social democracy to be a fully developed form of socialism.

With respect to Marxist-governed nations, a number of interesting developments occurred during the late 1990s and the early 2000s in Latin America, especially in Chile, Bolivia, Brazil, and Venezuela where left-leaning governments were elected to political power. These governments turned away from neo-liberal/conservative economic policies and implemented economic reforms and programs along the lines of those discussed in the section on Marxist economic beliefs earlier in this chapter (Cameron & Hershberg, 2010). Each of these countries had been hurt by neo-conservative economic policies associated with globalization and carried out by the World Bank, the International Monetary Fund, and the World Trade Organization. This trend of economic reform occurred from 1998 until approximately 2010 during which time three out of four people of a population of 350 million lived in South American countries ruled by Marxist or quasi-Marxist governments. Since then, several of these countries have encountered economic problems (as have many bourgeois governments) brought about by corruption, falling oil and commodity prices, and overspending on the part of some governments (Blei, 2016).

The classical Marxist view that capitalist societies comprise two monolithic classes and that all conflict in society runs along class lines has been criticized on the basis of being incompatible with the realities of contemporary societies (George & Wilding, 1994; Mishra, 1984; O'Connor, 1973). The working class is divided along white collar and blue collar, private and public sector, rural and urban workers, skilled and unskilled workers, managerial and professional status, and so on. And it is very questionable whether all conflicts in society are based on class or capitalist oppression. For example, is the enemy of oppressed women capitalism or patriarchy? Are all racial conflicts or religious conflicts actually class conflicts? It should be noted here, however, that since at least the late 1970s, neo-Marxist analyses of society and social welfare have incorporated gender and race dimensions. Both Ferguson, Lavalette, and Mooney (2002) and O'Brien and Penna (1998), for example, consider how other world views, such as feminism, anti-racism, and postmodernism, have supplemented Marxism and reduced the charge against it of being a totalizing and Eurocentric grand narrative. There have also been recent attempts (e.g., Ferguson et al., 2002; Mullaly, 2002) to use Marxist theory to analyze and explain oppression. And there has long been an alternative Marxist tradition to that of early Marxism, which emphasized structural determinism to the exclusion of the role of human agency in the "making of history."

The traditional Marxist claim—that the state is the representative of the capitalist class and that all issues dealt with by the state are directly or indirectly relevant to the stability and reproduction of the capitalist system—is doubtful. As George and Wilding (1985) point out, a group of policy issues, including abortion, adoption, divorce, capital punishment, and drug addiction, are mainly moral in nature and have nothing to do with the survival of capitalism. These authors present other considerations that have to be accounted for when assessing the autonomy of the state to act against the interests of the capitalist class:

- the political ideology of the government (a social democratic government is more likely to pursue anti-capitalist policies than a conservative government);

- the nature of public opinion (public opinion, such as the public's wish for anti-pollution legislation, will often set limits on pro-capitalist policies);
- the power of the working class (when the working class is well organized, governments have to take notice of the demands of trade unions).

With respect to its view of the welfare state, Marxism is in the unenviable position of trying to balance both sides of a contradiction. "Social welfare may help shore up capitalism, materially and ideologically, but it also represents a gain for the working class in its struggle against exploitation" (Mishra, 1984, p. 81). This is the classical dilemma for Marxists. During good times, Marxists have tended to focus on the broader political implications of the welfare state, often neglecting or denigrating its benefits to individuals and families. However, during periods of attack on the welfare state from the right, Marxists become its staunchest champions. "In this sense, Marxism represents a paradoxical theory of emancipation" (O'Brien & Penna, 1998, p. 74).

Table 6.2 shows that Marxism and social work ideology share many of the same values and ideals. It will be recalled from the previous chapter that there was also a high degree of compatibility between social democratic and social work ideologies. Because the social democrats and the Marxists both want the same thing—a socialist state—they naturally share many of the same primary values. There is much consistency among social democracy, Marxism, and social work in terms of their primary values. Each has egalitarianism as a central value, and both social democracy and social work have humanitarianism as an explicit central value while Marxism has it as an implicit central value (i.e., Marxism seeks to abolish capitalism for humanitarian reasons). The major difference among the three sets of belief systems is that whereas social democracy and social work perceive the welfare state to be a stepping stone toward a better society, Marxists tend to perceive it as a mechanism that props up capitalism, although they concede that it has, in part, come about through the efforts of the working class.

Contributions of Marxism to Social Work in Anglo-democracies

Before dismissing Marxism as a possible course of action for social work, we should be cognizant of the contributions it has already made through such earlier writings as Ian Gough's *The Political Economy of the Welfare State* (1979), the Macmillan series of *Critical Texts in Social Work and the Welfare State*, edited by Peter Leonard in the late 1970s and early 1980s, Paul Corrigan and Peter Leonard's *Social Work Practice under Capitalism* (1978), Bailey and Brake's *Radical Social Work* (1975), three American books—Piven and Cloward's *Regulating the Poor: The Public Functions of Welfare* (1972) and Jeffrey Galper's *The Politics of Social Services* (1975) and *Social Work Practice: A Radical Perspective* (1980)—a Canadian book by Steven Wineman, *The Politics of Social Services* (1984), and, from Australia, Harold Throssell's *Radical Essays in Social Work* (1975). As Ferguson et al. (2002) point out, these books represented an important break from the tradition of social administration (as an approach to social policy) and its essential empirical assumption that all we needed to do to combat social problems was to obtain more and better services. In short, they broke with the liberal or psychosocial approaches of social work. George and Wilding (1994) contend that Marxism remains the most insightful and satisfactory model in explaining the development of the welfare state. Box 6.3 outlines the influences of Marxism on progressive or radical social work in the 1970s and early 1980s.

In varying degrees, most social work programs in Anglo-democracies incorporated some of these progressive ideas and analyses into parts of their curriculum, but for the most part they occupied token or marginal positions alongside mainstream social work ideas and practices.

Ferguson and Woodward (2009) point out that like many other social movements that developed in the 1960s and 1970s (e.g., growth of the trade union movement and the welfare state following a "rediscovery" of poverty, civil rights movements in the southern US and in Northern Ireland, the women's liberation movement, the gay rights movement, and the student rights movement), radical social work experienced a decline. The main reasons for this decline were the worldwide economic crisis that began in 1973 along with the inflation-fuelling Vietnam War and the election of right-wing governments (principally the Conservatives under Margaret Thatcher in Britain, the Republicans under Ronald Reagan in the US, and the Progressive Conservatives

Box 6.3 *Marxist Influences on Progressive Social Work (1970s–Early 1980s)*

- Critically analyzed capitalism to show its oppressive features and contradictions, which was used to develop the levers and latitude for the practice of radical social work.
- Critiqued and showed how mainstream social work practices actually covered up many of the oppressive features of capitalism by helping people cope with, adjust to, or fit back into an oppressive society.
- These critical analyses of capitalism and mainstream social work were used to develop radical/progressive theories and practices of social work at both the personal and political levels.
- This progressive agenda included raising the awareness of service users of how capitalism oppressed and exploited them and encouraging them to organize and mobilize against it.
- Encouraged social workers to join with the trade union movement rather than elitist and self-serving professional associations, since it (the trade union movement) was seen as the vehicle for overthrowing capitalism.
- Established building up the welfare state as a major goal because it had need rather than profit as its criterion for the production and distribution of goods and services.
- Advocated for the election of socialist political parties because they were viewed as more committed to social justice than were bourgeois political parties.
- Responded to the criticism of feminist social workers that it ignored gender in its theory and practice and to the criticism, mainly from black social workers, that it ignored colour in its theory and practice.

under Brian Mulroney in Canada). Led by big business and bourgeois governments, economic restructuring occurred to address a worldwide recession and inflation (i.e., stagflation). Principal targets of this restructuring included trade unions and the welfare state. We witnessed, as Leonard (1997) pointed out, the ascendency of neo-conservatism and neo-liberalism on a global scale and the virtual collapse of Left (i.e., progressive) politics, a reduced welfare state, increasing disparities between rich and poor, national trade unions in disarray, and massive economic uncertainty. Capitalism was transformed from a rigid and centralized postwar form to a flexible (for the capitalists at least) and global form (Harvey, 1989), thus making much of the earlier analyses of capitalism outdated and irrelevant. In the face of these attacks, which included attacks on social programs and social workers, "the social work profession became increasingly defensive and sought to play down its radicalism" (Ferguson & Woodward, 2009, p. 28).

Despite these attacks and changes, however, radical and Marxist ideas have survived, although in somewhat different forms. Addressing these different forms of radical social work Ferguson and Woodward observe that "[I]n the UK, for example, the late 1980s saw the growing of influence of anti-racist social work, feminist social work and anti-oppressive practice, while in Australia and Canada, 'critical' (or structural) social work became the generic term for what were often very similar approaches" (2009, p. 28). Anti-oppressive perspectives in the UK figured prominently in the new diploma in social work, and in Canada the Canadian Association of Schools of Social Work requires university-based social work programs to demonstrate how oppression and structural factors are dealt with in their curriculum. The fact that students are now required to explore the ways in which different forms of structural oppression shape the lives of people who use social work services is a step forward in moving social work beyond individual explanations of social problems, which ascribe all of the problems that service users experience to defects in personality development and family relationships (Powell, 2001). These newer forms of progressive or radical or Marxist social work have been important in increasing awareness of the multiple oppressions experienced by service users in ways that earlier versions of radical social work sometimes failed to do (Ferguson & Woodward, 2009).

In assessing the potential of Marxism for social work today, we should also be cognizant that many contemporary writers (e.g., Donna Baines, 2011; Iain Ferguson et al., 2002; Iain Ferguson & Rona Woodward, 2009; Jim Ife, 1997; Peter Leonard, 1997; Bob Mullaly, 2010) are attempting to reconstruct, reformulate, and revitalize Marxist theory informed by feminist, anti-racist, postmodern, and other critiques. We and many, many others believe that a Marxist view of the dynamics of advanced capitalism, class, the state, culture, alienation, and oppression can help us to make sense of a range of current social welfare and social work issues and debates. But unlike three or four decades ago, we do not believe that Marxism by itself holds the key to social transformation and emancipatory forms of social work practice.

Conclusion

This chapter presented an overview of Marxism as one of two prominent schools of socialism (the other being social democracy). An attempt was made to establish the historical and social context within which Marx lived and wrote and to extend some of his ideas and analyses about such things as social welfare, capitalism, oppression, and social problems to today's realities. An attempt was made to dispel some of the negative myths and stereotypes held by many in North America about Karl Marx and Marxist thought. The chapter examined Marxist beliefs about human nature, the nature of society, the role of the state, the meaning of social justice, and social change. It also looked at Marxist ideology and how Marxists would view and treat social problems, and it described the nature and role of social work in accordance with the Marxist paradigm and presented an outline of the contributions made by Marxism to social work theory and practice. As well, it compared Marxist ideals with those of progressive social work and concluded that there was much more convergence between the two than exists between progressive social work and either neo-conservative or liberal ideals. It also concluded that since both are socialist paradigms, there is much in common between social democracy and Marxism. One of the major areas in which they differ is the means for transforming capitalism to a socialist society. A critique of the Marxist paradigm was also outlined.

Critical Questions

1. Which approach do you believe that socialism, in general, and social work, in particular, should adopt in pursuing the transformation of capitalist society to one of socialism—evolution or revolution? Why?

2. Marx believed that capitalism contained internal contradictions that would eventually lead to its demise. Can you think what some of these contradictions might be?

3. The United States is probably the only Western democracy without a socialist political party. Why do you think this is?

4. An idea inspired by Marxism to help eliminate or reduce intergenerational inequality and families building up huge fortunes is to do away with inheritance. What do you think of this idea?

5. A few key Marxist concepts or ideas are "alienation," "internalization of a socially constructed identity," "social production and reproduction," and "the control of society not by an army or police but by the ideas of the ruling class." What do these ideas mean, and how are they related to social problems?

7 Feminist, Anti-racist, and Postmodern Critiques

The overall impact of postmodernism is that many other groups now share with black folks a sense of deep alienation, despair, uncertainty, loss of sense of grounding even if it is not informed by shared circumstance.

—bell hooks (1990)

Introduction

In the previous chapters, four paradigms were presented—two that support capitalism and two that seek its transformation to some form of socialist or collectivist society. Although these paradigms were presented as different from one another, some similarities and overlaps were also indicated. These four paradigms and their respective ideological bases were the major world views for much of the nineteenth and twentieth centuries, and they have formed the basis for most social theory and practice. There have been other perspectives, such as ultra-right-wing ideologies of fascism and Nazism and ultra-left-wing ideologies of anarchism and communism. However, these latter perspectives and/or movements have not been as long-standing or as popular in Western democracies and, therefore, are not discussed here.

Over the past two decades or so, two significant developments have brought the relevance of paradigms or political ideologies as world views into question. First, as noted in Chapter 2, capitalism has been transformed from its rigid and centralized postwar form to a flexible (for the capitalists at least) and global form, thus making much of the earlier analysis of capitalism irrelevant. We have witnessed the declining power of nation-states to intervene in their own economies, the spread of terrorism, increasing disparities between rich and poor, the fall of many state socialist regimes, national trade union movements in disarray, the virtual collapse of leftist politics in the developed nations, and continuing oppression on the basis of class, gender, culture, sexuality, age, race, ability, and so on. Given these and other events, many people today are skeptical about the relevance of the dominant paradigms in the face of the rapid social, economic, political, and cultural changes that have occurred since the early 1970s.

The second development that has questioned the legitimacy of paradigms and ideological foundations has been the emergence of postmodern and post-structural thought. They have challenged many of the theories, universalistic ideals, and discourses that underpin the traditional paradigms. For example, discourse theorists reject any claim that ideologies or paradigms have core characteristics that give them a "true" and independent meaning "outside" of the interpretation given by their specific discourses (Rorty, 1999; Bastow & Martin, 2003). It has been suggested that the era of grand theoretical perspectives (such as social paradigms) is over. Some of the reasons for the current skepticism with respect to traditional ideological analysis are explored below. As well, a summary of some postmodern and post-structural critiques of paradigms, political ideologies, and the modern welfare state are presented.

Certainly, legitimate and substantive criticisms were made of the dominant paradigms and ideological frameworks from other perspectives prior to the more recent postmodern critiques. These criticisms have come from a number of sources, but the major critiques have emanated from various forms of feminism and from anti-racist writers. Feminists have criticized the paradigms for not addressing women's issues, thus rendering women invisible, while those writing from a critical race perspective have faulted them for being colour-neutral. An overview of the feminist and anti-racist critiques of the dominant paradigms is presented in this chapter, followed by the postmodern/post-structural critique. The examination here is not exhaustive. For example, the political ecology or "green" critique (e.g., Dominelli, 2012) and the Indigenous critique (e.g., Baskin, 2016) continue to be developed.

The purpose of this chapter is not to discard ideological analysis as a tool for understanding social phenomena or to reject the analytical value of the paradigms outlined in the previous chapters, in particular social democracy and Marxism. Rather, feminism, anti-racism, postmodernism, and other critiques can help to correct, inform, and revitalize the paradigms and political ideologies, which in turn will contribute to our understandings of social theory, social welfare formations, and social work practice.

Feminist Critique

Although postmodernism provides a powerful critique of the traditional paradigms, many contemporary scholars concur with Knuttila (2002, p. 224), who says that:

> The most important and systematic critique of the analytical and explanatory capacities of the older theoretical approaches has come from scholars and activists associated with various schools of feminist thought. As new questions were posed concerning the nature and role of the state, especially as it relates to sex and gender relations, the existing approaches were found wanting in two related, but different aspects.

These two aspects are: (1) there is overwhelming evidence that the state plays a central role in the domination of men and the subordination of women; and (2) this evidence has led to demands that the existing ideological and theoretical frameworks be revised to account for the role of the state in maintaining dominant patriarchal and heterosexual relations that characterize Western society. This section looks at the analysis of gender inequality and the critiques that have been made of the traditional paradigms for ignoring gender.

Although there are different forms or groupings of feminism, the common thesis is that the relationship between the sexes is one of inequality or oppression. All schools of feminism attempt to identify the causes of gender inequality and to remedy it, but they differ in terms of their beliefs as to which agency produces and reproduces inequality (Macey, 2000). Feminist critiques are primarily concerned with two themes: (1) the ways in which the gendered nature of social institutions and practices have been ignored and gender neutrality has been assumed in traditional social science literature; and (2) the ways in which issues of particular importance to women have been marginalized or excluded from the social welfare agenda (Woodward, 1997).

Feminists draw attention to the fact that women experience a different social world—including the welfare state—than men. The differences experienced by women in the Canadian context are very similar to those of other Anglo-democracies.

- Women have the greatest responsibility for the family, including child care and elder care (i.e., women are "cradle-to-the-grave" caregivers) (Gazso, 2010).
- Women are disproportionately the victims of male violence (Rosenberg & Duffy, 2010).
- Women are among the poorest groups in Canadian society. Women over 65, women living with disabilities, Aboriginal women, and lone mothers are among Canada's poorest (Statistics Canada, 2014).
- In 2014, women comprised 50.1 per cent of the population of Canadians 55 to 59 years of age, increasing to 63 per cent for people 85 to 89 years of age and 72 per cent for those 90 years of age and over (Statistics Canada, 2015).
- Women still experience occupational segregation in many sectors of the labour force and receive lower earnings, benefits, and pensions (Statistics Canada, 2017).
- Women remain significantly under-represented in legislatures, cabinets, the courts, and senior levels of public services and business corporations. In the 2015 federal election, Canadian voters elected 88 female Members of Parliament (MPs), putting female representation in the House of Commons at 26 per cent—only a 1 per cent increase over the 2011 election results (*Globe and Mail*, 2016).
- There are gender inequalities with respect to access to social programs, benefit levels, rights, and redistributive outcomes. For example, the neo-liberal state views women as principally responsible for social reproduction yet fails to provide the necessary supports to engage in this work (access to publicly funded daycare, a public prescription/medication plan, pay equity, and so on) (Smith-Carrier, 2017).
- Women experience more adversely the results of cutbacks to social services.

The paradigms and political ideologies presented in Chapters 3–6 were, of course, all constructed by men and reflect the world as seen and experienced by men. This male construction includes the four welfare models as well. For example, although the four welfare models fall along the traditional left-to-right political ideological spectrum, they all feature a male breadwinner, a female bread-maker, and a dependent family. One of the key contributions of the feminist movement has been its recognition that "the personal is political" (and vice versa), which has helped to break down the traditional treatment of separating the private individual or family from political influences. Another common assumption underpinning all four paradigms is the belief in the maintenance of the family as integral to society's stability. This belief forms part of what feminists call the ideology of "familism" (Neysmith, 1991; Williams, 1989), which comprises a set of ideas that characterize the "'normal' or 'ideal' family form as one where the man was the main breadwinner and his wife's main contribution to the family was through her role as mother, carer, and housewife rather than as a wage-earner and who was therefore, along with her children, financially dependent upon her husband" (Williams, 1989, p. 6). Families not conforming to this normal family model are thus viewed as somewhat deviant and potentially problematic.

Although all feminists may agree on the existence of gender inequalities, they are fundamentally divided on the causes of these inequalities and on the strategies for effecting social change. They also differ on the nature and extent of women's subordination. It is possible to subdivide feminism into a large number of categories or schools. Williams (1989), for example, uses six categories. Here, three schools of feminism are outlined: liberal feminism, socialist feminism, and radical feminism. These groupings are consistent with the categorization that many other writers use (e.g., Armitage, 2003; Knuttila & Kubik, 2000; Mandell & Johnson, 2017).

It should be noted here that there is no school of "conservative feminism," since the essence of feminism is to do something to rectify women's inequality. There are, of course, conservative women who advocate for a return to the days when women remained in the home as homemakers, abortion was illegal, and feminism did not exist (e.g., a Canadian group that calls itself "REAL Women").

Liberal Feminism

"First-wave" feminism of the nineteenth and early twentieth centuries used the language of liberalism to demand formal equality (equal opportunities and equal civil rights) with men. This first wave focused on social issues, such as temperance, and on gaining the vote for women. Since the 1960s, "second-wave" feminism has sought equality and civil rights, with the emphasis on reforming existing institutions. Calixte, Johnson, and Motapanyane (2010, p. 3) summarize the essence of liberal feminism:

> Liberal feminists take the core principles of liberalism and apply them to inequalities between men and women; they espouse the idea that women should be equally integrated into existing social, political, religious, and economic institutions and that they should enjoy the same benefits that accrue to men. First, liberal feminists, past and present, are concerned with establishing women's capacity for rational thought and thus their shared humanity with men. Second, liberal feminists endorse the concept of meritocracy. These first two principles have been particularly important in shaping the goal of achieving access to formal education for women, largely achieved in Western societies in the early 20th century. Third, liberal feminists are concerned with establishing equality of opportunity for women in all areas of social, economic, legal, and political life. . . . Fourth, freedom of choice is a principle of liberal feminism.

The liberal feminist remedy for gender inequality is to reform (not transform) social and political institutions. Biological differences between men and women are not viewed by liberal feminists as a significant barrier to gender equality. The legal integration of gender into the Canadian Charter of Rights and Freedoms in 1985 was regarded by liberal feminists in Canada as an important milestone for establishing equality rights. However, in 2006 the newly elected Harper Conservative government made significant changes to Status of Women Canada (SWC), the main government organization responsible for ensuring the full participation of women in Canadian society, and the Court Challenges Program (CCP), which ensured disadvantaged groups access to the courts.

> The government has reduced the SWC's overall budget by $5 million; eliminated the $1 million Status of Women Independent Research Fund; removed the term "advancement of equality" from the mandate of the organization; and closed 12 of its 16 regional offices. In addition, for-profit organizations have been granted eligibility for funding, but advocacy and research organizations have been classified as no longer eligible (Knight & Rodgers, 2012, p. 267).

Pam Palmater, a Mi'kmaq lawyer, professor, and activist from Mi'kma'ki, New Brunswick, believes that the Canadian government must amend the Indian Act to end gender and racial discrimination (2014). Indigenous women have experienced some success in using litigation to reverse the discriminations contained in the Indian Act, but litigation is lengthy and costly and even strong claims do not always result in successful outcomes in court. A key problem with using litigation (a key tool of liberal feminism) is that, because courts are tasked with deciding particular conflicts in particular circumstances at particular times, litigation does not lead to consistent incremental progress in a particular direction (Peach, 2011, p. 113).

For example, in December 2017 the Liberal government passed Bill S-3, which was designed to address gender discrimination in the Indian Act. Bill S-3: An Act to Amend the Indian Act (Elimination of Sex-Based Inequities in Registration) was a response to a Supreme Court of Quebec ruling in *Descheneaux v. Canada* (2015), which found that the Indian Act violates the Canadian Charter of Rights and Freedoms based on gender discrimination (https://chiefsofontario.wordpress.com, 2017). The provisions of Bill S-3 are designed to eliminate the gender inequality in the Indian Act, but there is no fixed date for implementation. The Liberal government believes that more consultation is needed with First Nations and other Indigenous groups about issues related to Indian registration, band membership, citizenship, and the future of the Indian Act. For many First Nations women, "equality delayed is equality denied" (McIvor, Palmater, & Day, 2017).

Criticisms of Liberal Feminism

Other schools of feminist thought have levelled criticism against liberal feminism (see Mandell & Johnson, 2017; Williams, 1989). (1) Liberal feminism is said to be naive and simplistic because it overlooks the capitalist and patriarchal nature of the state. (2) Liberal feminism fails to see that the status quo, which disadvantages women, benefits men, who are unlikely to surrender their privileged position without resistance. (3) Historically, liberal feminists have restricted their analysis of gender inequality to the public sphere, and by simply pursuing the extension of opportunities in the public sphere they overlook a crucial part of women's lives and ignore the truism that the personal is political. Williams (1989) points out that contemporary liberal feminism has drawn on work (social learning theories) done on the socialization of girls within the private sphere of the home. (4) Liberal feminists seek equality of opportunity in male terms, which fails to account for current gender differences and other structural forces. Women are simply not able to compete equally with men because of the prevailing domestic division of labour and patriarchal assumptions about their caring role. (5) Liberal feminist strategies are criticized as primarily benefiting white, highly educated middle-class women and having little relevance to women living in poverty and/or racialized women. (6) Both socialist and radical feminist groups point out that although women have proved the irrationality of women's inequality in the face of liberal ideas of justice, equality, and liberty, very little change has been achieved by law or state reform.

Although liberal feminism is criticized by other feminist schools, its strongest point might be its commitment to action for social justice. It has brought about reforms in the public sphere such as the workplace, education, wages, pensions, civil and social rights, and so on. It has developed various strategies for social change that have been adopted by other feminist groups (although for different reasons). However, while such reforms are necessary to improve women's lives in the here and now, they are not sufficient in themselves. They have helped to ameliorate the position of (some) women in society, but as with liberalism in general, liberal feminism has done very little to address such structural forces as classism, patriarchy, and racism in society. "Reforms and laws cannot undermine the institutionalization of women's oppression within the very structures of the labour market, the family, education system and the welfare state" (Williams, 1989, p. 47). These shortcomings have resulted in many feminists looking elsewhere for analyses, theories, and strategies that address structural causes of gender inequality.

Socialist Feminism

Socialist feminism covers a range of political strategies, but in general it is influenced by social democratic and Marxist thought as well as by liberal feminist ideas. Socialist feminism provides a materialist analysis of gender inequality by identifying the relationship between patriarchal oppression and class relations in capitalist economic systems (Calixte et al., 2010). However, it does not consider women's oppression a simple subset of the overall oppression of the working class. Williams (1989, p. 57) articulates the caution socialist feminists have about classical Marxism:

> socialist feminists have also been critical of classical Marxism for ignoring the significance of the specific oppression of women, and of the practices of socialist groups and organizations representing the working class, especially the trade unions, for seeing the struggles by women against aspects of oppression as irrelevant or "dividing the working class."

Marxist feminists examine women's relationship to work, both in the home and in the labour market, since one of the central functions of capitalism is to take advantage of the labour of workers for profit. Although Marxist feminism explains the gendered division of labour, it does not explain why these gendered roles occurred in the first place. Socialist feminists seek to explain the oppression of women to include an analysis of gender inequality. For example, contemporary socialist feminist analyses have focused on the role of gender in globalization (Calixte et al., 2010). Socialist feminists critique the "global care chain," which is characterized by the migration of women from less economically developed regions of the world because of the negative consequences of structural adjustment programs (a set of stringent economic policies often introduced as a condition for gaining a loan from the International Monetary Fund), to wealthy countries such as Canada to work in the agricultural, sex, and domestic service industries. "A complicated set of dynamics, involving rigid immigration and labour rights restrictions, perpetuates and compounds the vulnerability of women in these domains" (Calixte et al., 2010, p. 20). The development of information-oriented economies has also led to more precarious work for women, characterized by lack of job security, part-time employment, temporary work, on-call work, low wages, few benefits, and the absence of union representation.

There is contentious debate within socialist feminism about the forms of practice it ought to take. However, with respect to theoretical development, Williams (1989) summarizes a few areas of general agreement: the importance of understanding that the differences between men's and women's behaviour are socially constructed and not biologically caused; the necessity of recognizing the personal as political; and the significance, for solidarity, of recognizing the different as well as shared experiences of oppression of women of different classes, races, ages, sexual orientation, and so on. With respect to forms of practice, she notes the following types of advances made by socialist feminists:

- In relation to welfare strategies, many socialist feminists have put their energies into women's groups and organizations fighting for improved health, housing, income security, child and elder care, education, and employment services.
- Many socialist feminists have joined social democratic political parties and have campaigned for women's issues to become part of their socialist party's platform.
- Many socialist feminists have been elected to work within trade unions, especially within the public sector. For example, in Canada Shirley Carr, who became the first female president of the Canadian Labour Congress (and the first woman in the world to head a national labour organization), championed legislation to address women's equality, maternity leave, child care, sexual harassment, and concerns about health and safety in the workplace.

Williams (1989, p. 68) argues that socialist feminism is the most fruitful of the feminist approaches because it draws attention to women's dual role and demands "the reorganization of the sexual division of labour and an end to the divisions between paid and unpaid work." In terms of the welfare state, this means changing the concept of welfare so that it no longer underpins female dependency or the sexual division of labour whereby caring is viewed as women's natural work and it no longer privileges the male breadwinner/head of household model of the family. Socialist feminists do disagree as to the greatest source of women's oppression—capitalism or patriarchy or the interface of the two—and they also differ in their analyses as to the root of patriarchy (see Williams, 1989, pp. 57–69, for a discussion of these important questions).

Radical Feminism

One group—radical feminists—believes that neither the liberal feminist nor the socialist feminist approach is radical enough. Liberals focus on reforming social institutions and practices by changing sexist values, norms, and ideas; socialists argue for a fusion of class analysis with an understanding of female oppression in a patriarchal social system. Radicals, however, believe that they both miss the fundamental form of oppression experienced by women—that women as a class or group are oppressed by men as a class or group (Robbins, Chatterjee, & Canda, 1998). The term "sexual politics" (Millett, 1970) has been used to describe unequal power relations between men and women, and patriarchy is considered the primary source of women's oppression both personally and institutionally.

Patriarchy has been defined in two ways by radical feminists—male power and control over women's sexuality and male power and control over women's biology in terms of their reproductive capacity (Williams, 1989). Regarding sexuality, radical feminism holds that throughout history men have constructed and controlled women's bodies to serve their own needs and interests. The possibility of male violence serves as the perpetuation of male domination over women by force. This analysis has been behind feminist campaigns against male violence (e.g., "take back the night" marches), war, nuclear proliferation, pornography, and incest (Williams, 1989).

> Radical feminists see our societies as violent and male-dominated, a world in which cultural representations of women include those of prostitution, pornography, and rape. Radical feminists argue that eliminating patriarchal society is the only viable solution to ending inequality. Patriarchy is sustained by men maintaining relationships with one another and thus ensuring that their power and privilege is maintained through interlocking systems of oppression such as racism, classism, and women's sexual oppression. Radical feminists, especially lesbian and cultural feminists[1] suggest that women divest themselves of patriarchy by strengthening bonds among women and by removing themselves from patriarchy's grip (Calixte et al., 2010, p. 25).

The second radical definition of patriarchy, which sees it as the fundamental class oppression giving rise to other forms of oppression, was first discussed in Shulamith Firestone's powerful treatise, *The Dialectic of Sex: The Case for Feminist Revolution* (1970). For Firestone, the basis of class is biological, and one class (males) has dominated the other class (females) throughout history largely because of women's biological role in species reproduction. Because of the biological processes of childbirth, women are forced to depend on men for long periods of time, which has resulted in the emergence of larger patterns of male domination and female subordination. Thus, the abolition of patriarchy can only be possible by relieving women of their biological reproductive role by every means possible—family planning, abortion, 24-hour childcare centres, artificial reproduction (Firestone, 1984).

Radical feminism has made important contributions to feminist theory and political action. It has drawn attention to problems that other feminist perspectives do not emphasize—for example, rape, domestic violence, sexuality, and reproductive technologies. It emphasizes "the personal is political" analysis as a guiding principle more than other feminisms. Some radical feminist positions developed out of what is called the "woman-centred" stage of second-wave feminism (Lerner, 1979, cited in Woodward, 1997). This position gave priority to women's experience as the focus of all study and the source of social and cultural values. For example, a critique of motherhood was a major concern of some radical feminists in the 1970s (e.g., Rich, 1977) who, on the one hand, celebrated motherhood as an essentially female experience but, on the other hand, critiqued it as a social institution under patriarchy that distorted women's experiences. In the 1980s and 1990s, radical feminists extended Millet's concept of patriarchy as sexual politics to include heterosexism as a source of female oppression (Rich, 1980; Jeffreys, 1986, cited in Woodward, 1997). The women-centred approaches of radical feminists have been instrumental in establishing separate social services provided by women for women, such as women's shelters, and in challenging the sexism of the medical profession by establishing "well-women" clinics and health centres where women can be treated by a female doctor and where the emphasis is on the provision of information to women about their own bodies. Radical feminism has also been important in terms of establishing women-only counselling services for victims of male violence, and these services, in turn, have been important for exposing the patriarchal assumptions held by the police and the courts about female sexuality (Williams, 1989).

Patriarchy in Social Welfare Organizations

Radical feminists (along with socialist feminists) have also critiqued the internal culture of social welfare organizations for its patriarchal nature. Wendy Weeks (1992), a leading feminist social welfare writer in Australia, points out that most public and private welfare organizations have been structured by men and, therefore, tend to be characterized by such male characteristics as: male dominance rather than gender equality; competition and independence rather than cooperation and interdependence; hierarchical rather than flat structures; rational control with an emphasis on technology; and a devaluing of subjective experience (cited in Armitage, 2003). Alternative social services organizations established by feminist social service workers are characterized in varying degrees by a democratic organizational culture:

- participation of workers and service users in decision-making;
- a shared or agreed-upon model of leadership;
- the accommodation of caring responsibilities within the organization's operations and employment policies;
- consensus and discussion as the basis of decision-making rather than decisions being made by those in senior positions within the organization or by majority vote;
- a respectful workplace free from harassment.

The incorporation of these feminist concepts and values has not been easy, since they fly in the face of the patriarchal nature and structure of social services organizations in Western society. However, as Armitage (2003, p. 183) states, "the goal of a more equal and democratic workplace for workers and service users represents an important challenge. If human service organizations cannot produce a more equal and equitable environment in their own sphere of activity, how can they expect to introduce these values to the wider community?"

Criticisms of Radical Feminism

In spite of its contributions to social theory, political action, and the social welfare state and social work practice, radical feminism has been the subject of wide-ranging criticism. A major criticism is that by defining patriarchy in terms of biological differences, radical feminism may have distanced itself from the economic reductionism of Marxism (i.e., explaining women's oppression in terms of the needs and operation of capitalism). Rather, it has fallen victim to biological reductionism, which traps women back into their biology. In other words, radical feminism tends to reduce the complex issue of women's inequality to a simple single explanation—biology. Radical feminism has been accused of creating a "false universalism" by assuming a commonality of interests and positions among women that is at odds with the differences of interest among them with respect to race, culture, class, and so on. The other "false universalism" is derived from the radical feminist definition of patriarchy whereby all men are considered oppressors. Finally, radical feminism has been criticized for being naive or idealist in the extreme because it rests on the hope of social change through the encouragement of woman-centred values and practices to counter and overcome society's dominant male values and practices.

Conclusion

Feminism exposes the glaring omission inherent in all four dominant paradigms—that of a gender analysis of women's inequality in society and of how the state contributes to women's oppression. Included in this analysis is the role that the welfare state has played in this oppression. Feminism challenges the assumed gender neutrality of the paradigms and of the postwar welfare state. "There can be no doubt, then, that the state in capitalist society is vitally important to the construction, production, and reproduction of sex and gender relations" (Knuttila & Kubik, 2000, p. 193). The three feminist perspectives presented above all focus on this common concern but offer different analyses and explanations of women's subordination in society and different strategies for correcting it. In addition to its gender analysis, feminism has developed social theory that includes social and political practice. "It is through campaigns that feminists have put women and women's concerns on the public agenda, and the explanations which feminists offer for what their research and struggles reveal derive from listening to women's voices" (Woodward, 1997, p. 92).

Feminist theory, along with other modernist social theories, has been criticized on a number of fronts. Racialized groups, in particular black feminists, have referred to the above feminist perspectives as "white feminism" because of their omission of race and racism in their analyses of women's oppression. Postmodernism, in general, and postmodern feminists, in particular, have criticized feminism as being a historically and theoretically modernist movement based on such universalisms as a unitary image of woman and for espousing grand narratives in their theory-building. The next section looks at the anti-racist critique of the dominant paradigms, which includes a critique of "white feminism" and the modernist welfare state.

Anti-racist Critique

Just as white feminists critiqued the traditional paradigms and older social theory for being male-dominated, racialized groups have criticized the paradigms and theories for their failure to account for racism. Because the ideologies of conservatism, liberalism, socialism, and Marxism were developed largely in Europe during a period of history when the population of Europe was mainly white and the dominant group (including those who developed these ideologies) consisted mainly of white males, it is little wonder that the ideologies reflect gender and race biases. And just as white feminists criticized these ideologies and their derived social theories for being gender-exclusive, so did racialized women criticize both the ideologies and white feminism for ignoring colour. Although questions about race had bothered feminists through the 1970s, it was not until the 1980s that racialized women became an organized force and introduced a new "radical women of colour" perspective into the feminist public culture (Seidman, 1998). They criticized the dominant political paradigms for reflecting the interest of white, bourgeois males, and they (particularly black women, Latina women, and Indigenous women) criticized the women's movement for focusing on the experiences, values, and interests of white, middle-class women (e.g., Lorde, 1984; Davis, 1981; Moraga & Anzaldua, 1983).

Defining Race and Racism

From the time of the Enlightenment and with the popularization of Darwinian theories of evolution, race became associated with visible biological differences. Physiological characteristics, such as skin colour, facial features, and brain size, were used to identify and/or categorize different "races," and with the development of social Darwinian ideas these characteristics were often used to rank the peoples of the world in an assumed order of superiority and inferiority (Penketh & Ali, 1997). This kind of thinking led to the implementation of eugenicist immigration policies in such countries as the United States and Sweden, which discriminated against certain social groupings such as Jews and racialized groups. Today, we know from the science of genetics that comparative studies of various population groups have shown that there is much more statistically significant genetic diversity within these groups than among them. "To geneticists, the physiological differences associated with 'race' have no more significance than hair or eye colour" (Penketh & Ali, 1997, p. 103).

Because the use of race as a way of categorizing people lacks scientific validity and any evidence from biology, then it is a social construction, a way of making sense of the world by dividing people into assumed biological categories (Thompson, 2016). If there is no scientific basis for the concept of race, why does the term continue to be used? Husband (1987, p. iii) answers this by writing that "one reason for its continuing vitality is that, beneath its apparent simple reduction of complex individuals and societies to self-evidently basic units there lies a highly complex body of emotive ideas." These ideas constitute "racism."

Elsewhere (Mullaly & West, 2018), I (Bob) have described racism as the belief that human abilities are determined by race, that one race is superior to all others and, therefore, has the right to dominate all other races. The assumption that racial classifications can be made based on biological differences underpins racism. Skin colour, for example, may be associated with other biological differences such as intelligence. A partial answer to the question of why we still have such categorizations when there is no scientific validation for doing so is that such classifications carry out certain ideological political functions for the racially dominant group (i.e., white people).

Effects of Racism

The assumption of racial superiority has had substantial negative effects on racialized groups within most European societies and the countries they colonized. Racialized groups are subject to disparaging stereotypes and are oppressed at the personal, cultural, and structural or institutional levels of society (Mullaly & West, 2018). The effects of racism at the personal level include the imposition of an identity by the racially dominant group that is often stereotyped, essentialist, and inferior. On the surface, there appears to be no escape from this negative identity, since racialized individuals are reminded of it every day in their interactions with the dominant white group. There is also a tendency on the part of non-white groups to accept and internalize this socially constructed and imposed identity and to act in ways that reinforce the stereotypical identity in the eyes of white people.

In today's society, there are many cultures but one dominant culture that reflects the norms, values, shared patterns of thinking, and world views of the dominant group (i.e., a white, male, bourgeois group). All other cultures are viewed as inferior, and, therefore, the solution to the problems members of these groups experience could be resolved if they would assimilate into the dominant culture. And, of course, it is rather difficult for a racialized individual to assimilate into the racially dominant white group (see Mullaly & West, 2018, for more discussion on oppression and anti-oppressive social work practice at the cultural level). At the institutional or structural level, recent research on racism in the United States indicates that structural racism and discrimination occurs through mutually reinforcing systems of housing, education, employment, earnings, benefits, credit, media, health care, and criminal justice. "These patterns and practices in turn reinforce discriminatory beliefs, values, and the distribution of resources" (Bailey et al., 2017, p. 1453). Elsewhere (Mullaly & West, 2018), I (Bob) summarize the effects of racism experienced by Indigenous people in Canada and make the argument that racism in particular and oppression in general at the structural level constitute a form of *socially sanctioned violence*. This "structural violence" leads to a slow, agonizing, unpunished, and premature death for countless numbers of subordinate people all over the world on a daily basis. In Chapter 9 we elaborate on this concept of "structural violence."

There are three major responses to race and racism in the literature: assimilation, multiculturalism, and anti-racism (or the politics of difference). The first two are based on an assumed notion that the dominant white culture is superior to all others. Assimilation would have all other cultures and races reject their own cultures and accept and integrate, as much as possible, into the dominant culture. Multiculturalism accepts and may even celebrate the idea of a plurality of cultures in today's society, but there is still a superior culture to which all others must defer. This is reflected, for example, in the Canadian Constitution, which specifically recognizes the languages of the two "founding" peoples—French and English—as "official" while "the preservation and enhancement of the multicultural heritage of Canadians" is also claimed as a societal value (Constitution Act, 1982, sections 16, 27). Similarly, the anti-racist approach accepts that there are many different cultures in society, but it differs from multiculturalism in that the fundamental belief is that there are no superior or inferior cultures. Cultural differences should be celebrated, and cultural equality must be pursued. These approaches are discussed in more detail and in the context of structural social work practice in Chapter 8.

Criticisms of Black Feminism

The criticisms of white-dominated feminism from black feminists in the 1980s were important for the development of feminist theory, feminist strategy, and, therefore, for the feminist critique of the welfare state. Williams (1989, p. 69) notes that

> [a] significant amount has been written articulating the experiences of Black women, how their relationship to work, the family, men, sexuality, reproduction, the state, including the welfare state, is structured by *"race"* as well as by gender, and how this renders their experiences different from those of white women.

Racialized women argued that they not only suffered from oppression as women but also as racialized individuals and often as people living in poverty as well. The simultaneous experiences of black women with respect to sexism, racism, and classism not only compounded these oppressions but reconstituted them in specific ways. For example, white feminists who enjoy the privileges of "whiteness" and bourgeois social standing could afford, economically and politically, to pursue a separatist agenda. Black women, however, cannot pursue a separatist agenda, since they must forge bonds of solidarity with black men to fight racism and classism (Seidman, 1998).

Black feminists have criticized how the concept of patriarchy has been used in a number of ways.

- It emphasizes women being oppressed as women, which overlooks the differences of power between women, particularly the racism of some white women and the racism of the state along with its sexism.
- White women have greater access to society's power structure (e.g., to the courts) than do racialized women.
- The patriarchy of black men cannot be equated with that of white men. There is more solidarity between white men and white women than there is between white males and black males.
- The white feminist criticism of the family as a site of oppression is not as appropriate to the experience of blacks, where the black family has been the site of resistance in struggles against slavery and current struggles such as against police brutality, discrimination in housing and employment, and so on (Williams, 1989).

Black feminists did not wish to subvert the core status of the category of women but sought to make it more inclusive by expanding the range of legitimate identities that women could claim (Seidman, 1998). Instead of a unitary female identity, black feminism led to a diversity of feminist standpoints—each reflecting a particular class and racial positioning of women. Racialized feminist women sought to expand the category of "women" to include them by viewing gender, class, and race as interconnected.

Conclusion

Just as feminism exposed the glaring omission in the dominant paradigms of a gender analysis of women's inequality and the ways that the state contributed to women's oppression, so, too, did racialized groups (particularly black feminists) expose the omission of a race analysis of inequality along lines of race and how the state contributed to the oppression of racialized groups. Furthermore, while black feminism criticized mainstream feminism for assuming colour neutrality, the 1980s lesbian feminism also criticized mainstream feminism for its heterosexual leanings and argued against the dichotomous nature of female and male sexual values and for expanded sexual expression and choice for women. By the mid-1980s, a multitude of voices spoke about women's social differences. "New feminist identities surfaced: women of colour, working class women, sadomasochistic lesbians, and postcolonial women" (Seidman, 1998, p. 263). They all criticized mainstream feminism for repressing women's differences and for imposing controls on women's bodies and behaviours. Third-wave feminism continues to deconstruct the category of "woman" and seemingly clear-cut notions of identity. Many feminists argue that third-wave feminism in the West has come about because of black women's critiques of white feminism (Karaian & Mitchell, 2010, p. 64). The third wave of feminism still considers many of the issues politicized by the second wave, such as violence against women, job equity, reproductive rights, and poverty, but third-wave feminists believe that there is also a need to examine complexities, intersectionality, and fluidity within the feminist movement.

> Mainstream feminism was criticized for functioning as a disciplining, normalizing force that reinforced dominant Eurocentric, middle class, White social norms. Drawing on the poststructural critique of essentialism and foundationalism, a new social and cultural force in feminist cultural politics was born: postmodern feminism (Seidman, 1998, p. 264).

Postmodern Critique

Postmodernism, Social Welfare, and Social Work

The application of postmodern ideas to institutions such as the welfare state, which define modernism, can cause confusion. The position taken here is similar to that of other writers, including Ben Agger (1992; 1998), Peter Leonard (1997), and John Rodger (2000). In this view, postmodernism is not a fully developed or coherent or singular theoretical perspective but a critique of modernity and modernist thought. This does not mean a total condemnation and rejection of modernism. Rather, postmodernism provides an essential ingredient to inform and revitalize progressive social thought such as social democracy, Marxism, feminism, and anti-racism. The modernist project of emancipation (i.e., to resist and overcome domination) is not over. It continues, as Leonard (1997, p. xiii) states, "under changed historical conditions—economic, cultural, social—and with a newly reflective ability . . . to understand the contradictions of emancipatory projects of the past as well as that of the present." A major purpose here, then, is to show how postmodernism can contribute to a reconstructed project of emancipation as it is still expressed within socialist, feminist, anti-racist, anti-oppressive, and other struggles against domination. In other words, although postmodernism does not replace modernist progressive thought, it supplements, corrects, informs, and revitalizes modernism.

Unfortunately, there has been a general reluctance among social work and social policy writers to engage with postmodernism. Carter (1998) has suggested that social policy is just about the last social science to take up the postmodern challenge. Commenting on the lack of postmodern material in social policy studies, John Rodger (2000, p. 15) writes:

> Ideological concepts common in the lexicon of social policy analysis such as neo-liberalism, democratic socialism, welfare pluralism and collectivism all lack a referent to the wider social and cultural influences which are at work in determining the shape of a future welfare society. While students of social policy have become accustomed to making sense of the welfare state debate through the clash of neo-liberal and socialist politics, they have been slow to recognise that the debate has moved on from a polarised choice between state or market.

Both Carter and Rodger call for social policy students to engage with the substantial postmodern literature that describes contemporary social change and sensitizes us to the social, economic, political, and, especially, cultural context within which social policies are being formulated for the twenty-first century. The nature of society and politics is changing, and we need to engage with ideas that until recently have not been familiar to students of social policy and social work. Writers in Britain (e.g., Howe, 1994; Parton, 1994) and Australia (e.g., Pease & Fook, 1999) took up the postmodern challenge earlier than their North American counterparts. Notable exceptions in Canada are Adrienne Chambon and Allan Irving (1994), Chambon, Irving, and Epstein (1999), and Peter Leonard (1994; 1995; 1997).

Surprisingly, many contemporary social welfare and social work writers openly reject postmodernism as having any potential for understanding social welfare formations or contributing to social work knowledge. Writing from Australia, Fitzpatrick (2002, p. 14) and Mendes (2003, p. 5) argue that postmodernism is relegated "to sit on the sidelines of social conflicts, rather than promoting collective campaigns for social and economic justice." Similarly, some British writers (e.g., Ferguson & Lavalette, 1999; Philo & Miller, 2000) have accused postmodernism of being in vogue, but "increasingly [it is] recognized as contributing to a moral relativism and a stance of 'ironic detachment' which is untenable in the face of the economic and ecological crisis facing humanity" (Ferguson, Lavalette, & Mooney, 2002, p. 15). The noted Canadian social welfare writer Andrew Armitage (2003) claims that postmodernism is a recent form of socialism, which I am sure horrifies postmodernists, since one of their fundamental beliefs is the rejection of all grand narratives or totalizing ideological schemes such as capitalism and socialism. Armitage says of postmodernism, "The critique of welfare institutions by the postmodernists is searching but the conclusions tend to endorse an anarchy that would be a complete contradiction to the concept of a just and peaceful society" (p. 180). Colleen Lundy (2004, p. 43), in her book on structural social work practice, states that it

> remains to be seen the degree to which postmodernism can contribute to the emancipatory project and offer a "solution" to social work practice and social problems in our society. In my view, broad-based social change and social justice are more likely to occur through a collective struggle. . . . A focus on subjectivities while retreating from the broader structures will neither serve our profession nor the people we serve.

The second edition of her book (2011) is just as dismissive of postmodernism as the first edition.

Although each of the above writers acknowledges some of the legitimate criticisms that postmodernism has made of the traditional social policy and social work approaches to social change, they all dismiss postmodernism without showing how they would address these criticisms. At the very least, the positions of these writers appear to be based on a lack of awareness that there is more than one form of postmodernism, including a critical postmodernism in which the intention is not to reject all modernist thought or abandon the modernist project of emancipation but to forge links between critical theory (Marxism, feminism, anti-racism, etc.) and postmodernism. It is this critical postmodern perspective that is adopted here. Some of the major criticisms that postmodernism and post-structuralism make of modernist concepts such as paradigms and ideological formations are identified below. Rather than rejecting these criticisms and insights, it is my intention to use them in an attempt to inform and help revitalize modernist progressive social welfare and social work thought.

Postmodern Critique of Modernism

Although a full discussion of modernism and postmodernism is well beyond the purview of this book, a brief outline of some of the major postmodern criticisms of the concept of paradigms is presented here. More discussion of postmodernism will follow in Chapter 8, where postmodernism is brought into a theory of structural social work. The project of modernity, which came into focus toward the end of the eighteenth century, promised that the domination of nature by science and the accumulation of objective, pure knowledge acquired by a rational subject using impartial scientific means would yield freedom from want, scarcity, and so on (Harvey, 1989). Doctrines of equality, liberty, and faith in human intelligence (once educated) abounded. "[T]he intellectual foundation of modernity was a belief in the power of reason over ignorance, order over disorder, and science over superstition that would allow humanity to achieve progress and emancipation" (Mullaly, 2001, p. 307). A selected list of postmodern and post-structural criticisms of modernist thought (including paradigms and ideologies) are contained in Box 7.1 and discussed below.

The rejection of modernist beliefs by postmodern writers, perhaps most notably Michel Foucault, is by now well known. Social theories and philosophical traditions that envisage a universal subject (e.g., the working class, the rational individual), an essential human nature (e.g., self-interested, altruistic), and a global human destiny in which human history is claimed to represent a unilinear and progressive development are rejected by postmodernists (Lemert, 1994, cited in O'Brien & Penna, 1998). Claims to universality, reason, and order often mask the interests of those making them. "Imperialist nations, ruling classes, males, whites, heterosexuals, doctors, psychiatrists [social workers] and criminologists have all claimed that their perspective defines a universal and rational outlook. By doing so they have effectively silenced other nations, other classes, other genders, other races, those of other sexual orientation, patients, the mad and prisoners" (Smith, 1993, p. 31). Because the pursuit of scientific truths in

Box 7.1 *Postmodern/Post-structural Critique of Modernist Ideas*

Postmodernism/Post-structuralism:

- Rejects the idea that there is objective social knowledge containing an absolute truth
- Rejects the idea of an objective, value-free scientific method that makes reality accessible
- Rejects the notion of universalism, such as a universal human subject or a universal set of human needs
- Rejects a belief in "essentialism," such as an essential human nature
- Rejects the myth that modern history reflects a progressive road towards humanist goals
- Rejects attempts to develop overarching frameworks (paradigms, ideologies) or all-encompassing theories (e.g., Marxism) that attempt to establish an underlying reality
- Rejects the notion that there exists a fixed human identity characterized by coherence and unity rather than by fragmentation
- Rejects the binary or oppositional structure of modernist thought
- Criticizes modernist use of language and dominant discourses that reflect dominant–subordinate relationships
- Rejects the notion that power is concentrated (rather than dispersed) and rests within certain areas of the social structure (e.g., the ruling class)

human affairs has at times led to repression and control, postmodernists reject all totalizing belief systems or grand narratives that seek to impose some kind of ideal order on society in the interests of society.

Postmodernism joins with critical social theorists and feminists in criticizing the assumptions that underpin positivism and thus rejects positivism—the collection and analysis of observable "objective" data—as the pre-eminent method for carrying out research. The claim that the only valid research occurs from objective, impartial, unbiased, neutral, rational observation of social phenomena that reveals or creates innocent knowledge, verifiable thanks to rigorous scientific tests, was rejected by critical theorists of the Frankfurt School in the 1950s, by second-wave feminists, by postmodernists, by critical race theorists, by Indigenous scholars, and by researchers from other marginalized groups. These groups have all argued that traditional research draws from a narrow foundation of knowledge based on the social, historical, and cultural experiences of bourgeois white males who have overseen the research enterprise since the beginning of the Enlightenment. The researcher's social location and political commitments are obscured by methodological claims to objectivity and neutrality. Brown and Strega (2005, p. 11) address this point:

> The histories, experiences, cultures, and languages (the "ways of knowing") of those on the margins have been devalued, misinterpreted, and omitted in the academy, where . . . only certain conceptualizations of information are counted as "valid" (objective and therefore authoritative) knowledge. In this process, many ways of knowing, which Foucault (1980) referred to as "subjugated knowledges," have been excluded or trivialized.

Although critical social theory, which is associated with progressive forms of socialism and underpins progressive forms of social work, shares with postmodernism many of the same criticisms of positivism, Strega (2005) criticizes it for its continuing commitment to the idea that reality can be uncovered (e.g., socialism is superior to capitalism; people are social animals rather than desert islands). Thus, it implicitly continues to support hierarchical dualisms and the inequities engendered in these dualisms.

Bastow and Martin (2003) point out that global warming along with environmental disasters such as Chernobyl undermined the belief in the mastery and control of nature by science and led many to believe that unfettered economic production and consumption were leading to ecological devastation. Furthermore, the whole premise of uninterrupted economic growth, which all traditional paradigms require to fund either the expansion of business (neo-conservatism) or the expansion of the welfare state (liberalism and social democracy), has been called into question by postmodernists and others.

The notion of an essential "human nature" is rejected by postmodernists and poststructuralists. The dominant modernist paradigms, adherents claim, have positive essences or core characteristics that give them a true and independent meaning and/or identity outside the interpretation of a specific discourse (Rorty, 1999, cited in Bastow & Martin, 2003). Postmodernists argue that an essential human nature exists only within the discourse of each paradigm and that this essential human nature varies from paradigm to paradigm. Such essentialist thought makes all human beings the same, and, therefore, they should all be treated the same, no matter what differences may exist with respect to time, social context, culture, or other social characteristics. Postmodernists argue that ways of thinking and acting are produced by a network of social forces within which we are immersed rather than by some innate characteristic of the individual. The individual or subject is not an autonomous self-producing agent but a product of changing culture and discursive fields (Ashe, 1999). Post-structuralism starts from the assumption that no fully formed or complete identities pre-exist social interactions. Rather, individuals occupy a plurality of shifting and overlapping identities (the workplace, the home, political struggle, the legal system, gender, class, age, sexuality, race, and so on) that construct them in relation to others through different discourses and changing conditions. Workers, for example, have modified the meaning of what it is to be an employee through struggles that have changed social relations in the workplace (Bastow & Martin, 2003). Similarly, various social service–user movements have changed the meaning of what it is to be a "client" of certain social services organizations.

Postmodern Critique of Modernist Epistemology

The modernist notion that a (different) set of rational assumptions underpins each paradigm is also rejected by postmodernists. For example, each paradigm assumes in a different manner that the totality of society can be objectively understood and that social division or conflict exists because of a failure to recognize the rational order beneath the surface of the conflict. Postmodernists reject such assumptions because they contain oppressive political implications. The idea that there is some "true" understanding of society "legitimises the coercion of those unwilling to recognise the validity of such claims" (Bastow & Martin, 2003, p. 148). This can lead to the logic that people must be forced to be free (e.g., the Marxist concept of "dictatorship of the proletariat" or the neo-conservative goal of freeing people from government providing health and education services to them).

Post-structural critics of modernist epistemology have highlighted and critiqued the "binary" or "oppositional" structure of Western thought, arguing that it is based on a series of prejudicial dualisms, such as mind/body, public/private, reason/emotion, culture/nature, human/animal, white/non-white, man/woman, rich/poor, straight/gay, and so on. The terms contained in these dualisms are held to be opposites, mutually exclusive, and logically contradictory, since one cannot be both at once. Dualisms thus exclude all kinds of other possibilities that do not fall neatly into one of the two fixed meanings of the dualism. And, as Lloyd (1999) points out, they also contain an implicit value judgment whereby the first term is more highly valued than the second. Thus, binary oppositionals not only restrict our thinking and our identities, they do so by establishing hierarchies. Post-structuralists call for more fluid understandings of these concepts. For example, the post-structural feminist Judith Butler (1990) suggests that instead of the binary structure of gender (male/female), we work with the notion of a multiplicity of genders, which introduces these concepts as social constructions rather than as natural constructions. Deconstructionism would be the tool used to expose the hierarchical, binary oppositions and rhetorical devices that produce claims to truth and reality. Some examples of binary oppositions that form part of the dominant paradigms are: capitalism/socialism, competition/cooperation, statutory welfare/voluntary welfare, individualism/community, and free market/government intervention.

For example, the dominant discourse in many schools of social work in Canada, the US, and Australia, and among many social work educators, includes "general systems theory" and/or "ecological models" as core social work knowledge in spite of 30 years of damning critique (more about this in Chapter 8). Use of these borrowed concepts represents an appropriation of material from biology that appeals to the authority of "science" (i.e., an incontestable, authoritative truth) to create the appearance that social work is based on hard science. In this way, the possibility of developing alternative theories and practices (such as structural social work or feminist social work) is reduced because they are not scientific enough.

Traditional social science tended to believe that language simply reflected reality and that knowledge was obtained and/or given through language. However, postmodernism and post-structuralism have helped to show us that there are many realities, not one universal reality, and that language does not have the properties of absolute truth but is historically, culturally, socially, and politically contextualized. Language is not politically neutral, as evidenced by Howe's (1994, p. 522) summary of the relationship between power and language. Whereas modernist beliefs contended that increasing knowledge of the essential and true nature of things produced power, postmodernism reversed the process: "Those with power can control the language of the discourse and can therefore influence how the world is to be seen and what it will mean. Language promotes some possibilities and excludes others; it constrains what we see and what we do not see."

A Postmodern Analysis of Disability

A postmodern analysis of disability reveals how changing social and cultural forces work to "construct" the concept of the "disabled" person. Oliver and Barnes (2012) cite the work of Foucault and his analysis of mental health issues to demonstrate how the idea of disability as individual pathology becomes possible only when there is an idea of individual ablebodiedness/mindedness. "A key feature of medicalization and the personal tragedy theory[2] of disability is the assertion that 'able-bodied/mindedness' is 'normal'" (Oliver & Barnes, 2012, p. 88). To become more normal, the disabled person is expected to undergo medical treatment, rehabilitation, or psychotherapy. The issue of adjustment then becomes the focus of professional intervention at the individual level and serves to reinforce ideological and cultural constructions of disability by rooting them in practice, ignoring issues of social prejudice and discrimination (Oliver, 1990).

The concept of normalcy originates in the development in the nineteenth century of the concept of the "normal man" by Adolphe Quetelet (1796–1874), a social statistician (DePoy & Gilson, 2011, p. 23) and in the development of measures of central tendencies in statistics by Sir Francis Galton, a cousin of Charles Darwin (Davis, 2014). Davis argues that Galton devised the notion of quintiles in which the fourth and fifth quintiles became the location of desirable human traits; height, strength, and intelligence. It was Galton who first coined the term "eugenics" to refer to the science of improving the human germ plasm through better breeding (Kerr & Shakespeare, 2002, cited in Oliver & Barnes, 2012, p. 92).

Galton utilized the concept of the normal curve and normality to camouflage what he actually wanted, which was a bigger, smarter, stronger, more dominant human being that corresponded to the putative traits of the dominant social and political classes in a racialized and sexist society. Seeming to be an ideology of democracy and utilitarianism, the norm actually acted as a rationale for rule by elites. . . . The mythos of the normal body has created the conditions for the emergence and subjection of the disabled body, the raced body, the gendered body, the classed body, the geriatric body—and so on (Davis, 2014, p. 3).

Perceptions of disabled people's abnormality were later countered with the idea of "normalization" in which disabled people were encouraged to adopt the patterns and conditions of everyday life as closely as possible to established societal norms and patterns. In North America, Wolf Wolfensberger (2003) drew on deviance and labelling theory to develop a more theoretical and scientific discourse referred to as "Social Role Valorization." Oliver and Barnes (2012, p. 91) contend that the emphasis on changing the appearance and behaviour of people with impairments in order for them to "fit in" to society met with extensive criticism for a number of reasons: (1) normalization theory ignores differences in terms of age, gender, class, and race within and across marginalized groups; (2) emphasis on changing the behaviour and attitudes of marginalized individuals so that they can appear more "normal" does not question the prevailing assumption of normalcy; and (3) normalization does not diminish the impact of professional authority over the lives of disabled people.

Discourse

A related concept to language is that of "discourse." Discourse is a term widely used and variously interpreted. In modernist usage, it usually refers to talking or to a way of talking within a circumscribed area of discussion, as in a "discourse about the economy," or is used to delineate how a topic is discussed, as in "social work or other professional discourse" (Strega, 2005). Discourse, in this way, is considered a way for people to discuss a particular topic, with its role in producing, reproducing, or transforming social structures, relations, and identities being overlooked (Fairclough, 1992, cited in Strega, 2005). Discourse, however, includes not only language but the rules governing the choice and use of language and how the ideas and language will be framed (Mullaly & West, 2018). A discourse is a framework of thought, meaning, and action (Thompson, 1998) that does not reflect knowledge, reality, or truth but creates and maintains them. "Knowledge," according to Foucault, is produced by discourse—it is "the way in which power, language, and institutional practices combine at historically specific points to produce particular ways of thinking" (Featherstone & Fawsett, 1994, cited in Stainton & Swift, 1996, p. 77).

With respect to ideology, each ideology or paradigm has its own discourse that consists of a set of assumptions about the social world. And although there is always more than one discourse at any particular time, one discourse usually dominates. The dominant discourse(s) today largely reflects the interests of global capitalism, patriarchy, and people of European descent. And, as Agger (1989) points out, even our textbooks are largely written within this dominant discourse.

The knowledge presented in the social science literature assists in the reproduction of the existing social order through: (1) the incorporation of ideas that support the current socio-economic-political-cultural order; and (2) the suppression and/or marginalization of scholarship that seeks to challenge or transform it (Wachholz & Mullaly, 2000).

> By virtue of being developments of modernist thought, the welfare state and social work have also been subject to postmodern critique. Because the world is characterized by diversity, multiplicity, pluralism, and conflict rather than by sameness, unity, monism, and consensus, postmodernists believe that no group should try to define the reality, needs, interests, or experiences of another group. The welfare state and social work have tended to overlook differences and diversity and have, instead, carried out policies and practices of homogenization, exclusion, bureaucratic control and surveillance, hierarchical decision-making and professional expertise. A cornerstone of postmodernism is its concern for language and discourse. It criticizes modernism for its use of dominant discourses that reflect class, gender, race, and other forms of dominant–subordinate relationships and it criticizes professions, such as social work, for controlling the discourse of their practices by using pathological, diagnostic, and professional vocabularies that exclude and disempower service users (Mullaly, 2001, p. 307).

Queer Theory and Discourse

During the gay and lesbian civil rights movement in America in the 1970s and 1980s, activists began to question essentialist identity categories based on sexuality, which ignored other social factors such as class, age, race, ethnicity, or ability (Motschenbacher & Stegu, 2013). Queer Theory challenges the essentialist assumptions underlying identity categories, such as male/female and homosexual/heterosexual and is concerned with changing the dominant discourses that shape our understanding of gender and sexuality. The term "queer" has been reclaimed from being a pejorative word to one denoting a distinct culture and a politicized way of representing marginalized groups who do not wish to assimilate into mainstream heteronormative culture (Mulé, 2015). "Although not fully agreed upon within queer communities, *queer* is defined here as inclusive of non-normative sexual orientations and gender identities and expressions" (Mulé, 2015, p. 18).

Assignment of gender categories such as homosexual and heterosexual emerged out of scientific discourses on sexuality in the late nineteenth century (Auger & Krug, 2013). At that time, scientific discourse on sexuality was developed to divide humanity into two exclusive categories, male and female, with opposite but complementary characteristics. These essentialist assumptions were used to formulate an understanding of sexual relationships and how sexual behaviour associated with each gender contributed to the continuation of the species. Aberrant behaviour became indicative of aberrant individuals, and scientific discourses on "normal" and "perverted" sexual practices linked sexuality and biology as essential components of identity (Foucault, 1978, cited in Auger & Krug, 2013). Auger and Krug (2013) point out that contemporary sociobiologists continue to follow the same chain of assumptions by examining chromosomes and hormones to find explanations for diverse human behaviours.

Queer Theory is an umbrella term for various approaches that have a critical focus on heteronormativity. "The long-term goal of Queer Theory is the reconceptualizing of dominant discourses which shape our understanding of gender and sexuality, often to the detriment of people who, for various reasons, are judged as not meeting the heteronormative ideal" (Motschenbacher & Stegu, 2013, p. 520). The linguistic construction of heteronormativity favours heterosexuality in general, as well as specific forms of heterosexuality that normatively structure people's behaviours. For example, in heterosexual relationships the two partners are normatively required to be a female and male but also may include normative assumptions about the ages of the individuals who should be in a relationship, race, religion, and so on. Queer Theory views all identity categories as problematic, since they regulate and exclude people, and asks the question: why must anyone construct an identity out of behavioural patterns or a person's biological makeup in the first place (Motschenbacher & Stegu, 2013)?

Postmodernism, Paradigms, and Ideology

In the past three decades, a revival of interest in ideologies has occurred, which reflects the fact that ideology has not come to an end, as Daniel Bell (1965) had argued in the 1960s. Nor have we reached the "end point of mankind's [*sic*] ideological evolution" (i.e., that capitalist or liberal democracy has won the competition for ideological pre-eminence for all times), as Fukuyama (1992, p. xi) argued in the 1990s. "Instead, the ideological frames through which people interpret and experience their world are recognised increasingly as an ever-present feature of modern life. . . . As such, ideologies are rooted in social relations of power, and seek either to legitimise existing social orders or to delegitimise them" (Bastow & Martin, 2003, p. 15).

Part of the revival of interest in ideologies, however, has been the emergence of *discourse theory*, which offers a way of studying ideologies different from the traditional analysis of major political concepts. Instead of analyzing ideological formations according to how they look at such notions as "human nature" (e.g., individual vs social), universal values (e.g., cooperation vs competition), and "great books" (e.g., *Das Kapital* vs *The Wealth of Nations*), discourse theory does not limit itself to dominant political traditions and the theoretical arguments over preferred social and political arrangements derived from these traditions. Discourse theory recognizes "that the world is made meaningful not simply by political concepts and ideals but also by popular notions, common sense values, and often quite irrational prejudices about peoples and their innate characteristics that are rarely formulated as ideologies" (Bastow & Martin, 2003, p. 4). Proponents of discourse theory such as Bastow and Martin (2003, pp. 16–17) argue that the focus of analysis is "more on the contingent, open-ended and contestable features of discourse than on stable, relatively closed and incontestable features of ideologies."

It would seem, then, that discourse analysis enables us to rethink the nature of political ideologies and paradigms. Rather than being guided by fixed and immutable symbolic frameworks, discourse analysis opens up further possibilities for defining the world and seeing how to change it. In brief, discourse analysis requires us to "think outside the box" to discover new connections and relationships between ideas. Discourse theory allows us to deconstruct ideologies to see how their assumed essentialisms are in fact contingent and relational. This helps us to consider possibilities that fall outside traditional ideological frameworks. It also helps us to examine the relationships (i.e., shared ideas and patterns of understanding) among them. For example, an assumption of economic progress and rationality underpins both socialist and liberal ideologies (Bastow & Martin, 2003). Discourse theory is useful, as well, in exposing any discriminatory or oppressive ideas and beliefs that may underpin a dominant discourse. And we can develop "counter-discourses" based on the ideals of equality, fairness, and social justice.

Other postmodern correctives to our progressive (socialist and Marxist) paradigms include using postmodern thought to inform and revitalize the modernist ideal of emancipation. Peter Leonard (1997, p. 28) argues that, consistent with postmodernism, the narrative or discourse of emancipation must be one of uncertainty—"a story without guarantees as to the outcome." However, a universal discourse of justice and equality has always been central to the historical emancipatory struggles against domination. Leonard counters the postmodern rejection of these universalisms by pointing out that they are socially constructed and culturally produced within a specific historical period of short duration. "They are, therefore, culturally relative and are not necessarily shared, even as ideals, by other cultures." Postmodernism fosters the idea that other culturally produced conceptions of human well-being, such as African, Indigenous, Asian, and so on, can take their place alongside those of the Euro-centred West. Of this Leonard says:

> we slowly start to learn that it is possible to think differently than we have previously thought, perceive the world differently, even feel differently. But the fact that the narrative of emancipation is a ship which sails in a sea of different cultures and diverse social conditions enables us, at least, to envisage a process of arriving at some agreed values, which we can call *universal by consent*, and which are established as a result of political struggle which resolves itself in a consensus amongst those striving for emancipation (Leonard, 1997, p. 28).

What might be agreed? Leonard uses the example of the "value of diversity," which immediately provides a critique of social forces in any particular paradigm or otherwise whose objective or function is to attain homogenization or Oneness by disregarding the fact of difference.

Thompson (1998) points out that the postmodern concept of difference has two meanings. First, it is often used to refer to change, development, or movement, or, what Thompson calls difference, flux. In this respect, difference is in opposition to essentialism. Second, it also refers to the multiplicity of social divisions that characterize present-day society. Difference here is seen to be in opposition to normalization—the tendency to impose restrictive social norms at the expense of diversity. Thompson (2016) affirms the value of difference as a source of learning, stimulation, variety, and interest rather than as a source of unfair discrimination against people for being different from the perceived mainstream of society.

The postmodern emphasis on difference includes "cultural diversity" as a value, not just as a concept. Although culture (values, norms, and shared patterns of thought) is discussed in more detail in Chapter 8, it is important to note here that progressive social workers, along with feminists and social activists, have tended to lump culture in with other structural forces as part of the "personal is political" model of social analysis. However, thanks to postmodernism and cultural studies, we now have a better understanding of how culture mediates the effects of the person on the political and the effects of the political on the person. Without a solid understanding of culture and how it mediates these relationships, there is a danger of endorsing an assumed superior culture, thus elevating William Ryan's concept of "blaming the victim" for social problems from the individual level to the cultural level. The "personal is political" model of analysis is extended to include culture as a working model of structural and anti-oppressive social work in Chapters 8 and 9.

Box 7.2 *The Personal Is Political: An Insurmountable Leap of Faith?*

If there is a social work "mantra" at all, it has to be that "the personal is political." This slogan was popularized by the women's movement in the 1970s, although it was first used by African Americans in the 1960s in their struggle for civil, political, and social rights. The profession of social work during the late 1960s and early 1970s was characterized by a tension-filled, often acrimonious split between the clinical stream and the policy stream, the micro and the macro, direct practice and indirect practice, counselling and community development, and so on. Desperate for unification and a common identity, the profession made several attempts at unification: development of a unitary framework or theory base; imposition of a concept borrowed from biology (general systems theory) as core or fundamental knowledge for *all* social work; and implementation of a generalist model of social work education at the BSW level. All attempts failed to unite the profession, which has at one end of its continuum the individual as the unit of analysis and intervention and at the other end all of society (national or global). It is no wonder that social work in the late 1970s and early 1980s latched onto the phrase "the personal is political" like a hungry dog to a bone. Borrowing (a favourite social work pastime) the analysis from the women's movement, social work thought that it had finally secured the unifying mechanism.

"The personal is political" analysis exposed (if not clarified) the link between the individual and society. The individual influenced society and, in turn, was influenced by society. The individual and society were not isolated entities; there was a clear relationship

Continued

of interdependence. You could not understand one without understanding the other. The slogan became a social work homily that permeated (with varied intensity) the social work curriculum. Its recitation could be heard in the classroom, at faculty meetings, at student events, at demonstrations, in general conversation, in arguments, at thesis defences, and so on. Because feminists took the leadership in developing the analysis and putting it into practice, social work courses that focused on gender issues tended to be more advanced in terms of incorporating the analysis into everyday social work practice.

In spite of all this, many social workers, once in the field, still do not put "the personal is political" into practice. To expect social workers to do so is an insurmountable leap of faith—this leap from analysis to practice is too great. By extending "the personal is political" analysis to include the cultural level, the insurmountable leap of faith between the personal and the political perhaps can be reduced. The cultural level is located between the personal and the political and is the cement that reinforces oppression at the personal and structural levels (Mullaly & West, 2018; Thompson, 2016).

Moosa-Mitha (2005) identifies an important post-structural contribution to the theory supporting the traditional socialist paradigms and earlier progressive social work. The binary thinking that is part of the dominant paradigms can be *deconstructed* to move beyond simple dichotomous relationships. For example, binary thinking about oppression assumes the existence of an oppressed and an oppressor. However, a more complex notion of oppression recognizes and acknowledges that a person can be both an oppressor and oppressed at the same time (Mullaly & West, 2018; Razack, 1998, cited in Moosa-Mitha, 2005). This recognition of multiple relationships is associated with the fact that persons occupy more than one social identity and challenges the tendency to essentialize people on the basis of a singular social location or identity, such as class or gender or race. And, as discussed above, essentializing has been part of the dominant paradigms and has been manifest in social policies and social work practices.

As the title of his 1997 book, *Postmodern Welfare: Reconstructing an Emancipatory Project*, suggests, Peter Leonard argues that postmodernism can contribute to a reconstruction of the welfare state as an emancipatory project:

An emancipatory project of welfare under the conditions of late capitalism must turn its face against the kind of totalizing programme which was the ideal of many of the protagonists who established the old welfare state. It cannot be based upon some overall grand *plan*, some new, complete *reorganization* of welfare, because the over-ambitious planning, programming and organization of welfare institutions, its professionals and subjects, produced the paradox that a commitment to welfare resulted, to a large degree, in a system of domination in the interests of exclusion, homogenization and the defence of expert power (p. 163).

Leonard deconstructs the modernist welfare state (a precondition for reconstruction) to reveal our knowledge and beliefs as historically and culturally specific products, which can no longer be legitimated by reference to the universal authority of *reason*. Then, in a most "unpostmodern" way (by his own admission), he suggests some elements of reconstruction:

- "The obligation to acknowledge and, whenever possible, to celebrate difference is a fundamental ethical assumption of a reconstructed welfare project" (p. 164).
- The experiences of clients, patients, and welfare recipients being subjected to the professional gaze of experts with assumed superior knowledge must be de-pathologized and renamed as the effects of racism, classism, sexism, and other discourses and practices of domination.
- To counteract the homogenizing tendency of the welfare state, co-authorship of joint narratives about problems, needs, and claims must be emphasized. Because every narrative is open to interpretation, a dialogue of the interpretations gives priority to the recognition of a diversity of subjects.
- The dominant discourse of welfare is laden with binary classifications such as good mothers and bad mothers, workers and shirkers, deserving and non-deserving, independent and dependent. Discourses on these binaries must be deconstructed to show their exclusionary and oppressive consequences and reconstructed within welfare discourses of emancipation. For example, interdependence is a common experience in all human societies. "A politics of welfare, . . . if it is to be emancipatory, demands a rejection of discourses on dependence and independence and in their place argues for a discourse on *interdependence*" (p. 158).

In sum, postmodernism has much to contribute to our understandings of paradigms or ideological formations, to the idea of welfare as an emancipatory project, and to social work as a vital part of that project. Postmodern contributions to structural social work are the subject of subsequent chapters.

Conclusion

In this chapter, three different critiques of the dominant paradigms and/or ideological formations were presented. Different schools of feminism have criticized all four paradigms for being gender-exclusive. As well, feminism has contributed to the development of critical or progressive social theory in general and to social welfare and social work theory in particular. Similarly, anti-racist or critical race theorists have criticized the paradigms for not including the lived experiences of racialized individuals. They too have contributed to progressive social theory and social work thought and practice. Feminist and critical race theories and analyses have benefited from postmodern insights and ideas with respect to informing, complementing, and supplementing many of their earlier modernist ideas and concepts. Hopefully, progressive social work and social welfare theorists will also benefit from postmodern insights and ideas.

Critical Questions

1. Which school of feminism—liberal, socialist, or radical—do you think that progressive social work should adopt?

2. An argument sometimes heard is that only members of a particular oppressed group can really understand the hardships and problems experienced by that group. Therefore, only members of any particular oppressed group should practise social work with that group. In other words, only female social workers should work with women, only Indigenous social workers should work with Indigenous persons, only social workers from racialized groups should work with persons from racialized groups, and so on. What do you think of this position?

3. Conversely, can social workers from subordinate groups work with members of dominant groups, such as female social workers working with men, Indigenous workers with white people, and so on?

PART II

Structural Social Work Theory and Oppression

8 A Reconstructed Theory of Structural Social Work

We can be for theory or we can be against theory,
but we can never be without theory.

—bob mullaly (2007)

Introduction

A number of elements are presented in this chapter, which, taken together, constitute the theoretical basis and framework for the new structural social work: its socialist ideology; its radical social work heritage; its critical social theory base; its social change perspective; its dialectical analysis; and its conceptual framework that incorporates and integrates these components into a transformative and emancipatory form of social work practice. In the present edition, these elements are reconceived in light of the postmodern, feminist, and anti-racist ideas discussed in Chapter 7.

Socialist Ideology

Returning to the four societal paradigms discussed in Chapters 3–6, we will now try to answer the question posed at the end of Chapter 1: "Which of the societal paradigms is most congruent with a progressive view of social work?" That is, which of the major societal paradigms is most congruent with a concept of social justice premised on creating societal conditions in which people are free from oppression and domination, with a social belief in the individual as a social being, with an economic belief whereby societal decisions dominate economic decisions, with a political belief in participatory democracy, and a social welfare system that emphasizes equality, solidarity, and community?

To help answer the question posed in the introduction of this chapter, a schematic outline of the four paradigms is presented in Table 8.1. Both neo-conservatism and liberalism adhere to the basic values of capitalism, with the former advocating a purer form (less government intervention) than the latter does. Conversely, both social democracy and Marxism adhere to the basic values of socialism, although they differ on the means to achieve a socialist state. While a major goal of the capitalist paradigms is to maintain basic capitalist structures in North America, the socialists would have as their major goal the transformation of these capitalist structures to socialist structures. The implication for the social work profession is that by deciding which societal paradigm is most congruent with its ideology, social work is also deciding its position with respect to preserving or changing the society within which it is located.

Table 8.1 Overview of Four Paradigms

	Neo-Conservatism	Liberalism	Social Democracy	Marxism
Social Beliefs	Freedom (or liberty) Individualism Inequality	Freedom Individualism Inequality (all of the above modified by humanitarianism and pragmatism)	*Primary Values* Freedom Collectivism Equality *Derivative Values* Humanitarianism Democratic participation	Freedom Collectivism Equality
Economic Beliefs	Laissez-faire Competitive capitalism Private ownership	Mixed economy or welfare capitalism	Government intervention Public control of economy Equitable distribution of income and opportunities	Public ownership of economy Industrial democracy Distribution according to need Planned economy
Political Beliefs	Elite rule Dominance of economic system Law, order, and stability Paternalism	Representative democracy Pluralism	Participatory democracy Capitalism can be transformed by a social democracy The state has a positive role to play in society	Participatory democracy Government planning enhances democracy Transformation of capitalism by class conflict
View of Social Problems	Caused by individual weakness, deviance, or heredity	Caused by social disorganization, which is inherent in a capitalist system	Caused by various social conflicts inherent in a capitalist society	Caused by social relationships (owners vs workers) inherent in capitalism
View of Social Welfare	Hostile to a well-developed welfare state Goal is to relieve destitution Ideal social welfare model = residual system	Used to modify the negative effects of capitalism Goal is to provide a social minimum Ideal social welfare model = institutional system	Welfare capitalism can be used as a stepping stone toward socialism Ideal welfare system = structural model (goal is to promote egalitarianism)	Welfare capitalism props up capitalism but also represents the efforts of the working class Ideal welfare system = structural model
Nature of Social Work Practice	Coerce people to look after themselves Social control Poor Law treatment Emphasize investigations to prevent abuse	Personal reform Limited social reform Advocacy	Provide practical, humanitarian care to casualties of capitalism Restructure society along socialist lines	Revolutionary: no social change possible in a capitalist society Evolutionary: essentially the same as social democracy

As we have already seen, and as is clear from Table 8.1, social work ideology has much more in common with the socialist paradigms than it does with the capitalist paradigms.[1] If social workers truly believe in the values and ideals they espouse, then they cannot subscribe to and try to maintain a social order that contradicts and violates many of these same values and ideals. If the social work profession is to be true to itself, it must, first of all, realize that in North America at least, it embodies one of the contradictions of capitalism. The profession is based on humanitarian and egalitarian ideals but operates within a social order based on an inequality whereby a minority dominates (controls and exploits) the majority. Second, in light of this awareness, social workers must do something about it. They must try to change the present social order to one that is more compatible with their own world view. To bring about this transformation, they must go beyond critical analysis of our capitalist social system and develop transformational theory or what is termed here structural social work theory.

Although structural social work may align itself with socialism, it must be a *revitalized socialism* and not the "old" socialism of the twentieth century, which reflected a project of emancipation rooted in domination. This revitalized socialism must engage with postmodernism, as well as with feminist, anti-racist, and other struggles against domination, and demand the acknowledgement and celebration of diversity in cultures, sexualities, races, ages, abilities, and other human characteristics that were excluded, suppressed, or discriminated against within an unreconstructed modernist version of socialism (Leonard, 1997). In other words, structural social work must align itself with a form of socialism that is informed and reconstituted by the feminist, anti-racist, postmodern, and other anti-oppressive critiques outlined in Box 8.1.

Box 8.1 *Toward a Reconstructed Socialism*

- Move beyond the preoccupation of the old socialism with class as the primary source of oppression, and include the voices and experiences of all oppressed groups.
- Deconstruct the gender neutrality of old socialism and its oppressive assumptions about women's responsibilities in society to eliminate its gender exclusion and its patriarchal base.
- Deconstruct the colour neutrality of old socialism and its oppressive assumptions about white superiority to eliminate its preoccupation with pursuing mainly the interests of white persons in general and white, bourgeois males in particular.
- Deconstruct the role of the state in maintaining dominant patriarchal and heterosexual relations and replace this narrow politics with a politics of difference that seeks true social equality.
- Deconstruct assumptions of normalcy and its focus on disability as a site of otherness and marginality to examine how these assumptions construct categories of social and cultural exclusion based on human diversity.

- Reorganize the sexual division of labour by breaking down the separation between the private sphere of home, family, and unpaid work and the public sphere of paid work, the market, and state.
- Deconstruct the assumptions about traditional family forms and gender systems that underpin much public policy and most welfare models and reconstitute socialism so that it reflects the multiple forms of families that are present today.
- Be cognizant of the claim of many socialist feminists that there is a relationship between capitalism and patriarchy and that socialism and feminism complement and need each other.
- Deconstruct the (Eurocentric) dominant culture, and reconstruct the concept of culture so that cultural differences are celebrated and cultural equality is a value of a reconstituted socialism.
- Bridge positive and liberating aspects of socialism's modernist critical theory tradition with those of postmodernism by:
  - retaining ideals of social justice, emancipation, and equality in a way that respects difference, diversity, and inclusion;
  - working on the interstices of materialist philosophies and critical postmodernism;
  - avoiding totalizing belief systems and essentialisms, on the one hand, and politically disabling fragmentation along with witless relativism, on the other.
- Challenge fatalistic ideas, such as the belief that today's situation is evolutionary and inevitable—what was made by a small elite can be unmade and/or remade.

It must be acknowledged that many persons today, both inside and outside social work, are skeptical of socialism as a working model for society. Given the fall of the Berlin Wall, the dictatorial nature and subsequent failure of Soviet socialism, and the rise of neo-conservatism, many people have given up on any notion of a socialist alternative. This skepticism has been reinforced by a nihilistic school of postmodern thinking that dismisses meta-narratives or broad interpretive schemas like those employed by Marx or Freud and thus rejects socialism and most other forms of Enlightenment reason. However, it must also be acknowledged that many persons today, inside and outside social work, including many (critical) postmodernists, still subscribe to such socialist values as social justice, equity, collective care, and structured opportunities so that all classes, races, genders, cultures, sexualities, ages, and abilities may attain personal and social fulfillment. Although socialism as an ideology, or as a meta-narrative, may have fallen out of favour with many progressive thinkers, its ideals and values have not. Structural social work, like any other radical social work approach, has always been underpinned by socialist ideology, but today it must be a reconstructed or reconstituted socialism.

The Heritage of Structural Social Work Theory

Historical Overview

Structural social work is part of the larger radical social work movement and, therefore, adheres to certain themes common to all schools of radical social work. These themes are outlined in the "radical social work" section below. Structural social work theory is the term adopted here for a number of reasons. First, the term "structural" is descriptive of the problems that confront social work in that they are an inherent, built-in part of our present social order. Our social institutions function in such a way that they discriminate against people along lines of class, gender, race, sexual orientation, ability, and so on. Second, the term "structural" is prescriptive for social work practice because it indicates that the focus for change is mainly on the structures of society and not solely on the individual. Third, structural social work theory appears to be more flexible and inclusive, and in many cases more realistic, than most other radical theories. For example, it is not only concerned with one group of oppressed people, such as people living in poverty, but with all groups who are survivors of the present social order. Also, it does not restrict social work practice to either inside or outside the existing social welfare system. And, finally, much of the developmental work of structural social work theory has been carried out in Canada, where it has assumed the status of a major social work perspective.

"Structural social work" is a term first used by Middleman and Goldberg in 1974. However, although these authors identified the social environment as the source of social problems, they attributed them to the liberal notion of social disorganization. Nowhere do they call for whole-sale social change, nor do they present a social or ideological analysis of capitalism. Instead, their prescription for social problems falls within the ecological approach. Middleman and Goldberg (1974, p. 26) state that "the assumption that inadequate social arrangements are predominantly responsible for the plight of many clients of social agencies suggests the need for social workers who can *help people to modify the social situations that limit their functioning*" (emphasis added). Although Middleman and Goldberg point out much that is wrong with capitalism (without mentioning capitalism, using instead the term "social environment"), nowhere do they call for its overthrow. There are many radical social work writers in the United States, but none, other than Middleman and Goldberg (see also Middleman & Goldberg-Ward, 1974), have used the term "structural social work" to describe their particular radical approach.

Arguably, most radical social work literature has originated in Britain. As with the American literature, however, very few radical writers use the term "structural social work." Ann Davis (1991, p. 71) is one exception. In "A Structural Approach to Social Work," she presents two contrasting approaches of structural social work that are offered in the literature:

These two broad approaches which offer a contrasting analysis of, and ways of working with structural issues, provide different starting points for social workers in training and practice. The first, in arguing for maintenance within given conditions, promotes a consensual view of practice in which recognition of the discrimination suffered by vulnerable groups is dealt with through advocacy within organizational and political givens. The second, in arguing for change of existing structures which perpetuate inequality, promotes an adversarial view of practice which simultaneously seeks to alleviate and transform the conditions in which oppressed clients find themselves.

The latter approach corresponds to the view of structural social work presented in this book.

Structural Approach to Social Work in Canada

Most of the developmental work on the structural approach to social work has been carried out in Canada. It was pioneered by Maurice Moreau (1979; 1990; Moreau & Leonard, 1989) at the School of Social Work at Carleton University in the mid-1970s with the help of many of his colleagues at Carleton,[2] the University of Montreal,[3] and the Université du Québec à Montréal.[4] This approach was presented by Moreau as an umbrella for the major radical themes of Marxism, feminism, radical humanism, and radical structuralism (Carniol, 1992; LeComte, 1990). One of the unique features of this structural approach was that it did not attempt to prioritize different forms of oppression—classism, racism, patriarchy, heterosexism, ableism, ageism, and so on—into some kind of hierarchical listing of most to least fundamental or most to least debilitating (Moreau & Leonard, 1989). Rather, the structural approach views various forms of oppression as intersecting with each other at numerous points, creating a total system of oppression (see Sklar et al., 1986; Wineman, 1984). Another notable feature of the structural approach is that it does not restrict itself to working only with social institutions. Instead, it is a generalist model of practice requiring knowledge and skills for working with individuals, families, groups, and communities, always making the connection between the personal and the political (Carniol, 1992; LeComte, 1990).

The structural social work approach has continued to develop in Canada since the mid-1970s. Moreau continued researching and writing on the subject until his death in 1990. Although there was a lull in structural and radical social work publications during most of the 1980s, there has been a significant resurgence since 1989.[5] The radical/structural social work literature of the 1990s, for the most part, attempted to deal with one of the major criticisms of the previous radical social work—that it was long on analysis but short on practice. Fook's (1993) book on radical casework, Ife's (1995) book on community development, and Martin's (1990) and Williams's (1989) books on social policy are examples of applying structural concepts and analyses to particular areas of practice. Today, structural social work is well represented within many social work textbooks in Canada—for example, Lundy's (2011) book on social work, social justice, and human rights and an edited book by Hick, Peters, Corner, and London (2009), which focuses on structural social work in various practice contexts. As well, much of anti-oppressive social work has developed from structural social work (see Mullaly & West, 2018; Baines, 2011).

Radical Social Work

Clark and Asquith (1985) have noted that social workers who are committed to some type of socialist vision, ranging from "mild social reformism to revolutionary Marxism," are attracted to the radical social work perspective. Langan and Lee (1989a) contend that many social workers (socialist and non-socialist) are attracted to this perspective as well because they have found that conventional theory is inappropriate for dealing with the social reality of so many people. This perspective chastises conventional social work for failing to develop a critical self-awareness and for often pathologizing oppressed people by offering individualistic explanations for social problems. The radical perspective also "urges social workers to get involved in socialist political action as much in their own interests as in the interests of those who depend upon their services" (Langan & Lee, 1989a, p. 4). The progressive view of social work discussed in Chapter 1 corresponds to the radical perspective. Davis (1991, p. 70) summarizes the radical argument:

> social workers need to understand the nature of state power and the role of social work as an element of state control and oppression, and to construct an approach to practice which is underpinned by this understanding. Such practice must be directed at challenging and changing structures which oppress.

Beginning with the Settlement House movement, social work has always had a radical element. Bertha Reynolds, an American Marxist social work academic and activist during the 1930s and 1940s, argued that to be a good social worker, one had to be a radical (Withorn, 1984). "Like many other radical social workers, Bertha Reynolds . . . viewed the rise of radical social work as consistent with the ethics and values of the profession" (Wagner, 1990, p. 6). In spite of its long history, however, radical social work has only developed a substantial literature and following since 1975 with the publications of Bailey and Brake's *Radical Social Work* in Britain, Jeffry Galper's *The Politics of Social Services* in the United States, and Harold Throssell's *Social Work: Radical Essays* in Australia. That these three publications were written independently of one another, in three different English-speaking countries, but at the same time and with similar alternative approaches to conventional social work practice, and that they corresponded with the emergence of the world economic crisis and the fiscal crisis of the state should not be surprising. It is completely consistent with one of the features of the concept of a paradigm that when the dominant paradigm is no longer able to evade anomalies or to explain crises, competing paradigms will begin to emerge or re-emerge.

Because of radical social work's association with socialism, which is an extremely broad tendency, there is a wide range of opinion among radical social workers (Clark & Asquith, 1985). Different shades of socialism coexist under the radical social work label.[6] Evidence of these differences is found in the following list of names that have been applied to radical social work: critical social work (Allan et al., 2003; Carniol, 1979; Hick, Fook, & Pozzuto, 2005); Marxist social work (Corrigan & Leonard, 1978; Longres, 1986; Wineman, 1984); political social work (Withorn, 1984); progressive social work (Jones, 1983; Smid & van Krieken, 1984); radical social work (Bailey & Brake, 1975; Galper, 1975; Langan & Lee, 1989b; Pritchard & Taylor, 1978; Simpkin, 1979; Statham, 1978); socialist social work (Galper, 1980); socialist welfare work (Bolger, Corrigan, Docking, & Frost, 1981); and structural social work (Davis, 1991; Middleman & Goldberg, 1974; Moreau, 1979; Moreau & Leonard, 1989). These nominal differences suggest that there is less homogeneity among radical social workers than is often believed by both enthusiasts and critics. Mullaly and Keating (1991) contend that the above schools of radical thought tend to fall into one of three traditional schools of socialist thought—social democracy, revolutionary Marxism, and evolutionary Marxism—and that these three perspectives differ on: (1) the place of radical social workers in the capitalist welfare system and whether they work within or outside it; (2) the fundamental source of oppression in a capitalist society; and (3) the priority given to the personal versus the political in a strategy of social transformation. These differences reflect disagreement on the means for transcending capitalism rather than any disagreement on the goal of social transformation itself. The legacy of radical social work theory is that it has the advantage of almost 40 years of theoretical insight to inform a new vision for social work. Jones (2011, p. 42) points out that radical social work has always been grounded in a commitment to social work practice that was informed by:

> a far superior understanding of the plight of clients and their continual reproduction under capitalism. It was social work that was not afraid to learn and to think and saw how rigorous and deep analysis of society strengthened rather than undermined people. It was a social work based on solidarities and alliances.

The Imperative of Theory for Social Work

We often use theories in our everyday lives without even being aware that we are doing so. Sears and Cairns (2010, p. 13) point out that our thoughts and actions are based on sets of assumptions about the way that the world works and that we act on the basis of our expectations, generalizing from past experiences to model new situations and develop appropriate responses.

> Gramsci used the term *common sense* to describe everyday philosophizing as opposed to conscious theoretical thinking. Our common-sense assumptions tend to be an eclectic blend of personal tastes and opinions; wisdom received from family, friends, or other influential individuals; and knowledge obtained from schools, religious institutions, political leaders, media, and other social institutions.

Just as we use theories in our everyday life, often without realizing it, social workers, too, often use theories in their everyday professional lives without realizing it. David Howe (1987) takes to task those "practical-folk" social workers who declare that their practice is not related to theory by showing that all practice is theory-based. Social workers who appeal to common sense or declare themselves to be pragmatists or announce they are eclectics see people and their situations in one way or another. Perceptions are never theory-free because they are based on certain fundamental assumptions about the nature of people, society, and the relationship between the two. These assumptions enable social workers to make sense of any situation, and making sense is what Howe (1987) calls a "theory-saturated activity." And just because a social worker cannot imagine how else to view a particular situation does not mean that it is not related to theory. It just means that this one taken-for-granted reality (theory) is the social worker's entire world of sense. In other words, those persons who call themselves common-sense, pragmatic, or eclectic social workers base their practice on personally constructed theory rather than on scientifically constructed theory.

Without going into a discussion of them, theory carries out four basic functions: description; explanation; prediction; and control and management of events or changes. Social work is a practice-based profession that pursues all four of these functions: it describes phenomena; it attempts to explain what causes them; it predicts future events, including what will happen if certain interventions occur; and it attempts to control and manage events or changes at all levels of human and social activity (Reynolds, 1971). "If drift and purposelessness are to be avoided, practice needs to be set within a clear framework of explanation, the nature of which leads to a well-articulated practice" (Howe, 1987, p. 17).

Order and Conflict/Change Perspectives

There is no shortage of social work knowledge. Many students, in fact, often believe there is an overabundance of knowledge. Most of us have come to believe that the world is comprised of "facts" that can be put together into a coherent package known as "the truth." However, there is usually more than one explanation or theory for the same set of phenomena. Within sociological theory it is generally accepted that there are two broad perspectives that provide a basis for the plethora of theories and theoretical positions found within social work textbooks and professional journals. Understanding the differences between the order and conflict perspective of social theory is particularly important for social work because it helps to delineate conventional theories and practice approaches from more progressive theories and practice approaches. For example, Lundy (2011) uses the order and conflict frameworks to situate various social work approaches along a continuum according to the degree to which they support radical change or regulation of society.

Order and change perspectives represent two competing views on the nature of people, society, and social problems. The former views society as orderly, stable and persistent, and unified by shared culture and values, with a consensus on the desired form of society and its institutions. The latter views society as a continually contested struggle among groups with opposing views and interests. From a change perspective, society is held together not by consensus but by differential control of resources and political power. The neo-conservative and liberal paradigms, as well as conventional social work, are based on the order view (i.e., maintenance of the capitalist system). "As a generalization, groups or individuals committed to the maintenance of the status quo employ order models of society. . . . Dissident groups, striving to institutionalize new claims, favour a conflict (change) analysis of society" (Horton, 1966, p. 703). Sears and Cairns (2010) believe that by contrasting these two very different theoretical perspectives, it is easier to detect patterns in theoretical thinking and to draw together major theoretical trends in social theory.

Order Perspective

The order perspective, which currently dominates North American social thought, is associated with Durkheim and Weber and more recently with Talcott Parsons. Parsons is usually regarded as the founder of an explicitly functionalist theory of society (McDaniel & Agger, 1984), which is synonymous with a systems analysis (i.e., structural-functional analysis) of society and social problems (Horton, 1966). The main assumption about theory within the order perspective is that it should be developed as a tool to help us understand how to maintain order (Sears & Cairns, 2010).

Society

Any society is comprised of people who are by nature competitive, acquisitive, self-absorbed, individualistic, and therefore predisposed toward disorder. To establish and maintain order, enduring social institutions are created and rules (laws) established so that human interaction can be regulated. In this way, all parts of society can be coordinated so that members of society and society's organizations and institutions all contribute to the support, maintenance, and stability of the social system. The basic assumption is that there is agreement on the values and rules of society so that they, along with the social institutions regulating the system, must be learned, respected, and revered by everyone. "We learn what is expected of us in the family, at school, in the workplace and through the media" (Howe, 1987, p. 35). While it may seem that a society based on common values would be threatened by social stratification, advocates of the social order model argue that people will accept social hierarchy provided that they view the system as generally fair. "Indeed, stratification can be the basis for an efficient division of labour and a source of motivation for hard work as people seek advancement" (Sears & Cairns, 2010, p. 19). Economic, technological, and cultural innovation may initiate a call for social change in modern industrial society, but Sears and Cairns contend that the pluralist state is able to maintain order in society by using processes of negotiation and reconciliation.

Social Problems

If a person does not behave in ways expected of, say, a parent, a wage-earner, or a law-abiding citizen, it is assumed that something went wrong in that person's socialization process. To ensure itself against disequilibrium, society will attempt to return the person to normal functioning through its social institutions. If society's official agents, such as teachers, social workers, or police, fail to correct or control the malfunctioning or out-of-step person, then that person may have to be removed from society and the individual's behaviour neutralized by institutionalization. This removes a threat to social stability and also serves as an example to other would-be non-conformists and deviants.

Because it is assumed that there is essential agreement among members of society on the nature of prevailing institutions and supporting ideology, their existence is taken for granted and the existing order legitimated (Reasons & Perdue, 1981). And because institutions and their supporting ideology fend off disequilibrium, discontinuity, and disorder of the system, their preservation becomes a social imperative. These assumptions about social institutions being good, necessary, and agreed to, as well as the belief that people are contentious and must be controlled, lead order theorists to conclude that social problems are best described and understood by focusing on lower levels or plateaus of society than on the societal or structural level. In other words, order theorists look at three levels of society for describing, analyzing, and explaining social problems: (1) the individual level; (2) the family level; and (3) the subcultural level (Reasons & Perdue, 1981).

Social Problems at the Individual Level

At the individual level, the source of social problems is found within the person: a person is not conforming to the rules, norms, and expectations of society because of some individual trait. Poverty, mental health issues, drug addiction, and criminal activity are blamed on supposed personal defects. As Reasons and Perdue point out, at the individual level social problems are personalized. Poverty and crime, for example, are blamed on some defect of the person, and what emerges is "a biographical portrait that separates the individual from society" (Reasons & Perdue, 1981, p. 8). Individuals are carefully scrutinized (diagnosed, assessed) to discover the explanation for the problem. One of the most clear-cut examples of an order theory at the individual level is "biological determinism," which locates the explanation for human behaviour in some aspect of human biology (i.e., genes, chromosomes, anatomy, etc.). If social behaviour is biologically based rather than socially based, then the focus is on changing the person rather than changing society.

Examples of the above type of explanation would include Cesare Lombroso's explanation of criminal activity as being caused by persons who are physically distinct from non-criminals. Freud's psychoanalytic theory whereby intrapsychic phenomena were hypothesized as the determinants of maladjusted behaviour is another example. Much of social work's earlier casework and psychodynamic practices were based on individual explanations for social problems. Sociobiology is a contemporary development of a theory that holds that genetic information explains social behaviour. As recently as 1988, a psychology professor from the University of Western Ontario created international controversy when he published an article alleging that race was connected to intelligence, sexual restraint, and personality, among other personal characteristics (Rushton, 1988).

Most order theorists and most social workers, because they operate from a systems perspective or employ an ecological model when dealing with social problems, are not satisfied with individual levels of explanations of social problems. From this comes the liberal concept of social disorganization. As detailed in Chapter 4, this concept is based on the notion that the present liberal-capitalist social order contains some defects that create disorganization and bring harm to some people, and the job of social work (and other occupations) is to rectify these defects (i.e., to fix the parts of society not working properly so that society works better and is able to persist). Systems theory and an ecological approach to social work, however, do not try to change the essential nature of the system but deal with individuals and/or environmental influences within the system. The types of environmental influences most frequently dealt with by social workers practising from an order perspective are the family and the subculture.

Social Problems at the Family Level

The family as an important social unit has received enormous attention from social workers and others since the early 1960s. Family disorganization has been cited as an explanation for most social problems that social workers deal with. The family is routinely analyzed in an attempt to find its contribution to situations of poverty, juvenile delinquency, mental health issues, alcoholism, family violence, poor school performance, and so on. Family therapy was viewed as almost a panacea to society's problems, and "family dysfunction" replaced "individual pathology" as the popular explanation for social problems (but did not eliminate individualistic explanations). Rather than blaming social problems on some defect of the person, problems are attributed at the family level to poor parenting, undeveloped communication skills, and the like. Rather than a "sick" individual being blamed for social problems, as neo-conservatives contend, problems are blamed on "maladaptive" or "dysfunctional" families. Social problems become family problems.

Social Problems at the Subcultural Level

Explanations of social problems at the subcultural level of society focus on various categories of people who are distinct from the larger majority population by reason of such features as race, ethnicity, and class. Subculture theorists believe these distinctive groups have distinctive subcultural values that put them at a disadvantage or in conflict with the larger or dominant culture (Reasons & Perdue, 1981). Social problems are not blamed on the individual or the family at the subcultural level but are attributed to one's culture.

An example of a subcultural theory is the "culture of poverty" or what is often termed "the cycle of poverty theory," which attempts to explain poverty. The culture of poverty theory assumes there are common traits among people living in poverty (feelings of inferiority, apathy, dependence, fatalism, no sense of deferred gratification). These traits are passed on to subsequent generations through the process of socialization so that by the time children living in poverty are of school age, they have internalized the basic traits of poverty and are not psychologically prepared to take advantage of the opportunities available to them. No thought is given to the possibility that many of these so-called traits of people living in poverty are actually adaptations and adjustments on the part of people to cope with poverty rather than actual causes of poverty. This explanation persists in social science literature.

In 2015 a popular book about the generational nature of poverty documented the experiences of an American economist who became a Big Brother to a black child in a family where one parent was in prison and the parent at home was receiving income assistance from the state. In the book, a white, well-educated, middle-class economist contrasts his own upbringing with that of the black family and finds that they generally have inferior parenting traits and that the children are apathetic and unmotivated to improve their lot in life, choosing petty crime and welfare benefits over education and paid employment. The author claims that his research into poverty, based largely on his one experience with this family over a period of 10 years, indicates that too-generous social welfare policies in the United States have contributed to a dependency that encourages and perpetuates generational poverty (Vass Gal, 2015). The book also discusses how poverty is closely tied to black cultural influences, which is linked to "cultural deprivation theory."

Another subcultural theory is the "cultural deprivation theory," which attempts to explain the situation of North American Indigenous people and other minority groups. This theory attributes the second-class status of Indigenous people and other minorities to an inferior culture. In other words, Indigenous culture is inadequate to prepare persons to function properly (successfully) in the larger society. Examples include: Indigenous parents do not read to their children; they do not take vacations abroad to expand their children's horizons; there is low motivation for school achievement or for work; there is no concept of the importance of time; welfare and alcoholism are part of this inferior culture. The end result is that children of Indigenous ancestry are culturally deprived. Once so labelled, of course, they are expected to fail in school and often do. Any country with an Indigenous population, such as Canada and Australia, has committed terrible acts of injustice and cultural genocide with respect to these populations that were influenced by the beliefs underpinning this "cultural deprivation theory." A "residential school system" was implemented by the Canadian government and began in the 1880s. Of this system the *Summary of the Final Report* of the Truth and Reconciliation Commission of Canada states:

> Canada's residential school system for Aboriginal children was an education system in name only for much of its existence. These residential schools were created for the purpose of separating Aboriginal children from their families, in order to minimize and weaken family ties and cultural linkages, and to indoctrinate children into a new culture—the culture of the legally dominant Euro-Christian Canadian society, led by Canada's first prime minister, Sir John A. Macdonald. The schools were in existence for well over 100 years, and many successive generations of children from the same communities and families endured the experience of them (2015, p. v).

The main purpose of the residential school system was to eradicate all aspects of Indigenous culture and to interrupt its transmission from one generation to the next. Indigenous children were educated according to Euro-Canadian and Christian values so that they could be more easily assimilated into mainstream society.

The above subcultural explanations for social problems are part of a larger process of "blaming the victim." William Ryan (1976) outlines this process:

1. Identify the problem.
2. Study those affected by the problem, and discover how they are different from the rest of society.
3. Define the differences, which are in fact the effects of injustice and discrimination, as the causes of the social problem.
4. Assign a government bureaucrat to invent a humanitarian action program to correct the differences by changing the people affected by the problem.

Thus, the solution to social problems originating at the subcultural level is to try to untangle, correct, and make up for the deficiencies of these inferior cultures by changing the people from them. This strategy involves counselling, resocialization, cultural enhancement services, upgrading, rehabilitation, and community education programs. In effect, people are worked on so that they can better fit into the mainstream, into the culture of the majority. This process of acculturation leaves society's social institutions unchanged. It is better to change a minority culture than to change social institutions so that they can accommodate the minority culture.

Social Work and the Order Perspective

Within the order perspective, social work would operate at the three levels where social problems are seen to occur—the individual, family, and subcultural levels. Because the social order is assumed to be accepted by members of society, then the primary function of the social worker is to preserve it. Both the neo-conservative and the liberal paradigms subscribe to the goal of preserving the capitalist system. In the case of neo-conservatism, social work preserves the capitalist society by coercing and controlling persons who stray from the capitalist way of life. From a liberal perspective, social work preserves the capitalist system by helping people to adjust and cope, or by modifying the immediate environments of persons, or by advocating on behalf of certain groups that have been disadvantaged by capitalism.

Most current social work theories and practices today are based on the order perspective. Major activities are personal reform, limited social reform, and advocacy, all of which are carried out in an effort to humanize capitalism, not to change it. The major theories— psychoanalytic, family therapies, general systems theory, and the ecological approach—all emanate from the order perspective. In the case of psychoanalytic theory, the major task is clearly personal reform. In the case of family therapy and general systems theory, the major task is to repair the harm or disruption that has upset the healthy functioning of the family or the equilibrium of the system. The ecological approach aims to find the best fit between the person and the system. In none of these theories or approaches is any thought given to the possibility that the source of the problem lies not within the system but is the system itself. This critical omission is the Achilles heel of conventional, mainstream social work carried out in the order tradition.

This is not to say that structural social workers would never use general systems theory or the ecological approach. These perspectives are useful in that they provide the social worker with a snapshot of the situation with which they are dealing. They identify the relevant actors and organizations in an individual's life and help to clarify the relationships among them. However, by themselves they only describe situations and do not provide any causal explanations for a problem or situation. Unlike critical social theories such as structural social work that contain analyses and explanations for social problems, they offer no theoretical explanation whatsoever for any social phenomena such as poverty, social inequality, or differential levels of power, prestige, and influence in society. Although systems and ecological approaches may include a person's immediate environment (i.e., one's family, school, workplace, community), they do not deal with larger-order structural phenomena. By emphasizing only those aspects of the social environment considered amenable to social work practice, systems theory and the ecological approach ignore broader structural social forces, which in effect reinforces social inequality (Gould, 1987, cited in Pease, 1991).

Major Criticisms of Theories in the Order Perspective

Pease (1991) has summarized some of the major criticisms and the structural variables that are unaccounted for in systems and ecological models of social work practice:

- They are focused more on stability and preserving the status quo than on social change (Moreau & Leonard, 1989).
- They assume no conflict among the goals of different groups and no clash of interests between marginalized and dominant groups (Gould, 1987).
- They consider existing power inequalities in society to be the norm (Marchant, 1986).
- They ignore the roles of power and wealth in maintaining inequality and exploitation (Gould, 1987).
- They fail to challenge class, gender, race, and other forms of oppression based on social, economic, and political arrangements (Moreau & Leonard, 1989).

For the structural social worker, these variables are critical for understanding social problems and developing emancipatory forms of social work practice. To this list of criticisms of systems and ecological approaches to social work practice, Finn and Jacobson (2003) add the following: they are so vague and general that they give little specific guidance for practice; the approach's focus on the "here-and-now" situation and intervention contributes to a neglect of history; while the language offers a metaphor for conceptualizing the person–environment relationship, the translation into practice is not so clear (Rossiter, 1996); feminist scholars such as Walters, Carter, Papp, and Silverstein (1988, cited in Finn & Jacobson, 2003) have noted that systems certainties such as boundaries, roles, and balance actually encode and reinforce the gender stratification of the larger society rather than challenge it; the emphasis on the "fit" of persons within a social context tends to support rather than question the dominant order and accentuates strategies for adaptation to rather than transformation of existing structural arrangements (Coates, 1991); the approach is reliant on an uncomplicated view of both the person and the environment because it assumes that both are stable, knowable, and non-problematic (Rossiter, 1996); and, finally, the approach adheres to liberal notions of the person as an autonomous individual and assumes a basic distinction between the individual and society rather than acknowledging the dialectical relationship between them.

The Change Perspective

The basic premise of the change, or conflict, perspective is that society is arranged around fundamental inequalities that can only be overcome by a substantial transformation of social relations (Sears & Cairns, 2010). The change perspective is strongly identified with Karl Marx (and therefore with socialism) and a variety of later writers loosely associated under the umbrella labels of "critical," "political economy," "progressive," and "radical."

Society

Change theorists accept the view of society as a system of interrelated parts but do not believe the parts are held together by consensus and shared interests and values. Rather, they see society comprising inherently opposing groups with respect to interests, values, and expectations. These groups compete for resources and power, and those who win exercise their control and power by imposing an ideological world view that holds capitalism as the best of all economic systems (McDaniel & Agger, 1984). Part of the ideological climate or hegemony established by the dominant group is the formulation of laws, the creation of social institutions, and the distribution of ideas that favour the dominant group.

> The state, in this conflict model, does not serve the interests of all by defending the social order against chaos but rather acts on behalf of the most powerful by protecting a particular inequitable order against the claims of the disadvantaged. The state might appear to be a neutral referee as contending interest groups stake their claims on a level playing field, but according to the conflict model the rules of the game favour the powerful every time. The representation of subordinate groups within the corridors of power might create the illusion of full participation but generally does not result in a significant change in the condition of the bulk of the disadvantaged population (Sears & Cairns, 2010, p. 22).

Change theorists do not accept the present social order. They want radical change. A truly just order can come about only through the radical reorganization of society, not through the extension of social control (Horton, 1966). From the perspective of the change model, the resources and privileges of the powerful can only have one source: the exploitation of subordinate groups (Sears & Cairns, 2010). Change theorists' vision of society is one in which a new economic order of production is realized that would bring with it new social relations, with no one group dominating another (Howe, 1987).

Social Problems

Horton (1966) tells us that conflict analysis is synonymous with historical analysis, an interpretation of intersystem processes that brings about the transformation of social relations. A key concept in this analysis is alienation (Naiman, 1997), which means a separation from the social system and a separation of people from each other in a society that reduces them to commodities (i.e., the only value they have is what they can obtain in the labour market). To the order theorist, this situation is known as "anomie," which occurs when people lose their sense of collective consciousness. The role of the state, from the order perspective, is to promote this collective consciousness in order to protect and preserve the status quo. To the change theorist, this situation is known as "alienation," and the progressive response would be change. In sum, the order theorist perceives anomie as synonymous with deviance and disorganization, and the task is to bring people who have been separated from society and from each other back into society. The change theorist views the same situation as alienation, and the task is to change the society that creates and perpetuates inequality and alienation.

Change theorists do not believe that social problems normally originate within the individual, the family, or the subculture, as do order theorists, but "arise from the exploitive and alienating practices of dominant groups" (Horton, 1966, p. 704). Given the nature of a society marked by inequality and structured along lines of class, gender, race, age, and so on, the explanation for social problems must lie at a higher societal plane than those perceived by order theorists. For change theorists, the societal plane where social problems are more realistically described, analyzed, and explained is at the structural level (Reasons & Perdue, 1981). This level includes society's institutions and its supportive ideology. At this level, a social problem is defined as:

> a condition that involves the social injury of people on a broad scale. The injury may be physical in manifestation (as with disease stemming from a health service geared to income), social-psychological (as with alienation), economic (as with poverty), political (as with the oppression of dissident groups), or intellectual (as with nonexistent or inadequate education). Social problems ensue from institutional defects and are not to be best interpreted or understood through individuals, families, or subcultures. Thus, the social problem as such is not an aberration but rather a normal consequence of the way in which a society is organized (Reasons & Perdue, 1981, p. 12).

Reasons and Perdue (1981) point out that the above definition of social problems does not mean that change theorists ignore individuals, families, and subcultures as areas for study. The difference is that change theorists will always connect these societal planes with the broader structural order of society. In other words, the change theorist will always look to public issues (i.e., social institutions and their supportive ideology) as the source of private troubles. And because social problems are rooted in the social order, they cannot be resolved by technical or administrative reforms. They can only be resolved by a massive reorganization or transformation of the social system. In sum, the major postulates of the social change or conflict perspective are:

1. Society is the setting within which various struggles occur among different groups whose interests, values, and behaviours conflict with one another.
2. The state is an important agent participating in the struggle on the side of the powerful groups.
3. Social inequality is a result of coercive institutions that legitimate force, fraud, and inheritance as the major means of obtaining rights and privileges.
4. Social inequality is a chief source of conflict.
5. The state and the law are instruments of oppression controlled and used by the dominant groups for their own benefit.
6. Classes are social groups with distinctive interests that inevitably bring them into conflict with other groups with opposed interests. (Reasons & Perdue, 1981, pp. 13–14)

Social Work and the Change Perspective

The change or conflict social worker must fight for change at all social, economic, and political levels. A conflict analysis of society reveals who is benefiting from established social arrangements; it shows how domination is maintained; and it suggests what must be done to bring about changes in power and resources. To assist the victims of an oppressive social order, the social worker needs to know who holds the power, whose interests are being served by maintaining the status quo, and what devices are being used to keep things as they are (Howe, 1987).

Table 8.2 Assumptions of Order and Conflict/Change Perspectives

	Order	Conflict/Change
Nature of Human Existence	Competitive, contentious, individualistic, and acquisitive	Cooperative, collective, and social
Nature of Social Institutions	Must endure and regulate human interactions (political, economic, educational, religious, family) to avoid disorder	Dynamic with no sacred standing; facilitate cooperation, sharing, and common interests
Nature of Society	Consists of interdependent and integrated institutions and a supportive ideological base; viewed as an organism or system with each part contributing to the maintenance of the whole	In a society of structural inequality, the social nature of human existence is denied, with social institutions serving private rather than public interests
Continuity of Social Institutions	Prevail because of agreement (consensus) among society's members	Prevail in a class-divided society because of control and coercion
Nature of Relationship between People and Society	Members are expected to conform and adapt to consensus-based social arrangements	Acceptance, conformity, and adaptation to a coercive social order is questioned
Nature of Social Problems	Socialization will occasionally fail whereby reverence for institutions and respect for rules will not be learned; such occurrence on a large scale is a social problem	Faulty socialization is more a matter of defective rules than of defective control; rules are problematic
Approach to Social Problems	Behaviour must be changed through resocialization (rehabilitation, counselling, etc.) or neutralized through formal systems of state control (criminal law, prisons, asylums, etc.). Social change can only involve minor adjustments that are consistent with the nature of the existing system.	Institutions and ideology must be changed to protect social nature of human existence

Behavioural change can only involve minor adjustments consistent with cooperative and collective nature of society; massive commitment to behavioural change is a form of blaming the victim |
| Paradigms | Neo-conservatism Liberalism | Social democracy Marxism |

Because social democracy and socialism are based on social change thought, social work from a change perspective would be very similar to the nature and type of social work practice outlined in Chapter 5 (social democratic social work) and in Chapter 6 (evolutionary Marxist social work). Social work would have a dual function: (1) to provide practical humanitarian care to the casualties of a capitalist social order; and (2) at the same time, to further the democratization and restructuring of society along socialist lines.

The change-based dual function of social work does not preclude intervention at the individual, family, and subcultural levels. The difference is that instead of dealing with each of these levels by itself, the connection between people's private troubles and the structural source of these troubles would be made in every case. Rather than looking within the individual or within one's family or within one's subculture for the source of distress, the way in which the larger social order perpetrates and perpetuates people's problems would be identified and discussed with the person or group experiencing the distress. Although change social workers would do many of the same things that order social workers would do, many differences emanate from the different explanations each holds about the nature of society and of social problems. These differences will be discussed in the next three chapters.

Structural Social Work as a Critical Social Theory

Structural social work is part of a school of social theory known as critical theory. Critical theory provides criticisms and alternatives to traditional, mainstream social theory, philosophy, and science. It is motivated by an interest in the emancipation of those who are oppressed, is informed by a critique of domination, and is driven by a goal of liberation (Kellner, 1989). Critical theory concerns itself with moving from a society characterized by exploitation, inequality, and oppression to one that is emancipatory and free from domination.

Karl Marx is arguably the founder of critical theory. His ideas and emancipatory intentions have been extended and developed by the Frankfurt School (most notably Theodore Adorno, Max Horkheimer, and Herbert Marcuse) and by its heir apparent, Jürgen Habermas (see Jay, 1973). "The basic idea of their 'critical theory' is that since persons cannot be free from that about which they are ignorant, liberation depends in the first instance on recognition of that which imprisons the human mind or dominates the human person" (Sabia & Wallulis, 1983, p. 4).

In *Critical Theory in Political Practice* (1990, p. 3), Stephen Leonard defines critical theory:

A critical theory of society is defined as a theory having practical intent. As its name suggests, it is critical of existing social and political institutions and practices, but the criticisms it levels are not intended simply to show how present society is unjust, only to leave everything as it is. A critical theory of society is understood by its advocates as playing a crucial role in changing society. In this, the link between social theory and political practice is perhaps the defining characteristic of critical theory, for a critical theory without a practical dimension would be bankrupt on its own terms.

Critical theory, then, is different from most social science theory constructed according to the canons of scientific inquiry. Traditional social theory may describe and explain social processes, but it is quite independent of political practice. Its commitment is to the advancement of object-ive knowledge by attempting to understand the world as it really is. Conversely, critical theory is committed to changing the world "in ways that can help 'emancipate' those on the margins of society by providing them with insights and intellectual tools they can use to empower them-selves" (S. Leonard, 1990, p. xiii).

Leonard (1990) contends that there are three requirements or undertakings of a critical theory: (1) it must locate the sources of domination in actual social practices; (2) it must present an alternative vision (or at least an outline) of a life free from such domination; and (3) it must translate these tasks in a form that is intelligible to those who are oppressed in society. Current examples of theory that satisfy these requirements and, therefore, are critical theories (by defin-ition) in practice are Paulo Freire's "pedagogy of the oppressed," "liberation theology," and some forms (i.e., transformative forms) of feminist theory (S. Leonard, 1990).

In accordance with the above requirements of a critical theory, structural social work theory is a critical theory. It is critical of existing social, economic, and political institutions and prac-tices and seeks to change them. It articulates an alternative social vision (or at least an outline) consistent with progressive social work values in which life is free from domination. And, as will be seen in the following chapters, its major thrust is to involve people in its social analysis and in its political practice. Other forms of social work theory are also critical theories accord-ing to the above criteria—transformative forms of feminist social work, anti-racist social work, anti-oppressive social work, and Indigenous anti-colonial social work.

Kincheloe and McLaren (2011, pp. 288–291) have identified themes important for a "revital-ized" critical social theory (CST):

- CST analyzes competing power interests between groups and individuals within society—identifying who wins and who loses in specific situations. Privileged groups have an interest in supporting the status quo to protect their advantages, and this dy-namic becomes a central focus of critical analysis and research.
- CST acknowledges that there are multiple forms of power and domination but recog-nizes that economic factors can never be separated from other axes of oppression.
- CST views language as an unstable social practice with shifting meanings depending on the context in which it is used. Linguistic descriptions are not simply about the world but also serve to construct it.
- CST supports the belief that culture is a domain of struggle. For example, diversity awareness is often constituted in social work practice as "cultural competence." This terminology focuses on cultural difference at the expense of examining the inherent as-sumption that the dominant white culture provides a universal standard against which all other cultures are compared (Pease, 2010).

Many of these themes identify the important role of culture in addressing oppression (dis-cussed in Chapter 9), and they have been developed under the growing influence of postmod-ern theory. Baines (2011) explains that by the mid-to-late 1990s much of the focus on multiple forms of oppression had turned to a blend of critical postmodernism and intersectional class analysis.

> Postmodernism and poststructuralism offered ways of understanding multiple oppressions such as identity, social location, voice, diversity, borders, anti-essentialism, inclusion, exclusion, and difference, while simultaneously emphasizing the importance of everyday experience . . . both the older and the newer [modern and postmodern] frameworks explore the individual and his/her place in the world recognizing, for example, that one's identity is shaped by their class, race, gender, etc.—in short, that we all have multiple and socially constructed identities. The older and newer frameworks also recognize that the ways that we interpret our identities and experiences are also buffered and shaped by class, race, gender, etc. (Baines, 2011, p. 10).

Competing Perspectives: Modernism and Postmodernism

There are two competing perspectives of critical theory—modernist and postmodernist—and there are a number of versions of postmodernism, with the critical postmodern school containing emancipatory purpose. Both the modernist and postmodernist views are committed to a conception of social theory that is emancipatory in intent and politically engaged, but neither has been able to make good this commitment (S. Leonard, 1990). The major difference between the two is that whereas modernism believes it has the potential for overcoming domination and oppression in all its forms, postmodernism indicts this belief and views modernism as another form of enslavement. It is a false dichotomy or binary opposite to choose one or the other as a basis for structural social work theory and practice; both are necessary.

It should be noted at the outset that a substantial literature on postmodernism has developed over the past few decades in both the humanities and the social sciences. However, some still tend to impose a clear, complete, and time-defined break—what could be called a "great divide"—between anything written in the period now known as modernity (from the Age of Enlightenment around the end of the eighteenth century up to the present or recent past, which includes most critical social theory writings) and writings in the era of postmodernity (from around 1970 to the present, according to David Harvey [1989]). Such a position is uninformed, uncritical, and non-scholarly. Although there are major differences between the two, often overlooked or not known in the first place is the fact that postmodernism and critical social theory share a common intellectual heritage. The postmodern writers Baudrillard, Derrida, Foucault, and Lyotard all wrote within the period of modernity, did not reject progressive causes, and based their critiques of the Enlightenment on the thinking of Nietzsche and Heidegger. The latter is seen by many to be the archetype and trend-setter of postmodernism. Both Heidegger and Nietzsche influenced the Frankfurt School's critique of civilization. Both sets of critiques reject the Cartesian philosophy of identity (with its omission of the Other), the emancipatory myth of teleology, and positivism (Nietzsche declared not only God dead but all imposter gods such as philosophy and science).

Modernism

Habermas (1983) contends that the project of modernity came into focus in the eighteenth century even though the preconditions of modernity were put in place much earlier, during the Renaissance transition from the Middle Ages to the modern world. Enlightenment thinkers of the eighteenth century sought "to use the accumulation of knowledge generated by many individuals working freely and creatively for the pursuit of human emancipation and the enrichment of daily life" (Harvey, 1989, p. 12). The increased domination of nature by the scientific revolution promised freedom from scarcity and want and reduced the risks of natural calamities. The project of modernity was to develop rational forms of social organization and to use rational thought to liberate people from the irrationalities of myth, religion, and superstition and to release them from the arbitrary use of power that characterized European life prior to that time (Harvey, 1989; S. Leonard, 1990). Doctrines of equality, liberty, faith in human educated intelligence, and universal reason abounded, and it was expected that "the arts and sciences would promote not only the control of natural forces but also understanding of the world and of the self, moral progress, the justice of institutions and even the happiness of human beings" (Harvey, 1989, p. 13).

In this modernist project, human beings were freed from the beliefs that everyone and everything belonged to a preordained place in the grand scheme of things and that all they could do was contemplate the wonder of it all. Prior to modernism, no one should question, let alone attempt to change, the world as it was given to us by Divine Providence (Howe, 1994). Modernist thinkers detached themselves from the universe "in order to examine it, probe it, penetrate it, fathom it, see of what it is made, understand how it works, explain it, control it, use it, and exploit it [for the betterment of all people]" (Howe, 1994, pp. 514–515).

On the surface, it would seem that the project of modernity would be a worthwhile endeavour. However, its commitment to reason as the sole determinant of knowledge has proved problematic because scientific reasoning became the model. Given the success of science in understanding and dominating the natural world in the interests of human welfare, modernists adopted scientific rationality, objective knowledge, and the development of grand theories (including socialism and capitalism) as the way of understanding the social world and as the means of attaining human emancipation. By the nineteenth century, the newly established social sciences (the inheritors of the Enlightenment project) had adopted positivism as the dominant and legitimate means of pursuing knowledge. Thus, the demand for objective, empirically verifiable knowledge led to the dismissal of normative concerns and, more important, to a dogma that knowledge for its own sake ought to be pursued. Legitimate knowledge was restricted to that most closely resembling natural and universal laws, which guided the physical sciences (S. Leonard, 1990). The twentieth-century experience, with its holocausts, two world wars, militarism, devastation of the environment, threat of nuclear annihilation, and the nuclear bombing of Nagasaki and Hiroshima, shattered the emancipatory ideal of modernism.

Modernist thought contained a host of difficult problems and contradictions. For example, who could claim to possess superior reason and knowledge, and under what conditions would this reason and knowledge be exercised as power? Whose Utopian plan should be adopted, and what guarantees existed that it would not become oppressive? What should be the relationship between the means of obtaining knowledge and the ends to which it would be put (Harvey, 1989)? Questions like these are ignored in traditional social science with its focus on developing knowledge for the sake of knowledge and with no attempt to connect theory to any political practice.

Modernist critical theory departs from traditional social theory in a number of areas and, in so doing, has attempted to address (but not necessarily resolve) a number of the above criticisms of modernism. It is normative in nature and practical in intent; it rejects such scientistic elements of positivism as "science is the only means of obtaining knowledge" and that objectively verifiable facts constitute the only legitimate form of knowledge; it does not believe that the subjects who create the knowledge can be distinguished from the objects of that knowledge; and it subscribes to the belief that knowledge and a commitment to human emancipation (i.e., theory and practice) cannot be separated. The best-known critical theorists—Marx,[7] members of the Frankfurt School, and Jürgen Habermas—all have addressed these issues in varying degrees.[8] In spite of the problems associated with the project of modernity—its crimes against humanity in the name of progress and order, its grand theories of individual and social development that are Eurocentric and androcentric, and its professional discourses and practices that actually homogenize, monitor, and control subordinate populations (supposedly in their own interests) (Leonard, 1995)—its emancipatory intent would still appear to be a laudable goal for those concerned with human well-being and social justice. There is consensus that Marx, the Frankfurt thinkers, and Habermas were unable to conceptualize the practical intent of their critical theories. However, rather than abandoning modernist critical theory altogether, maybe the means for achieving the Enlightenment ideal of human emancipation has to be rethought. To assist in this task, the ideas, ideals, and practices of postmodernism are examined below to see what, if any, insights it might hold for critical theory.

Postmodernism

Although Marx, the Frankfurt School, and Habermas have had a tremendous influence on critical social theory scholars, a rival perspective to modernist thought has assumed major attention in the past few decades. This rival perspective belongs to a tradition of rejectionist criticism of modernity that calls for a "total break with the Enlightenment" (Fraser, 1985, pp. 165–166). This tradition, as noted above, goes back to Nietzsche and Heidegger, and more recently it includes the French post-structuralists (e.g., Lyotard) and arguably its most influential proponent, Michel Foucault. Foucault presents a compelling critique of many modernist ideas and concepts, even though he describes his work as having emancipatory intent (S. Leonard, 1990).

It is important to understand that postmodernism is not restricted to postmodern social theory (Agger, 1998). It includes postmodern architecture, art, and design as well as postmodern literary and cultural theory. With respect to postmodern social theory, a range of perspectives will deeply affect the kind of politics that might emerge from them. At one end of the continuum, postmodernism is a conservative, individualistic, and nihilistic doctrine that believes there is no potential for solidarity among oppressed persons or for social change efforts because every person is their own moral agent—a position that Ife (1997) calls an "anything goes brand of politics" and what Geertz (1986) calls "witless relativism." At the other end of the postmodern social theory spectrum are those writers who have taken postmodern analyses and criticisms of modernity as essential ingredients in an attempt to revitalize critical social theory. Examples of these latter theorists include Ben Agger, Stanley Arnowitz, Terry Eagleton, Nancy Fraser, David Harvey, Frederic Jameson, Douglas Kellner, and Timothy Luke. Examples of such theorists within social work and social welfare include Jim Ife, Peter Leonard, Bob Mullaly, Bob Pease, and Jan Fook. This book and its development of the new structural social work follow this "critical postmodernist" approach.

Although there is no agreement about when the world entered its postmodern phase, David Harvey, in his celebrated book, *The Condition of Postmodernity: An Enquiry into the Origins of Cultural Change* (1989), contends that it emerged as a full-blown though still incoherent movement somewhere between 1968 and 1972. He documents how this cultural transformation from modernism to postmodernism occurred in such areas as architecture, art, literature, urban planning, philosophy, theology, and all other arenas of intellectual activity. Although the nature and depth of this transformation is debatable, there is no doubt that, in the words of Huyssens (1984), "in an important sector of our culture there is a noticeable shift in sensibility, practices and discourse formations, which distinguishes a post-modern set of assumptions, experiences and propositions from that of a preceding period" (cited in Harvey, 1989, p. 39).

Summary of Postmodernist Assumptions and Critiques of Modernism

- Postmodernists[9] reject the claim that modernism has brought about material and social progress for some populations because, at the same time, it has also meant exploitation, impoverishment, cultural destruction, and death for others through its association with modern imperialism, colonialism, economic development, and warfare (Leonard, 1994).
- Modernism's pursuit of scientific truths in human affairs has at times led to totalitarianism and Utopian visions that, in turn, have repeatedly led to repression and control. Therefore, postmodernists reject all totalizing belief systems or meta-narratives, such as Marxism and socialism, that seek to impose an ideal order on society (Howe, 1994).
- Instead of believing in a single reality derived from a single rationality, discourse, or meta-narrative, postmodernists believe that different realities exist at any one time and that they are constantly being defined and redefined by different actors in different contexts (Ife, 1997).
- Postmodernists believe that the world is characterized by diversity, multiplicity, pluralism, and conflict rather than sameness, unity, monism, and consensus. No group should try to define the reality or experience of another group (Howe, 1994, p. 524).

- Postmodernists believe that power is to be found in different localities, contexts, and social situations. The prison, the school, the asylum, the hospital, and the social worker's office are all examples of places where power is dispersed and built up independently of any systematic strategy of class or gender or ethnicity. What happens at each locality cannot be explained by some overarching theory (Harvey, 1989).
- A cornerstone of postmodernism is its concern for language and discourse. It severely criticizes modernism for the totalistic nature of its use of dominant discourses because they reflect class, gender, race, and other forms of dominant relationships (Leonard, 1994).
- Postmodernists believe that "all groups have a right to speak for themselves, in their own voice, and have that voice accepted as authentic and legitimate" (Harvey, 1989, p. 48).

Limitations of Postmodernism

In its concern for difference, for the difficulties of communication, for the complexity and diversity of cultures, interests, and the like, postmodernism exercises a positive influence. The theories and language of modernism tended to gloss over important differences and failed to pay attention to important details and disjunctures. Postmodernism has been especially important in acknowledging the multiple forms of otherness as they emerge from differences in subjectivity, gender, class, race, and so on. It is this aspect of postmodernism that Stephen Leonard (1990) says gives it a radical edge.

Although postmodernism offers a useful critique of the oppressive aspects of modernism, it also contains contradictions and limitations with respect to realizing its emancipatory intent. Postmodernists seem to overlook the fact that much of the world is still modernist and that ideology is still a driving force for many people and groups. Much of the postmodern rhetoric appears to avoid confronting the realities of political economy and global power. While postmodernists have argued for otherness, difference, localism, and fragmentation, capitalism has taken another course—globalization of capital accumulation that is being used to subjugate the very groups and localities for which postmodernism expresses its concern. By denying the existence of universal phenomena and by fragmenting people under the banner of localism, is postmodernism not aiding and abetting this subjugation?

Harvey (1989) asks that if, as the postmodernists insist, we cannot aspire to any unified representation of the world, or see it as a whole with connections and differentiations rather than as constantly shifting fragments, how can we ever act coherently with respect to changing it? The simple postmodernist answer is that we should not even try to engage in a global project because any coherent representation or action is either illusory or repressive. This leaves the question open as to what path localized struggles should take to add up to a progressive, rather than regressive, attack on the central forms of capitalist and other structural sources of oppression.

Postmodernism does not accept the notion of historical progress because the very idea of progress implies an acceptance of a meta-narrative. History and experience are reduced to a series of pure, fragmented, and unrelated presents. Such a breakdown of the temporal order abandons all sense of historical continuity and memory, which means that a pursuit of better futures cannot take place (Harvey, 1989). To the extent that our identities are the creation of our histories, and to the extent that our historically constituted identities are a matter of power/ knowledge constraints, postmodernism "eludes the difficult task of articulating the kind of collective action required to transform our relationships with others in emancipatory ways" (S. Leonard, 1990, p. 79). Although postmodernism allows for the development of alternative realities, it does not suggest what they might be, and its absence of normative elements precludes any direction to take (Ife, 1997).

Ife (1997) points out a few other contradictions and limitations of postmodernism. It does not account for structural oppressions such as race, class, and gender, since its pluralist perspective sees power as being dispersed throughout society and not concentrated in the hands of a few. By emphasizing difference and localism, it reduces any potential for solidarity among groups experiencing the commonality of oppression (whatever its source). A related criticism made by Ife is that, by its rejection of universal meta-narratives, postmodernism is also rejecting the importance of universal discourses that are at the foundation of most social justice movements, such as the peace movement, the environmental movement, the women's movement, and the human rights movement. By drawing attention away from structural issues and universal notions of social justice, postmodernism appears to have an essential conservative element that can be used as a convenient legitimization for an "anything goes" brand of politics; it allows for a multiplicity of visions, not just those concerned with social justice. And its emphasis on relativism could be used to justify many human rights violations (e.g., those in China). A final limitation noted here, again taken from Ife, is that by advocating universal skepticism and a universal discourse of difference while indicting all universal truths, postmodernism is self-contradictory.

Implications of Modernism and Postmodernism for Structural Social Work Theory

Modernist and postmodernist critical theory obviously differ in many respects. In fact, each almost represents the very antithesis of the other. However, there are also commonalities between the two. Both stand against domination and oppression, and both have failed to reach their emancipatory intent. As well, both fulfill the three criteria of critical theories outlined by S. Leonard (1990). (1) They are both critical of our present social order and locate the sources of domination in actual social practices (although each may identify different practices). (2) They both have, or in the case of postmodernism allow for, many different, alternative visions of society. Modernist critical theory seeks a society based on socialist or collectivist principles, and although critical postmodernism allows for many alternative visions, only those concerned with human liberation are legitimate, given its emancipatory intent. (3) Both perspectives have a practical intent because both see the involvement of marginalized populations as a necessary part of this praxis, albeit in different ways. Critical social theory (both modernist and postmodernist) is a partisan enterprise because it involves standing alongside oppressed and marginalized populations against exploitation and domination, and both perspectives claim to do this.

Structural social work does not perceive these two perspectives on critical theory as completely dichotomous or polarized. Instead, it views each as having strengths and limitations that the other does not and seeks to use the strengths of each as a corrective for some of the limitations and contradictions of the other. The following are some examples that reflect this attempt.

Modernist and Postmodernist Contributions to Structural Analysis and Practice

One of the major strengths of modernist critical theory is that it attends to pervasive structural issues of oppression and domination, particularly in the areas of class, gender, and race. It recognizes commonalities among all forms of oppression, such as the nature of dominant/subordinate relations, the dynamics and consequences of oppression, and the hegemony of the view of the dominant group and how it is reinforced by social institutions. For example, the deficit situation and sufferings of people may result from social forces of which they are unaware or about which they have little knowledge or understanding. Such is the global nature of capitalism, patriarchy, racism, and the like. A structural analysis helps them to understand and normalize their position in a capitalist, patriarchal, racist society. In turn, understanding and normalization help to free them from feelings of guilt and blame for a situation that they did not cause and to open possibilities for solidarity and collective action with other oppressed persons and groups. In other words, a structural analysis links the personal with the political by enabling people to relate their personal experience with oppression to a broader political understanding.

The contribution of critical postmodernism to a structural analysis is to help us recognize that although oppression and exploitation may be universal phenomena, they will be experienced differently by different people living in different places in different contexts. For example, a person living on the streets of Toronto would experience poverty differently from a person living in rural Newfoundland. An understanding of these differences, along with their meanings for people, would be obtained by the structural social worker through dialogue with those experiencing oppression and then used to inform the larger structural analysis to determine what action should be taken to combat this oppression. Consistent with Foucault's belief, by fighting local practices of oppression in a multi-faceted way, while recognizing that they are attached to broader practices, global oppressions are challenged.

Modernist critical theory emphasizes solidarity among oppressed people but does so through various meta-narratives. For example, Marxism calls for solidarity of the working class against capitalism, and feminism calls for solidarity among women against patriarchy. Solidarity among those who have had common experiences of oppression has been the essence of modernist critical theory's political practice. Solidarity underpins all significant social movements. It is the glue that holds coalitions and alliances together and provides them with their strength, as measured by the numbers of people acting for change. Without solidarity among oppressed people, resistances to the dominant social order are dispersed and weakened. However, the politics of solidarity have often neglected the politics of difference and have reflected in their own organization and culture the very forms of domination and exclusion that existed in the wider societies (Leonard, 1995). Postmodernism helps the structural social worker develop a new politics of solidarity—one that pursues the idea of fractured identities in which differences within particular oppressed groups "are always given attention, contextualized with reference to their specific geographical location in the world, their class position, and their place within the structures of race and ethnicity . . . age, sexuality, and differences of ability" (Leonard, 1995, p. 7). In sum, solidarity within and among oppressed groups is crucial in the quest for emancipation, but to avoid various forms of oppressive inclusions and exclusions that have occurred in the past, it must incorporate a progressive politics of difference.

Another important area for the structural social worker is that of language and discourse. Most social work activity is carried out through language and discourse, whether counselling, writing reports, reading research and journal articles, or articulating analyses of personal and social problems. Like everyone, social workers are immersed in language (Howe, 1994). The modernists believed that language simply reflected reality and that knowledge (obtained or given through language) was empowering. The task of progressive social workers, then, was to increase their own knowledge of oppression and use their knowledge and analyses when working with marginalized groups. However, the postmodernists have shown us that there is no one universal reality but many realities and that language does not have the properties of absolute truth but is historically, culturally, and socially contextualized and largely reflects the interests and world views of dominant groups. Thus, any discourse will include some pieces of information and exclude others.

As well, the messages received may be different from what was intended by the sender. The knowledge historically used by social workers has been that of "expert" knowledge derived from objective, scientific, and professional sources and has reflected a Eurocentric, patriarchal, and bourgeois bias rather than the lived reality of oppressed persons (Leonard, 1994). This expert knowledge has been disempowering for marginalized populations because it reproduces relationships of hierarchy and subordination and excludes the voices of the very people with whom social work claims to be concerned. Structural social workers would facilitate the authentic voices of marginalized groups to be heard (Ife, 1997) and use this communication to inform and modify their professional knowledge and analyses. This process (called dialogical communication) would be used by both the social workers and the oppressed persons to gain a fuller and more accurate understanding of the particular historical, cultural, and social situation they are confronting. It not only is empowering for oppressed persons to be heard, but it provides social workers with fuller, more accurate information than the traditional privileged, and assumed objective, universal knowledge. This approach recognizes the centrality of language and communication in developing emancipatory theories and practices. Structural social work is committed to respecting the plurality of ways in which human beings find their own voices, while also being committed to solidarity with those who are struggling, against the imposition of others, to find those voices.

In sum, the structural social worker does not perceive modernist and postmodernist critical theory as totally dichotomous. This approach is similar to that of some other writers (Ife, 1997; Leonard, 1994; 1995) in that it seeks to use the strengths of each to correct the limitations and contradictions of the other. Allan (2003a, p. 50) argues that critical social work must find a way of keeping the two approaches together but "maintain the tension between the two and work with the contradictions, debates and uncertainties that emerge from taking this position." This view of two opposing sets of forces or theoretical positions acting upon each other constitutes what is called a dialectical relationship (to be discussed in a subsequent section of this chapter). Structural social work as a critical theory is best summarized by Stephen Leonard (1990, p. 269):

> Domination and oppression take a variety of forms, and because of this, enlightenment and emancipation will also take a variety of forms. From this it should be clear that any adequate account of critical theory must be cognizant of the need to be sensitive to the plurality and difference that defines our identities and characterizes our lives, and it must also be attentive to the need to open a philosophical and political space in which individuals can find their own voices, however plural and different they may be. At the same time, a critical theory cannot ignore the harsh reality of those who are victims of history; it must be in solidarity with those victims, or it risks seeing its aims and conclusions transformed into idle posturing and hopeless despair. Plurality and solidarity: these must be the watchwords of critical theory.

The Dialectic in Structural Social Work

One of the most prominent aspects of structural social work is its dialectical analysis and approach to practice. The concept of dialectic is an essential component of structural social work theory. It sensitizes practice to the opposing and contradictory forces within capitalism,[10] the welfare state, and social work, and it helps social work avoid the construction of false dichotomies or dualisms that have been part of the social work tradition. This tradition is actually two traditions—an idealist tradition that persuades individuals they can effect great changes through self-determination and a structural determinist tradition that sees individuals as the victims of a deterministic social environment that cannot be changed. Neither tradition comprehends the dialectic between the individual and the social world—the individual both is the creator of the social world and is created by the social world.

Naiman (1997, pp. 13–14) summarizes the main principles of "dialectics":

- *Everything is related.* Nothing in the universe is isolated, but, rather, all things are dependent on each other. This relationship may be direct or indirect, and therefore, nothing can be understood in isolation.
- *Change is constant.* Nothing in the universe is final, absolute, or immutable. Everything is in a continual process of change, with the replacement of old forms by new forms preserving the viable elements of the earlier form. Change is neither linear nor circular but more like a spiral.
- *Change proceeds from the quantitative to the qualitative.* Change usually occurs gradually and cumulatively over time. At some point, however, the cumulative or quantitative changes result in a qualitatively (i.e., radically) different nature or form. In other words, small changes eventually add up to something quite different from what existed in the first place.

- *Change is the result of the unity and struggle of opposites.* We tend to think in terms of binary opposites—good or bad, right or wrong, beautiful or ugly, true or false, capitalist or socialist, and so on. Dialectics emphasizes the unity of these binary opposites— things can contain within them two opposing forces at the same time. The tensions or contradictions between these opposing tendencies eventually become the basis for social change.

Dialectical analysis is based on a view of society and social processes as containing contradictory opposites that must be unravelled and understood. A dialectical social work theory recognizes the false dualisms of orthodox social work theory and attempts to replace them by recognizing the symbiotic relationship between contradictory elements with all their attendant mutuality. For example, the welfare state has both social care and social control functions, it contains both liberating and oppressive features, and it represents both the fruits of the struggles of oppressed people and a mechanism used by the dominant group to "cool out" the powerless.[11] Without a dialectical understanding of social process, false dichotomies or dualisms are constructed and incorporated into social work theory and practice. The social welfare state and social work may be viewed by one group as solely part of the state apparatus that controls and oppresses people (e.g., orthodox Marxists), while another group may view them as instruments of human liberation representing only humanitarian concerns (e.g., conventional social workers). A dialectical perspective recognizes that social welfare and social work contain both of these contradictory forces. Given this dialectical perspective, the strategy for structural social work is to maximize the emancipatory potential of social welfare and social work and to neutralize or minimize their repressive elements.

The modernist versus postmodernist debate is another example of a duality or false dichotomy that a dialectical analysis can help to clarify. Modernism, with its emphasis on universalisms, historical continuity, and solidarity, is often contrasted with postmodernism's emphasis on difference, present realities, and fragmentation. A dialectical analysis helps one to see the world as possessing some universal truths (e.g., capitalism, oppression of subordinate groups) but with different people in different localities with different ethnicities, social positions, and so on experiencing universal phenomena differently. Dialectical analysis helps one to connect the personal with the political. The aim here is to make an attempt to integrate parts of modernism (the *thesis*) with parts of postmodernism (the *antithesis*) and arrive at a *synthesis* of the two, although it will be an incomplete synthesis. Without a dialectical analysis, the temptation would be to opt for either modernism or postmodernism as a perspective on which to base one's critical theory (as too many have). This would, of course, result in the potential contributions of one or the other being omitted, which in turn would render a disservice to those suffering exploitation and subordination.

Two Fundamental Questions in Structural Social Work

Mullaly and Keating (1991) contend that many of the philosophical, theoretical, and practical disagreements that exist among radical or progressive social workers are actually due to the inadvertent acceptance on the part of many of certain false dichotomies. They further argue that a dialectical approach would lead to greater integration of theory and better informed radical practice. In the chapters on social democracy and Marxism, three schools of socialist thought were identified—social democracy, evolutionary Marxism, and revolutionary Marxism. These three schools differ with respect to their individual prescriptions for social transformation. Two questions fundamental to structural social work and that would elicit disagreement among the socialist schools are:

1.   Should structural social workers work inside or outside the social welfare system?
2.   Do structural social workers concentrate on changing people's consciousness as a prerequisite to social change (i.e., radical humanism), or do they concentrate on changing material conditions and structural patterns as a prerequisite to changing people's consciousness (i.e., radical structuralism)?

The following responses to these questions should help to explain and clarify the dialectical nature of structural social work.

1.   *Where should structural social workers work—inside or outside the social welfare system?* Social democrats appreciate the welfare state within a capitalist society for providing people with a minimum standard of living, but they believe it should also promote greater equality and social justice. They view the capitalist welfare state as a stepping stone toward a socialist society and, therefore, advocate working within the system. Revolutionary Marxists believe that the capitalist welfare state promotes the survival, not the transformation, of capitalism. Therefore, they maintain that structural social workers should work outside the welfare system and support welfare rights groups, co-operatives, self-help groups, and other alternative services and organizations that challenge capitalism. The evolutionary Marxists join the social democrats in their belief that the welfare state can be used to transform capitalism but agree with the revolutionary Marxists that many welfare state activities support and preserve capitalism. Thus, they would work within the system but would separate the forces for socialist change from the forces that preserve capitalism.

A dialectical analysis recognizes the place of human consciousness in the creation and recreation of human circumstances but also recognizes that circumstances affect people and shape their consciousness. The state is shaped both by the logic of capitalism, patriarchy, and racism and by the conscious struggles of people along lines of class, gender, and race. Modern states contain both emancipatory and repressive forces (Frankel, 1979). This requires structural social workers to work both inside and outside the welfare state.

2.   *Radical humanism vs radical structuralism: which comes first, the personal or the political?* Although radical social workers recognize the connection between private troubles and public issues, there is disagreement on which should come first in a strategy of political transformation, the personal or the political. Should changing people (by consciousness-raising) be a prerequisite to changing society, or is the redistribution of wealth and power necessary to change people's consciousness? The former approach is known as "radical humanism" and the latter as "radical structuralism" (Burrell & Morgan, 1979). Each reflects a different set of ontological (the nature of being) and epistemological (the nature of knowledge) assumptions.[12]

Radical humanism is a subjectivist orientation to social change, and radical structuralism is an objectivist orientation. Each provides a different answer to the question "Are we creators of or created by our social reality?" Subjectivist radical humanism holds that knowledge and social reality are created in people's minds through personal experience (Howe, 1987) and that no social facts exist because we create our own social reality. Conversely, objectivist radical structuralism holds that knowledge and social reality are external to the individual, that social reality is composed of concrete structures, and that this external social reality has a deterministic impact on an individual's development and circumstances (Burrell & Morgan, 1979; Howe, 1987).

Obviously, radical humanists and radical structuralists favour different means (i.e., social work practices) to achieve a society free from inequality. The former, who believe that personal consciousness-raising precedes political change, focus their efforts on raising people's consciousness about how inequalities shape, limit, oppress, and dominate their experiences (Howe, 1987). By understanding how capitalist hegemony operates to make people accept their subjugation, they can free themselves to regain control over their present experiences and their destiny (Carniol, 1984; Howe, 1987). Paulo Freire's work in consciousness-raising among oppressed persons is relevant to the subjectivist approach of radical humanists. Radical structuralists, who believe that reality resides in the social world rather than in the person, focus their efforts on changing material conditions and structural patterns along socialist lines. With enough changes, a socialist society would become the new reality. Radical structuralists would organize and mobilize social service users, trade unions, and other social activist groups to achieve this transformation. This approach involves consciousness-raising focused on the reality of unfair social structures and how they are perpetuated rather than on constrained individual reality. Each of these approaches to social transformation contains limitations.

> Radical humanism naively and optimistically assumes that raising people's consciousness will effectively address social problems and expose an exploitative social system. It ignores the fact that power and privilege, whether rooted in class, gender, or race, is [*sic*] not likely to be relinquished without a struggle and that part of this struggle would involve supporting the ideological hegemony required to continue to control people's consciousness. Radical structuralism is overly simplistic and deterministic in its understanding of the complexity of human need and the depth of oppression. It is difficult to understand how describing external power empowers people to change it (Mullaly & Keating, 1991, p. 67).

A dialectical analysis would view these two different approaches to radical practice as a false dichotomy. Although both link private troubles and public issues, they dichotomize praxis (political practice) along personal–political lines. Subjective reality and objective reality are irrevocably locked into a dialectical relationship. We are conscious creators of our surroundings, using thought, information, and emotion to act and to choose. At the same time, we are created by our surroundings. A dialectical approach to structural social work avoids the simplistic linear cause–effect notion of historical materialism and the naive romanticism associated with the notion of totally free human will (Mullaly & Keating, 1991). Dialectical analysis helps to illuminate the complex interplay between people and the world around them and to indicate the role of social work within society. "We are not only objects of the prevailing social order, we must also be subjects who are able to move beyond it" (Mullaly & Keating, 1991, p. 72). In short, structural social work incorporates both these radical traditions into its theory base, recognizing that they constitute a dialectical whole rather than distinct and contradictory approaches. It is not a question of which comes first, the personal or the political. Neither is a prerequisite to the other; both must occur conjointly (Allan, 2003b).

As marginalized groups make their voices heard, one hopes with some help from structural social work, their experiences with and analyses of their subordinate positions in society, including their exploitation and oppression, will be incorporated into structural social work theory, as were the feminist and anti-racist experiences and analyses. Obviously, the theory base of structural social work is not static. It will continue to grow and develop as more information on the experiences of all oppressed groups is received from the oppressed themselves. This will assist in the development of a dialectical politics of difference and solidarity within structural social work theory and practice.

Box 8.2 *Development of a Theoretical Orientation*

Early in my academic career, if someone had asked me (Bob) what my theoretical orientation was, I would have answered unhesitatingly—"Marxist." However, with the critique of Marxism that accompanied the emergence and development of feminist scholarship and that included a progressive feminist analysis of social welfare and social work, I adjusted my theoretical orientation and became a "pro-feminist Marxist." Subsequently, as racialized groups criticized Marxism and feminism for being colour-neutral and omitting race as a source and form of oppression, I became an "anti-racist, pro-feminist, Marxist social worker."

The problem for me was obvious. As more groups would develop and articulate an analysis of their respective sources and forms of oppression, my theoretical label would continue to expand. Thus, I was relieved when Maurice Moreau began to develop his idea of structural social work. This view concerned all forms and sources of oppression and did not regard any particular oppression as primary or more important than others. That is not to say that all oppressions are equally severe; rather, it recognizes that many groups in society find themselves in a position of second-class citizenship, not because of anything they did but because of some group characteristic or trait that they possess and over which they have no control. When people ask me today what my theoretical orientation is, I answer by saying that I am a "critical" social worker. "Critical," today, of course, has a meaning quite different from what it did 35 years ago. It has moved from a narrow Marxist view to an all-inclusive view of oppression—as have I.

Structural Social Work:
A Conceptual Framework

Based on a reconstituted socialist ideology, located within the radical social work camp, grounded in critical theory, structural social work views social problems as arising from a specific societal context—liberal/neo-conservative capitalism—rather than from the failings of individuals. The essence of socialist ideology, radical social work, critical theory, and the change perspective is that inequality: (1) is a natural, inherent (i.e., structural) part of capitalism; (2) falls along such lines as class, gender, race, sexual orientation, age, ability, and geographical region; (3) excludes groups from opportunities, meaningful participation in society, and a satisfactory quality of life; and (4) is self-perpetuating. Writing from Britain, Pond (1989, cited in Davis, 1991, p. 65) presents some reasons why social workers should attend to inequality as a major part of the structural context in which they practice:

> The distribution of economic rewards between different groups in the population and different parts of the country is an important determinant of the nation's economic and social structure. Economic and social inequality are inextricably intertwined, and the distribution of income and wealth, the extent of poverty and privilege, have their effects on living standards, life chances and opportunities. Individuals' health and well-being are influenced by their position in the labour market, income and access to economic resources. Thus, class differences in health (for example) have persisted, despite an overall improvement in national standards.
>
> Moreover, inequalities in wealth have political implications, providing the wealthiest individuals with access to economic, social, and sometimes political power. For this reason, inequalities can become self-perpetuating, having an influence on the institutions that reinforce the class structure.

Given this view of social problems, structural social workers seek to change the social system and not the individuals who receive, through no fault of their own, the results of defective social arrangements.[13] Thus, the goal of structural social work is twofold: (1) to alleviate the negative effects on people of an exploitative and alienating social order; and (2) to transform the conditions and social structures that cause these negative effects. This goal involves a two-tiered process: immediate relief or tension reduction on one level accompanied by longer-term institutional and structural change.

As mentioned previously in this chapter, the term "structural" in structural social work is both descriptive and prescriptive. It is descriptive in the sense that the major source of social problems is identified as the way our society is structured. It is prescriptive in the sense that because social problems are rooted in our social structures, then the structures must be changed, not the individual, the family, or the subculture adversely affected by social problems. Even if it were possible to change everyone currently harmed by our social structures, the source of these problems—our social structures—would still be there to harm, oppress, and alienate more people along lines of class, gender, race, and so on.

The dominant ideology or belief system of a society constitutes the "hidden" or "invisible" structures that are part of the larger concept of social structures. The social institutions of a society maintain the dominant ideology of that particular society, and the social relations of society, in turn, are supported by these social institutions. Because each of these three levels—the dominant ideology, supporting social institutions, and social relations—is an integral part of the structure of society, they must all be changed in the work of social transformation. If the foundation of society is comprised of liberalism, for example, the social institutions of that society will rest on, reflect, and carry out liberal beliefs, values, and ideals. In turn, the social relations will also reflect liberal beliefs, values, and ideals so that they (the social relations) will be characterized by inequality, individualism, capitalism, and so on. In other words, the social institutions and social relations of a particular society will be determined by the dominant ideology and, in turn, will operate in a manner consistent with and supportive of the dominant ideology.

Fundamental social change presents a difficult challenge. Each level of the social structure is interdependent and mutually reinforcing of the other levels, which suggests that a serious approach to social change must occur at all three levels. At the substructural level, the dominant ideology must be challenged by engaging in consciousness-raising—exploring with people the alienating and oppressive features of our present liberal-capitalist system, which is characterized by oppression falling along lines of race, class, gender, culture, age, and so on.[14] At the level of social institutions, not only must the social welfare institution be changed so that its control functions are minimized and its liberating features maximized, but all social institutions must change in a similar manner. At the level of social relations, we must not only attempt to break down the superordinate–subordinate relations around us, we must also attend to the way we live our own personal lives so that we do not contribute to the reproduction of our present social relations, which are often based on classism, sexism, racism, and so on.[15]

The ultimate goal of structural social work is to contribute to the transformation of our current society to one that is more congruent with our reconstituted socialist principles. Carniol (1990, p. 22) says of this transformation:

> A new form of intervention would call for a restructuring of our major institutions, so that they become answerable to the public rather than being strictly controlled by a relatively small class of people composed primarily of white wealthy males. Without such transformation those social problems now experienced will be perpetuated endlessly into the future, with bandaids being busily applied by a profession that should know better.

We now turn to this dual task of helping people while simultaneously working toward the transformation of the liberal and/or neo-conservative paradigm. Given the inroads that neo-conservatism has made in the past several decades with respect to replacing liberalism as the dominant paradigm, it is imperative that structural social work develop theory and praxis for its commitment to socialist principles.

Conclusion

Box 8.3 summarizes some of the major theoretical assumptions and ingredients of the new structural social work that were presented and discussed in this chapter.[16]

Box 8.3 *Major Elements of the New Structural Social Work*

....

- Social problems are built into the structures (social institutions, social processes, social practices, and social relationships) of society.
- Focusing on the individual as the cause of social problems is blaming the victim. For social problems to be resolved, social structures must change.
- Social inequalities are mainly structural in nature and not the result of innate differences.
- Society functions in ways that discriminate against people along lines of class, gender, race, age, ability, and so on.
- The state's institutions, such as the law and educational system, function as instruments of oppression and benefit the privileged groups.
- The traditional dichotomy between the individual and society needs to be challenged; individual problems cannot be understood separately from the social context.
- Social structures, ideology, and personal consciousness are interrelated—each element or component of society affects the others.
- Knowledge is not objective, and the knowledge of the dominant group forms the ruling ideas in society and reflects the interests of the dominant group, often at the expense of subordinate groups.
- Culture, from a critical theory perspective, can be used to further our understanding of oppression and anti-oppressive social work practice.
- A social change perspective must be adopted as a response to social problems and oppression.
- Conventional social work perpetuates social problems by focusing on personal change and/or limited social reform rather than fundamental social change.
- Capitalism should be rejected in favour of some kind of reconstituted democratic socialism.
- No single source or form of oppression can claim primacy. All sources and forms of oppression are to be rejected and no hierarchy of oppression is to be developed.
- The welfare state in a capitalist society props up capitalism and operates in a way to reproduce all oppressive social relations.
- The positive and liberating aspects of modernist critical social theory and of critical postmodern theory are both of central importance.

Continued

- Emphasizing either "individual agency" or "structural forces" as the focus for social change is overly reductionist. To understand social problems and develop structural approaches, both are necessary.
- The dominant order must be challenged and resisted by developing counter-discourses to victim-blaming, free-market glorification, welfare dependency, etc.
- An anti-oppressive and anti-privilege approach to social work should be adopted (see Chapters 9 and 10).

To conclude, all societies establish organizations to carry out certain functions that are essential for their maintenance. Examples include an economic system to ensure the production, distribution, and consumption of needed and desired goods and services; an education system to provide persons with the knowledge and skills needed to participate in the workforce; and a welfare system to attend to the needs of economically deprived persons. These organizations are called social institutions. These institutions, along with their procedural rules of operating, the policies governing their operations, and their social practices, are known as "social structures." These structures affect everyone in society.

Traditional critical social theory has always emphasized social structures as the major source of social problems. Because these social structures were initially established by and continue to be dominated by a particular social group—bourgeois, white, Christian, heterosexual males of European descent—they primarily reflect and reinforce the assumptions, views, ideals, culture, social position, and interests of this group. Furthermore, this group enjoys its privileges and power at the expense of subordinate groups, such as the working class; racialized individuals; non-Christians; people with disabilities; lesbian, gay, bisexual, transgender, queer, intersex, and asexual persons; women; and so on (Mullaly, 2010). Our social structures are imbued with sexism, racism, patriarchy, and classism in that there is a privileged or dominant group within each of these social divisions that has more social, political, and usually economic power than the subordinate groups. The domination of men over women, affluent persons over people living in poverty, white people over racialized individuals, heterosexual persons over gay, lesbian, and transgendered people, and so on has "been so internalized into the structures of society that [it has] also become intrinsic to the roles, rules, policies and practices of [social] institutions" (Haney, 1989, p. 37).

This domination is not usually a conscious or intentional choice on the part of the dominant group, since few people would consider themselves oppressors. Paulo Freire (1994) argues that it is more a case that the dominant group is not aware of any viable alternative social, economic, or political structure. Members of the dominant group perceive their situation of having more not as a privilege that may dehumanize others but as their God-given right for having taken advantage of the opportunities that are available to everyone (in their view). Little thought is given to the possibility that access to opportunities and resources is largely based on one's social position or location (i.e., one's class, gender, race, etc.) rather than strictly on merit or effort. Awareness of the oppressive nature and functions of our present social structures is an essential element of structural social work theory and practice. To that end, the next chapter focuses on the nature, dynamics, causes, and consequences of oppression.

Critical Questions

1. When you hear that someone is a "radical," what is the image that first comes to your mind? Where does this image come from? Can you think of any political purpose that such an image might serve?

2. A tenet of structural social work is that oppression often originates from within or is caused by social structures because they treat people differently (favourably or unfavourably) according to their race, gender, class, age, sexuality, and so on. Furthermore, some of these structures are invisible. What are some examples of invisible structures of privilege, and how do they contribute to oppression?

3. One group of young people lives in comfortable homes in a crime-free and mostly white neighbourhood. These young people all attend the finest schools, have extra money from their parents when they want it, wear the latest teen fashions, and will make use of family connections to get good jobs when they are finished school. Another group of young people lives in a neighbourhood with slum housing, heavy traffic, and a high level of street crime. The schools they attend lack resources and have a high annual rate of teacher turnover, and their parents cannot afford extra help for them. They wear second-hand clothes and spend most of their time on the streets because there is always tension at home and a steady stream of bill collectors, social workers, and the police at their doors. Which group do you think tends to see society as stable, orderly, and full of opportunities, and which group do you think sees society as chaotic and crisis-ridden with no legitimate opportunities?

4. Give some examples of where or how our social structures or institutions are racist, sexist, ageist, classist, ableist, and so on.

9 Oppression: The Focus of Structural Social Work

The oppressed are allowed once every few years to decide which particular representatives of the oppressing class shall represent and repress them.

—Vladimir Lenin (1918), paraphrasing Karl Marx

Introduction

Much mention was made in the previous chapter of oppression and subordinated populations. Indeed, the primary focus of structural social work to date has been oppression. Its socialist ideology, its social change perspective, its critical theory base, its dialectical analysis, and its inclusion of multiple forms of oppression all point to oppression, not to individual deficiency or to social disorganization, as the major source of social problems. Most structural social work practice is carried out with, or on behalf of, oppressed people.

It is crucial for structural social workers to have an understanding of the nature of oppression, its causes and sources, its production and reproduction, its dynamics, its effects on the oppressed, including its internalization, and the social functions it carries out in the interests of the dominant groups (i.e., the oppressors) in society. These are some of the topics discussed in this chapter along with an overview of a model of oppression (the PCS model) that locates oppression at three interrelated levels—personal, cultural, and structural or institutional. As with the preceding and following chapters, this chapter is informed by critical social theory, particularly that of Marx, the Frankfurt School, Habermas, critical postmodernism, feminism, and critical race theory.[1] It is worth noting here that although this chapter focuses mainly on oppression, we agree with Peggy McIntosh (2012) in believing that although oppression may be the *source* of social problems, it is privilege that is the underlying *cause* of social problems, and so we have devoted the next chapter (Chapter 10) to the concept of privilege and the practice of *anti-privilege*.

The Nature of Oppression

To understand what oppression is, it is necessary to know what oppression is not. Since people are social beings and live in societies, no one is free from social structures. Such structures consist of boundaries, barriers, expectations, regulations, and so on. One could make a loose argument that everyone in society is oppressed because one's choices or freedoms are restricted by the simple existence of social structures. For example, when a person drives an automobile, they are obliged to buckle up the seat belt, to drive (in North America) on the right-hand side of the road, and to obey all traffic laws and regulations. These restrictions on our freedom cannot be regarded as oppressive. Not everything that frustrates or limits or hurts a person is oppressive. So if one wishes to distinguish between what oppression is and is not, one has to look at the social context of a particular restriction, limit, or injury (Frye, 1983).

Everyone suffers frustrations, restrictions, and hurt. What determines oppression is when they happen to a person not because of individual talent, merit, or failure but because of their membership in a particular group or category of people—for example, black people, women, people living in poverty, and gay and lesbian persons. "If an individual is oppressed, it is by virtue of being a member of a group or category of people that is systematically reduced, molded, immobilized. Thus, to recognize a person as oppressed, one has to see that individual as belonging to a group of a certain sort" (Frye, 1983, p. 8). Of course, not all groups in society are oppressed. Nor are all oppressed groups equally oppressed. Those in the dominant mainstream of our society are less likely to be oppressed and more likely to be among the oppressors. Women are oppressed (by men) as women. Men are not oppressed as men. Non-whites are oppressed (by whites) as non-whites. Whites are not oppressed as whites. Gay and lesbian persons are oppressed (by heterosexuals) as gay and lesbian persons. Heterosexuals are not oppressed as heterosexuals. This is not to say that oppression is a simple matter of dividing society into two groups: bad people (i.e., the oppressors) and victimized people (i.e., the oppressed). It is much more complex, since most people are oppressed in some aspects of their lives and oppress others in other aspects of their lives.

In addition to being group-based, oppression is described by almost all writers on the subject as relational. There must be a dominant group who oppresses and a subordinate group who is oppressed. The former occupies positions of power, influence, and privilege that are used to maintain their position, often at the expense of the subordinate group(s). Gil (1998, p. 11), for example, argues that once oppression is "integrated into a society's institutional order and culture, and into the individual consciousness of its people through socialization, oppressive tendencies come to permeate almost all relations." Gil points out, however, that the intensity of oppression is not constant but will vary over time. In other words, oppression occurs among (groups of) people in their everyday relations with each other.

Besides being group-based and relational, another feature of oppression is that it is not accidental (nor is it usually intentional).

> The experience of oppressed people is that the living of one's life is confined and shaped by forces and barriers which are not accidental or occasional and hence avoidable, but are systematically related to each other in such a way as to catch one between and among them and restrict or penalize motion in any direction (Albert et al., 1986, p. 19).

Since oppression is perpetrated and perpetuated by dominant groups and is systematic and continuous in its application, a logical question is: why does it occur? The simple and correct answer is that oppression occurs because it benefits the dominant group. Oppression protects a kind of citizenship that is superior to that of the oppressed. It protects the oppressors' access

> # Box 9.1 *Misuse of the Concept of Oppression*
>
> Unfortunately, some writers feel pressure to seek the approval of their peers and attempt to "jump on the bandwagon" of certain frameworks that may be popular at certain times and in certain places (Naiman, 1997). Because "anti-oppressive social work" currently enjoys theoretical popularity, as evidenced by an extensive coverage of the subject in the social work literature since the 1990s, some writers have made claims about oppression that violate its relational nature. For example, a 2003 (later editions in 2010 and 2017) Canadian social work textbook on working with people experiencing addictions was entitled by its authors (Rick Csiernik and William Rowe) *Responding to the Oppression of Addiction: Canadian Social Work Perspectives*. My (Bob's) question is, who is the dominant group that is oppressing another group, and who is the subordinate group that is being oppressed by a dominant group? Which groups are involved in an oppressive relationship? People experiencing problems with addictions may be oppressed along lines of class, race, gender, ability, and so on, but they cannot be oppressed by addictions. No group is enjoying a position of power, privilege, influence, and opportunity because it is oppressing people who are addicted. Addiction may be an outcome of oppression, and although addiction to alcohol or drugs or gambling involves hardship and misfortune, it does not determine oppression. Oppressed groups disproportionately experience certain problems because of their second-class or inferior position in society, but the problem itself is not oppressive. Subordinate group members may be more susceptible to health and social problems than members of the dominant group, but the health or social problem is not the cause of oppression. Health and social problems may be symptoms or outcomes of oppression, but they are not causes of oppression. Only people oppress people.

to a wider range of better-paying and higher-status work. It protects the oppressors' preferential access to and preferential treatment from our social institutions. The oppressed serve as a ready supply of labour to carry out the menial and dangerous jobs in society, and they also serve as scapegoats during difficult times for the dominant group, often being blamed for inflation, government deficits, recessions, social disruptions, and the like. In short, oppression carries out certain social functions for the dominant group by ensuring that society reproduces itself and maintains the same dominant–subordinate relationships.

Although oppression may be group-based, this does not mean that all groups in society are oppressed or that oppressed groups are all equally oppressed. Those in the dominant mainstream of society are less likely to be oppressed and more likely to be among the oppressors. As indicated above, given the relational nature of oppression, people may be oppressed in some relations and oppressors in others, while some relations may involve mutual oppression (Gil 1998).

Just as not all groups are oppressed, persons within an oppressed group are not all equally oppressed. In other words, not all persons within an oppressed group will experience everything the same way. For example, although all women may be oppressed as women, there is great diversity among women that will result in more oppression for some women and less oppression for others. It is true that all women are oppressed by patriarchy (although there is no agreement among feminists as to how much), but many women are also oppressed by race, class, age, sexuality, standards of beauty, and so on. And many women may assume the role of oppressor along these same lines. Oppression, then, is a complex and multi-faceted social phenomenon.

In one of the few American textbooks on anti-oppressive social work, the authors, Morgaine and Capous-Desyllas (2015, pp. 19–20) identified five separate features of oppression that highlight its complexity and multi-faceted nature:

- Pervasiveness: social inequality is woven throughout social institutions, as well as being embedded within individual consciousness.
- Restrictiveness: oppression represents structural and material limitations that significantly shape individual opportunities and one's sense of possibility.
- Hierarchical: oppression denotes a hierarchical relationship in which members of privileged groups have unearned advantages at the expense of disadvantaged groups.
- Complex: power and privilege are relative, because individuals hold multiple, complex, and intersectional social group memberships that give relative privilege and disadvantage in different ways, depending on different contexts.
- Internalization: oppression also resides in the human psyche where oppressive beliefs are internalized.

Oppression, then, is not a static concept but a dynamic, multi-dimensional, and relational one. Dominelli (2002) points out that although relations of domination divide people into superior and inferior groups, these relations occur as interactions between people not only at the personal level but at the cultural and institutional or structural levels as well (to be discussed further in a subsequent section of this chapter entitled Levels of Oppression). The dominant group in society may not really subscribe to oppressive behaviour as a means of protecting its favourable position. Most people do not consider themselves oppressors. In fact, most people probably believe that oppressive behaviour should not be a part of a democratic society. Why, then, do they engage in oppressive practices? Paulo Freire (1970, p. 45) eloquently answers this question:

> The oppressors do not perceive their monopoly on having more as a privilege which dehumanizes others and themselves. . . . For them, having more is an inalienable right, a right they acquired through their own "effort," with their "courage to take risks." If others do not have more, it is because they are incompetent and lazy, and worst of all is their unjustifiable ingratitude towards the "generous gestures" of the dominant class. Precisely because they are "ungrateful" and "envious," the oppressed are regarded as potential enemies who must be watched.

Thus, the view the oppressors hold of the oppressed is that they constitute a dangerous class that must be controlled for the good of the whole society. The ways this social control is carried out are discussed below.

Box 9.2 *Myths That Perpetrate and Perpetuate Oppression*

···

- *Myth of scarcity.* There is not enough to go around, which deflects attention away from the fact that a small minority owns most of the world's resources.
- *Myth of might makes right.* The majority rules even if it means tyranny of the minority.
- *Myth of objective information.* It is possible for one group (mainly white, bourgeois males) to observe humanity objectively, thus becoming the authoritative knowers.
- *Stereotyping.* All members of a group are the same.
- *Blaming the victim.* People are the architects of their own misfortune and oppression.
- *Competition and hierarchy.* Human beings are competitive by nature and aspire to be ahead/above others. (From Anne Bishop, 2002)

To this set of myths that supports oppression, Haney (1989) adds two others:

- *Myth of supremacy.* The dominant educational system, with its emphasis on Western civilization, leads to a belief in the supremacy of a white, Western, male culture.
- *Myth of class.* Most people believe they belong to the middle class, which lives in harmony with a "higher" (superior) class. This belief mandates and then sanctions a dominant and a subordinate class.

We would add one more myth to the above list—the myth that underpins liberal ideology: the myth of equal opportunity (or meritocracy). Because civil and political rights have been equalized under the law, it is believed that if one works hard and takes advantage of the opportunities (in education and in the job market, for example) available to all, one can succeed in life. If a person fails, the judgment is that the person did not take advantage of available opportunities (and therefore should not be helped). This myth overlooks or does not recognize the fact that not all people are in the same position to take advantage of so-called opportunities, since social position and resources give some people preferred access to these so-called "equal" opportunities. And, of course, since the majority of the people who "fail" are disproportionately from historically disadvantaged and subordinate groups, the notion of superior/inferior groups is reinforced—an example of a process that Ryan (1976) calls "blaming the victim."

Oppression as a Social Justice Issue

Most anti-oppressive social work writers base their ideas and writings on some notion of "social justice." However, there is no agreement on the meaning of this concept in the literature. David Gil (1994) makes the point that although social work professional codes of ethics require social workers to "promote social justice," these codes do not specify the meaning of social justice, instead treating it as if it were self-evident. Yet social justice cannot be promoted unless its meaning is first clarified. One of the oldest and most ubiquitous concepts of social justice is that of distributive justice, which focuses on distribution and redistribution issues with respect to how rights, opportunities, and material resources are allocated in society (Morgaine & Capous-Desyllas, 2015). However, if we are to adopt a social justice form of social work, we must recognize the severe limitations of the distributional view of social justice.

The particular concept of social justice that we favour is that developed by Iris Marion Young. In *Justice and the Politics of Difference* (1990), she defines social justice as "the elimination of institutionalized domination and oppression" (p. 15). She contends that contemporary philosophical theories of justice do not conceive justice so broadly. Instead, they restrict themselves to an interpretation of social justice as the morally proper distribution of benefits and burdens among all of society's members. The benefits to be distributed would include both material resources, such as wealth and income, and non-material social goods, such as rights, opportunities, and power. Issues of distributive justice are analogous to persons dividing a stock of goods and comparing the amount or size of the portions. Injustice, according to this distributive notion of social justice, would be defined as a situation in which one group has a monopoly over a particular good. Even explicitly socialist discussions of social justice fall within the distributional theory because the principles of distribution (need vs market) are paramount to social justice. What distinguishes the distributive perspective of social justice, then, is the tendency to see social justice and distribution as co-extensive concepts (Young, 1990).

Welfare capitalism and conventional social work have also adopted the distributional concept of social justice in that their focus has been on the distribution and redistribution of income and other resources (often defined in terms of some kind of social minimum such as a "minimum wage"). Discussion has tended to centre on inequalities of wealth and income and the extent to which the state can or should alleviate the suffering of the poor and disadvantaged. Even progressive social work and social welfare writers tend to equate social justice with a redistribution of goods and services. An example is Lena Dominelli, who has written landmark progressive books on feminist social work (Dominelli & McLeod, 1989), on anti-racist social work (Dominelli 1988), and on anti-oppressive social work (Dominelli, 2002). She asserts that "those endorsing an emancipatory approach to social work have an explicit commitment to social justice" (2002, p. 4). She then criticizes the law as limited in pursuing social justice: "Its [the law's] tendency to individualise collective problems can only mean that *redistributive justice* remains beyond its scope. Yet it is precisely *this form of justice* which black activists, women, and other oppressed groups are demanding" (1988, p. 14; emphasis added). It may be that some oppressed groups are demanding this form of justice, but again, it is limited justice because it does nothing to alter the processes and practices that allow for an unjust share of society's resources to go to one group in the first place.

Obviously, the immediate provision of basic goods and services for people suffering severe deprivation must be a first priority for any group or program seeking social justice. Any conception of justice must take into account the vast differences in the amount of material goods that exist in our society, where thousands starve and live on the streets while others can have anything they want (Young, 1990). From a structural perspective, however, a major limitation of the distributional theory of social justice is identified by Iris Marion Young in *Justice and the Politics of Difference* (1990). Equating the scope of social justice only with distribution is misleading in two ways: (1) the social processes and practices that caused the maldistribution in the first place are ignored; and (2) the limits of the logic of extending the notion of distribution to such non-material goods and resources as rights and opportunities are not recognized.

Ignoring Social Processes and Practices

Young notes that the distributional view of justice assumes a social atomist or individualist perspective of people in that they are externally related to the goods they possess and only related to one another in terms of a comparison of the amounts of goods they possess. The institutional contexts within which distribution occurs are ignored. These institutional contexts go beyond a narrow Marxist account of the mode of production and include all social structures and practices, the rules and norms that guide them, and the language and symbols that mediate social interactions within them. This context affects distribution—what is distributed, how it is distributed, who distributes it, who receives it, and what the outcome is. An example presented by Young (1990, p. 23) is economic inequality. Discussions of distribution often omit the decision-making structures that determine economic relations in society.

> Economic domination in our society occurs not simply because persons have more wealth and income than others, as important as this is. Economic domination derives at least as much from the corporate and legal structures and procedures that give some persons the power to make decisions about investment, production, marketing, employment, interest rates, and wages that affect millions of other people. Not all who make these decisions are wealthy or even privileged, but the decision-making structure operates to reproduce distributive inequality and the unjust constraints on people's lives.

Limits of Extending Distribution to the Non-material

Advocates of the distributive theory of justice claim that any issue of justice, including such non-material things as rights and opportunities, may be treated as "goods" or some aggregate of things to be possessed and/or distributed and redistributed. Young argues that such treatment produces a misleading conception of the issues of justice involved, since it reifies aspects of social life that are better understood as functions of rules, relations, and processes than as things.

Distributing or redistributing rights and opportunities is not the same as distributing or redistributing income because rights and opportunities are not possessions. Some groups may have rights and opportunities that other groups do not have, but extending them to the groups that do not have them does not entail that the formerly privileged group must surrender some of its rights and/or opportunities as it does in the case of a redistribution of income. Rights are not things but relationships; rights are institutionally defined rules specifying what people can do in relation to others. "Rights refer to doing more than having, to social relationships that enable or constrain action" (Young, 1990, p. 25). In other words, people may have certain rights but be unable to exercise them because of particular constraints based on class, gender, race, and so on. For example, a person living in poverty may have a right to a fair trial but be unable financially to hire proper legal counsel.

Similarly, opportunity refers to doing rather than to having. It is a condition of enablement rather than of possession and usually involves a system of social rules and social relations as well as an individual's skills and abilities. Having opportunities may lead to securing material goods such as food, shelter, and a job, but it is no guarantee that these goods and services will be secured. Just as people may have certain rights but are unable to exercise them, so, too, might people have certain opportunities but be constrained from using them because of particular social relations and practices. For example, in Canada we may say that Indigenous persons have the opportunity to obtain an education, but education occurs in a complex context of social relations. Indigenous people tend to have inferior schools, fewer material resources, and less access to tutors and computers, as well as the experience of culture shock in off-reserve schools. This is not to say that distribution is irrelevant to educational opportunities but that opportunity has a wider scope than distribution (Young, 1990).

Certainly, then, the distributive theory of social justice contains a major limitation. By focusing on something that must be identifiable and assignable, it reifies social relations and processes and institutional rules. It gives primacy to substance over relations, rules, and processes by conceiving of people as social atoms, thus failing to appreciate that individual identity and capacities are themselves the products of social relations and processes (Taylor, 1985, cited in Young, 1990). Such an atomistic social ontology ignores or obscures the importance of institutional contexts and rules and social relations and processes for understanding issues of social justice. An adequate conception of social justice must understand and evaluate these social phenomena as well as the substance of distribution (Young, 1990).

Heller (1987) suggests a conception of justice that includes social phenomena. She views justice as primarily the virtue of citizenship wherein persons collectively consider problems and issues facing them within their institutions and actions, under conditions free from oppression and domination, with reciprocity and mutual tolerance of differences. Young argues that this conception of justice shifts the focus from distribution issues to procedural issues of participation in deliberation and decision-making. A norm would be just only if people who follow it have an effective voice in its consideration and acceptance. A social condition would be just only if it enabled all people to meet their needs and exercise their freedoms. A social process would be just only if it were an inclusive process with respect to different social groupings. A social practice would be just only if it is in accordance with how people carrying it out would like to be treated themselves. Social injustice from this perspective entails not only an unfair distribution of goods and resources but includes any norm, social condition, social process, or social practice that interferes with or constrains one from fully participating in society—that is, from becoming a full citizen.

This concept of social justice is empowering because it goes beyond a concern with distribution to include the institutional conditions necessary for the development and exercise of individual capacities and collective communication and cooperation (Young, 1990). Oppression consists of institutional conditions that inhibit or prevent one from becoming a full participant in society. A society may be evaluated as just to the degree that it contains and supports the institutional conditions necessary for the promotion of the universal value that everyone is of equal intrinsic worth. For all those concerned with developing an adequate conception of social justice and for those committed to social justice in practice, oppression must be a central concern. This contention is consistent with such anti-oppressive social work writers as Donna Baines (2011) in Canada, Lena Dominelli (2002) in the UK, and Karen Morgaine and Moshoula Capous-Desyllas (2015) in the US.

The Origins of Modern-Day Oppression and the Politics of Identity

Modern-day classism, sexism, racism, homophobia, ageism, ableism, and other forms of oppression are not superstitious carry-overs from the Dark Ages. On the contrary, Young (1990) states that nineteenth- and early twentieth-century scientific and philosophical discourse explicitly proposed and legitimated formal theories of race, sex, age, and national superiority. Also, she contends that the methods of science and the attributes of the scientist have, in part, contributed to the formulation of these theories of superiority/inferiority. The social construction of these theories that present a white, bourgeois male as the perfection of human form and equate the virtues of manliness with the virtues of respectability is discussed below.

There has been much criticism of modern scientific reason by critical theorists, feminists, and postmodernists. These criticisms, which were summarized in the previous chapter, have, in part, punctured the authority of modern scientific reason. A major part of this criticism has been directed at the construction of the scientist and philosopher as knowers or subjects standing outside the objects of knowledge—autonomous, objective, and neutral. The subject is a socially detached observer, standing in the immediate presence of reality but without any involvement in it. Moreover, as Foucault (1977) notes, these observations are not mere passing looks but normalizing gazes that assess their object according to some hierarchical standard. Some of the particulars or attributes of the object are then defined as deviant or are devalued in comparison to the norm.

Young (1990) cites scholarship that has revealed the white, bourgeois, male, European biases attached to the notion of a rational subject or knower. That is, the virtues of the scientist have also become the virtues of masculinity—detachment, careful measurement and the manipulation of instruments, comprehensive generalizing and reasoning, and authoritative speech supported by evidence (Keller, 1985; Merchant, 1978, both cited in Young, 1990). Those articulating and carrying out the code of modern scientific reason were white, bourgeois males speaking for themselves and unmindful that there might be other positions. In other words, they became not only the knowers or truth-seeking subjects, they also created or embodied the standards against which all other groups (objects) were measured. This already privileged group assumed the privilege of the authoritative subject of knowledge, and groups that they defined as differing became the objects of their distancing and mastering observations.

> The imposition of scientific reason's dichotomy between subject and object on hierarchical relations of race, gender, class, and nationality . . . has deep and abiding consequences for the structuring of privilege and oppression. The privileged groups lose their particularity; in assuming the position of the scientific subject they become . . . agents

of a universal view from nowhere. The oppressed groups, on the other hand, are locked in their objectified bodies, blind, dumb, and passive. The normalizing gaze of science focused on the objectified bodies of women, Blacks, Jews, homosexuals, old people, the mad and feeble-minded. From its observations emerged theories of sexual, racial, age, and mental or moral superiority (Young, 1990, p. 127).

Nineteenth-century theories of race that explicitly assumed white, male, bourgeois, European body types and facial features as the norm were given legitimation and naturalized by scientific discourse (Young, 1990). Using this norm as the measuring stick, these theories posited that all other bodies were considered either degenerate or less developed. This superior body type by nature also determined directly the intellectual, aesthetic, and moral superiority of persons in this group over all other types (West, 1982).

In addition to a superior body type, the nineteenth-century ideal of beauty was primarily an ideal of manly virtue—a strong, self-controlled, rational man distanced from sexuality, emotion, and everything disorderly or disturbing (Mosse, 1985; Young, 1990). "In much nineteenth-century scientific discourse . . . whole groups of people are essentially and irrevocably degenerate: Blacks, Jews, homosexuals, poor and working people, and women" (Young, 1990, pp. 128–129). Women were considered physically delicate and weak, childlike mentally, and prone to irrationality and madness. The notion of whiteness was identified with reason, while blackness was associated with body (Kovel, 1970). This allowed people who were white to identify themselves as possessing reason and, therefore, to be the subject of knowledge and to identify racialized individuals as the objects of knowledge (Said, 1978). Nineteenth-century discourse often extended the concept of "black" to depict Jews and gays and lesbians. A new discourse on old age occurred in this time period too, shifting it from an association with wisdom and endurance to an identification with frailty, incontinence, and senility (Cole, 1986, cited in Young, 1990). All groups that did not meet the norm of the young, white, bourgeois man were objectified in varying degrees as degenerate others.

This normal/abnormal or good/bad distinction did not guarantee respectability and superiority for all white bourgeois men, however, because even they were subject to disease and deviance, especially if they succumbed to sexual impulse. The nineteenth-century medical and moral literature is replete with male fears of becoming effeminate. Therefore, manly men must protect their health and beauty by exercising control over sexual urges. Bishop (1994) contends that during this period every oppressed group was assigned at least one negative sexual myth, usually that the oppressed group was sexually out of control, immoral, or perverted. Thus, all women secretly want to be raped; gays and lesbians are perverts who engage in unnatural sex acts and want to seduce children; people living poverty breed like rabbits; black men want to rape white women; black women are more highly sexed than white women; Indigenous women cannot say "no"; individuals with disabilities and older persons have no sexuality. These stereotypic attributes reinforced the socially constructed and "scientifically" legitimated belief that groups other than young, white, bourgeois males were inferior and degenerate.

Once a social definition (including stereotypes) is constructed, various social practices and psychological responses come into play to contribute to its institutionalization. In effect, an aggregate of differentiated individuals is categorized (constructed) as a distinct group and consequently share a common status assigned to them by others and are subject to categorical treatment. They become united only by a negative identity.

The Dynamics of Oppression

It could be argued that the racial, gender, class, mental, and other theories of superiority generated by nineteenth-century scientific reason have been discredited by twentieth-century research and social movements. Numerous pieces of social legislation and social rules in the form of proclaimed civil, political, and human rights are now available to oppressed persons, as are affirmative action and employment equity programs that express a commitment to equality among social groups. Ideologies of natural superiority and group domination no longer seem to hold the influence they once did in our society. However, the position taken here is that various forms of oppression still are rooted in contemporary society, but they appear in different manifestations having both continuities and discontinuities with past structures.

Oppression does not usually occur today through some coercive rule of law or because of the evil intentions of a dominant group, although sometimes it does, as in cases of anti-union legislation or in the recent law—referred to as the "bathroom bill"—passed and enacted by North Carolina on 23 March 2016 that discriminates against transgender people by requiring them to use public washrooms based on the biological gender noted on their birth certificates as opposed to their preferred and more recently acquired gender. North Carolina's reputation was stained, and the state was hurt financially because many businesses left and major sporting events and concerts were moved out of the state in protest against this discriminatory bill. A year later, the part of the bill that required transgender people to use public washrooms based on the gender noted in their birth certificates was repealed, but no protections were enacted to protect transgender people from other discriminations such as in the areas of housing, employment, and education. Oppression today occurs mostly through the systemic constraints on subordinate groups that take the form of unquestioned norms, behaviours, and symbols and in the underlying assumptions of institutional rules. In other words, modern-day oppression is structural.

> In this extended structural sense oppression refers to the vast and deep injustices some groups suffer as a consequence of often unconscious assumptions and reactions of well-meaning people in ordinary interactions, media and cultural stereotypes, and structural features of bureaucratic hierarchies and market mechanisms—in short, the normal processes of everyday life. We cannot eliminate this structural oppression by getting rid of the rulers or making new laws, because oppressions are systematically reproduced in major economic, political, and cultural institutions (Young, 1990, p. 41).

To understand the meaning and practice of oppression, Foucault (1977) suggests that we go beyond viewing oppression as the conscious and intentional acts of one group against another. Instead, oppression is often found in such areas as education, the production and distribution of goods and services, public administration, the delivery of health and social services, and the like. In other words, many people contribute to maintaining and reproducing oppression in carrying out many of their day-to-day activities, yet they do not understand themselves to be agents of oppression (Young, 1990). This is not to say that members of oppressed groups are never intentionally harmed, as evidenced by rapes of women, physical attacks on gay men, lockouts of workers, and harassment of racialized individuals. Nor does it mean that members of oppressed groups never oppress others, as evidenced by verbal attacks of the working poor on the non-working poor, physical attacks by youth gang members belonging to one oppressed group against youth belonging to another oppressed group, racial biases held by people in some ethnic or religious communities, or attacks by members on others belonging to the same oppressed group. In spite of these acts of intentional oppression, the contention here is that most oppression today is systemic and unintentional, built into our social institutions, and carried out unconsciously in our day-to-day activities.

What are some of the systemic and unintentional daily activities that contribute to oppression in today's society? Bishop (2002) outlines several components that appear to be common to all forms or sources of oppression and help to maintain oppression.

- First, a position of supremacy is held by the dominant group and is backed by "power over" others. This power can include greater material resources, physical strength, weapons, information, decision-making, and control of the media. Both groups internalize this hierarchy and act it out, thus reproducing the hierarchy with minimal resistance.
- Second, all social groups incur stereotypes. Although stereotypes can be positive, they are most often hurtful and used in a damaging way against subordinate groups. The more powerful groups in society cannot be hurt by stereotypes as much as those with little power.
- Third, all oppressed groups are susceptible to violence or its threat in society. Beatings, threats, vandalism, and harassment are activities sometimes perpetrated on subordinate groups to keep them in their place whenever they step out of it or think of doing so.
- Fourth, as mentioned above, all oppressed groups have been assigned at least one negative characteristic about their sexuality. Usually it is a belief that members of the oppressed groups are sexually out of control, perverted, or immoral and, therefore, unworthy of any positive regard or treatment.
- Fifth, subordinate groups are at greater risk of being separated from their children than are members of the dominant group. People living in poverty, Indigenous persons, single mothers, black people, gay and lesbian individuals, and immigrants are all suspect in terms of their ability to care properly for their children, and consequently they experience more surveillance and intrusions and have less protection of their rights than those in the dominant group. Fear of losing one's children is, of course, a powerful social control mechanism for obtaining compliance or conformity from subordinate group members.

Levels of Oppression

Oppression occurs at three levels: the personal or individual level, the cultural level, and the structural or institutional level (Dominelli, 1997; Mullaly, 2002; Thompson, 1997; 2001; 2002). Each of these three levels or locations is interdependent, interactive, and mutually reinforcing with respect to the other levels and, in turn, is supported, reinforced, and influenced by the other two levels. In other words, each level of oppression influences and reinforces oppression on the other two levels. Thompson (1997) has named this multi-dimensional perspective the "PCS" (personal, cultural, structural) model of analysis.

The personal or individual level is located within the cultural and structural contexts of society, and the cultural level is located within the structural context (see Figure 9.1). Although we may examine oppression at only the personal level or at one of the other two levels, it will be an incomplete examination because one's thoughts, attitudes, and actions can only be understood in the larger context(s) with an awareness that the three levels continuously interact with one another. In some respects, the PCS model of analysis is an elaboration of the "personal is political" analysis of feminists, social activists, and progressive social workers (Mullaly, 2002). It retains the "personal" and the "political" by recognizing that social problems are political or structural by nature and that they cause personal difficulties for many people. Furthermore, just as structural forces affect people, so, too, do people affect structures. This insight has been behind all social change movements, from small acts of individual resistance to large social movements. The PCS model adds to this perspective an intermediate level, which is the cultural level. Culture (values, norms, and shared patterns of thinking) tended to be lumped in as part of the structural level in the "personal is political" model (see, for example, Baines, 2007; 2011; Dominelli, 2002). However, today, thanks to the development of contemporary cultural studies, we have a greater understanding of how the dominant culture of a society reflects and reinforces the oppression of subordinate cultures on the other two levels.

Oppression at the personal level comprises those thoughts, attitudes, and behaviours that depict a negative prejudgment of a particular subordinate group. It is usually based on stereotypes and

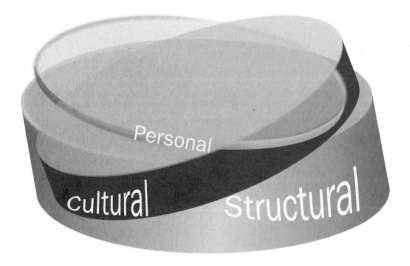

FIGURE 9.1 PCS Model of Oppression: Dynamic Interaction between Levels

Source: Mullaly & West (2018, p. 30).

may be overt or covert. Oppression at the cultural level consists of those values, norms, and shared patterns of thinking and acting, along with an assumed consensus about what is right and normal, that, taken together, endorse the belief in a superior culture. It acts as a vehicle for transmitting and presenting the dominant culture (i.e., the culture of the dominant group) as the norm, the message being that everyone should conform to it. Oppression at the structural level refers to the means by which oppression is institutionalized in society. It consists of the ways that social institutions, laws, policies, and social processes and practices all work together primarily in favour of the dominant group at the expense of subordinate groups. At this level, oppression is given its formal legitimation.

The Multiplicity and Persistence of Oppression

A person's identity is associated with physical, psychological, social, and cultural variables such as appearance, personality, social status or class, social roles, and race or ethnicity (Mullaly, 2002). One's identity is seldom, if ever, determined solely by one characteristic, although one characteristic may be a major marker in most situations (e.g., one's gender or skin colour). The individual does not possess a single social identity but multiple identities that shift and change over time or in different contexts. Persons may be identified in various ways because they tend to be members of many affinity groups. Black persons, for example, may be rich, poor, old, or gay. These differences produce different identities as well as potential conflicts with other black people and affinities with some white people. Oppressed people are seldom oppressed along one dimension only but tend to be multiply oppressed.

Given the fact of multiple identities and the wide array of forms and sources of oppression, most oppressed people belong to more than one category of oppression. Anne Bishop (2002, p. 78) states, "we are oppressors in some parts of our identity, and oppressed in others." She suggests that it would be easier to fight oppression if a line could be drawn between oppressors and oppressed. This means that most oppressed people also have access to some form of superiority and domination. Because many disadvantaged people have at least one form of domination as part of their identity, it is very difficult to wage a campaign to eliminate oppression. Although the individual may want to see the end of oppression in those parts of their identity that are subordinate (e.g., poverty, homosexuality), they may be very reluctant to surrender the power and privilege that come with that part of personal identity that is dominant (e.g., maleness, affluence).

The net effect of defending those parts of our identity that give us relatively favourable treatment in society while contributing to the oppression of others is to keep the whole system of oppression in place. As long as separation, competition, and hierarchy among subordinate groups exist, there is no potential for solidarity and collective action on the part of oppressed groups, which leaves the status quo protected. Only a complete and complex understanding of our own contradictory roles as oppressors and oppressed will allow us to recognize our shared interests and to resist rather than cooperate with oppression (Bishop, 1994). Mullaly and West (2018) present an overview of a few models that attempt to depict the intersecting and multiple nature of oppression.

Forms of Oppression

Although all oppressed groups, such as people living in poverty and working-class people, women, racialized individuals, LGBTTQ individuals, persons with disabilities, elderly people, Jews, and Indigenous persons, experience some obstacles to developing their capacities and to participating fully in society, it is impossible to give one essential or universal definition of oppression. Iris Marion Young (1990) has developed a set of five categories or forms of oppression that encompass both distributive issues of injustice and social structures, relations, and practices that go beyond distribution. Although not all oppressed groups experience all five forms of oppression, they do experience at least one of them and usually more than one. A summary of each is presented below.

Exploitation

Exploitation refers to those social processes whereby the dominant group is able to accumulate and maintain status, power, and assets from the energy and labour expended by subordinate groups. Exploitation is primarily experienced by working-class persons, women, and racialized individuals.

With respect to workers, capitalism systematically transfers powers from workers through the private ownership of the means of production and through markets that allocate labour and the ability to buy goods. As well, the powers of workers are diminished by more than the amount transferred because workers also suffer material deprivation and a loss of control over their work, which results in a loss of self-respect.

The injustice of class division goes beyond the fact that a few people have enormous wealth while many people have little. Exploitation is realized through a structural relationship between the have and have-not groups. Social rules about what work is, who works for whom, how work is to be compensated, and how the results of work are to be distributed and used all operate through a systematic process to produce and reproduce relations of power and inequality.

Women are exploited not only in the Marxist sense that they are wage workers or that their domestic labour is simply subsumed in the wages a family receives but also in terms of their nurturing, caring, and smoothing over of workplace tensions (Alexander, 1987; Young, 1990). Women expend energy and expertise that are most often unnoticed and unacknowledged (while they simultaneously perform their work in their paying jobs) in ways that enhance the wealth, status, or comfort of others, usually of men who thereby are released to carry out work considered more important and creative, both aspects of which are more highly rewarded than the work of the subordinate women. In other words, the power, freedom, and status enjoyed by men are attributable significantly to women who work for them and in a way that constitutes a systematic and unreciprocated transfer of power and energy from women to men (Young, 1990).

Along with class and gender, Young (1990) argues that there is also a race-specific form of exploitation. It is carried out by members of non-white groups performing menial tasks for white people. Wherever racism exists in a predominantly white society, there is an expectation that members of non-white groups will carry out servant roles for the dominant white group—domestics, bellhops, maids, non-professional nannies, porters, busboys, janitors, dishwashers, and the like. In addition to servile, unskilled, minimum-wage, and low-status work with little autonomy, these jobs involve a transfer of energy whereby the servers enhance the status of the served.

To Young's contention that menial labour constitutes a form of exploitation, another form of work—dangerous work—can also be considered exploitative. During times of war, it has traditionally been working men living in poverty, both white and black, who are usually on the front lines of the battlefield while white bourgeois males—high-ranking officers and officials in departments of defence—direct operations far from the front lines and take credit for victory. The coal-mining industry and the fisheries have historically employed (in the former case) or relied on (in the latter case) resource-poor people to go into the mines to dig and extract the coal or to go on the waters to catch the fish, while the owners of the mines or the fish-processing plants, who determine wages or the price of the fish catch, seldom leave their safe and comfortable corporate headquarters. Female workers are subject to sexual harassment on the job, a type of corporate violence to which men typically are not exposed. (One in 13 women in the Canadian military reported that they had been sexually assaulted during the period from April to August 2013, according to a 2014 Statistics Canada survey reported in the *Halifax Metro*, 15 August 2014). The "#MeToo" movement arose and spread virally in October 2017 because of the widespread prevalence of sexual assault and harassment, especially in the workplace.

The above forms of exploitation cannot be eliminated by a redistribution of material resources. As long as current structural relations and institutionalized practices remain unaltered, the process of transferring energy and labour from the exploited to the dominant group will reproduce an unequal distribution of goods and benefits. "Bringing about justice where there is exploitation requires reorganization of institutions and practices of decision-making, alteration of the division of labor, and similar measures of institutional, structural, and cultural change" (Young, 1990, p. 53).

Marginalization

Marginalization primarily affects racialized individuals, some old and young persons, many single mothers and their children, people with physical and mental disabilities, unskilled workers, and North American Indigenous peoples. These groups constitute a growing underclass permanently confined to the margins of society because the labour market cannot or will not accommodate them.

Young (1990) suggests that marginalization is perhaps the most dangerous form of oppression because it excludes whole groups of people from useful and meaningful participation in society, which, in turn, may lead to severe material deprivation. Even though advanced capitalist societies have put in place modern welfare systems to deal with material deprivation, in North America at least, welfare redistribution has not eliminated large-scale suffering, and in the present political climate there is no assurance that the welfare state will continue. As well, the welfare state in liberal democracies has been criticized for denying those who become dependent on it of certain rights and freedoms that others take for granted (Galper, 1975; 1980). Welfare bureaucracies have often treated people living in poverty, old persons, and individuals with disabilities who rely on them for support and services with punitive, demeaning, patronizing, and arbitrary policies and regulations that interfere with their basic rights to privacy, respect, and autonomy. Black youths are an example of a marginalized group that has been treated in a punitive and violent manner, as evidenced by the dozens of black youth who are shot and killed every year by police officers in the US.

Even when material deprivation is not present, marginalization may still occur. Many older people, for example, have the material means to live comfortable lives, but they are excluded from meaningful social participation and cannot exercise their capacities in socially defined and recognized ways. Most of society's productive and recognized activities are related to age and work. Thus, in their marginality older people are often subject to feelings of uselessness, boredom, and a lack of self-respect.

Marginalization constitutes a basic feature of injustice and oppression. To overcome it requires both a restructuring of productive activity to address a right of participation within the wage system and establishing some socially productive activity outside the wage system.

Powerlessness

Powerlessness consists of inhibitions in the development of one's capacities, a lack of decision-making power in one's working life, and exposure to disrespectful treatment because of the status one occupies. It affects primarily non-professional workers but also racialized individuals and women to a lesser extent. It is based on the social division of labour but is more complex than the traditional Marxist model of class exploitation in that it recognizes the distinction between the "middle class" and the "working class" as a social division of labour between professionals and non-professionals.

Most workplaces in advanced capitalist societies are organized hierarchically, with direct participation of workers being rare and decisions (in both the private and public sectors) being imposed on workers and citizens. However, this decision-making power is often mediated by agents who may have no say in the decision but do exercise power and authority over others in carrying out decisions and policies. The powerless are those who do not have power or authority even in this mediated sense; they "exercise little creativity or judgement in their work, have no technical expertise or authority, . . . and do not command respect" (Young, 1990, pp. 58–59). Non-professionals suffer this type of oppression; professionals (white males at least) do not.

The status privilege of professionals has three aspects (Sennett & Cobb, 1972, cited in Young, 1990). First, professionals develop their capacities and gain recognition by obtaining a university education and through subsequent professional advancement with an accompanying rise in status. Second, professionals have considerable work autonomy relative to non-professionals and usually have some authority over others, whether subordinate workers or clients. Third, the privileges of the professional extend beyond the workplace to a whole way of life or culture that has respectability associated with it. The norms of respectability in our society—in terms of dress, speech, tastes, and demeanour—are those of a professional culture. If one wishes to make a good impression, whether in seeking a bank loan or applying for a job, one likely will try to look "professional" or "respectable" as part of one's efforts. Typically, professionals receive more respectful treatment in our society than non-professionals.

The power and respectability that accompany the privileged status of being a professional also involve racist and sexist dynamics. Racialized individuals and women who are professionals must prove their respectability again and again. When it is not known that they are professional persons, they are often not treated with respect or deference, but when others become aware that the individual is, for example, a university instructor or a business executive, the person will often receive respect. Conversely, working-class white men are often accorded respect until their working-class status is discovered.

Although the injustices of powerlessness have distributional consequences, they are more fundamentally issues of the division of labour and bring into question the social division of those who make decisions and those who carry out these decisions. This social division of labour provides a plausible explanation for the fact that so many social workers are being co-opted by our present social system, which oppresses so many people. As professionals, social workers are able to exercise their capacities through their university training and through the professional development that occurs throughout their careers. In addition, they are able to exercise considerable power over others and receive the respect that goes with the privilege of professionalism. It requires considerable commitment as well as energy to work at transforming the society that has given the social worker some degree of power and privilege. Privilege, along with social workers dealing with their own privilege, is presented in more detail in the next chapter.

Cultural Imperialism

Exploitation, marginalization, and powerlessness all refer to relations of oppression that occur through the social division of work. Feminists and black liberation theorists, among others, have identified a further form of oppression—cultural imperialism. This form of oppression comes about when the dominant group universalizes its experience and culture and uses them as the norm. Through a process of ethnocentrism, the dominant group, most often without realizing it, projects its experience and culture as representative of all humanity. Our social institutions are based on the culture and experiences of the dominant group, and our educational system, the media, the entertainment industry, literature, and the marketing of products reinforce this notion of a universal culture. We are socialized into this ethnocentric view of the world. Cultural imperialism is experienced in varying degrees by all oppressed groups.

The dominant group reinforces its position by measuring other groups according to the dominant norms. Thus, the differences of women from men, black people or Indigenous people from white people, Jews from Christians, gay men and lesbians from heterosexuals, and workers from professionals become largely constructed as deviance and inferiority. These "other" groups experience a double and paradoxical oppression. Stereotypes are used to mark them at the same time that their own experiences and perspectives are rendered invisible.

The stereotypes applied to the culturally imperialized brand them as deviant and inferior and are so pervasive in society that they are seldom questioned. Examples are that Indigenous persons are alcoholic and lazy, gay men are promiscuous and perverted, women are good with children, black people are drug addicts and criminals. The fact that culturally dominated groups tend to be defined from the outside not only renders their own experiences and perspectives invisible to the dominant group but forces oppressed groups to look at themselves through the eyes of a dominant group that views them with contempt or amusement (Du Bois, 1969, cited in Young, 1990). "This, then, is the injustice of cultural imperialism: that the oppressed group's own experience and interpretation of social life finds little expression that touches the dominant culture, while the same culture imposes on the oppressed group its experience and interpretation of social life" (Young, 1990, p. 60). To overcome cultural imperialism, it would seem that a necessary step would be for culturally oppressed groups to take over the definition of themselves and assert a positive sense of group difference.

Violence

Almost all oppressed groups suffer systemic violence simply because they are members of a subordinate group. Violence includes not only physical attack but harassment, ridicule, or intimidation, which serves the purpose of stigmatizing group members. The oppression of violence lies not only in direct victimization but in the constant fear that violence may occur, solely on the basis of one's group identity.

Women have reason to fear rape; racialized individuals have reason to fear harassment; gay men and lesbians have reason to fear unprovoked assaults; striking workers have reason to fear attacks by police or strikebreakers. Violence is structural when it is tolerated, accepted, or found unsurprising by the dominant group or when perpetrators receive light or no punishment. Violence is a social practice when people from the dominant group seek out people from oppressed groups to beat up, rape, or harass. To reform institutions and social practices that encourage, tolerate, or enable violence against members of specific groups will require a change in cultural images, stereotypes, and the day-to-day reproduction of dominance and aversion.

The above summary of Young's (1990) five faces of oppression avoids the problems associated with both the unified and the pluralistic accounts of oppression. The former tends either to leave out groups that even the theorist thinks oppressed or to ignore important ways in which groups are oppressed. The latter fails to accommodate the similarities and overlaps in the oppression of different groups, on the one hand, and, on the other hand, falsely represents the situation of all group members as the same.

Young's framework avoids the above reductions and exclusions. Rather than a full theory of oppression, the five forms of oppression function as objective criteria for determining whether or not individuals and groups are oppressed. Each criterion can be operationalized and applied through the assessment of observable behaviour, status relationships, distributions, texts, and culture. Although the presence of any one of these five conditions is sufficient for calling a group oppressed, different oppressed groups exhibit different combinations of them, as do different individuals within these groups. Comparisons can be made of the ways a particular form of oppression occurs in different groups or of the combinations of oppression that groups experience. Obviously, this framework has significant potential for helping social workers to better understand the oppression of people with whom they work in their professional practice.

Oppression as Structural Violence

We believe that the term "social or structural inequality" is part of an academic and professional discourse that reduces its political charge and impact by "covering over" the structural violence experienced by members of subordinate groups all over the world. Furthermore, by not including the violent consequences and correlates of social inequality in its discourse and practice, the profession of social work is, in effect, an unwitting agent in limiting healthy and productive living and in contributing to premature rates of death. Structural social workers and anti-oppressive social workers view social inequality as more than notions of deprivation, disadvantage, and redistribution. It is part of a socially sanctioned process whereby people are hurt, maimed, and killed in ways that are unseen and unpunished. Elsewhere (Mullaly, 2010), I (Bob) have argued that social inequality is a form of (social) terrorism perpetrated by privileged groups on subordinate groups at the structural level.

Oppression at the structural level refers to the means by which oppression is institutionalized in society. It consists of the ways that our social structures (i.e., social institutions, laws, public policies, social processes and practices) all work together primarily in favour of the dominant group at the expense of subordinate groups. Structural oppression may be overt and visible, such as when the state does not recognize gay and lesbian marriages or does not allow these persons to have other family rights (e.g., inheritance, pension benefits, the right to visit a partner in a hospital when only family members are allowed). However, most oppression at the structural level today is covert or hidden.

Covert Oppression at the Structural Level

Covert structural oppression occurs when our social institutions, laws, policies, and practices disproportionately allocate goods, services, and opportunities with a positive social value (e.g., good health care, decent housing, a good job) to dominant group members and disproportionately allocate goods, services, and limited opportunities with negative social value (e.g., inadequate housing, incarceration, poor health care) to members of subordinate groups. Some of the ways that this inequitable distribution occurs will be looked at below.

Covert oppression at the structural level is a powerful force in maintaining group-based hierarchies. First, it appears to contradict the spirit and intention of the civil and human rights legislation and the principles of liberty and equality that have been developed over the past 100 years to prohibit institutional discrimination and to extend citizenship status to previously excluded groups. Second, its hidden nature results in many dominant and subordinate group members not recognizing it, which may result in subordinate group members blaming themselves for their own oppression (i.e., internalizing their oppression). Even if recognized, its hidden and subtle nature makes it very difficult for subordinate groups to employ collective action to bring it to an end. The belief that modern Western democracies are largely free from discrimination and oppression at the structural level is not only held by the lay public but is widespread among political commentators, public intellectuals, and a number of scholars (Sidanius & Pratto, 1999). However, the evidence overwhelmingly contradicts this belief. Rather than social equality and equal opportunity, widespread institutional or structural oppression affects all the major areas of an individual's life—employment, housing, health, education, financial opportunities, and treatment by the criminal justice system. Structural oppression constitutes a total environment or what Sidanius and Pratto (1999, p. 129) call a "circle of oppression."

The term "social inequality" is widely used by social work and social policy personnel to refer to a differential or inequitable distribution of goods, services, and opportunities whereby members of dominant groups enjoy satisfactory levels of living while members of subordinate groups live in states of deprivation. As mentioned above, one of the traditional tasks of the social welfare state and social work has been to attempt to reallocate or redistribute goods and services to members of subordinate groups so as to reduce deprivation and disadvantage. However, this activity, sometimes referred to as distributive or redistributive justice, does nothing about the social, economic, and political processes and practices that disproportionately allocate goods, services, and opportunities in the first place. Furthermore, by focusing on the reduction of deprivation and disadvantage as the goal, we tend to overlook or not even recognize the fact that the deprivation and disadvantage, which are associated with social inequality, lead to higher rates of morbidity and to premature death for countless numbers of subordinated people all over the world.

The social inequalities that occur because of oppression at the structural level go beyond an inequitable distribution of society's resources. The African-American psychiatrist and scholar Hussein Bulhan (1985) argues, for example, that structural oppression is a form of violence because it negatively affects human growth and development, it interferes with the inherent potential of individuals, it limits productive and healthy living, and it brings about premature death. Bulhan's (p. 135) definition of violence links it with structural oppression: "Violence is any relation, process, or condition by which an individual or a group violates the physical, social, and/or psychological integrity of another person or group."

Violence at the personal level is relatively easy to detect and control because it usually involves direct action in which the act of violence and its consequences are observable. The perpetrator and the victim are normally distinguishable, and the purpose of the violence can be verified and its effects can be assessed. Structural violence is a much more complex and higher-order phenomenon. It is a feature of social structures and social institutions. The social processes, relations, and practices associated with social inequities often span generations. They are deeply ingrained in people and dominate everyday living. "Structural violence involves more than the violation of fairness and justice. . . . [it] leads to hidden but lethal inequities, which can lead to the death of those who lack power or influence in the society" (Bulhan, 1985, p. 136).

Thus, rather than a quick death by state execution or a personal act of lethal violence, structural oppression in the form of such inequities as inadequate income, substandard or no housing, unemployment, and lack of health care leads to a slow, agonizing, unpunished, and premature death for countless numbers of subordinated people all over the country, not to say the world, on a daily basis.

To better understand the concept of structural violence and its relationship to social inequality, we turn to two other sources: (1) a landmark study by Sidanius and Pratto (1999) that presents an impressive amount of international empirical evidence of the existence of social inequality and social discrimination in six areas of everyday living, along with their resultant violent consequences; and (2) overviews of the structural violence and social inequities experienced by three subordinate groups in Canada.[2]

Structural Violence in Six Areas of Everyday Living

Although the Sidanius and Pratto study is by now about 20 years old, anyone working in the social services area knows that many of the findings remain true today—a testament to how slowly and unevenly social change occurs. Also, it is the same groups who experience discrimination in these areas today who have historically suffered from the same forms and processes of discrimination in the same areas. Social work and social policy textbooks have always contained coverage of social problems in these six areas and have presented the same groups of people in these areas—people living in poverty, racialized individuals, women, Indigenous people, older and younger persons, immigrant groups, persons with disabilities, and LGBTTQ persons, among members of other subordinate groups.

The six areas in which the study focused—the housing, retail, and labour markets as well as the education, health care, and criminal justice systems—are still the subjects of the social work and social problems literature some 20 years after the study by Sidanius and Pratto was published. The link between structural violence and discrimination in these six areas should be obvious, since the people who experience social inequality have higher rates of morbidity and mortality than do members of the general population. A deficit in any of these areas contributes to a threat to one's health, safety, and security. Another finding of the study was that social policies that address problems of discrimination, such as affirmative action, employment equity, social housing, parole and probation, group homes, and social assistance, are the very policies that are most unpopular with the dominant group and, therefore, are constantly under threat of being discontinued, which adds more uncertainty and stress to persons who depend upon them.

Structural Violence Experienced by Indigenous Peoples in Canada

In Canada, as with all countries with an Indigenous population, Indigenous people, by all indicators, experience the highest levels of social inequality and, therefore, suffer the most from structural violence, as shown below:

- Half of all status First Nations children live below the poverty line (MacDonald & Wilson, 2013), and First Nations people living in First Nations communities experience four times the Canadian unemployment rate. For those employed, First Nations individuals earn half the annual income of the rest of Canadians (Health Canada, 2014).
- First Nations and Inuit families have an infant mortality rate two to four times that of the national average (Truth and Reconciliation Commission of Canada, 2015).
- The average life expectancy for First Nations adults is 6.0 years less than that of non–First Nations Canadians (Health Canada, 2011).

- Suicide rates for Aboriginal youth are among the highest in the world (Health Canada, 2013)—the rates for adolescent girls is about seven times higher than the national rate, and for Aboriginal adolescent boys it is more than five times higher (Kirmayer et al., 2007).
- While alcohol consumption among First Nations people and Inuit is lower than the Canadian average, those who drink tend to drink more heavily (Health Canada, 2006). In general, alcohol and drug abuse is higher among Aboriginal populations than in the general Canadian population (Statistics Canada, 2012; Guarnotta, 2016).
- Death caused by alcohol and illegal drugs is, respectively, two and three times the rate for the general population, with Aboriginal youth facing two to six times the risk for alcohol-related problems (Chansonneuve, 2007).
- Aboriginal women are three times more likely to experience violence from their spouses than non-Aboriginal women (Chansonneuve, 2007).
- First Nations children are involved in child welfare investigations at a rate 4.2 times that for non-Aboriginal children (Truth and Reconciliation Commission of Canada, 2015) and are apprehended at rates of six to eight times those of non-Aboriginal children (Auditor General of Canada, 2008). First Nations children make up 40 per cent of children in the Canadian child welfare system (Blackstock, Trocmé, & Bennett, 2004).
- Incarceration rates for Aboriginal people are more than eight times that for the non-Aboriginal population (Office of the Correctional Investigator, 2012).
- The 1200 missing and murdered Indigenous women in Canada at last is the focus of a long-awaited and demanded inquiry—that is, the National Inquiry into Missing and Murdered Indigenous Women and Girls.

Structural Violence Experienced by Older Canadians and by Women

Among other subordinate groups experiencing structural oppression and violence are older Canadians and women. Although Canadians on average are living longer these days, the high rate of mental health problems among the elderly cannot all be attributed to old age. Poverty, loneliness, and a sense of uselessness contribute to depression and exacerbate other mental disorders such as Alzheimer's and related dementias (Hall & Havens, 2008). Suicide among elderly people is a major concern in Canada, with males aged 85 to 89 having a suicide rate second only to men aged 40 to 59 (Statistics Canada, 2015). Over-prescription and overuse of medications is also a major concern, with older Canadians accounting for 60 per cent of public program prescription drug spending (Canadian Institute for Health Information, 2014).

The rate of violence against women is disturbingly high in Canada. A wife is three times more likely to be murdered by her husband than husbands are by their wives, with one woman on average being murdered by her current or former husband every seven days (Beattie & Cotter, 2010). Women in general are four times more likely to be assaulted in intimate heterosexual relationships than men are by their female partners. The assaults experienced by women are more frequent and result in more severe injuries (Sinha, 2013). Immigrant women, women with disabilities, young women, single women, Indigenous women, and queer women are particularly vulnerable to violence (Sinha, 2013). Furthermore, poverty rates for women in Canada are significantly high among various subordinate groups: 21 per cent of single mothers (Williams, 2010); 36 per cent of First Nations women living off-reserve (O'Donnell & Wallace, 2011); 22 per cent of visible minority women and 28 per cent of recent immigrant women (Hudon, 2015); 33 per cent of women with disabilities (Canadian Women's Foundation, 2015); and 13 per cent of women seniors (Hudon & Milan, 2015). Discrimination against women has also been documented in the workplace with respect to wages, occupational segregation, training, and pensions (McInturff, 2016). This discrimination is an example of structural oppression, which of course makes women more vulnerable to structural violence.

Structural Violence Leads to Violence at Other Levels

An examination of the living situation of almost any subordinate group anywhere in the world is likely to show it experiencing oppression in all or most of the above areas. That is, subordinate groups will, for the most part, suffer directly from lack of adequate employment, low income and poverty, inadequate housing, discrimination in the retail market, lack of educational opportunities, inferior health care, and overrepresentation within the criminal justice system. These inequities constitute structural violence in that people such as Indigenous persons, older persons, and women who experience them along with their attendant social inequality will consequently suffer from disproportionate levels and incidences of stress, anguish, frustration, alienation, and exclusion, and these factors result in differential rates of mortality (i.e., lowered life expectancies), morbidity, incarceration, homicide, suicide, and infant mortality. There can be no doubt, as Bulhan (1985) argues and as did Fanon (1968) before him, that oppression at the structural level leads to violence at the intrapersonal level (e.g., suicide and self-mutilation), at the interpersonal level (e.g., homicide and domestic violence), and at the institutional level (premature death because of social inequalities). What makes this type of violence so insidious is the fact that no recognized perpetrator or intention is normally identified as responsible for the violence. Commenting on structural violence elsewhere (Mullaly, 2010, pp. 275–276), I (Bob) concluded that:

> structural inequalities often have violent effects or outcomes. Terms such as "social inequality" and "structural inequality" tend to cover up the violent outcomes that many people from subordinate groups experience. Structural inequalities are much more than one person or one group having a greater quantity of or more access to social goods, rights, and opportunities. They are more than violations of philosophical notions of fairness, equity, and justice. Structural inequalities are socially sanctioned forms of physical and psychological violence, which over time will lead to hurtful discrimination and slow, agonizing, premature, and unpunished death. The term "structural violence," I contend, more accurately reflects the realities of oppressed persons. "Structural inequality" is a somewhat abstract, technical, bourgeois, and polite term that covers up its violent outcomes. We should call it what it is—*socially sanctioned structural violence.*

Responses of Oppressed People to Their Oppression

There are two major sets of responses that oppressed people may make with respect to the oppression they experience: (1) accommodation and compliance through a process of inferiorization; or (2) rejection through a process of assimilation, multiculturalism, or collective resistance through a politics of difference (Adam, 1978; Young, 1990). Both sets of responses are discussed below.

Accommodation and Compliance through Inferiorization

Members of oppressed groups are defined in ways by the dominant group that often devalue, objectify, and stereotype them as different, deviant, or inferior. Their own experiences and interpretation of social life find little expression that touches the dominant culture (Young, 1990). Because they find themselves reflected in literature, the media, formalized education, and so forth either not at all or in a highly distorted fashion, they suffer an impoverished identity (Adam, 1978). The paradox of this situation for oppressed populations is that at the same time that they are rendered invisible by the dominant group, they are also marked as different.

This lack of a strong self-identity will, in many cases, lead to an internalization of the dominant group's stereotyped and inferiorized images of subordinate populations (Young, 1990). This internalized oppression, in turn, will cause some oppressed people to act in ways that affirm the dominant group's view of them as inferior and, consequently, will lead to a process of inferiorized persons reproducing their own oppression. Through a process of cultural and ideological hegemony, many oppressed people believe that if they cannot make it in our society, if they are experiencing problems, then it is their own fault because they are unable to take advantage of the opportunities the dominant group says are available to everyone. It is, as Paulo Freire (1970) said, as if the oppressor gets into the head of the oppressed. People understand their own interests in ways that reflect the interests of the dominant group.

When people internalize their oppression, blaming themselves for their troubled circumstances, they will often contribute to their own oppression by considering it as unique, unchangeable, deserved, or temporary (Adam, 1978) or else blame other significant people in their lives such as parents or family. Oppressed persons also often contribute to their own oppression by psychologically or socially withdrawing or engaging in other self-destructive behaviours, which causes them to be rejected by others. This, in turn, confirms the low image they may have of themselves (Moreau & Leonard, 1989). The radical psychiatric movement considers all alienation the result of oppression about which the oppressed have been mystified or deceived. That is, the oppressed person is led to believe that they are not oppressed or that there are good reasons for the oppression (Agel, 1971).

Paulo Freire (1970) discusses several stances oppressed people may adopt that either reinforce or contribute to their own oppression. Fatalism may be expressed by the oppressed about their situation—"There is nothing I can do about it" or "It is God's will" are common expressions of fatalism. However, this fatalistic attitude is often interpreted as docility or apathy by the oppressor, which reinforces the view of the oppressed as lazy, inferior, and getting all that they deserve. Horizontal violence often occurs among oppressed people—an Indigenous person, for example, may strike out at another Indigenous person for petty reasons (which again reinforces the negative images held by the dominant class of subordinate groups). Self-deprecation also occurs when a group hears so often that they are good for nothing that, in the end, they become convinced of their own unfitness. Another characteristic of some oppressed persons is that they feel an irresistible attraction toward the oppressor and their way of life. This affirms, of course, the belief that oppression is legitimate and that it is more desirable to oppress than to be oppressed.

Rejection of Oppression through Assimilation, Multiculturalism, and a Politics of Difference

In contrast to the above inferiorized coping mechanisms that comply with or accommodate oppression, three emancipatory sets of politics attempt to overcome oppression: assimilation through a politics of integration; multiculturalism through a politics of cultural pluralism; and collective resistance through a politics of difference. These three sets of politics are discussed below with respect to each of their relationships to oppression.

Assimilation

Assimilation would render equal social status to everyone according to the same principles, rules, and standards. Wasserton (1980, cited in Young, 1990) outlines three reasons for choosing the assimilationist ideal of liberation. First, by imagining a society in which class, race, gender, and so forth have no special social significance, one sees more clearly how these categories unnecessarily limit possibilities in our existing society for some people. Second, a clear and unambiguous standard of equality and justice for all is promised, and any group-related differentiation or discrimination would be suspect. That is, any social benefits distributed differently according to group membership would be viewed as unjust. Third, the assimilationist ideal eliminates the situation of group differences resulting in social differences. Thus, people would be free to develop themselves as individuals. In sum, assimilationism promises a "deal." The identities, cultures, and values of oppressed groups are to be surrendered for the promise or opportunity of improved life chances. Submission to the social rules of the superordinate group supposedly mitigates the barriers confining subordinate groups (Adam, 1978).

Some writers, such as Agger (2013) and Johnson (2006), have criticized assimilation as a goal of liberation politics. Today in North American society and in many other societies, there is widespread agreement that no person should be excluded from political, economic, or social activities because of ascribed characteristics. However, group differences continue to exist, and certain groups continue to be advantaged. Although some persons from disadvantaged groups have succeeded in improving their overall life chances, the general scheme of allocating privilege and resources has remained unchanged (Agger, 2013; Johnson, 2006).

Young (1990) outlines three ways that assimilationism, by ignoring group differences, has oppressive consequences. First, assimilationism entails bringing formerly excluded groups into the mainstream, but this means coming into the game after the rules and standards have already been set and having to prove oneself according to these rules and standards. The privileged group, of course, defines the standards against which all will be measured, and because their privilege involves not recognizing these standards as culturally and experientially specific, they are perceived as the ideal of a common, universal, and neutral humanity in which all can partici- pate regardless of race, class, gender, and so on. Because the standards are in fact group-specific to the dominant class, they put subordinate groups at a disadvantage in trying to measure up to them, and for that reason assimilationist policies perpetuate their disadvantage.

Second, the notion of a universal humanity devoid of group differences allows dominant groups to overlook or not recognize their own group specificity. The assimilationist's blindness to difference perpetuates cultural imperialism because the subordinate groups are the ones that must drop their culture and adopt the dominant culture, which is assumed as a common, uni- versal humanity.

Third, assimilationism often produces an internalized devaluation by members of subordin- ate groups. Assimilationist participation means accepting an identity other than one's perceived own and being reminded by others and by oneself of one's other identity. As a result, children of non–English-speaking groups may become ashamed of the accents of their parents, and LGBTTQ couples avoid displaying affection to each other in public.

Multiculturalism

Multiculturalism as a concept and as a public policy issue dates back to the 1970s in most Western industrialized countries. Although there have been many progressive activists and supporters of multiculturalism, Agger (1998) contends that the concept of multiculturalism has been appro- priated to some extent by some schools of postmodernism and that, consequently, a change in meaning has occurred. Basically, Agger argues that multiculturalism is a recognition and accept- ance of cultural pluralism but does nothing to change the situation of there being one dominant culture with all others subordinate to it. This situation violates the position of earlier multicul- tural activists that there not be a hierarchy of cultures (this position has now been adopted in the "politics of difference" approach as outlined below). Multiculturalists today acknowledge and accept cultural pluralism and often equate multiculturalism with annual ethnic celebrations. Although many self-proclaimed advocates of multiculturalism may enjoy these annual exotic festivities, some of them show little interest in or knowledge of the struggles, blocked opportun- ities, and second-class citizenship that members of these subordinated cultures experience on a daily basis (Mullaly, 2010).

The dominant theory of multicultural social work in Canada, the US, and Australia is that of cultural sensitivity. The aim of this theory is to increase worker and agency awareness of and sensitivity to different cultural norms and to reduce (but not eliminate) institutional racism. Cultural sensitivity enables white social workers to better establish a "helping relationship" with members of other races and cultures, to make services more accessible, and to advocate for the enactment of equal rights legislation. Although the cultural sensitivity model represents an ad- vance over the assimilationist (melting-pot) approach to issues of race and culture, it can ac- tually, without intending it, allow racism to persist but in a more "respectable" form (Ahmad, 1991; Thompson, 1997). The cultural sensitivity model ignores the fact that cultures and races are ranked in order of perceived merit, and it ignores the power relations in Western society between racialized individuals and white people, both historically and in the present (Ahmad, 1991; Williams, 1989).

The Politics of Difference

As an alternative to assimilation and multiculturalism, Adam (1978) argues for collective resistance to assimilation and/or to an acceptance of a dominant culture on the part of subordinated groups. He emphasizes the importance of community for developing self-identity, solidarity, and resistance to domination. Communication among members of a subordinate group over time engenders social networks and language that nurture collectivization and a new understanding of their life situation—one defined by the group itself.

> Shared experiences identify effective strategies for coping with social limitations, methods of survival and self-betterment, sources of freedom and joy. Brotherhood or sisterhood is not the simple correlate of, for example, physical resemblances; it is the mutual creation . . . of each member by the other (Adam, 1978, p. 122).

Young (1990) elaborates on this notion of community by calling for a "politics of difference" as the means of overcoming oppression. Rather than attempting to transcend group differences as the assimilationist approach would do or simply accepting them as the multicultural approach would do, the politics of difference seeks equality among all socially and culturally differentiated groups whereby mutual respect and affirmation of one another in their differences would occur. Group differences are considered positive and desirable rather than a liability or disadvantage or simply a fact. The positivity of group difference is liberating and empowering in that the identity the dominant group has taught them to despise would be reclaimed, affirmed, and celebrated. This positive view of one's specific culture and experience makes it increasingly difficult for the dominant group to parade its values and norms as universal and neutral.

The politics of group difference also promotes a notion of group solidarity against the individualism of liberal humanism. It is recognized that a positive view of one's specific group requires separate organizations that exclude others. This does not eliminate the need for coalitions among groups or the need for oppressed groups to combat other types of oppression (e.g., white people against racism or men against sexism), but it is a recognition that group autonomy is an important vehicle for empowerment and the development of a group-specific voice and perspective (Young, 1990).

Young notes that many fear that asserting group differences will lead to a justification of subordination. However, she contends that a politics of difference confronts this fear because it presents group difference not as essential, other, or exclusively opposed but as ambiguous, relational, and shifting, marked by specificity and variation. In this way, group differences are conceived as relational rather than defined by substantive categories and attributes (Minow, 1985; 1987; 1990, cited in Young, 1990). A relational view of difference does not focus on the attributes of groups as the measure of difference but on the interaction of groups with institutions (Littleton, 1987, cited in Young, 1990).

In this relational view, the meaning of difference becomes contextualized (Scott, 1988, cited in Young, 1990). Group differences are conspicuous, depending on the groups compared, the purposes of the comparison, and the point of view of those making the comparison. Such contextualized understandings of difference undermine essentialist assumptions. Young (1990) provides the following example to underscore this point. Persons using mobility devices are different from other people in terms of athletics, health care, and social service support, but they are not different in many other respects. At one time, persons with disabilities were excluded and segregated from society because the differences between able-bodied and disabled were conceptualized as extending to all or most capacities.

A relational understanding of group difference rejects exclusion. Differences among groups do not mean they are different in all respects. They have overlapping experiences, common goals, and shared attributes. The assumption that oppositional categorization is inherent in group differences must always be challenged. A relational and contextualized understanding of difference also undermines the notion of an essential individual identity. "In our complex, plural society, every social group has group differences cutting across it, which are potential sources of wisdom, excitement, conflict, and oppression" (Young, 1990, pp. 172–173).

A politics of difference, of course, has serious implications for policy-making. A goal of social justice (and structural social work) is social equality. As discussed previously, social equality not only refers to an equitable distribution of social goods but to full participation of everyone in society's major institutions and to the socially supported opportunity for all to develop and exercise their inherent capacities. Although in Canada and in many other Western societies, formal legal equality exists for most groups, these societies are still marked by extreme social inequality. Instead of policies that are universally formulated and thus oblivious to differences of class, race, gender, age, and so forth, a politics of difference would require policies that reflect the specific situations of oppressed groups. "Groups cannot be socially equal unless their specific experience, culture, and social contributions are publicly affirmed and recognized" (Young, 1990, p. 174).

A politics of difference would require a dual system of rights: a general system of rights for all and a more specific system of group-conscious rights and policies (Young, 1990). We already have a precedent for such a system in the form of civil, political, and human rights for all citizens, along with some affirmative action and employment equity programs for some groups that have historically been disadvantaged in our society. To extend this dual system of rights to the point that there would be effective recognition and representation of the voices and perspectives of oppressed groups (as opposed to interest groups), Young proposes the implementation of institutional mechanisms and public resources supporting: (1) the self-organization of subordinate groups whereby group members could achieve collective empowerment and a reflective understanding of their collective experiences and interests in the context of society; (2) group analysis and generation of policy proposals in institutionalized settings whereby decision-makers are obliged to demonstrate that their deliberations have taken relevant group perspectives into consideration; and (3) group veto power regarding specific policies and decisions that affect a group directly, such as land use for Indigenous communities or reproductive rights for women.

Structural Social Work with Oppressed Groups

An understanding of oppression has several major implications for structural social workers. First, recognizing the limitations of a distributional model of justice is important because this helps in avoiding the pursuit of a more equitable distribution of goods and services without attending to (and thereby reifying) the institutional rules and the social processes and practices that caused the maldistribution in the first place. The goal of structural social work is not simply to compensate and care for victims of oppression. It is to transform the entire constellation of oppressive rules, processes, and practices. Only a theory of social justice that has oppression as its central concern can accommodate this goal.

Second, an understanding of how oppression and its dominant–subordinate relations have been socially constructed is important if social work is to avoid notions and practices of "blaming the victims." Only by knowing that oppression is a social construction can social work embark on a deconstruction of oppressive practices and a reconstruction of society characterized by true social equality.

Third, only an understanding of oppression as a systemic situation that is produced and re-produced in everyday social processes and practices—and an awareness that oppression carries out several important social functions for the dominant group—will lead to structural solutions. Otherwise, social work will continue to treat oppression as a technical problem (e.g., as a lack of "goodness of fit" between the individual and society) amenable to technical solutions rather than as the moral and political (i.e., structural) problem that it is.

Fourth, an understanding of the various forms of oppression allows structural social workers to make more sense of the situation of oppression of those they serve. All forms of oppression are not the same and will, therefore, require attuned responses and actions. This knowledge will also enable the social worker to engage in a more meaningful way in consciousness-raising and normalization activities with oppressed persons.

Fifth, at a micro level of social work practice, an understanding of personal or individual oppression and the various types of internalized oppression will enable the structural social worker to better understand how oppressed persons may be experiencing and coping with their situation of oppression. Through dialogue, this knowledge will assist the worker in sorting out with members of subordinate groups helpful and counterproductive responses to their oppression.

Sixth, at the macro level of social work practice, an understanding of the politics of difference will help the structural social worker to encourage and support group-specific organizations and groups or the establishment of new ones. These are important mechanisms for oppressed people discovering themselves, reclaiming their identity, creating community and solidarity, and developing a group-specific voice and perspective. The politics of difference will also encourage structural social workers to advocate for policies and decision-making mechanisms that give full recognition and representation to the voices of oppressed groups.

These, then, are some implications that a theory of justice, based on a politics of difference and having oppression as its central concern, would hold for structural social work. They may be viewed as the "what is to be done" aspect of combatting oppression. The elements of "how to do it" are the subjects of Chapters 11 and 12.

Conclusion

This chapter looked at the concept of oppression along a number of dimensions. Oppression was described as a type of second-class citizenship that is assigned to people not on the basis of lack of merit or failure but because of their membership in a particular group or category of people. Oppression exists and persists because of the number of positive functions it carries out for the dominant group at the expense of subordinate groups. A number of myths that help to rationalize and perpetuate oppression were presented. It was argued that the (re)distributional model of justice that has historically underpinned the modern social welfare state and social work practice only compensates victims of oppression and does nothing to alter the causes of inequality. Furthermore, it was argued that structural inequality goes beyond a simple notion of an inequitable distribution of society's resources, because social inequalities lead to higher rates of morbidity and to slow, agonizing, premature, and unpunished death for countless numbers of subordinate persons all over the world on a daily basis.

Although there are different forms, sources, levels of severity, and experiences associated with oppression, a common set of dynamics is engaged between dominant and subordinate groups. Iris Marion Young's five categories of oppression, of which all oppressed groups experience at least one, were presented. This categorization is adopted here because it includes both distributive issues of social justice and social practices that go beyond distribution. A model of oppression that located oppression at three levels—personal, cultural, and structural or institutional—was outlined. The multiple nature and persistence of oppression were discussed, and two sets of responses (acceptance and resistance) to oppression by subordinate groups were outlined. Finally, some implications of adopting oppression as the major explanation for social problems for structural social workers were presented.

Critical Questions

1. Studies have shown that members of dominant groups are often unaware of their many privileges and take them for granted. Furthermore, the studies show that members of subordinate groups tend to be more aware of the privileges that members of dominant groups enjoy. Why is this? What are the implications of this for social workers, who are usually members of dominant groups working with members of subordinate groups?

2. Identify the characteristics that make you a member of dominant groups (e.g., class, gender, race, age, religion, sexuality, ableness). Make a list of privileges that you have in society that are associated with each of your dominant group characteristics.

3. Compare your lists of privileges with the lists compiled by those in your class who are not part of the dominant groups of which you are a member. In other words, if you are a male, how

does your list of privileges compare to the lists that were compiled by the female members of your class? Similarly, if you are white, how does your list of privileges compare to the lists compiled by the non-white members of your class?

4. Take any source or form of oppression, such as poverty, racism, sexism, homophobia, or ageism, and identify some of the ways it is carried out at the personal, cultural, and structural levels. What would structural social workers do with this information in their social work practice?

5. A black single mother living in poverty with her three small children is experiencing problems in several areas of her life. She is often turned down by employers for jobs for which she is qualified. She has difficulty finding (being accepted by landlords) decent housing for her family. She often receives derogatory treatment from store clerks, her children's teachers, hospital/medical personnel, employees delivering public services, and others with whom she interacts as a consumer or customer. Is there one subordinate characteristic (single parent, race, class, gender) that is most responsible for the degrading and insulting treatment that she receives on a daily basis?

6. Does the composition of the profession of social work in Canada reflect the diversity of the country's population? Should it? Why or why not?

10 Overview of Privilege

I am convinced that studies of oppression will not go anywhere toward ending oppression unless they are accompanied by understanding of the systems of privilege that cause systems of oppression.

—Peggy McIntosh (2012)

Introduction

One might wonder why we have devoted an entire chapter to the subject of "privilege." After all, as social workers are we not most concerned with people experiencing social problems that are derived from oppression? Is this not the major group with whom we work? Would not a focus on privilege direct our attention away from oppression and its negative effects on the individuals and groups who suffer from it? While it is true that social work has historically focused on oppressed persons as its primary target group, there are several reasons why privilege and privileged people should be a major concern, not just for social work but for all people who occupy at least one position of privilege. The major reason that social work ought to be concerned with privilege is that a singular focus on oppression ignores or overlooks the fact that oppression and privilege go hand in hand. You cannot have one without the other. Together they form a symbiotic relationship.

The flip side of the coin of oppression is privilege. However, compared to oppression in general and anti-oppressive social work in particular, not much has been written on privilege in the social work literature. And what has been written usually focuses on a single source or form of privilege such as "white privilege" or "male privilege" or "class privilege," which ignores the multiplicity and intersectionality of privilege. The fact that not much has been written in the social work literature on privilege is most unfortunate because the main reason we have oppression is that we have privilege. It is similar to the relationship between poverty and wealth—we have poverty because we have wealth. If we want to truly understand poverty, we must understand wealth. If we want to do something serious about poverty, we must do something serious about wealth. And if we want to truly understand oppression and do something about it, we must understand what privilege is and what it is not and how it manifests in all its rarely visible but always intersectional ways. And if we want to challenge oppression, then we must confront our own privilege (McIntosh, 2012).

An earlier and more extensive version of this chapter appears in Challenging Oppression and Confronting Privilege, *third edition, by Bob Mullaly and Juliana West (2018). (See Chapter 2 of that publication.)*

Just as privilege opens doors of opportunity, oppression slams them shut (Johnson, 2006). Just as poverty will always be with us until we do something about wealth, we will always have oppression until we do something about privilege. As articulated by Harry Brod (1989, p. 89), "privilege is not something we take; it is given to us by society if we possess the characteristics that society values, such as being male, white, heterosexual, affluent, and non-disabled." Ferber (2003) offers two major reasons why we have tended to ignore the issue of privilege. First, it implicates those with power, and second, it is far easier to explore the problems faced by oppressed groups than it is to explore our own roles in perpetuating inequality. This is unfortunate because we are all implicated in systems of oppression. "Although as individuals we may not believe that we are oppressive people, we still participate in relations of oppression and gain various privileges from that relationship" (Ferber 2003, p. 320). As stated by Alison Bailey (2004, p. 307), "privilege is *granted* and birth is the easiest way of being granted privilege."

Although members of dominant groups enjoy privileges and benefits that are not available to non-privileged people, it should be noted that privilege usually comes with a penalty to the privileged person. There is no doubt that I (Bob) have benefited from male privilege, but I have also been hurt by it because I have been locked inside a tiny box of masculinity—a box that Jamie Utt calls the "Act Like a Man" box. I want to be free and independent of those aspects of masculinity that hurt both men and women, and I want to be free from such rules of masculinity as "big boys don't cry," men are the lords and masters of their own households, men must know everything even when they don't, and violence may be acceptable for solving problems. Privilege hurts both the victims and the beneficiaries of privilege even as it pays a dividend to the latter group.

Given the fact that privilege negatively affects both privileged and non-privileged people, it seems important that we as people in general and as social workers in particular know as much as possible about privilege and how it works. This chapter will explore the concept and the structural nature of privilege, some of its major characteristics (including its invisibility to privileged persons), the dynamics of privilege or how systems of privilege work, reasons why privileged persons become defensive and uncomfortable in talking about it, and why dominant groups do not see privilege as a problem. We will also discuss the myth of meritocracy, and some of the specific privileges that are attached to various positions of domination will be outlined. Finally, we will explore what all this has to do with us as individuals and as social workers, along with what we can do about privilege to make a difference.

The Nature of Privilege

In the previous chapter on oppression, it was noted that all of us suffer from some kind of frustration, hurt, and restriction at some point in our lives, but this does not mean that we are oppressed. What determines oppression is when a person is blocked from opportunities to self-development or is excluded from full participation in society or is assigned a second-class citizenship not because of a lack of individual talent or merit but because of membership in a particular group or category of people. Similarly, what determines privilege is not any particular advantages a person might have but whether these advantages were earned or conferred systematically by society on the basis of membership in a particular social group (Heldke & O'Connor, 2004; McIntosh, 2003).

Just as all oppression counts as harm but not all harms count as oppression, all privilege is advantageous, but not all advantages count as privilege (e.g., having a driver's licence, holding political office, becoming a naturalized citizen, which are all *earned* advantages).

Thus, there are two kinds of advantages—earned and unearned—and those that are unearned are considered privileges. The corollary is that advantages that are earned (e.g., a quality education, skills, a good reputation) are not considered privileges (although one could argue that some advantages or assets are more easily earned if they are accompanied by class, race, gender, or other privileges). Bailey (2004) argues that failure to recognize the differences between earned and unearned assets allows privileged groups to equate all privilege with earned advantages. If one were looking for a definition of privilege, Marsiglia and Kulis (2009, p. 17) offer the following: "Privilege is the unearned advantages of special group membership." Privileges make people more powerful and profitable because they have more opportunities, advantages, access, and status attached to them (Hays, Chang, & Dean, 2004). That is why white, able-bodied, heterosexual, married males continue to own most of the wealth in Anglo-American societies, occupy the most prestigious positions, and control the media and other forms of popular communication (Mullaly, 2007).

As suggested above, privilege is often explained in terms of natural abilities or given traits of the individual. Persons with privilege often appeal to these traits or personal characteristics as justification for having privilege in the first place (Heldke & O'Connor, 2004). However, privilege is not an individual phenomenon. Oppression will not go away even if we change the attitudes, personalities, and behaviours of all privileged people because such changes will not end the dominance that has been conferred on members of privileged groups (McIntosh, 2003). It is the nature of society and of social systems that must change. "Individualistic thinking also makes us blind to the very existence of privilege, because privilege, by definition, has nothing to do with individuals, only with social categories we wind up in" (Johnson 2006, p. 77).

Another explanation for privilege by those with privilege is that it is an outcome of human nature in that it is only natural for different groups to compete with each other for power, dominance, and privilege. In this competition, there will be winners and losers, with those groups who are smarter, stronger, more able and capable coming out on top and getting more than anyone else. Other variations of the human nature argument as presented by Johnson (2006) are that people cannot help but fear the unfamiliar and therefore must be able to keep other groups in their place, or that existing social groups such as men and women are so dissimilar that it is as though they came from different planets (Mars and Venus?) and it is a wonder that we can get along as well as we do, or that there is only one natural orientation (e.g., sexual, religious) and all the rest are unacceptable and bound to cause conflict whenever they become obvious. Although such arguments about human nature may be popular or persuasive among some, Johnson (2006, p. 3) makes the point that "the only way to hold on to them is to ignore most of what history, psychology, anthropology, sociology, biology, and, if people look closely, their own experience reveal about human beings and how they live."

Myths about Privilege

If privilege does not exist because of individual traits or characteristics or because of human nature, then why does it exist? The answer to this question can be found in the relationship between oppression and privilege. As discussed in Chapter 9, oppression occurs because it benefits the dominant group in that it protects a kind of citizenship that is superior to that of oppressed groups. Privilege occurs for the same reason. Similarly, oppression and privilege conjointly protect the privileged group's access to a wider range of better-paying and higher-status work as well as preferential access to and treatment from our social institutions. A correlate to the invisible nature of privilege is that privileged persons believe that having more is an inalienable right that accompanies hard work, vigilance, the courage to take risks, and superior intelligence and capabilities. That oppressed persons do not have more is proof that privilege is earned and not given. Supporting these beliefs about privilege are the same myths that support oppression, as outlined in Chapter 9—namely, the myths of scarcity, of objective information, of might is right or the belief in majority rule even if it tyrannizes the minority, of supremacy or the belief in a superior culture, of class, of equal opportunity or meritocracy, of stereotyping or the belief that all members of a group are the same, of blaming the victim or the belief that individuals are responsible for their own oppression, and of competition and hierarchy.

Johnson (2006) adds two more myths supporting the existence of privilege (and oppression) to the above list. As with the other myths, the two additions ignore history. First is the myth or belief that things have always been the way they are and will not change. Second is the myth of "no effect," which is based on the belief that nothing we do can change the system because it is just too big and powerful. These myths are part of a larger ideology that rationalizes privilege and oppression as necessary for the preservation of society. In examining these myths, it is instructive to keep in mind the definition of a myth—a popular belief or idea that is fictitious or imaginary and does not reflect reality.

Intersectional Nature of Privilege

Johnson (2006) asserts that if one looks at privilege or oppression as intersectional, it simplifies and clarifies the nature of privilege. He states that by understanding that each form of privilege is related to all the others, we can dispense with the useless exercise of trying to determine which is the least or most privileged or least or most oppressive. It also helps us to avoid the trap of thinking that privilege falls along binary lines in that you are either privileged or you are not because in reality you are usually both. In other words, we can belong (and usually do) in both privileged and oppressive categories. The intersectional model also reveals how different dimensions of privilege are connected to one another and that if we are to work for change, we need to focus on privilege in all the forms it takes (Johnson 2006). "We won't get rid of racism, in other words, without doing something about sexism and classism, because the system that produces the one also produces the others and connects them" (Johnson 2006, p. 53). Obviously then, part of the nature of privilege is that all its various forms are connected and interact with one another.

Ferber and Herrera (2013) maintain that while intersectionality has been intertwined in our understanding and conceptualization of oppression, it is still relatively new terrain when thinking about privilege. As an invisible package of unearned assets and unexperienced disadvantages (Carbado, 2002), privilege has tended to be depicted as occupying distinct domains—white privilege, male privilege, heterosexual privilege. Just like oppression, however, privilege is intersectional, and our understanding of the intersectional nature of privilege should be "not just wide but deep" (Ferber & Herrera, 2013, p. 97). We should be willing to examine the many dimensions of privilege and explore and stay present with our emotional reactions as we uncover the layers.

Privilege Is Everywhere Yet Invisible

Another major feature of privilege is the fact that it is ubiquitous at the same time that it is invisible to privileged persons (Kimmel & Ferber, 2003).[1] Everywhere we look, privileged people are the standard against which everyone else is measured. Most of our political leaders, most of our corporate leaders, most people in the mainstream media and in advertising, most spokespersons, most professional people tend to be white, non-disabled, middle- and upper-class males. Privilege is all around us, and for many of us, it is us. However, privilege also tends to be invisible to those who are privileged. We are not schooled to recognize our privileges in the same way that we are schooled to recognize and be wary of people who are members of subordinate groups. People will tell us that they went to see a "female doctor," or they will say they went to see "the doctor." Very few will say that they went to see the "male doctor." People will tell us they have a "gay friend," or they will tell us about a "friend." Very few will tell us about having a "heterosexual friend." If I (Bob), as a white person, talk about a colleague at work, people will assume I am talking about a "white colleague." By identifying the race, gender, or sexual orientation of subordinate persons, we draw attention to the markers that explain why these persons are not privileged. By not identifying the markers that are associated with privileged persons, we help to keep privilege invisible.

When I look in the mirror, I do not see my privileges, but when oppressed persons look in the mirror, they see their gender or their race or their disability because these characteristics are visible to them every day as the reasons why they are not privileged. When we look at the wage difference between men and women, we always express the difference in terms of what the woman earns compared to the man (which makes the man's wage the standard); for example, women on average earn about 70 cents for every dollar a man earns. This statistic makes the discrimination against women visible. If we were to express the difference in terms of men's wages as a function of women's wages, we would say that for every dollar a woman earns, a man earns about $1.43. That way, it would not be the discrimination that is made visible but the privilege. Just by being a male, a worker receives an extra 43 cents, which represents what Connell (2001) calls the "masculine or patriarchal dividend"—the unearned benefit accruing to a male just for being male.

Allan Johnson (2006, p. 7) makes the case that to do something about privilege is not only a moral imperative but a matter of survival:

> The trouble we're in privileges some groups at the expense of others. It creates a yawning divide in levels of income, wealth, dignity, safety, health, and quality of life. It promotes fear, suspicion, discrimination, harassment, and violence. It sets people against one another. It builds walls topped with broken glass and barbed wire. It weaves the insidious and corroding effects of oppression into the daily lives of tens of millions of women, men, and children. It has the potential to ruin entire generations and, in the long run, to take just about everyone down with it.

Dynamics of Privilege

Johnson (2006) contends that the ease of not being aware of privilege is an aspect of privilege itself, or what he refers to as "the luxury of obliviousness." The fact that oppressed groups must be fully attentive to the privileged groups without the latter having to give attention in return is a key aspect of privilege. Because privileged people tend to control the political system, the police, jobs, the education system, and most resources, oppressed groups have to get to know them well in order not to displease them. Privileged persons, on the other hand, have little reason to pay attention to subordinate groups or to how privilege affects them. To be privileged is not having to think about it. "So strong is the sense of entitlement behind this luxury that males, whites, and others can feel put upon in the face of even the mildest invitation to pay attention to issues of privilege" (Johnson, 2006, p. 22). Sisneros et al. (2008) point out that one of the hidden characteristics of membership in a privileged group is the assumption that the privileged status is the norm whereas the status of the oppressed group is not. As an example, the authors note that the assumption that growing up in a multiracial family or a family with gay or lesbian parents (or a single-parent family) can harm children is not based on any data. The consequences of accepting myths such as these can be disastrous in social workers' work with children and their families.

According to Johnson (2006), one of the reasons why privileged persons pay little attention to the issue or reality of privilege or do not see it as a problem is that they tend to compare themselves with other privileged persons and not with members of oppressed groups. This is so because people make comparisons on the basis of what is valued in society. White people, for example, will compare themselves with other white people because being white is seen as a valued characteristic. Similarly, men will compare themselves with other men and not with women. The effect of this dynamic is that white people do not feel privileged by their race because their comparison group is also white. Likewise, men do not feel privileged by their gender because their comparison group is other men.

The paradoxical situation of being privileged without knowing it reinforces the invisible nature of privilege. And, of course, there are consequences to this invisibility. Two major consequences identified by Kimmel and Ferber (2003) are: (1) it is difficult to create or develop a politics of inclusion from invisibility; and (2) the invisibility of privilege means that many privileged persons become defensive and irritated when they are confronted with the statistical realities and human consequences of privileges based on racism, sexism, and so on. Anyone who has ever attempted to have a classroom or other discussion on privilege knows that many privileged persons feel like victims themselves. We certainly agree with Alison Bailey (2004, p. 14), who argues that "silence about privilege is itself a function of privilege and it has a chilling effect on political discourse. Conversations that focus exclusively on oppression reinforce the structured invisibility of privilege." Kimmel and Ferber (2003) contend that a major task for anyone concerned with social justice and anti-oppression is to make visible the privilege that masks that invisibility. One way of doing this, which will be discussed below, is to dump out the contents of what Peggy McIntosh (2003) calls our invisible knapsacks of privilege.

As suggested in the preceding paragraph, one reason that privilege is not dealt with constructively or at all by privileged people is that the thought of benefiting from racism, sexism, classism, and so on or behaving in ways that are racist, sexist, classist, and so on can cause a broad range of unpleasant emotions, such as anger, shame, guilt, fault, and frustration (Schmitz, Stakeman, & Sisneros, 2001, cited in Sisneros et al., 2008). Or they may not get it at all (Johnson, 2006). Even people who see themselves as non-prejudiced can be guilty of holding prejudices (Tatum, 1994). The uncomfortable feelings resulting from confronting one's prejudices can create barriers to self-examination or social analysis or other types of learning. And, of course, if we fail to examine our belief systems, world views, and ways of knowing, we will not be adequately prepared for engaging in healthy (i.e., respectful, egalitarian) relationships in a multicultural environment.

> We enter this world lacking assumptions. Through socialization by family, friends, and other people we respect and trust, we learn stereotypes, misinformation, myths, and partial histories that glorify some, vilify others, and erase people and events by making no mention of them at all. Misinformation acquired through early learning is reinforced by institutional and cultural structures such as the media, schools, religion, and governmental and legal systems, as well as traditions and customs (Sisneros et al., 2008, p. 25).

These myths and misinformation shape how we see ourselves and others and can either bolster or deflate our self-identity depending on our social position. If we do acquire new learnings that puncture the old assumptions we were taught, we are presented with a choice. We can decide to pass on the old misinformation and behave in ways that continue to marginalize people, or we can break the cycle and become allies with oppressed groups in confronting and challenging both privilege and oppression. How to break the cycle will be discussed in the last section of this chapter.

As with oppression, one of the features of privilege is that various privileges intersect and interact with other privileges and with different forms of oppression at the same time. Categories that define privilege exist simultaneously and in relation to one another. In other words, a person can belong to more than one category of privilege (e.g., a white, bourgeois male). Categories that define privilege also exist in relation to categories that define oppression. For example, a person can belong to a category (or categories) of privilege and to a category (or categories) of oppression (e.g., a black male) at the same time. Usually, the more categories of privilege to which one belongs, the more privileged one is apt to be, although not necessarily. For example, a white, unemployed male belongs to two categories of privilege but may not feel any privilege because of his unemployed status. His inability to earn a living may get in the way of his enjoying the unearned benefits that go with being a white male.

As Johnson (2006) points out, each of us is a package deal. People never see me (Bob), for example, only in terms of my race, or sex, or class but as a white, middle-class, non-disabled, heterosexual, and so on professor. It is tempting to attempt to calculate some kind of cost-benefit analysis of one's privilege by counting the number of privileged categories one falls within, subtracting the number of oppressive categories one belongs to, and arriving at a "privilege score." Unfortunately, privilege (and life) is not that simple. The dynamics of multiple privilege or multiple oppression are so bound up with each other that it is impossible to tell where one ends and the next begins. If we are looking at gender and race, for example, how much gender or race counts (i.e., contributes to either privilege or oppression) by itself cannot be determined.

Participating in Systems of Privilege

In explaining how systems of privilege work, Allan Johnson (2006) argues that privilege and oppression exist through systems such as family, schools, and workplaces and people's participation in them. The systems are organized around three key characteristics: they are (1) dominated by privileged groups (positions of power tend to be occupied by members of privileged groups); (2) identified with privileged groups (privileged groups represent the cultural standard of comparison for all groups); and (3) centred on privileged groups (because systems are identified with privileged groups, the tendency is to focus attention on them, which makes other groups feel invisible). All three characteristics reinforce the notion that privileged groups are superior to all others and therefore deserve their privilege.

In terms of people's participation in the systems of privilege, Johnson identifies three behaviours or activities that prop up and help to maintain these systems. The first is what he calls following the "paths of least resistance." In every social situation, we face an almost endless number of choices. For example, in class a student could sing, yell at the instructor, eat lunch, whistle, carry on a loud conversation, and so on. All these choices vary in terms of the level of resistance that is inherent in each choice, as we would soon discover if we chose an inappropriate path. Singing in class would quickly provoke resistance from other students (and the instructor) in the form of condemnation. By comparison, behaving in a way that is expected in a classroom would be the path of least resistance, which is the one we are most likely to take.

We usually follow the path of least resistance for a number of possible reasons. It might be the only one we see. Or we may be aware of other paths but are afraid of the consequences if we do not follow the path of least resistance. For example, we may feel uncomfortable when we hear a friend or colleague tell a racist joke, but we are afraid of being ridiculed or ostracized if we object to it, so we take the path of least resistance and smile or laugh or just remain silent. Another example would be a woman taking the path of least resistance by remaining silently attentive to a male colleague taking up air space and expressing opinions on something that he obviously knows little or nothing about (a not uncommon male tendency, which privilege allows). Another path, one that is likely to meet resistance, would be to challenge the man for what he is saying and doing, which in effect would also raise the possibility of alternative paths, such as the man learning about silence and listening, about supporting others, and about sharing space (Johnson, 2006). "Patterns of dominance and the paths of least resistance that sustain them show up in every system of privilege" (Johnson, 2006, p. 94).

Remaining silent is the second behaviour of people participating in systems of privilege that reinforces privilege identified by Johnson. He (2006, p. 106) refers to silence as "passive oppression," which he defines as "making it possible for oppression to happen simply by doing nothing to stop it." Oppression depends upon silence in order to continue. When privileged people do not act or say anything about observed or known acts of oppression at the personal, cultural, or structural level, they are perpetuating privilege and oppression by contributing to a social environment that makes it easy for oppression to occur and for so many to stand by and let it happen. Privileged people may privately disapprove of acts of racism or sexism or gay-bashing and may console themselves with the thought that they themselves would never do such things, but by remaining silent they are in effect reinforcing and condoning oppression. As long as the vast majority of men remain silent on the issue of sexual harassment and domestic violence or as long as issues of racism in the community or the workplace or the classroom are not addressed by white persons, any social justice intentions or anti-oppressive sentiments are irrelevant to the fact and future of sexism and racism as patterns of inequality and the suffering they cause.

Silence is just as oppressive as a visible act of oppression. Most privileged people engage in oppression, not by acting out of hostility or ill-will toward a subordinate group but because they acquiesce in the face of a cultural order that continues the work of oppression. This is all that is required of most privileged people for oppression to continue—that they not notice, that they do nothing, and that they remain silent (Johnson, 2006). For those concerned with social justice and anti-oppression, an obvious course of action is to "speak out." This will be discussed in the final section of this chapter.

"Othering" subordinate groups is the third behaviour noted by Johnson (2006) that is carried out by privileged people in systems of privilege, which reinforces privilege and oppression. The concept of "other" was presented in previous chapters with respect to oppressed persons being considered outside and different from the dominant group. That is, representative entities outside one's own gender, social group, class, culture, or civilization are considered to be the Other. The creation of this binary opposite by privileged groups is known as "othering." All non-Western cultures are seen as the Other of the West, while within Western society, women, gay and lesbian persons, and immigrants are often seen as the Other (Sardar & Van Loon, 2004). "The most common representation of the Other is as the darker side, the binary opposite of oneself: we are civilized, they are barbaric; the colonists are hard-working, the natives are lazy; heterosexuals are good and moral, homosexuals are immoral and evil" (Sardar & Van Loon, 2004, p. 13).

For oppression to exist, two basic ingredients are required—a group that is being oppressed and an oppressor or privileged group that benefits from oppression. Moraga (2004) argues that in the process, the oppressor/privileged groups externalize their fears by projecting them onto the people who seem to best fit the category of the "other." Johnson (2006, p. 96) claims that "Other is the key word in understanding how systems are identified with privileged groups. The privileged group is the assumed 'we' in relation to 'them.' The 'other' is the 'you people' whom we regard as problematic, un-acceptable, unlikable, or beneath our standards." For example, in a white-dominated system, white is the assumed race, and all *others* are viewed as non-white. This in effect lumps together a considerable diversity of ethno-racial groups into a single category of "other" in relation to a white standard.

Personal, Cultural, and Structural Levels of Privilege

It was presented in the previous chapter that oppression occurs at three levels. Just as oppression occurs at the personal or individual level, the cultural level, and the structural or institutional level, so too does privilege. These three levels or locations of privilege are in dynamic interaction with one another, with each level supporting, reinforcing, and influencing privilege on the other two levels and in turn are supported, reinforced, and influenced by the other two levels. And, as presented earlier in this chapter, whenever oppression or privilege occurs, so too does its equal and opposite effect occur. In other words, if privilege occurs at any one of these three levels, so too does oppression, since privilege exists at the expense of those who are oppressed.

The term given to the multi-dimensional perspective of oppression by Thompson (1997; 2002) is the "PCS model of analysis" (P for personal, C for cultural, and S for structural). Not only have we adopted this model of analysis of oppression, but we have extended it to include an analysis of privilege as well. Just as Thompson (2002, pp. 44–45) has stated with respect to oppression, "The basis of PCS analysis is that any approaches to the questions of discrimination and oppression which do not take into account all three of these levels, and their inter-relationships, is in danger of oversimplifying a very complex set of issues," we (Bob and Marilyn) make the same claim with respect to privilege. That is, any approach to the question of privilege and advantage that does not take into account all three levels of privilege, and their interrelationships, is in danger of over-simplifying a very complex set of issues with respect to privilege. This PCS model is adopted here as the working model for both oppression/anti-oppression and privilege/anti-privilege.

Similar to oppression, the personal or individual level of privilege is located both within the cultural and structural contexts of society, and the cultural level is embedded within the structural context (see Figure 9.1). Thus, if we examine privilege at only one of the three levels, it will be an incomplete analysis because the total context within which privilege occurs can only be understood in the larger context of society and with an awareness that the three levels continuously interact with one another. Along with the interactions that occur among the three levels of oppression and among the three levels of privilege, respectively, there should be a continuous "reaction" between the forces of oppression and those of privilege that resist and conflict with each other at each of the three levels.

Privilege at the personal level comprises those thoughts, attitudes, and behaviours that depict a negative prejudgment (on the part of the dominant group) of particular subordinate social groups and/or a favourable prejudgment of the dominant social group (by the dominant group). These prejudgments in the first instance are usually based on stereotypes of the subordinate group that may be overt or covert and in the second instance are usually based on images of superiority, meritocracy, and respectability associated with the dominant group. Without institutional or structural backing, these thoughts, attitudes, and behaviours constitute a prejudice against subordinate groups (Dominelli, 1997; Thompson, 1998) and an admiration for the dominant group. An example of privilege at the personal level would be when an affluent person secures the services of a prominent (and expensive) lawyer to represent them in a legal matter or when a professional person uses their dominant social position to get a preferred rate on a bank loan or a bank account or makes the decision to send their children to a private and well-resourced school.

Privilege at the cultural level consists of the values, norms, and shared patterns of seeing, thinking, and acting, along with an assumed consensus about what is right and normal, that taken together endorse the belief in a superior culture. An example of cultural privilege occurs when the dominant religious group (i.e., Christians) has its religion recognized and celebrated with a host of religious holidays such as Christmas and Easter, which non-Christians are often forced to observe and even participate in some of the celebrations and activities. Every day, dominant group members see their identity groups (males, white people, heterosexuals, etc.), their religion, their social systems, their language, their history, and so on presented as the "norm" in the mass media, in their government bodies, in public school curricula, in advertising, and in other cultural arenas. In effect, they see themselves as the "official culture" of society, which makes them the beneficiaries of cultural privilege.

Privilege at the structural level refers to the means by which privilege is institutionalized in society. It consists of the ways that social institutions, laws, policies, social processes and practices, and the economic and political systems all work together primarily in favour of the dominant group at the expense of subordinate groups. An example of structural privilege is that I (Bob) can be reasonably assured that I will be paid more than many other people (e.g., women, immigrants) for doing the same kind of work. At a minimum, I will not be paid less than others who do the same kind of work. I can also be reasonably assured that I will be treated fairly by the police and other government services.

Just as the above examples at each level of privilege (individual, cultural, and structural) demonstrate how I (Bob) benefit at each level, I also benefit because these levels continuously interact with one another. For example, on a personal level I know that when I book my economy air ticket using my title of "Doctor" (Mullaly), I am likely to be treated well by those making the reservations. And when I fly I know that because of my gender, colour, Anglo-Saxon name, and professional title, I will be treated with courtesy and respect when I check my bags and when I go through security and board the plane. I also know that I will experience cultural privilege because the media and other agents of culture portray professional, white males as valuable and upstanding members of society, which makes me a valuable and upstanding airline passenger by airline staff without having to prove or demonstrate my worthiness. Although I experience privilege at three levels in this example, and as illustrated in Figure 9.1, privilege at the personal level is usually the most apparent of the three levels because it is the most visible, but it exists in large part because of its interplay with the less visible but equally sustaining cultural and structural privileges. In other words, although having the title of "Doctor" on my boarding pass does not alone guarantee preferential or privileged treatment, being a white male with an Anglo-Saxon name helps significantly. This is an illustration of how these three levels of privilege interact and mutually reinforce each other.

Why Dominant Groups Do Not See Privilege as a Problem

Very few people would like to think that they are oppressive or that they are connected to someone else's misery, no matter how remote the connection. If privileged groups were to see and accept oppression and privilege as their issues, they might want to do something about them. If middle-class people saw poverty as their issue, or if white people saw racism as their issue, or if males saw sexism as their issue, or if non-disabled persons saw ableism as their issue, there would be more engagement by privileged groups in confronting and eliminating relationships of domination and oppression. But this is not happening. Privileged groups are not engaged with these issues, and when they are, it is usually for a short time and with little effect. The fact that they have privilege allows them to avoid the responsibility they have for the perpetration and perpetuation of oppression. They avoid this responsibility because there are so many ways they can fool themselves into thinking that they are not part of the problem. Allan Johnson (2006) outlines a number of these ways, which are summarized here.

1. *Deny and minimize.* One of the easiest ways to "get off the hook" is to deny that a problem of oppression exists (e.g., "racism and sexism used to be problems, but they aren't anymore

because of the laws and programs that address them"). Closely associated with denial is the minimization of experiences with oppression (e.g., "those Indigenous people should just quit whining about colonization all the time and get over it"). When the reality of oppression is denied, so too is the reality of the privilege that underpins it, which is just what it takes to avoid responsibility. When privileged people practise this kind of denial and minimization, they are in effect acting as though they know better than oppressed persons do about what they are experiencing and up against, which is the kind of presumption that privilege fosters and allows.

2. *Blame the victim.* Blaming the victim means acknowledging that harm has been done but holding the victim responsible. White people might say, for example, that if Indigenous people would drop their traditional culture, stop drinking, get an education, and go to work, they would not have the number and severity of social problems that they currently experience. Similarly, when a woman says that she was sexually harassed, men can tell themselves that it was her own fault because she should not have dressed provocatively or she should not have been where she was. "The result of such thinking is that oppression is blamed on the people who suffer most from it, while privilege and those who benefit remain invisible and relatively untouched" (Johnson, 2006, p. 111).

3. *Call it something else.* A more subtle way of avoiding responsibility for oppression and privilege is to call them something else. For example, gender inequality is often referred to as "the battle of the sexes" or as an anthropological curiosity based on the notion that males and females are from different cultures (if not from different planets) even though they may grow up in the same families, attend the same schools, and watch television together. Any problems or misunderstandings are seen as the result of different ways of communicating. And while there are gender differences in styles of talk, they are more significant than the differences, say, between Chinese and Canadian styles of talk because they serve the purpose of ensuring male privilege. For example, every time a man interrupts a woman and she defers by keeping quiet, a pattern of male dominance and male centredness is acted out once again.

4. *It's better this way.* The ideology that surrounds privilege includes all kinds of claims that the status quo is preferred. White people often claim that racialized individuals prefer to live with their own or that they cannot afford to live among white people. Both claims are incorrect, since research shows that most racialized individuals prefer to live in integrated neighbourhoods and that it is racism, not income, occupation, or education, that gets in the way of integrated living for most racialized individuals, especially those in the middle class (Massey & Denton, 1998, cited in Johnson, 2006; Wise, 2015). Similarly, patriarchal culture conveys all kinds of messages to the effect that women prefer strong men to dominate them. The truth does not matter in these situations because the purpose of the ideology of inequality is to reinforce the status quo (of privilege) by making it appear normal and legitimate. Even when oppressed persons call attention to the divisions and inequalities caused by privilege, they are often accused of creating divisions and problems themselves, with the result that talking about privilege rather than privilege itself is defined as the problem.

5. *It doesn't count if you don't mean it.* We have all experienced a member of a privileged group (including ourselves) saying something or doing something that has racial or sexist or classist overtones. Examples include a man who makes repeated sexual comments to a female colleague or a middle-class person who makes a joke about people living in poverty. When confronted (usually by subordinate group members), the privileged person often responds by becoming defensive and saying something like "I didn't mean anything." This kind of response

is intended to get the person off the hook, the reasoning being that because the person did not mean any offence, then the action did not happen, since the only thing that connects the person to the consequences of what was said or done is conscious (i.e., bad) intent. This reaction fails to acknowledge that regardless of the intent, the woman or the person living in poverty has been harmed and must deal with it on their own. In effect, "I didn't mean it" or "It was just a joke" comes very close to saying, "I didn't say it" or "I didn't do it," which is not true. Most of the time, the true message should be that "I said it" or "I did it" but "I did not think about it beforehand." In most social situations, this kind of response does not get one off the hook. If I steal something and tell the judge that I did not mean anything by it, I will still be held responsible for my actions, and I will have an awareness of the consequences of what I do or do not do. But privilege works against such awareness for privileged persons in all kinds of social situations. As Johnson (2006, p. 117) says, "the luxury of obliviousness makes a lack of conscious intent a path of least resistance that's easy to follow without knowing it. The sense of entitlement and superiority that underlies most forms of privilege runs so deep and is so entrenched that [privileged] people don't have to think about it in order to act from it." People who say, "I didn't think about it," are often telling the truth, which makes it so disarming and such an effective way of defending privilege. The fact that people do not have to think about saying or doing hurtful things to subordinate persons is precisely the problem with privilege and the damage it causes.

6. *I'm one of the good ones.* Another way of avoiding responsibility for oppression and privilege is to make a case that because I am not a bad person (only bad people oppress others), the problem could not have anything to do with me. I can argue that I have no problem with gay and lesbian people in my workplace, that I have an "End Racism" button on my office door, and that I never park in handicapped parking places. And part of my being a good person is that I strongly disapprove of all those bad or flawed people who discriminate against others and I sympathize with people who suffer as a result. However, my silence, inaction, and passive acceptance of the everyday privilege that goes along with people like me makes me part of the problem. When social categories work to my advantage, I must consider that these same categories are working against others through no fault of their own, which then becomes my business because I am being privileged at their expense. If people are being oppressed because of racism, sexism, and so on, other people are receiving privileged treatment because of racism, sexism, and so on. If privileged people do nothing, they are in effect supporting and perpetuating oppression. There is no such thing as a neutral position because doing or saying nothing is a choice that has political consequences.

7. *Sick and tired.* When it comes to the problem of oppression and privilege, privileged persons often do not want to hear about it because it upsets the luxury of obliviousness that comes with their privilege. A common response is saying or making facial gestures that imply "Here we go again." Privileged people often become annoyed or irritated with the person who raises issues of oppression and privilege, not because they do not believe that these issues are real but because they feel that they are being put upon or bashed or made to feel guilty. They may feel that a great weight has been placed on their shoulders or that open season on privileged persons has just been declared. However, it is one thing to hear about problems associated with social inequality and oppression, but it is quite another to live with them every day. Yes, life is hard these days for

almost everyone, and almost everyone may feel exhausted, but white persons who feel exhausted are not exhausted because they are white. Heterosexual persons are not having a tough time because they are heterosexual. Subordinate group members have to do all the things that make privileged group members tired (from raising families to earning a living to growing older and so on), but on top of that, they have to struggle with the accumulated stress that oppression piles on them simply because, through no fault of their own, they are in the wrong social categories.

In sum, a number of avoidance mechanisms are available to privileged groups that allow them to avoid feeling any guilt, shame, or responsibility for the deleterious effects of oppression. This option "puts members of privileged groups inside a tight little circle that cuts them off from what it means to be alive" (Johnson, 2006, p. 124). It means that privileged groups have to distance and insulate themselves from much of humanity—men from women, white persons from racialized individuals, affluent people from people living in poverty—because if they were to get too close to these people, they would find it more difficult to maintain the denial and illusion and would have to deal with the troubles that surround privilege and oppression. Given this situation, it would seem more desirable for dominant groups to accept responsibility for privilege and oppression and view it as a challenge and an opportunity rather than as an affliction or a source of guilt and shame.

A Taxonomy of Everyday Examples of Unearned Privilege

In her ground-breaking and celebrated work, Peggy McIntosh (1990) referred to what she calls the "invisible knapsack." The invisible knapsack contains all the benefits or privileges that come to us every day simply because we are white, or middle-class, or straight, or a member of any other privileged group in society. In the boxes below, we outline selected privileges that are associated with being middle- or upper-class, a member of the white race, male, heterosexual, non-disabled, a member of a two-parent family, and of adult age that precedes old age. We (Bob and Marilyn) limited the number of privileges in each category to around 10, although some of the lists compiled by others are quite lengthy. McIntosh's original list of "white privileges," for example, contains 46 items. These lists do not reflect the privileges of every person who falls into a particular category. They are both under- and over-inclusive. Other social categories have an impact on each set of privileges. For example, a black male does not have the same number of privileges or the same qualitative extent of privileges as a white male.

Carbado (2004) tells us that we have to be careful not to universalize any category of privileged persons or present them as a "cohesive identity" in ways that deny or obscure the fact of multiplicity or heterogeneity *within* categories of privileged persons. At the same time, people who fall into categories of privilege must do more than identify the privileges that have been conferred upon them. They must also realize how they actively re-enact these privileges interpersonally, culturally, and institutionally. In other words, privileged persons must come to recognize their own complicity in the normalization of privilege.

Box 10.1 *Middle- or Upper-Class Privilege*

- I do not worry about going hungry or being homeless.
- I can live where I choose and move when and where I choose.
- I do not have to shop around for the best buy or wait for sales.
- I can be sure that my children will not be mistreated by teachers and staff at school.
- I can get discounts on major purchases and preferred interest rates on my investments because I am seen as a valuable customer.
- I am not presumed to be immoral, lazy, evil, unmotivated, stupid, incompetent, work-shy, alcoholic, or promiscuous because of my social class.
- I can leave my children with an inheritance to make things a little easier for them.
- I can assume that I am entitled to these privileges because of the dominant social beliefs.
- I can take advantage of all the income tax breaks that are not available to those with lower incomes.

Thanks to the Women's Theological Center in Boston for several of the above privileges.

Box 10.2 *White Privilege*

- If I should need to move, I can be pretty sure of renting or purchasing housing in an area that I can afford and in which I would want to live.
- I can go shopping alone most of the time, pretty well assured that I will not be followed or harassed.
- I can be sure that my children will be given curricular materials that testify to the existence of their race.
- Whether I use cheques, credit cards, or cash, I can count on my skin colour not working against the appearance of financial reliability.
- I can swear or dress in second-hand clothes or not answer letters without having people attribute these choices to the bad morals, the poverty, or the illiteracy of my race.
- If a traffic cop pulls me over or if my tax return is audited, I can be sure that I haven't been singled out because of my race.
- I can choose public accommodation without fearing that people of my race cannot get in or will be mistreated in the places I have chosen.
- I can be sure that if I need legal or medical help, my race will not work against me.
- I can choose blemish cover or bandages in "flesh" color that more or less matches my skin.

Taken from Peggy McIntosh, *White Privilege: Unpacking the Invisible Knapsack* (1990).

Box 10.3 *Male Privilege*

- I am praised for spending time with my children and for cooking and doing household chores.
- I am not expected to change my name when I get married.
- I can walk alone in public without fear of being harassed or sexually violated.
- Prospective employers will never ask me whether I plan to have children.
- I am confident that I will never be accused of sleeping my way to the top in my workplace.
- When I get dressed in the morning, I never worry about whether my clothing will invite sexual harassment.
- If I am sexually active, even promiscuous, I can largely count on not being called a slut or a whore. In fact, I will be seen as a stud in some circles and held in high regard.
- I can count on my wife or partner doing most of the housework and child care even if she has a job outside the home.
- I can express anger or outrage without being seen as irrational, emotional, or too sensitive.

Thanks mainly to Devon Carbado (2004) and also to Steven P. Schacht (2003) for most of the above male privileges.

Box 10.4 *Heterosexual Privilege*

- I can be assured that I will not be blamed for creating or spreading the AIDS virus.
- I don't have to worry about people trying to cure me of my heterosexuality.
- My partner and I can display affection in public without fear of ridicule or harassment.
- I can be assured that I will never be denied medical treatment because I am heterosexual.
- My children will never have to explain why they have parents of different genders.
- I can take a job with almost any employer and be assured that my partner will be included in the benefits package.
- My heterosexuality will be affirmed in every religious tradition.
- I do not have to struggle with "coming out" or worry about being "outed."
- I can display my partner's photos at work without causing office gossip or hostility.
- I don't have to worry about being bashed after leaving a social event with other heterosexuals.
- If a child is sexually abused by a heterosexual person, I do not have to worry about being suspected as a pedophile because of my heterosexuality.

Thanks to Devon Carbado (2004) for most of the above privileges.

The next set of privileges was originally developed by Peggy McIntosh as examples of heterosexual privilege. It seems to us, however, that these privileges could just as easily be applied to the traditional form of family that is still considered the norm in North America and in other Anglo-democracies—that is, a heterosexual couple with children. This type of family is, of course, a form of heterosexism, but it is also a family type that enjoys certain privileges that are not available to other family forms—single-parent and two-(same-sex)-parent families. The fact that a heterosexual "different-sex" couple lives together under the same roof triggers all kinds of societal assumptions about their individual worth, politics, life, and values and triggers a host of unearned advantages and powers for each of them (McIntosh, 2003).

Box 10.5 *Traditional Family Privilege*

- My children do not have to answer questions about why they have two different-sex parents.
- I have no difficulty finding neighbourhoods where people approve of our household.
- I will never be turned down on an application for housing because there are two parents.
- Most people I meet will see my marital arrangements as an asset to my life or as a favourable comment on my likeability, my competence, and my mental health.
- I will feel welcomed and "normal" in the usual walks of public life, both institutional and social.

Box 10.6 *Non-disability Privilege*

- I can be assured that most people do not assume I am incapable of a sex life or of having children.
- I am not likely to be singled out at school based on stereotypes that underestimate my abilities and be put in a special education class that doesn't allow me to develop my potential.
- I am not likely to be shuttled into some dead-end, menial job, given inadequate job training, paid less than I am worth regardless of my ability, or separated from other workers on the job.
- When I go out in public, I can be pretty sure that I will not be stared at or looked at as odd or not belonging and that most buildings will be accessible to me.
- I assume that when I need to travel, I will have access to buses, trains, airplanes, and other means of transportation.
- I am assured that wherever I go, most people will not feel awkward or uncomfortable around me.
- I am assured that I can participate actively in mainstream society and will not be segregated into living situations such as nursing homes or into special schools and sports programs.

Thanks to Allan G. Johnson (2006) for the above examples of non-disability privileges.

Box 10.7 *Young Adult and Middle-Age Privilege*

- I do not have to endure people yelling at me because they assume I cannot hear.
- I can be assured that people will not infantilize me by talking "baby talk" to me.
- I am not likely to be viewed as a burden on society and draining the country's resources.
- I do not have to endure receiving endless advertisements in the mail for funeral arrangements, estate planning, pension and insurance schemes, nursing-home care, and specials on incontinence supplies.
- I am not likely to feel useless, lonely, and suicidal because of my age or have people pity me because they assume I am lonely and useless.
- I can be assured that people will not equate my age with illness and infirmity.
- I am assured that people will not consider me as incapable of having a sex life.

Social Work and Privilege

Because everyone in society is affected by oppression and privilege and because everyone grows up within and participates in systems of privilege and oppression, privilege is an issue for social workers personally and professionally and for social work organizations. Social workers generally are members of privileged groups. This is not to say that many social workers have not experienced oppression or are not members of oppressed groups. Overall, however, they enjoy many of the privileges outlined earlier in this chapter by virtue of their race, job, education, middle class, professional status, economic status, age, non-disability, and so on. In addition, a service user quickly learns that the social worker often has control over the resources that the service user needs and has decision-making power over certain aspects of the service user's life that the service user does not have over the social worker's (Marsiglia & Kulis, 2009). Unfortunately, just as privilege is not handled very well by privileged people generally, so too are social workers and social work organizations often oblivious to or in denial of privilege issues in the course of their social work practice. As argued earlier, members of privileged groups are not only more likely than subordinate groups to believe that existing inequalities are legitimate and natural, they also are more likely to act in their own self-interests and are encouraged to do so (Sidanius & Pratto, 1999). So a crucial question for social work and for those who believe in social justice is what would encourage people with privilege to give up their privilege and seek greater social equality.

Strategies to Reduce Privilege

Just as oppressed groups have a range of strategies available to them to respond to their oppression, so too do privileged people have a range of strategies to help neutralize or reduce their privileges. Dominelli (2002) points out that privileged people (including social workers) have three strategies available to them to deal with their position of dominance over others (including service users):

- a demarcationist option;
- an incorporationist option; and
- an egalitarian option.

These three positions can coexist and overlap with each other, and a person may hold more than one of them simultaneously or at different points in time. Only the egalitarian position is not exclusionary. People who subscribe to the *demarcationist* strategy tend to have a hierarchical view of the world and orient their actions toward keeping power and resources in their own hands. They follow a "we–them" demarcation between privileged and inferior people. The *incorporationist* option allows for collaboration between privileged and subordinate groups, with those who are "othered" being allowed to permeate the ranks of the privileged group but only if they know their place and maintain a respectful distance. Low-level reform aimed at improving what is deemed to be a basically sound system is the goal of the incorporationists, which they achieve through the selective inclusion of people drawn from the ranks of the "other." This group of selected people are those whom the dominant group thinks they can trust to be true to the values and traditions of the dominant group, and they are given honorary status in the dominant group. However, this honorary status can be withdrawn at any time if the behaviour of the person who is designated as inferior displeases the dominant group.

Those in the dominant group who reject the current social system because they consider it unfair and unjust follow the *egalitarian* option. They seek transformation of a society characterized by inequality and oppression to one that is egalitarian and inclusive of difference on equal terms. Anti-oppressive social workers, even though they may be members of privileged groups, would obviously opt for the egalitarian strategy because they recognize the injustice associated with a social order that grants them privileges that are based on certain characteristics that the person has and, for the most part, were born with. The parallels between the demarcationist and neo-conservative social work positions, between the incorporationist and liberal-humanist social work positions, and between the egalitarian and critical social work positions should be obvious at this point.

Standpoint Theories

Although Dominelli ends her discussion of strategies to deal with privilege by advocating for the egalitarian approach, Pease (2010) argues that the egalitarian model is easily compromised in that it is not so easy in practice for egalitarians to reject the social order that grants them privileges and that any rejection may not be total rejection. To address this limitation, he proposes a fourth strategy: that privileged groups develop a critical distance from their privilege. For this to occur, he believes that privileged persons must turn to standpoint theory, which has its origins in Marxism and was adopted by feminists, gay and lesbian theorists, Indigenous scholars, disability activists, critical race theorists, and post-colonial writers. Referring to the celebrated work of S. Harding (2004), he points out that these groups were able to develop "knowledge grounded in their own experiences as oppressed groups, which was used to provide a critical stance against the dominant Eurocentric, patriarchal, class elitist, heterosexist, and ableist conceptual frameworks" (Pease, 2010, pp. 28–29).

Standpoint theories have, of course, been used by many practising critical social workers who have worked with members of these groups. They serve a couple of important purposes—one primarily for oppressed group members and another primarily for privileged group members. First, standpoint theories are based on the premise that there is a direct relationship between one's social location in the world and one's understanding of the nature of the world. The further away one is from the centre of power, the more comprehensive one's analysis of society or the world will be because those who are oppressed have to understand the viewpoint of dominant or privileged groups in order to survive within them, while members of privileged groups have no need to understand the perspective of subordinate groups. This allows oppressed or subordinate groups to develop knowledge grounded in their own experiences, which enables them to adopt a critical stance against those dominant knowledge bases of privileged groups that contribute to the oppression of subordinate groups.

A second important purpose of standpoint theories is that while they validate the experiences of oppressed groups and encourage collective resistance against oppressive thought and practice (Harding, 2004, cited in Pease, 2010), they are useful for privileged groups to critically reflect on the ways in which their own world views contribute to the oppression of others. In this way, dominant group members potentially can develop the capacity to see themselves from the perspective of members of oppressed groups and to develop knowledge that serves the interests of oppressed groups (Harding, 1995, cited in Pease, 2010). In this way, it is possible that members of privileged groups might challenge the taken-for-granted self-interests of their own group (Pease, 2010). For example, financially well-off people might challenge poverty, and white people might challenge racism, and heterosexual people might challenge homophobia, and so on. While social work practitioners and students may learn all about oppression, we believe it is equally if not more important to learn about privilege—especially our own. Standpoint theories allow us to do this.

Privilege and Social Workers

Marsiglia and Kulis (2009) speak to a few problems with respect to the issue of privilege and social work practice. They claim that the social worker's privilege, if left unchecked, can be a barrier to empathy and an obstacle to culturally grounded practice (i.e., anti-oppressive practice). This is so because privilege makes professionals assume certain things about service users, such as having what the worker has (a car or a comfortable home) or sharing similar experiences (being able to eat a hot breakfast before coming to the agency). Service users are usually aware of privileges enjoyed by the social worker even if the social worker is not.

If left unaddressed, this perceived privilege can become an obstacle to effective communication and rapport building, as clients [sic] may assume that the professionals cannot understand what they are going through due to their lack of experience with certain oppressive situations. Social workers, including those from minority groups, may be in denial about the privileges they enjoy that their clients [*sic*] do not. Self-awareness about privilege increases social workers' effectiveness and, in the end, enhances their professional and personal growth. Ignoring privilege or minimizing its impact on the client–worker relationship may compromise rapport and trust, leading to ineffective practice (Marsiglia & Kulis, 2009, p. 17).

In a study of how a group of (self-defined) left-of-centre social workers dealt with issues of class, race, and gender in their everyday work, Donna Baines (2002) reported on a number of observations made by the study participants on some negative ways that some social workers and social work supervisors handled issues of privilege. First, one participant noted that many people feared that if they began to talk about giving up their privilege, they would become subordinated, which had the effect of shutting down all discussion on confronting privilege. Another participant observed that there is a tendency not to acknowledge one's own power; rather, everyone wants to be part of an oppressed group. This sentiment, which is called the "flight to innocence" by Sharene Razack (1998, cited in Baines, 2002), is a way for people to avoid the responsibility for changing relationships of dominance–subordination by "hiding behind some facet of their identity that locates them close to, or within, subordinated groups" (1998, cited in Baines, 2002, p. 192).

This is a revealing observation that supports what Johnson asserts about privilege in that it shows that people are more willing to confront their subordinate status than they are their privileged positions. Baines speculates that because many social work models emphasize seeing the world through the eyes of service users and fail to recognize (or at least address) the power and privileges that social workers possess on the basis of their education, class, employment, race, and so on, the need to identify oneself as a member of an oppressed group is the logical extension of such models. We think it is also a way of denying that part of one's identity is associated with the harm others experience because of oppression, and it gets people off the hook in terms of taking any responsibility for doing something about it. I (Bob) agree with Baines (2002, p. 192) when she says that "little is achieved by privileged people sharing powerlessness while much can be achieved by redistributing power and building politicized, affirming identities. Learning how to use power and privilege, rather than denying it [*sic*], is part of the challenge of the anti-racist [and anti-oppressive] project."

Prevalence of Privilege in Organizations

In addition to how it affects people, the trouble that surrounds privilege also affects organizations such as workplaces (including social work agencies) and universities (including social work programs). The prevalence of privilege and oppression in organizations is one of our best-kept secrets for those with privilege and one of our worst-kept secrets for members of subordinate groups. Most of the time, people act as though there were no issues of privilege and oppression, and the organization either denies that anything is wrong or is oblivious to it—until a crisis occurs and the typical reaction is panicked efforts at damage control to minimize bad publicity or legal exposure (Johnson, 2006). If left unattended, privilege makes organizations increasingly dysfunctional and vulnerable.

In a society such as ours that is characterized by relationships of privilege and oppression, the assumption cannot be that because no one has complained, there is no problem with oppression in an organization. The workplace and the university are part of the larger society. People in the workplace or in the university have grown up and been socialized in the larger society. To some degree, the organization has to reflect the larger society, which includes the existence of oppression and privilege. Privilege and oppression must become a part of the organization's agenda, and it must be discussed. The silence must be broken. Otherwise, white men, for instance, will see little reason to examine themselves in relation to the racism and sexism that haunt the lives of so many people or to see how living in a racist and sexist society has influenced them with respect to how they see the world or how they regard women, racialized individuals, persons with disabilities, and so on (Johnson, 2006).

It is not enough for the boss or the instructor to treat women as they would men or racialized individuals as they would white people because sexism and racism go beyond one person's intentions or behaviours. If privilege and subordination are not discussed in the organization, it becomes very difficult or risky for a member of a subordinate group to raise issues of privilege. If subordinate group members become uncomfortable working or studying in an organization because critical issues are not addressed, the organization will become known as a place where they are not fully welcome. Persons who are not white, heterosexual, male, non-disabled, and so on will realize that they can do better elsewhere, "someplace where you can look at those with power and influence and see people who look like you" (Johnson, pp. 64–65). Over time, these other places will do better because of their diverse population of students or workers and because they are able to attract and keep talent from a larger pool of individuals.

What Can We Do?[2]

There are no easy answers to the question of what we as social workers can do about the problem of privilege and oppression. There is no recipe book or how-to-do-it manual or 12-step program. Nor is there any way around or over the problem. We must confront it head-on and go through it if we are to make a difference. The following are some of the tasks that can be carried out in confronting privilege and unsettling systems of privilege. More tasks and strategies can be found in Chapter 9 of *Challenging Oppression and Confronting Privilege*, third edition, by Mullaly and West (2018).

1. *Reclaim the words.* One of the inherent characteristics of professionalism is that each profession develops a professional discourse or vocabulary. For a long time, social work had a clinical or therapeutic discourse, mainly because it aligned itself with the medical model and adopted counselling or therapy as ways of dealing with social problems and people experiencing social problems. Much of our discourse today, it seems to us, is a consequence of trying to avoid politically charged words so that we do not offend the public, our employers, mainstream social workers, and so on. In the previous chapter, we made the argument that the term "social inequality" is one of those bourgeois, technical, polite, and professional terms that tend to reduce the political charge or the imperative of doing something about the violent outcomes of oppression. We should identify social inequality for what it is—socially sanctioned social terrorism

and structural violence. Then maybe we will take it more seriously and try to do more about eliminating it.

Similarly, social work has developed a discourse about difference that has little political charge and does not make people feel uncomfortable when they hear the words in the discourse—words like diversity, tolerance, cultural sensitivity, appreciating difference. Contrast these words with the following: racism, sexism, patriarchy, domination, privilege, oppression, subordination, anti-Semitism, classism. The latter group of words actually names problems, and these words tend to be the vocabulary of people hurt by the problems. People from privileged groups are often uncomfortable with such words because they do not want to look at what they point to. White men, for example, tend not to want to look at sexism or racism. Heterosexual persons do not want to look at heterosexism. Privileged persons would rather hear words such as diversity, appreciating difference, tolerance, and cultural sensitivity because they are good things to talk about and the language is polite (Johnson, 2006). The political function of using terms such as these, however, is that they cover over the troubles associated with racism and other forms of oppression and privilege. And if we cannot talk about a trouble, then we cannot do much about it.

One thing we can do, then, as anti-oppressive or structural social workers is to reclaim the words of oppression and privilege and recognize that a word like "racist" does not mean "bad white people," or "sexist" does not mean "bad men," or "feminism" does not mean being a lesbian or man-hater. We can use words like oppression and domination and sexism without being oppressive or dominant or sexist. If we are going to be part of the solution with respect to eliminating oppression and all the harm it causes, then we must drop our defensive sensitivity to that difficult discourse and the reality to which it points.

2. *Acknowledge that oppression and privilege exist.* Most systems of privilege maintain oppression by denying or minimizing its existence, by blaming people experiencing oppression, by calling it something else, or by diverting attention away from it. There would be much more opposition to privilege if people with privilege were aware of how it affects the everyday lives of subordinate groups. Awareness by itself is not enough, however. We must maintain this awareness in the face of a system characterized by paths of least resistance that lead away from critical awareness of how systems of privilege and oppression work.

The crucial task for structural social workers is to apply our understanding of how systems of oppression and privilege work and to change the systems themselves—social, economic, cultural, political, religious, familial, and so on. Maintaining a critical awareness of privilege takes commitment and work, and to hang on to this awareness we must make it part of our everyday lives.

3. *Pay attention.* Developing an understanding of what privilege and oppression are and how they operate and how we participate in them is the first step in working for change. The simplest way to develop an understanding is to make reading about privilege part of our lives. It is easy to have an opinion, but it takes work to know what you are talking about. Some people assume that because privilege and oppression are part of everyday life or because they have experienced oppression, they know all they have to know. However, one person cannot possibly experience all that is involved in oppression and privilege. As well, our experiences are so deeply shaped by privilege and oppression that often, what we think we know misses the mark.

There is a vast literature on issues of privilege available in any decent library system, although, as Johnson (2006) observes, you would never know it, judging from its invisibility in the mass media and mainstream bookstores. The mass media would rather discuss whether or not men and women are from different planets or have different brains than examine the reality of male privilege. Reading is just the beginning, however, because at some point we have to look at ourselves and society and see whether we can identify what we are reading about. For example, once we have included the concept of "paths of least resistance" into our everyday consciousness, we begin to see them everywhere. If privileged groups are to take their share of responsibility for dealing with issues of privilege, then we must listen, observe, ask, read, and listen again—we must make it our business to find out for ourselves.

4. *Learn to listen.* Johnson (2006, p. 141) says it best in the following passage:

> Attentive listening is especially difficult for members of dominant groups. If someone confronts you with your own behaviour that supports privilege, step off the path of least resistance that encourages you to defend and deny. Don't tell them they're too sensitive or need a better sense of humor, and don't try to explain away what you did as something else than what they're telling you it was. Don't say you didn't mean it or that you were only kidding. Don't tell them what a champion of justice you are or how hurt you feel because of what they're telling you. Don't make jokes or try to be cute or charming, since only access to privilege can lead someone to believe these are acceptable responses to something as serious as privilege and oppression. Listen to what is being said. Take it seriously. Assume for the time being that it's true, because given the power of paths of least resistance, it probably is. And then take responsibility to do something about it.

5. *Little risks: Do something.* The more we pay attention to privilege and oppression, the more we will see opportunities to do something about them. Opportunities exist everywhere, beginning with ourselves. We can become cognizant of the paths of least resistance that we follow and our relationship to them that makes it so easy to follow them. For most men, it can mean trying to stop hogging air time and interrupting others (especially women) and learning new ways of listening more and talking less. Or it can mean to stop avoiding looking at or communicating with persons who have noticeable disabilities and learn to get over feelings of discomfort and awkwardness. There is no limit to the number of paths of least resistance that we can step off.

It is not just a matter of changing personal behaviour, however, because the choices we make are connected to the systems in which we participate. By *openly* changing how we participate in a system, we not only change our behaviour but also contribute to changing how that system operates. Changing the world involves the dynamic relationship between personal and social change. Other ways that we can help to make a difference include the following:

- *Make noise and be seen.* Every system of privilege and oppression depends on silence. Rather than collude in it, we should show up, stand up, speak out, sign petitions, write letters, volunteer.

- *Find little ways of getting off the paths of least resistance.* It can be as simple as not laughing at a racist or sexist or heterosexist joke or stepping it up a notch and saying that you do not find such jokes funny. It can be writing to the editor of your local newspaper to protest any instances of sexism or racism or any other form of oppression that appeared in the paper.

- *Dare to make people feel uncomfortable, starting with yourself.* One could ask about the profile of employees in one's workplace if, for example, most of the clerical staff are women and most of the managerial staff are men or if there is a sea of white faces in a university admissions or faculty office to greet members of a diverse society with many faces that are not white. Some people would object to making others feel uncomfortable, but there is nothing comfortable about being a member of an oppressed group, and systems of privilege do a lot more than make people feel uncomfortable. Almost any significant social movement (e.g., the suffragette movement, the civil rights movement, the trade union movement) has depended on discomfort and disruption to bring about social change.

- *Openly choose and model alternative paths.* As we identify the paths of least resistance that we tend to follow, we can identify alternative paths and openly follow them so that people can see what we are doing. Paths of least resistance become more visible when people follow alternatives, just as rules become more visible when they are broken. Any university instructor will tell you that students tend to sit in the same seat every time they attend class and that it is extremely noticeable when the seating pattern is broken on just one occasion.

- *Openly promote change in how systems are organized around privilege.* The possibilities are almost endless because privilege is everywhere. We could, for example, advocate for equality in the workplace, not support businesses that engage in unfair labour practices or that are inaccessible to people with disabilities (and tell the businesses why we do not support them), support fair trade businesses, join international organizations such as the anti-globalization movement or the peace movement or the environmental movement or Amnesty International, support "end legislated poverty" organizations. Openly support and compliment people when they take an alternative path to that of the least resistance.

- *Make anti-privilege part of the agenda.* Whether it is in the workplace or an educational social work program, put privilege on the agenda of agency or unit meetings and as part of the curriculum and classroom discussions. For starters, here are a few topics for the agency or social work program: share with others the difficulties you have in recognizing and acknowledging the privileges you have; analyze how traditional/dominant social work theory and practices used in your workplace or found in your curriculum might be oppressive; discuss how alternative standpoint knowledge bases such as critical race theory, feminist approaches, queer theory, class analysis, Indigenous knowledge, critical disability theory, and post-colonial theory could replace traditional knowledge and approaches that contribute to the maintenance of privilege and, conversely, to the oppression of subordinate groups; and problem-solve ways of not reproducing privilege when we speak or when we make case notes or recordings.

The first five of the above activities for confronting and challenging privilege were developed by Allan Johnson (2006), and the final activity was developed by us based on our experiences of teaching in structural and anti-oppressive social work programs. Although we emphasize social work and social workers, these activities are for anyone in society who might be concerned with issues of privilege and oppression. Obviously, they have relevance for all social workers who follow a social justice mandate. In Chapter 8 we outlined a number of principles of anti-oppressive social work practice that are consistent with the above activities in confronting and resisting privilege—everything from having a goal of social transformation to the constructive use of anger.

A number of writers advocate that members of privileged groups become "allies" of subordinate groups and work collectively to overcome relationships of privilege and oppression (e.g., Sisneros et al., 2008; Bishop, 2002). In her book *Becoming an Ally: Breaking the Cycle of Oppression*, Anne Bishop presents a portrait of allies as persons who are socially aware, are connected with *all* other people, have a critical analysis of social structures, possess a collective orientation as opposed to one that is individualistic, have an acceptance of struggle and a sense of process, have an understanding of "power with" as opposed to "power over," and have a high degree of self-understanding, a knowledge of history, and an understanding that good intentions do not matter if there is no action against oppression. She makes the point that the same characteristics are typical of people who are well advanced in their own liberation process. Bishop (2002, p. 110) says of allies:

> allies understand that, as part of various oppressor groups (white, male, able-bodied, heterosexual, middle or above in the class structure), they did not individually bring the situation [of oppression] about and they cannot just reach out with goodwill and solve it. They understand that they must act with others [not for others or on behalf of others] to contribute to change. They believe that to do nothing is to reinforce the *status quo*; . . . They take responsibility for helping to solve problems of historical injustice without taking on individual guilt. Most look for what they can do, with others, in a strategic way, and try to accept their limitations beyond that.

Allies would carry out most if not all of the activities outlined above with respect to confronting and trying to change systems of privilege. Bishop presents an extensive list of questions and guidelines that someone considering becoming an ally to oppressed groups should ask themselves. The most important guideline for being an ally, in our view, is that the role of the ally is to help or assist oppressed groups in any way one can in their struggle for liberation. Under no circumstances should one assume that one knows better or should be the leader just because one is a member of a privileged group—this is probably the worst thing one could do. Becoming allies and/or doing something else to combat social injustice and inequality in our society is critical. Although not powerless to affect their own living conditions, oppressed groups cannot, by themselves, do away with entrenched systems of privilege. What is needed is for privileged persons to make the problem of privilege *their* problem and to do something about it (Johnson, 2006). Becoming an ally is one way of doing this.

The final action to be mentioned here that we can take to undo our privilege is for each of us to take what Peggy McIntosh calls our "invisible knapsack" and remove all of its contents. This invisible knapsack contains all the benefits that come to us simply because we are white, or male, or straight, or middle-class, or non-disabled. We have to open that knapsack, dump out the contents, and take a look at all the different ways that these ascribed characteristics (those we are born with) have become so obscured and invisible that we have come to believe that the privileges we have in our lives are the result of some kind of achievement on our part. In other words, we have to dispel the myth of meritocracy. We must use our unearned advantages to weaken hidden systems of privilege and our arbitrarily awarded power to reconstruct power systems on a broader base.

Pedagogy of Privilege

In recent years, there have been a number of researchers and writers (almost exclusively outside of social work) who have been developing a literature on privilege. Many of these writers have been mentioned in this chapter. One major area of concern to those who write about and those who teach about privilege is the fact that while courses focusing on prejudice and oppression flourish, "classroom discussions of privilege consistently meet with student resistance and a variety of additional pedagogical challenges" (Tatum, 1994, cited in Case, 2013, p. 3). In dealing with student (and other people's) resistance while discussing privilege and in addressing other pedagogical obstacles, Kim Case (2013, pp. 4–5) has developed a "Model of Privilege Studies Pedagogy" that should inform instructional approaches and classroom strategies of faculty who teach in the area of privilege studies as well as maximize student learning and raise awareness of privilege across disciplines. This model of privilege incorporates the following 11 elements:

- *analyzes privilege and power* in teaching about privilege, pushing the boundaries of teaching multiculturalism, diversity, or oppression and discrimination;
- *emphasizes the definition of privilege* (unearned group advantage) and how it affects lived experiences and dominant group psychology;
- *focuses on the invisibility of privilege*, the consequences of that invisibility for the privileged [persons] and the oppressed [persons];
- *teaches privilege across a wide variety of oppressions*;
- frames learning about privilege through an *intersectional theory perspective*;
- *involves educator personal reflection on privilege*, biases, assumptions, and the ways in which instructor social identity may impact the learning community;
- encourages critical analysis through *student reflection and writing about their own privileged identities*;
- *promotes social action to dismantle privilege* through student learning that extends beyond the classroom walls;
- *values the voices of the marginalized and oppressed people* by avoiding claims of equal validity awarded to all perspectives; and
- *infuses learning about privilege across the curriculum*, including core liberal arts courses not traditionally associated with diversity content (e.g., biology, introduction to psychology, economics, marketing, and math).

To this list of 10 elements of anti-privilege work we would add one more:

- *includes in our structural social work practice an engagement with anti-privilege work on a personal level* wherever privilege is used to oppress people. Rather than colluding with privilege and oppression by remaining silent, we should show up, stand up, and speak out.

We have tried to follow and adhere to this Model of Privilege Studies Pedagogy in writing this chapter (and this book). And, in turn, we think that the material in our book has, in some small way, contributed to this model by extending some of its ideas into areas beyond education into social work and into our personal lives as social workers. It is our hope that more social work writers and practitioners will focus on privilege in their writing and their practice. For, as argued by Peggy McIntosh (2012), we will not get anywhere in fighting oppression without confronting privilege—our own and others'.

Conclusion

This chapter focused on privilege, which is the flip side of oppression. The relationship between the two is direct and unambiguous. We have oppression because we have privilege. Privilege benefits one group at the expense of many groups. In discussing the nature of privilege, we saw that it is surrounded by a paradox in that those who have privilege tend not to know it or know how privilege happens from one moment to the next. It is invisible to most privileged persons but not to oppressed groups. For the most part, privileged persons believe that the unearned advantages attached to their special group membership are the outcome of their hard work, vigilance, and cultural superiority. This belief is reinforced by a number of myths, such as the myth of meritocracy. Together, oppression and privilege protect the privileged group's access to a wider range of better-paying and higher-status positions as well as preferential access to and treatment from our social institutions. Like oppression, privilege is multi-dimensional and can only be understood if viewed as an intersectional phenomenon.

When we looked at the dynamics of privilege, we saw that it is not considered a problem by the dominant group because of the "luxury of obliviousness"—that because they own or control most of society's resources, its social institutions, and political power, they do not have to think about how their privilege negatively affects subordinate groups. Dominant group members tend to compare themselves to other dominant group members and not to members of oppressed groups. We looked at the way systems of privilege operate, and we saw how the behaviours of following "the path of least resistance," remaining silent, and "othering" subordinate groups are used to prop up these systems. We examined a number of mechanisms that allow persons with privilege to avoid any responsibility for oppression and its deleterious effects. We presented specific examples of privileges associated with a number of social groups and argued that privilege has not been handled very well by social work to date. We also presented a transformative and intersectional "Model of Privilege Studies Pedagogy" that frames and informs our work as writers and the work of all persons concerned with social inequality and other harmful outcomes that occur at the intersections between oppression and privilege. Here we offer an excerpt from one of our favourite writers on the subject of privilege, Allan Johnson (2006, p. 107).

Having privilege doesn't mean that someone is a bad person. But it does mean that there isn't a single member of a dominant group who doesn't have issues of privilege to deal with both internally and externally, in relation to the world around them. It was handed to them when they were children with no sense of what was wise and good to take unto themselves and what was not. And, so they accepted it, uncritically, unknowingly, even innocently, but accept it they did. It wasn't their fault. They have no reason to feel guilty about it, because they didn't *do* anything. But now it is there for them to deal with, just as it's there for women, poor people, people of color, people with disabilities, lesbian, gay, bisexual, transsexual persons, older people, and so on who *also* didn't do anything to deserve the oppression that so profoundly shapes their lives.

To end this chapter on a hopeful and positive note, we quote Michael Kimmel (2003, p. 9):

the struggles against inequality are collective struggles, enormous social movements that unite people across geography, race, religion, class, sexuality, and gender. Participating in these struggles to end inequality brings one into the long history of those who have stood alongside the victims of oppression, those who have added their voices to the voices of those who have been silenced. Examining our privilege may be uncomfortable at first, but it can also be energizing, motivating, and engaging.

Critical Questions

1. How does privilege also hurt privileged persons or groups?
2. I (Bob) remember observing a situation recently in which a man held a door open for a woman, who reacted by saying, "I can open the door myself, thank you." The man said in a surprised tone, "I was only being polite." What do you make of this door-opening ceremony? Is there more going on than the man might realize? What cultural messages are being conveyed about men and women? Do you think the same man might be as "polite" at home, sharing equally in the housework and child care?
3. Identify any critical incidents in your life that led to your increased awareness of privilege enjoyed by members of your group.
4. Discuss how the "invisibility of privilege" might be made evident to other social workers or fellow students who are from privileged backgrounds without making them feel guilty or defensive.
5. How would you open people up to the idea of male or gender or heterosexual privilege without turning them off?
6. Does your agency or school have a diversity training program? If not, why not? If so, does it include white privilege? If not, how can you help it to provide a safe forum for the exploration of the realities and challenges of white privilege?

PART III

Structural Social Work:
Practice Elements

11 Working within (and against) the System: Radical Humanism

They sentenced me to twenty years of boredom, for trying to change the system from within.

— From "First We Take Manhattan," by Leonard Cohen (1988)

Introduction

The ultimate goal of structural social work is to contribute to the transformation of society. To accomplish this goal, social work must operationalize an ideology within a society where another ideology dominates. To carry out this task, the social worker should possess the following attributes:

- an awareness of the limitations of our present society as a satisfactory social system;
- a vision of society in which the satisfaction of human need is the central value;
- an awareness that social work is a political activity that either reinforces or opposes the status quo;
- an awareness that social problems are not amenable to individual, family, or subcultural solutions;
- an awareness that critical social analysis is itself an important social work skill;
- an awareness that structural social work is much more than an approach to practice—it is a way of life.

The guiding principle for structural social work practice is that everything we do in some way contributes to the goal of social transformation. This does not mean that the legitimate, here-and-now needs of people are ignored. Rather, structural social work practice comprises a simultaneous two-pronged approach: (1) to provide practical, humanitarian care to the victims and casualties of our inherently oppressive liberal-capitalist society; and (2) to restructure society along socialist lines. This two-pronged approach to practice is consistent with the concept of dialectic discussed in Chapter 8.

The purpose of this chapter is to present certain practice elements that characterize structural social work practice and that therefore distinguish it from mainstream, conventional social work practice. Although these practice elements are presented and analyzed separately here, in reality they cannot be separated so easily, for they are all interrelated, functionally intertwined, and mutually reinforcing. These elements of practice operationalize structural social work theory. Through the practice of this structural social work theory, social workers will contribute to the long-term transformation of our present society by tending to the short-term needs of people within the social welfare institution—the very system that oppresses both those who depend on it and those who work within it.

The theory of structural social work does not consider any level of social work practice as inherently conservative or oppressive. Nor does it consider that one level of practice is inherently more progressive and liberating than another. For example, Galper (1975) has shown how community organization, as it has traditionally been practised, is just as conservative as traditional casework. A substantial literature (see Agel, 1971; Allan, Pease, & Briskman, 2003; Caspary, 1980; Fook, 1993; Forbes, 1986; Longres & McLeod, 1980; Lundy, 2004; Vazala-Martinez, 1985) shows how casework or clinical work can be emancipatory as opposed to oppressive for the service user. The major distinction between liberal mainstream social work practice and structural social work practice is that the former reflects and perpetuates the present social order whereas the latter attempts to transform it.

The approach to structural practice within the social welfare system emanates from the radical humanist school of thought. As presented in Chapter 8, this approach is based on the belief that changing people by personal consciousness-raising on a massive scale is a prerequisite for changing society. This consciousness-raising, which is carried out by structural social workers with service users and with co-workers, focuses on raising people's awareness of how a society characterized by dominant–subordinate relations shapes, limits, and dominates the experiences of members of subordinate groups, thus alienating them from social structures, from each other, and from their true selves. Only by becoming aware of how others define us to suit their own interests and by understanding how ideological hegemony makes our subjugation appear acceptable can we become free to begin to regain control over our lives and our destiny (Carniol, 1984; Howe, 1987; Mullaly & Keating, 1991). In sum, radical humanism is predicated on the belief that before social transformation can occur, personal transformation must take place. This assumption is rejected by structural social workers, who believe that it is not a case of personal change coming first or of social change coming first (the latter comes from the radical structural school of social change—discussed in Chapter 8 and further discussed in the next chapter). Rather, both approaches carried out simultaneously (in a dialectic) are necessary. The women's movement is one of the clearest examples in which both approaches were carried out simultaneously. In combatting sexism and patriarchy, much use was made of women's consciousness-raising groups that helped large numbers of women become aware of the pervasiveness, oppressive effects, and dynamics of gender discrimination in society. With this awareness, women put pressure on the system to change its gender biases. At the same time, leaders in the women's movement put pressure on the political structures to enact legislation and policies that addressed gender inequality. Many people (mainly men) then adjusted to the new social reality (i.e., legislation and policies promoting gender equality) before they had a real understanding or awareness of gender oppression in society.

The remainder of this chapter is divided into two major sections. The first section discusses certain elements of structural social work practice that help to operationalize radical humanist

> **Box 11.1** *Common Myths Held about Structural Social Work*
>
> ....
>
> - It is a militant, unreasonable, and irresponsible approach to practice—a relic of the 1960s and 1970s.
> - One must work at the macro level and carry out large-scale social changes; otherwise, one is not working structurally.
> - There is nothing that an individual social worker can do to change the system.
> - It denies all conventional social work practice such as counselling, micro skills, direct practice, and family therapy.
> - Social work should be about people and not about politics.
> - Structural social work is strong on critique but short on practice.
> - By focusing on social structures and forces, structural social work absolves people of all personal responsibility for their actions.
> - You will lose your job if you practice structural social work in an agency.
> - Structural social work is just too hard for the average person. It alienates one from other workers and leads to burnout and self-destruction.

thought when working with users of various social agencies, services, and programs. The second section focuses on ways that help social workers not only to survive working in mainstream social work bureaucracies but to change them from within as well. The material in this chapter also addresses a number of myths (see Box 11.1) often associated with progressive social work approaches in general but structural social work in particular.

Working with Service Users

As noted in Box 11.1, one of the myths held by many about structural social work is that such work ignores all conventional social work activities such as working with people who are in crisis or who are hurting in the "here and now." Nothing could be further from the truth! Structural social workers are keenly aware that: (1) over time, oppression results in damaging psychological effects in a person's intrapsychic and interpersonal areas; and (2) before one can take action against social structures that are negatively affecting their social position and functioning, work has to be carried out with individuals that encompasses intrapsychic and interpersonal processes. As well, crisis situations, including a lack of material necessities such as food, shelter, and clothing, and safety issues must be alleviated before political action can be contemplated.

Intrapsychic Work

Geraldine Moane (2011), a critical psychologist, reviewed a series of studies and summarized the effects of oppression on psychological functioning: a sense of inferiority or low self-esteem, loss of personal identity, fear, powerlessness, suppression of anger, alienation and isolation, and guilt or ambivalence (see Mullaly, 2010, for a discussion of these factors). The main aim of structural social work in the intrapsychic area is to: (1) counteract these damaging effects of oppression; and (2) build strengths in the individual for developing a community of solidarity with others and for taking individual and/or collective action against oppression. Individual work, group work, or community work may be used separately or in some combination to pursue these goals.

Box 11.2 *A Psychology of Liberation*

Psychological approaches to social problems have been criticized as, at best, unrealistic and, at worst, as contributing to the maintenance of social problems. Earlier versions of progressive social work have accused clinical or counselling social workers, psychologists, psychiatrists, and other helping professionals of supporting the status quo by: controlling or managing the dangerous (i.e., oppressed) classes; cajoling or coercing victims of social problems to accept and adjust to the very systems that victimized them in the first place; diverting attention away from the real source of social problems—an oppressive society; attempting to humanize an inhumane society; and promoting personal development through 12-step and other programs. Too often, critics have charged, people experiencing social problems have entered therapy or counselling because of problems associated with their oppression only to focus on their childhood, family, and endless analysis of their feelings. Psychotherapy and personal development become substitutes for political action.

The above "anti-psychological" position overlooks not only the obvious psychological consequences of oppression but also the psychology of both dominant group and subordinate group members. As well, it homogenizes all perspectives in psychology and overlooks the critical and liberation schools of psychological thought that also criticize mainstream psychology for its inattention to social variables. The critical and liberation schools of psychology start with the premise that psychological patterns can only be understood by analyzing the social context in which individuals live their lives. Members of this school, such as Moane (1999; 2011) and Fox and Prilleltensky (1997), seek "to develop a political explanation of psychological phenomena, and to harness psychological insights for the purposes of political activism" (Moane, 1999, p. 182). "Internalized oppression" is a focus of liberation psychologists in that they analyze psychological patterns associated

Continued

with internalized oppression and develop psychological processes for breaking out of internalized oppression and bringing about social change. Moane calls this a *psychology of liberation*.

In sum, structural social work is not anti-psychological. It is "anti-mainstream psychological" and "pro-liberation psychology." The latter recognizes that breaking out of the oppression associated with social problems, whether at the psychological or at the political level, requires changes in both psychological and social patterns. Not attending to the need for social change means that social conditions will continue to affect individuals and shape psychological functioning in oppressive ways, and not attending to psychological change means that any desired social change will be undermined by negative psychological patterns. Both are necessary.

Often, an individual requires counselling to deal with the psychological effects of oppression and to become emotionally ready to participate in a group. This can take the form of introspective counselling or behavioural therapy or any other type of individual work that helps to stabilize a victim of oppression, relieve some hurt, change some symptoms and behaviours, and build some strengths. The important point for structural social work is that, regardless of the individual approach used, it must not de-contextualize human activity or treat it in a de-socialized or ahistorical way (Bulhan, 1985). Otherwise, personal changes may become concessions to the current social order whereby the person has been helped to adjust to it rather than to change it. "As well, individual work is not an end in itself, but the means to connecting or reconnecting with other persons similarly oppressed so that they might together reflect on their situation and engage in collective actions to change it" (Mullaly, 2010, p. 224).

One of the criticisms made of any kind of social work (including structural social work) is that it is potentially oppressive, especially at the one-to-one intrapsychic level. This type of criticism was articulated best by Bulhan (1985, p. 271), who, with respect to any kind of therapeutic intervention or helper–helpee relationship, asked, "[F]or how can an intervention liberate the patient from the social oppression when the 'therapist–patient' relationship itself is suffused with the inequities, nonreciprocity, elitism, and sado-masochism of the oppressive social order?" Bulhan is referring to inequities such as the power of the professional (therapist, social worker) and the powerlessness of the service user, the comfort of the professional's office (often alien to the service user), the professional's values (often foreign to the service user), and the professional's discourse that differentiates expert from layperson or professional from client. Given this power imbalance, Bulhan asks, "Is it therefore surprising that the oppressed have not come in droves to seek help from mental health professionals, and, if a few of them turn to 'therapy' as a last resort, that they soon drop out and return to their own travails?"

To avoid reproducing oppressive patterns and relationships while working with oppressed persons, two essential themes of structural social work must be kept in mind at all times. First, people experiencing social problems or oppression must be the agents of their own change, whether it is personal, cultural, or social. Of this Moane (1999, p. 183) says, "Change is a process which individuals undergo in their social context and through their own processes. It is fundamental that this process of change is experienced by individuals as one in which they are in control, rather than as a re-enactment of patterns of domination." The second theme to help avoid the reproduction of oppression is to ensure that one's structural social work practice is *critically reflective*. This takes the form of the social worker engaging in a reflective conversation with the situation, which, as Thompson (1998, p. 204) argues, "can be used to promote an ethos in which equality issues [including the relationship between the social worker and the service user] are openly and explicitly on the agenda." He further argues that the reflection must be critical with respect to not taking any existing social arrangement or structure for granted. Otherwise, the reflection becomes another routine, uncritical form of practice that legitimates existing relations of social inequality. Critical reflection is discussed more in a subsequent section of this chapter.

Interpersonal Work

There is widespread agreement in the literature that to become part of a group process with other persons who are experiencing similar problems or are in similar situations is the most effective way for them to: (1) develop political awareness; (2) self-define a more genuine identity than the one imposed on them by the dominant group (e.g., "welfare bum," "lazy Aboriginal," "inferior black culture"); (3) develop the confidence to assert their more authentic identity (e.g., Indigenous persons as a resilient group of people who have survived hundreds of years of colonization and policies of assimilation); and (4) establish solidarity with similar others to take action against their oppressors (Bishop, 2002; Freire, 1994; hooks, 1993; Leonard, 1997; Mullaly & West, 2018; Pharr, 1988). Consciousness-raising is a critical element in the process of liberation, and the most effective way for engaging in consciousness-raising is in groups. These two elements of structural

---

Box 11.3 *Where Do I Start as a Structural Social Worker?*

As an exercise for a class of students in Australia, I (Bob) asked them where they would begin with service users—given a structural explanation for social problems. One student wrote the following passage that I think helps to answer this question that so many students new to structural social work have.

Because the explanation for social problems goes far beyond the individual, structural social work becomes much more than just dealing with the problems of individuals. It is about challenging the dominant order, and doing what we can on the personal, cultural, and structural levels to work towards a society that is free

Continued

of oppression. So then, given our understanding that oppression (domination, subordination, and privilege) is the root cause of social problems, what will our practice look like?

Whichever way we look at society, it is made up of individuals. Much of social work practice involves dealing with individual people, and taking a wider view of society does not exclude working with people on the personal level. I believe one of the most important things we can do for people at the personal level is simply to listen to them. Everyone has their story, and everyone's story deserves to be heard. Everyone's story will be different, as we all experience our lives in our own unique way.

We need to explore the oppression in people's lives and allow them to verbalize how they are feeling. We mustn't assume that we understand what someone has experienced because we have heard similar stories before, or have had similar experiences ourselves. Nor should we assume that because we can identify one form of oppression in someone's life, that it is the main reason for concern. We need to respect the people we are dealing with, and their views of what is happening in their lives.

The act of listening in itself can be part of the healing process. It indicates that you consider the person worth listening to, and that she or he has value. By listening carefully to the service user, a dialogue can develop, where ideas and knowledge can be shared and assumptions challenged. Listening to someone's story also gives the opportunity of naming the oppression or oppressions, and placing them in a political framework. Making these connections and normalizing the experiences can all be part of a powerful process. It may not solve someone's structural problems, but it can give a greater understanding of what is happening to her/him, and why.

The fact that persons have survived the various forms of oppression in their lives indicates that they have strengths, and that they have used these strengths to develop strategies. By identifying what strategies have worked for them in the past, an indication may be given as to what direction they may move to in the future. If strategies haven't been successful, it may be possible to relate this to structural objects, and a political dialogue can follow.

An important aspect of structural social work is to respond to the psychological damage that oppression causes. This will involve building up self-esteem and confidence. The act of listening and of identifying strengths that people possess is the beginning of this. People also need to express their feelings of shame, guilt, and repressed anger. It may be possible to redirect this anger and for it to be used in a constructive way, just as our own anger can be used constructively.

— Reproduced with thanks to Liz Deutscher

social work (i.e., consciousness-raising and collectivization) are discussed in this chapter along with a number of factors that assist in the process of consciousness-raising. Taken together, they provide the framework and guidelines of a structural approach to interpersonal work.

The Personal Is Political

One of the myths held about structural social work is that such work is carried out only at the macro level. Most progressive social work writers today (e.g., Baines, 2011; Gil, 1998; Morgaine & Capous-Desyllas, 2015; Mullaly & West, 2018; Thompson, 2016) agree that social work interventions are limited if they focus on only the individual level or the structural level. Bulhan (1985) points out that the former, which focuses only on the here and now and individual problems of people, tends to lose sight of people's shared victimization and the need for social transformation and often results in a minimalist view of change or a conservative outlook that blames the victim. The latter, which works toward social transformation, tends to become a paternalistic imposition of change from the top and disengages the person on whose behalf the changes are sought. Both approaches fail to adopt a dialectical perspective whereby interventions at both the individual/personal level and the societal/ political level are carried out simultaneously, with each informing and influencing the other.

Although social work has always espoused an awareness of the connection between the personal and the political,[1] the emphasis for the most part has been on personal change, adjustment, and/or coping. This emphasis, of course, is consistent with the order view of society discussed earlier. In fact, a dichotomy emerged in social work practice in that most social workers chose and worked within the areas of casework, group work, and family therapy (i.e., intervention on a personal level), leaving the larger socio-political issues to a minority of community organization and social policy social workers. Social workers who subscribe to a change or conflict analysis of society view this split as a false dichotomy (Mullaly & Keating, 1991) and would point to what C. Wright Mills (1959, p. 3) said about the relationship between the individual and society: "Neither the life of an individual nor the history of a society can be understood without understanding both."

The traditional split between micro and macro social work practice has served to weaken the link between the personal and the political, which is at the heart of social work. This split is often reinforced by the ways the curriculum is organized in schools of social work and by the structures within which social workers are employed. Curriculum tends to be divided along micro–macro lines; most social agencies are mandated to provide personal services without engaging in political or macro-level practice; and agencies that focus on social policy, social action, or larger social change tend not to see the provision of personal services as part of their mandate. The artificiality of such organizational constraints needs to be challenged. Although they may reflect the current political reality of separating the personal from the political, they do not reflect the social reality of people's lives or the reality of good social work practice. How can a direct practitioner be effective if they omit the cultural or community or societal context of the people with whom they work? Similarly, how can a social policy or community practitioner be effective if they lack interpersonal, listening, and communication skills? In terms of skills, the differences between micro and macro social workers are much less than might appear on the surface (Ife, 1997).

"The personal is political" stands for a method of analysis developed and refined by feminists for "gleaning political insights from an analysis of personal experience—in particular, female experience" (Collins, 1986, p. 215). Most writers today use this statement when analyzing or discussing how the socio-economic–political context of a society is critical in shaping who we are in terms of our personality formation and what we are in terms of our personal situation (Mullaly & Keating, 1991). Social work deals with many personal issues, troubles, and situations. If the personal is political, then social work is also political.

Major Implications for Structural Social Work

The premise that the personal is political has two major implications for social work practice. First, it signals that a social worker's individual practice has certain political ends. This applies to all social workers. Personal practices inevitably contain political ends. For conventional social work, the political end is to maintain the status quo. This is done by personalizing social problems. For structural social work, the political end is to change the status quo and leave oppression behind. This does not preclude intervention at the individual or family level, but instead of dealing with each of these levels by itself, the connection between private troubles and the structural source of these troubles is made in every case. Each structural social worker must see their individual work as an integral element of the larger movement of social transformation.

The second major implication that "the personal is political" has for social work practice is that it forces the worker beyond carrying out mere psychosocial manipulations, which in effect pathologize the people who are forced to use social work services. Understanding that private troubles are often linked to political (structural) forces enables the worker to begin a discussion of the relationship between the personal and the political (i.e., consciousness-raising) with the persons experiencing difficulties and to explore the personal situation of the person within its larger social context to see if there are connections between the two (i.e., normalization). This activity often has the effect of reducing some of the internalized guilt and blame (i.e., internal oppression) that many people experience as part of their troubled situations. This has to be carried out with a high degree of both personal and social empathy on the part of the structural social worker. These processes, along with some of the techniques that facilitate them, are considered below.

As discussed in Chapter 7, structural social work owes a great deal to feminist analysis. It has shown us the nature and extent of patriarchy in our society, and it has given us ways of dealing with women's oppression that do not further contribute to it. Too much of conventional social work practice locates the source of many problems women face within the person herself. This psychologizing of what are essentially problems of the larger society contributes to women's oppression by failing to see a woman in the context of a patriarchal society and by placing the blame for all her troubles squarely on the shoulders of the woman experiencing them. Because of the many social workers who have been actively involved in and/or influenced by the feminist movement, there is now a major social work perspective and practice based on feminist theory and analysis.[2] In addition, feminist social work writers have shown us that sexism exists within the welfare state and within our own profession (Walker, 1977; Weeks, 1992; Williams, 1989). And, of course, becoming aware of, identifying, and analyzing sexism in social work are prerequisites to purging us of it.

A "personal is political" (i.e., structural) analysis holds the potential to be a powerful force for change. If people are helped to relate their disempowerment and experiences of oppression at a personal level to a broader political understanding, there is a basis for moving beyond "coping and adjustment social work practice" to a practice that attacks the alienating and oppressive institutional and thought structures of our current society.

The Personal Is Political as a Method of Analysis and a Force for Change

"The personal is political" as a method of analysis has relevance and utility for dealing with all sources of oppression in our society. It can be used to better understand the nature and extent of racism in our society and how it contributes to the oppression of racialized groups. It can be used to better understand the nature of colonialism and how it contributes to the oppression of Indigenous persons in our society and to the oppression of developing countries by the industrial and post-industrial societies. It can be used, as well, to better understand oppression based on classism, ageism, physical disability, mental disability, heterosexism, and so on. However, the concern expressed in Chapters 7 (see Box 7.2) and 9 about the difficulty in translating "the personal is political" analysis into social work practice should be kept in mind. The practice problem is that it seems to be a giant leap between the personal and the political, so much so that many practitioners retreat to working at the personal level only (and some at the political level only) so that the dialectic between personal problems and their structural causes is lost. However, we believe that if the "personal is political" analysis is made personal to a service user, it will reduce the perceived distance between the two levels of practice and help to make the connections between personal problems and their political or structural causes. A set of "personal is political" questions can be asked of any group that is afflicted by any particular social problem, which will help them to make this connection. For example, if we are working with an unemployed person or group of people, we can ask: "Why do you think there are so many unemployed people in today's society?" This can be followed by a discussion about the problem being a lack of jobs rather than that so many people lack the work ethic. Follow-up questions could be: "What has been your experience in looking for a job?" "How are you treated (by society) as an unemployed person?" "What judgments are made of you?" (which gets at issues of self-blame and stereotypes). This type of dialogue is a form of "critical questioning," which is discussed more fully in the section on consciousness-raising in this chapter.

This connecting the personal with the political kind of social work is not to suggest that the structural social worker excuses irresponsible behaviour or bad choices by adopting a simplistic "it's all society's fault" approach when dealing with the situations of service users. However, a distinction must be made between "excusing" and "explaining" irresponsible behaviour. Personal responsibility is discussed in more detail in a subsequent section of this chapter. The PCS model of oppression presented in Chapter 9 helps us out of this dilemma because it separates culture from social structure and reminds us that oppression also occurs at the cultural level situated between the personal and structural levels. "The personal is political" is still a powerful analytical tool, but an awareness that a dominant culture helps to legitimize and institutionalize oppression provides the structural social worker with specific targets to change—oppressive stereotypes, dominant discourses, norms, values, and shared patterns of thinking (see Mullaly & West, 2018, for an overview of anti-oppressive social work at the cultural level).

Empowerment

Power, Powerlessness, and Empowerment

From the discussion in Chapter 9, it is obvious that oppression leads to the alienation and powerlessness of the subordinate classes. Most definitions of power or powerlessness refer to the control or lack of control persons have over their environment and their destiny. Oppressed people, as individuals, have limited choices over most aspects of their lives and are often ruled by forces of which they are not even aware. A tenet of mental health is that "Throughout life, the feeling of controlling one's destiny to some reasonable extent is the essential psychological component of all aspects of life" (Basch, 1975, cited in Pinderhughes, 1983).

One of the insights of postmodernism is that everyone has some measure of power and that it was a limitation of earlier modernist forms of progressive social work to assume that members of subordinate groups had no power. Yet although no one is without power, it is equally wrong to assume that power differentials do not exist—including the power difference between social workers and their service users. At a societal level, dominant groups not only have more power than subordinate groups, they also frequently use it to maintain this power differential and the privileges that come with it. Gil (1976) argues that the lack of control that oppressed people experience over their life situation and their destiny robs them of their essential human dignity, for without any real control, life becomes meaningless. We drift through it, controlled by others, used by others, and devalued by others for the interests of others. Oppression, then, violates or contradicts such important social work values and beliefs as self-determination, personal growth and development, the inherent dignity and worth of persons, social equality, and democracy.

A key concept of structural social work is "empowerment." However, empowerment is a contested concept and one that has been appropriated by neo-conservatives. With respect to its contested nature, Allan (2003) points out that earlier forms of mainstream social work and some progressive perspectives regarded it as a process whereby social workers would give power to the people with whom they worked. And, with respect to its appropriation, empowerment takes on another meaning for neo-conservatives. For example, many neo-conservative politicians have promised to empower oppressed persons to look after themselves by reducing the scope of and/ or taking away the benefits of the welfare state. These two meanings of empowerment are quite different from that of structural social workers, who view it as a process through which members of subordinate groups reduce their alienation and sense of powerlessness and gain greater control over all aspects of their lives and their social environments. The definition and concept of empowerment that are most consistent with structural social work were developed by Gilles Rondeau (2000, p. 218):

I define empowerment as a process that enables the transition from a state of passivity to one of activity and control over one's life. . . . [I]t essentially means a process of change where people stop being passive and become active, that is, they take charge and become active players in their own lives. By becoming active, they attempt to take, or take back, control of themselves and their environments.

Empowerment as a Goal and a Process

Empowerment, as a goal and a process, has been a recurrent theme in social work (Freedberg, 1989). However, since the 1980s it has been receiving increasing attention in social work theory and practice (Simon, 1990). Some writers view empowerment as the major goal of social work intervention (e.g., Gutierrez, Parsons, & Cox, 1998; Pinderhughes, 1983; Rondeau, 2000), while another "calls for a revision of social work practice theory in a way that defines the major function of social work as empowering people to be able to make choices and gain control over their environment" (Hasenfeld, 1987, p. 487). Empowerment is typically understood as a process through which people reduce their powerlessness and alienation and gain greater control over all aspects of their lives and their social environment. Simon (1990) points out that (1) empowerment has its basis in the self-help or mutual aid traditions and in the civil and human rights activities of the 1960s; and (2) because of the many groups, organizations, and professions involved with empowerment in all its dimensions, it should be considered social movement. "Empowerment, in short, is a series of attacks on subordination of every description—psychic, physical, cultural, sexual, legal, political, economic, and technological" (Simon, 1990, p. 28).

As a dialectical process, empowerment occurs in two ways. Consistent with radical structuralism, empowerment for some disciplines and groups is essentially a political and economic process whereby these structurally oriented groups will actively attempt to gain more power and influence over those organizations and institutions, such as schools, hospitals, and the workplace, that have an impact on their lives. This area of empowerment will be examined in more detail in the next chapter. Consistent with radical humanism, the empowerment process involves the psychological, educational, cultural, and spiritual dimensions involved when individuals are helped to understand their oppression and to take steps to overcome it.

Simon (1990) points out that empowerment is a compelling topic for social work for three major reasons. First, the people that social workers work with tend to be in marginal and disadvantaged positions and are among the most oppressed, alienated, and powerless. Second, social work is a profession disproportionately staffed by women, who themselves comprise a group that historically has been oppressed and powerless, even within the profession of social work (Cummings, 1980). And third, "Social workers of both genders are no strangers to the experiences of being discounted, scapegoated, dislodged, underpaid, and overlooked by legislatures, public administrators, executive directors of agencies, colleagues in other professions, academics, clients, and the public" (Simon, 1990, p. 34). We know first-hand the meaning of occupational subordination.

This trinity of interests in empowerment should serve as a catalyst for social work to continue to devise theory and strategies for working with oppressed and disempowered groups, including the profession itself. Hasenfeld (1987) contends that empowerment must occur on at least three levels in social work: (1) at the worker/service user level, where activities are carried out to increase the service user's power resources; (2) at the agency level, where organizational policies should be aimed at increasing people's power resources rather than conformity to prescribed behaviours; and (3) at the social policy level, where the formulation and enactment of policy decisions are influenced by those directly affected by them. Consistent with the PCS model of anti-oppressive social work, Mullaly and West (2018) and Thompson (2001) contend that empowerment as a practice must occur at three levels—the personal, cultural, and structural levels. At the personal level, which is the major focus in this chapter, the emphasis is on helping individuals to gain greater control over their own lives through intrapsychic and interpersonal work by, for example, alleviating the psychological damages caused by oppression and enhancing confidence. At the cultural level, assumptions, stereotypes, and discourses of the dominant groups that perpetuate dominant–subordinate relations are deconstructed and challenged. And at the structural level, power relations rooted in the institutions of society are resisted and challenged. Empowerment at the cultural and structural levels is discussed in the next chapter.

Three Considerations for Carrying out Empowerment-Based Structural Social Work

Should empowerment take place at the personal level before structural empowerment can occur? Dalrymple and Burke (1995) believe that this should be the case. However, as suggested earlier, crisis situations might have to be resolved or some intrapsychic damage might need to be repaired before proceeding to structural analyses or social action. We concur with June Allan (2003) when she argues that in order to avoid the traps of creating dualisms, structural social workers need to work with persons at all levels of empowerment and that this may be done simultaneously (but not always). Many inherent difficulties are involved in empowerment work, but if three considerations are kept in mind at all times, the process of empowerment will be greatly facilitated. First, social workers cannot empower others but can only aid and abet in the empowerment process. Service users "who are empowered by their social workers have, de facto, lost ground . . . in their battle for autonomy and control over their own environment and existence." The role of social work is to provide "a climate, a relationship, resources and procedural means through which people can enhance their own lives" (Simon, 1990, p. 37). The relationship between social worker and user is one of collaboration, with the latter retaining control of the purpose, pace, and direction of the collaborative effort.

A second important aspect of the empowerment process is that instead of being an expert problem-solver, the social worker becomes engaged in a mutual learning situation with the service user (Moreau & Leonard, 1989). The worker should not assume that a compatibility of interests exists between service user and worker (Hasenfeld, 1987). What could be more presumptuous and more disrespectful on the part of a social worker than to think that they know exactly what the problem is and what the solutions are? To avoid this elitist, expert, disempowering practice, social workers should: (1) continually update their knowledge of the history of race, gender, class, and other relations of subordinate groups (i.e., know as much as possible about the groups one is working with) (Simon, 1990); and (2) help the service user to define and contextualize their situation and problems while always encouraging service users to question and to express disagreement or reservations about particular interventions that the social worker might suggest (Moreau & Leonard, 1989).

A third aspect of empowerment for social workers is to avoid exploiting the helping encounter for our own benefit (Pinderhughes, 1983). It was mentioned that social work experiences subordination as an occupation. Also, we are often stigmatized because of our association with marginalized groups. Thus, we may be vulnerable in terms of compensating for the powerlessness we experience at work and may use our professional role to gain a sense of power. Rather than empowering the people with whom we work, we may actually reinforce their victim status by playing the role of benefactor and exploiting the power differential between ourselves and service users.

Consistent with the principle of linking the personal with the political, empowerment-based social work transcends the micro and macro levels of practice and today includes work at the cultural level as well. At the micro level, the social worker helps the individual not only to take more control of their life, to set goals, to access resources, and to articulate needs and ambitions but also to create or join associations or organizations of members of similar social groupings. These organizations (e.g., anti-poverty groups, women's organizations, Indigenous groups) constitute the focus of macro social work discussed in Chapter 9 and further discussed in the next chapter. The fact that there were (and still are in many workers' minds) two major levels of social work practice has historically created tension between micro and macro practitioners (Ife, 1997). Social workers at the micro level have often believed that the larger aims of social change pursued by macro workers are unattainable and thereby have devalued the importance of social change. Conversely, social workers at the macro level have often believed that individual approaches to helping are simply affirmations of the status quo, thus devaluing the skilled work of many social workers.

The "old" structural social work model incorporated both approaches to empowerment within the day-to-day work of each social worker and within the social work profession as a collective (Ife, 1997). Individual empowerment is not possible unless the individual understands the connection between individual powerlessness and its structural/political sources through a reflection on their own experiences not only as an individual but as a member of one or more oppressed groups. Similarly, at the macro level empowerment work must incorporate the lived experiences, the personal stories, and the impact of oppression on the individual lives of the people who constitute the membership of the various groups or organizations of oppressed persons. The link between the personal and the political is made not just at the analytical or theoretical levels but at the practice level of empowerment-based structural social work. And, of course, empowerment work today must include an awareness of how the dominant culture both oppresses subordinate groups and supports and reinforces social institutions that serve the dominant group through dominant discourses, stereotypes, and popular or mass culture (see Mullaly & West, 2018). The medium in which these links are made is through a consciousness-raising dialogical relationship.

Ife (1997) makes an important point about empowerment when he calls on social workers not to speak on behalf of oppressed groups but to facilitate the voices of marginalized persons themselves to be heard. In the current socio-economic–political climate, marginalized persons do not have a legitimate voice, and what voice they do have tends to be devalued by politicians, who are themselves also overwhelmed by the corporate sector. Well-intentioned advocacy by social workers who speak on behalf of marginalized groups is actually disempowering. It only reinforces marginalization in that oppressed people still do not speak for themselves and, thus, are further excluded from political discourse. As well, the perception may be that social workers are using marginalized people to represent their own views and interests rather than those they claim to represent.

Structural social workers must work alongside oppressed groups to help them find their own voices and make them heard. This involves helping them to define their own needs, to develop the skills and vocabulary required to articulate these needs, to gain access to public forums to address the structures of power and domination, and to help legitimize these authentic voices by supporting them in every way possible. The role of the social worker in empowerment-based social work is one of facilitator and supporter, not leader. The ideal of empowerment connects the personal with the political. It requires both good interpersonal skills and political and organizational awareness and understanding.

Empowerment is not a technique but a goal and a process. As a goal, it will not be reached overnight, just as the oppressive conditions within our current social order will not suddenly disappear. As a process, it is ongoing. Components of empowerment work are feelings and beliefs about self-efficacy, ideas and knowledge and skills for critical thinking and action, knowledge and skills (including the process of reflection, learning, and relearning) to influence invisible and external structures (Dalrymple & Burke, 1995; Gutierrez et al., 1998, cited in Allan, 2003). This process of empowerment is not linear, and no one area is considered more important than another (Gutierrez et al., 1998). It applies just as much to community development projects, policy formulation and implementation, and social action campaigns as it does to work with individuals and groups. "Hence there is a broad range of strategies that could be drawn on to facilitate empowerment" (Allan, 2003). Some of the elements of empowerment work are presented below.

Consciousness-Raising

Although the idea of revolutionary praxis involving both subjective and objective elements was formulated by Marx, the more recent versions have come from Paulo Freire, the contemporary women's movement, and a host of recent writers concerned with social justice and anti-oppression (Baines, 2011; Gil, 1998; Dominelli, 2002; Freire, 1994; Leonard, 1997; Moane, 2011, Mullaly & West, 2018; Thompson, 1998; 2001; Young, 1990). Consistent with the precept that the personal is political, consciousness-raising is legitimized on the basis of the relationship between the social order and human misery. "Thus, consciousness-raising involves the politicization of people" (Longres & McLeod, 1980, p. 268). As awareness of social injustice and oppression grows, oppressed people are more able to identify the causes of their oppression and are less likely to blame themselves (Longres, 1986; Midgely, 1982). Freire developed a total pedagogy based on the "conscientization" of the peasant population living in Latin America. With a similar set of ideas and purposes, the women's movement has used consciousness-raising as a powerful tool for combatting gender oppression and empowering women.

There are two elements to consciousness-raising:

> First, consciousness-raising is reflection in search of understanding dehumanizing social structures. Second, consciousness-raising is action aimed at altering societal conditions. The two must go hand in hand; action without reflection is as unjustifiable as reflection without action (Longres & McLeod, 1980, p. 268).

The techniques used in consciousness-raising are similar to those used in conventional social work, with one significant difference. Conventional social work is introspective, often motivating people to change their behaviour and adjust to their circumstances. Consciousness-raising, on the other hand, encourages people to gain insights into their circumstances with a view to changing them (Midgely, 1982).

Consciousness-raising is obviously an important part of intrapsychic and interpersonal work in that with increased awareness of injustice and oppression, oppressed people are better able to identify the structural causes of their negative emotions and interpersonal difficulties. Part of the intrapsychic and interpersonal work may involve personal development through individual counselling or by taking a course such as assertiveness training or leadership development, which have been found to increase self-confidence and assertiveness (Mulvey, 1994, cited in Moane, 2011), two characteristics needed for social change activities. However, without a social analysis, such courses may reinforce and perpetuate a "blaming the victim" ideology by overemphasizing human agency and cultivating the belief that problems in living can only be solved through personal change (Kitzinger & Perkins, 1993; Mulvey, 1994). Thus, although personal development may be a first step for many in an ongoing process of empowerment and change, it should be framed within a structural analysis of oppression and social injustice.

Obviously, consciousness-raising is part of the radical humanist school, since it is predicated on the belief that reflection must precede action. Although it sees practical action as an outcome, consciousness-raising places its initial emphasis on the understanding of oneself in the context of the social order. As Leonard (1984, pp. 210–211) points out, "The hegemony of the ruling class involves the domination of its world view, a view which drenches individual consciousness and which must therefore be actively struggled against at the level of consciousness." Thus, changes of consciousness regarding social relations are a precondition of the transformation of those relations.

Although a certain amount of consciousness-raising may occur in individual counselling sessions (e.g., providing statistics to the oppressed individual with whom one is working, providing some factual information about some aspect of their oppression, asking questions that connect the personal and the political, exploring some of the functions that a particular form of oppression carries out for the dominant group), most effective consciousness-raising occurs in groups of persons who share the same form of oppression (Longres & McLeod,

1980; Young, 1990). Elsewhere (Mullaly, 2010), I (Bob) pointed out that there is widespread agreement among many anti-oppressive writers and progressive social work writers that to become a member of a group process with other persons who are similarly oppressed is the most effective way for oppressed persons to develop political awareness of their situation. In such a group context, the members can self-define a more authentic identity than the one imposed on them by the dominant group, develop the self-confidence to "come out" and assert their more authentic identity, and establish solidarity in order to take action against their oppression (Adam, 1978; Bishop, 2002; Dominelli, 1997; Freire, 1994; Herman, 1992; hooks, 1993; Ife, 2001; Leonard, 1984; Pharr, 1988; Withorn, 1984).

Consciousness-Raising as Political Education

Much of consciousness-raising occurs in the form of political education whereby structural social workers, in the course of their daily service efforts, explore with service users their experiences with oppression and how to challenge and resist it. Consciousness-raising can occur by linking people's personal problematic situations with their political causes so that oppressed people "become more aware of the structures and the discourses that define and perpetuate their situations of oppression" (Ife, 2001, p. 151).This type of education is not a process of depositing knowledge (i.e., the banking concept of education) into the head of a service user (Bock, 1980), nor is it a process of haranguing people about social injustice (Longres, 1986). Allan (2003, p. 65) cautions us that although consciousness-raising may open up possibilities for action, it can also be "oppressive and patronizing if it is based on the assumption that the practitioner's consciousness is superior and is to be imposed on the people with whom they are working." First and foremost, consciousness-raising must involve reflection based on the service user's experience and individual consciousness, not solely the worker's. This does not mean that the structural social worker will not introduce new ideas or challenge beliefs held by the service user, however. Rather, the political education process takes the form of a dialogue in which both the social worker and the service user assume roles of mutual sharing and learning.

The service user will present their world view and where they see themselves fitting into this view. The social worker, in turn, will ask questions that might expose any of the service user's stereotypical or socially conditioned assumptions. This type of questioning is called "*critical questioning*," which is different from "normal questioning" (Fook, 1993) because it focuses on any socially conditioned answer. An example is a response a social worker might give to a woman who says, "If I just tried harder to be a good wife and mother, I might still have my family." The worker could say, "And why do you think that?" Such a response, however, might imply that there is one correct answer, and the woman could respond, "Because it is the woman's job to look after her family." Alternatively, a structural social worker would respond by asking a critical question such as "Is that what you think or what you think is expected of you?" This use of critical questioning has the potential for persons to explore their expectations and how they feel they have to act. It may also provide the opportunity for the woman to understand the extent to which her life may represent her own personal choices on the one hand or social conditioning on the other (Fook, 1993).

To facilitate this process of dialogue, mutual learning, and critical questioning, the social worker must express empathy to signal to the service user that their world view and explanation for any difficulty is understood by the social worker. Empathy "is a large part of the substance of critical consciousness for a social worker" (Keefe, 1980, p. 389). In her classic book *Radical Casework,* my friend and former colleague Jan Fook (1993) extends the concept of empathy beyond "personal empathy" to include "social empathy." The former refers to a social worker's ability to understand by experiencing or merging with the experience of another with respect to their perceptions, feelings, and ideas of their own personal world. Social empathy refers to the worker's ability to empathize with the service user's perceptions, feelings, and ideas about the social world. This is a valuable tool to link the personal and the political in the service user's situation. What Fook has called "social empathy," Jessup and Rogerson (1999) call "structural empathy." Examples of translating these concepts into practice are contained in Box 11.4.

A major topic of dialogue between social worker and service user is how our present society works, including the social functions carried out by poverty, sexism, racism, heterosexism, and so on. If members of various subordinate groups realize that their personal difficulties are related to their membership within a particular oppressed group and that their oppression is socially useful

---

Box 11.4 *Social or Structural Empathy*

Social Empathy

"Take the following exclamation by a bored and frustrated housewife: 'Men always get what they want!' This can be empathically reflected [back to the woman] in at least two ways. The first picks up the personal experience: 'You feel you never get what you want?' The second highlights her perceptions of the social condition: 'You think men get a better deal than women?' A socially empathic response would ideally combine the two and draw attention to the links about them: 'You don't think you ever get what you want because men always get a better deal than women?'" (Fook, 1993, p. 112)

Structural Empathy

Working with a woman who has abused drugs and alcohol and is now separated from her children and her partner, who was physically abusive, a social worker might ask, "Can you tell me what rights you believe you have as a mother, wife, and individual?" and "What resources do you need to get your children back?" (Jessup & Rogerson, 1999, p. 173, cited in Allan, 2003, p. 66). Other structural empathic questions in this situation are: "Tell me, what do you think the role of mother and partner should be?" "Where do these expectations come from?" "How do you differ from these?" (Jessup & Rogerson, 1999, p. 174, cited in Allan, 2003, p. 66).

to the dominant groups, this awareness should alleviate much of the internalized guilt and blame that exist. In turn, awareness of their oppression, coupled with the energy unleashed from not feeling guilty or responsible for their subordinate status any more, should lead to some kind of social action against that oppression. For this consciousness-raising to be successful, however, it must be based on people's experiences and not on some foreign, academic critical analysis imposed on people in sophisticated quasi-Marxist jargon. "Consciousness-raising methods require the same sensitivities to self-determination and relationship-building that traditional . . . [social work] requires" (Longres, 1986, p. 31).

Often, service users demonstrate what Marxists call "false consciousness" or what anti-oppressive writers call "internalized oppression" (Ruth, 1988) in that they understand their troubles and behave in ways that promote the interests of the dominant groups in society (Longres, 1986). At the same time, a part of all of us tells us that society is not working in a way that supports a satisfying and enriching life for large numbers of people. From a structural social work perspective, we should look for and reinforce that part of the service user's perspective that is aware of social oppression (Galper, 1980; Gil, 1998). In this way we are not imposing a brand of politics unrelated to the normal events of service users. Instead, we are focusing on their experiences in an empathic, respectful, and relevant manner.

Some examples may help to clarify the discussion so far. People who are forced to apply for welfare benefits often express humiliation, guilt, and shame because they have been socialized into believing that everyone in society should be able to make it on their own. One of the ideological myths of capitalism is that equal opportunity exists and that only the lazy, the inferior, and the weak do not take advantage of opportunities available to everyone. To be on social welfare is a sign of weakness, inferiority, and laziness. When people seek social welfare benefits or any other kind of social service, we must help them to deal with their pressing, immediate problems. Most people cannot develop a larger critical perspective of their distress until they experience some symptomatic relief.

However, we have an obligation as structural social workers to move beyond symptomatic relief, since we know the symptoms will likely reappear (Galper, 1980). We must participate in the consciousness-raising experience of the welfare recipient by discussing why poverty exists in a capitalist society (i.e., the social functions it carries out), why the receipt of social welfare is seen as a failure in our society, the social control functions of social welfare, and how it operates in the best interests of capitalism and the dominant groups in society. In other words, a structural analysis of the welfare recipient's situation and experiences is discussed in an empathic manner at a level and in a language that the recipient understands. As mentioned previously, although most people are victims of false consciousness or internalized oppression, everyone knows to some extent that society is not working in the interests of large numbers of people. Similarly, many social welfare recipients have some awareness that their situation is not necessarily or completely of their own doing. It is these thoughts that the structural social worker uses to begin the consciousness-raising process.

Consciousness-raising should always be based on the service user's situation and experiences. Oppression is group-based, so consciousness-raising should focus on a structural analysis of the position the service user's group occupies in society. If we are working with senior citizens, then the structural social worker must know all about ageism. If this analysis is discussed in a meaningful way with senior citizens, part of that discussion will include how many of the problems experienced by senior citizens—limited housing options, inadequate or non-existent home care, the high cost of drugs, meagre pensions, transportation difficulties—are not caused by senior citizens but stem from a society that treats people as commodities whereby, if you are a non-producer and have no market value as a worker, you have no social value.

Longres and McLeod (1980) make two additional points about consciousness-raising as social work practice. First, because consciousness-raising focuses on the negative features of society and politicizes people around these features, structural social workers who engage in this practice will not be favoured by politicians, by administrators, and by many conventional social workers. Consciousness-raising will not make life easier for the social worker. Second, although consciousness-raising should be a cornerstone of social work practice, it does not represent the totality of practice; giving support, dealing with crises, providing hard services, advocacy, making referrals, and helping to make people's immediate lives more bearable are also important activities. It should also be noted here that consciousness-raising is greatly enhanced when it occurs on a group basis. More will be said about this later. Four activities that are part of the consciousness-raising process—normalization, collectivization, reframing or redefining situations, and dialogical relationships—are presented below.

Normalization

Normalization assists in the consciousness-raising process. Its purpose is to dispel any notion that any particular difficulty experienced by an oppressed individual is unique and idiosyncratic only to that individual when in fact the difficulty is a logical outcome of oppression and is experienced by many members of a particular subordinate group. It is a way of learning that many others of the same social grouping, whatever it might be, also experience the same problems and that in their situation it is not unusual to have such problems. Many oppressed persons will internalize feelings of guilt, shame, and self-blame about their oppressive living conditions because they have been socialized into accepting the dominant culture's message that they are the architects of their own misfortune. In other words, they believe that they are responsible for causing the social problems they are experiencing. Normalization breaks with that part of conventional social work that does not look at an individual as part of a social group subject to all the vagaries involved in a dominant–subordinate relationship. Normalization is an activity consistent with Piven and Cloward's (1993, pp. xiii–xiv) contention that:

> we have to break with the professional doctrine that ascribes virtually all of the problems that clients experience to defects in personality development and family relationships. It must be understood that this doctrine is as much a political ideology as an explanation of human behaviour. It is an ideology that directs clients to blame themselves for their travails rather than the economic and social institutions that produce many of them. . . . This psychological reductionism—this pathologizing of poverty and inequality—is, in other words, an ideology of oppression.

Structural social work understands that the political, cultural, and economic context of our present society, which is characterized by dominant–subordinate relationships, favours the dominant group at the expense of the subordinate groups. Unlike conventional social workers, structural social workers never overlook class, gender, race, and the like as possible sources of personal problems.

One of the first normalization activities is to deal with the service user's notion that the problem or situation being experienced is something unique to that service user. This may be done in two ways: individually and collectively. First, giving some factual information to the service user may help them to see that other people are in the same situation. For example, people are socialized into believing that those who are not working in the labour market are in some way defective and, therefore, are responsible for their unemployed status. However, if the unemployment rate for a community is 10 per cent, there obviously are more workers than there are jobs, so some people, through no fault of their own, will not be able to find work. And if there are 1 million unemployed people within a labour force of 11–12 million (as there were in Canada during the recession of the early 1980s), this does not mean that there are 1 million unique problematic situations caused by 1 million individual workers. Rather, there is one social problem affecting 1 million workers and their families, and a problem of this magnitude is well beyond the control of any individual negatively affected by it. If persons experiencing unemployment are able to place their situation in the wider political and economic context and understand that there are many other people like them, much of the guilt and blame that have been internalized should be alleviated. Unemployment is a structural problem that negatively affects lower socio-economic groups but is encouraged by the dominant group so that the latter will benefit by having an available workforce to compete among themselves for carrying out dangerous and menial jobs at subsistence wages, which of course contributes to larger profits for the dominant group.

Feminist social workers are able to provide female service users with all kinds of information on how our patriarchal society oppresses women, how it causes problems for them, and how it then convinces them that they, themselves, are responsible for the emotional, financial, marital, and family problems they might encounter. Normalizing information helps them to combat internalized oppression and to reject blaming-the-victim explanations. An example is that of an abused woman who believes that she is one of a very tiny minority of women and that because this happens to so few, there must be something she is doing to cause her partner to abuse her. Providing some basic statistical information, such as abuse rates of women, should help to normalize this woman's situation and dampen her internalized belief that, somehow, she has brought this abuse on herself. Once the internalized guilt, shame, and blame are eliminated or alleviated, a certain amount of energy is freed up that can be used to take a deeper and broader look at the situation and deal with it in a more fundamental way (Galper, 1980).

A second and more effective normalization activity is to link the service user with others experiencing similar situations and problems. One of the difficulties of trying to normalize a service user's situation on an individual basis is that "the weight is too strongly distributed in favor of individual uniqueness and private troubles" (Longres & McLeod, 1980, p. 273). The collective sharing and consciousness-raising that occur within these types of self-help groups show people that their situations and problems are not idiosyncratic but are part of a larger social dynamic.

In sum, normalization puts situations and problems in their proper political, economic, cultural, and social context. The emphasis is not on the uniqueness or individuality of a service user's situation but on the sameness and common ground of the service users. It is a way of reducing guilt and raising self-esteem and opens the possibility of analyzing the structural causes, dynamics, and consequences of social problems and oppression. A precondition for carrying out normalization activities is that the social worker is able to move beyond the traditional diagnostic mindset that ascribes all social problems to personality defects and family dysfunction. If this diagnostic mentality remains in place, chances are greatly reduced that the service user will be able to move beyond the traditional "personal inadequacy" perception of social problems.

Collectivism

Collectivism is a primary social value of both of the socialist paradigms. Collectivism recognizes that people are social beings who depend on one another for the satisfaction of most of their primary and social needs. It is the antithesis of individualism and, therefore, should be reflected in structural social work practice. As far back as 1975, Galper (1975) pointed out that because we live and experience problems within a social context, the analysis of the causes of problems, the development of awareness of the extent to which problems are widely shared, and the mobilizing of activity toward the solutions of these problems must take place in conjunction with others. Thompson (1998, p. 147) supports Galper's position when he says, "because inequality is a political issue, responses to it are often of a collective nature. That is, people band together to tackle the problem by challenging the ideologies and social practices that sustain it."

Longres and McLeod (1980, p. 273) conclude that "The first step to consciousness-raising is forming groups based on common social statuses" and that "consciousness-raising in a holistic way is only possible within groups" because such a medium is free of what Corrigan and Leonard (1978) call the "cult of individualism." This does not deny the necessity for individual work with service users, for it is recognized that many people feel overwhelmed in a group or that a group focus overshadows their immediate personal needs. Some individualizing is necessary to show care, respect, support, and encouragement to participate in a group process. As mentioned above, initially the situation may call for the relief of any pressing and immediate stress as well as a demonstration of personal and social empathy for the service user. Once the initial crisis is dealt with and a trusting relationship is established, the service user will be in a better position to look at their situation in a broader but more fundamental way with others.

Groups of service users may serve a number of different purposes: therapy, consciousness-raising, political action, or a combination of these. If such groups already exist, the structural social worker should refer all service users they come into contact with to these groups. For example, a structural social worker should refer anyone in receipt of, or applying for, social welfare to any welfare rights or anti-poverty organizations that might exist in the community. As well, structural social workers should support such groups however they can, including alerting such groups to policy developments that have the probability of negatively affecting them (Galper, 1980). Although structural social workers should support mutual aid groups of service users, they should not violate the social work value of self-determination by attempting to lead them. Withorn (1984, p. 110) underscores this point when she discusses the functions of mutual aid groups:

> Political practice means establishing groups of clients, not staff-led therapy groups, but "mutual aid" groups, in the best sense. Such groups can discuss common concerns and organize joint demands on workers. They can also provide support and assistance to each other. We do not live in a socialist society: we cannot organize real "mass organizations." Any efforts will be compromised and feel contrived. But the presence of such groups could help articulate client demands: They may be a safe place for sharing "bootleg" information about the agency, and they may give clients a place to do their own "power analysis."

To these functions of the collective process Leonard (1984, pp. 210–211) would add two psychological benefits: (1) positive changes in the conception of the self occur; and (2) people are able "to move away from the cult of individualism which dominates people's lives within capitalist societies." These groups can also be consciousness-raising groups in which members are involved in social analysis of their oppressive conditions and dynamics. They can also be social or political action groups in which members strategize, plan, and carry out campaigns to challenge and change oppressive social conditions, policies, and practices. Groups are usually dynamic, change over time, and may shift from one focus or purpose to another, as illustrated in Box 11.5.

In working with groups organized on the basis of a common status, the social worker ideally is assigned to groups that share their gender, race, class of origin, and so on. Maurice Moreau (n.d.) cites research showing that if the social worker is of the same social group as that with whom they are working, (1) the worker is better able to empathize with the group members, and (2) the group members tend to explore themselves much more than when the social worker has a different background. The caution for the worker, however, is not to project their own life experience onto the service users.

Eight practices that Moreau and Leonard (1989, p. 124) use for the operational definition of collectivization are useful here:

1. Drawing a service user's attention to the links between their personal difficulties and the similar problem situations of other service users.
2. Putting service users of the same agency who are living in similar problem situations in touch with each other.
3. Grouping service users for the purpose of mutual aid.
4. Grouping service users for the purpose of creating necessary resources the agency itself should provide.
5. Grouping service users for the purpose of creating necessary resources other agencies should provide.
6. Grouping service users for the purpose of changing problematical aspects of the agency.

7. Grouping service users for the purpose of changing aspects of other agencies and organizations that are problematic to service users.
8. Referring service users to larger social movements directly related to their situations.

Adam (1978) makes an important point with respect to the collective process by showing that it is not always (if ever) a linear process. He acknowledges that when individuals who are similarly oppressed come together, a dialectical movement toward integration of the group occurs whereby group members discover each other and, in the process, discover themselves. However, for this discovery to occur, a certain withdrawal from the inhospitable environment controlled by the dominant group may be necessary. Thompson (1998) argues that greater progress can often be made by the subordinate group if members of the dominant group (including the social worker) are not present at or involved with the meetings, planning, etc. of the subordinate group. He gives the examples of some women's groups and some groups of black people who deliberately exclude men and white persons, respectively, from meetings. Leonard (1997) also notes that some degree of segregation is a necessary element for emancipation and symbolic community identity. He points out that some groups have developed their own social services, which are more relevant to their needs than are many mainstream agencies, but they still participate in the larger social services network. Adam (1978) issues a caution with respect to segregation. He points out that it could lead to a ghetto-type situation, which, although it may offer some degree of comfort and safety from the dominant group, could also be stifling and confining to oppressed individuals.

Box 11.5 *The Brisbane Women's Reading Group*

Several years ago, I (Bob) was invited to speak to a class of social work students at the University of Queensland in Brisbane, Australia. The students in this class were taking a specialization in radical/structural social work coordinated and taught by Dr Bill DeMaria. On this day, a few graduates of the program were also in attendance to speak to the students about some of their experiences as structural social workers. One of the graduates related a work experience that I think illustrates several essentials of collectivist structural social work.

She had recently graduated and obtained a job with the Commonwealth (i.e., federal government, which is responsible for social security in Australia) in the Department of Income Assistance (Centrecare). She was given the task of working with a group of single-parent mothers who were regarded by the department as potential "child protection" cases (simply because they were lone parents and in receipt of welfare). The young structural social worker managed to obtain some funds from the department for child care and transportation so that the women could attend a weekly group meeting. The social worker

Continued

set the meeting up as a reading club in which the women would read a book selected from a number of books suggested and then purchased by the worker. The group would then discuss the book at their weekly meeting. This program was sold to Centrecare as a way for the women to get out of the house once a week for a needed break.

Initially, the books were of general interest, but over time, as the group bonds became established and the worker gained the trust of the women, feminist books were introduced. The women would read these books, some of which critically analyzed the place of women in a patriarchal society such as Australia and others that looked critically at such topics as discriminatory (to women) spousal and child support legislation, gender-discriminatory welfare legislation and policies, and so on. The women were encouraged by the worker to talk about their own lived experiences with respect to the texts that they read.

The worker described the process of consciousness-raising and normalization that occurred with the women in the group. Initially, the group operated along the lines of a therapy group, but over a short period of time anger set in, which was directed toward adding a political dimension to the group's activities. The group developed and carried out strategies to change some of the moralistic and punitive legislation and regulations that negatively affected them as a group of oppressed persons (i.e., as women with children who were dependent on welfare).

The segregation process does not mean that the social worker has no involvement with the group. Mullaly (2010, p. 232) makes two points in this regard:

> First, social workers who have had some prior involvement with some group members should not feel rejected if they are not invited to or are excluded from such groups. Letting group members know that you are available to them on an individual or group basis may be all that you can do at this time. Second, knowing the importance of the liberating functions carried out by segregated groups, the anti-oppressive social worker should encourage the formation of such groups and support them in every way possible. There will still be plenty of opportunities to work with oppressed persons on a group basis.

Redefining

Redefining is a consciousness-raising activity in which personal troubles are redefined in political terms, exposing the relationship between objective material conditions and subjective personal experiences. Society, as discussed earlier, is characterized either by order or by change, and each view defines social problems differently. According to the order view, social problems emanate from individual defects, family dysfunction, or subcultures outside the mainstream. The social change view ascribes most social problems to the present set of social relations whereby the dominant group controls the subordinate groups. Because social agencies are established within the present liberal-patriarchal-capitalist system, they tend to embody the ideology and thought structure of the larger system—that is, an order perspective. This includes the problem definition that underlies all services and social work–service user interactions. Rose and Black (1985) argue that the thought structure of operating assumptions that typically characterizes social agencies validates the North American political economy and invalidates users of social services. Contributing to an entrenchment of a personalist definition of social problems within social agencies is the fact that this thought structure produces several effects on service users (Rose & Black, 1985). (1) It invalidates the service user by validating the larger system. (2) It decontextualizes the service user because it severs their subjectivity from the objective and materialist context that frames and shapes all social life. (3) It shapes people's behaviour to correspond to the given social reality, and the more one deviates from this "proper and appropriate" behaviour, the more severe is society's treatment. (4) It saturates service users with pejorative vocabulary, a language of pathology and deviance that contains such concepts as diagnosis, treatment, symptoms, acting-out behaviour, resistance, and so on. (5) It forces service users to accept the problem definition imposed on them—in other words, to accept a false reality. If one were seeking an operational definition of oppression, these five effects of the prevailing definition of problems on service users would be a good starting point.

Redefining represents an alternative social reality, an alternative definition of problems. Validation is derived from reconnecting people to their objective social and historical context. The task, rather than working on personal change and accommodation to society, is to engage people as producers and participants in comprehending and acting on their contextual environment. Redefining involves the social worker and service user in a process of deconstruction and reconstruction. In every instance, explanations of problems that are self-blaming are challenged, deconstructed, and examined in terms of the service user's specific situation and reconstructed or redefined in terms of their connection with the larger socio-economic-political system. As with consciousness-raising and normalization, priority is given to group rather than individual work because the former is consistent with collectivization and mutual sharing among persons with similar social statuses, which produces more meaningful consciousness-raising.

Moreau (n.d.) outlines a number of redefining or "reframing" techniques. These techniques include: critical questioning (discussed above); dialectical humour (Frayne, 1987, cited in Moreau, n.d.); metaphors and storytelling (Gordon, 1978); cognitive dissonance (Festinger, 1957); the checking of inferences (Middleman & Goldberg, 1974); mental imagery (Rosen, 1982); persuasion (Simons, 1982); and the use of silence (Bourgon, 1988). Such techniques help to contextualize not only the service user's problem situation but often the service user's behaviour. Behaviour that may be labelled as inappropriate and self-destructive according to the personalist problem definition may be relabelled as perfectly appropriate and normal with an alternative problem definition. Lundy (2004, p. 139) offers the following simple ways of operationalizing the concept of "redefining" or "reframing." She says that service users are often hard on themselves and may accept responsibility for a situation that is structurally caused.

The structural social worker will, in such instances, engage the service user in a process of reflection and, in a tentative fashion, offer another way of looking at the situation by saying something like "Do you think another explanation might be . . .," or "Another way of looking at it could be . . .," or "I see it another way." Narrative therapists use a number of techniques to help people see situations in ways that are not self-blaming. Externalizing the problem in conversation helps to remove the problem from the identity of the service user and to see it differently (Lundy, 2004).

An example may help to make this discussion more concrete. Many graduates from the social work program at St Thomas University (a structural program) in New Brunswick, where I (Bob) had been a faculty member and where Marilyn is currently the director, are employed in departments of social services in which one of the services is "child protection." They report that the problem definition of child abuse and neglect is that these occur because of inappropriate behaviours and attitudes on the part of parents. Case recordings of non-structural social workers highlight personal inadequacies, emotional immaturity, poor coping skills, and family dysfunction as the areas to focus on in working with child abuse and/or neglect situations. Large amounts of money are spent each year on providing family therapy training to the social workers so that they might work more effectively with child protection families. If there is any mention that maybe the service users' problems are largely material and structural or institutional, it is dismissed either as incorrect or by stating that "There is nothing we can do about that. Our job is to work with these families."

The problem definition of the social agency is that child abuse and neglect are problems of personal inadequacy when, in fact, child abuse and neglect are in large part a class problem. Contrary to the myth of classlessness, which is part of the current system's thought structure, both evidence and reason lead to the unmistakable conclusion that the incidence and severity of child abuse and neglect is often a function of poverty (Swift, 1995). This is not to say that child abuse and neglect do not occur among other socio-economic classes; the evidence does indicate, however, that the great preponderance of abuse and neglect and the greatest severity of abuse and neglect occur among those who have the fewest resources to work with, who are struggling the most to secure the basic necessities of life, and who have the greatest number and most sustained pressures on them—that is, people living in poverty—especially women living in poverty (Swift, 1995). This is not an excuse for child abuse or neglect, but it is an explanation. The job of the structural social worker, then, is to redefine the problem from one of personal pathology to one of class. This should be done not only with the service user but should be stated at case conferences, and the case recordings should be redressed to reflect the service users' problems as largely material and institutional.

This is not to imply that child abuse and neglect are only matters of class. Physical abuse, emotional abuse, and sexual abuse each have their own distinct set of dynamics. The argument here is that class has an impact on these dynamics and that adequate material conditions are often a more realistic solution than sending people to parenting courses when they may not know where their next meal will come from, or if they will have a roof over their heads, or even if they will still have children to parent.

One of the myths about structural social work (see Box 11.1) is that it does not allow for personal responsibility. That is, in linking all personal situations to larger social or political structures and forces, it removes all blame from the person for any seemingly irresponsible or bad behaviour. The criticism of structural social work is that when people make bad choices, it adopts a "society made me do it" response, which is similar to the "it's all a capitalist plot" critique of critical social theory explanations for social problems. Structural social work does not overlook or accept irresponsible or bad behaviours on the part of individuals. However, it does not blame or pathologize people for such social phenomena as poverty, racism, sexism, and so on.

Unlike mainstream "blame the victim" explanations for social problems, structural social work recognizes that the reasons for people's behaviours are much more complex than a simple dichotomy of the person being good or evil. When people suffer from all the injustices and indignities of oppression over a long period of time and must struggle to obtain the basic necessities of life, they will often develop coping behaviours that help them to survive day to day that, on the surface, might seem morally wrong or self-destructive. As well, when individuals lack the resources or opportunities to live their lives in productive and socially acceptable ways, they often use ways and means to get by that are not socially acceptable. And as in the case of child abuse or neglect, these are not excuses for seemingly bad or irresponsible behaviours; they are explanations. Thus, structural social workers would not accept or overlook personal irresponsibility, but they would not condemn the person as bad or evil because of it. They would work with the individual to extinguish or neutralize such behaviour, but in their work they would recognize that such behaviour is linked to larger oppressive forces in society and, therefore, would take a broader approach than simply "fixing up" the person.

Dialogical Relationships

Normalization, collectivization, and redefinition are the means of carrying out consciousness-raising. The medium within which these activities are carried out is dialogue, between the social worker and the service user and among service users. Dialogue is the vehicle for uncovering people's subjective reality and opening it to critical reflection.

> Dialogue cannot be professional interviewing, application of therapeutic technology, instructions for improved functioning, or casual conversation. It is purposive in both process and focus. It directs itself to validation of the oppressed as persons, attempting to demonstrate their capacity to inform you, and it struggles to direct the content towards depiction and analysis of the objective situation (Rose & Black, 1985, p. 45).

To be able to engage in meaningful dialogue, the structural social worker must develop a dialogical relationship with service users—a relationship based on horizontal exchange rather than vertical imposition (Freire, 1970). A dialogical relationship is one wherein *all participants in the dialogue are equals*, wherein each learns from the other and teaches the other. Power is shared as much as possible between worker and service user, and each is considered to have different but equivalent wisdom and experience so that they mutually engage in theory-building and action (Allan, 2003). Professional knowledge is not privileged over knowledge gained from lived experiences (Ife, 2001). Of course, the social worker will have some skills and insights that the service user does not have, but the service user has experiences and insights that the worker lacks. The structural social worker must make conscious efforts to dispel any myths of expert technical solutions to fundamental political problems. Wisdom, experience, and expertise are accepted and validated "from below" as well as "from above" (Ife, 1997). The worker may pose problems but not solve problems, since this latter activity must be shared between worker and service user(s). Both work together so that they can ask the questions as well as think about the answers. As a result, both will come to a better understanding of the issue, both will learn, and both will act (Ife, 1997). Criticism of conventional social work practice has often centred on its elitist, impersonal, and overly technical approach. "In essence, a dialogical relationship is exchanging, comparing and communicating, rather than indoctrinating, proselytizing and generally issuing a 'communiqué'" (Moreau, 1979, p. 89).

As structural social workers, we do not want to reproduce with service users the kinds of social relations that have oppressed them in the first place. One of the contradictions of social work practice is that it attempts to provide practical humanitarian care for people in distress, yet it often provides this care in a superordinate (helper–helpee), authoritarian (worker has the answers), and mystical (helping process is not explained) way. A dialogical relationship minimizes these aspects. Burghardt (1982, p. 215) points out that "one of our pivotal, potentially 'insurrectionary' roles can be to produce relationships between client and worker that run counter to the dominant social relationships produced elsewhere." Such relationships not only are conducive to structural social work practice, but they challenge the ideological hegemony of the larger society.

To demystify social work activities, techniques, and practices, social workers must not be possessive of them but must make them broadly available to people at large as part of their job. For instance, the use of any technique, skill, or process is an opportunity to demystify it by discussing its origins and purpose, as well as other situations in which it might prove useful, and by encouraging the service user to ask questions. The content of service users' files should be made available to them, and they should have the right to be present at all conferences that affect them. Hidden strategies and manipulative approaches are not used, and the rationale behind all questions asked by the worker is explained (Moreau, n.d.).

In discussing empowerment, Moreau and Leonard (1989, pp. 82–87) present the following dialogical practices:

- sharing with the service user the content of case recordings;
- directly involving service users in the decisions that affect them;
- directly involving the service user in providing feedback on the kinds and quality of services provided;
- reducing the social distance between worker and service user by use of self-disclosure, casual dress, giving the rationale for techniques and questions, personal empathy, home visits, first names, direct clear speech, and use of body language;
- sharing with the service user one's personal biases and limits as part of the "helping" contract;
- providing information on the role of the agency and the rights of the service user and letting them know the worker is there to serve them.

Box 11.6 *Interviewing Skills for Structural Social Workers*

1. Capacity to *engage* clients at the beginning.
2. Demonstration of *warmth*, *empathy*, *sensitivity*, and *respect* to all clients in the group.
3. Management of *shared* air time.
4. Ability to facilitate a broad *definition* of the problem.*
5. Attention to the *different perspectives* held by various members in the client group.*
6. Appropriateness of probes and questions to facilitate a consideration/reflection that the impact of *class/gender/race/sexuality/ability/age* might have on the problem.*
7. Interviewer's use of non-judgmental and *non-pathologizing* language.*
8. Overall ability to elicit discussion that explores problems from a *critical perspective*.*
9. Ability to demonstrate confident handling of proceedings without becoming *dogmatic* or *authoritarian*.*

In conclusion, consciousness-raising is the approach used for working with service users, just as empowerment is the goal and process of structural social work for challenging oppression, and "the personal is political" provides the critical analysis at this level. Normalization, collectivization, and redefining are the techniques used in consciousness-raising. All structural social work at the personal level is carried out through the medium of dialogical communication and relationships. Two Australian structural social work educators (Fraser & Strong, 2000) developed a set of interviewing skills that provided the focus of a course they taught on structural social work skills. These skills, which capture much of the discussion above, are presented in Box 11.6. The skills that the authors identified as traditional are listed from 1 to 3, and the remaining six skills (with an asterisk) are broadly identified as structural interviewing skills. All students were assessed on how well they were able to demonstrate competence on these skills in role-playing situations.

In the Belly of the Beast: Surviving and Changing the Workplace

Most social workers work in agencies, whether they are public or private. The question most often asked of me (Bob) by social work students and practitioners is *"How can I practice structural social work and not get in trouble with my agency or even lose my job?"* Although the short and glib answer is "by being smart (i.e., strategic) about what you do," there is, of course, much more to it than that. There are a number of ways a structural social worker can survive within and challenge or change social agencies that hold the same oppressive thought and ideological structures as the larger society. Although social work by itself cannot eliminate oppression and injustice, it can help to erode oppressive structures and practices starting within its own arena for struggle—the workplace.

Contradictions of Agencies as a Basis for Radicalization

Jeffry Galper articulated the basic contradiction of most mainstream or conventional social agencies and services as far back as 1975 in his celebrated book *The Politics of Social Services*: they "deny, frustrate and undermine the possibilities of human liberation and a just society, at the same time that they work toward and, in part, achieve greater degrees of human well-being" (p. 45). Social agencies and services provide social care and social control at the same time. This is their basic contradiction, and within this contradiction we can carry out structural social work practice.

Agencies and services are organized so that "they support and reinforce conformity, among both clients and workers, to the very institutions and values that generate the problems to which the services were addressed in the first place" (Galper, 1975, p. 46). To receive services, people are often forced to accept roles and behaviours for themselves that reinforce and support the status quo.[3] And social workers are constrained in a variety of ways by various means, such as being subject to traditional individual supervision, a reward structure based on conformity to agency need rather than on service user need, heavy caseloads that yield little opportunity to step back and consider the larger picture, requirement to use "risk assessments" that focus on individual traits as an explanation for social problems rather than on structural factors, and computerization with programmed problem definitions and solutions.

While structural social workers recognize that conventional social agencies do not offer sufficient solutions to social problems, are too often inadequate within their own terms, frequently constrain workers to behave in ways that are deleterious to service users, and offer limited opportunities for a rewarding social work career, the vast majority of social workers find themselves working somewhere in "the system." Structural social workers need to support one another, and because there are limited opportunities for employment with alternative social agencies (to be discussed in the next chapter), with radical unions, or in other positions geared to undermine the system, most social workers will continue to be employed by mainstream agencies. Thus, the challenge to the structural social worker is to remain true to one's structural mission while not alienating oneself from management and from other workers in the agency.

Most social workers enter their work because of a concern for people and an interest in responding to social problems. However, studies show that "it is adjustment to the bureaucratic reality of the job that causes the most discomfort among new workers and is the most responsible for the loss of 'idealism'" (Withorn, 1984, p. 160). Understanding the contradictory functions of social agencies helps one to make sense of the frustrations, limitations, and obstacles experienced by the worker. Many progressive social workers believe their only option for structural social work practice is that of "protecting the poor, the sick, the criminal, and the deviant against the agencies" (Piven & Cloward, 1993, p. xii). Their belief is that they must become "guerrillas in the bureaucracy" and undermine the agency at every turn from their political underground position (Withorn, 1984). But not all agencies are alike, and, as Withorn notes, not all the negative aspects of social service work can be attributed to the social control functions of mainstream social agencies. Some of the features of mainstream agencies that tend to control and/or pacify its social workers are presented in Box 11.7.

Box 11.7 *Control and Pacification Features of Mainstream Social Agencies*

- The dominant assumption of mainstream social work is that agencies carry out no political functions.
- All oppressive features of the larger society are reproduced in social agencies (i.e., classism, racism, sexism, ageism, heterosexism, etc.).
- Agency-based definitions of social problems and solutions tend to personalize social problems and pathologize service users.
- Success orientation encourages workers to toe the line and not rock the boat.
- Most social agencies are organized hierarchically, with top-down management, and provide little opportunity for input by front-line workers.
- Day-to-day demands on workers detract from looking at the larger picture of how the agency functions to support dominant–subordinate relations of the larger society.
- Traditional supervision is carried over from student field instruction days when supervisors review all cases with the worker to ensure they are practising within agency expectations.
- The service orientation of agencies has been replaced by "rule orientation" in many cases.
- Radicalism, radicals, and progressive forms of social work are discounted as unrealistic and naive.
- There is always the implicit threat of unemployment if one steps outside the agency rules.

Given a structural understanding of the nature, operations, and political functions of social agencies, social workers should be able to operate above the political underground in combining social care with our structural social work goals. (Guidelines for carrying out a structural analysis of one's field placement or workplace can be found in Box 11.11 near the end of this chapter.)

> The overriding goal must always be to politicize the workplace so that activists, clients, and fellow workers understand the political dimensions of the work and take the greatest advantage of the contradictions of the system. This can only be done by a self-conscious strategy that is sensitive to specific workplaces with their particular personalities, structures, and political imperatives and is aware of broader bureaucratic, economic, and social realities (Withorn, 1984, p. 200).

The contradictions present in most social agencies and the fact that social workers always have some measure of autonomy permit us to undertake more intra-organizational change than is often believed possible. And as Scurfield (1980) and Patti and Resnick (1972) point out and according to the previous (1994) CASW *Code of Ethics*, our primary obligation is to the people we serve and not to the agency that employs us. The legitimation for radicalizing the agency is derived from our ethical obligation to place professional values above organizational allegiance. The challenge for structural social workers is to work within the "social care–social control" contradiction and maximize the agency's emancipatory potential while neutralizing its control function. Some of the ways to do this are presented below.

Radicalizing and Democratizing the Agency

The purpose of politically radicalizing the agency is to emphasize its service function and to de-emphasize its control function. In order to carry out this purpose, it is necessary to engage in "anti-capitalist practice" within the agency (Burghardt, 1982, p. 191). This opposes those assumptions of professional social organizations that flow from the prevailing thought and ideological structures of our liberal-capitalist society. If one of the goals of structural social work is to transform society from capitalism to socialism, then a logical place to begin is with the social welfare institution of which we are a part and, more specifically, with the social agency within which we work. Thus, as we practise anti-capitalist social work we are also practising socialist or structural social work. We de-emphasize capitalist values and practices while emphasizing socialist values and practices. This means we must challenge the agency's traditional definitions of problems and their resultant oppressive policies, attempt to democratize the agency, strive for more egalitarian relationships within the agency, and defend the service user from the agency. Of course, as structural social workers concerned with all forms and sources of oppression, we would extend the concept of "anti-capitalist practice" to "anti-oppressive practice." We would challenge all sexist, racist, ageist, etc., definitions of problems and policies and practices that occur within the agency. Box 11.8 presents some "overt" activities that structural social workers can carry out to protect service users from regressive agency policies and practices and that contribute to changing the workplace.

> **Box 11.8** *Overt Structural Social Work Activities to Challenge Oppression in the Agency*
>
> - Push for definitions of problems and solutions that are grounded in people's lived realities and do not blame victims.
> - Ensure that case recordings reflect these realities.
> - Every staff meeting or supervisory session is an opportunity to raise questions about traditional assumptions and conventional approaches.

- Circulate articles that contain structural analyses of problems dealt with by your agency.
- Bring in structural speakers who will have analyses different from those of the agency.
- Work through your union and/or professional association to raise concerns about work requirements that force workers to harm service users.
- Develop brochures outlining the rights and entitlements of service users, and distribute them routinely.
- As a regular and routine part of your practice, refer all service users to existing alternative groups and organizations (to be discussed in next chapter).
- Push for more peer and group supervision and decision-making.
- Seek out and network with sympathetic co-workers. Develop collective approaches and support others.
- Confront any behaviour or comments that defame/demean service users or reflect negative stereotypes.
- Have realistic expectations; accept that change takes time but is nonetheless worth pursuing.

In calling for social workers to become "organizational operators" (i.e., those who seek to have a positive influence on the organization), Thompson (1998) would add the following to the above list:

- Promote practice that is critically reflective.
- Make the value base of equality and the affirmation of difference open and explicit.

When agency policies and definitions of people's problems are based on assumptions of individual deficiencies, family dysfunction, or cultural inferiority, the structural social worker has an obligation to confront these oppressive assumptions. Workers can press for definitions of these problems that are grounded in people's social, economic, and political circumstances. When to press and how to press are two considerations when challenging personalist interpretations of structural problems. With respect to the first consideration, Galper (1980, p. 198) says, "Every staff meeting offers an opportunity to raise questions, to challenge conservative assumptions, and to encourage coworkers to do the same. Every supervisory session provides an opportunity for political encounter." The most effective strategy for presenting these challenges is not based on confrontation but focuses on asking questions about current practices while presenting information that leads to a different definition of the problem. For example, at a staff meeting of a child protection unit of a provincial department of social services that views child abuse/neglect problems as essentially family problems to be solved by family therapy, one could ask, "Why are we doing all this family therapy work when we know from our own experience that if most of the families we work with had a decent job with a decent income they wouldn't be having so many problems? Also, these articles that I have here [and which are then distributed] clearly show that most child abuse and neglect situations are problems related to poverty and not to bad parents."

Most social agencies are managed from top to bottom. The social work literature is replete with accounts of how this hierarchical management model works against the front-line worker's attempts to deliver an adequate and quality service to people (see, e.g., Baines, 2011; Carniol, 2005; Withorn, 1984). Policies are formulated at the top of the organization with little or no input from workers, let alone service users, and are passed down the line for implementation. This type of management is anti-democratic because it excludes worker or service-user participation. It promotes inequality in that a small elite makes the decisions and imposes them on workers and results in oppressive policies because the decision-making is based on the myths, assumptions, and stereotypes inherent to capitalism, patriarchy, etc. Thus, part of the struggle for structural social workers is to democratize the workplace. This may take various forms, such as union activity to build and increase service-user participation in the decision-making process, more peer supervision, development of a consultative relationship with supervisors rather than a boss–subordinate relationship, and a struggle to implement more democratic means of sharing decisions, responsibilities, and information. Much more research and many more written accounts of democratic collective experiences of administering and delivering services are needed.[4]

In addition to challenging personal pathology definitions of social problems and attempting to democratize social agencies, structural social workers must also confront all agency policies and practices that oppress or negatively affect service users in other ways. Major areas of concern are to maximize the service user's access to resources, benefits, or services provided by the agency, to link service users together and support service-user advocacy groups, and to combat any behaviour that demeans or defames service users. It is preferable, of course, for the structural social worker to use overt means in performing these tasks, but in many situations workers are forced to use covert strategies. This presents a dilemma for social workers, but the previous (1994) CASW *Code of Ethics* was clear in this regard. It stated unambiguously that the social worker's primary responsibility is to the service user, and when the needs of the service user conflict with the needs of the agency, the social worker has an ethical and professional responsibility, first and foremost, to the service user. The fact that the most recent (2005) *Code of Ethics* omits this obligation is another sign of the depoliticization of the social work profession in Canada.

Moreau and Leonard (1989) call the maximizing of service-user use of an agency's services or benefits "defence of the client." The aim of this defence is to maximize the service user's use of resources while minimizing their negative effect. Moreau and Leonard outline five (covert) practices that defend the service user within the worker's own agency and two practices that defend the service user in relation to outside agencies. The five practices within the worker's agency are:

1. Provide service users with confidential inside information on how best to present a request for service from the agency.
2. Alter or falsify statistics to satisfy organizational requirements, all the while giving more time to needy service users. (For example, an agency may require that each service user receive a monthly home visit, which is virtually impossible because of the heavy caseloads. A worker may report that they have fulfilled this requirement but in fact has not because they have chosen to give more attention to service users who are most in need. At the same time,

the worker has the obligation to protest the heavy caseload to the agency, to their union, and so on.)

3. Deliberately avoid recording certain facts. For example, a welfare recipient has received some money from an outside source that, if reported, would be deducted from their welfare or result in the disqualification of the service user from benefits.

4. Overlook a service user's violation of policies, rules, or procedures of the agency that are harmful to the service user—for example, residency requirements for eligibility for a service.

5. Become involved in making efforts to change organizational rules, regulations, or practices that work against the needs or interests of service users.

The two practices of defending the service user in relation to outside agencies are:

1. Provide service users with confidential "inside" information on how to present a request for service from another agency.

2. Overlook a service user's violation of rules, policies, or procedures of an outside organization—for example, violation of a probation order or illegally receiving a financial benefit.

[**NOTE:** At no time should a social worker become involved in breaking rules or altering or falsifying agency-required statistics unless the well-being of the service user is compromised by not doing so. It is only when the well-being of a service user is threatened by some penalty or sanction by the agency that these practices should be considered. A structural social worker always weighs the risks associated with any action that may be outside the normal way of operating. As the Australian social work writer B. Lane (1997, p. 39) says, using an Aussie metaphor, "perhaps as social workers, we need to become skilled at swimming with the crocodiles while accomplishing our tasks. Being an advocate for social justice requires the talent to know when to risk and when to wait." When engaging in such action, it must be done in a thoughtful and considered manner. Otherwise, there is a danger of getting caught or having your action backfire, and you could be responsible for all kinds of negative results—including giving the rest of us structural social workers a "bad name." On the other hand, it should be remembered that many social workers, without telling anyone, break rules on a daily basis mainly because of bureaucratic priorities that interfere with social workers performing their jobs.]

Another way of enhancing the service user's power and influence within the agency is to link service users with one another and to outside advocacy groups. Just as groups enhance consciousness-raising, so, too, do they enhance the ability of service users to challenge destructive agency policies. Groups of service users should be supported in every way the social worker is able to do so, such as providing information (including so-called confidential information), referring other service users to the group, forewarning the group of destructive policy discussions being held within the bureaucracy so that they might prepare to counter them, and identifying workers within the agency the group can trust and those who should be avoided.

Finally, in carrying out anti-oppressive or structural work within the agency, social workers must confront any behaviour that demeans or defames service users. Derogatory remarks about service users by workers are far more common than they should be. Blair's classic study of welfare workers (1973, cited in Withorn, 1984, p. 202) found that anti-client statements served as a way of affirming social solidarity among workers and were part of the normative culture of the workplace in that these derogatory remarks were often used by workers to show others that they were not "naive or sentimental about clients." Just as racist or sexist remarks or jokes are unacceptable, so, too, are anti-client statements because all such statements perpetuate stereotypes and devalue people. Such behaviour can be initially dealt with in subtle ways, such as not laughing or responding to it, or by silence, or by disapproving looks, or by a general discussion at a staff meeting about such behaviour and what it represents. If, as Withorn (1984) notes, subtle tactics do not work, then structural workers may have to resort to overt disapproval such as taking the offending person aside and telling them that you are offended by this person's derogatory humour, that you have given all the non-verbal and indirect cues you could to get that message across but to no avail, and that if it continues you will have no choice but to report or complain to management about the behaviour.

Protecting Ourselves

Social agencies are often repressive because they enforce service-user conformity to capitalist values and relations. Also, they "enforce worker conformity through direct coercion, subtle pressures and ideological indoctrination" (Galper, 1975, p. 196). Therefore, any attempts at democratizing or radicalizing the agency put the worker at risk. However, the risks to the worker are probably not as great as is often assumed. It was pointed out earlier in this chapter that the inherent contradictions of agencies give the worker some latitude for structural work. Although most agencies contain repressive elements, usually their goals are couched in terms of equality, democracy, social justice, human need, and optimal service. These stated goals, along with a certain degree of autonomy that the worker enjoys, give the worker a foothold for structural practice within the agency. Furthermore, by keeping certain guidelines in mind, structural social workers can minimize the likelihood of any kind of serious reprisal from the agency. Some of these guidelines are found in Box 11.9.

Box 11.9 *Protecting Ourselves from Reprisals*

- Form a caucus of "like-minded" people, and use it for peer support and collective action.
- Know your agency—legislation affecting it, agency policies, formal and informal power relations, points of vulnerability, who can and cannot be trusted—and use this knowledge strategically to promote anti-oppression.
- Become valuable to the agency by doing your work in a competent manner.
- Avoid adventurism and martyrdom.

- Work through your union and/or professional association to promote anti-oppression.
- Avoid militant confrontations. Searching questions are usually more effective than accusations or attacks.

Thompson (1998) presents a number of guidelines for "elegant challenging" by social workers. If challenging the actions or attitudes of others that are punitive, moralistic, and/ or oppressive in the workplace is to be effective, it needs to:

- Be tactful and constructive rather than a personal attack.
- Avoid "cornering people" and allow them to save face.
- Pay attention to an appropriate time and place to challenge rather than immediately challenge at all times.
- Not be punitive—the aim is to promote equality and anti-oppression and not to create unnecessary tensions and hostilities.
- Acknowledge explicitly or implicitly the vulnerability of all of us with respect to oppressive practices.
- Be undertaken in a spirit of compassion and social justice rather than a spirit of taking the high moral ground.

Galper (1980) originally presented some of the above guidelines for radical or structural practice in social agencies and argued that, if followed, they would minimize the risks of reprisal by the agency against the worker. He says that the first step is to be competent in carrying out the agency's assigned tasks. If a worker is competent, they will be of value to the agency. In turn, the agency will be more tolerant of efforts at democratization and radicalization than it would be if the worker was not competent. If a structural worker is incompetent, then the agency has an easy reason for getting rid of them. Galper also cautions us to avoid "adventurism or isolation." The structural activities we carry out within the agency should not be overly militant, irrational, or destructive. What is the sense of making a public scene over a principle if your action gets you fired (unless this is your strategy)? For example, what is the sense of jumping on top of the coffee table and yelling Marxist slogans such as "Social workers of the world unite! Capitalism sucks!" We already know that. What good comes from making the "big splash" if it means you are gone tomorrow? More realistically, challenging the entire belief system of a supervisor in a strident, face-to-face confrontation can only alienate. Martyrs are of limited practical use for ongoing structural work within agencies.

There is consensus in the literature that the most important way of protecting ourselves, not just from agency reprisal but also from burnout, is to have peer support. Withorn (1984) contends that a "workplace caucus" of "politically compatible people" is essential to combat the bureaucracy's inherent tendency to divide workers through hierarchy and specialization. Such caucuses provide support to members, facilitate consciousness-raising of the workers' situation, enable planning to radicalize the agency, and give members a sense of collective and individual efficacy to change their agency. Galper (1980) echoes the need for a caucus of radical/structural workers and says that the process of establishing such a caucus does not have to start in a grandiose way but may begin with two or three like-minded workers meeting informally. Sherman and Wenocur (1983, p. 377) believe that a mutual support group of workers "weakens the impact of the disempowering socialization process in an organization by creating an alternative subculture governed by workers' values." And, finally, a study of graduates from a structural social work program in Canada found that peer support either from within or from outside the agency was the most important factor in carrying out structural social work practice (Moreau & Leonard, 1989). Donna Baines (1997), a progressive social work writer, provides the clearest example of the functions that can be carried out by a caucus (see Box 11.10).

It was mentioned above that to carry out structural social work within your agency, an important guideline is to know your agency—its history, policies, points of vulnerability, and the people in it—who is likely to be supportive, who is not to be trusted. Box 11.11 provides us with

---

Box 11.10 *The Conspiracy*

The following example is taken from Donna Baines's practice as a social worker in a culturally diverse, impoverished inner-city community in the United States where she was part of a caucus of progressive social workers.

> Jokingly referring to ourselves as "the conspiracy," we shared stories and our outrage over lunch. Without the support of these colleagues, I would have found it difficult to resist the dominant discourse that blames individuals for all their problems. Instead, we continually reframed our problems and our clients' problems to be the result of structural and systemic forces and sought solutions that went beyond those just for individual cases.

Baines goes on to talk about the importance to the group of the practice principle:

> Build ties to oppositional groups outside the workplace. . . . This principle is especially important for maintaining a sense of social solidarity. It concretizes certain aspects of the personal-is-political equation and provides alternatives for clients and practitioners, as well as resources and important information on specific and broader struggles for social justice. It is seen as essential for social workers to remain grounded in a social-movement sense of services, rather than an individualized view of clients' problems. For time to time, members of "the conspiracy" at the hospital fed information to community groups, spoke at public meetings, and tried to connect clients to activist organizations. These tiny efforts helped us tie our everyday concerns and struggles to larger strategies and visions for social justice and social change (Baines 1997, pp. 314–315).

a set of structural guidelines that will help us to gain a good understanding of our workplace or field placement in terms of its mandate, the problems with which it deals, the interventions the agency expects us to use, the conditions and expectations that the agency has of service users in order for them to receive its services or benefits, the expectations and rules the agency has for its workers, and some of the control mechanisms the agency has for its employees.

Box 11.11 *Structural Analysis of an Employing Agency and/or a Student Field Placement*

Almost all social agencies in our (liberal/neo-conservative) society contain an inherent contradiction. On the one hand, they work toward and, in part, achieve greater degrees of well-being by providing resources or services to people who would otherwise have less. On the other hand, the services provided by social agencies are organized and delivered in a manner that supports and reinforces "conformity" among users and workers to the very social institutions, beliefs, and values that generate the problems that agencies were established to deal with in the first place.

- Make a list of contradictions that you have identified within your agency/placement (e.g., its mission statement talks about respecting the dignity of the people it serves, but some of the activities it asks social workers to do are social control functions).
  In order for us to function effectively as structural social workers, we must be aware of the social control and people-denying functions of our agency and the methods used to carry out this social control and/or system- (society-) preserving function.

- Do you think that the social control functions of social agencies and services are accidental? Or do they serve a purpose? Whom do they benefit?

1. Origin, Mandate, and Purpose of Employing Agency (Field Placement)

Origin: Why was the agency established in the first place (i.e., what problem[s] existed, who defined them as problems, and how were they dealt with before the agency [or service] was established)?

Mandate: Where does the agency get its mandate to exist? Where does it get its funding?

Purpose: Does the agency have a stated purpose, a mission statement? If so, what is it? If unstated, what is it, and how is it communicated? Is there a philosophical statement of purpose that is supposed to guide agency practices? (If so, is it consistent with the CASW *Code of Ethics*?)

Continued

2. Problem Definition and Focus

- How are problems defined by the agency (i.e., what are the causes or sources of the problems as perceived by the agency)? What is the agency's explanation for the problems?
- Are there limitations or false assumptions in the agency's definition or explanation of the problems it deals with?
- What are the agency's solutions for the problems (i.e., what must happen in order for the problems to be eliminated)?
- What is the prevailing thought of workers toward the problems and the people they are dealing with? What is their explanation for the problems? Is it consistent with the agency's views?
- If the problems the agency deals with were left unattended, what would be the impact on service users and on society as a whole?

3. Interventions Used by Agency Personnel

- What type of social work interventions are used in your agency?
- Are they the most appropriate for resolving problems, or do they simply keep a lid on the situation and the service users?
- What is the rationale behind each type of intervention used? That is, are they consistent with the way the agency has defined the problems? (For example, if the problems are basically ones of poverty, counselling for relationship problems may be inappropriate.)
- In your opinion, is the service or benefit adequate to deal with the problems? If not, what kind of message do you think this gives the service users?

4. Relationship between Agency and Service Users

- Are there any conditions of eligibility for receiving services other than need? If so, what are they, and why do they exist?
- Does the agency promote conformity on the part of the services user in any way?
- What are the conditions and expectations that users must carry out and/or meet in order to continue to receive services? What are the reasons for disqualifying or terminating a person from receiving service?
- Is there any connection between eligibility for receipt of services and the labour market? If so, what are they, and why do they exist?
- Do service users have access to their files or records? If not, why not?
- What happens if a service user is dissatisfied with the service or the treatment they receive? (For example, are there established appeal procedures?)
- Are there any mechanisms for service-user input into the policies or operations of the agency?

5. Relationship between Agency and Employees

- Who decides on policy for the agency? Do staff persons have any formal input into policy formulation and/or administrative decisions?
- Who defines the working conditions? Do employees have any say?
- How are people supervised or held accountable for their work?
- What are promotions and pay raises based on? In other words, what is the system of rewards and punishment, and what criteria are used?
- If workers are unionized, what input does the union have on: (i) policy; (ii) administrative decisions; and (iii) conditions of work?
- How are disagreements and grievances dealt with in the agency? That is, who is involved, and who usually settles them?
- What is the prevailing mood and thought of workers toward the problems they deal with, and do they agree with the agency's interpretations of causes and solutions?
- What is the prevailing mood and thought of workers toward their work? That is, do they think the interventions the agency asks them to carry out are appropriate? Do they think their efforts are having an impact on reducing or resolving the problems they are dealing with?
- What is the general morale of the workers, and to what do you attribute it (good or bad)?
- How have you as a worker or student been treated generally within the agency? List the things you appreciated hearing or having been done for you as a worker/student.
- For students—make an inventory of the things you appreciated and did not appreciate (e.g., hearing comments about naiveté, idealism, etc.) when starting your placement. What do you think lies behind any negative treatment or comments?

6. Conclusion

- What are some of the control mechanisms used by or available to your agency to keep you in line?
- What structural social work do you think could be carried out in this agency (with service users; with employees; other)?
- What are some of the ways that we can protect ourselves while carrying out structural social work in the agency?

Conclusion

This chapter presented an overview of structural social work practice that emanates from the radical humanist school of thought. The focus is on working directly with individuals, families, groups, and communities as well as working within conventional or mainstream social agencies. Several practice elements were presented that should facilitate the ultimate goal of structural social work—to contribute to the social transformation of society while carrying out practical, day-to-day, humanitarian care to victims and casualties of social problems and oppression. These practice elements, which emerge from the critical or social change explanation for social problems, help to differentiate conventional practice from structural social work practice. Structural social work does not consider any level of social work practice inherently conservative or oppressive, nor does it consider any level to be inherently progressive or emancipatory. A number of myths regarding structural social work were examined and debunked.

The second part of the chapter addressed the most contentious aspect of structural social work—how can it be carried out in a mainstream workplace without the social worker receiving some kind of reprisal, including the loss of one's job? A number of guidelines and strategies were presented for democratizing and changing the culture and practices of workplaces that define social problems in individual terms and that hold the same oppressive thought and ideological structures as the larger society. Issues and strategies for protecting oneself from reprisal were discussed. There are risks involved in attempting to change the social agency from within, yet a number of ways exist for protecting ourselves and our jobs. An analytic framework for understanding the workplace and its conservative and controlling assumptions was presented, which should help the social worker find ways to work in a structural and liberating fashion within the agency. The alternative to working within and against the agency is to work within and *for* the agency. The former entails risks of retaliation by the agency. The latter entails risks of cynicism, despair, and burnout because we deny much of the social, economic, and political reality around us (Galper, 1980). Put in these terms, it would seem that working within and against the system/agency is the better choice.

Critical Questions

1. Identify as many stereotypes as you can with respect to the following oppressed groups: people living in poverty, Indigenous persons, women, immigrants, LGBTTQ persons, black persons, people with disabilities, older people. Where do these stereotyped views come from? What functions do you think they carry out for the dominant group?

2. Why did you originally choose social work as an occupation? What were your initial beliefs about the place of social work in society? Have they changed at all? If so, in what way? What has been your biggest surprise about social work?

3. Most people recognize the relevance that sociology and psychology hold for social work practice, but why should social work students have to study economics, politics, culture, women's studies, and Indigenous studies?

4. What is your idea about "good communication" between a social worker and a service user? Can you identify any class or cultural assumptions in your answer?

5. How do you usually deal with conflict? Is there anything in particular that makes it easier or more difficult for you to deal with or manage conflict?

6. Structural social workers do not blame people for the social problems that they may experience. However, structural social workers do not adopt an "anything goes" approach to people's behaviour or attitudes; they do hold people accountable for their actions. What kinds of responses would you make to service users who are abusing or neglecting their children, who lie to you, or who are breaking the law for personal gain?

12

Working outside (and against) the System: Radical Structuralism and Working within Ourselves

The question people should ask is not "Is there life after death?," but "Is there life after birth?"

—Saul Alinsky (1972)

Introduction

The previous chapter presented and discussed a number of structural social work practice elements that may be carried out in the course of one's work within the traditional social welfare system. This chapter considers a number of modes and forms of structural practice outside the social welfare system and outside the formal practice of social work. The reason for carrying out structural practice outside the system is that the system places institutional limits on much of our social work practice. Although much good work may be carried out within the system, it "must be linked to struggles for structural change outside agency walls. In practice, this means the worker should keep in touch with and support parallel social change movements going on outside of social agencies" (Moreau, 1979, p. 89). As well as structural social work practice outside the system, this chapter presents several strategies and guidelines that should help us on a personal level as we encounter the myriad obstacles and issues associated with structural social work.

Structural social work practice within the system is based mainly on the radical humanist school of changing people's consciousness on a massive scale as a prerequisite to changing society. Structural practice outside the system is based mainly on the radical structural school of changing material conditions and oppressive structural patterns such as patriarchy, racism, and ageism. These would be replaced by a socialist society that, once in place, would become the new social reality for people. By itself, each approach has limitations, which were discussed in Chapter 8. Both are necessary.

This chapter discusses each of the following as arenas for carrying out structural social work practice outside the social welfare system: alternative services and organizations; coalitions, social movements, and new social movement theory; unions; professional associations; electoral politics; a revitalized public sector; challenging and resisting the dominant order; and the moral premise of social welfare—universal human needs. It also looks at the following personal aspects of the worker in carrying out structural social work practice and in living our lives as structural social workers: critical self-reflection; self-care; having realistic expectations; using anger in a constructive way; and making the political personal in our own lives.

Working outside and against the System

Alternative Services and Organizations

If we are to contribute to social transformation, a logical starting point is the workplace. However, structural social workers should not focus on the workplace to the exclusion of overall social change efforts outside their agency walls. Changing the social relations within agencies does not, by itself, change the basic elements of our dominant–subordinate social order with its severe discrepancies of wealth and power, domination by giant corporations, a dependence on industrial production that pollutes our environment, and patriarchy, sexism, racism, ageism, etc. One of the ways for structural social workers to contribute to social transformation is to create, develop, and/or support alternative social service organizations.

Alternative services and programs are counter-systems to mainstream social agencies and can be used ultimately to develop "a base from which larger social changes can be eventually effected" (Moreau, 1979, p. 87). These kinds of organizations usually come about because traditional, mainstream social services have been set up by the dominant group and tend to operate in accordance with dominant norms, values, and expectations. In other words, mainstream agencies and organizations are culturally specific (i.e., to the dominant culture) and sometimes will unintentionally contribute to the oppression of subordinate populations.

Alternative services and organizations are founded on principles, values, and ideals different from those of our traditional liberal services and organizations. They provide opportunities for subordinate groups to come together and engage in collective action. "Joining a group can help shift people from individual views toward the development of collective views" (Allan, 2003b, p. 70)—that is, personal issues are discussed in their political context. Alternative services and organizations facilitate consciousness-raising, solidarity and alliances, and lobbying to change oppressive rules, practices, conditions, and institutions (Allan, 2003b). They attempt to institutionalize new forms of social relationships by incorporating community control, mutual social support, and shared decision-making. These function to meet the needs of people in the community and are growth-producing for those working within them. For example, alternative services for Indigenous people, such as Native Friendship Centres or Aboriginal Peoples Councils for off-reserve Indigenous people, represent an alternative to mainstream social services that are enmeshed in colonial practices (Carniol, 2010).

> Indigenous approaches to building upon cultural conditions are not restricted to a particular agency in a specific region, but rather reflect the construction of alternatives to the continuing, pervasive, colonial domination that exists in Canada. When alternative social services are based on Indigenous knowledge they become important supports to the movement towards self-determination by Indigenous people (Carniol, 2010, p. 118).

Independent Living Centres are another good example of an alternative organization that is founded on values and principles quite different from the dominant individual pathology approach to disability. Stienstra (2012) explains that these self-advocacy organizations began in the

1980s out of opposition to the groups of medical and rehabilitation experts who had been speaking on behalf of people with disabilities. The initial goal of these self-advocacy organizations was to ensure that no decisions were made about people with disabilities unless they were involved in the decision-making (Stienstra, 2012). People with disabilities adopted a philosophy, known as independent living, based on respect and self-determination, and they created a model of service provision managed and directed by the recipient, recognizing the inherent expertise people with disabilities have as a result of their own life experiences. This philosophy is exemplified by the slogan—"Nothing about us without us."

Other examples of alternative services are welfare rights groups, tenant associations, rape crisis centres, transition homes for women and their children who have experienced intimate partner violence, LGBTTQ associations, ex-psychiatric groups, Alcoholics Anonymous, and prisoners' societies.

Structural social workers do not see alternative services and organizations as competitive with or disruptive to the operations of mainstream services and organizations. They understand that alternative services represent attempts by people associated with them to connect the personal with the political and to gain control over their own destiny. Structural social workers would support alternative services in a variety of ways:

- by becoming involved with them to the extent that they can without endangering their employment in mainstream agencies;
- by providing material resources, since alternative organizations are usually strapped for funds (e.g., money, stationery, photocopying);
- by providing inside information from one's own organization (e.g., notice of a pending policy that will negatively affect the alternative organization so that it can prepare to rebut or fight it);
- by referring users of a mainstream service to an alternative service (e.g., most persons applying for public assistance would benefit from membership in a welfare rights group);
- by encouraging the formation of such services or organizations where none exist.

Alternative services and organizations have some limitations. By themselves they will not bring about the transformation of the welfare state (contrary to revolutionary Marxist thought), but they do make an essential contribution to this goal. They embody the values, beliefs, principles, and practices of structural social work. They provide building blocks by which we learn workplace democracy. "They invite a questioning of top-down structures, and point to a better model of how social programs could be delivered" (Carniol, 2010, p. 122).

Social Movements, New Social Movement Theory, and Coalition-Building

As has been emphasized, one of the major goals of structural social work is to transform our present patriarchal, liberal-capitalist society to one based on a different set of values and social arrangements. However, by itself social work cannot transform society; it can only contribute to its transformation. The previous chapter focused on ways and means that structural change can be carried out on a daily basis within the social welfare system generally and within our agencies in particular. On a more macro scale, social work can contribute to social transformation by forming coalitions and alliances with other groups and organizations also committed to changing the destructive social relationships and operating principles of our present society. Social work must become part of a social movement.

> It is social protest movements and their capacity to generate significant social change in a way that no longer seems possible for more conventional politics or for that matter the more conventional casework and case management approach that can help renew and refresh social work's value base and inspire a new outrage at past and present injustices (Noble, 2015, p. 522).

Carniol (2010) explains that when many people come together to focus on personal and systemic abuses that have a direct impact on their lives, and when they organize themselves to demand social justice, they become a social movement. The goal of a social movement is to bring about some kind of social change. It is important, however, to distinguish between two different types of social change: social reform and structural change. The former refers to improving or altering existing laws, policies, and social conditions without changing the fundamental nature of society. The latter refers to fundamental changes in the very nature of the social, economic, and/or political order of society. The former is concerned with changes within the present social order and is usually associated with liberal social work based on the order view of society. The latter is concerned with changes of the present social order and is usually associated with social democratic or Marxist social work based on the conflict or change view of society. Obviously, given its goal of social transformation, structural social work is more concerned with movements of structural change than with social reform movements (though it does not ignore or necessarily refuse to work with reform groups).

Social Movements

An integral part of social movement work is to build coalitions that seek structural social change. The biggest obstacle to building coalitions is that many groups with potentially shared political interests focus solely on their respective single issues. This tendency has some obvious problems, which Biklen (1983, pp. 210–211) delineates in his discussion of self-help groups: (1) social issues are defined in a narrow parochial fashion; (2) single-issue groups often fail to make alliances with other groups whose interests they share because there is no awareness of the common causes of the oppression that each group experiences; (3) when single-issue groups focus on single issues, they may even compete with each other for resources, attention, acceptance, and political dominance; and (4) even when a single-issue group effects change in a particular area, it is not likely to bring about broad social change. For example, the Women's March on Washington on 21 January 2017 took place in protest against the inauguration of Donald Trump as president of the United States because of his right-wing agenda to "turn back the clock" on many women's issues that previous generations of women had fought to gain. Women-led marches also took place in more than 600 locations and in six countries in a protest meant to highlight women's rights, to protest the dehumanization of Muslim women, to end the systematic murder of black men and women, and to protect reproductive rights and the rights of LGBTTQ families (Democracy Now, 2017). However, there was much criticism within the media, and within the movement, that the organizers of the march were primarily white women who had appropriated the name of the movement from the 1997 Million Women March, which was a demonstration in support of black women's unity and self-determination (*The New Yorker*, 2017).

New Social Movement Theory

Social movements have evolved in advanced capitalist society to move beyond the simple class analysis of the early labour movement. The peace, environmental, gay and lesbian, people with disabilities, and women's movements differ in structure, type of constituents, and ideology from the old social movements of industrial society. While economic concerns remain a focus of new social movements, new concerns are being raised about quality of life, democratic participation, culture, and collective identity (Staggenborg, 2012). A major inherent weakness in traditional coalition-building and social movements was that they were organized mainly around class issues to challenge the excesses of capitalism. Thus, while the old social movements may have achieved power as the voice for disadvantaged workers, they also silenced the voices of women, racialized individuals, minorities, and young people entering the workforce (Fisher & Kling, 1994). The global economy without national regulation and control has undermined the old-style social movements.

An example of the limitations of old social movement theory can be found in the Occupy Wall Street movement. A recent book by Canadian activist Micah White, *The End of Protest* (2016), examines the Occupy Wall Street movement and how it revealed the limitations of contemporary ideas about protest and collective action. White is an editor at *Adbusters*, a Vancouver-based magazine promoting anti-consumerism through peaceful demonstrations and boycotts. In July 2011, an *Adbusters* blog post advocated for the peaceful occupation of financial districts everywhere to emphasize the undue influence of money over democracy. In the United States, the movement focused on a financial system in which greedy Wall Street investment bankers who, with the tacit approval of the United States Treasury and the Federal Reserve, successfully exploited the world financial system to the tune of hundreds of billions of dollars (Myers, 2012). However, as the Occupy movement grew, it became more of a loose-knit coalition among activists with a variety of different concerns: labour conditions, fracking and energy policies, financial regulation, and inequality (Calhoun, 2013).

White views the Occupy movement as a "constructive failure" (*Globe and Mail*, 2016). He explains that the main idea underlying contemporary protest—getting millions of people into the street with a unified message so that elected representatives are forced to listen and make real change—no longer works because protests have become an accepted, and part of "politics as usual" in Western democracies (White, 2016, p. 27). However, if the Occupy Wall Street movement had started a few months into the US presidential election campaign, White believes that the outcome of the campaign may have been very different. More recently, political activists in the United States are mobilizing for action based on the growing outrage against the Trump political agenda. The emergence of a counter-movement of political resistance to the Republican agenda has been aided by a number of congressional staffers who developed a guide, *Indivisible: A Practical Guide for Resisting the Trump Agenda* (2017). The guide is intended to serve as a resource for all individuals to be able to participate in the democratic process. It provides a step-by-step guide for grassroots advocacy tactics for promoting an alternative, positive agenda to counter the Trump agenda for change by:

- stalling the agenda of the majority Republican Congress and redirecting energy away from their priorities;
- demanding answers and explanations from local members of Congress on position statements;
- promoting the voices of those most affected by the right-wing agenda so that people are aware of the harm being caused.

However, new social movement theorists contend that the real problem with traditional forms of political protest is that political opportunities for change, such as the Occupy movement, have not yet included examination of the cultural dimensions of collective action.

> According to these critics, the structural focus neglects the agency of movement activists, who respond to opportunities and in some cases create them, as well as cultural elements of movements and their environments. Social networks, for example, are treated as structures that mobilize participants, but the ideas and emotions transmitted through networks are often overlooked. Culture is subsumed under framing activities, while a broader understanding of how culture constrains and facilitates collective action is underdeveloped (Staggenborg, 2012, p. 26).

Although new social movement theory gives social work more diversity by expanding the number of participants and the number of struggles being fought, it presents a significant challenge as well. How, in a postmodern context, do we continue to promote diversity and polyvocal discourse and, at the same time, find the commonalities needed to challenge global capitalist politics and culture? In other words, how do we combine a politics of difference with a politics of solidarity in practice? A politics of difference approach would view difference as a political resource (Young, 2000). Groups formed on the basis of social relations constituting gender, race, class, sexuality, and so on are best understood as structural, as distinct from cultural. "The social movements motivated by such group-based experiences are largely attempts to politicize and protest structural inequalities that they perceive unfairly privilege some social segments and oppress others" (Young, 2000, p. 92). According to Young, most political claims are not claims for recognition of identity but rather are claims for fairness, equality, and political inclusion. By using narratives to communicate the experiences and perspectives of different social groups, the biases derived from the dominant perspective are corrected, and the public is able to construct a more comprehensive account of why change is needed (Young, 2000, p. 83). Narrative is a means of relating both the history of socially differentiated groups and their perceptions of the history of the whole society in its relationships (Young, 2000, pp. 119–120).

Mutual identification of one another's oppression, by itself, is insufficient to generate a strategy and process that effectively challenge all forms of oppression. Mutual identification may lead to various oppressed groups supporting each other in the struggles of each against the immediate source of their respective oppressions. For example, groups oppressed by classism may identify with the oppression experienced by groups oppressed by racism or sexism. But this identification with other oppressed groups may not go any further than sympathetic understanding unless it is recognized that all forms of oppression are related. It may be true that sexism is at the base of gender inequality and that racism is at the base of racial inequality and that classism is at the base of economic inequality, but it is also true that inequality is a value and an established practice in our present patriarchal, liberal-capitalist society. It makes no political sense for workers to demand economic equality but to ignore gender inequality as someone else's problem or for women to demand gender equality but ignore racial inequality. Although each oppressed group may fight oppression on its own front, the recognition that we live in a society that requires inequality for its very survival will cultivate coalitions among groups by providing them with a common goal—the transformation of our present society based on inequality to one based on true equality, not just equal opportunity.

A goal of social transformation necessitates a shared ideological position among various oppressed groups. This common base provides the cement for building and maintaining coalition structures. Without a common ideology there is no common cause, issues are viewed in a parochial fashion, and single-issue reform becomes the goal of each group. The net result is that if any change occurs it is only a minor change within the system and not a fundamental change of the system itself. System-tinkering is liberal-style social change. For example, many activists within the Black Lives Matter movement have viewed mass protest as their sole imperative while others have focused on developing specific policy demands. This approach may lead to substantive reform or merely to a conservative transition from "protest to politics" (Rickford, 2016, p. 39).

The Black Lives Matter movement, which was born out of a Twitter hashtag, was founded by black women demanding accountability for racist violence and the murder of black people at the hands of the state (Rickford, 2016). The activists involved in the movement were determined to remain autonomous from the American political establishment and old-guard leaders such as Jesse Jackson and Al Sharpton. However, the movement also chose not to engage in alliances with progressive trade unions or political parties, and it did not articulate a clear analysis of the social, economic, and political underpinnings of white privilege. Questions of gender and sexuality also generated significant fissures within Black Lives Matter. Although in the beginning black women were at the forefront of the movement, some supporters continued to frame the struggle in terms of a "putatively masculine prerogative of self-defense" (Rickford, 2016, p. 39).

> Black Lives Matter, though still young has entered a decisive phase. Whether it can expand its popular base will depend on its capacity to strengthen links to other embattled groups and grassroots movements, explicitly address the spate of violence against transgender people of color, and develop a firm ideological foundation while retaining its resiliency and élan. If it can do so, the movement may well pose a deeper challenge to existing social and political arrangements, prefiguring a more humane future and fording a theory and practice of mass struggle for our time (Rickford, 2016, p. 40).

Coalition-Building

Not unrelated to a goal of social transformation is a shared political analysis as a prerequisite for coalition-building. Whatever the original causes of various forms of oppression, the fact is that they have become culturally ingrained into our present society and have themselves become mutually reinforcing. Coalition-building for purposes of broad structural change becomes more crucial but more realistic when oppressed people understand that the same political and economic elite that pursues globalization as an economic goal and allows the devastation of our environment for profit is also responsible for the immoral and gross inequalities of living conditions between rich and poor; that the same political and economic elite that promotes imperialist policies abroad for economic gain is also responsible for policies at home that discriminate against people living in poverty, women, racialized individuals, gay, lesbian, and bisexual persons, and so on; and that the same political and economic elite that promotes militarism for political and economic domination is also responsible for consumerism whereby people measure their own and others' worth and social standing in terms of what they own. This kind of awareness makes it imperative for structural social workers to join with the women's movement, the peace movement, the environmental movement, the human rights movement, and any other movement seeking a transformation of society in order to end oppression of any kind.

The Idle No More movement began in 2012 when the Harper Conservative government tried to push through an omnibus bill, Bill C-45, which had two provisions of concern to Indigenous people in Canada: a reduction in the number of federally protected waterways and a fast-track process for surrendering reserve lands (Kinew, 2014). Many have called the Idle No More movement a failure because it was poorly organized, unfocused, and without a real point (Coates, 2015). However, what started as a protest by four Indigenous women from Saskatchewan quickly developed into a demonstration of Indigenous solidarity against colonialism. The Idle No More movement now encompasses recognition of treaty rights, the revitalization of Indigenous cultures, and an end to legislation imposed without meaningful conversation (Kinew, 2014). The ideals underlying the movement are important for all Canadians (Kinew, 2014):

1. Idle No More is about engaging youth in political activism.
2. Idle No More is about finding meaning in life by preserving cultural and spiritual practices.
3. Idle No More is about rights and meaningful consultation.
4. Idle No More is about the environment and protecting natural resources for future generations.
5. Idle No More is about a democracy in which people are actively engaged, information is shared, and many voices are being heard.

An important dynamic of oppression that should facilitate coalition-building is that "no category of oppression, however distinct, creates an irreducible group which is only oppressed in one way" (Wineman, 1984, p. 167). Racism does affect racialized individuals, but these individuals include the working class, women, LGBTTQ persons, the young and old, and people with disabilities. In turn, classism affects the working class, but the working class consists of women, racialized individuals, LGBTTQ persons, young and old people, and people with disabilities. Most oppressed people are multiply oppressed both individually and in groups. This dynamic should help oppressed groups overcome any tendency toward single-constituency movements if there occurs within oppressed groups what Wineman (1984, p. 220) calls "a flowering of internal caucuses based on sex, race, class, sexual orientation, age, disability, and various combinations of these characteristics." An internal caucus is a recognition of the fact that people bring their particular identities of oppression with them into various struggles. A caucus of women within an anti-poverty group's struggle against economic exploitation becomes a link between women's organizations and organizations for people living in poverty. An Indigenous women's caucus within an anti-poverty group becomes a link between Indigenous, women's, and anti-poverty organizations. These internal caucuses not only manifest overlapping oppressions among single-constituency organizations but become the points of contact between various oppressed organizations and spearhead common goals and joint actions (Wineman, 1984, p. 221). This notion of "internal caucuses" is discussed further within the "Professional Associations" section of this chapter.

Progressive Unionism

Social workers' growing awareness of social injustice may lead to the feeling that they are alone in the battle of ideas for social change (Baines, 2011). Fortunately, there are other groups and social movements that pursue similar goals. An effective practice of structural social work must include the trade union movement as a major vehicle for carrying out its social transformation mandate. Most people are aware that unions have struggled historically to improve working conditions and pay for union members. What is less known is the fact that the trade union movement has been at the forefront in urging governments to introduce and improve social programs such as old age pensions, employment insurance, public health care, and daycare. During periods of cutbacks, the trade union movement has led the resistance and opposition to attacks on the welfare state (Carniol, 2010, p. 108). In the 1940s and 1950s, social workers shied away from unions because they viewed a fight for increased wages and improved working conditions as contradictory and unethical, portraying any such gains as drawing resources away from their clients (Jennissen & Lundy, 2011). However, unions provide social workers with opportunities for worker empowerment in the workplace, for better understanding of class issues, for contributing to the development of economic and social alternatives, and for participating in coalitions with other workers, consumer groups, and progressive social movements. To realize these potentialities, however, social workers must be familiar with the two opposing views of the nature and purpose of unionism that exist within and outside the trade union movement.

Jeffry Galper (1980, p. 157), in his landmark differentiation, used the concepts "class-conflict" and "class-collaborationist" to differentiate radical and non-radical unionism. The former, based on workers' awareness that they constitute a distinct class in society, views the role of unions as protecting and advancing the interests of the "total" working class and that to do so necessitates the eventual abolition of capitalism. The latter, based on a lack of workers' awareness that they constitute a distinct class in society, views the role of unions as protecting and advancing only the interests of the union membership by fighting for a larger share of the wealth that workers produce within the context of capitalism. The trade union movement in Sweden typifies (although not exactly) the class-conflict view of unions, and unions in the United States represent the case closest to a pure class-collaborationist viewpoint. Great Britain and Canada fall between these two types, with Britain closer to the class-conflict view. Canada, because of its proximity to the United States and because many unions in Canada were once (and some still are) controlled by American unions, is closer to the class-collaborationist view than most trade union movements in other countries (Heron, 1996).

Class-Conflict View of Unionism

Obviously, if unions are to become an effective vehicle for promoting the welfare state and for socialist transformation, they must adopt a class-conflict view. A class-collaborationist view is based on the conservative-liberal belief that there is a harmony of interests between capital and labour. American unions often opposed social welfare schemes such as social insurance because they were seen as a rival to the protection unions had secured for their members through bargaining (Fraser, 1979). As a result, they obtained an extensive but inequitable occupational welfare system instead of an adequate public welfare system that would cover more people (Mishra, 1981). Piven and Cloward (1977), and David Wagner (1990) argue that the American trade union movement has not been a force for social welfare concessions in the postwar era. And in view of the fact that the proportion of the US labour force that is unionized has been declining for the past several decades, it is unlikely that the trade union movement in that country will be a significant political force in the near future.

A class-conflict view is based on the belief that there is an inherent conflict of interests between capital and labour. Whatever one group gets is at the expense of the other group (i.e., profits vs wages). This view also recognizes that the welfare state in capitalist societies has benefited the working class, but it has benefited the capitalists even more by subsidizing certain costs of production, such as maintaining an educated and healthy workforce and guaranteeing a certain level of consumption of goods and services purchased with social welfare benefits. As long as capitalism exists, there will never be a true welfare state based on the principle of distribution according to need.

The progressive class-conflict concept of unionism has much in common with structural social work. Both reject capitalism as a social and economic system and seek to replace it with a social order in which human need is the central organizing principle. Both reject narrow, self-interested individualism in favour of collective association, rights, and responsibilities. Both reject elitist, hierarchical decision-making and advocate active participation in and control over all aspects of one's living and working conditions. And both reject exploitation and oppression based on such grounds as class, gender, and race, with the progressive union movement focusing on its elimination specifically in the workplace.

Progressive Class-Conflict Unionism: Unifor

One example of progressive class-conflict unionism is Unifor, Canada's largest private-sector union, which "was officially formed on August 31, 2013, at a Founding Convention in Toronto,

Ontario. It marked the coming together of the Canadian Auto Workers union (CAW) and the Communications, Energy and Paperworkers Union of Canada (CEP)—two of Canada's largest and most influential labour unions" (www.unifor.org). Unifor develops alliances with multiple political parties, social justice movements, equity-seeking movements, and other organizations that can advance their political, economic, and social goals. Unifor recognizes the historical relationship between labour movements and the NDP, and they share mutual goals. However, Unifor has its own analysis, policies, and strategies:

> For decades, union membership (as a share of total employment) had been in steady decline—particularly in the private sector. Running parallel to this decline in union density had been a sharp rise in income inequality, growing threats to retirement security, chronic unemployment and underemployment (particularly for young people) and a noticeable rise in insecure, precarious forms of work, especially among newcomers. The decline of union influence coincided with the rise of grossly imbalanced business-friendly policies, starting in the 1980s, that included tax cuts, labour market deregulation and corporate-led free trade deals. Unifor was a bold answer to the question: "How do Canadian unions respond to the changing economy and these challenging times?" (www.unifor.org).

Unifor would like to get workers more involved in the political process, since politics plays a central role in the outcomes that affect quality of life. Unifor points to the success of global social movements such as the Arab Spring, the Spanish Indignados, and the Brazilian Landless movements to demonstrate that protest movements are starting to mobilize people around the world. The overall mission of Unifor is to build an active, effective, and universal workers' movement in which political action moves beyond casting a ballot every four years:

- Formulating and articulating demands of broader economic, social, and environmental issues that affect all working people.
- Organizing and mobilizing members and other Canadians into active campaigns in support of those demands.
- Lobbying and pressuring political leaders and representatives at all levels in support of those goals and demands.
- Participating in election campaigns to raise issues, and to support candidates who agree with them (Unifor, 2014, p. 15).

Another major reason for structural social workers to become involved with the trade union movement is that the growth of the welfare state is, in part, a product of the union movement (Carniol, 2010; Flora & Heidenheimer, 1981; Fraser, 1979; Furniss & Tilton, 1977; Mishra, 1981; Wilensky, 1975). International comparisons show that countries with extensive and well-organized labour movements, such as Austria, Germany, and the Scandinavian countries, tend to have extensive and well-developed welfare states. And, conversely, countries without a high percentage of the workforce unionized tend to have primitive welfare states.

Mishra (1981, p. 113) outlines four ways in which organized labour has contributed to the development of the welfare state. First, the growth of labour movements is often perceived by the ruling classes as a threat to capitalism, and to reduce this threat the ruling classes have often conceded social programs to the working class. Otto von Bismarck's social legislation in Germany in the latter part of the nineteenth century is a good example. Second, ruling classes and liberal and conservative governments have often implemented social welfare programs being promoted by socialist parties and that were very popular with the working class. An example would be Canada's public health care program, which was originally a socialist party idea but was legislated by bourgeois governments to dampen the rising popularity of the socialist (CCF/NDP) party. Third, labour movements have themselves demanded social legislation as a means of improving the life situation of working-class people. And fourth, social democratic governments, as in Sweden and Great Britain, have aligned themselves with labour movements as a means of transforming capitalist societies to socialism.

In addition to its contributions to the development of the welfare state, unionism holds many benefits for social workers. Several writers have commented on these benefits (see Baines, 2011, and Carniol, 2010, for some examples). Carniol (2010) believes that unionism provides a counter-balance to the elitist, exclusionary, and self-serving tendencies that characterize the "ideology of professionalism." Carniol (2010) suggests that active union membership has potential for social workers to empower themselves in the workplace by working toward greater industrial democracy, by linking broader issues such as employment equity, better pension legislation, and day-care to the more traditional "bread and butter" issues, and by forming important links with other workers and other social movements.

Although it is imperative that structural social workers recognize the strength of the union movement as the most economically well-organized working-class organization with potential for taking on capitalism, the weaknesses and limitations of the current union movement must also be understood. Unions have become large bureaucracies preoccupied with technocratic procedures at the expense of mass mobilization and consequently fail to see the state as a constituent part of capitalist domination (Carniol, 2010). Nor are workers free from the racism, sexism, and conservatism that are part of the larger societal consciousness. Feminists have criticized unions for being dominated by white males who are often homophobic, for being focused on product rather than process, and for ignoring the needs of women, racialized individuals, and other sexual/cultural/ethnic identities (Carniol, 2010). To realize the revolutionary potential of the union movement, union members must understand how social transformation is in their best interests and how it has a direct material importance.

Professional Associations

In the 1940s in Canada, the Canadian Association of Social Workers (CASW) was unwilling to promote the collective bargaining function of unions for social workers (Jennissen & Lundy, 2011). The CASW was primarily concerned with issues such as qualifications and professional development. Social workers tended to work through staff associations to improve salary standards, conditions of work, and personnel policies (Jennissen & Lundy, 2011, p. 106). However, unlike unions, staff associations were comprised of members of individual agencies, and there were no clear lines drawn between front-line workers and management. Some social workers viewed unions as too radical or too "blue-collar" and not appropriate for "professionals." Jennissen and Lundy (2011, p. 108) explain: "In 1948 the CASW recognized the rights of professional workers to join unions, but it stopped short of promoting unions as the agency of choice for advancing the interests of social workers."

Unlike unions, professional associations, as a form of organization, are not the product of an inherent conflict among particular groups in society. They are, in fact, created by society to carry out particular functions for society and not to oppose society. Given the fact that professional associations are part of the current social structure, the critical question for structural social workers is: Can professional associations of social workers be used as another means of social transformation?

Mullaly and Keating (1991) have summarized the main radical social work criticisms of professionalism. First, professionalism emphasizes technical aspects of helping, such as impartiality, emotional neutrality, and apolitical service. Thus, it masks the political component of social work practice and perpetuates the notion that capitalist social relations are natural and normal functions of an industrialized society. As well, professionalism promotes technical solutions to problems, implying that these problems are individual rather than larger social and political problems.

Second, because professionalism focuses on organizing an exclusive group based on academic credentials, it divides social workers from other workers and from persons who use social work services. By requesting certification from the state, professional social workers implicitly align themselves with the state. In exchange for state recognition, social workers are required to deliver services that contain elements of oppression and control. In effect, professionalism blinds social workers to issues of class, particularly their own class position and class function.

Third, by organizing themselves into social and occupational hierarchies, professional social workers are practising inequality. By treating social problems as individual misfortunes, they promote individualism. And by accepting an ethic of "service to others," they disempower those they would serve. The messages conveyed are that intervention should focus on people and not on social structures and that the best source of helping rests with the "expert" social worker and not within the service user.

Finally, the history of professionalism, such as in law and medicine, indicates that such hierarchical organizations benefit the professionals, not the service users. Despite its "service to others" ethic, professionalism becomes self-serving, since professionals tend to seek personal, social, economic, and political power for themselves. For example, a review of the major activities of the CASW in the 1960s and 1970s reveals that the association chose to work closely with governments as a way to promote itself as a professional body. "But by so doing, social workers' capacity as a group to present more critical strategies and options by advancing social welfare was seriously compromised. Moreover, the CASW did not support its members who confronted serious work-related problems" (Jennissen & Lundy, 2011, p. 161).

The above criticisms of professionalism have led many radical social work writers (Carniol, 2010; Ferguson, Lavalette, & Mooney, 2002; Galper, 1980; Hardy, 1981a, 1981b; Laursen, 1975;

Wagner & Cohen, 1978; Wilding, 1982; Withorn, 1984) to reject professionalism and/or to opt for unions as the most appropriate form and means for social workers to organize to pursue social transformation. However, not all radical writers and certainly not all social workers believe that there is necessarily an incompatibility between unionism and professionalism as means of engaging in collective forms of organization. The position taken here is that structural social workers should join professional associations for the same reason they should join unions—to engage in collective action with the purpose of social transformation. Given the present class-collaborationist nature of most unions in North America and the evidence cited above, which suggests that professionalism by itself does not deter social activism, it is a false dichotomy to present unionism as the radical form of social work organization and professionalism as the conservative form. Most social workers belong to both a union and a professional association. Just as structural social workers work within the social welfare institution to radicalize it and to use it as a means of social transformation, so, too, should they join professional associations for the very same purposes.

A progressive professional association should also have liaison committees as linkages to other social movement groups that seek the transformation of society—the peace movement, the environmental movement, the human rights movement. One other necessary committee, if a professional association is to avoid becoming a self-serving, status quo organization, is an active social action committee led by members who have a structural (as opposed to a reformist) outlook. This committee must be supported by the membership and the executive in carrying out analyses of social programs, policies, legislation, government actions, and corporate interests. In sum, the various caucuses and the social action committee can preserve the social conscience of social work in the face of its professionalization.

Box 12.1 *Twelve-Step Recovery Program for Professionals*

My name is _____ and I am a recovering professional.
          (fill in name)

1. I admit to believing that I had no useful skills or knowledge—unless I called myself a "professional."
2. I came to believe that professionalism was not a way to distance myself from my clients.
3. I came to believe that as a "professional," I could fix people and solve their problems.
4. I admit to calling myself a "professional" in an attempt to cover up my insecurities and self-doubt.
5. I came to believe that the professional relationship is not hierarchical. Just because I am the expert doesn't mean that we are not equals—right?

Continued

6. I came to believe that aspiring to a "professional image" by wearing dress clothes, carrying a briefcase, distributing business cards, and driving a car of recent vintage did not separate me from the resource-poor people with whom I work.
7. I admit to signing my name and adding my professional credentials to everything I write.
8. I admit to using my voicemail to screen out certain difficult people.
9. I admit to sending a memo (with my name and credentials) to people rather than bothering to talk to them.
10. I admit to saying, "Call me and we'll do lunch."
11. I admit to using professional jargon, acronyms, and my prolific propensity for vocabulary to impress, overpower, and distance people.
12. I admit to embracing professionalism without taking into account its effects on my stated beliefs in social justice, egalitarianism, and other social work values and ideals.

Unfortunately, as was outlined in Chapter 1, the CASW took a drastic turn to the political right in 2005. A new code of ethics was produced that emphasizes residual ideas and regressive practices while de-emphasizing most of the progressive elements that were contained in its 1994 predecessor. The new code has no philosophical or vision statement to inspire social work and give it a sense of direction toward progressive practices. The code has been almost completely depoliticized. Among other major limitations (see Chapter 1), there is no outline of the kind of society social work should pursue; there is no statement that the service user's interests ought to be social work's primary obligation (it is now just one of many obligations); it contains a limited view of social justice; and it advocates for a practice of professional impartiality whereby it is assumed that all people in society should be treated equally even though some groups have greater or lesser need (i.e., social inequalities among social groups are not recognized).

Electoral Politics

Little social work literature addresses electoral politics as an arena for struggle for social workers. A great deal has been written on advocacy and on lobbying and influencing governments, but almost nothing exists on supporting a particular political party as a way of dealing with social problems, let alone as a way of transforming our current neo-conservative/liberal society.

The reasons for this lack of attention to electoral politics are partly historical and partly methodological. Historically, social work has perceived involvement in party politics as unprofessional. To become involved in politics was to meddle in the preserve of the politicians. Not only is conventional social work emotionally neutral, it is also politically neutral. Involvement in party politics was considered a personal choice, certainly not a professional choice. Methodologically, conventional models of social work practice, such as systems theory and the ecological approach, preclude electoral political activity. One might assess the negative impact of government policy on people, but the social worker is limited to helping people adapt to the policy or to lobby government to ameliorate the policy. In view of the fact that governments ultimately decide on the nature, shape, size, and quality of social programs, it hardly makes sense for social work not to involve itself in attempting to get the political party most sympathetic to a progressive welfare state elected. If political decisions determine the fate of the welfare state and the nature of our social relationships, social work must involve itself in the political arena.

In political democracies, political parties constitute an important means by which social classes or social groups organize to pursue their collective interests (Wolfe, 1989). In other countries, such as the Scandinavian nations, the working classes have been able to offset the greater power resources of capital by electing social democratic governments. These governments, in turn, have implemented policies favourable to the working class, such as full employment and the

---

Box 12.2 *All Social Work Is Political—There Is No Escape*

I (Bob) remember a number of years ago attending a meeting of the Canadian Association of Deans and Directors of Schools of Social Work. This group met (and continues to meet) on a semi-annual basis to discuss common interests and concerns with respect to social work education in Canada. At this particular meeting, someone raised a concern about a proposed piece of federal legislation that, if passed, would result in further cutbacks to welfare programs. Discussion ensued, and a motion was made to send a letter from the deans and directors to the Canadian government protesting the legislation. One dean who was new to the group and to Canada, since he had just recently arrived from the United States to take up his position, said that he did not think that the group should do anything of a political nature because that was not our job. Well, you could have heard a pin drop as others in the room looked at each other in disbelief. After a relatively long and uncomfortable silence, the newly arrived dean said, "I seem to have said something wrong."

This is not necessarily a Canadian–American difference because, unfortunately, I (Bob) have heard many, many social workers in Canada adopt this same position, arguing that social work is about people and should not be about politics. Such a position indicates a lack of awareness that social work, by its very nature, is and must be a highly political activity. That is, if I decide to do nothing to challenge the current situation, in effect I am supporting it because there is no resistance or protest coming from me. And *this is a political choice*. My intention may not be political, but the outcome or result of my decision to do nothing is political. I have, unwittingly perhaps, actually supported the status quo by not challenging, protesting, resisting, or trying to change it. *There is no neutral political ground in social work*. I would much rather adopt the political position of trying to change the current system of dominant–subordinate relations than support it by claiming that social work is above politics and doing nothing.

pursuit of a welfare state that promotes an equality of the highest standards (Esping-Andersen, 1989). Conversely, countries that have elected mostly liberal or conservative governments, such as the United States and Canada, have developed political economies favouring the interests of capital over those of the working class, as evidenced by policies that accept high unemployment and a residual welfare state. Clearly, then, social work cannot remain at arm's length from electoral politics. Social work is not politically neutral; it is a political act or practice. If it does nothing politically, it has removed itself as a force for change, which in effect supports the status quo. Given the inherent political nature of social work, it must organize and declare its political hand. It must align itself with other groups and organizations that share similar goals. This includes supporting political parties committed to social, political, and economic justice for all and not just for a privileged minority.

American social workers committed to social transformation do not have a national socialist party to work with. In fact, the majority of Americans do not have the background and experience they need to discuss the nature of capitalism and socialism objectively and critically. Many people espouse an uncritical and unexamined commitment to the "free enterprise system" and to the "American way" (Galper, 1980, p. 90). In the absence of a national socialist or radical party, Wineman (1984, p. 224) advocates radical activity at the local level as a means of building a "bottom-up approach to constructing a national radical presence in electoral politics." Such activity not only pushes mainstream politicians to the left as they scramble for the votes of women, minorities, people living in poverty, and so on, it also helps to mobilize and consolidate multi-constituency and multi-issue coalitions as "they begin to create a foundation for the eventual emergence of a national third party" (Wineman, 1984, p. 225).

In Canada there is a social democratic national party, the New Democratic Party. However, it is seldom mentioned in most Canadian social work and social welfare textbooks,[1] even in those books with a leftist perspective.[2] Andrew Armitage pays tribute to the contributions made to the Canadian welfare state by the NDP and its predecessor, the Co-operative Commonwealth Federation.

> The New Democratic Party has been the most consistent advocate of social welfare in the Canadian political spectrum. The party's political statements, more clearly than those of other parties, have committed it to the welfare ideal of the redistribution of income, wealth, and power. When elected to office (in British Columbia, Saskatchewan, Yukon, Manitoba, and Ontario), New Democratic governments have shown a willingness to introduce social welfare programs not legislated anywhere else in Canada or, indeed, in North America. . . . Long before Liberal or Progressive Conservative governments have introduced social welfare legislation, members of Parliament from the New Democratic Party and its predecessor, the Co-operative Commonwealth Federation, have brought the need of Canadians for such programs as pensions, medicare, housing, and income guarantees before the House of Commons (Armitage, 1996, pp. 141–142).

However, NDP governments have also been criticized for behaving more like bourgeois (conservative and liberal) governments once elected to office (in British Columbia, Saskatchewan, Manitoba, and Ontario, at least) in that although there were small improvements with respect to the living conditions for the people living in poverty, the NDP governments failed to make good on their promises to challenge inequality and poverty and seemed to capitulate to the "corporate agenda" (Armitage, 2003; Ralph, 1993).

During the twentieth century, very few major policy differences existed between Canada's two major national political parties, the Liberals and the Progressive Conservatives.[3] Both parties were located near the centre of the political spectrum, with the Conservatives leaning more to the right. The Progressive Conservative Party had a tendency to disavow the progressive rhetoric of some of it leaders (Armitage, 1988, p. 93), and the Mulroney Conservative government systematically retrenched the Canadian welfare state during its term in power (1984–93) through a policy of grad-ualism (Mishra, 1990). In the twenty-first century, as was discussed in Chapter 2, the Conservative government under Stephen Harper (the word "Progressive" was dropped from its official party name) enacted a number of draconian economic, social, environmental, and political policies.

Most of Canada's social programs have been legislated under Liberal governments, yet the motivation has often been to undermine the popularity of the NDP, to avert labour unrest, or, in the event of a minority government (such as that in 2004), to agree to NDP demands for social reform and/or improved social programs to avoid being unseated as government. There have been periods of neglect and disinterest on the part of Liberal governments, and on occasion Liberal spokespersons have appealed to the alienating aspects of welfare transfers in their quest for political support (Armitage, 1988, p. 92). Both the Liberal and (Progressive) Conservative parties accept the free market as the preferred socio-economic system, and both have a history of being more responsive to the needs of capital than to the needs of subordinate groups. This is the major reason for the persistence of residualism with respect to Canada's welfare state.

Given the history, ideology, and approaches of Canada's political parties to the welfare state, it makes no sense for structural social workers to support either the Liberals or the Conservatives. To do so would be the same as supporting an arsonist's bid to become fire chief. Social work is not above politics—it is a political activity. If it does not have a progressive agenda, it will auto-matically become part of the conservative forces in society. The warped professional notion of political neutrality must be rejected and replaced with the knowledge that electoral politics is a major arena where the struggle for social justice and social transformation occurs.

A Revitalized Public Sector

The above call for involvement in electoral politics was one of the strategies of the old social movements—to win state power and to use that power to transform society. However, post-modernists and others have expressed a legitimate concern with any proposal that the state pro-vide the leadership, structure, and resources to meet the common (and culturally relevant) needs of people. After all, the modern nation-state was originally established as the collective expres-sion of ideals of universal reason and order and resulted in structures of domination, control, exclusion, homogenization, and discipline (Leonard, 1997). In spite of these criticisms, more and more writers (e.g., Fisher & Karger, 1997; Fisher & Kling, 1994; Leonard, 1997; Mullaly, 2001; 2002; 2010) have argued that at some point we must turn our attention to the state and attempt to relegitimize it.

Contrary to neo-conservative dogma, the demands of a global economy require more rather than less government involvement in human, social, and economic affairs. The resources, structure, and legislation needed to ensure that people's common needs are met can only be provided, at this point in our history, by the state. Neither the market nor the voluntary sector can guarantee rights—only the state, with its ability to formulate and implement legislation, is in a position to do so. Despite its relative weakening in the face of globalization, no other institution has the capacity or the resources to rebuild our neglected social and public infrastructure. The promised benefits of a global economy have not been delivered. "Without a legitimate public sector there are no public citizens, only private consumers" (Fisher & Karger, 1997, p. 177). Government policies of privatization have undermined government legitimacy and responsibility, which has resulted in fewer public services and a loss of access to a potentially accountable and responsible public sector.

Contradictions of globalization continue to grow (e.g., increasing disparities of wealth) at the same time that it appears to be collapsing. In Canada at least, before the recession of 2007 the national deficit had been eliminated, the debt was being paid down, and we were experiencing record government surpluses that could have been used to revitalize the public sector. Although the recession interrupted this economic growth, it has returned to a limited extent since 2009 to the point where the current Liberal government under Justin Trudeau is now formulating a significant infrastructure program, more money and attention have been directed toward some of the long-standing Indigenous issues, attention is once again being focused on environmental issues, and so on (see "Hopeful Signs" in Chapter 2 for more examples).

Challenging and Resisting the Dominant Order

We are taught to accept the world as it is, and, thus, we unthinkingly reinforce and reproduce it, but we can challenge this discourse of economic determinism. Marx argued that we enter a social world not of our own making but we are able to act upon it provided we understand how it is made and, in doing so, we can develop a revolutionary "praxis" to free ourselves, at least to some degree, from the hegemony of ruling discourses. Foucault, in his later writings, argued that power is never exercised without resistance, insubordination, and obstinacy. How, then, can structural social work challenge and resist the current order? This is one of the key questions that we have attempted to answer throughout this book.

Resistance and challenge can occur at all levels of social work activity. At the political or societal level, Leonard (1997) argues that there is a need to develop a fully articulated alternative discourse, one that provides a powerful critique of the "globalization thesis" and the current ruling discourse that says no one has control over the determining effects of global market forces because they are the products of impersonal economic relations, new technologies, and new means of communication. Writers such as John Ralston Saul (2004; 2005) and Manfred Steger (2002; 2003) have developed powerful critiques of the globalization thesis and exposed it for what it is—an ideological social construction rather than some economic law of inevitability. Based on such critiques, the counter-discourse to the globalization thesis is that economies are the results of acts of will and the will of capitalists has become increasingly dominant since the mid-1970s.

Reisch (1995) argues that we need to become "responsible extremists" (such as Saul and Steger) by vilifying those who espouse the dominant discourse, not by engaging in character assassination but through the targeted use of facts to counter their use of the dominant discourse.

An example of a counter-discourse that has challenged and significantly altered the dominant discourse of patriarchy is feminism. Although more than a discourse, feminism is regarded as an alternative discourse that resists and challenges the hegemony of male domination. Similarly, the dominant discourse of white supremacy has been challenged by black nationalists, black liberation philosophers and theologians, black academics, and anti-racist social workers. And the dominant discourse of heterosexuality has been confronted by the discourse of the gay and lesbian movement.

At the agency and individual worker levels, we need to practise acts of individual and collective resistance. It has already been mentioned that several university social work programs in Canada, Australia, and the US base their curriculum on critical or progressive social work frameworks that include resistance. Faculty and students discuss how the contradictions that are part of all agencies—contradictions between their social care and social control functions—provide the opportunities for acts of resistance and challenge. Tiny efforts are sought that help us connect our everyday concerns and struggles to larger strategies and visions for social justice and social change (Baines, 2011). Studies on the experiences of many graduates from progressive social work programs in Canada show that practices and strategies of resistance (e.g., defence of the service user practices, increasing the service user's power in the worker–service user relationship, materialization and collectivization practices) are very useful in challenging the dominant discourse that blames individuals for all their problems (LeComte, 1990; Moreau & Leonard, 1989; Moreau et al., 1993). Foucault's (1988) work on the mutual interplay of power and resistance opens up unlimited opportunities for acts and strategies to undermine discursive practices of domination. This is evidenced by Ken Moffatt's study of the micro-mechanisms of power in a social assistance office and the strategies developed by workers to oppose the controlling technologies of "surveillance and government of the welfare recipient" (Moffatt, 1999, p. 219).

The Moral Premise of Social Welfare: Universal Human Needs

The attempt to define and meet human needs in the past sometimes led to domination whereby the dominant group was able to exercise its control over ideas and convince people to perceive their needs in ways that were compatible with the interests of the dominant or ruling group (Gil, 1998). As well, postmodernists have criticized notions of common needs and needs identification given the role that mass culture plays in manufacturing desire, which is often translated into needs. They view needs as individually determined, culturally specific, and highly interpretive.

Acknowledging these criticisms of any identification of a universal set of human needs, Doyal and Gough (1991) assert that a notion of objective human need is still morally necessary and that meeting such need must take precedence over the satisfaction of wants or desires. If we lack any notion of objective human need as the basis of solidarity for political struggle for justice and equality in the distribution of welfare, Doyal and Gough contend that we are left with the neo-conservative belief that there is only one universal need: the need for the market.

Producing an impressive amount of cross-cultural indicators and measures, Doyal and Gough suggest that it is possible to identify universal, transcultural human needs. Every human being has two basic needs: the need for physical health and the need for autonomy. These are the preconditions for any individual action or interaction in any culture. When physical health and autonomy are identified as needs required for individuals to act as autonomous agents, we are provided with a sound basis for social policy and for moral judgments on our own and other societies (Doyal & Gough, 1991, cited in Leonard, 1997). We are also provided with a moral premise for progressive social welfare. The need for (and public right to) physical health requires adequate health care, nutrition, housing, non-hazardous work and physical environments, economic and physical security, basic education, and safe birth control and child-bearing. The need for (and public right to) personal autonomy consists of freedom of agency and political freedom, including self-development, mental health (e.g., a sense of self-worth), and personal opportunity (Fisher & Karger, 1997). The optimal satisfaction of health and autonomy is a fundamental right of all individuals. To pretend otherwise is morally incoherent and politically disabling.

Table 12.1 summarizes ways in which the progressive social worker can and should become involved in the larger society beyond the immediate workplace, as discussed above. Although we can lay substantial groundwork for fundamental social change in our workplaces and in our work with individuals, groups, communities, and so on, only by reaching out into the wider world can we hope to effect real change. In this regard, a slogan from the environmental movement—think globally, act locally—is a useful place to begin.

Table 12.1 Overview of Elements for Working outside and against the System

Locations/Factors in Working outside and against the System	Selected Characteristics of Practice
Alternative services and organizations	Create, develop, and/or support alternative organizations founded on different principles from those of mainstream agencies. Provide prototypes of future democratic workplaces.
Coalitions, social movements, and new social movements theory	Create, develop, and join coalitions and social movements. At the global level, support and develop transnational organizations such as Greenpeace and Amnesty International.
Progressive unions	Adopt a class-conflict union perspective and approach to social justice issues. Use the union to promote and negotiate such workplace conditions as caseload sizes, more worker participation in developing agency policies and practice, etc.
Professional associations	Avoid the traditional trappings of professionalization, such as elitism, conservatism, and self-serving behaviour. Politicize the association from within. Encourage the association to join coalitions and social movements.

Electoral politics	Support progressive political parties (not bourgeois parties such as the Canadian Liberal and Conservative parties) by providing them with your vote, money, and inside work.
	Provide information to progressive parties that they can use for political purposes and to improve their social welfare policies.
The public sector	Challenge such fatalistic ideas as that today's situation is evolutionary, inevitable, and irreversible. What was made by an elite few can be unmade and remade.
	Develop a counter-discourse of why we need government.
The dominant social order	Develop counter-discourses to victim-blaming, free-market glorification, welfare dependency, etc. (e.g., wouldn't the rich feel better about themselves if they had to work for their money?).
	Become more aware of the micro-mechanisms of power that can be used to minimize the harm, surveillance, and degradation that many service users feel because of agency policies and practice.
Human need	Although needs are largely individually determined, culturally relevant, and highly interpretive, everyone has the need for (and right to) physical health and personal autonomy.

Working within Ourselves

Critical Self-Reflection

Originating with Argyris and Schon (1976), critical self-reflection is referred to in the literature by various terms: self-reflexive practice, critical reflection, self-reflexivity, and critically reflective practice. In essence, structural social workers integrate theory and practice through a process of "reflection in action," questioning their knowledge claims in an ongoing way (Allan, 2003a). Fook (1999, p. 199) contends that critical self-reflective practice involves "the ability to locate oneself in a situation through the recognition of how actions and interpretations, social and cultural background and personal history, emotional aspects of experience, and personally held assumptions and values influence the situation." Its use prevents us from taking things for granted and encourages us to reanalyze situations in ways that provide for new actions and changes in power relations. As a way of knowing, critical reflection allows marginalized aspects of experience, such as emotions and personal histories, to be valued. As a process, it focuses attention on the social worker's influence on situations and how this might affect power relations or how it might perpetuate existing structures and beliefs. Critical reflection is also based on, and integrates, elements of deconstructive thinking, which can provide a means for reconstructing and changing the ways in which individuals view their social worlds (Fook, 2004, p. 16).

Critical self-reflection is an element of the tradition of critical social theory, which Leonard (1997) argues provides a link to postmodern critique. Because we all internalize in varying degrees parts of the dominant ideology, it is important to develop reflexive knowledge of the dominant ideology to see how it constrains us and limits our freedom. Reflexive knowledge, which is derived through critical reflection, is knowledge about ourselves. It helps us to understand how our identities are largely determined by the dominant ideology. It tells us where we are within the social order in terms of our positions of domination and subordination and how we may exercise power in our professional and personal lives to either reproduce or resist social features that limit the freedoms or agency of others. Reflexive knowledge is also knowledge about the source and substance of our social beliefs, attitudes, and values. This kind of knowledge has the potential of helping us to free ourselves from self-imposed constraints that are derived from the massive power of the dominant ideology.

There are trends within social work policy and practice that follow certain ideological and political stances and may promote values and attitudes that work against social work principles (Askeland & Fook, 2009). Social workers need to critically examine these trends underlying theories and values and whether or not they promote or undermine the values of progressive social work. Social workers should reflect on the following questions (Askeland & Fook, 2009, p. 288):

- Do the trends leave space for the practice of social work, making use of the social workers' competence?
- Since empowerment is an aim of social work, how is the power embedded in these different trends?
- Who or what is the source for the knowledge on which the trends are based?

Processes of critical reflection, and the ability to think critically, are an integral part of critical (structural) social work practice. Critical thinking or practice (thinking or working with others by adhering to critical principles), in combination with critical reflection, encourages social workers to examine their own social location in relation to experience and actions and to make meaning from that experience (Askeland & Fook, 2009). David Gil (1998) provides a checklist of areas for critical self-reflection:

- the images of social reality that we presently hold;
- the ideas, beliefs, and assumptions we now take for granted about people, society, and the relationship between the two;
- the perceptions we hold of individual and collective needs and wants that underpin the actions, thoughts, and social relations of most people;
- our values and ideologies, which derive from our perceptions of needs and interests and affect our choices, actions, thoughts, and social relations.

Anne Bishop (2002) discusses the importance for anyone who wishes to become an ally of oppressed groups to reflect critically on his or her own experiences as both a member of an oppressed group and as a member of an oppressor group. She argues that learning about one's oppression is much different from and less difficult than learning about oneself as an oppressor because the process of becoming an oppressor is hidden from the person. This is so because the oppressor role is equated with normalcy, universal standards and values, and political and cultural neutrality. Nothing adverse is perpetrated on the person to make them aware of their role of oppressor. Understanding one's position as an oppressor requires an understanding that one is a member of a particular social group and not just an individual member of society. Structural social workers engage in ongoing critical self-reflection of their roles as oppressor and oppressed in both their personal lives and in their social work practice.

Self-Care

Structural social work is one form of struggle against oppression and in pursuit of liberation. This struggle can be painful and discouraging at times; it can become even more so because structural social work is marginalized within our own profession. Mainstream social workers often write us off as "out of touch" and "unrealistic radicals." Anyone who has lived or worked on the edge of or outside the mainstream knows all about marginalization, isolation, ridicule, and defamation on a personal level. In addition, social work today is fraught with pressures that can lead to incredible stress, particularly when staff are not adequately supported in meeting the complex and demanding challenges of social problems and societal dysfunction. In turn, the stress can become so overwhelming that we function below the level of our competence to the point where our practice becomes dangerous work (Thompson, 1998). Prolonged exposure to stress can lead to burnout—a psychological condition in which the worker "functions 'on automatic pilot'—that is, in an unthinking, unfeeling way, cut off from the sensitive issues involved in his or her work" (Thompson, 1998, p. 226).

Self-care consists of strategies and practices aimed at caring for oneself by oneself. Self-care concerns the "purposeful use of practices to enhance personal well-being and healthful functioning" (Profitt, 2011, p. 279). Four themes have been identified as integral to the concept of self-care (Profitt, 2011):

1. *The interrelation between the personal and the professional.* Reinterpretation of past experiences in a critical light will lead to personal/professional growth that expands and enriches social work practice. Subjectivity is an invaluable source for deepening social workers' understanding of social processes. Subjectivity means that we have an understanding of how we are socially constructed within social relations of power and privilege.

2. *Institutional parameters.* Many social workers struggle with institutional ideologies, structures, and rules that are a part of mainstream casework. To maintain integrity, some social workers choose to resist in strategic ways to educate and politicize others, advocate for service users' rights, and find alternative spaces in which to foster political potential.

3. *Ongoing negotiation of boundaries.* Contrary to conventional social work practice in which the boundaries between the personal and the professional are kept separate, social workers understand that the lines are fluid, complex, and overlapping. "Cherished values for caring for people and social fairness that infuse personal life also permeate professional practice and cannot simply be separated, repressed, or dismissed in social work practice" (Profitt, 2011, p. 284).

4. *Responses to working with victims of violence.* Social workers are affected somatically, emotionally, and spiritually by the work they do. Responses to witnessing pain and suffer can coexist with appreciation for the strength and resilience of service users and a renewed commitment to healing and social change.

It has already been emphasized that mutual support and cooperation among structural social workers is crucial if we are to avoid being co-opted by the system or agency or if we are to cope with the negative attitudes and behaviours that supervisors and mainstream colleagues may possess and exhibit. There is consensus in the literature and with people's experience of structural social work that the most important element in carrying out acts of resistance and in protecting oneself from the risks inherent in structural social work practice is to establish and work with caucuses or support groups of like-minded colleagues. Profitt (2011, pp. 287–288) outlines the importance of moving toward a more politicized, collective notion of self-care. First, social workers must interrogate the professional assumption that it is normal, as compassionate beings, to witness structural injustice, oppression, and violence without being affected (see Weinberg, 2009, on "moral distress"). Engaging in political activism may help social workers to counter feelings of frustration, anger, powerlessness, and vicarious trauma. Second, the need for self-care is often generated by the very social, political, and economic systems that cause suffering for service users and place unrealistic workload demands on social workers. Social workers collectively need to be able to question current managerial discourses. Third, social workers must resist internalizing this managerial strategy, or blaming others, by joining unions or professional associations to challenge systemic factors in the workplace. Finally, social workers need to recognize that self-care is a form of resistance and an important dimension of ethical social work practice:

> Although self-care is a dimension of ethical practice intended to ensure quality service to clients, we must also claim it for ourselves as a social work practice directed at well-being and interconnectedness of social workers with our communities and struggles for social justice (Profitt, 2011, p. 288).

Realistic Expectations

A question we are frequently asked by students when discussing the ultimate goal of structural social work—social transformation—is whether we think it will happen. Of course, the subtext of this question is whether or not we think that structural social work will bring about some kind of social transformation in the foreseeable future. The short answer is no, we do not believe structural social work will, by itself, bring about social transformation. The longer answer is to suggest that some social workers equate social transformation with overnight revolution and believe that the absence of militant or cataclysmic, large-scale changes is proof that fundamental structural change is unrealistic. Gil (1998) reminds us that oppressive institutions have evolved over many centuries and, therefore, are often perceived to be natural, normal, legitimate, and unchangeable. There are no quick and easy strategies for eliminating oppression.

Life might be a whole lot simpler if we just accepted the way things are, but mainstream social workers are more susceptible to burnout than structural social workers. Their analysis and explanations of social problems do not explain the persistence of problems, nor does their analysis explain why their interventions and practices seem so ineffectual. Over time, with limited successful outcomes from their interventions, they will naturally begin to question themselves and their competencies. Structural social workers at least have an analysis that explains why mainstream interventions and "solutions" to social problems do not work. People who live in poverty did not invent poverty. Racialized groups did not create racism. Gay, lesbian, bisexual, and transexual persons did not invent homophobia. Women did not ask to be treated in a sexist way. These are structural problems that can only be satisfactorily resolved by structural change (recognizing that some personal change may be associated with structural interventions). The struggle against oppression can be painful and discouraging at times, but anyone who has ever participated in it knows that it also brings great comradeship, which is deeply rewarding. If we do nothing about oppression, we lose our basic humanity, and, we suggest, we will have difficulty living with ourselves.

The social transformation of a society characterized by relations of domination and subordination will require a lengthy and difficult process, one that could take decades or centuries. This does not mean that we have to accept the status quo. It merely means that we have to be realistic about the outcomes of structural social work. The question is not "How can I start the revolution to end oppression?" Rather, it is *"How can I contribute to undermining and resisting oppression in my everyday practice?"*

Our task is to contribute to social transformation in any way we can—in our professional practices and in our personal lives. Although complete social transformation may not occur in the lifetimes of most of us, we will see some fundamental changes. The women's movement has brought about fundamental change in the relations between males and females. Part of this change is the common usage today of gender-inclusive language as opposed to the male-dominated discourse of a couple of decades ago. This change, of course, is much greater than a simple vocabulary alteration. It has both symbolic and real effects. Language is part of culture. It both reflects and contributes to dominant–subordinate relationships. One way of helping to change the culture (such as patriarchy) is to change the language.

Everyone in their day-to-day living experiences can contribute to language changes. For example, instead of using the term "client," which denotes a relationship of inequality between the social worker (the helper) and the "helpee," many social workers today (including ourselves—Bob and Marilyn) use the term "service user." An example of where a structural social worker can make a contribution to undermining some of the oppressive aspects of social work practice is in the area of case recordings and agency files. Traditionally, case recordings were written in a diagnostic discourse that tended to pathologize the service user by attributing problems to deficiencies within the individual, the family, the culture, and so on. These recordings were guarded like Fort Knox and could only be seen by selected agency personnel. The structural social worker could help to de-pathologize the experiences of service users by identifying problems for what they are—outcomes of racism, sexism, classism, and/or other forms of oppression rather than using some victim-blaming explanation. Today, because of "freedom of information" legislation, service users do have access to their files, which provides them with

> ## Box 12.3 *Making Waves in the Billabong*
>
> In the late 1990s and early part of the new century, I (Bob) was head of a structural social work program at Victoria University in Australia. One day in class we were discussing the nature of social transformation and what we could do as individual social workers to bring it about. I attempted to make the point that it was unrealistic to think that we could bring about some kind of overnight revolution, that we had to join with other groups who were also seeking fundamental transformation of our current society, and that it would take a long time and a lot of effort by many people before we would realize substantial structural changes. One student, much more creative than I, said that she viewed social transformation in a similar vein to making big waves in a billabong (i.e., a large pool of water). She said that if one or two people threw pebbles into the billabong, you would hardly see any movement, but if you had many, many people throwing pebbles you would see considerable turbulence in the billabong. Her point, of course, was that as more and more people practise structural social work and contribute to fundamental structural changes, social transformation will occur.

the opportunity to disagree with what is written and to offer their own stories. However, not all service users are informed about their right to look at their files. Structural social workers would ensure that this right is made known. Some agencies have a policy of co-authorship of a joint narrative about problems, needs, and claims (Leonard, 1997). This practice recognizes that narratives are open to interpretation and that the service user's knowledge is just as valuable as is some piece of universal expert knowledge, which by itself has a tendency to homogenize people within a professional discourse.

The Constructive Use of Anger[4]

Obviously, structural social work practice will not be easy. It requires an examination and deconstruction of social work's most cherished assumptions so that we can learn and become part of the resurgence of social critique in the newer forms of political movements that challenge the dominant order in the name of equality and diversity (Leonard, 1997). It requires a view of the reality of oppression, not as a closed world from which there is no exit but as a limited situation that can be transformed (Freire, cited in Rees, 1991). It also requires an understanding of the nature and causes of the new social, economic, and political conditions of globalization and the current worldwide reactionary political climate. We cannot theorize and analyze from a distance, however, because most of all, structural social work requires a personal and collective commitment to social justice. It is not enough to know that we should involve ourselves in struggle or even to want to become involved in social struggle.

But what is it that would drive a person to take on such an onerous commitment to literally take on the world as we now know it and attempt to transform it? The answer is to capitalize on a feeling that most social workers concerned about social injustice possess—anger at the degrading material and social conditions experienced on a daily basis by millions of people in the less-developed countries and in capitalist countries; anger at governments that cater to the wishes of the wealthy at the expense of women, children, racialized groups, and other marginalized groups; anger at a social welfare system that homogenizes, controls, and monitors people who are forced to go to it for assistance and that has turned its workers into bureaucratic ciphers; and anger at the discrimination, exploitation, and blocked opportunities that so many people experience today, not because of anything they might have done or who they are as individuals but simply because they belong to particular social groups, which for the most part they did not choose.

Feminists have used the construction of anger as a catalyst to attack sexism and patriarchy. According to feminist therapy, women need to get in touch with their anger and turn it outward rather than inward (Goldhor-Lerner, 1985) because the latter results in depression, despair, and anxiety, which, in turn, reproduce women's traditional roles of passivity and submission under patriarchy (Baines, 1997). A similar dynamic is experienced by social workers who internalize their anger caused by social and workplace injustice. Leonard (1997, p. 162) contends that anger can be mobilized from internalization as anxiety and depression into externalization as collective resistance: "Collectively, anger emerges as a moral protest at injustice." Herman (1992, p. 189) argues that anger has been the driving force behind all great social movements. It can move oppressed people and their allies from feelings of "helpless fury" to "righteous indignation." Bishop (2002, p. 101) identifies anger as a source of power if it is used as "an expression of our will directed against injustice."

Peter Leonard argues that a sense of moral outrage at the structures of domination and oppression manufactured and reproduced within the current set of oppressive social arrangements provides the basis for progressive discourses and practices. "Not intellectual detachment but anger is the human attribute which has the most possibility of generating the kind of individual and collective resistance which is a necessary precondition of emancipation" (Leonard, 1997, p. 162). Thompson (1998) issues an important caution about anger, however. He asserts that anger can be a positive force for change if it is channelled constructively, but if it gets out of control or is misdirected or used as a blanket approach to struggles for liberation, it can be used ideologically by the dominant group to pathologize and stigmatize subordinate group members and their anti-oppressive allies.

Anger is a gift (Lim, 1996, cited in Leonard, 1997). It is what will enable those of us who are committed to anti-oppressive social work to translate our social justice ideals into practice and to continue the struggle for liberation. If, in our personal lives and in our social work practice, we assist in making oppression acceptable by helping people to cope with it or adjust to it, we not only fail them, we fail ourselves, and we become part of the problem. Social workers who are committed to social justice must join the struggle against oppression in all its forms and at all levels at which it occurs. There is no choice.

Making the Political Personal in Our Own Lives

The most important arena for radical change is ourselves. Moreau and Leonard (1989, p. 238) contend that one of the central factors conducive to the practice of structural social work is to attain congruence between our personal/political beliefs and the way we live our lives. Withorn (1984, p. 82) states that socially committed social workers need "to achieve harmony among their politics, their work, and their personal lives." In other words, it is not enough to espouse structural ideology and to carry it out in our professional work—we must live it. To do otherwise is not only contradictory and hypocritical, it is self-defeating.

It was argued in the previous chapter that to avoid reproducing dominant–subordinate social relationships and oppressive behaviours that are part of our society, a structural social work practice must be carried out. So, too, in our personal lives must we avoid reproducing social relationships and behaviours at the root of so many of our social problems—inequality, excessive competition, exploitation of people and resources, profit-driven production, distribution, and consumption, sexism, racism, homophobia, ageism, individualism, militarism, and so on. By carrying out our ideological beliefs in our daily lives, we supplement our structural work by contributing to social transformation outside of our professional practice.

Our personal relationships represent one area for personal and social transformation. Just as we strive for egalitarian and participatory relationships in the workplace, so should we practise equality in all our relationships. We must work at eliminating traditional roles and divisions based on gender in our homes and in our associations with others. Structural social workers must examine their own lives and interactions with others to determine whether or not they are contributing to a social atmosphere of oppression, aggression, and even violence. Are sexist, racist, or homophobic jokes and slurs condoned or tolerated? Does violence in any form occur? Are environmentally harmful products purchased and used? Are war toys purchased for children, or do we allow them to watch violent television shows? Structural social work requires more than a nine-to-five workplace effort; it requires a commitment to personal evaluation, challenge, and change.

Do our consumer patterns support capitalism, or do we take advantage of the collective, more democratic, and non-exploitative alternatives that exist in the midst of our capitalist society? With respect to our personal finances, do we use private banks that make enormous profits for a few people, often have investments in countries that violate human rights, have oppressive labour policies, and often exploit their own workers, most of whom are women? Or do we join credit unions, which are collectively owned and operated by their memberships and invest their money in the local community? Do we purchase goods and services made or delivered by non-unionized companies, or do we support the trade union movement by purchasing union-produced goods and services? Do we patronize profit-driven businesses when there are opportunities to support the development and expansion of the co-operative movement where, as with credit unions, the enterprises are membership-owned and operated in the best interests of its members and not for a few shareholders? Do we purchase environmentally friendly products and boycott products from establishments with poor environmental track records?

North Americans consume billions of dollars of goods and services yearly. The market is the heart of capitalism, but it is also an arena where the traditional capitalist principles of production, distribution, and consumption can be altered.

To live structurally in our hierarchical society is not easy, however. Most of the rewards—promotions, acceptance, respect—are given to those who conform to our present social order. By engaging in structural social work, we run the risk of retaliation from the status quo. This retaliation can range from persons being nervous in our presence to overt efforts to discredit us by applying labels such as "troublemaker." Galper (1980) and Withorn (1984) have written about the risks involved in radical work and some of the ways of coping with and reducing the risks—avoid adventurism and martyrdom; be competent in your work; work collectively; realize that all radicals experience some degree of ambivalence about their radicalism by virtue of having been socialized into a society marked by dominant–subordinate relations. The greater risk, however, is to capitulate to the status quo and not carry out our structural ideology in our work and in our personal lives. The risk in this case is that we do nothing to bring about progressive structural change and, thus, fail the people we serve. Thereby, we fail ourselves. We become part of the problem and not the solution as we join the conventional social work group delivering services and practising in ways that blame victims for their troubles. And we run the risk of cynicism, despair, and burnout because we know that in the long run what we are doing is simply perpetuating the system that causes people troubles in the first place.

In sum, to be effective as structural social workers we need a political analysis that distinguishes the causes and the consequences of social problems. We need a vision of a humanized society to give us direction in our efforts. We need knowledge to enable us to work effectively both inside and outside our social agencies. We need to have harmony between our political beliefs and our personal lives. And we need a commitment to carry out the difficult task of social transformation. Structural social work is more than a theory or a technique or a practice modality. It is a way of life.

Critical Questions

1. We are all socialized into social institutions and organizations that are characterized by hierarchy and top-down management. What would an alternative organization characterized by collective or horizontal management look like? How would decisions be made? Who would speak for the organization? And how would other organizations relate to it—i.e., who would they communicate with?

2. Unions are concerned with the working conditions of their members. Caseload size is often an issue in social work settings and one that unions should address at the bargaining table (i.e., bargain for a reasonable ceiling on the number of cases a social worker should carry). Can you identify other workplace issues that social work unions should address?

3. Examine the official policies of each of the federal political parties in the areas of income taxation, public health care, social housing, daycare, and Indigenous self-government. Which

party has policies closest to those of progressive or structural social work? Which political party in your province has the most social workers (past or present) among its members? How can we as a profession use or influence political parties to pursue progressive social policies?

4. Do you have any rules for yourself that help you to deal with any anger you might experience in the workplace? For example, earlier in my career I (Bob) often reacted immediately to my anger by writing a letter or email or telephoning the person (and sometimes others) responsible for my anger. This often got me in trouble because my communiqué tended to be knee-jerk and confrontational rather than thoughtful and strategic. Now I have a rule that I wait at least one day to respond. I ask myself before acting—is my anger in check?

5. What are some of the ways you look after yourself? Can you think of other forms of self-care or strategies you might consider adopting on an individual level and on a collective level with people inside your workplace and outside?

Notes

Chapter 1

1. This is not to say that casework must be, or that all casework is, residual or victim-blaming. Jan Fook's *Radical Casework* (1993) is an example of casework practice that links the personal with the political. That is, it links public issues with personal difficulties by including social analysis as part of its practice. Nor is this to say that all community organization is radical. No area of social work is inherently mainstream or radical. More is said about these issues in subsequent chapters.

2. Of course, many perspectives, models, theories, and so on exist within social work. With respect to our present social order, however, two basic views are held by social workers. Some believe our present society is capable of righting any social wrongs that may occur. Others believe that our present society is not capable of righting social wrongs because the social order itself produces these wrongs and, therefore, limited reform of the system will do nothing to resolve social problems. The first group of social workers, called here conventional workers, seeks to make our social order work better. The second group, called here progressive workers, seeks to transform our present social order into one that works better for larger numbers of people. Another term for progressive social work is radical social work, which is discussed in some detail in Chapter 8.

3. The conventional social work view of egalitarianism is that of "equal opportunity." This notion of egalitarianism and others will be discussed in the chapters that focus on the four different paradigms. See Benn and Peters (1959) for an overview and discussion of different meanings of egalitarianism.

4. For fuller coverage of collectivism as an organizing principle for an idealized social work society, see Galper (1975, pp. 140–152).

5. This is not to suggest that the conflation of the two terms in the literature is not confusing and, in some regards, misleading. According to the *Encyclopaedia of Social Sciences* (Selizam, 1944, pp. 544–548), the doctrine of humanism espouses that the person has two natures, good and bad, and that there is constant tension between the two. Humanitarianism denies this dualism within the individual and claims that people are innately good and reasonable. Humanism is an intellectual-philosophical stance dating back to the Renaissance that puts humankind at the apex of creation and presumes, if not a godless world, then a world in which God or some supernatural or divine presence is not or cannot be an active agent in human well-being. Humanitarianism, on the other hand, consists of the efforts of humans to better the life situations of those who are less fortunate and to treat others in a humane way, and many humanitarian organizations and NGOs, rather than operating outside the spiritual realm, work from within specific ethical-religious traditions. Humanists tend to explain the spiritual essence of humans through psychological and other human-centred theories; humanitarians often reflect their concept of a divine presence in their actions toward and for others and in their belief in the presence of God in all humanity.

6. For American examples, see Galper (1975); Gil (1976; 1998); Withorn (1984); and Harrington (1962). For Canadian examples, see Banting (1982); Djao (1983); McQuaig (1993; 2001); Moscovitch and Drover (1981); and Naiman (1997).

7. For example, Michael Harrington's *The Other America* (1962) is often cited as the major work that brought to the attention of affluent America the fact that poverty was real and pervasive in the United States in the early sixties and was followed by President Lyndon Johnson declaring war on poverty in 1964. In its *Fifth Annual Review* (1968), the Economic Council of Canada revealed disturbing evidence on the extent of poverty in Canada, which led to a special Senate committee chaired by David Croll to investigate poverty and make recommendations to remedy it. Biehal and Sainsbury (1991, p. 250) state that poverty was rediscovered in Britain in the 1960s by non-social workers.

8. This theme will be explored in more detail in subsequent chapters. See especially Chapters 4, 8, and 11.

Chapter 2

1. "Taylorism" is a term derived from F.W. Taylor's seminal book, *The Principles of Scientific Management* (1911). This treatise described how labour productivity could be dramatically increased by breaking down each labour process into component motions and organizing fragmented work tasks according to rigorous standards of time

and motion study. Assembly-line production is an example of Taylorism in the workplace.

2. "Fordism" is consistent with but more complex and far-reaching than Taylorism. The term is derived from Henry Ford, who applied principles of scientific management to his automated automobile assembly line in 1913. He used technology and an existing division of labour in his auto plant, but his major innovation was to flow the work to a stationary worker, which resulted in radical gains in productivity. What separates Fordism from Taylorism was Ford's recognition that mass production meant mass consumption, a new system for the reproduction of labour power, a new politics of labour control and management, a new aesthetics and psychology—in short, a new kind of society, one based on mass production and mass consumption (Harvey, 1989). The name often applied to pre–World War II society is "Fordist capitalism" as industry and the labour process were organized around Ford's ideas about a rationalized workplace and a rationalized society.

3. Keynesianism refers to the economic theory of the British economist John Maynard Keynes (1883–1946). This theory argues for a high level of government intervention into the economy to ensure a high level of economic activity and high levels of employment. It is based on the assumption that there is a direct relationship between inflation and employment—that is, there is a supposed trade-off between the two. When unemployment levels are unacceptably high, governments are to cut taxes and increase public spending to stimulate the economy and increase the number of jobs. Conversely, when the economy is overstimulated and dangerous levels of inflation occur, governments are to raise taxes and reduce public spending, which in turn would reduce inflation but also employment.

4. For fuller and more elaborate explanations of the "crisis of legitimation," see George and Wilding (1984); Mishra (1984); Gough (1979); and Riches (1986).

5. A word on terminology is necessary. "Neo" is a prefix that means "new" or "different from." It also means the reappearance of a tradition or perspective after a period of decline or abandonment (Marshall, 1998). "Neo-liberalism" and "neo-conservatism" are often used interchangeably in the literature, which causes some confusion to students of social work and social policy. McBride (in Burke, Mooers, & Shields, 2000) contends that either term is correct when used to describe the ideology driving the current process of globalization. "Neo-conservatism" is the name given to the current re-emergence of conservative thought, and "neo-liberalism" is the term given to the reappearance of classical liberalism. Both ideologies are the subjects of later chapters where they will be explained more fully. The term used in this book when discussing the ideology underpinning globalization is "neo-conservatism." Much of the literature on globalization and social welfare uses "neo-liberalism" in the same way that "neo-conservatism" is used here. Neo-conservatism (or neo-liberalism) is a loosely knit body of ideas premised on a slight rethinking and a substantial reassertion of nineteenth-century conservatism or classical liberalism. It emphasizes market solutions rather than collective decisions to solve or deal with social and economic problems and a reduced role for the state with respect to human affairs (McBride, 2001).

6. Discourse includes not only language but the rules governing the choice and use of language and how the ideas and language will be framed. A discourse is a framework of thought, meaning, and action (Thompson, 1998) that does not reflect knowledge, reality, or truth but creates and maintains them. "Knowledge, according to Foucault, is produced by discourse—it is 'the way in which power, language and institutional practices combine at historically specific points to produce particular ways of thinking'" (Featherstone & Fawsett, 1994, cited in Stainton & Swift, 1996, p. 77). Although there is always more than one discourse at any point in time, usually one discourse is dominant. The current dominant economic discourse consists of a set of assumptions about the social and economic world that largely reflect the interests of global capitalism. The concept of "discourse" is an important tool for understanding phenomena such as globalization and for developing social work practices that deal with the negative causes and consequences of the current globalization process. By understanding a dominant discourse, we can deconstruct it and expose any discriminatory or oppressive assumptions, ideas, and beliefs that may underpin it. Also, we can develop *counter-discourses* based on the ideals of equality, fairness, and social justice. These ideas will be discussed more fully in subsequent chapters.

7. Thomas Hobbes was a seventeenth-century British philosopher who assumed that human beings were by nature isolationist and greedy creatures driven by their desires and aversions and who were inescapably engaged in a perpetual struggle for power and control over others and for resources and privilege. He viewed society as a collection of individuals who agree to surrender some natural freedoms in order to live in a formally organized state that affords people the security necessary to satisfy their needs. He viewed government as a

necessary evil without which life would be "solitary, poor, nasty, brutish, and short." Charles Darwin was a nineteenth-century British naturalist who became famous for his theories on evolution and natural selection. Social Darwinism is a social theory in which its proponents apply Darwin's biological ideas and theories, such as "survival of the fittest" and "evolutionary change," to human social institutions. This school of social thought gave a false scientific credence to laissez-faire and anti-welfare policies on the part of governments.

8.   International trade during the 25-year rise of globalization (1970–95) was governed by a system of international trade agreements, collectively known as the GATT (the General Agreement on Tariffs and Trade). In 1995, the GATT was reconceived as a new, powerful body, the World Trade Organization (WTO). Saul (2004) claims that the creation of this body was the last triumph of globalization. The rules for international trade, for the most part, would be made by the WTO rather than by national governments. Saul argues that the context or the built-in assumptions behind the establishment of the WTO are especially significant in that civilization had been reconceptualized through the "prism of economics." That is, any international agreement that involved a commercial element would be treated as fundamentally a commercial transaction. For example, culture would be seen as a matter of industrial regulation, and food would be seen as a secondary outcome of agricultural industries. In other words, agriculture would not be seen as a food source but as an industry subject to trade rules of the WTO. Any restrictions that a country might impose on food imports concerning use of fertilizers, herbicides, pesticides, genetic manipulation, hormones, and antibiotics were regarded as protectionism by international trade rules without the hardest of hard scientific evidence.

The International Monetary Fund (IMF) was created in 1945 with the purposes of promoting international monetary cooperation and exchange stability, fostering economic growth and high levels of employment, and providing temporary financial assistance to countries in economic difficulty (primarily developing countries). Although these goals are laudable, the (punishing) approach used by the IMF during the period of globalization was to develop and implement structural adjustment programs (SAPs) based on what Saul calls "crucifixion economics" (i.e., free-market economics) and to impose them on poor countries to ensure debt repayment and economic restructuring. The "crucifixion economics" that underpinned the SAPs comprised "low wages, compliant unions, environmental deregulation,

privatization of public services, and diminished role of the state in social protection and social programs" (Lundy, 2004, p. 4).

The G-8 (Group of 8) was a group of the eight wealthiest nations: Canada, France, Germany, Italy, Japan, Russia, the United Kingdom, and the United States (Russia was suspended in 2014). Originally the G-6 (it did not include Canada or Russia), it was created in 1975 with the aim of bringing together the leaders of the biggest national economies to examine the world through the "prism of economics." The core relationship of this group was organized "around naked, commercial self-interest, without the positive and negative counterweights of social standards, human rights, political systems, dynasties, formal religions, and, at the negative extreme, supposed racial destinies" (Saul, 2004, p. 35). This group supported globalization and its regulatory institutions—the IMF and the WTO—and over time focused on trade as the solution to every problem, both economic and social.

9.   In personal correspondence with me (Bob) (11 June 1990), Robert D. Leighninger, Jr, editor of the *Journal of Sociology and Social Welfare*, stated that writers often use Kuhnian terms to give their work borrowed legitimacy and if the concept "paradigm" is not applied carefully, the legitimacy is bogus. Kuhn was dealing with the physical world and physical sciences, not the social world and social sciences. Leighninger did admit that one can apply the concept outside of the physical sciences and talk about multiple-paradigm sciences and paradigm shifts rather than single-paradigm social sciences and revolutions. Social work is, of course, well acquainted with borrowing concepts and knowledge and with the dangers inherent in this practice.

10. I (Bob) wish to thank my colleague Richard Sigurdson, dean of Arts at the University of Manitoba, for his assistance in conceptualizing the political ideologies discussed here. Particularly helpful was his book chapter, "Political Ideas and Ideologies," in Rand Dyck (Ed.), *Studying Politics: An Introduction to Political Science* (2002).

11. Dialectics is Marx's method of theorizing. In its broadest sense, it is the study of contradictions (Cornforth, 1953). It is based on the belief that all things are interconnected and that everything is in a state of continuous change (including society and theories about society). Change occurs through the interplay among these opposing or contradictory forces. According to the dialectic, there are three main elements: (1) a thesis, which is the dominant reality (e.g., modernist thought); (2) an antithesis (e.g., postmodernism), which arises to challenge the dominant thought; and

(3) a synthesis, which reconciles the thesis and antithesis. The synthesis then becomes the new reality or thesis that, in turn, will be challenged by a new antithesis and so on.

Chapter 3

1.   Several conservative American writers have attributed the growth of the underclass to the welfare programs of the 1960s War on Poverty. The welfare poor supposedly were lured away from self-sufficiency by these programs and lost the capacity to live independently. See, for example, Butler and Kondratas (1987); Gilder (1981); Mead (1986); Murray (1984).

Chapter 4

1.   For example, one heir of Jeremy Bentham and Adam Smith (two classical liberals) was John Stuart Mill, one of the pioneers of reform liberalism, and another was Herbert Spencer, a promoter of the ultra-conservative ideas of social Darwinism.
2.   The postwar welfare state in Britain developed from an amalgam of liberal and social democratic beliefs, values, and ideals and was based on the twin liberal pillars of Keynesian economics and Beveridge social policy. The Labour (social democratic) governments were responsible for the development of much of Britain's welfare state.
3.   Marsh, who in 1943 wrote the Canadian equivalent (*Report on Social Security for Canada*) to the Beveridge Report, was greatly influenced by Lord Beveridge's thoughts and liberal ideology.
4.   See Djao (1983) for an overview of this shift, and see Guest (1985) for a more detailed coverage of this shift from a residual to an institutional model of social welfare in Canada.
5.   See Galper (1975) for a definitive and insightful analysis of how and why the social welfare state reinforces liberal capitalism.

Chapter 5

1.   All provinces except New Brunswick, Prince Edward Island, and Newfoundland and Labrador have had social democratic governments in recent years (the NDP in all provinces except for the Parti Québécois in Quebec). At the time of this writing (2017), only one province, Alberta, has a majority social democratic (NDP) government, with the British Columbia NDP forming a minority government (with the BC Green Party), having been sworn in on 22 June 2017.
2.   We are indebted to M. Dickerson and T. Flanagan (1986) for their succinct chapter on "Socialism" in

their book, *An Introduction to Government and Politics: A Conceptual Approach*, which provided much of the material for my overview of some highlights of socialism.
3.   This notion of a "provisional government" caused the anarchist wing of socialism to split from the international socialist organization that existed (1864–1972) because they feared that this transitional government might become permanent.
4.   This method of radical change is called "radical structuralism." It is discussed in detail in Chapter 7.
5.   Mishra (1981) refers to this perspective as the "Social Administration School" of social policy (welfare).
6.   Even with respect to the British experience with social democracy, there is disagreement as to whether or not social democracy has moved Britain closer to a socialist state. There are also some who believe social democracy was not given a fair chance. See Pritchard and Taylor (1978) for a discussion of these issues.
7.   The best-known and most controversial reform is called "the wage-earners fund," which is intended to rectify the unequal distribution of wealth and influence created by private ownership of industry. For details on how this scheme works, see Himmelstrand et al. (1981).
8.   These commissions are somewhat similar to royal commissions in the British sense but usually comprise one member who is an acknowledged expert in the field of inquiry. These studies average two to three years' duration.

Chapter 6

1.   For a polemic discussion and critique of both the Marxist revolutionary and Marxist evolutionary approaches to radical social and political change and social work practice, see Pritchard and Taylor (1978, esp. ch. 7).

Chapter 7

1.   Radical cultural feminists view themselves as the successors of radical feminism and practise a "politics of disengagement" by concentrating on the positive features of women-only cultural spaces (e.g. care and nurturance). Cultural feminists believe that valuing women demands a women-centred culture (Calixte et al., 2010, p. 26).
2.   The personal tragedy theory of disability posits that people with impairments should strive to be as "normal" as possible (Oliver & Barnes, 2012, p. 91). The personal tragedy approach suggests that disability is some terrible chance event that occurs at random to unfortunate people (Oliver, 2009, p. 20).

Chapter 8

1. As discussed in Chapters 5 and 6, both social democracy and Marxism fall within the socialist camp. Both want the same type of society, but they differ on the means to get there.
2. Professors Jim Albert, Peter Findlay, Helen Levine, Roland Lecomte, and Allan Moscovitch, as well as visiting professors from Britain, Mike Brake and Peter Leonard.
3. Professors Gisele Legault and Pierre Racine.
4. Professor Michelle Bourgon.
5. Some examples are: Allan, Pease, and Briskman (2003); Carniol (1990; 1995); Fook (1993); Ife (1997; 2001); Langan and Lee (1989b); Lundy (2004); Moreau and Leonard (1989); Mullaly (1993); Pease and Fook (1999); Thompson (1993); Wagner (1990); Wharf (1990).
6. For an expository discussion of the commonalities and differences contained in the radical social work literature, see Mullaly and Keating (1991).
7. There have been some criticisms of Marxist theory being embedded in positivism in that Marx's theory of "historical materialism" has been interpreted by some as a scientific world view justifying domination. S. Leonard (1990) and Miliband (1977) argue that this interpretation is a distortion of Marx's work because it overlooks Marx's own watchwords, "Doubt all things."
8. See S. Leonard (1990) for an excellent overview of how each of these critical theorists has addressed these questions.
9. It is recognized here that postmodernism is a very diverse rather than a homogeneous body of thought. The characteristics ascribed to postmodernism in this chapter represent some of its major broad tendencies. Even these broad tendencies, however, have their proponents and dissenters among postmodern writers.
10. For a discussion of some internal contradictions of capitalism, such as the tendency of capitalism to overproduce and the fact that the majority of people (i.e., workers) actually produce the wealth but have no control over it, see Galper (1980).
11. For a discussion of some internal contradictions of the welfare state and of social work, see Galper (1975).
12. Mullaly and Keating (1991, p. 66) write: "Radical humanism is based on the ontological assumption that the human being is fundamentally set apart from everything else in existence because of its conscious and creative capacities. From this follows the epistemological assumption that the human mind does not receive objectivity from an external world. Rather it confers objectivity by imposing its own order on the world as it is perceived. What is 'known' or perceived about external reality is subjectively conferred by the knower."

    Further, "radical structuralism reflects the ontological assumption that the human person is merely one entity among many. While human conscious and creative capacities differentiate humanity, they do not set it apart from all else. From this follows the epistemological assumption that external reality is objective and as such tends to impose itself on our consciousness."
13. The structural approach does not deny the need for individual change. Changing social structures will naturally affect individuals, both materially and psychologically. To think otherwise is to deny the connection between the personal and the political. Unlike conventional social work, however, structural social work does not believe that the resolution of social problems lies solely or principally in individual change.
14. This particular approach to social change, called radical humanism, was discussed in the section "The Dialectic in Structural Social Work" and will be used as the theoretical basis for the structural social work practice described in Chapter 11.
15. The implications for structural social work of how we live our lives are discussed in Chapter 12.
16. I (Bob) am most grateful to Dr Katrina Brown of Dalhousie University's School of Social Work, who developed an earlier version of such characteristics.

Chapter 9

1. We are especially indebted to Iris Marion Young for a good deal of the material in this chapter. Young's book, *Justice and the Politics of Difference* (1990), is highly recommended for all progressive-minded social workers. We are also indebted to Barry D. Adam for his insightful analysis of internalized oppression (inferiorization) in his *The Survival of Domination: Inferiorization in Everyday Life* (1978).
2. I (Bob) am grateful to two American writers, Sidanius and Pratto (1999), who presented an impressive amount of empirical data and powerful evidence showing that covert structural oppression can be found in all the major areas of an individual's life in Western democratic nations. Below, I draw heavily from their work.

Chapter 10

1. We are indebted to Michael Kimmel for the analysis contained in his chapter "Introduction: Toward a Pedagogy of the Oppressor," found in Kimmel and Ferber, *Privilege: A Reader* (2003).

2. Some writers (e.g., Bishop 1994; Butler 1978) speak of liberation as a journey in which one starts out as a victim, moves on to become a survivor, and ends up as a warrior or activist fighting against oppression. However, it should not be interpreted as a linear, forward-moving, and uninterrupted journey.

Chapter 11

1. Schools of social work have always had as one of their major curriculum streams what was called the Human Behaviour in the Social Environment (HBSE) sequence.

2. The literature is too extensive to cite here, but since 1976 when *Social Work* published a "Special Issue on Women," a substantial literature has developed on such topics as "feminist counselling," "feminist therapy," and "feminist social work."

3. For an insightful and illuminating analysis of the control functions of social agencies and services, see Galper (1975, ch. 4), Thompson (1998), and Withorn (1984).

4. Most of the literature on democratic worker-run agencies focuses on alternative organizations and services. Very little has been written on democratizing the social agency as a workplace since Galper (1980) and Simpkin (1979). Most writings in the 1980s focused on stemming the tide of the deprofessionalization and/or the proletarianization of social work.

Chapter 12

1. For example, Dennis Guest's basic text, *The Emergence of Social Security in Canada* (1980; 1985), makes no reference to the NDP or its predecessor, the Co-operative Commonwealth Federation (CCF), nor does Frank McGilly in his overview of Canadian income and health programs, *Canada's Public Social Services* (1990), except to mention that the provincial CCF government of Saskatchewan was the first socialist government in North America and the first government to enact and implement public hospital insurance. Similarly, neither Allan Moscovitch and Jim Albert, co-editors of *The Benevolent State: The Growth of Welfare in Canada* (1987), nor Brian Wharf, editor of *Social Work and Social Change in Canada* (1990), makes any substantial reference to the NDP, while Rosalie Chappell (1997) in *Social Welfare in Canadian Society* gives only brief mention of the NDP as a social democratic party that pursues some social democratic ideals in its political agenda.

2. Angela Djao, a Canadian Marxist sociologist, makes no mention of the NDP in her book on Canadian social welfare, *Inequality and Social Policy: The Sociology of Welfare* (1983). Likewise, Ben Carniol, a radical social worker, says nothing about the CCF/NDP in his *Case Critical* (1987; 1990; 1995). It is only in his fifth edition (2005) that he makes passing reference to the NDP.

3. The Reform Party, which began as a western Canada protest party, achieved significant electoral success in the west in the 1993 federal election, but it remained primarily a party with regional strength and had no presence in provincial electoral politics. It was further to the right than the Progressive Conservative Party. Subsequently, the Reform Party became the Canadian Alliance under a "Unite the Right" movement, and in December 2003 the Canadian Alliance and the Progressive Conservative Party amalgamated to form the Conservative Party of Canada. In January 2006 the Conservatives under the leadership of Stephen Harper won a minority government.

4. Earlier versions of this section appeared in my (Bob's) article "Confronting the Politics of Despair," *Social Work Education*, 20(2) (2001), and in my 2002 book *Challenging Oppression: A Critical Social Work Approach.*

Bibliography

Preface

Canadian Association of Social Workers (CASW) (2005). *Code of ethics*. Ottawa, ON: CASW.

Carniol, Ben (1990). *Case critical*. Toronto: Between the Lines.

Fook, Jan (1993). *Radical casework: A theory of practice*. St Leonards, New South Wales: Allen & Unwin.

Harvey, David (1989). *The condition of postmodernity: An enquiry into the origins of cultural change*. Cambridge, UK: Basil Blackwell.

Langan, Mary, & Lee, Phil (Eds) (1989). *Radical social work today*. London, UK: Unwin Hyman.

Leonard, Peter (1997). *Postmodern welfare: Reconstructing an emancipatory project*. London, UK: Sage.

Martin, George (1990). *Social policy in the welfare state*. Englewood Cliffs, NJ: Prentice-Hall.

Williams, Fiona (1989). *Social policy: A critical introduction—Issues of race, gender and class*. New York, NY: Basil Blackwell.

Chapter 1

Baines, Donna (Ed.) (2011). *Doing anti-oppressive practice: Social justice social work*. 2nd ed. Winnipeg, MB: Fernwood.

Banks, Sarah (2008). Critical commentary: Social work ethics. *British Journal of Social Work, 38*(6), 1238–1249.

Banting, Keith G. (1982). *The welfare state and Canadian federalism*. Montreal, QC, and Kingston, ON: McGill-Queen's University Press.

Benn, S. I., & Peters, R. S. (1959). *Social principles and the democratic state*. London, UK: Allen & Unwin.

Biehal, Nina, & Sainsbury, Eric (1991). From values to rights in social work. *British Journal of Social Work, 21*, 245–257.

Canadian Association of Social Workers (CASW) (2005). *Code of ethics*. Ottawa, ON: CASW.

Carniol, Ben (2010). *Case critical*. Toronto, ON: Between the Lines.

CCSWR (Canadian Council of Social Work Regulators) (2012). Entry-level competency profile for the social work profession in Canada. Retrieved from: http://www.ccswr-ccorts.ca/publications-resources.

Chandler, Robert G. (1995). The profession of social work. In Joanne C. Turner & Francis J. Turner (Eds), *Canadian social welfare*. Scarborough, ON: Allyn & Bacon.

Clark, C. L., & Asquith, A (1985). *Social work and social philosophy*. London, UK: Routledge & Kegan Paul.

Djao, Angela (1983). *Inequality and social policy*. Toronto, ON: John Wiley & Sons.

Dominelli, Lena (2010). *Social work in a globalizing world*. Cambridge, UK: Polity.

Ferguson, Iain, Lavalette, Michael, & Whitmore, Elizabeth (2005). *Globalisation, global justice and social work*. London, UK: Routledge.

Finn, Janet L., & Jacobson, Maxine (2003). Just practice: Steps toward a new social work paradigm. *Journal of Social Work Education, 39*(1), 57–76.

Fook, Jan (1993). *Radical casework: A theory of practice*. St Leonards, New South Wales: Allen & Unwin.

Fraser, Heather, & Briskman, Linda (2004). Through the eye of a needle: The challenge of getting justice in Australia if you're Indigenous or seeking asylum. In Iain Ferguson, Michael Lavalette, & Elizabeth Whitmore (Eds), *Globalisation, global justice and social work* (pp. 109–123). London, UK: Routledge.

Friedmann, John (1973). The public interest and community participation: Toward a reconstruction of public philosophy. *Journal of the American Institute of Planners, 39*(1), 2–12.

Furniss, Norman, & Tilton, Timothy (1977). *The case for the welfare state*. Bloomington, IN: Indiana University Press.

Galper, Jeffry (1975). *The politics of social services*. Englewood Cliffs, NJ: Prentice-Hall.

Gandhi, Leela. (1998). *Postcolonial theory: A critical introduction*. St Leonards, New South Wales: Allen and Unwin.

Gil, David G. (1976). Social policies and social development: A humanistic-egalitarian perspective. *Journal of Sociology and Social Welfare, 3*(3), 242–263.

Gil, David G. (1990). Implications of conservative tendencies for practice and education in social welfare. *Journal of Sociology and Social Welfare, 17*(2), 20–21.

Gil, David G. (1998). *Confronting injustice and oppression: Concepts and strategies for social workers*. New York, NY: Columbia University Press.

Gil, David G. (2013). *Confronting injustice and oppression: Concepts and strategies for social workers* (updated with new preface). New York, NY: Columbia University Press.

Goroff, Norman (1981). Humanism and social work paradoxes, problems, and promises. *Journal of Sociology and Social Welfare, 8*(1), 1–9.

Hardy, Jean (1981a). *Values in social work*. London, UK: Routledge & Kegan Paul.

Hardy, Jean (1981b). *Values in social policy: Nine contradictions*. London, UK: Routledge & Kegan Paul.

Harrington, Michael (1962). *The other America*. New York, NY: Macmillan.

Heller, Agnes (1987). *Beyond justice*. New York, NY: Basic Books.

Hick, Stephen (2010). *Social work in Canada: An introduction*. Toronto, ON: Thompson Educational Publishing.

Howe, David (1987). *An introduction to social work theory*. Aldershot, UK: Wildwood House.

Ife, Jim (1997). *Rethinking social work: Towards critical practice*. Lance Cove, New South Wales: Addison Wesley Longman.

International Federation of Social Workers & International Association of Schools of Social Work (2005, 2012). *Ethics in social work, Statement of principles*. Berne, Switzerland. Retrieved from: www.ifsw.org.

Jennissen, Therese, & Lundy, Colleen (2011). *One hundred years of social work: A history of the profession in English Canada*. Waterloo, ON: Wilfrid Laurier University Press.

Lees, Ray (1972). *Politics and social work*. London, UK: Routledge & Kegan Paul.

McQuaig, Linda (1993). *The wealthy banker's wife: The assault on equality in Canada*. Toronto ON: Penguin Books.

McQuaig, Linda (2001). *All you can eat: Greed, lust and the new capitalism*. Toronto, ON: Viking.

Marx, K. (1844). Letter from Marx to Arnold Ruge in Dresden. Deutsch-Französische Jahrbücher (Zodiac, Trans.). Marxist Internet Archive. Retrieved from: https://www.marxists.org/archive/marx/works/1843/letters/43_09-alt.htm.

Mishra, Ramesh B. (1981). *Society and social policy*. 2nd rev. edn. London, UK: Macmillan.

Moreau, Maurice, & Leonard, Lynn (1989). *Empowerment through a structural approach to social work*. Ottawa, ON: Carleton University School of Social Work and Health and Welfare Canada.

Morgaine, Karen, & Capous-Desyllas, Moshoula (2015). *Anti-oppressive social work practice: Putting theory into action*. Los Angeles, CA: Sage.

Moscovitch, Allan, & Drover, Glen (Eds) (1981). *Inequality: Essays on the political economy of social welfare*. Toronto, ON: University of Toronto Press.

Mullaly, Robert (Bob) (2006). Forward to the past: The 2005 CASW Code of Ethics. *Canadian Social Work Review/Revue Canadienne de Service Social*, 23, 125–150.

Mullaly, Bob (2010). *Challenging oppression: A critical social work approach*. 2nd edn. Don Mills, ON: Oxford University Press.

Mullaly, Robert P., & Keating, Eric F. (1991). Similarities, differences and dialectics of radical social work. *Journal of Progressive Human Services*, 2(2), 49–78.

Naiman, Joanne (1997). *How societies work: Class, power and change in a Canadian context*. Toronto, ON: Irwin Publishing.

Pateman, C. (1970). *Participation and democratic theory*. Cambridge, UK: Cambridge University Press.

Payne, M. (1997). *Modern social work theory*. Chicago, IL: Lyceum Books.

Pease, Bob (2003). Rethinking the relationship between self and society. In June Allan, Bob Pease, & Linda Briskman (Eds), *Critical social work: An introduction to theories and practices* (p. 8). Crows Nest, New South Wales: Allen and Unwin.

Pincus, Allen, & Minahan, Anne (1973). *Social work practice: Model and method*. Itasca, IL: F.E. Peacock.

Rojek, C., Peacock, G., & Collins, S. (1988). *Social work and received ideas*. London, UK: Routledge & Kegan Paul.

Rubington, Earl, & Weinberg, S. Martin (Eds) (2010). *The study of social problems: Seven perspectives*. 7th edn. New York, NY: Oxford University Press.

Saiflin, Murad, & Dixon, Richard W. (Eds) (1984). *Dictionary of philosophy*. New York, NY: International Publishers.

Schneider, Robert L., & Lester, Lori (2001). *Social work advocacy: A new framework for advocacy*. Belmont, CA: Brooks/Cole.

Selizam, E. (Ed.) (1944). *Encyclopaedia of social sciences*. New York, NY: Macmillan.

Staggenborg, Susan (2012). *Social movements*. New York, NY: Oxford University Press.

Statham, Daphne (1978). *Radicals in social work*. London, UK: Routledge & Kegan Paul.

Taylor, Charles (1985). *Philosophy and the human sciences*. Cambridge, UK: Cambridge University Press.

Trainor, Brian T. (1996). *Radicalism, feminism and fanaticism: Social work in the nineties*. Aldershot, UK: Avebury.

Weinberg, Merlinda (2010). The social construction of social work ethics: Politicizing and broadening the lens. *Journal of Progressive Human Services*, 21(1), 32–44.

Wharf, Brian, & Cossom, John (1987). Citizen participation and social policy. In Shankar A. Yelaja (Ed.), *Canadian social policy*, 2nd edn (pp. 266–287). Waterloo, ON: Wilfrid Laurier University Press.

Wilensky, Harold L., & Lebeaux, Charles N. (1958; 1965). *Industrial society and social welfare*. New York, NY: Russell Sage Foundation.

Withorn, Ann (1984). *Serving the people: Social services and social change*. New York, NY: Columbia University Press.

Young, Iris Marion (1990). *Justice and the politics of difference*. Princeton, NJ: Princeton University Press.

Chapter 2

Ambrosino, Rosalie, Heffernan, Joseph, Shuttlesworth, Guy, & Ambrosino, Robert (2015). *Empowerment series: Social work and social welfare*. Toronto, ON: Nelson Education.

Armitage, Andrew (2003). *Social welfare in Canada*. 4th edn. Don Mills, ON: Oxford University Press.

Aronson, Jane, & Hemingway, Dawn (2011). "Competence" in neoliberal times. *Canadian Social Work Review 28,* (2), 281–285.

Aronson, J., & Sammon, S. (2000). Practice amid social service cuts and restructuring: Working with the contradictions of "small victories." *Canadian Social Work Review, 17*(2), 167–187.

Baines, Donna (Ed.) (2011). *Doing anti-oppressive practice: Social justice social work.* 2nd edn. Winnipeg, MB: Fernwood.

Bandopadhyay, Pradeep (1971). One sociology or many: Some issues in radical sociology. *Sociological Review, 19*(1), 5–29.

Bastow, Steve, & Martin, James (2003). *Third Way discourse: European ideologies in the twentieth century.* Edinburgh, UK: Edinburgh University Press.

Berg, Andrew G., & Ostry, Jonathan D. (2011). Equality and efficiency. *Finance and Development, 48*(3), 3 (International Monetary Fund, Sept 2011).

Berger, Peter L., & Luckmann, Thomas (1966). *The social construction of reality.* New York, NY: Doubleday.

Beveridge, W. (1942). *Social insurance and allied services* (the Beveridge Report). London, UK: HMSO, CMND 6404.

Bonneycastle, Colin R. (2006). From social equality to compassion: A critique of the 2005 CASW code of ethics. *Canadian Social Work Review, 23*(1–2), 77–93.

Borland, Jeff, Gregory, Bob, & Sheehan, Peter (2001). Inequality and economic change. In Jeff Borland, Bob Gregory, & Peter Sheehan (Eds), *Work rich, work poor* (pp. 1–20). Melbourne, Victoria: Victoria University.

Bricker-Jenkins, Mary (1997). Hidden treasures: Unlocking strengths in the public social services. In Denis Saleeby (Ed.), *The strength perspective in social work practice,* 2nd edn (pp. 133–150). New York, NY: Longman.

Burghardt, Steve (1982). *The other side of organizing: Resolving the personal dilemmas and political demands of daily practice.* Cambridge, MA: Schenkman.

Burke, Mike, Mooers, Colin, & Shields, John (Eds) (2000). *Restructuring and resistance: Canadian public policy in the age of global capitalism.* Halifax, NS: Fernwood.

Callaghan, J. (2000). *The retreat of social democracy.* Manchester, UK: Manchester: University Press.

Callahan, Marilyn, & Swift, Karen (2006). Back to the present: Rethinking risk assessment in child welfare. In Anne Westhues (Ed.), *Canadian social policy: Issues and perspectives.* 4th edn. Waterloo, ON: Wilfrid Laurier University Press.

Canadian Association of Social Workers (CASW) (2004a). *Women's income and poverty in Canada revisited.* Ottawa, ON: CASW.

Canadian Association of Social Workers (CASW) (2004b). *Gendering the poverty line.* Ottawa, ON: CASW.

Canadian Association of Social Workers (CASW) (2005). *Code of ethics.* Ottawa, ON: CASW.

Canadian Business (1985). Still nursing after all these years: A special report. Jan., 69–70.

Canadian Centre for Policy Alternatives (1995). *CCPA Monitor.* July–Aug., 12.

Carniol, Ben (1979). A critical approach in social work. *Canadian Journal of Social Work Education, 5*(1), 95–111.

Carniol, Ben (1984). Clash of ideologies in social work education. *Canadian Social Work Review, 2,* 184–199.

Carniol, Ben (2010). *Case critical.* Toronto, ON: Between the Lines.

Chappel, Rosalie (2013). *Social welfare in Canadian society.* 2nd edn. Scarborough, ON: Nelson.

Cornforth, M. (1953). *Materialism and the dialectical method.* New York, NY: International Publishers.

Corrigan, Paul, & Leonard, Peter (1978). *Social work practice under capitalism: A Marxist approach.* London, UK: Macmillan.

De Maria, William (1982). Fumbling with the kaleidoscope: World view clashes in social work. *Canadian Journal of Social Work Education, 8*(1–2), 31–44.

De Souza, Mike (2007). Harper's anti-Kyoto letter fuels Liberal counterattack. *Ottawa Citizen,* 31 Jan., A3; cited in Donald Gutstein (2014), *Harperism: How Stephen Harper and think tank colleagues have transformed Canada* (p. 140). Toronto, ON: James Lorimer.

Djao, Angela (1983). *Inequality and social policy.* Toronto, ON: John Wiley & Sons.

Dominelli, Lena (1996). Deprofessionalizing social work: Anti-oppressive practice, competencies and postmodernism. *British Journal of Social Work, 26,* 153–175.

Dominelli, L. (2007). Contemporary challenges to social work education in the United Kingdom. *Australian Social Work, 60*(1), 29–45.

Drover, Glen, & Woodsworth, David (1978). Social welfare theory and social policy. *Canadian Journal of Social Work Education, 4*(1), 19–41.

Dupre, Marilyn E. (2013). *Social work education and disability: A multicase study of approaches to disability in core and specialized curricula at three bachelor of social work programs.* Unpublished PhD Study, University of Manitoba, Faculty of Social Work.

Dykema, C. R. (1977). The political economy of social welfare: A perspective. *Journal of Sociology and Social Welfare, 4*(3–4), 439–469.

Esping-Andersen, Gotta (1989). The three political economies of the welfare state. *Canadian Review of Sociology and Anthropology, 26*(11), 10–36.

Fabricant, Michael B., & Burghardt, Steve (1992). *The welfare state crisis and the transformation of social service work.* Armonk, NY: M.E. Sharpe.

Ferguson, Iain (2008). *Reclaiming social work: Challenging neo-liberalism and promoting social justice.* London, UK: Sage.

Ferguson, Iain, & Lavalette, Michael (2005). Another world is possible. In Iain Ferguson, Michael Lavalette, & Elizabeth Whitmore (Eds), *Globalisation, global justice and social work* (pp. 207–223). London, UK: Routledge.

Ferguson, Iain, Lavalette, Michael, & Mooney, Gerry (2002). *Rethinking welfare: A critical perspective*. London, UK: Sage.

Ferguson, Iain, & Woodward, Rona (2009). *Radical social work in practice: Making a difference*. Bristol, UK: The Policy Press.

Financial Times (London) (2000). 4 February, 5.

Findlay, P. G. (1978). Theories of the state and social welfare in Canada. *Canadian Journal of Social Work Education, 14*(1), 109–128.

Finn, Janet L., & Jacobson, Maxine (2003). Just practice: Steps toward a new social work paradigm. *Journal of Social Work Education, 39*(1), 57–76.

Fisher, Robert, & Karger, Howard J. (1997). *Social work and community in a private world: Getting out in public*. White Plains, NY: Longman.

Fook, Jan (2000). Critical perspectives on social work practice. In I. O'Connor, P. Smyth, & J. Warburton (Eds), *Contemporary perspectives on social work and the human services: Challenges and change* (pp. 128–138). St Leonards, New South Wales: Pearson Education.

Fook, Jan (2002). *Social work: Critical theory and practice*. London, UK: Sage.

Fook, Jan (2011). The politics of competency debates. *Canadian Social Work Review, 28*(2), 295–298.

Ford, Julienne (1975). *Paradigms and fairy tales: An introduction to the science of meanings*. London, UK: Routledge & Kegan Paul.

Franklin, R. (1989). Wimps and bullies: Press reporting of child abuse; cited in P. Carter, T. Jeffs, & M. Smith (Eds), *Social work and social welfare yearbook*. Philadelphia, PA: Open University Press.

Freedland, Jonathan (2005). Enough of the love-in: Bush was a compassionate conservative too. *The Guardian*, 7 December.

Fukuyama, Francis (1992). *The end of history and the last man*. New York, NY: Free Press.

Galper, Jeffry (1975). *The politics of social services*. Englewood Cliffs, NJ: Prentice-Hall.

Galper, Jeffry (1980). *Social work practice: A radical perspective*. Englewood Cliffs, NJ: Prentice-Hall.

Garrett, P. (1999). Mapping child-care social work in the final years of the twentieth century: A critical response to the "looking after children" system. *British Journal of Social Work, 29*, 27–47.

George, Vic, & Wilding, Paul (1976). *Ideology and social welfare*. London, UK: Routledge & Kegan Paul.

George, Vic, & Wilding, Paul (1984). *The impact of social policy*. London, UK: Routledge & Kegan Paul.

George, Vic, & Wilding, Paul (1985). *Ideology and social welfare*. 2nd edn. London, UK: Routledge & Kegan Paul.

George, Vic, & Wilding, Paul (1994). *Welfare and ideology*. London, UK: Harvester Wheatsheaf.

George, Vic, & Wilding, Paul (2002). *Globalization and human welfare*. Basingstoke, UK: Palgrave.

Gough, Ian (1979). *The political economy of the welfare state*. London, UK: Macmillan.

Government of Canada (2005). *Economic and fiscal update*. Department of Finance, 14 Nov.

Gray, John (1998). *False dawn: The delusions of global capitalism*. London, UK: Granta Books.

Guest, Dennis (1997). *The emergence of social security in Canada*. 3rd edn. Vancouver: UBC Press.

Gutstein, Donald (2014). *Harperism: How Stephen Harper and think tank colleagues have transformed Canada*. Toronto, ON: James Lorimer.

Harmes, Adam (2004). *The return of the state: Protestors, power-brokers and the new global compromise*. Vancouver, BC: Douglas & McIntyre.

Harris, J. (1998). Scientific management, bureau-professionalism, new managerialism: The labour process of state social work. *British Journal of Social Work, 28*(6), 839–862.

Harris, J. (2003). *The social work business*. London, UK: Sage.

Hart, Michael Anthony (2002). *Seeking Mino-Pimatisawin: An Aboriginal approach to helping*. Halifax, NS: Fernwood.

Hart, Michael (2006). An Aboriginal approach to social work practice. In T. Heinonen & L. Spearman (Eds), *Social work practice: Problem solving and beyond*, 2nd edn. Toronto, ON: Irwin Press.

Hart, Michael (2007). *Cree ways of helping: An Indigenist research project*. PhD thesis, Faculty of Social Work, University of Manitoba.

Harvey, David (1989). *The condition of postmodernity: An enquiry into the origins of cultural change*. Cambridge, UK: Basil Blackwell.

Hattersley, R. (2001). It's no longer my party. *The Guardian*, 24 June.

Hay, C. (1999). *The political economy of New Labour: Labouring under false pretences?* Manchester, UK: Manchester University Press.

Haynes, Karen, & Mickelson, James S. (1992). Social work and the Reagan era: Challenges to the profession. *Journal of Sociology and Social Welfare, 19*(1), 169–183.

Head, S. (1996). The new ruthless economy. *The New York Review, 43*(4) (29 Feb.)

Healy, Karen (1999). Power and activist social work. In Bob Pease & Janis Fook (Eds), *Transforming social work practice*. Sydney, New South Wales: Allen and Unwin.

Healy, Karen (2000). *Social work practices: Contemporary perspectives on change*. London, UK: Sage.

Healy, Karen (2002). Managing human services in a market environment: What role for social workers? *British Journal of Social Work, 32*(5) (August).

Herbert, M. (2003). *Canadian Association of Social Workers Child Welfare Project: Creating conditions for good practice.* Ottawa: Canadian Association of Social Workers.

Howe, David (1994). Modernity, postmodernity and social work. *British Journal of Social Work, 24,* 513–532.

Hunsley, Terry (1987). *Future directions and challenges in social development.* Discussion paper. Ottawa: Canadian Council on Social Development.

Ife, Jim (1997). *Rethinking social work. Towards critical practice.* Lance Cove, New South Wales: Addison Wesley Longman.

Jeffrey, Brooke (2015). *Dismantling Canada: Stephen Harper's new Conservative agenda.* Montreal, QC: McGill-Queen's University Press.

Jenson, Jane (1989). Different but not "exceptional": Canada's permeable Fordism. *Canadian Review of Sociology and Anthropology, 20*(1), 69–94.

Jones, Howard (Ed.) (1975). *Towards a new social work.* London, UK: Routledge & Kegan Paul.

Karger, Howard Jacob (1987). Ideology and the crisis of the welfare state. *Quarterly Journal of Ideology: A Critique of Conventional Wisdom, 11*(1), 3–11.

Kerans, Patrick (1978). Social science and ideology in policy analysis. *Canadian Journal of Social Work Education, 4*(1), 129–141.

Kuhn, Thomas S. (1962; 1970). *The structure of scientific revolutions.* Chicago, IL: University of Chicago Press.

Leonard, Peter (1975). Explanation and education in social work. *British Journal of Social Work, 5*(3), 325–333.

Leonard, Peter (1994). Knowledge/power and postmodernism. *Canadian Social Work Review, 11*(1), 11–26.

Leonard, Peter (1995). Postmodernism, socialism and social welfare. *Journal of Progressive Human Services, 6*(2), 3–19.

Leonard, Peter (1997). *Postmodern welfare: Reconstructing an emancipatory project.* London, UK: Sage.

Leonard, Stephen T. (1990). *Critical theory in political practice.* Princeton, NJ: Princeton University Press.

Lightman, Ernie (2003). *Social policy in Canada.* Don Mills, ON: Oxford University Press.

Lightman, E., & Irving, A. (1991). Restructuring Canada's welfare state. *Journal of Social Policy, 20*(1), 65–86.

Lowenberg, Frank M. (1984). Professional ideology, middle range theories and knowledge building for social work practice. *British Journal of Social Work, 14,* 309–322.

Lundy, Colleen (2004; 2011). *Social work and social justice: A structural approach to practice.* Peterborough, ON: Broadview Press.

McBride, S. (2001). *Paradigm shift: Globalization and the Canadian state.* Halifax: Fernwood.

McGilly, Frank (1998). *An Introduction to Canada's public social services: Understanding income and health programs.* 2nd edn. Don Mills, ON: Oxford University Press.

McKenna, Francis (1985). Corporate welfare—Alive and well in the 1980s. *Perception, 8*(5), 25–26.

McLaren, P., & Leonard, Peter (Eds) (1993). *Paulo Freire: A critical encounter.* London, UK: Routledge.

McNally, David (2002). *Another world is possible: Globalization and anti-capitalism.* Winnipeg, MB: Arbeiter Ring.

Marquand, D. (1999). Premature obsequies: Social democracy comes in from the cold. In A. Gamble & T. Wright, *The New Social Democracy.* Oxford, UK: Blackwell.

Marshall, Gordon (Ed.) (1998). *A dictionary of sociology.* Oxford Reference Online [www.oxfordreference.com]. Oxford, UK: Oxford University Press.

Masterman, M. (1970). The nature of a paradigm. In I. Lakatos & A. Musgrave (Eds), *Criticism and the growth of knowledge* (pp. 59–89). Cambridge, UK: Cambridge University Press.

Mendes, Philip (2003). *Australia's welfare wars: The players, the politics and the ideologies.* Sydney, New South Wales: University of New South Wales Press.

Midgely, James (1992). Introduction: American social policy and the Reagan legacy. Special issue on the Reagan legacy and the American welfare state, *Journal of Sociology and Social Welfare, 19*(1), 3–11.

Mishra, Ramesh (1984). *The welfare state in crisis.* New York, NY: St Martin's Press.

Mishra, Ramesh (1989). Riding the new wave: Social work and the neo-conservative challenge. *International Social Work, 32*(3), 171–182.

Mishra, Ramesh (1990). *The welfare state in capitalist society.* Toronto, ON: University of Toronto Press.

Mishra, Ramesh (1999). *Globalization and the welfare state.* Cheltenham, UK: Edward Elgar.

Mitchell, Terry, & Curtis, Lori (2013). Canada, First Nations have a road map. It was the Kelowna Accord. *The Globe and Mail,* 13 January.

Moreau, Maurice, & Leonard, Lynne (1989). *Empowerment through a structural approach to social work.* Ottawa, ON, and Montreal, QC: Carleton University School of Social Work and École de service social, Université de Montréal.

Morgan, Kimberly J. (2013). America's misguided approach to social welfare: How the country could get more for less. *Foreign Affairs,* Jan./Feb.

Mullaly, Robert (1984). Social welfare: Vigilante style. *Perception, 8*(2), 23–25.

Mullaly, Robert (1994). Social welfare and the New Right: A class mobilization perspective. In Andrew F. Johnson, Stephen McBride, & Patrick J. Smith (Eds), *Continuities and discontinuities: The political economy of social welfare and labour market policy in Canada* (pp. 76–94). Toronto, ON: University of Toronto Press.

Mullaly, Robert (Bob) (2001). Confronting the politics of despair: Towards the reconstruction of progressive social work in a global economy and postmodern age. *Social Work Education, 20*(3), 303–320.

Mullaly, Robert (Bob) (2002). *Challenging oppression: A critical social work approach.* Don Mills, ON: Oxford University Press.

Mullaly, Bob (2007). *The new structural social work.* 3rd edn. Don Mills, ON: Oxford University Press.

National Council of Welfare (1975). *The hidden welfare system.* Ottawa, ON: Minister of Supply and Services.

National Council of Welfare (1979). *The hidden welfare system revisited.* Ottawa, ON: Minister of Supply and Services.

Oxfam International (2016). *An economy for the 1%.* A report published by Oxfam GB for Oxfam International. Cowley, UK: Oxfam House.

Parton, Nigel (1994). Problematics of government, (post) modernity and social work. *British Journal of Social Work, 24,* 9–32.

Parton, Nigel (1999). Reconfiguring child welfare practices: Risk, advanced liberalism, and the government of freedom. In Adrienne Chambon, Allan Irving, & Laura Epstein (Eds), *Reading Foucault for social work.* New York, NY: Columbia University Press.

Pease, Bob, & Fook, Janis (Eds) (1999). *Transforming social work practice: Postmodern critical perspectives.* St Leonards, New South Wales: Allen and Unwin.

Perspectives (1991). Editorial: A bleak year for social progress. *15*(2), 4–6.

Picard, André (2012). Harper's disregard for Aboriginal health. *The Globe and Mail,* 9 April.

Pritchard, Colin, & Taylor, Richard (1978). *Social work: Reform or revolution?* London, UK: Routledge & Kegan Paul.

Rees, S., & Rodley, G. (Eds) (1995). *The human costs of managerialism: Advocating the recovery of humanity.* Leichhardt, New South Wales: Pluto Press.

Riches, Graham (1986). *Food banks in Canada.* Ottawa: Canadian Council on Social Development.

Rossiter, Amy, & Heron, Barbara (2011). Neoliberalism, competencies, and the devaluating of social work practice. *Canadian Social Work Review, 28*(2), 305–309.

Saul, John Ralston (2004). The collapse of globalism and the rebirth of nationalism. *Harper's Magazine,* (March), 33–43.

Saul, John Ralston (2005). *The collapse of globalism and the reinvention of the world.* Toronto, ON: Viking Canada.

Sigurdson, Richard (2002). Political ideas and ideologies. In Rand Dyck (Ed.), *Studying politics: An introduction to political science* (pp. 97–121). Toronto, ON: Nelson Education.

Simpkin, Mike (1979). *Trapped within welfare: Surviving social work.* London, UK: Macmillan.

Stainton, Tim, & Swift, Karen (1996). "Difference" and social work curriculum. *Canadian Social Work Review, 13*(1), 75–87.

Steger, Manfred B. (2003). *Globalization: A very short introduction.* New York, NY: Oxford University Press.

Stephenson, M., Rondeau, G., Michaud, J. C., & Fiddler, S. (2000). *In critical demand: Social work in Canada. Volume 1 – final report.* Ottawa, ON: Canadian Association of Social Workers and Canadian Association of Schools of Social Work.

Teeple, Gary (2000). *Globalization and the decline of social reform: Into the twenty-first century.* 2nd edn. Aurora, ON: Garamond Press.

Thompson, Neil (1998). *Promoting equality: Challenging discrimination and oppression in the human services.* London, UK: Macmillan.

Titmuss, Richard M. (1963). *Essays on the welfare state.* Lincoln, UK: Unwin.

Tornebohm, Håkan (1977). *Paradigms in fields of research.* Report no. 93. Gothenburg, Sweden: University of Gothenburg, Dept. of Theory of Science.

Tudiver, N. (1993). Employee assistance plans: Who benefits? *Canadian Review of Social Policy/Revue canadienne de politique sociale, 32,* 74–81.

Vincent, A. (1998). New ideologies for old? *Political Quarterly, 69*(1), 48–58.

Wiggins, Cindy (1996). Dismantling unemployment insurance: The changes, the impacts, the reasons. *Canadian Review of Social Policy, 37,* 75–84.

Williams, Fiona (1989). *Social policy: A critical introduction—Issues of race, gender and class.* New York, NY: Basil Blackwell.

Wineman, Steven (1984). *The politics of human services.* Montreal, QC: Black Rose Books.

Zucman, G. (2014). Taxing across borders: Tracking personal wealth and corporate profits. *Journal of Economic Perspectives, 28*(4), 121–148.

Chapter 3

Butler, Stuart, & Kondratas, Anna (1987). *Out of the poverty Trap.* New York, NY: Free Press.

Coates, John (1991). Putting knowledge for practice into perspective. *Canadian Social Work Review, 8*(1), 82–96.

De Schweinitz, Karl (1943). *England's road to social security.* Philadelphia, PA: University of Pennsylvania Press.

Dickerson, Mark O., & Flanagan, Thomas (1986). *An introduction to government and politics: A conceptual approach.* Agincourt, ON: Methuen.

Djao, Angela (1983). *Inequality and social policy.* Toronto, ON: John Wiley & Sons.

Friedman, M. (1962). *Capitalism and freedom.* Chicago, IL: University of Chicago Press; cited in Djao (1983).

Furniss, Norman, & Tilton, Timothy (1977). *The case for the welfare state.* Bloomington, IN: Indiana University Press.

George, Vic, & Wilding, Paul (1976). *Ideology and social welfare.* London, UK: Routledge & Kegan Paul.

George, Vic, & Wilding, Paul (1985). *Ideology and social welfare*. 2nd edn. London, UK: Routledge & Kegan Paul.

George, Vic, & Wilding, Paul (1994). *Welfare and ideology*. London, UK: Harvester Wheatsheaf.

Gilder, George (1981). *Wealth and poverty*. New York, NY: Basic Books.

Green, Joyce (2000). Neoliberalism and neoconservatism. In Lorraine Code (Ed.), *The encyclopedia of feminist theories* (p. 364). New York, NY: Routledge.

Hobbes, Thomas (1981 [1651]). *Leviathan*, ed., C. B. MacPherson. Harmondsworth, UK: Penguin English Library.

Iatridis, Demetrius (1983). Neo-conservatism reviewed. *Social Work, 28*(2), 101–107.

Jeffrey, Brooke (2015). *Dismantling Canada: Stephen Harper's new conservative agenda*. Montreal, QC: McGill-Queen's University Press.

Lavalette, Michael, & Pratt, Alan. 1997. *Social policy: A conceptual and theoretical introduction*. London, UK: Sage.

Marchak, M. Patricia (1981). *Ideological perspectives on Canada*. 2nd edn. Toronto, ON: McGraw-Hill Ryerson.

Mead, L. (1986). *Beyond entitlement*. New York, NY: Free Press.

Mendes, Philip (2003). *Australia's welfare wars: The players, the politics and the ideologies*. Sydney, New South Wales: University of New South Wales Press.

Mill, John Stuart (1866). Letter to the Conservative MP Sir John Pakington (March). Retrieved from: http://myweb.uiowa.edu/jlcox/151millbrit.htm.

Mills, C. Wright (1959). *The sociological imagination*. New York, NY: Oxford University Press.

Mishra, Ramesh (1984). *The welfare state in crisis*. New York, NY: St Martin's Press.

Mishra, Ramesh (1989). Riding the new wave: Social work and the neo-conservative challenge. *International Social Work, 32*(3), 171–182.

Mullaly, Robert (1994). Social welfare and the new right: A class mobilization perspective. In Andrew F. Johnson, Stephen McBride, & Patrick J. Smith (Eds), *Continuities and Discontinuities: The political economy of social welfare and labour market policy in Canada* (pp. 76–94). Toronto, ON: University of Toronto Press.

Murray, Charles (1984). *Losing ground: American social policy 1950–1980*. New York, NY: Basic Books.

Naiman, Joanne (1997). *How societies work: Class, power and change in a Canadian context*. Toronto, ON: Irwin Publishing.

Porter, Ann (2012). Neo-conservatism, neo-liberalism and Canadian social policy: Challenges for feminism. *Canadian Women Studies, 29*(3), 19–31.

Pritchard, Colin, & Taylor, Richard (1978). *Social work: Reform or revolution?* London, UK: Routledge & Kegan Paul.

Resnick, P. (1984). The ideology of neo-conservatism. In Warren Magnussen et al. (Eds), *The new reality: The politics of restraint in British Columbia*. Vancouver, BC: New Star Books.

Rice, James J., & Prince, Michael J. (2000). *Changing politics of Canadian social policy*. Toronto, ON: University of Toronto Press.

Riches, Graham (1986). *Food banks in Canada*. Ottawa, ON: Canadian Council on Social Development.

Roberts, Geoffrey K. (1971). *A dictionary of political analysis*. New York, NY: St Martin's Press.

Rossiter, Clinton (1968). Conservatism. In David L. Sills (Ed.), *International encyclopaedia of the social sciences*, vol. 3 (pp. 290–294). New York, NY: Macmillan and The Free Press.

Rubington, Earl, & Weinberg, S. Martin (Eds) (2010). *The study of social problems: Seven perspectives*. 7th edn. New York, NY: Oxford University Press.

Scruton, Richard (1982). *A dictionary of political thought*. London, UK: Macmillan.

Sigurdson, Richard (2002). Political ideas and ideologies. In Rand Dyck (Ed.), *Studying Politics: An Introduction to Political Science* (pp. 97–121). Toronto, ON: Nelson Education.

Standing Committee on the Environment and Sustainable Development. Parliament Canada (2014). *Fall 2014 report of the Commissioner of the Environment and Sustainable Development*. Retrieved from: http://www.oag-bvg.gc.ca/internet/English/parl_cesd_201410_e_39845.html.

Stoez, D., & Karger, H. (1990). Welfare reform: From illusion to reality. *Social Work, 35*(2), 141–147.

Wilensky, Harold L., & Lebeaux, Charles N. (1958; 1965). *Industrial society and social welfare*. New York, NY: Russell Sage Foundation.

Chapter 4

Baines, Donna (Ed.) (2011). *Doing anti-oppressive practice: Social justice social work*. 2nd edn. Winnipeg, MB: Fernwood.

Bastow, Steve, & Martin, James (2003). *Third Way discourse: European ideologies in the twentieth century*. Edinburgh, UK: Edinburgh University Press.

Bell, David, & Tepperman, Lorne (1979). *The roots of disunity: A look at Canadian political culture*. Toronto, ON: McClelland & Stewart.

Campbell, Colin, & Christian, William (1999). *Parties, leaders, and ideologies in Canada*. Toronto, ON: McGraw-Hill Ryerson.

Carniol, Ben (1984). Clash of ideologies in social work education. *Canadian Social Work Review, 2*, 184–199.

Coates, John (1991). Putting knowledge for practice into perspective. *Canadian Social Work Review, 8*(1), 82–96.

Curtis, James, Grabb, Edward, Guppy, Neil, & Gilbert, Sid (1988). *Social inequality in Canada: Patterns, problems, policies*. Scarborough, ON: Prentice-Hall Canada.

Dickerson, Mark O., & Flanagan, Thomas (1986). *An introduction to government and politics: A conceptual approach*. Agincourt, ON: Methuen.

Djao, Angela (1983). *Inequality and social policy.* Toronto, ON: John Wiley & Sons.

Freeden, M. (1978). *The new liberalism: An ideology of social reform.* Oxford, UK: Clarendon.

Galper, Jeffry (1975). *The politics of social services.* Englewood Cliffs, NJ: Prentice-Hall.

George, Vic, & Wilding, Paul (1976). *Ideology and social welfare.* London, UK: Routledge & Kegan Paul.

George, Vic, & Wilding, Paul (1985). *Ideology and social welfare.* 2nd edn. London, UK: Routledge & Kegan Paul.

Germain, Carol (Ed.) (1979). *Social work practice: People and environment: An ecological perspective.* New York, NY: Columbia University Press.

Gil, David G. (1976). *The challenge of social equality.* Cambridge, MA: Schenkman.

Government of Canada. Office of the Correctional Investigator (2014). *Annual Report (2013–2014).* Retrieved from: http://www.oci-bec.gc.ca/cnt/rpt/pdf/annrpt/annrpt20132014-eng.pdf.

Gray, John (1998). *False dawn: The delusions of global capitalism.* London, UK: Granta Books.

Guest, Dennis (1985). *The emergence of social security in Canada.* 1st and 2nd edns. Vancouver, BC: University of British Columbia Press.

Heinonen, Tuula, & Spearman, Len (2009). *Social work practice: Problem solving and beyond.* 3rd edn. Toronto, ON: Nelson Education.

Hobhouse, L. T. (1994). *Liberalism and other writings,* ed. J. Meadowcroft. Cambridge, UK: Cambridge University Press.

Horowitz, Gad (1968). *Canadian labour in politics.* Toronto, ON: University of Toronto Press.

Horowitz, Gad. (1996). Conservatism, liberalism and socialism in Canada: An interpretation. *Canadian Journal of Economics and Political Science, 32*(2), 143–171.

Ives, Nicole, Denov, Myriam, & Sussman, Tamara. (2015). *Introduction to social work in Canada.* Toronto, ON: Oxford University Press.

Karger, Howard Jacob (1987). Ideology and the crisis of the welfare state. *Quarterly Journal of Ideology: A Critique of Conventional Wisdom, 11*(1), 3–11.

Lee, Bill (1986). *Pragmatics of community organization.* Mississauga, ON: Common Act Press.

Lees, Ray (1972). *Politics and social work.* London, UK: Routledge & Kegan Paul.

Liberal Party of Canada. 2015. *Real change: A fair and open government.* Available at: https://www.liberal.ca/files/2015/06/a-fair-and-open-government.pdf.

McCready, John (1980). *The context for Canadian social policy.* Working Papers on Social Welfare in Canada Series. Toronto, ON: University of Toronto Faculty of Social Work.

Marchak, M. Patricia (2011). *Ideological perspectives on Canada.* 6th edn. Montreal, QC: McGill-Queen's University Press.

Marsh, Leonard C. (1950). The welfare state: Is it a threat to Canada? In *Proceedings of the Canadian Conference on Social Work.* Ottawa, ON: Canadian Conference on Social Work.

Naiman, Joanne (1997). *How societies work: Class, power and change in a Canadian context.* Toronto, ON: Irwin Publishing.

O'Brien, Martin, & Penna, Sue (1998). *Theorising welfare: Enlightenment and modern society.* London, UK: Sage.

Pritchard, Colin, & Taylor, Richard (1978). *Social work: Reform or revolution?* London, UK: Routledge & Kegan Paul.

Roberts, Geoffrey K. (1971). *A dictionary of political analysis.* New York, NY: St Martin's Press.

Rubington, Earl, and Martin S. Weinberg (Eds) (1989; 1995). *The study of social problems.* 2nd and 3rd edns. New York, NY: Oxford University Press.

Sigurdson, Richard (2002). Political ideas and ideologies. In Rand Dyck (Ed.), *Studying politics: An introduction to political science* (pp. 97–121). Toronto, ON: Nelson Education.

Smith, David G. (1968). Liberalism. In David Sills (Ed.), *International encyclopaedia of the social sciences,* vol. 3 (pp. 276–292). New York, NY: Macmillan and The Free Press.

Trudeau, P.E. (1967, December 21). There's no place for the state in the bedrooms of the nation. CBC Television News [Video file]. Retrieved from http:www.cbc.ca/archives/entry/omnibus-bill-theres-no-place-for-the-state-in-the-bedrooms-of-the-nation.

Wilensky, Harold L., & Lebeaux, Charles N. (1965). *Industrial society and social welfare.* New York, NY: Russell Sage Foundation.

Chapter 5

Bastow, Steve, & Martin, James (2003). *Third Way discourse: European ideologies in the twentieth century.* Edinburgh, UK: Edinburgh University Press.

Becker, Howard, & Barnes, Harry Elmer (1978). *Social thought from lore to science, II.* Gloucester, MA: Peter Smith.

Berry, Christopher J. (1986). *Human nature.* Atlantic Highlands, NJ: Humanities Press International.

Dickerson, Mark O., & Flanagan, Thomas (1986). *An introduction to government and politics: A conceptual approach.* Agincourt, ON: Methuen.

Djao, Angela (1983). *Inequality and social policy.* Toronto, ON: John Wiley & Sons.

Esping-Andersen, Gotta (1990). *The three worlds of welfare capitalism.* Princeton, NJ: Princeton University Press.

Ferguson, Iain, Lavalette, Michael, & Mooney, Gerry (2002). *Rethinking welfare: A critical perspective.* London, UK: Sage.

Ferguson, Iain, & Woodward, Rona (2009). *Radical social work in practice: Making a difference.* Bristol, UK: The Policy Press.

Furniss, Norman, & Tilton, Timothy (1977). *The case for the welfare state.* Bloomington, IN: Indiana University Press.

George, Vic, & Wilding, Paul (1985). *Ideology and social welfare.* 2nd edn. London, UK: Routledge & Kegan Paul.

George, Vic, & Wilding, Paul (1994). *Welfare and ideology.* London, UK: Harvester Wheatsheaf.

Giddens, Anthony (1994). *Beyond left and right: The future of radical politics.* Cambridge, UK: Polity.

Gil, David. 1976. *The challenge of social equality.* Cambridge, MA: Schenkman.

Himmelstrand, Ulf, Ahrne, G., Lundberg, L., & Lundberg, L. (1981). *Beyond welfare capitalism.* London, UK: Heinemann.

Horton, John (1966). Order and conflict theories of social problems as competing ideologies. *American Journal of Sociology, 72*(May), 701–713.

Hughes, J. (1973). Nationalization and the private sector. In J. Urry & J. Wakeford (Eds), *Power in Britain.* London, UK: Heinemann.

Jacques, Martin (1990). After capitalism: What now? *Social Policy, 21*(2), 12–16.

Jordan, Bill, with Charlie Jordan (2000). *Social work and the Third Way: Tough love as social policy.* London, UK: Sage.

Leonard, Peter (1995). Postmodernism, socialism and social welfare. *Journal of Progressive Human Services, 6*(2), 3–19.

Leonard, Peter (1997). *Postmodern welfare: Reconstructing an emancipatory project.* London, UK: Sage.

Meacher, Michael (1977). The socialist alternative. In K. Coates and F. Singleton (Eds), *The just society* (pp. 135–148). Nottingham, UK: Spokesman Books.

Mendes, Philip (2003). *Australia's welfare wars: The players, the politics and the ideologies.* Sydney, New South Wales: University of New South Wales Press.

Mishra, Ramesh B. (1981). *Society and social policy.* 2nd rev. edn. London, UK: Macmillan.

Mishra, Ramesh (1999). *Globalization and the welfare state.* Cheltenham, UK: Edward Elgar.

Mullaly, Robert P., & Keating, Eric F. (1991). Similarities, differences and dialectics of radical social work. *Journal of Progressive Human Services, 2*(2), 49–78.

Naiman, Joanne (1997). *How societies work: Class, power and change in a Canadian context.* Toronto, ON: Irwin Publishing.

Nove, A. (1989). Socialism—Why? In H. B. McCullough (Ed.), *Political ideologies and political philosophies.* Toronto, ON: Thompson Educational Publishing.

Olsen, Gregg M. (2002).*The politics of the welfare state: Canada, Sweden, and the United States.* Don Mills, ON: Oxford University Press.

Pritchard, Colin, & Taylor, Richard (1978). *Social work: Reform or revolution?* London, UK: Routledge & Kegan Paul.

Reasons, Charles E., & Perdue, William D. (1981). *Ideology of social problems.* Scarborough, ON: Nelson Canada.

Roberts, Geoffrey K. (1971). *A dictionary of political analysis.* New York, NY: St Martin's Press.

Rule, J. B. (1971). The problem with social problems. *Politics and Society, 2*(1), 47–56.

Rundle, G. (1999). Break-out from the giggle palace: Social democracy, the postmodern economy and the prospects for political renewal. In G. Patmore & D. Glover (Eds), *New voices for social democracy: Labor essays 1999–2000* (pp. 159–172). Annandale, New South Wales: Pluto Press.

Scruton, Richard (1982). *A dictionary of political thought.* London, UK: Macmillan.

Sears, Alan, & Cairns, James (2015). *A good book, in theory.* 3rd edn. Toronto, ON: University of Toronto Press.

Sigurdson, Richard (2002). Political ideas and ideologies. In Rand Dyck (Ed.), *Studying politics: An introduction to political science* (pp. 97–121). Toronto: Nelson Education.

van Houton, Gerry (1992). Socialism today: Renewal or retreat? In J. Roberts & J. Vorst (Eds), *Socialism in crisis? Canadian perspectives* (pp. 117–146). Halifax, NS, and Winnipeg, MB: Fernwood Publishing and Society for Socialist Studies.

White, S. (2001). The ambiguities of the Third Way. In S. White (Ed.), *New Labour: The progressive future?* Basingstoke, UK: Palgrave.

Chapter 6

Bailey, Roy, & Brake, Mike (Eds) (1975). *Radical social work.* New York, NY: Pantheon Books.

Baines, Donna (Ed.) (2011). *Doing anti-oppressive practice: Social justice social work.* 2nd edn. Winnipeg, MB: Fernwood.

Berry, Christopher J. (1986). *Human nature.* Atlantic Highlands, NJ: Humanities Press International.

Blalock, Hubert M. (1967). *Toward a theory of minority group relations.* New York, NY: Wiley.

Blei, Daniela (2016). Is the Latin American Left dead? *New Republic,* 18 April. Retrieved from: https:/newrepublic.com/article/132779/latin-american-left-dead.

Buchbinder, H., Burstyn, V., Forbes, V., & Steedman, M (1987). *Who's on top? The politics of heterosexuality.* Toronto, ON: Garamond Press.

Cameron, Maxwell A., & Hershberg, Eric (Eds) (2010). *Latin America's left turn: Politics, policies, and trajectories of change.* Boulder, CO: Lynne Reinner Publishers.

Corrigan, Paul, & Leonard, Peter (1978). *Social work practice under capitalism: A Marxist approach.* London, UK: Macmillan.

Djao, Angela (1983). *Inequality and social policy.* Toronto, ON: John Wiley & Sons.

Ferguson, Iain, Lavalette, Michael, & Mooney, Gerry (2002). *Rethinking welfare: A critical perspective.* London, UK: Sage.

Ferguson, Iain, & Woodward, Rona (2009). *Radical social work in practice: Making a difference.* Bristol, UK: The Policy Press.

Finn, Ed (1979). Ontario's Bill 70 a major step in workplace safety: Unionist. *Toronto Star,* 19 Feb., quoted in Howard Buchbinder, Inequality and the social services, in Allan Moscovitch & Glen Drover (Eds) (1981), *Inequality: Essays on the political economy of social welfare.* Toronto, ON: University of Toronto Press.

Galper, Jeffry (1975). *The politics of social services.* Englewood Cliffs, NJ: Prentice-Hall.

Galper, Jeffry (1980). *Social work practice: A radical perspective.* Englewood Cliffs, NJ: Prentice-Hall.

George, Vic, & Wilding, Paul (1985). *Ideology and social welfare.* 2nd edn. London, UK: Routledge & Kegan Paul.

George, Vic, & Wilding, Paul (1994). *Welfare and ideology.* London, UK: Harvester Wheatsheaf.

Gough, Ian (1979). *The political economy of the welfare state.* London, UK: Macmillan.

Harvey, David (1989). *The condition of postmodernity: An enquiry into the origins of cultural change.* Cambridge, UK: Basil Blackwell.

Ife, Jim (1997). *Rethinking social work: Towards critical practice.* Lance Cove, New South Wales: Addison Wesley Longman.

Laski, H. (1925). *A grammar of politics.* London, UK: Allen & Unwin.

Leonard, Peter (1997). *Postmodern welfare: Reconstructing an emancipatory project.* London, UK: Sage.

Marx, Karl (1970 [1875]). Critique of the Gotha Program. In K. Marx and F. Engels, *Selected works,* vol. 3 (pp. 13–30). Moscow, USSR: Progress Publishers.

Marx, Karl. (1975 [1845]). Theses on Feuerbach. In K. Marx, *Early writings* (p. 423). Harmondsworth, UK: Penguin.

Marx, Karl, & Engels, Friedrich (1976). Reproduced from The ruling class and ruling ideas. In *Karl Marx, Friedrich Engels: Collected works,* vol. 5 (pp. 59–62), tr. Richard Dixon. New York, NY: International Publishers.

Mishra, Ramesh B. (1981). *Society and social policy.* 2nd rev. edn. London, UK: Macmillan.

Mishra, Ramesh (1984). *The welfare state in crisis.* New York, NY: St Martin's Press.

Mullaly, Robert (Bob) (2002). *Challenging oppression: A critical social work approach.* Don Mills, ON: Oxford University Press.

Mullaly, Bob (2010). *Challenging oppression: A critical social work approach.* 2nd edn. Don Mills, ON: Oxford University Press.

Mullaly, Bob, & West, Juliana (2018). *Challenging oppression and confronting privilege: A critical approach to* anti-oppressive and anti-privilege theory and practice. 3rd edn. Don Mills, ON: Oxford University Press.

O'Brien, Martin, & Penna, Sue (1998). *Theorising welfare: Enlightenment and modern society.* London, UK: Sage.

O'Connor, James (1973). *The fiscal crisis of the state.* New York: St Martin's Press.

Piven, Frances Fox, & Cloward, Richard A. (1972). *Regulating the poor: The public functions of welfare.* New York, NY: Random House.

Powell, Fred (2001). *The politics of social work.* London, UK: Sage.

Pritchard, Colin, & Taylor, Richard (1978). *Social work: Reform or revolution?* London. UK: Routledge & Kegan Paul.

Strachey, J. (1936). *The theory and practice of socialism.* London, UK: Victor Gollancz.

Throssell, Harold (Ed.) (1975). *Social work: Radical essays.* St Lucia, Queensland: University of Queensland Press.

Wineman, Steven (1984). *The politics of human services.* Montreal, QC: Black Rose Books.

Chapter 7

Agger, Ben (1989). *Socio(ontology): A disciplinary reading.* Urbana, IL: University of Illinois Press.

Agger, Ben (1992). *Cultural studies as critical theory.* London, UK: Falmer Press.

Agger, Ben (1998). *Critical social theories: An introduction.* Boulder, CO: Westview Press.

Armitage, Andrew (2003). *Social welfare in Canada.* 4th edn. Don Mills, ON: Oxford University Press.

Ashe, Fidelma (1999). The subject. In Fidelma Ashe, Alan Finlayson, Moya Lloyd, Iain MacKenzie, James Martin, & Shane O'Neill (Eds), *Contemporary social and political theory.* Buckingham, UK: Open University Press.

Auger, Jeanette A., & Krug, Kate (2013). *Under the rainbow: A primer on queer issues in Canada.* Halifax, NS: Fernwood.

Bailey, Z. D., Krieger, N., Agenor, M., Graves, J., Linos, N., & Bassett, M. T. (2017). Structural racism and health inequalities in the USA: Evidence and interventions. *The Lancet, 389*(10,077), 1453–1463.

Baskin, Cyndy (2016). *Strong helpers' teachings: The value of Indigenous knowledges in the helping professions.* Toronto, ON: Canadian Scholars' Press.

Bastow, Steve, & Martin, James (2003). *Third Way discourse: European ideologies in the twentieth century.* Edinburgh, UK: Edinburgh University Press.

Bell, Daniel (1965). *The end of ideology: On the exhaustion of political ideas in the fifties.* New York, NY: Free Press.

Brown, Leslie, & Strega, Susan (Eds) (2005). *Research as resistance: Critical, Indigenous, and anti-oppressive approaches.* Toronto, ON: Canadian Scholars' Press.

Butler, Judith (1990). *Gender trouble: Feminism and the subversion of identity.* New York, NY: Routledge.

Calixte, Shana L., Johnson, Jennifer L., & Motapanyane, J. Maki (2010). Liberal, socialist and radical feminism: An introduction to the three theories about women's oppression and social change. In Nancy Mandell (Ed.), *Feminist issues: Race, class and sexuality*. Toronto, ON: Pearson Canada.

Carter, J. (1998). Postmodernity and welfare: When worlds collide. *Social Policy and Administration, 32*(2), 101–105.

Chambon, Adrienne S., & Irving, Allan (Eds) (1994). *Essays on postmodernism and social work*. Toronto, ON: Canadian Scholars' Press.

Chambon, Adrienne S., Irving, Allan, & Epstein, Laura (Eds) (1999). *Reading Foucault for social work*. New York, NY: Columbia University Press.

Davis, A. (1981). *Women, race and class*. London, UK: Women's Press.

Davis, Lennard. 2014. *The end of normal: Identity in a bio-cultural era*. Ann Arbor, MI: University of Michigan Press.

DePoy, Elizabeth, & French Gilson, Stephen. (2011). *Studying disability: Multiple theories and responses*. Thousand Oaks, CA: Sage.

Dominelli, Lena (2012). *Green social work: From environmental crisis to environmental justice*. Cambridge, UK: Polity.

Fairclough, Norman (1992). Discourse and text: Linguistic and intertextual analysis within discourse analysis. *Discourse and Society, 3*(2), 193–217.

Ferguson, Iain, & Lavalette, Michael (1999). Social work, postmodernism and Marxism. *European Journal of Social Work, 2*, 1.

Ferguson, Iain, Lavalette, Michael, & Mooney, Gerry (2002). *Rethinking welfare: A critical perspective*. London, UK: Sage.

Firestone, Shulamith (1970). *The dialectic of sex: The case for feminist revolution*. New York, NY: Bantam Books.

Firestone, Shulamith (1984). The dialectic of sex. In Alison M. Jaggar & Paula S. Rothenberg (Eds), *Feminist frameworks*. New York, NY: McGraw-Hill.

Fitzpatrick, Tony (2002). In search of a welfare democracy. *Social Policy and Society, 1*(1), 11–20.

Foucault, Michel (1978). *The history of sexuality, Volume I: An introduction*. New York, NY: Penguin.

Foucault, Michel (1980). *Power/knowledge: Selected interviews and other writings 1972–1977*, ed. Colin Gordon. New York, NY: Pantheon.

Fukuyama, Francis (1992). *The end of history and the last man*. New York, NY: Free Press.

Gazso, A. (2010). Mothers' maintenance of families through market and family care relations. In M. Mandell (Ed.), *Feminist issues: Race, class, and sexuality*. 5th edn. (pp. 219–246). Toronto, ON: Pearson Canada.

Globe and Mail (2016). Jane Taber: "Women are under-represented in all levels of government." 2 June. Retrieved from: https://www.theglobeandmail.com/news/politics/women-are-under-represented-in-all-levels-of-government/article30255608.

Harvey, David (1989). *The condition of postmodernity: An enquiry into the origins of cultural change*. Cambridge, UK: Basil Blackwell.

hooks, bell (1990). Postmodern blackness. *Postmodern Culture, 1*(1).

Howe, David (1994). Modernity, postmodernity and social work. *British Journal of Social Work, 24*, 513–532.

Husband, Charles (1987). Introduction: "Race," the continuity of a concept. In Charles Husband (Ed.), *Race in Britain: Continuity and change*. London, UK: Hutchison.

Jeffreys, S. (1986). *The spinster and her enemies*. London, UK: Pandora Press.

Karaian, Lara, & Mitchell, Allison (2010). Third-wave feminisms. In Nancy Mandell (Ed.), *Feminist issues: Race, class, and sexuality*, 5th edn. Toronto, ON: Pearson Canada.

Kerr, Anne and Shakespeare, Tom (2002). *Genetic politics: From eugenics to genome*. London, UK: New Clarion Press.

Knight, Melanie, & Rodgers, Kathleen (2012). "The government is operationalizing neo-liberalism": Women's organizations, Status of Women Canada, and the struggle for progressive social change in Canada. *NORA—Nordic Journal of Feminist and Gender Research, 20*(4), 266–282.

Knuttila, Murray (2002). *Introducing sociology: A critical perspective*. 2nd edn. Don Mills, ON: Oxford University Press.

Knuttila, Murray, & Kubik, Wendee (2000). *State theories: Classical, global and feminist perspectives*. 3rd edn. Halifax, NS: Fernwood.

Lemert, Charles (1994). Post-structuralism and sociology. In Steven Seidman (Ed.), *The postmodern turn: New perspectives on social theory* (pp. 265–281). Cambridge, UK: Cambridge University Press.

Leonard, Peter (1994). Knowledge/power and postmodernism. *Canadian Social Work Review, 11*(1), 11–26.

Leonard, Peter (1995). Postmodernism, socialism and social welfare. *Journal of Progressive Human Services, 6*(2), 3–19.

Leonard, Peter (1997). *Postmodern welfare: Reconstructing an emancipatory project*. London, UK: Sage.

Lerner, Gerda (1979). *The majority finds its past: Placing women in history*. New York, NY: Oxford University Press.

Lloyd, Moya (1999). The body. In F. Ashe, A. Finlayson, M. Lloyd, I. MacKenzie, J. Martin, & S. O'Neill (Eds), *Contemporary social and political theory: An introduction*. Buckingham, UK: Open University Press.

Lorde, A. (1984). *Sister outsider: Essays and speeches*. New York, NY: The Crossing Press.

Lundy, Colleen (2004; 2011). *Social work and social justice: A structural approach to practice*. Peterborough, ON: Broadview Press.

Macey, David (2000). *The Penguin dictionary of critical theory*. London, UK: Penguin Books.

McIvor, S., Palmater, P., & Day, S. (2017). Equality delayed is equality denied for Indigenous women. *Policy Options*. Retrieved from: http://policyoptions.irpp.org/magazines/december-2017/equality-delayed-is-equality-denied-for-indigenous-women.

Mandell, Nancy, & Johnson, Jennifer (Eds) (2017). *Feminist issues: Race, class, and sexuality*. 6th edn. Toronto, ON: Pearson Canada.

Mendes, Philip (2003). *Australia's welfare wars: The players, the politics and the ideologies*. Sydney, New South Wales: University of New South Wales Press.

Millett, K. (1970). *Sexual politics*. New York, NY: Avon Books.

Moosa-Mitha, Mehmoona (2005). Situating anti-oppressive theories within critical and difference-centered perspectives. In Leslie Brown & Susan Strega (Eds), *Research as resistance: Critical, Indigenous, and anti-oppressive approaches*. Toronto, ON: Canadian Scholars' Press.

Moraga, C., & Anzaldua, G. (Eds) (1983). *This bridge called my back: Writings by radical women of color*. New York, NY: Kitchen Table Press.

Motschenbacher, H., & Stegu, M. (2013). Queer linguistic approaches to discourse. *Discourse & Society, 24(5)*, 519–535.

Mulé, N. (2015). The politicized queer, the informed social workers: Dis/re-ordering the social order. In B. O'Neill, T. Swan, & N. Mulé (Eds), *LGBTQ people and social work* (pp. 17–36). Toronto, ON: Oxford University Press.

Mullaly, Robert (Bob) (2001). Confronting the politics of despair: Towards the reconstruction of progressive social work in a global economy and postmodern age. *Social Work Education, 20(3)*, 303–320.

Mullaly, Bob, & West, Juliana (2018). *Challenging oppression and confronting privilege: A critical approach to anti-oppressive and anti-privilege theory and practice*. 3rd edn. Don Mills, ON: Oxford University Press.

Neysmith, Sheila M. (1991). From community care to a social model of care. In Carol Baines, Patricia M. Evans, & Sheila M. Neysmith (Eds), *Women's caring: Feminist perspectives on social welfare*. Toronto, ON: McLelland & Stewart.

O'Brien, Martin, & Penna, Sue (1998). *Theorising welfare: Enlightenment and modern society*. London, UK: Sage.

Oliver, Michael (1990). *The politics of disablement: A sociological approach*. New York, NY: St Martin's Press.

Oliver, Michael, & Barnes, Colin (2012). *The new politics of disablement*. Basingstoke, UK: Palgrave Macmillan.

Palmater, Pamela (2014). Genocide, Indian policy, and legislated elimination of Indians in Canada. *Aboriginal Policy Studies, 3(3)*, 27–54.

Parton, Nigel (1994). Problematics of government, (post) modernity and social work. *British Journal of Social Work, 24*, 9–32.

Peach, Ian (2011). Finding your allies where you can: How Canadian courts drive Aboriginal recognition in Canada. *Aboriginal Policy Studies, 1(1)*, 106–131.

Pease, Bob, & Fook, Janis (Eds) (1999). *Transforming social work practice: Postmodern critical perspectives*. St Leonards, New South Wales: Allen and Unwin.

Penketh, Laura, & Ali, Yasmin (1997). Racism and social welfare. In Michael Lavalette & Alan Pratt (Eds), *Social policy: A conceptual and theoretical introduction*. London, UK: Sage.

Philo, G., & Miller, D. (Eds) (2000). *Market killing*. London, UK: Longman.

Razack, S. (1998). *Looking white people in the eye: Gender, race, and culture in courtrooms and classrooms*. Toronto, ON: University of Toronto Press.

Rich, Adrienne (1977). *Of woman born: Motherhood as experience and institution*. London, UK: The Women's Press.

Rich, Adrienne (1980). Compulsory heterosexuality and lesbian existence. *Signs 5(4)*, 389–417.

Robbins, Susan P., Chatterjee, Pranab, & Canda, Edward R. (1998). *Contemporary human behavior theory: A critical perspective for social work*. Boston, MA: Allyn and Bacon.

Rodger, John J. (2000). *From a welfare state to a welfare society: The changing context of social policy in a postmodern era*. London, UK: Macmillan.

Rorty, Richard (1999). *Philosophy and social hope*. New York, NY: Penguin.

Rosenberg, Lisa, & Duffy, Ann (2010). Violence against women. In M. Mandell (Ed.), *Feminist issues: Race, class, and sexuality*, 5th edn. (pp. 161–196). Toronto, ON: Pearson Canada.

Seidman, Steven (1998). *Contested knowledge: Social theory in the postmodern era*. 2nd edn. Malden, MA: Blackwell.

Smith, T. (1993). Postmodernism: Theory and politics. *The Activist, 3(7)*, 31–34.

Smith-Carrier, Tracy (2017). Reproducing social conditions of poverty: A critical feminist analysis of social assistance participation in Ontario, Canada. *Journal of Women, Politics & Policy, 38(4)*, 498–521.

Stainton, Tim, & Swift, Karen (1996). "Difference" and social work curriculum. *Canadian Social Work Review, 13(1)*, 75–87.

Statistics Canada (2014). *Immigration, low income and income inequality in Canada: What's new in the 2000s?* Analytical Studies Branch Research Papers Series. Ottawa, ON: Statistics Canada.

Statistics Canada (2015). Study: Women in Canada: Female population (2014). *The Daily*. Ottawa, ON: Statistics Canada.

Statistics Canada (2017). Women and paid work. In *Women in Canada: A gender-based statistical report*. Ottawa, ON: Statistics Canada.

Strega, Susan (2005). The view from the poststructural margins: Epistemology and methodology reconsidered. In Leslie Brown & Susan Strega (Eds), *Research as resistance. Critical, Indigenous, and anti oppressive approaches*. Toronto, ON: Canadian Scholars' Press.

Thompson, Neil (1998). *Promoting equality: Challenging discrimination and oppression in the human services*. London, UK: Macmillan.

Thompson, Neil (2016). *Anti-discriminatory practice: Equality, diversity and social justice*. 6th edn. London, UK: Palgrave Macmillan.

Wachholz, Sandra, & Mullaly, Robert (2000). The politics of the textbook: A content analysis of feminist, radical and anti-racist social work scholarship in American introductory social work textbooks published between 1988 and 1997. *Journal of Progressive Human Services, 11*(2), 51–75.

Weeks, Wendy (1992). Gender in the social and community services: Implications for management. Human Services Management Network Conference, April. Brisbane, Queensland: Queensland University of Technology.

Williams, Fiona (1989). *Social policy: A critical introduction—Issues of race, gender and class*. New York, NY: Basil Blackwell.

Wolfensberger, Wolf (2003). *Leadership and change in human services: Selected readings from Wolf Wolfensberger*. London, UK: Routledge.

Woodward, K. (1997). Concepts of identity and difference. In K. Woodward (Ed.), *Identity and difference*. Milton Keynes, UK: Open University.

Chapter 8

Agger, Ben (1998). *Critical social theories: An introduction*. Boulder, CO: Westview Press.

Allan, June (2003a). Theorizing critical social work. In June Allan, Bob Pease, & Linda Briskman (Eds), *Critical social work: An introduction to theories and practices*. Crows Nest, New South Wales: Allen and Unwin.

Allan, June (2003b). Practicing critical social work. In June Allan, Bob Pease, & Linda Briskman (Eds), *Critical social work: An introduction to theories and practices*. Crows Nest, New South Wales: Allen and Unwin.

Allan, June, Pease, Bob, & Briskman, Linda (Eds) (2003). *Critical social work: An introduction to theories and practices*. Crows Nest, New South Wales: Allen and Unwin.

Bailey, Roy, & Brake, Mike (Eds) (1975). *Radical social work*. New York, NY: Pantheon Books.

Baines, Donna (Ed.) (2011). *Doing anti-oppressive practice: Social justice social work*. 2nd edn. Winnipeg, MB: Fernwood.

Bolger, Steve, Corrigan, Paul, Docking, Jan, & Frost, Nick (1981). *Towards socialist welfare work*. London, UK: Macmillan.

Burrell, G., & Morgan, G. (1979). *Sociological paradigms and organizational analysis*. London, UK: Heinemann.

Carniol, Ben (1979). A critical approach in social work. *Canadian Journal of Social Work Education, 5*(1), 95–111.

Carniol, Ben (1984). Clash of ideologies in social work education. *Canadian Social Work Review, 2*, 184–199.

Carniol, Ben (1990; 1995). *Case critical*. Toronto: Between the Lines.

Carniol, Ben (1992). Structural social work: Maurice Moreau's challenge to social work practice. *Journal of Progressive Human Services, 3*(1), 1–20.

Clark, C. L., & Asquith, A. (1985). *Social work and social philosophy*. London, UK: Routledge & Kegan Paul.

Coates, John. 1991. Putting knowledge for practice into perspective. *Canadian Social Work Review, 8*(1), 82–96.

Corrigan, Paul, & Leonard, Peter (1978). *Social work practice under capitalism: A Marxist approach*. London, UK: Macmillan.

Davis, Ann (1991). A structural approach to social work. In Joyce Lishman (Ed.), *Handbook of theory for practice teachers in social work*. London, UK: Jessica Kingsley.

Finn, Janet L., & Jacobson, Maxine (2003). Just practice: Steps toward a new social work paradigm. *Journal of Social Work Education, 39*(1), 57–76.

Fook, Jan (1993). *Radical casework: A theory of practice*. St Leonards, New South Wales: Allen & Unwin.

Frankel, B. (1979). On the state of the state: Marxist theories of the state after Leninism. *Theory and Society, 7*, 199–242.

Fraser, Neil (1985). Michel Foucault: A young conservative? *Ethics, 96*, 165–184.

Freire, Paulo (1994). *Pedagogy of the oppressed*. 1st and 2nd edns. New York, NY: Continuum Publishing.

Galper, Jeffry (1975). *The politics of social services*. Englewood Cliffs, NJ: Prentice-Hall.

Galper, Jeffry (1980). *Social work practice: A radical perspective*. Englewood Cliffs, NJ: Prentice-Hall.

Geertz, C. (1986). The uses of diversity. *Michigan Quarterly Review, 25*(1), 105–123.

Gould, K. (1987). Life model versus conflict model: A feminist perspective. *Social Work* (May–June), 346–351.

Habermas, Jurgen (1983). Modernity: An incomplete project. In Hal Foster (Ed.), *The anti-aesthetic: Essays on postmodern culture* (pp. 3–15). Port Townsend, WA: Bay Press.

Haney, Eleanor H. (1989). *Vision and struggle: Meditations on feminist spirituality and politics*. Portland, ME: Astarte Shell Press.

Harvey, David (1989). *The condition of postmodernity: An enquiry into the origins of cultural change.* Cambridge, UK: Basil Blackwell.

Hick, Steven, Fook, J. and Pozzuto, R. (Eds) 2005. *Social work: A critical turn.* Toronto, ON: Thompson Educational Publishing.

Hick, Stephen, Peters, Heather I., Corner, Tammy, & London, Tracy (Eds) (2009). *Structural social work in action: Examples from practice.* Toronto, ON: Canadian Scholars' Press.

Horton, John (1966). Order and conflict theories of social problems as competing ideologies. *American Journal of Sociology, 72*(May), 701–713.

Howe, David (1987). *An introduction to social work theory.* Aldershot, UK: Wildwood House.

Howe, David (1994). Modernity, postmodernity and social work. *British Journal of Social Work, 24*, 513–532.

Huyssens, A. (1984). Mapping the postmodern. *New German Critique, 33*, 5–52.

Ife, Jim (1995). *Community development: Creating community alternatives—Vision, analysis and practice.* Melbourne, Victoria: Longman.

Ife, Jim (1997). *Rethinking social work: Towards critical practice.* Lance Cove, New South Wales: Addison Wesley Longman.

Ife, Jim (2001). *Human rights and social work: Towards rights-based practice.* Cambridge, UK: Cambridge University Press.

Jay, M. (1973). *The dialectical imagination: A history of the Frankfurt School and the Institute for Social Research, 1932–50.* Boston, MA: Little, Brown.

Jones, Chris (1983). *State social work and the working class.* London, UK: Macmillan.

Jones, Chris. (2011). The best and worst of times: Reflections on the impact of radicalism on British social work education in the 1970s. In Michael Lavalette (Ed.), *Racial social work today: Social work at the crossroads.* Bristol, UK: The Policy Press.

Kellner, Douglas (1989). *Critical theory, Marxism, and modernity.* Baltimore, MD: Johns Hopkins University Press.

Kincheloe, J. L., & McLaren, P. (2011). Rethinking critical theory and qualitative research. In Kecia Hayes, Shirley R. Steinberg, & Kenneth Tobin (Eds), *Key works in critical pedagogy* (pp. 285–326). Rotterdam, The Netherlands: Sense Publishers.

Langan, Mary, & Lee, Phil. (1989a). Whatever happened to radical social work? In Mary Langan & Phil Lee (Eds), *Radical social work today* (pp. 1–18). London, UK: Unwin Hyman.

Langan, Mary, & Lee, Phil (Eds) (1989b). *Radical social work today.* London, UK: Unwin Hyman.

Lecomte, Roland (1990). Connecting private troubles and public issues in social work education. In Brian Wharf (Ed.), *Social work and social change in Canada* (pp. 31–51). Toronto, ON: McClelland & Stewart.

Leonard, Peter (1994). Knowledge/power and postmodernism. *Canadian Social Work Review, 11*(1), 11–26.

Leonard, Peter (1995). Postmodernism, socialism and social welfare. *Journal of Progressive Human Services, 6*(2), 3–19.

Leonard, Peter (1997). *Postmodern welfare: Reconstructing an emancipatory project.* London, UK: Sage.

Leonard, Stephen T. (1990). *Critical theory in political practice.* Princeton, NJ: Princeton University Press.

Longres, John (1986). Marxian theory and social work practice. *Catalyst, 5*(4), 13–34.

Lundy, Colleen (2004; 2011). *Social work and social justice: A structural approach to practice.* Peterborough, ON: Broadview Press.

McDaniel, Susan A., & Agger, Ben (1984). *Social problems through conflict and order.* Don Mills, ON: Addison-Wesley.

Marchant, H. (1986). Gender, systems thinking and radical social work. In H. Marchant & B. Wearing (Eds), *Gender reclaimed: Women in social work* (pp. 14–32). Sydney, New South Wales: Hale & Iremonger.

Martin, George (1990). *Social policy in the welfare state.* Englewood Cliffs, NJ: Prentice-Hall.

Middleman, Ruth R., & Goldberg, Gale (1974). *Social service delivery: A structural approach to social work practice.* New York, NY: Columbia University Press.

Miliband, Ralph (1977). *Marxism and politics.* Oxford, UK: Oxford University Press.

Moreau, Maurice J. (1979). A structural approach to social work practice. *Canadian Journal of Social Work Education, 5*(1), 78–94.

Moreau, M. (1990). Empowerment through advocacy and consciousness-raising: Implications of a structural approach to social work. *Journal of Sociology and Social Welfare, 17*(2), 53–67.

Moreau, Maurice, & Leonard, Lynn (1989). *Empowerment through a structural approach to social work.* Ottawa, ON: Carleton University School of Social Work and Health and Welfare Canada.

Mullaly, Robert (1993). *Structural social work: Ideology, theory and practice.* Toronto, ON: McClelland & Stewart.

Mullaly, Bob (2007). *The new structural social work.* 3rd edn. Don Mills, ON: Oxford University Press.

Mullaly, Bob (2010). *Challenging oppression: A critical social work approach.* 2nd edn. Don Mills, ON: Oxford University Press.

Mullaly, Robert P., & Keating, Eric F. (1991). Similarities, differences and dialectics of radical social work. *Journal of Progressive Human Services, 2*(2), 49–78.

Mullaly, Bob, & West, Juliana (2018). *Challenging oppression and confronting privilege: A critical approach to anti-oppressive and anti-privilege theory and practice.* 3rd edn. Don Mills, ON: Oxford University Press.

Naiman, Joanne (1997). *How societies work: Class, power and change in a Canadian context*. Toronto, ON: Irwin Publishing.

Pease, Bob (1991). Dialectical models versus ecological models in social work practice. In *Proceedings of the 11th Pacific Regional Seminar on Social Work* (pp. 107–112). Hong Kong: International Federation of Social Workers.

Pease, B. (2010). *Undoing privilege: Unearned advantage in a divided world*. New York, NY: Zed Books.

Pease, Bob, & Fook, Janis (Eds) (1999). *Transforming social work practice: Postmodern critical perspectives*. St Leonards, New South Wales: Allen and Unwin.

Pond, C. (1989). The changing distribution of income, wealth and poverty. In C. Hammet (Ed.), *The changing social structure*. London, UK: Sage.

Pritchard, Colin, & Taylor, Richard (1978). *Social work: reform or revolution?* London, UK: Routledge & Kegan Paul.

Reasons, Charles E., & Perdue, William D. (1981). *Ideology of social problems*. Scarborough, ON: Nelson Canada.

Reynolds, Paul Davidson (1971). *A primer in theory construction*. New York, NY: Bobbs-Merrill.

Rossiter, Amy (1996). A perspective on critical social work. *Journal of Progressive Human Services, 7*(2), 23–41.

Rushton, J. Philippe (1988). Race differences in behaviour: A review and evolutionary analysis. *Personality and Individual Differences, 9*(6), 1009–1024.

Ryan, W. (1976). *Blaming the victim*. 2nd edn. New York, NY: Vintage.

Sabia, David R., Jr, & Wallulis, Jerald (1983). *Changing social science: Critical theory and other critical perspectives*. Albany, NY: State University of New York Press.

Sears, Allan, & Cairns, James (2010). *A good book in theory: Making sense through inquiry*. 2nd edn. Toronto, ON: University of Toronto Press.

Simpkin, Mike (1979). *Trapped within welfare: Surviving social work*. London, UK: Macmillan.

Sklar, H., Albert, M., Cagan, L., Chomsky, N., Hahnel, R., King, M., & Sargent, L. (1986). *Liberating theory*. Boston, MA: South End Press.

Smid, G., & van Krieken, R. (1984). Notes on theory and practice in social work: A comparative view. *British Journal of Social Work, 14*, 11–27.

Statham, Daphne (1978). *Radicals in social work*. London, UK: Routledge & Kegan Paul.

Throssell, Harold (Ed.) (1975). *Social work: Radical essays*. St Lucia, Queensland: University of Queensland Press.

Truth and Reconciliation Commission of Canada (2015). *Honouring the truth, reconciling for the future: Summary of the final report of the Truth and Reconciliation Commission of Canada*. Retrieved from http://www.trc.ca/websites/trcinstitution/File/2015/Honouring_the_Truth_Reconciling_for_the_Future_July_23_2015.pdf.

Vass Gal, Adam D. (2015). *Generational poverty: An economic look at the culture of the poor*. Wilmington, DE: Vernon Press.

Wagner, David (1990). *The quest for a radical profession*. Lanham, MD: University Press of America.

Walters, M., Carter, B., Papp, P., & Silverstein, O. (1988). *The invisible web: Gender patterns in family relationships*. New York, NY: Guildford.

Wharf, Brian (Ed.). *Social work and social change in Canada*. Toronto, ON: McClelland & Stewart.

Williams, Fiona (1989). *Social policy: A critical introduction—Issues of race, gender and class*. New York, NY: Basil Blackwell.

Wineman, Steven (1984). *The politics of human services*. Montreal, QC: Black Rose Books.

Withorn, Ann (1984). *Serving the people: Social services and social change*. New York, NY: Columbia University Press.

Chapter 9

Adam, Barry D. (1978). *The survival of domination: Inferiorization and everyday life*. New York, NY: Elsevier.

Agel, Jerome (Ed.) (1971). *The radical therapist*. New York, NY: Ballantine Books.

Agger, Ben (1998). *Critical social theories: An introduction*. Boulder, CO: Westview Press.

Agger, Ben. (2013). *Critical social theories*. 3rd edn. New York, NY: Oxford University Press.

Ahmad, B. (1991). Developing anti-racist social work education practice. In CD Project Steering Group (Ed.), *Setting the context for change*. London: CCETSW.

Albert, M., Cagan, L., Chomsky, N., Hahnel, R., King, M., Sargent, L., & Sklar, H. (1986). *Liberating theory*. Boston, MA: South End Press.

Alexander, David (1987). Gendered job traits and women's occupations. PhD dissertation, University of Massachusetts.

Auditor General of Canada (2008). *First Nations child and family services program—Indian and Northern Affairs Canada. 2008 May: Report of the Auditor General of Canada*. Ottawa, ON: Retrieved from http://www.oag-bvg.gc.ca/internet/docs/aud_ch_oag_200805_04_e.pdf.

Baines, Donna (Ed.) (2007). *Doing anti-oppressive practice: Building transformative politicized social work*. Halifax, NS: Fernwood.

Baines, Donna (Ed.) (2011). *Doing anti-oppressive practice: Social justice social work*. 2nd edn. Winnipeg, MB: Fernwood.

Beattie, S., & Cotter, A. (2010). Homicide in Canada, 2009. *Juristat, 30*(3), 1–27. Retrieved from http://www.statcan.gc.ca/pub/85-002-x/2010003/article/11352-eng.pdf.

Bishop, Anne (1994; 2002). *Becoming an ally: Breaking the Cycle of Oppression*. 1st and 2nd edns. Halifax, NS: Fernwood.

Blackstock, C., Trocmé, N., & Bennett, M. (2004). Child maltreatment investigations among Aboriginal and non-Aboriginal families in Canada. *Violence against Women, 10*(8), 901–916.

Bulhan, Hussein A. (1985). *Frantz Fanon and the psychology of oppression*. New York, NY: Plenum Press.

Canadian Institute for Health Information (2014). *Drug use among seniors on public drug programs in Canada, 2012*. Retrieved from: https://secure.cihi.ca/free_products/Drug_Use_in_Seniors_on_Public_Drug_Programs_2012_EN_web.pdf.

Canadian Women's Foundation. (2015). *The facts about women and poverty*. Retrieved from: http://www.canadianwomen.org/facts-about-women-and-poverty.

Chansonneuve, D. (2007). *Addictive behaviours among Aboriginal people in Canada*. Ottawa, ON: Aboriginal Healing Foundation.

Cole, Thomas R. (1986). Putting off the old: Middle class morality, antebellum Protestantism, and the origins of ageism. In David Van Tassel & Peter N. Stearns (Eds), *Old age in a bureaucratic society*. New York, NY: Greenwood.

Csiernik, Rick, & William Rowe. (2003). *Responding to the oppression of addiction: Canadian social work perspectives*. Toronto, ON: Canadian Scholars' Press. [Subsequent editions published 2010 and 2017].

Dominelli, Lena. (1988). *Politics, culture, philosophy: Interviews and other writings 1977–1984*. New York, NY: Routledge.

Dominelli, Lena. (1997). *Anti-racist social work*. 2nd edn. London, UK: Macmillan.

Dominelli, Lena. (2002). *Anti-oppressive social work theory and practice*. Basingstoke, UK: Palgrave MacMillan.

Dominelli, Lena, & McLeod, Eileen (1989) *Feminist social work*. Hampshire, UK: Macmillan Education.

Fanon, Frantz (1968). *The wretched of the Earth*. London, UK: Temple Smith.

Foucault, Michel (1977). *Discipline and punish*. New York, NY: Pantheon.

Freire, Paulo (1970). *Pedagogy of the oppressed*. 1st and 2nd edns. New York, NY: Continuum Publishing.

Frye, Marilyn (1983). *The politics of reality: Essays in feminist theory*. Trumansburg, NY: Crossing Press.

Galper, Jeffry (1975). *The politics of social services*. Englewood Cliffs, NJ: Prentice-Hall.

Galper, Jeffry (1980). *Social work practice: A radical perspective*. Englewood Cliffs, NJ: Prentice-Hall.

Gil, David (1994). Confronting injustice and oppression. In Frederic G. Reamer (Ed.), *The foundation of social work knowledge* (pp. 231–263). New York, NY: Columbia University Press.

Gil, David G. (1998). *Confronting injustice and oppression: Concepts and strategies for social workers*. New York, NY: Columbia University Press.

Guarnotta, Emily. (2016). Native Americans and alcoholism. Retrieved from: www.Recovery.org.

Hall, M., & Havens, B. (2008). *The effect of social isolation and loneliness on the health of older women*. Winnipeg, MB: Prairie Women's Health Centre of Excellence. Retrieved from: http://www.pwhce.ca/effectSocialIsolation.htm.

Haney, Eleanor H. (1989). *Vision and struggle: Meditations on feminist spirituality and politics*. Portland, MA: Astarte Shell Press.

Health Canada. (2006). *The human face of mental health and mental illness in Canada 2006*. Retrieved from: http://www.phac-aspc.gc.ca/publicat/human-humain06/15-eng.php.

Health Canada. (2011). *A statistical profile on the health of First Nations in Canada: Vital statistics for Atlantic and western Canada 2001/2002*. Ottawa, ON: Health Canada.

Health Canada. (2013). *National Aboriginal youth suicide prevention strategy (NAYSPS): Program framework*. Ottawa, ON: Health Canada.

Health Canada. (2014). *A statistical profile on the health of First Nations in Canada: Determinants of health, 2006 to 2010*. Retrieved from: http://www.hc-sc.gc.ca/fniah-spnia/pubs/aborig-autoch/2010-stats-profil-determinants/index-eng.php.

Heller, Agnes (1987). *Beyond justice*. New York, NY: Basic Books.

Hudon, T. (2015). Immigrant women. In Statistics Canada, *Women in Canada: A gender-based statistical report 7th edition*. Retrieved from: http://www.statcan.gc.ca/pub/89-503-x/2015001/article/14217-eng.htm#a30.

Hudon, T., & Milan, A. (2015). Senior women. In Statistics Canada, *Women in Canada: A gender-based statistical report 7th edition*. Retrieved from: http://www.statcan.gc.ca/pub/89-503-x/2015001/article/14316-eng.htm.

Johnson, Allan G. (2006). *Privilege, power, and difference*. 2nd edn. New York, NY: McGraw-Hill.

Kirmayer, L. J., Brass, G. M., Holton, T., Paul, K., Simpson, C., & Tait, C. (2007). *Suicide among Aboriginal people in Canada*. Ottawa: Aboriginal Healing Foundation.

Kovel, Joel. (1970; 1984). *White racism: A psychohistory*. New York, NY: Columbia University Press.

Lenin, Vladimir I. (1918). *State and revolution: The Marxist theory of the state and the tasks of the proletariat in the revolution*, tr. Zodiac and Brian Baggins. Lenin Internet Archive (marxists.org). Retrieved from: https://www.marxists.org/ebooks/lenin/state-and-revolution.pdf.

MacDonald, D. & Wilson, D. (2013). *Poverty or prosperity: Indigenous children in Canada*. Ottawa, ON: Canadian Centre for Policy Alternatives.

McIntosh, Peggy (2012). Reflections and future directions for privilege studies. *Journal of Social Issues, 68*(1), 194–206.

McInturff, K. (2016). Women's work: What's it worth to you? *Monitor Canadian Centre for Policy Alternatives*, (January/February), 42–43. Retrieved from: https://www.policyalternatives.ca/publications/monitor/women%E2%80%99s-work-what%E2%80%99s-it-worth-you.

Merchant, Carolyn (1978). *The death of nature.* New York, NY: Harper & Row.

Moreau, Maurice, & Leonard, Lynn (1989). *Empowerment through a structural approach to social work.* Ottawa, ON: Carleton University School of Social Work and Health and Welfare Canada.

Morgaine, Karen, & Capous-Desyllas, Moshoula (2015). *Anti-oppressive social work practice: Putting theory into action.* Los Angeles, CA: Sage.

Mosse, George (1985). *Nationalism and sexuality.* New York, NY: Fertig.

Mullaly, Robert (Bob) (2002). *Challenging oppression: A critical social work approach.* Don Mills, ON: Oxford University Press.

Mullaly, Bob (2010). *Challenging oppression: A critical social work approach.* 2nd edn. Don Mills, ON: Oxford University Press.

Mullaly, Bob, & West, Juliana (2018). *Challenging oppression and confronting privilege: A critical approach to anti-oppressive and anti-privilege theory and practice.* 3rd edn. Don Mills, ON: Oxford University Press.

Naiman, Joanne (1997). *How societies work: Class, power and change in a Canadian context.* Toronto, ON: Irwin.

O'Donnell, V., & Wallace, S. (2011). First Nations, Métis and Inuit women. In Statistics Canada, *Women in Canada: A gender-based statistical report.* Ottawa: Statistics Canada. Retrieved from: http://www.statcan.gc.ca/pub/89-503-x/2010001/article/11442-eng.pdf.

Office of the Correctional Investigator. (2012). Spirit matters: Aboriginal people and the Corrections and Conditional Release Act. Retrieved from: http://www.oci-bec.gc.ca/cnt/rpt/index-eng.aspx.

Ryan, W. (1976). *Blaming the victim.* 2nd edn. New York, NY: Vintage.

Said, Edward (1978). *Orientalism.* New York, NY: Pantheon.

Scott, Joan (1988). Deconstructing equality-versus-difference: Or the uses of post-structuralist theory for feminism. *Feminist Studies, 14,* 33–50.

Sennett, Richard, & Cobb, Jonathan (1972). *The hidden injuries of class.* New York, NY: Vintage.

Sidanius, Jim, & Pratto, Felicia (1999). *Social dominance: An intergroup theory of social hierarchy and oppression.* Cambridge, UK: Cambridge University Press.

Sinha, M. (2013). Measuring violence against women: Statistical trends. *Juristat: Canadian Centre for Justice Statistics.* Retrieved from: http://www.statcan.gc.ca/pub/85-002-x/2013001/article/11766-eng.pdf.

Statistics Canada (2012). *Aboriginal people's survey.* Ottawa, ON: Statistics Canada.

Statistics Canada (2015). Study: Women in Canada: Female population (2014). Ottawa: *The Daily.*

Taylor, Charles (1985). *Philosophy and the human sciences.* Cambridge, UK: Cambridge University Press.

Thompson, Neil (1997). *Anti-discriminatory practice.* 1st and 2nd edns. London, UK: Macmillan.

Thompson, Neil (2001). *Anti-discriminatory practice.* 3rd edn. Basingstroke, UK: Palgrave Macmillan.

Thompson, Neil (2002). Developing anti-discriminatory practice. In Dylan Ronald Tomlinson & Winston Trew (Eds), *Equalising opportunities, minimising oppression: A critical review of anti-discriminatory policies in health and social welfare* (pp. 41–55). London, UK: Routledge.

Truth and Reconciliation Commission of Canada (2015). *Honouring the truth, reconciling for the future: Summary of the final report of the Truth and Reconciliation Commission of Canada.* Retrieved from: http://www.trc.ca/websites/trcinstitution/File/2015/Honouring_the_Truth_Reconciling_for_the_Future_July_23_2015.pdf.

Wasserton, Richard (1980). *Philosophy and social issues.* South Bend, IN: Notre Dame University Press.

West, Cornel (1982). *Prophesy deliverance! An Afro-American revolutionary Christianity.* Philadelphia, PA: Westminster.

Williams, C. (2010). *Women in Canada: A gender-based statistical report. Economic well-being.* Ottawa, ON: Statistics Canada. Retrieved from: http://www.statcan.gc.ca/pub/89-503-x/2010001/article/11388-eng.pdf.

Williams, Fiona (1989). *Social policy: A Critical introduction—Issues of race, gender and class.* New York, NY: Basil Blackwell.

Young, Iris Marion (1990). *Justice and the politics of difference.* Princeton, NJ: Princeton University Press.

Chapter 10

Bailey, Alison (2004). Privilege. In Lisa Heldke & Peg O'Connor (Eds), *Oppression, privilege, and resistance: Theoretical perspectives on racism, sexism, and heterosexism* (pp. 301–316). New York, NY: McGraw-Hill.

Baines, Donna (2002). Radical social work, race, class, and gender. *Race, Gender, and Class, 9*(1), 145–167.

Bishop, Anne (1994; 2002). *Becoming an ally: Breaking the cycle of oppression.* 1st and 2nd edns. Halifax, NS: Fernwood.

Brod, Harry (1989). Work clothes and leisure suits: The class basis and bias of the men's movement. In Michael Kimmel & Michael A. Messner, (Eds), *Men's lives* (p. 289). New York, NY: MacMillan.

Butler, Sandra (1978). *Conspiracy of silence: The trauma of incest.* San Francisco, CA: Volcano Press.

Carbado, D. (2002). Straight out of the closet: Race, gender, and sexual orientation. In F. Valdes, J. McCristal-Culp, & A. Harris (Eds), *Crossroads, directions, and a new*

Critical Race Theory (pp. 220–242). Philadelphia, PA: Temple University Press.

Carbado, D. (2004). Straight out of the closet: Men, feminism, and male heterosexual privilege. In Lisa Heldke & Peg O'Connor (Eds), *Oppression, privilege, and resistance: Theoretical perspectives on racism, sexism, and heterosexism* (pp. 395–419). New York, NY: McGraw-Hill.

Case, Kim A. (Ed.) (2013). *Deconstructing privilege: Teaching and learning as allies in the classroom.* New York, NY: Routledge.

Connell, R. W. (2001). *Gender.* Oxford, UK: Polity Press.

Dominelli, Lena (1997). *Anti-racist social work.* 2nd edn. London, UK: Macmillan.

Dominelli, Lena (2002). *Anti-oppressive social work theory and practice.* Basingstoke, UK: Palgrave MacMillan.

Ferber, Abby L. (2003). Defending the culture of privilege. In Michael Kimmel & Abby Ferber (Eds), *Privilege: A reader* (pp. 319–330). Boulder, CO: Westview Press.

Ferber, A., & Herrera, A. (2013). Teaching privilege through an intersectional lens. In K. Case (Ed.) *Deconstructing privilege: Teaching and learning as allies in the classroom* (pp. 83–101). New York, NY: Routledge.

Harding, S. (1995). Subjectivity, experience and knowledge: An epistemology for rainbow coalition politics. In J. Roof & R. Wiegman (Eds), *Who can speak? Authority and critical identity.* Chicago, IL: University of Illinois Press.

Harding, S. (2004). Standpoint theory as a site of political, philosophical and scientific debate. In S. Harding (Ed.), *The feminist standpoint theory reader: Intellectual and political controversies.* New York, NY: Routledge.

Hays, D. G., Chang, C. Y., & Dean, J. K. (2004). White counselors' conceptualization of privilege and oppression: Implications for counselor training. *Counselor Education and Supervision, 43*, 242–257.

Heldke, Lisa, & O'Connor, Peg (2004). *Oppression, privilege, and resistance: Theoretical perspectives on racism, sexism, and heterosexism.* New York, NY: McGraw-Hill.

Johnson, Allan G. (2006). *Privilege, power, and difference.* 2nd edn. New York, NY: McGraw-Hill.

Kimmel, Michael (2003). Toward a pedagogy of the oppressor. In Michael Kimmel & Abby Ferber (Eds), *Privilege: A reader.* Boulder, CO: Westview Press.

Kimmel, Michael, & Ferber, Abby (Eds) (2003). *Privilege: A reader.* Boulder, CO: Westview Press.

McIntosh, Peggy (1990). White privilege and male privilege: A personal account of coming to see correspondences through work in women's studies. Reprinted in *Independent School, 49*(2), 31–36.

McIntosh, Peggy (2003). White privilege and male privilege. In Michael Kimmel & Abby Ferber (Eds), *Privilege: A reader.* Boulder, CO: Westview Press.

McIntosh, Peggy (2012). Reflections and future directions for privilege studies. *Journal of Social Issues, 68*(1), 194–206.

Marsiglia, Flavio Francisco, & Kulis, Stephens (2009). *Diversity, oppression, and change: Culturally grounded social work.* Chicago, IL: Lyceum Books.

Massey, Douglas S., & Denton, Nancy A. (1998). *American apartheid: Segregation and the making of an underclass.* Cambridge, MA: Harvard University Press.

Moraga, C. (2004). La guera. In M. L. Andersen & P. H. Collins (Eds), *Race, class and gender,* 5th edn. (pp. 28–35). Belmont, CA: Wadsworth Press.

Mullaly, Bob (2007). *The new structural social work.* 3rd edn. Don Mills, ON: Oxford University Press.

Mullaly, Bob, & West, Juliana (2018). *Challenging oppression and confronting privilege: A critical approach to anti-oppressive and anti-privilege theory and practice.* 3rd edn. Don Mills, ON: Oxford University Press.

Pease, B. (2010). *Undoing privilege: Unearned advantage in a divided world.* New York, NY: Zed Books.

Razack, S. (1998). *Looking white people in the eye: Gender, race, and culture in courtrooms and classrooms.* Toronto, ON: University of Toronto Press.

Sardar, Ziauddin, & Van Loon, Borin (2004). *Introducing cultural studies.* Thriplow, Royston, UK: Icon Books.

Schacht, Steven P. (2003). Teaching about being an oppressor. In Michael Kimmel & Abby Ferber (Eds), *Privilege: A reader* (pp. 161–172). Boulder, CO: Westview Press.

Schmitz, C. L., Stakeman, C., and Sisneros, J. (2001). Educating professionals for practice in a multicultural society: Understanding oppression and valuing diversity. *Families in Society, 82*(6), 612–622.

Sidanius, Jim, & Pratto, Felicia (1999). *Social dominance: An intergroup theory of social hierarchy and oppression.* Cambridge, UK: Cambridge University Press.

Sisneros, Jose, et al. (2008). *Critical multicultural social work.* Chicago, IL: Lyceum Books.

Tatum, B. D. (1994). Teaching white students about racism: The search for white allies and the restoration of hope. *Teachers College Record, 94*(4), 462–476.

Thompson, Neil (1997). *Anti-discriminatory practice.* 1st and 2nd edns. London, UK: Macmillan.

Thompson, Neil (1998). *Promoting equality: Challenging discrimination and oppression in the human services.* London, UK: Macmillan.

Thompson, Neil (2002). Developing anti-discriminatory practice. In Dylan Ronald Tomlinson & Winston Trew (Eds), *Equalising opportunities, minimising oppression: A critical review of anti-discriminatory policies in health and social welfare* (pp. 41–55). London, UK: Routledge.

Wise, Tim (2015). *Under the affluence: Shaming the poor, praising the rich and sacrificing the future of America.* San Francisco, CA: City Lights Books.

Chapter 11

Adam, Barry D. (1978). *The survival of domination: Inferiorization and everyday life.* New York, NY: Elsevier.

Agel, Jerome (Ed.) (1971). *The radical therapist*. New York, NY: Ballantine Books.

Allan, June. (2003). Practicing critical social work. In June Allan, Bob Pease, & Linda Briskman (Eds), *Critical social work: An introduction to theories and practices*. Crows Nest, New South Wales: Allen and Unwin.

Allan, June, Pease, Bob, & Briskman, Linda (Eds) (2003). *Critical social work: An introduction to theories and practices.* Crows Nest, New South Wales: Allen and Unwin.

Baines, Donna (1997). Feminist social work in the inner city: The challenges of race, class, and gender. *Affilia, 12*(3), 297–317.

Baines, Donna (Ed.) (2011). *Doing anti-oppressive practice: Social justice social work*. 2nd edn. Winnipeg, MB: Fernwood.

Basch, Michael (1975). Toward a theory that encompasses depression: A revision of existing causal hypotheses. In E. James Anthony & Theresa Benedek (Eds), *Depression and human existence*. Boston, MA: Little, Brown; cited in Elaine B. Pinderhughes (1983), Empowerment for our clients and for ourselves, *Social Casework, 64*(6), 331–338.

Bishop, Anne (2002). *Becoming an ally: Breaking the cycle of oppression*. 1st and 2nd edns. Halifax, NS: Fernwood.

Blair, Peter (1973). Orientation towards clients in a public welfare agency. In Elihu Katz & Brenda Danet (Eds), *Bureaucracy and the public: A reader in official-client relations*. New York, NY: Basic Books; cited in Ann Withorn (1984), *Serving the people: Social services and social change*. New York, NY: Columbia University Press.

Bock, Scott (1980). Conscientization: Paulo Freire and class-based practice. *Catalyst, 2*(2), 5–26.

Bourgon, Michelle (1988). How feminism can take the crazy out of your head and put it back into society. In Geraldine Finn (Ed.), *Women's studies: A Canadian perspective*. Ottawa, ON: Garamond Press.

Bulhan, Hussein A. (1985). *Frantz Fanon and the psychology of oppression*. New York, NY: Plenum Press.

Burghardt, Steve (1982). *The other side of organizing: Resolving the personal dilemmas and political demands of daily practice*. Cambridge, MA: Schenkman.

Carniol, Ben (1984). Clash of ideologies in social work education. *Canadian Social Work Review, 2*, 184–199.

Carniol, Ben (2005). *Case critical*. Toronto, ON: Between the Lines.

Caspary, William R. (1980). Psychotherapy and radical politics. *Catalyst: A Socialist Journal of the Social Services, 7*, 27–36.

CASW (Canadian Association of Social Workers) (1994). *Preamble to the Canadian Association of Social Workers code of ethics*. Ottawa, ON: CASW.

CASW (Canadian Association of Social Workers) (2005). *Code of ethics*. Ottawa, ON: CASW.

Cohen, Leonard. (1988). First we take Manhattan. From *I'm Your Man* album. Copyright © 1988 Leonard Cohen and Sony/ATV Music Publishing Canada Company. Retrieved from: http://www.leonardcohensite.com/songs/first.htm.

Collins, Barbara G. (1986). Defining feminist social work. *Social Work, 31*(3), 214–219.

Corrigan, Paul, & Leonard, Peter (1978). *Social work practice under capitalism: A Marxist approach*. London, UK: Macmillan.

Cummings, Joan E. (1980). Sexism in social work: Some thoughts on strategy for structural change. *Catalyst, 8*, 7–34.

Dalrymple, J., & Burke, B. (1995). *Anti-oppressive practice: Social care and the law*. Buckingham, UK: Open University Press.

Dominelli, Lena (1997). *Anti-racist social work*. 2nd edn. London, UK: Macmillan.

Dominelli, Lena. (2002). *Anti-oppressive social work theory and practice*. Basingstoke, UK: Palgrave MacMillan.

Festinger, Leon (1957). *A theory of cognitive dissonance*. Stanford, CA: Stanford University Press.

Fook, Jan (1993). *Radical casework: A theory of practice*. St Leonards, New South Wales: Allen & Unwin.

Forbes, David (1986). Counselling in crisis. *Catalyst, 20*, 53–84.

Fox, D. R., & Prilleltensky, Isaac (Eds) (1997). *Critical psychology: An Introduction*. London, UK: Sage.

Fraser, Heather, & Strong, Desma (2000). Teaching structural social work skills to beginning students. *Advances in Social Work Education*, (spring), 24–32.

Frayne, G. (1987). Tape-analysis grid for the action research on the structural approach to social work. Unpublished material, Montreal, Université de Montréal, École de service social; cited in Maurice Moreau (n.d.), Practice implications of a structural approach to social work, Unpublished paper, Université de Montréal.

Freedberg, Sharon (1989). Self-determination: Historical perspectives on current practice. *Social Work, 34*(1), 33–38.

Freire, Paulo (1970; 1994). *Pedagogy of the oppressed*. 1st and 2nd edns. New York, NY: Continuum Publishing.

Galper, Jeffry (1975). *The politics of social services*. Englewood Cliffs, NJ: Prentice-Hall.

Galper, Jeffry (1980). *Social work practice: A radical perspective*. Englewood Cliffs, NJ: Prentice-Hall.

Gil, David G. (1976) *The challenge of social equality*. Cambridge, MA: Schenkman.

Gil, David G. (1998). *Confronting injustice and oppression: Concepts and strategies for social workers*. New York, NY: Columbia University Press.

Gordon, D. 1978. *Therapeutic Metaphors*. Cupertino, CA: Meta Publications.

Gutierrez, L., Parsons, R., & Cox, E. (1998). *Empowerment in social work practice: A sourcebook*. Pacific Grove, CA: Brooks/Cole.

Hasenfeld, Yeheskel (1987). Power in social work practice. *Social Service Review, 61*(3), 469–483.

Herman, J. L. (1992). *Trauma and recovery*. New York, NY: Basic Books.

hooks, bell (1993). *Sisters of the yam: Black women and self-recovery*. Boston, MA: South End Press.

Howe, David (1987). *An introduction to social work theory*. Aldershot, UK: Wildwood House.

Ife, Jim (1997). *Rethinking social work: Towards critical practice*. Lance Cove, New South Wales: Addison Wesley Longman.

Ife, Jim (2001). *Human rights and social work: Towards rights-based practice*. Cambridge, UK: Cambridge University Press.

Jessup, H., & Robertson, S. (1999). Postermodernism and the teaching and practice of interpersonal skills. In B. Pease & J. Fook (Eds.), *Transforming social work practice* (pp. 161–178). St Leonards, New South Wales: Allen & Unwin.

Keefe, Thomas (1980). Empathy skill and critical consciousness. *Social Casework, 61*(7), 387–393.

Kitzinger, C., & Perkins, R. (1993). *Changing our minds: Lesbian feminism and psychology*. London, UK: Onlywomen.

Lane, B. 1997. A question of justice. *Australian Social Work, 50*(4), 37–39.

Leonard, Peter (1984). *Personality and ideology: Towards a materialist understanding of the individual*. London, UK: Macmillan.

Leonard, Peter (1997). *Postmodern welfare: Reconstructing an emancipatory project*. London, UK: Sage.

Longres, John (1986). Marxian theory and social work practice. *Catalyst, 5*(4), 13–34.

Longres, John F., & McLeod, Eileen (1980). Consciousness raising and social work practice. *Social Casework, 61*(5), 267–276.

Lundy, Colleen (2004). *Social work and social justice: A structural approach to practice*. Peterborough, ON: Broadview Press.

Middleman, Ruth R., & Goldberg, Gale (1974). *Social service delivery: A structural approach to social work practice*. New York, NY: Columbia University Press.

Midgely, J. (1982). *Professional imperialism: Social work in the Third World*. London, UK: Heinemann.

Mills, C. Wright (1959). *The sociological imagination*. New York, NY: Oxford University Press.

Moane, Geraldine (1999). *Gender and colonialism: A psychological analysis of oppression and liberation*. New York, NY: St Martin's Press.

Moane, Geraldine (2011). *Gender and colonialism: A psychological analysis of oppression and liberation*. 2nd edn. Basingstoke, UK: Palgrave Macmillan.

Moreau, Maurice (n.d.). Practice implications of a structural approach to social work. Unpublished paper, Université de Montréal.

Moreau, Maurice J. (1979). A structural approach to social work practice. *Canadian Journal of Social Work Education, 5*(1), 78–94.

Moreau, Maurice, & Leonard, Lynn (1989). *Empowerment through a structural approach to social work*. Ottawa, ON: Carleton University School of Social Work and Health and Welfare Canada.

Morgaine, Karen, & Capous-Desyllas, Moshoula (2015). *Anti-oppressive social work practice: Putting theory into action*. Los Angeles, CA: Sage.

Mullaly, Bob (2010). *Challenging oppression: A critical social work approach*. 2nd edn. Don Mills, ON: Oxford University Press.

Mullaly, Robert P., & Keating, Eric F. (1991). Similarities, differences and dialectics of radical social work. *Journal of Progressive Human Services, 2*(2), 49–78.

Mullaly, Bob, & West, Juliana (2018). *Challenging oppression and confronting privilege: A critical approach to anti-oppressive and anti-privilege theory and practice*. 3rd edn. Don Mills, ON: Oxford University Press.

Mulvey, C. (1994). *Evaluation report on the Allen Lane Foundation's funding programme in Ireland, 1989–1991*. Dublin, Ireland: Allen Lane Foundation.

Patti, Rino J., & Resnick, Herman (1972). Changing the agency from within. *Social Work, 17*(4), 48–57.

Pharr, Suzanne (1988). *Homophobia: A weapon of sexism*. Inverness, CA: Chadron Press.

Pinderhughes, Elaine B. (1983). Empowerment for our clients and for ourselves. *Social Casework, 64*(6), 331–338.

Piven, Frances Fox, & Cloward, Richard (1993). *Regulating the poor: The functions of public welfare*. New York, NY: Vintage.

Rondeau, Gilles (2000). Reflection—Empowerment and social practice, or the issue of power in social work. *Social Work and Globalization*, special issue, July, 216–220.

Rose, Stephen M., & Black, Bruce L. (1985). *Advocacy and empowerment: Mental health care in the community*. Boston, MA: Routledge & Kegan Paul.

Rosen, S. (Ed.) (1982). *My voice will go with you: The teaching tales of Milton H. Erickson, M.D.* New York, NY: Norton.

Ruth, Sean (1988). Understanding oppression and liberation. *Studies: An Irish Quarterly Review*, (winter), 434–443.

Scurfield, Raymond (1980). An integrated approach to case services and social reform. *Social Casework, 61*(10), 610–618.

Sherman, Wendy Ruth, & Wenocur, Stanley (1983). Empowering public welfare workers through mutual support. *Social Work, 28*(5), 375–379.

Simon, Barbara Levy (1990). Rethinking empowerment. *Journal of Progressive Human Services, 1*(1), 27–39.

Simons, Ronald L. (1982). Strategies for exercising influence. *Social Work, 27*(3), 268–273.

Simpkin, Mike (1979). *Trapped within welfare: Surviving social work*. London, UK: Macmillan.

Swift, Karen (1995). *Manufacturing "bad mothers": A critical perspective on child neglect*. Toronto, ON: University of Toronto Press.

Thompson, Neil (1998). *Promoting equality: Challenging discrimination and oppression in the human services.* London, UK: Macmillan.

Thompson, Neil (2001). *Anti-discriminatory practice.* 3rd edn. Basingstoke, UK: Palgrave Macmillan.

Thompson, Neil (2016). *Anti-discriminatory practice: Equality, diversity and social justice.* 6th edn. London, UK: Palgrave Macmillan.

Thompson, Neil (2017). *Social problems and social justice.* London, UK: Palgrave.

Vazala-Martinez, Iris (1985). Toward an emancipatory clinical practice in human services. In David G. Gil & Eva Gil (Eds.), *Toward social and economic justice* (pp. 55–62). Cambridge, MA: Schenkman.

Walker, Gillian (1977). *The status of women in social work education.* Brief prepared for the Canadian Association of Schools of Social Work Task Force on the Status of Women in Social Work Education. Ottawa: CASSW.

Weeks, Wendy (1992). Gender in the social and community services: Implications for management. Paper presented at Human Services Management Network Conference, April. Brisbane, Queensland: Queensland University of Technology.

Williams, Fiona (1989). *Social policy: A critical introduction—Issues of race, gender and class.* New York, NY: Basil Blackwell.

Withorn, Ann. (1984). *Serving the people: Social services and social change.* New York, NY: Columbia University Press.

Young, Iris Marion (1990). *Justice and the politics of difference.* Princeton, NJ: Princeton University Press.

Chapter 12

Alinsky, Saul (1972). Playboy Interview: Saul Alinsky. *Playboy,* March.

Allan, June (2003a). Theorizing critical social work. In June Allan, Bob Pease, & Linda Briskman (Eds), *Critical social work: An introduction to theories and practices.* Crows Nest, New South Wales: Allen and Unwin.

Allan, June (2003b). Practicing critical social work. In June Allan, Bob Pease, & Linda Briskman (Eds), *Critical social work: An introduction to theories and practices.* Crows Nest, New South Wales: Allen and Unwin.

Argyris, C., & Schon, D. (1976). *Theory in practice: Increasing professional effectiveness.* San Francisco, CA: Jossey-Bass.

Armitage, Andrew (1988). *Social welfare in Canada: Ideals, realities, and future paths.* 2nd edn. Toronto, ON: McClelland & Stewart.

Armitage, Andrew (1996). *Social welfare in Canada revisited: Facing up to the future.* 3rd edn. Toronto, ON: Oxford University Press.

Armitage, Andrew (2003). *Social welfare in Canada.* 4th edn. Don Mills, ON: Oxford University Press.

Askeland, Gurid Aga, & Fook, Jan. (2009). Critical reflection in social work. *European Journal of Social Work, 12*(3), 287–292.

Baines, Donna (1997). Feminist social work in the inner city: The challenges of race, class, and gender. *Affilia, 12*(3), 297–317.

Baines, Donna (Ed.) (2011). *Doing anti-oppressive practice: Social justice social work.* 2nd edn. Winnipeg, MB: Fernwood.

Biklen, Douglas P. (1983). *Community organizing. Theory and practice.* Englewood Cliffs, NJ: Prentice-Hall.

Bishop, Anne (2002). *Becoming an ally: Breaking the cycle of oppression.* 1st and 2nd edns. Halifax, NS: Fernwood.

Calhoun, Craig (2013). Occupy Wall Street in perspective. *The British Journal of Sociology, 64*(1), 26–38.

Carniol, Ben (2010). *Case critical.* Toronto, ON: Between the Lines.

Coates, Ken (2015). *#Idle No More and the remaking of Canada.* Regina, SK: University of Regina Press.

Democracy Now (2017). Women's March on Washington: Historic protest three times larger than Trump's inaugural crowd. 28 January. Retrieved from: http://www.democracy now.org/2017/1/23/womens_march_millions_take_to_streets.

Doyal, L., & Gough, I. (1991). *A theory of human need.* New York, NY: Guilford Press.

Esping-Andersen, Gotta (1989). The three political economies of the welfare state. *Canadian Review of Sociology and Anthropology, 26*(11), 10–36.

Ferguson, Iain, Lavalette, Michael, & Mooney, Gerry (2002). *Rethinking welfare: A critical perspective.* London, UK: Sage.

Fisher, Robert, & Karger, Howard J. (1997). *Social work and community in a private world: Getting out in public.* White Plains, NY: Longman.

Fisher, Robert, & Kling, J. (1994). Community organization and new social movement theory. *Journal of Progressive Human Services, 5,* 5–24.

Flora, Peter, & Heidenheimer, Arnold (Eds) (1981). *The development of welfare states in Europe and America.* New Brunswick, NJ: Transaction Books.

Fook, Jan (1999). Critical reflectivity in education and practice. In B. Pease & J. Fook (Eds), *Transforming social work practice.* St Leonards, New South Wales: Allen & Unwin.

Fook, Jan (2004). Critical reflection and transformative possibilities. In Linda Davies & Peter Leonard (Eds), *Social work in a corporate era: Practices of power and resistance.* Burlington, VT: Ashgate.

Foucault, M. (1988). *Politics, culture, philosophy: Interviews and other writings 1977–1984.* New York, NY: Routledge.

Fraser, Neil (1979). The labor movement in the explanation of social service growth: The United States and Britain. *Administration in Social Work, 3*(3), 301–312.

Furniss, Norman, & Tilton, Timothy (1977). *The case for the welfare state*. Bloomington, IN: Indiana University Press.

Galper, Jeffry (1980). *Social work practice: A radical perspective*. Englewood Cliffs, NJ: Prentice-Hall.

Gil, David G. (1998). *Confronting injustice and oppression: Concepts and strategies for social workers*. New York, NY: Columbia University Press.

Globe and Mail (2016). Micah White: "Occupy Wall Street was a constructive failure." 18 March. Retrieved from: http://theglobeandmail.com/opinion/munk-debates/micah-white-occupy-wall-street-was-a-constructive-failure/article29294222/?service=print.

Goldhor-Lerner, H. (1985). *The dance of anger*. New York, NY: Harper & Row.

Hardy, Jean (1981a). *Values in social work*. London, UK: Routledge & Kegan Paul.

Hardy, Jean. (1981b). *Values in social policy: Nine contradictions*. London, UK: Routledge & Kegan Paul.

Herman, J. L. (1992). *Trauma and recovery*. New York, NY: Basic Books.

Heron, Craig (1996). *The Canadian labour movement: A brief history*. 2nd edn. Toronto, ON: James Lorimer.

Indivisible Team (2017). Indivisible: A practical guide for resisting the Trump agenda. 27 January. Retrieved from: www.IndivisibleGuide.com.

Jennissen, Therese, & Lundy, Colleen (2011). *One hundred years of social work: A history of the profession in English Canada*. Waterloo, ON: Wilfrid Laurier University Press.

Kinew, Wab (2014). Idle No More is not just an "Indian Thing." In Kino-Nda-Niimi Collective (Eds), *The winter we danced: Voices from the past, the future, and the Idle No More movement*. Winnipeg, MB: Arbeiter Ring Publishing.

Laursen, Kay (1975). Professionalism. In Harold Throssell (Ed.), *Social work: Radical essays* (pp. 47–71). St Lucia, Queensland: University of Queensland Press.

Lecomte, Roland (1990). Connecting private troubles and public issues in social work education. In Brian Wharf (Ed.), *Social work and social change in Canada* (pp. 31–51). Toronto, ON: McClelland & Stewart.

Leonard, Peter (1997). *Postmodern welfare: Reconstructing an emancipatory project*. London, UK: Sage.

Lim, O. (1996). *Anger is a gift*. Unpublished research paper, McGill University.

Mishra, Ramesh B. (1981). *Society and social policy*. 2nd rev. edn. London, UK: Macmillan.

Mishra, Ramesh (1990). *The welfare state in capitalist society*. Toronto, ON: University of Toronto Press.

Moffatt, K. (1999). Surveillance and government of the welfare recipient. In Adrienne Chambon, Allan Irving, & Laura Epstein (Eds), *Reading Foucault for social work*. New York, NY: Columbia University Press.

Moreau, Maurice J. (1979). A structural approach to social work practice. *Canadian Journal of Social Work Education, 5*(1), 78–94.

Moreau, Maurice, Frosst, Sandra, Frayne, Gwyn, Hlywa, Mary, Leonard, Lynn, & Rowell, Marilyn (1993). *Empowerment II: Snapshots of the structural approach in action*. Ottawa, ON: Health and Welfare Canada.

Moreau, Maurice, & Leonard, Lynn (1989). *Empowerment through a structural approach to social work*. Ottawa, ON: Carleton University School of Social Work and Health and Welfare Canada.

Mullaly, Robert (Bob) (2001). Confronting the politics of despair: Towards the reconstruction of progressive social work in a global economy and postmodern age. *Social Work Education, 20*(3), 303–320.

Mullaly, Robert (Bob), (2002; 2010). *Challenging oppression: A critical social work approach*. Don Mills, ON: Oxford University Press.

Mullaly, Robert P., & Keating, Eric F. (1991). Similarities, differences and dialectics of radical social work. *Journal of Progressive Human Services, 2*(2), 49–78.

Myers, Thomas A. (2012). Open letter from Thomas A. Meyers to Occupy Wall Street. *Journal of International Business Ethics, 5*(1), 50.

The New Yorker (2017). The somehow controversial Women's March on Washington. 18 January. Retrieved from: http://www.newyorker.com/culture/jia-tolentino/the-somehow-controversial-womens-march-on-washington.

Noble, Carolyn (2015). Social protest movements and social work practice. *International Encyclopedia of the Social & Behavioural Sciences, 22*, 518–524.

Piven, Frances Fox, & Cloward, Richard A. (1977). *Poor people's movements*. New York, NY: Pantheon.

Profitt, Norma Jean (2011). Self-care, social work, and social justice. In Donna Baines (Ed.), *Doing anti-oppressive practice: Social justice social work*. Halifax, NS: Fernwood.

Ralph, Diana (1993). Anti-poverty policy under NDP governments. *Canadian Review of Social Policy, 31*, 63.

Rees, S. (1991). *Achieving power: Practice and policy in social welfare*. North Sydney, New South Wales: Allen and Unwin.

Reisch, M. (1995). If you think you're not political, guess again: The 1994 elections. Keynote Address, NASW California Legislative Days Conference, 12 February, Sacramento, CA; cited in Robert Fisher & Howard J. Karger (1997), *Social work and community in a private world: Getting out in public*. White Plains, NY: Longman.

Rickford, Russell (2016). Black Lives Matter: Towards a modern practice of mass struggle. *New Labor Forum, 25*(1): 34–42.

Saul, John Ralston (2004). The collapse of globalism and the rebirth of nationalism. *Harper's Magazine* (March), 33–43.

Saul, John Ralston. (2005). *The collapse of globalism and the reinvention of the world*. Toronto, ON: Viking Canada.

Staggenborg, Susan (2012). *Social movements*. New York, NY: Oxford University Press.

Steger, Manfred B. (2002). *Globalism: The new market ideology*. Lanham, MD: Rowman & Littlefield.

Steger, Manfred B. (2003). *Globalization: A very short introduction*. New York, NY: Oxford University Press.

Stienstra, Deborah (2012). *About Canada disability rights*. Halifax: Fernwood.

Thompson, Neil (1998). *Promoting equality: Challenging discrimination and oppression in the human services*. London, UK: Macmillan.

Unifor, the Union (2014). Politics for workers: Unifor's political project. Unifor in Motion: Canadian Council, 13–15 September, Vancouver, BC. Retrieved from: www.unifor.org.

Wagner, David (1990). *The quest for a radical profession*. Lanham, MD: University Press of America.

Wagner, David, & Cohen, Marcia B. (1978). Social workers, class and professionalism. *Catalyst, 1*(1), 25–55.

Weinburg, M. (2009). Moral distress: A missing but relevant concept for ethics in social work. *Canadian Social Work Review/Revue canadienne de service sociale, 26*(2), 139–151.

White, Micah (2016). *The end of protest: A new playbook for revolution*. Toronto, ON: Knopf Canada.

Wilding, P. (1982). *Professional power and social welfare*. London, UK: Routledge & Kegan Paul.

Wilensky, H. L. (1975). *The welfare state and equality*. Berkeley, CA: University of California Press.

Wineman, Steven (1984). *The politics of human services*. Montreal, QC: Black Rose Books.

Withorn, Ann (1984). *Serving the people: Social services and social change*. New York, NY: Columbia University Press.

Wolfe, David (1989). The Canadian state in comparative perspective. *Canadian Review of Sociology and Anthropology, 26*(1), 95–126.

Young, Iris Marion (2000). *Inclusion and democracy*. Oxford University Press.

Credits

Index

Scotland, 61

Scruton, Richard, 77

Sears, Allan and James Cairns, 203, 204

segregation: collectivization and, 319–20

self-care, 363–4

self-deprecation, 259

self-determination, 11, 19–20

self-reflexive practice. *See* critical self-reflection

senior citizens: consciousness-raising and, 314–15; *see also* older people

service users: access to files, 365–6; behaviour that demeans or defames, 331–2; collectivization and, 316–17; consciousness-raising and, 312–15; dialogical relationships and, 323–4; empowerment and, 308–9; groups and, 317–18, 331; maximizing use of resources, 330–1; power and, 299; primary obligation to, 328, 330; as term, 365; working with, 298–310

Settlement House Movement, xii, 2, 3–4, 202

sexual harassment, 249

Sharpton, Al, 346

shelters, emergency, 56

Sherman, Wendy Ruth and Stanley Wenocur, 334

Sidanius, Jim and Felicia Pratto, 254, 255

Sigurdson, Richard, 133

silence, 273–4, 289, 321

Simon, Barbara Levy, 307

Singh, Jagmeet, 143

Sisneros, Jose et al., 271, 272

Smith, Adam, 79

social agencies: contradictions of, 326–8, 335; control and pacification features of, 327; democratizing, 330; hierarchical management of, 330; knowing one's, 334–5; overt structural social work activities, 328–9; radicalizing, 328–9; radical or structural practice in, 332–3; social workers protecting themselves, 332–5; structural analysis of, 335–7

social change: liberalism and, 102, 103; Marxism and, 149, 150, 153; neo-conservatism and, 84–5; paradigms and, 74; social democracy and, 125, 126, 129; social reform, 343; social work and, 6; structural change, 343; structural social work and, 230, 231, 232

social Darwinism, 177

social democracy, 122; in Canada, 109, 142–4; capitalism and, 128; change (conflict) perspective and, 214; critique of, 135–8; economic beliefs of, 127–8, 138, 197; evolutionary socialism and, 119–20; governments, 355–6; human nature and, 123–4, 126; inequality and, 136–7; overview of, 122–3, 138, 197; participatory decision-making and, 128, 129, 136; political beliefs of, 128–9, 138, 197; social beliefs of, 125–7, 138, 197; social change and, 125, 126; socialism and, 196; social justice and, 126; social problems and, 129–30, 132, 197; social work and, 133–4; social work practice and, 133–4, 138, 197; society and, 124, 126; state and nation-state and, 124, 126, 128–9, 132; summary of views, 126; in Sweden, 123; in United Kingdom, 122–3, 139–40; in United States, 140–2; welfare and, 130–2, 138, 197; welfare state and, 125, 226

Social Democratic Party of Canada, 142

social disorganization, 107, 109–10, 206

social engineering, 85

social insurance, 26; reforms in Germany, 351

socialism, 117–22, 196; in Canada, 110; change (conflict) perspective and, 214; common characteristics of thought, 118; evolutionary, 119–20, 142; ideology, 196–9; lack of working model of, 161–2; Marx on, 121; radical social work and, 125, 202–3; retreat of, 34; revitalized (reconstructed), xviii, 198–9; revolutionary, 119, 142; skepticism of, 199; social work ideology and, 198; United States and, 141, 356

Socialist Party of Canada, 142

socialization, 114, 205

social justice, 6, 14–15, 238–9; distributional view of, 14–16; liberalism and, 102, 103; Marxism and, 149, 150, 152; neo-conservatism and, 84, 85; oppression and, 238–42; social democracy and, 124–5, 126; social phenomena and, 16, 241

social location, 285

"social minimum," 15, 108, 113, 151, 239

social movements, 343–4, 360

social pathology, 90

social problems, 24–5; change (conflict) perspective and, 129, 211–12, 213; conservative-liberal perspectives on, 25; conventional view of, 4; family and, 89–90, 206–7; humanist liberal and liberal humanist views of, 108; at individual level, 206; liberalism and, 106–8, 197; Marxism and, 153–5, 197; neo-conservatism and, 89–90, 93, 197; new structural social work and, 231; oppression and, 234; order perspective and, 129, 205–9, 213; personal deficiency approach, 90, 107, 317, 321; personal disorganization and, 107; privilege as cause of, 234; progressive view of, 4–5; psychological approaches to, 299–300; social democracy and, 129–30, 132, 197; social disorganization and, 107, 109–10; at structural level, 212; at subcultural level, 207–9

social programs: cuts in Canada, 43–4, 63; cuts in Great Britain, 41–3; cuts in United States, 40–1; neo-conservatism and, 79

"Social Role Valorization," 187

social stratification, 205

social structures, 230, 231, 232, 234–5, 253

social theory, mainstream, xiv

Social Union Framework Agreement (SUFA), 44

social welfare. *See* welfare; welfare state

social work: advocacy and, 110; anti-capitalist, 328; autonomy and, 332; change (conflict) perspective and, 212–14; conventional, xvii, 5–7, 304, 311, 354–5; crisis in, 50–7; criticisms of, xii, 299; definition of, 14; demystifying, 324; deprofessionalization and, 52, 54; economic beliefs of, 95, 113; fundamental values of, 13–19; hopeful signs and, 57–65; ideals of, 161; ideology and, 20–4, 198; liberalism and, 112–13, 114–15, 209; Marxism and, 133, 161, 163–5; neo-conservatism and, 95, 209; occupational subordination and, 307, 309; order perspective and, 209; overview of paradigm, 138; as political, 5–7, 19, 355, 356, 357; political beliefs of, 95, 113; privilege and, 283–7; as profession, 4; progressive (critical) view, xvii, 4–5, 6; "reform-the-person" approach, 3, 4; social beliefs of, 95,